Love and Vulnerability

Love and Vulnerability: Thinking with Pamela Sue Anderson developed out of the desire for dialogue with the late feminist philosopher Pamela Sue Anderson's extraordinary, previously unpublished, last work on love and vulnerability. The collection publishes this work for the first time, with a diverse, multidisciplinary, international range of contributors responding to it, to Anderson's *oeuvre* as a whole and to her life and death.

Anderson's path-breaking work includes *A Feminist Philosophy of Religion* (1998) and *Re-visioning Gender in Philosophy of Religion: Reason, Love and Epistemic Locatedness* (2012). Her last work critiques, then attempts to rebuild, concepts of love and vulnerability. Reason, critical self-reflexivity, emotion, intuition and imagination, myth and narrative all have a role to play. Social justice, friendship, conversation, dialogue, collective work are central to her thinking.

Contributors trace the emergence of Anderson's late thinking, extend her conversations with the history of philosophy and contemporary voices such as hooks and Butler, and bring her work into contact with debates in theology; Continental and analytic philosophy; feminist, queer and transgender theory; postcolonial theory; African-American studies. Discussions engage with the Me Too movement and sexual violence, climate change, sweatshops, neoliberalism, death and dying, and the nature of the human.

Originally published as a special issue of the journal *Angelaki*, this large, wide-ranging collection, featuring a number of distinguished contributors, makes a significant contribution to the burgeoning interdisciplinary research on interpersonal relations, sympathy and empathy, affect and emotion.

Pelagia Goulimari (University of Oxford) co-directs the M.St. in Women's Studies and "Women in the Humanities" (TORCH). Her books include *Toni Morrison*, *Literary Criticism and Theory: From Plato to Postcolonialism*, *Postmodernism: What Moment?*, *Women Writing Across Cultures* and *Oxford Research Encyclopedia of Literary Theory*. She is the editor of *Angelaki*.

Love and Vulnerability
Thinking with Pamela Sue Anderson

Edited by
Pelagia Goulimari

Routledge
Taylor & Francis Group
LONDON AND NEW YORK

First published 2021
by Routledge
2 Park Square, Milton Park, Abingdon, Oxon, OX14 4RN

and by Routledge
52 Vanderbilt Avenue, New York, NY 10017

Routledge is an imprint of the Taylor & Francis Group, an informa business

© 2021 Taylor & Francis

All rights reserved. No part of this book may be reprinted or reproduced or utilised in any form or by any electronic, mechanical, or other means, now known or hereafter invented, including photocopying and recording, or in any information storage or retrieval system, without permission in writing from the publishers.

Trademark notice: Product or corporate names may be trademarks or registered trademarks, and are used only for identification and explanation without intent to infringe.

British Library Cataloguing-in-Publication Data
A catalogue record for this book is available from the British Library

ISBN13: 978-0-367-67871-5

Typeset in Minion Pro
by codeMantra

Publisher's Note
The publisher accepts responsibility for any inconsistencies that may have arisen during the conversion of this book from journal articles to book chapters, namely the inclusion of journal terminology.

Disclaimer
Every effort has been made to contact copyright holders for their permission to reprint material in this book. The publishers would be grateful to hear from any copyright holder who is not here acknowledged and will undertake to rectify any errors or omissions in future editions of this book.

Contents

Citation Information viii
Notes on Contributors xii

Editorial Introduction 1
Pelagia Goulimari

ANDERSON'S LAST WRITINGS

1 Towards a New Philosophical Imaginary 6
   Pamela Sue Anderson (edited by Sabina Lovibond and A.W. Moore)

2 Reorienting Ourselves in (Bergsonian) Freedom, Friendship and Feminism 21
   Pamela Sue Anderson (edited by Nicholas Bunnin)

3 Silencing and Speaker Vulnerability: Undoing an Oppressive Form of (Wilful) Ignorance 34
   Pamela Sue Anderson (edited by Nicholas Bunnin)

4 Creating a New Imaginary for Love in Religion 44
   Pamela Sue Anderson (edited by Paul S. Fiddes)

"LIVING A LIFE"

5 Pamela Anderson and "Vulnerability" 52
   Alan Montefiore

6 Vulnerability as a Space for Creative Transformation 56
   Laurie Anderson Sathe

7 Pamela Sue Anderson – Witness to the Gospel, Prophet to the Church: What Might the Church Hear from her Work? 61
   Susan Durber

8   Equality and Prophecy   66
    Michèle Le Doeuff

ANDERSON'S CONVERSATIONS WITH OTHERS

9   Vulnerable Selves and Openness to Love   78
    Nicholas Bunnin

10 Pamela Sue Anderson's Journeying with Paul Ricoeur   82
    Morny Joy

11 Mortal Vulnerabilities: Reflecting on Death and Dying with Pamela
    Sue Anderson   95
    Alison Jasper

12 Forgiveness, Empathy and Vulnerability: An Unfinished
    Conversation with Pamela Sue Anderson   107
    Paul S. Fiddes

13 The Concern with Truth, Sense, et al. – Androcentric or
    Anthropocentric?   124
    A.W. Moore

EXTENDING THE CONVERSATIONS

14 Vulnerable and Invulnerable: Two Faces of Dialectical Reasoning   133
    Sabina Lovibond

15 Wisdom, Friendship and the Practice of Philosophy   139
    Beverley Clack

16 The Disavowal of the Female "Knower": Reading Literature in the Light of
    Pamela Sue Anderson's Project on Vulnerability   154
    Dorota Filipczak

17 Anderson's Ethical Vulnerability: Animating Feminist
    Responses to Sexual Violence   163
    Emily Cousens

18 Conditioned Responsibility, Belonging and the Vulnerability of Our Ethical
    Understanding   179
    Chon Tejedor

19 Love's Luck-knot: Emotional Vulnerability and Symmetrical Accountability   193
    Carla Bagnoli

	CONTENTS	
20	The Three Faces of Vulnerability: My Vulnerability, the Vulnerability of the Other and the Vulnerability of the Third *Xin Mao*	207
21	Anderson on Vulnerability *Alison Assiter*	220
22	A Threshold for Enhancing Human Life: Anderson on Capability and Vulnerability *Kristine A. Culp*	229
23	Exploring Affectivity: An Unfinished Conversation with Pamela Sue Anderson *Andrea Bieler*	243
24	The Openness of Vulnerability and Resilience *Roxana Baiasu*	252
25	The Risks of Love and the Ambiguities of Hope *Günter Thomas*	263
26	On the Theme of Liberated Love and Global Feminist Discourse *Ashmita Khasnabish*	273
27	The Idea of Ethical Vulnerability: Perfectionism, Irony and the Theological Virtues *Stephen Mulhall*	281
	Index	295

Citation Information

The chapters in this book were originally published in *Angelaki*, volume 25, issue 1–2 (Feb–Apr 2020). When citing this material, please use the original page numbering for each article, as follows:

Introduction
Love and Vulnerability: Thinking with Pamela Sue Anderson
Pelagia Goulimari
Angelaki, volume 25, issue 1–2 (Feb–Apr 2020) pp. 3–7

Chapter 1
Towards a New Philosophical Imaginary
Pamela Sue Anderson (edited by Sabina Lovibond and A.W. Moore)
Angelaki, volume 25, issue 1–2 (Feb–Apr 2020) pp. 8–22

Chapter 2
Reorienting Ourselves in (Bergsonian) Freedom, Friendship and Feminism
Pamela Sue Anderson (edited by Nicholas Bunnin)
Angelaki, volume 25, issue 1–2 (Feb–Apr 2020) pp. 23–35

Chapter 3
Silencing and Speaker Vulnerability: Undoing an Oppressive Form of (Wilful) Ignorance
Pamela Sue Anderson (edited by Nicholas Bunnin)
Angelaki, volume 25, issue 1–2 (Feb–Apr 2020) pp. 36–45

Chapter 4
Creating a New Imaginary for Love in Religion
Pamela Sue Anderson (edited by Paul S. Fiddes)
Angelaki, volume 25, issue 1–2 (Feb–Apr 2020) pp. 46–53

Chapter 5
Pamela Anderson and "Vulnerability"
Alan Montefiore
Angelaki, volume 25, issue 1–2 (Feb–Apr 2020) pp. 54–57

Chapter 6
Vulnerability as a Space for Creative Transformation
Laurie Anderson Sathe
Angelaki, volume 25, issue 1–2 (Feb–Apr 2020) pp. 58–62

Chapter 7
Pamela Sue Anderson – Witness to the Gospel, Prophet to the Church: What Might the Church Hear from her Work?
Susan Durber
Angelaki, volume 25, issue 1–2 (Feb–Apr 2020) pp. 63–67

Chapter 8
Equality and Prophecy
Michèle Le Doeuff
Angelaki, volume 25, issue 1–2 (Feb–Apr 2020) pp. 68–79

Chapter 9
Vulnerable Selves and Openness to Love
Nicholas Bunnin
Angelaki, volume 25, issue 1–2 (Feb–Apr 2020) pp. 80–83

Chapter 10
Pamela Sue Anderson's Journeying with Paul Ricoeur
Morny Joy
Angelaki, volume 25, issue 1–2 (Feb–Apr 2020) pp. 84–96

Chapter 11
Mortal Vulnerabilities: Reflecting on Death and Dying with Pamela Sue Anderson
Alison Jasper
Angelaki, volume 25, issue 1–2 (Feb–Apr 2020) pp. 97–108

Chapter 12
Forgiveness, Empathy and Vulnerability: An Unfinished Conversation with Pamela Sue Anderson
Paul S. Fiddes
Angelaki, volume 25, issue 1–2 (Feb–Apr 2020) pp. 109–125

Chapter 13
The Concern with Truth, Sense, et al. – Androcentric or Anthropocentric?
A.W. Moore
Angelaki, volume 25, issue 1–2 (Feb–Apr 2020) pp. 126–134

Chapter 14
Vulnerable and Invulnerable: Two Faces of Dialectical Reasoning
Sabina Lovibond
Angelaki, volume 25, issue 1–2 (Feb–Apr 2020) pp. 135–140

Chapter 15
Wisdom, Friendship and the Practice of Philosophy
Beverley Clack

Chapter 16
The Disavowal of the Female "Knower": Reading Literature in the Light of Pamela Sue Anderson's Project on Vulnerability
Dorota Filipczak

Chapter 17
Anderson's Ethical Vulnerability: Animating Feminist Responses to Sexual Violence
Emily Cousens

Chapter 18
Conditioned Responsibility, Belonging and the Vulnerability of Our Ethical Understanding
Chon Tejedor

Chapter 19
Love's Luck-knot: Emotional Vulnerability and Symmetrical Accountability
Carla Bagnoli

Chapter 20
The Three Faces of Vulnerability: My Vulnerability, the Vulnerability of the Other and the Vulnerability of the Third
Xin Mao

Chapter 21
Anderson on Vulnerability
Alison Assiter

Chapter 22
A Threshold for Enhancing Human Life: Anderson on Capability and Vulnerability
Kristine A. Culp

Chapter 23
Exploring Affectivity: An Unfinished Conversation with Pamela Sue Anderson
Andrea Bieler

Chapter 24
The Openness of Vulnerability and Resilience
Roxana Baiasu
Angelaki, volume 25, issue 1–2 (Feb–Apr 2020) pp. 254–264

Chapter 25
The Risks of Love and the Ambiguities of Hope
Günter Thomas
Angelaki, volume 25, issue 1–2 (Feb-Apr 2020) pp. 265–274

Chapter 26
On the Theme of Liberated Love and Global Feminist Discourse
Ashmita Khasnabish
Angelaki, volume 25, issue 1–2 (Feb–Apr 2020) pp. 275–283

Chapter 27
The Idea of Ethical Vulnerability: Perfectionism, Irony and the Theological Virtues
Stephen Mulhall
Angelaki, volume 25, issue 1–2 (Feb–Apr 2020) pp. 284–296

For any permission-related enquiries please visit:
http://www.tandfonline.com/page/help/permissions

Contributors

Laurie Anderson Sathe is Associate Professor and Program Director for the Master of Arts in Holistic Health Studies at St. Catherine University, Minneapolis, USA. Her research focus is on transformative learning and the intersection of the mind, body and spirit in health and healing. She is published in the *Journal of Transformative Education*; *Journal of Qualitative Inquiry*; *Text Matters: A Journal of Literature, Theology and Culture*; *American Journal of Occupational Therapy*; and *Journal of Research on Leadership Education*, and in the book *New Topics in Feminist Philosophy of Religion: Contestations and Transcendence Incarnate* (Springer, 2010).

Alison Assiter is Professor of Feminist Theory at the University of the West of England, Bristol, UK. She has published many monographs and articles in a wide range of journals and with many publishers. Her most recent monograph is *Kierkegaard, Eve and Metaphors of Birth* (Rowman & Littlefield, 2015). She is also the editor of Rowman & Littlefield's book series "Reframing the Boundaries: Thinking the Political." The first title was published in December 2014, and a number of books have been published since then. She is a founder editor of the journal *Feminist Dissent*.

Carla Bagnoli is Professor of Theoretical Philosophy at the University of Modena, Italy. She had been Professor II at the University of Oslo, Norway, and has held visiting positions at Harvard University, Cambridge, USA; at the École Normale Supérieure de Lyon, France; at the Université Paris 1 Panthéon-Sorbonne, France; at the University of Oxford, UK; and the Center for Advanced Studies at the Ludwig Maximilian University of Munich, Germany. She was tenured Full Professor at the University of Wisconsin, Madison, USA, where she had taught since 1998. Carla has been President of the Italian Society of Analytic Philosophy, and is a founding member of the Italian Society of Women in Philosophy. In addition to articles in ethics, moral epistemology and moral psychology, she has published four monographs on moral dilemmas, the limits of ethical theory, the authority of morality and responsibility. She has edited *Morality and the Emotions* (Oxford UP, 2011), and *Constructivism in Ethics* (Cambridge UP, 2013).

Roxana Baiasu is Tutorial Fellow in Philosophy at the Stanford University Centre, Oxford, UK, and a member of the Philosophy Faculty at the University of Oxford, UK. She is writing in the areas of post-Kantian metaphysics and epistemology, philosophy of religion and feminist philosophy. She edited (with G. Bird and A.W. Moore) *Contemporary Kantian Metaphysics Today: New Essays on Time and Space* (Palgrave Macmillan, 2012), and published in, among others, the *Southern Journal of Philosophy*, *IJPS*, *Research in Phenomenology* and *Sophia*. She is a member of the Editorial Board of *Studia*

Phaenomenologica. Roxana is a Convener of the Oxford Forum which she co-founded with Pamela Sue Anderson in 2008.

Andrea Bieler is Professor of Practical Theology at the Divinity School of Basel University, Switzerland. She is the author/editor of 14 books and numerous essays, for example, *Verletzliches Leben. Horizonte einer Theologie der Seelsorge* (Vandenhoeck & Ruprecht, 2017).

Nicholas Bunnin is Emeritus Director of the Philosophy Project at the China Centre at the University of Oxford, UK, and a member of the Oxford Faculty of Philosophy. Since co-founding the Philosophy Summer School in China in 1988, he has worked to promote deeply creative engagements between Chinese and Western philosophers. He has brought his own analytic philosophical perspective to his reflections on both Chinese philosophy and phenomenology and its aftermath, as well as to his study of Plato, Aristotle, Kant and Wittgenstein. In his current project, he seeks to characterize a philosophy of the humanities to complement, rather than replace, philosophy of science as a fundamental framework for philosophical thinking.

Beverley Clack is Professor in the Philosophy of Religion at Oxford Brookes University, UK. Her publications include *Misogyny in the Western Philosophical Tradition* (Macmillan, 1999), *Sex and Death: A Reappraisal of Human Mortality* (Polity, 2002), *Freud on the Couch* (OneWorld, 2013) and *Philosophy of Religion: A Critical Introduction* (co-authored with Brian R. Clack; the third edition was published by Polity in 2019). With Pamela Sue Anderson she co-edited *Feminist Philosophy of Religion: Critical Readings* (Routledge, 2004). Her most recent publication is a collection of essays, co-edited with Michele Paule, titled *Interrogating the Neoliberal Lifecycle: The Limits of Success* (Palgrave Macmillan, 2019).

Emily Cousens is Early Career Researcher and Lecturer, specializing in feminism and queer theory. She has written articles and book reviews on feminist temporalities, Judith Butler and Sara Ahmed. Her doctoral thesis explored "Vulnerability and the Feminist Politics of Sexual Violence." Emily holds BA and MA degrees from the University of Oxford, UK, and completed her Ph.D. at Oxford Brookes University, UK. Emily currently teaches at the University of Oxford and the London School of Economics, UK. She has previously been Associate Lecturer at Oxford Brookes University, UK, and Visiting Lecturer at the University of Hertfordshire, UK. Emily is the Founder of the London School of Critical Feminisms, an annual intimate week-long summer school which charges no fees.

Kristine A. Culp teaches at the University of Chicago, USA, where she is Associate Professor of Theology in the Divinity School and in the Fundamentals: Texts and Issues programme in the College. Since 1991, she has been Dean of the Disciples Divinity House of the University of Chicago, USA, one of the university's oldest affiliates. She is one of 35 scholars in the interdisciplinary Enhancing Life Project, funded by the John Templeton Foundation; her research is on the experience of "aliveness" in relation to creaturely vulnerability and resilience. She is the author of *Vulnerability and Glory: A Theological Account* (Westminster John Knox, 2010), one of the first theological works to engage multidisciplinary analyses of vulnerability and risk, and the editor of *The Responsibility of the Church for Society and Other Essays* by H. Richard Niebuhr (Westminster John Knox, 2008). Her essays have addressed protest and resistance as theological themes, the use of fiction in theological thinking, feminist and womanist theologies and the appeal to "experience" in contemporary theology. She serves on numerous boards and advisory panels, including the Faith and Order Commission of the World Council of Churches.

Susan Durber first met Pamela in 1979, when they both became students at Mansfield College, Oxford, UK. As a direct result of their friendship, Susan went on to study at Luther Northwestern Seminary, USA, and later to work on a doctorate on the work of Jacques Derrida and its significance for biblical studies. Susan is a Minister of the United Reformed Church presently serving in Taunton in Somerset and is the present Moderator of the Faith and Order Commission of the World Council of Churches. She is a former Principal of Westminster College, Cambridge, UK, and a former Theology Advisor for Christian Aid.

Paul S. Fiddes is Professor of Systematic Theology at the University of Oxford, UK, and Director of Research at Regent's Park College, Oxford, UK. He is Principal Emeritus of the College and an Honorary Fellow of St Peter's College, Oxford, UK. His research interests include the interface between modern theology, literature and Continental philosophy. Among his many publications are *The Creative Suffering of God* (Clarendon, 1988), *Past Event and Present Salvation: The Christian Idea of Atonement* (Darton, Longman and Todd, 1989), *Freedom and Limit: A Dialogue between Literature and Christian Doctrine* (Macmillan, 1991), *The Promised End: Eschatology in Theology and Literature* (Blackwell, 2000), *Participating in God: A Pastoral Doctrine of the Trinity* (Westminster John Knox, 2000), *Seeing the World and Knowing God: Hebrew Wisdom and Christian Doctrine in a Late-Modern Context* (Oxford UP, 2013).

Dorota Filipczak teaches literatures in English and translation theory at the University of Łódź. She has published extensively on Canadian and British writers. Her most recent monograph is *Brian Moore's Eponymous Heroines: Representations of Women and Authorial Boundaries* (Lang, 2018). She founded and runs *Text Matters: A Journal of Literature, Theory and Culture*. She is the author of seven books of poetry and a member of the Association of Polish Writers.

Pelagia Goulimari is a member of the Faculty of English Language and Literature at the University of Oxford, UK, where she teaches women's writing, feminist theory and literary theory. She is the Co-Director of the interdisciplinary Oxford M.St. in Women's Studies, and of the Women in the Humanities programme at the Oxford Research Centre in the Humanities (TORCH). Her publications include the single-authored books: *Toni Morrison* (Routledge, 2009) and *Literary Criticism and Theory: From Plato to Postcolonialism* (Routledge, 2014), and the edited collections: *Postmodernism. What Moment?* (Manchester UP, 2007) and *Women Writing Across Cultures: Present, Past, Future* (Routledge, 2017). She is the Editor-in-Chief of *Angelaki: Journal of the Theoretical Humanities* (Routledge). Her publications in 2020 include *The Oxford Research Encyclopaedia of Literary Theory* (Oxford UP), co-edited with John Frow et al., where she is also contributing articles on "Genders" and "Feminist Theory," and the article "'Where Are You (Really) From?' Transgender Ethics, Ethics of Unknowing, and Transformative Adoption in Jackie Kay's *Trumpet* and Toni Morrison's *Jazz*" in the edited collection *Contemporary African American and Black British Women Writers: Narrative, Race, Ethics*, eds. Jean Wyatt and Sheldon George (Routledge).

Alison Jasper is Senior Lecturer in Religion and Gender at the University of Stirling, UK. Coming from a background in Religious Education teaching in England, since gaining her Ph.D. at Glasgow University, UK, she has integrated a range of disciplinary approaches in education, feminist theology and theory, and critical religion. At Stirling she was instrumental in setting up the Masters programme in Gender Studies and also contributed to the M.Sc. programme in Professional Education and Leadership, and the undergraduate programme in Religion. Recent publications include "Reflections on Reading the Bible: Flesh to Female Genius" in *The Bible and Feminism: Remapping the Field*, eds. Yvonne Sherwood and Anna Fisk (Oxford UP, 2017); "Collaborations and Renegotiations: Re-examining the 'Sacred' in the Film-Making of David Gulpilil and Rolf de Heer," *Literature and Theology* 31 (June 2017); and with John I'Anson, *Schooling Indifference: Reimagining RE in Multi-cultural and Gendered Spaces* ("Gender, Theology and Spirituality") (Routledge, 2017).

Morny Joy gained a Ph.D. from McGill University, Montreal, Canada, sand she spent a two-year postdoctoral fellowship studying with Paul Ricoeur at the University of Chicago, USA. She researches and publishes in the areas of philosophy and religion, postcolonialism and intercultural studies in South and Southeast Asia, as well as in diverse projects on women and religion. In recent years she has published two edited books, *Continental Philosophy and Philosophy of Religion* (Springer, 2011) and *Women, Religion, and the Gift: An Abundance of Riches* (Springer, 2017). In 2011 she received an Honorary Doctorate from the University of Helsinki, Finland, and she is also a Life Fellow at Clare Hall at the University of Cambridge, UK.

Ashmita Khasnabish is currently a Lecturer at Lasell College, Boston, USA, and was a Research Scholar of the Asiatic Society, India; a Visiting Scholar at MIT, Brandeis, Brown and Oxford Universities; taught at Emerson College, Lesley and Boston Universities; and lectured widely in Europe, North America and India. She is a Fellow of the Royal Asiatic Society, London. She has authored three monographs, namely *Jouissance as Ananda: Indian Philosophy, Feminist Theory, and Literature* (Lexington, 2006, 2003), *Humanitarian Identity and the Political Sublime: Intervention of a Postcolonial Feminist* (Lexington, 2009) and *Negotiating Capability and Diaspora: A Philosophical Politics* (Lexington, 2016, 2013), and many articles in refereed journals and book chapters. Forthcoming publications include the monograph *Virtual Diaspora: Postcolonial Feminism* and the edited anthology *Postcoloniality, Globalization, and Diaspora: What's Next?*

Michèle Le Doeuff grew up in Brittany and then read philosophy at the École Normale Supérieure de Fontenay and at the Sorbonne. A number of her articles have appeared in English, along with three books: *The Philosophical Imaginary* (Athlone, 1989; Continuum, 2002), *Hipparchia's Choice: An Essay Concerning Women, Philosophy, etc.* (Blackwell, 1990; Columbia UP, 2007); and *The Sex of Knowing* (Routledge, 2003). After being a Professeure Ordinaire at Geneva, she became a Director of Research at the CNRS in Paris. A pioneer of Simone de Beauvoir Studies, she also translated Bacon's *New Atlantis* and *Advancement of Learning* and Shakespeare's *Venus and Adonis*.

Sabina Lovibond is Emeritus Fellow of Worcester College, Oxford, UK, where she taught Philosophy from 1982 to 2011. She is the author of *Realism and Imagination in Ethics* (Basil Blackwell, 1983); *Ethical Formation* (Harvard UP, 2002); *Iris Murdoch, Gender and Philosophy* (Routledge, 2011); and *Essays on Ethics and Feminism* (Oxford UP, 2015).

Xin Mao is postdoctoral fellow in the Department of Philosophy at Sun Yat-Sen University, Zhuhai Campus, China. She was a student of Pamela Sue Anderson in the 2009 Philosophy Summer School in China. She received her Ph.D. from King's College London in 2017 with her thesis titled "Subjectivity, Infinite Ethical Responsibility and Null-Site Exposure:

A Constructive Exploration of Levinasian Subjectivity through the Lens of the Levinasian Concept of Utopia." Her recent publications include "A Levinasian Reconstruction of the Political Significance of Vulnerability," "Transformation from Real-Centredness to Other-Centredness: A Levinasian Re-appraisal of John Hick's Religious Pluralism" and "The Religiosity of Populism: The Sanctified and Abused Power of the People" in the journals, *Religions* and *Journal for the Study of Religions and Ideologies*.

Alan Montefiore was for more than 30 years a Fellow and Tutor in Philosophy at Balliol College, Oxford, UK. He is now an Emeritus Fellow of that College, and since the founding of the Forum for European Philosophy in 1996 has been its President. He has worked and published on a wide diversity of topics, including moral and political philosophy; contemporary French philosophy; philosophy of education; and, more specifically, on issues of identity and responsibility. His most recent book is *A Philosophical Retrospective: Facts, Values, and Jewish Identity* (Columbia UP, 2011).

A. W. Moore is Professor of Philosophy at the University of Oxford, UK, and Vice-Principal of St Hugh's College, Oxford, UK. He has published four books: *The Infinite* (Routledge, 1990, a third edition of which has just been published); *Points of View* (Clarendon, 1997); *Noble in Reason, Infinite in Faculty: Themes and Variations in Kant's Moral and Religious Philosophy* (Routledge, 2003); and *The Evolution of Modern Metaphysics: Making Sense of Things* (Cambridge UP, 2011). A collection of his essays titled *Language, World, and Limits: Essays in Philosophy of Language and Metaphysics* is forthcoming.

Stephen Mulhall is Professor of Philosophy and a Fellow of New College, Oxford, UK. His interests include Wittgenstein, Heidegger and Nietzsche; the relationship between philosophy and theology; and the relationship between philosophy and the arts, especially film and literature.

Chon Tejedor is Profesora de Filosofiá at the University of Valencia, Spain. Previously, she was Senior Lecturer in Philosophy at the University of Hertfordshire (2014–17) and, for 12 years, Lecturer in Philosophy at the University of Oxford (2002–14), UK. She read Philosophy, Politics, and Economics at the University of Oxford, UK, for her undergraduate degree, before completing a Masters and Doctorate in Philosophy at University College London, UK. Her publications include two books: *The Early Wittgenstein on Metaphysics, Natural Science, Language and Value* (Routledge, 2015) and *Starting with Wittgenstein* (Bloomsbury, 2011).

Günter Thomas is Professor of Systematic Theology at Ruhr-University Bochum, Germany, and Research Associate at the Faculty of Public Theology at the University of Stellenbosch, South Africa. His fields of research are constructive theology, systems theory, medical anthropology and religion and media. He has been (with William Schweiker) Principal Investigator of the Enhancing Life Project.

EDITORIAL INTRODUCTION

pelagia goulimari

LOVE AND VULNERABILITY
thinking with pamela sue anderson

Love and Vulnerability: Thinking with Pamela Sue Anderson grew around a critical dialogue with feminist philosopher Pamela Sue Anderson's extraordinary, unpublished last work on love and vulnerability – work interrupted by her early death from cancer in March 2017. The first part of the collection publishes this work, edited by close colleagues and friends, for the first time. The work consists of four interconnected pieces, entitled: "Towards a New Philosophical Imaginary"; "Reorienting Ourselves in (Bergsonian) Freedom, Friendship and Feminism"; "Silencing and Speaker Vulnerability: Undoing an Oppressive Form of (Wilful) Ignorance"; and "Creating a New Imaginary for Love in Religion."

In a second part, a diverse, multidisciplinary, international range of contributors respond to Anderson's last work, her oeuvre, and her life and death: philosophers working both in the Continental and Analytic traditions, theologians, literary and cultural critics, political theorists, and others. These include her sister, her former doctoral supervisor, former students, close friends, collaborators, colleagues, and those who knew her only through her written work.

Pamela Sue Anderson is perhaps best known for her path-breaking work in philosophy of religion, including: *A Feminist Philosophy of Religion* (1998) and *Re-visioning Gender in Philosophy of Religion: Reason, Love and Epistemic Locatedness* (2012). She was Tutorial Fellow in Philosophy and Christian Ethics at Regent's Park College, Oxford, from 2001, and in 2014 she was deservedly awarded the title of Professor of Modern European Philosophy of Religion by the University of Oxford.

She was awarded an honorary doctorate by the University of Lund as a Pioneer in Feminist Philosophy of Religion. Anderson was also, in exemplary fashion, a *friend* – to her students, colleagues, and collaborators: a source of generous support, fun and joy, profoundly interested and forever discussing and championing someone else's work, as many contributors to this volume attest. Michèle Le Doeuff, in her contribution, shares their "many studious holidays together":

> work until you drop! She was worse than me in that respect and sometimes I thought it necessary to try to moderate her, to no avail ever. At any rate, we both enjoyed ourselves a lot while at the same time believing in

what we were doing; fits of laughter were frequent.

Her former student Emily Cousens recalls in her contribution "Pamela's own performance of vulnerability-as-generosity [...] In both life and writing, she demonstrated the transformational character of vulnerability: its implication in violence but also in generative relationalities such as love and friendship too."

Anderson's death was a blow to many; in my own experience, it was a personal loss of a friend, but also a severe collective loss to the Oxford women's studies programme in and across the Humanities (including the interdisciplinary MSt in Women's Studies, the Women's Studies Steering Committee, and the TORCH Women in the Humanities programme). Many are contributing to this volume in order to continue their conversation with her. *Friendship, conversation, dialogue, collective work, collaboration*: these were constant themes and preoccupations in her work as well as a way of life for her; they are intricately connected to her understanding of love and vulnerability. She describes her conversion to a "relational ontology" in "Towards a New Philosophical Imaginary." Her friendship was not indiscriminate and unconditional, but she was not factional or cliquey. She was drawn to open and dynamic groups and communities, as she theorizes them in "Reorienting Ourselves in (Bergsonian) Freedom, Friendship and Feminism." Or, when these were lacking, she sought open and dynamic ways of relating to communities. She was an energetic but also very *critical* member of *several* communities – communities that might be deemed mutually exclusive. Was she working in the Continental tradition or the Analytic tradition, or seeking ways to bridge the two? What was the nature of her relationship to the Christian Church, the institution of philosophy, the Oxford Faculty of Philosophy, academic feminism, and so on? On these questions and others, there is no agreement among the contributors in this volume. But she was undoubtedly drawn to collaborations, and her late and last work, in particular, was connected to two collaborative research projects: The Enhancing Life project funded by the Templeton Foundation and the Love in Religion project at Regent's Park College. (See <http://enhancinglife.uchicago.edu/> and <loveinreligion.org>.)

Anderson's last work focused on reimagining love and vulnerability. Extending Michèle Le Doeuff's critique of the "philosophical imaginary" – the repertoire of unexamined myths and narratives underlying philosophical thinking, and acting as an unthought element within thought – Anderson critiques and then attempts to rebuild the concepts of love and vulnerability. We tend to fear vulnerability as an exposure to violence and suffering. We often project a vulnerability we all share onto "the vulnerable." We value our perceived invulnerability or strive for a goal of invulnerability. Such has been the nature of our philosophical imaginary but also our social imaginary, Anderson claims. She then proposes a bold reorientation. Let us think of vulnerability, also, as a capability we all share; an occasion, opportunity, or condition of possibility for a transformative and life-enhancing openness to others and mutual affection.

Granted, ontological vulnerability – whether personal or social, whether bodily or emotional – does not in itself necessarily lead to reciprocal affection. But we might envisage an "ethical" and, in some sense to be specified, rational vulnerability that aims to do so, under certain conditions of self-reflexive and reciprocal accountability. (On conditions and limits, see, for example, Paul Fiddes' discussion of Anderson's understanding of the limits of forgiveness and restorative justice in this volume.) "Ethical" vulnerability works closely with the project of identifying and eliminating social vulnerability and structural injustice. The task to reimagine love and vulnerability is enormous and all too clearly significant, especially in times of erecting borders between "us" and "them." Anderson discusses the "war on terror" in "Towards a New Philosophical Imaginary." She talks about attitudes to migrants and refugees in "Creating a New Imaginary for Love in Religion":

a dark social imaginary continues to stigmatize those needing to be cared for as a drain on an economy, carefully separating "the cared for" from those who are thought to be "in control" of their lives and of the world. As the political myth suggests, "we" do not want too many of "them," for example migrants and refugees.

But one might readily think of other examples. Anderson's overall project is, I believe, in the interest of social justice; one of its aims is to end the wilful ignorance of social vulnerability and structural injustice, as she explains in "Silencing and Speaker Vulnerability: Undoing an Oppressive Form of (Wilful) Ignorance." In this project, reason, critical self-reflexivity, emotion, intuition and imagination, concepts, arguments, myths, and narrative all have a role to play, according to Anderson, while also needing to be reimagined and rethought.

This volume and the conference that preceded it were conceived during the Thanksgiving and Memorial Service for Pamela Sue Anderson on 18 March 2017 at Mansfield College, Oxford – and quickly dubbed Pamela's conference and Pamela's edited collection. During the service, extracts from Anderson's last work on love and vulnerability, overflowing with life, were used by one of the speakers, Kate Kirkpatrick, to console the mourners in their grief. A dossier of Anderson's unpublished last work and selected, relevant published work was soon compiled by me – with generous help from Laurie Anderson Sathe, Nicholas Bunnin, Beverley Clack, Paul Fiddes, Kate Kirkpatrick, and A.W. Moore – and Anderson's collaborators and colleagues, over the course of her career, were invited to respond to this newly created dossier. An international conference soon materialized: "Love and Vulnerability: In Memory of Pamela Sue Anderson," at Mansfield College and Regent's Park College, on 16–18 March 2018. The conference organizing committee – Roxana Baiasu, Nicholas Bunnin, Paul Fiddes, Sabina Lovibond, and myself as chair – was supported by Laurie Anderson Sathe, Kate Kirkpatrick, A.W. Moore, and Katherine Morris. The running of the conference itself was supported by three students: Emily Cousens, Vanilla Parthiban, and Yaron Wolf. On an unusually snowy Oxford spring day, the unusual diversity of Anderson's different intellectual communities came together for the first time and in embodied form, triggering surprising interactions and conversations which this volume continues.

The conference was memorable, by all accounts, in that it brought life and academic work powerfully together. We are grateful to the following for providing funding and support: the Oxford Faculty of Philosophy, the Oxford Faculty of Theology and Religion, the Oxford Research Centre in the Humanities (TORCH), the Philosophical Fellowship Fund, Mansfield College, and Regent's Park College. Most conference papers were subsequently reworked and peer-reviewed for inclusion in this collection, and some additional pieces peer-reviewed or specially commissioned. Many thanks to our peer-reviewers for their thoroughness: Alison Assiter, Roxana Baiasu, Andrea Bieler, Nicholas Bunnin, Beverley Clack, Kristine A. Culp, Susan Durber, Paul Fiddes, Alison Jasper, Morny Joy, Kate Kirkpatrick, Sabina Lovibond, Xin Mao, Mari Mikkola, A.W. Moore, Katherine Morris, Chon Tejedor, Günter Thomas, and Heather Walton. Grateful thanks, also, to Paula Boddington, Elizabeth Frazer and Kimberly Hutchings, Heike Springhart, and Heather Walton, who enriched the conference with their papers but were unable to rework them for publication. Gerard Greenway and James Hypher provided unstinting in-house editorial support throughout the publication process.

The Contents pages opening this volume will, I hope, have already suggested the breadth and diversity of contributors, some of whom are highly distinguished – "at the top" of their field and needing no introduction – while others are at the beginning of promising careers. I will not be introducing all twenty-seven pieces individually, but let me sketch out the volume, in broad outline. Some contributors trace the emergence of Anderson's late thinking on love, vulnerability, and related concepts in her earlier work or offer synthetic accounts of her oeuvre around these concepts. Others rejoin and critically extend one or more of Anderson's own conversations with a number of fields and thinkers: Baruch Spinoza, Immanuel Kant, Henri Bergson, Emmanuel Levinas, Simone de Beauvoir, Paul Ricoeur, Gilles Deleuze, bell hooks, Patricia Hill Collins, Judith Butler, and Anderson's friends Paul Fiddes, Michèle Le Doeuff, and A.W. Moore. Some bring Anderson's work in contact with other thinkers and debates – debates in theology; Continental and Analytic philosophy; feminist, queer, and transgender theory; postcolonial theory; African-American studies; and wider debates about the future of the university, the Me Too movement, sweatshops, climate change, and so on. Thinkers, writers, artists, and activists brought into conversation with Anderson by contributors include: Hannah Arendt, Sri Aurobindo, John Broome, Wendy Brown, Tarana Burke, Havi Carel, Stanley Cavell, Ananya Chatterjea, Judy Chicago, Stefan Collini, George Eliot, Martha Fineman, Miranda Fricker, Thomas Fuchs, Jesus, Søren Kierkegaard, Margaret Laurence, Jonathan Lear, Niklas Luhmann, Maurice Merleau-Ponty, John Stuart Mill, Martha Nussbaum, Michael Oakeshott, Plato, Michèle Roberts, Matthew Sanford, Amartya Sen, Ludwig Wittgenstein, and Iris Marion Young.

To turn now to key concepts, themes, and topics, some contributors focus on vulnerability or aspects of it, including: emotional vulnerability; corporeal vulnerability, dying and death; illness and resilience; sexual violence; social vulnerability; the vulnerability of Jesus. Others discuss love and vulnerability, often as part of a larger constellation of concepts and themes, including: (symmetrical) accountability; affectivity; capability; empathy; epistemic justice; feminism; forgiveness; friendship; hope; the human; institutional critique; intuition; metaphysical and ethical unity; narrative; neoliberalism; philosophical nonsense; responsibility; restorative justice; risk; structural injustice; transformation; transformative justice; wilful ignorance; women in philosophy.

The unusually wide range of Anderson's interests and commitments was due partly to her determination to accept no intellectual master and to think for herself, in friendship and feminism. Anchoring all her interests and commitments was her feminism, particularly the issues of finding a place for feminist philosophy and a place for women in philosophy. This is why she personally made provisions for the Pamela Sue Anderson Studentship for the Encouragement of the Place of Women in Philosophy. In my view, these are strategic and pragmatic goals having to do with her particular time, place, and location. But what kind of feminist is Anderson? In addition to the aforementioned Beauvoir, Butler, Collins, Le Doeuff, and hooks, other important interlocutors were Sandra Harding, Julia Kristeva, and quite a few of the contributors to this volume. She was certainly not the kind of feminist who believed in the primacy of gender over race, sexual orientation, class, and other vectors. Nor was she only or primarily fighting discrimination against (white, cis, straight) women. As "Silencing and Speaker Vulnerability: Undoing an Oppressive Form of (Wilful) Ignorance" makes clear, she was committed to ending all forms of discrimination. I remember her closing her October 2017 Feminist Theory lecture on Simone de Beauvoir – in Room 11 of Examination Schools, a room adorned with portraits exclusively of "serious" and "respectable" men at the time – with enthusiastic discussion of Julia Serano's *Whipping Girl*. This was the last Feminist Theory lecture she ever delivered, and transfeminist issues were clearly high on her agenda. Her readings in feminists of colour (including queer theorists and transgender theorists) were perhaps somewhat limited in range, but the programmatic commitment was there. In another time and place, her intersectional and interdisciplinary inclinations might have had more scope to grow.

Anderson's last work is exceptionally good to think with, I believe. It casts a wide net, reaching out for help wherever she can find it. These last essays are fearlessly synthetic. They have a constructivist spirit, moving at speed, fleet of foot, from one ally to the next to build themselves. They are acts of the imagination at least as much as they rely on tight argumentation. As Anderson's former doctoral supervisor, Alan Montefiore, puts it in this volume: "This is a philosophy of 'Look at it in this way rather than in that.'" The pace and sketchiness of execution inevitably leave unanswered questions but effectively require the reader's collaboration. In their airiness and spaciousness, these last essays are good to think with. In painterly terms, they are a combination of impressionistic sketch, rooted in the moment, and high abstraction. Though Anderson's interest in vulnerability was life-long and preceded her cancer diagnosis and her experience of living with terminal cancer, her work must have found a testing ground in that experience. And yet there is nothing preachy about her voice, but much aliveness. It is a living voice vividly addressing its audience in an invitation to think together. It is a young voice, like the voice of the young girl, Dawn, that she reprises, following Le Doeuff, in "Towards a New Philosophical Imaginary."

In collectively thinking about how to edit Anderson's last writings, we (Anderson Sathe, Bunnin, Fiddes, Lovibond, Moore, and myself) decided to aim for the light touch. There was a quirkiness to the documents – for example, in Anderson's use of red, bold, and underline – that we decided to retain as much as possible. There is also an element of repetition in the four pieces. Most notably, a section of "Silencing and Speaker Vulnerability: Undoing an Oppressive Form of (Wilful) Ignorance" reappears in the middle section of "Creating a New Imaginary for Love in Religion," where it serves as an example.

Some of the contributors themselves were keen to emulate the unstuffy, unfinished, conversational quality of Anderson's last work. Some contributions are quite deliberately brief, bare, and intent on doing without the usual markers of "serious" academic scholarship, such as full, exhaustive referencing. Others have joined the conversation in lively critique of Anderson's work, determined to avoid numbing eulogy and deadening hagiography to keep her work alive. Yet others have honoured her commitment to fighting social vulnerability and structural injustice, including epistemic injustice, by reconnecting her work to ongoing institutional critique of philosophy, the university, the Church – and political activism. Some contributions were very much in the spirit of doing things with Pamela or going on a trip with Pamela. Nicholas Bunnin captures the hopes of many for this volume in his piece:

> When I outlined my plans for this essay to Adrian Moore, I confessed worries that I might be imposing my own preoccupations on Pamela's thinking. He reassured me that my worries were most likely fully justified, but at least the essay would show how talking with Pamela could stimulate fresh thinking in others.

introduction

It is my contention that a new philosophical imaginary – which would transform the myths we live by[2] – is needed to reconceive our affections, love and vulnerability. In this paper, I would like to appropriate Judith Butler's relational ontology for the purpose of transforming a patriarchal myth which projects onto "vulnerability" only negative affects, notably fear and shame. The result of this projection has been violence in the name of paternalistic control and/or excessive "protection" of a class, named "the vulnerable," who, as I will show, are treated as another class, or separate group; this control and so-called protection of the vulnerable merely generates more fear and/or greater inhibitions overall, undermining social and political relations.

My proposal for transformation aims at liberating love and vulnerability from the excessive fear and violence which has been conveyed mythically by our (Western) philosophical imaginary. This transformation would mean that, for instance, the affect of shame, which arises after intimate violence, could become reparative (or, in other words, redemptive) and not only negative (shameful). Moreover, there is the capability for mutual affection in vulnerability. Ultimately the aim of my current research is to set out possibilities for a new philosophical imaginary, in which *vulnerability is (re)conceived as a capability for an openness to mutual affection*; but developing this new (or, possibly renewed), more nuanced concept of vulnerability will require reciprocity in our affective, conative and cognitive relations. In particular, developing reciprocal affections in vulnerability would help to revise a weak

pamela sue anderson

edited by sabina lovibond and a.w. moore

TOWARDS A NEW PHILOSOPHICAL IMAGINARY[1]

concept of love: reciprocity would facilitate loving affection in mutual, self and other relations. But this affecting needs to be learnt by allowing ourselves to attend to each other – as I will try to show – "tenderly," respectfully, sincerely and so, lovingly.

In all seriousness, we would need to attend to politically induced "vulnerabilities" – what Butler might call "precarity" – for instance, homelessness. Insofar as concrete manifestations of these vulnerabilities are generated affectively by politically motivated patriarchal myth, they can be extremely difficult to recognize, in order to bring about new action-guiding concepts (of love and vulnerability). Negative affections are embedded in the differential privileging of (e.g., white Western; or Middle-Eastern...) fathers above all other social types; and mythical gender types have differentiated the vulnerable in this hierarchical and divisive manner. Instead, it will be crucial to see vulnerability as a universal, while its concrete manifestations will be socially and historically differentiated. In other words, I will follow Butler's lead with a relational ontology, in which vulnerability is a (universal) mode of relationality and not "the human condition."

(how) do religions interpret, or project, gender (on) vulnerability?

Religions can be agencies for care of "the vulnerable"; but if treating the latter as an inferior class, or problematic/pitiful people, we do an injustice: we reduce their humanity, giving them lesser social identities; we see this in demeaning on the grounds of "differences" in gender, race, sexual orientation, ethnicity and so on.

My focus might appear both abstract and ambitious when I claim that our (current/dominant) philosophical imaginary has configured, in its mythical images, narratives and symbols, a separate class of "the vulnerable." Yet a certain degree of abstraction is necessary for us, in order to gain the larger picture of how pejorative meanings of "the vulnerable" are often unwittingly attributed to "the feminine," when the latter is conceived as weak and woundable; this is especially the case in (general) descriptions of women, children, the disabled, etc. In this rendering of vulnerability, the vulnerable/feminine is in need of protection, even when this means (more) violent acts; and love here tends to become a patronizing form of – to be honest – unhelpful, and possibly oppressive, control.

That this ideologically driven myth associates vulnerability with "the wound," affecting negative forms of (on the one hand) dependency and (on the other hand) over-protection, and issuing in controlling forms of violence (e.g., getting the upper hand in the global war on terror), is clearly apparent in a (major) paternalistic response to vulnerability; and this paternalistic response is supposedly made on behalf of the vulnerable. My points about paternalism and patriarchal control are not new; but I maintain them, in order to support my argument *that paternalism decisively damages the life-enhancing capability of the vulnerable.* Generally speaking, we can see how myth is implicit in our twenty-first-century lives, guided globally by the social media which now span political worlds; but this complex, global network often obscures the extent to which "we" are controlled by (mythical) gender impositions. Feminist philosophers are all too aware of how a philosophical imaginary of violence is "the shameful face" of (Western) philosophy.[3]

In response I am arguing that we begin to re-vision the gender implicit in that pervasive imaginary, hierarchically structured by myth concerning vulnerability; this re-visioning would aim to liberate the loving qualities, which freely emerge in response to a new narrative/myth. Inspired by Michèle Le Doeuff, I am considering how to reconfigure the vulnerability of a young girl, named "Dawn."[4] This new narrative about Dawn develops images for transforming the philosophical imaginary of gender/vulnerability and violence into a new philosophical imaginary of love, vulnerability and affection.

The renewed mythical, conceptual persona of the young girl, Dawn, helps to imagine the light of a new day, "Daybreak" – as Nietzsche describes it – generating imagery of affection which enlightens, rather than reactive fear which darkens, our lives and loves. In a relationally autonomous process, each of us in relation to Dawn, who reasons with her heart, can learn to cultivate our attentive, cognitive and conative capability. Dawn's pre-adolescent vulnerability – especially her heart which is vulnerable, yet motivates her reason – can be cultivated in mutual responses of reciprocal attentiveness and tenderness, in herself as much as in others. Instead of oppressive forms of control, fear and violence, our reciprocally cultivated relations to Dawn will allow her heart to remain free: she is and we are free to reason with one another, in order to grow up both loving freely and, at the same time, being tenderly loved. Thus Dawn symbolizes – for a new philosophical imaginary – love's capability to see reality, to know the world and to strive to love humanity. Both men and women, in becoming enlightened (by Dawn) would have to seek the reparative ground of vulnerability, if we are to recover love's capable vulnerability from humanity's self-inflicted incapability (to love and become open to mutual affection).[5]

Narrative imagery expresses Dawn's enlightening qualities. In particular, the imaginary portrays the movement of stories about appropriately attending to her "heart" which, in this mythology, would liberate love's capability.[6] The task will be to recognize that vulnerability as wound-ability conditions the possibility not only of hurting and healing, but of transforming fear and violence (that has been perpetuated out of excessive fear for oneself and for one's beloved) into loving affects allowing for our graceful differences.

Roughly, the myths implicit in our philosophical (social) imaginary motivate us either to retain or to reconceive the imagery, stories and values associated with vulnerability; rethinking those myths is a first step towards transforming our reciprocal affections – of either violence, and fear due to that violence, or love, and confidence in that love. In other words, we can learn new, reciprocal relations of love by attending to what is most precious – and here I am reminded of Saint-Exupéry's story of "the Little Prince" who not only learns how to "tame" the fox, but recognizes the sense in which regularly attending to his "rose" has made her unique in all the world.[7] Thus, in responding to vulnerability as an openness to mutual affection we create love and friendship, while still knowing that violence might disrupt this picture; and yet we are able to transform the affects which cut us off from love and from a life which counts (if lost, this life would be grieved); that is, this life would be liveable and grievable.

vulnerability as a mode of relationality

In Judith Butler's essay "Violence, Mourning, Politics" (chapter 2 of her *Precarious Life*), she aims to bring together corporeal vulnerability, political life, exposure to violence, and mourning loss of life, e.g., the death of a loved one. What connects these lived experiences is, according to Butler, "a constitutive sociality"; this means that our relationally or, if you like, "socially" constituted bodies exist prior to an "I"; and this means that relationality is prior to a self. In the past I have rejected the very idea of a relational ontology – assuming, instead, a fundamental ontology of a self was necessary on largely Kantian grounds. However, my more recent reading and thinking about vulnerability, its affects and connections to love, have made Butler's account of relationality – and vulnerability as "a mode of relationality" – a serious challenge to my previous thinking; so much so that I have had to allow myself to be transformed by a new understanding of affects and affections in motivating love, and in reconceiving vulnerability. In particular, Butler's proposals have motivated me to open up new insight on vulnerability as a mode of relationality, and to argue against certain myths of vulnerability by which we currently – largely unwittingly – live. Or, at least I would like to develop a cogent argument which would change our assumptions about vulnerability – and, by extension, change our assumptions about love. In the longer term, as imagined in the first section of my paper, my aim is a new philosophical imaginary.

Butler's main thesis, in "Violence, Mourning, Politics," is not exactly the heart of an "argument." Instead, what I take to be her main thesis is an assertion that bodily vulnerability's relation to loss (of love) – where loss is a form of (or, due to) violence – necessitates a political (where the political is also personal) task of mourning. Butler demonstrates our need for mourning loss of life, showing that this need is not a matter of choice. In mourning we *accept* the loss and a process; but we also accept (in the sense of an active passion, not a free choice) that, if we do not undergo this process, we are missing something... (Perhaps she means the revelation that the other had a role creating who "I am" in "we were"...)

In fact, Butler claims we "submit to" a transformation in the process of mourning. However, I would like to question two things which remain mysterious in the sense of (apparently) ineffable here:

(i) to what transformation do "we submit" in the process of mourning?
(ii) What exactly is missing, if we do not mourn loss of another's life?

The first of these is also twofold: to what do we submit; and what is the significance in submitting to a transformation? As Butler insists, we undergo this transformation in the process of mourning, once we accept, in the sense of allow, the loss (of a loved one) to change us forever. In brief, she says that we are undone by another. Notice that a crucial part of Butler's assertion (above) is provocative: we are led to ask the second question: what does it mean that if we are not undone by the loss of another, then we are missing *something*? What would we miss?

I think that her reply would be that we would miss the life that counts; and a life which counts is one that is grievable; and we grieve a life when loss leaves us beside ourselves: dispossessed. Butler's answer to what is missing seems to be: a life that counts is a life that is valued, and a life that is valued is a life we grieve because it was part of who "we" were; and this can be no one. So, she says, loss unites "us" in corporeal vulnerability; we see another matters for "the self who I was" prior to loss. And yet Butler is hesitant here because she does not want to make vulnerability "the human condition." Instead, vulnerability differentiates us socially, historically and materially – in complex, perhaps mysterious ways! We don't experience vulnerability as either simply one individual thing, or as one universal (a priori) condition: it is somewhere between these two poles of the specific and the universal; vulnerability seems to happen to us, since we are wound-able.

And yet Butler adds that, although recognition of loss and of vulnerability follows from our constitutive relationality (or sociality), it is not just grief which calls the "I" into question. Desire in sexual relations already does this. For this reason, Butler describes both gender and sex as modes of *dispossession*: and dispossession means that we are beside ourselves in desire, grief and, Butler also mentions here, rage. But her central examples are of loss/death – due to AIDS, due to terrorism, and so on.

Butler later admits that talking about vulnerability has been especially problematic for women, and for all those who have been treated like "a separate class": here "the vulnerable" is a label that discriminates. Butler boldly states that "Women have <u>too long been associated with vulnerability, and there is **no** clear way to derive an ethics, much less a politics, from that notion</u>" (*Notes toward a Performative Theory of Assembly* 123; underline and bold added).[8] This might seem to challenge what I have also elsewhere claimed was an argument for "ethical" vulnerability. Yet perhaps Butler means by "that notion" (from which "there is no clear way to derive an ethics, much less a politics") that "vulnerable," projected as an attribute onto women, has been given excessively negative meaning. "The vulnerable," in that context, is fixed to women, gays, lesbians, trans, the disadvantaged and so on. It is undeniable that this attribution has denigrated and patronized those identities called "vulnerable," as if a separate class of second-class citizens or worse.

Nevertheless, aiming to avoid this negative stereotype, Butler continues to advocate thinking of vulnerability as a mode of relationality which is differentially visible – according to historical, social and material (economic) conditions. And I am very intrigued by something more in Butler: that her ontology is relational, and that vulnerability is not ontological but rather is socially constitutive of our bodies, and so our corporeal vulnerability is socially and political significant for "us." The question is how do we think and act in light of this vulnerability? In the opening to this paper I suggested we consider a contemporary appropriation of an old (classical) myth about Dawn and daybreak.

ontology

I have been challenged to rethink my own ontological assumptions for my contributions to the Enhancing Life Project.[9] I have tended to assume a Kantian, or neo-Kantian, account of a primordial (or transcendental) self, existing prior to our knowledge and actively unifying our experiences, prior to any of our relations. Roughly speaking, a fundamental ontology of a capable (active, even if phenomenologically vulnerable) self would have been my ontological starting point; this ontology of the self would have been necessary first of all – for any capability – and notably for being able to understand vulnerable life in its affective, conative and cognitive relations. However, I have very recently been challenged to consider whether in fact I could have this fundamental ontology of a (unifying) self, by thinking and reading – as mentioned already – Butler on a relational ontology of socially constituted bodies!

Could I have been mistaken about the (autonomous) self and its relationality? Is it necessary to presuppose "a self" prior to (our) socially constituted bodies? In other words, Butler has ultimately forced me – and others, apparently – to question any ontological assumption of a self, on whose capable relations, relations of self to another have been built. Why begin this way with an a priori or transcendental self as a condition of all of our experience?

Over ten years ago I argued that Iris Murdoch's conception of "un-selfing" involved a contradiction in terms: *a self* – in Murdoch's conception – seemed to me to be both necessary and unnecessary, to be both "done" and "undone" by the reality of love.[10] Previously, I tried to indicate contradictions in her **self**-concerned search both to un-find herself and to find a non-illusory vision of the reality of selves.[11] I took the question to be, how could (do) we get out of our self, in order to find it or create it? At that time, I maintained that the very idea of un-selfing **presupposes *a self* who is capable of loving relationships:** that is, I thought that a self has to exist before it can "have" relationships. It seemed to me Murdoch, following Simone Weil, insisted that a self must "de-create" (Weil's concept), in order to either find herself in or connect herself to loving relations.

Yet in the past year or so I have been led to reconsider how we are socially constituted (bodies) in a relational ontology; this is an ontology by which "we" are both created and dispossessed by our relations to others. Of course, this raises a question about the very existence of an isolated or autonomous self. For Butler, the question is how do we find, in the sense of recognize, our self; and one of her answers (perhaps her only answer) is that we find our self in others; and we know this to be the case when we are "dis-possessed" by the loss of another: to repeat, in her examples, this is in grief, rage or desire. Why is this so significant for me? Clearly it is because it offers us more positive possibilities in being vulnerable, wounded, lost ... and in knowing that life counts when we are loved, or have been loved.

In turn, my recent study of Butler's relational ontology has led me to try to reconceive vulnerability today as an openness – an open wound – which is neither necessarily negative nor wholly positive. Instead, as a mode of relationality, vulnerability provides us with the capability for being affected by, and affecting, change. Not only do I think that I need to change my ontological assumption, in order to grasp an account of a love which is worth expressing, giving and receiving, but "we" need to be changed so that fear and violence are not what we first of all associate with life's vulnerabilities. Moreover, I think that both Butler and living a life have helped me see that it is denying one's vulnerability that is counter-productive to living and loving.

Basically, I am asking you to consider what it would mean to leave behind any resistance to the possibility of ontological relations being prior to selfhood, or what you and I might consider to be "the self." According to Murdoch, it is only by "un-doing" the self that we find it; and according to Butler, it is only in "un-doing" gender in the sense of unbinding what has bound us to social stereotypes – that we un-do self-deception, and so gender and sexual oppression. Such un-doing seeks to liberate our vision of social reality. In turn, this liberation frees the self to perceive "the real" as the genuine object or the subject of love.

Yet Murdoch adds that the un-doing of self should not leave the self "denuded."[12] I guess that "denuded" suggests something of the self is taken away, but something also remains ... Is the "something" which remains simply the capability of making sense of ourselves? If so, then what is taken away in denuding?

Appropriate attempts to confront self-contradiction, or possible confusion, in trying both "to un-self" and "to self" in specific, concrete situations have highly significant implications for philosophical critiques of ethics, religion and moral psychology, but also serious implications for what I am saying about love and vulnerability.[13] To approach this capability we seem to need to make sense of ourselves, notably of the myths which we live by. So, for the significant implications concerning how we understand ourselves as loving, but also vulnerable, I turned to further thinking on the level of myth.

myths by which we live: the dark and difficult symbolism of wisdom

Instead of focusing on everyday stories of love, family life and vulnerability, which normally go on without any philosophical reflection, I have sought to make sense of love's motivation in the philosophical imaginary. The stories which remain decisive for philosophy – as the wisdom of love rather than merely the love of wisdom – contain significant symbolic and mythical elements, especially narratives which in their telling bring together human and divine characters. If we add gender to the mix of the crucial attributes of these characters, then we come close to the necessary ingredients for configuring and, hopefully, reconfiguring the relations which have been crucial to "the myths we live by."[14] Basically, this means to undo the hierarchy and discrimination according to gender, sexuality, race, religion, ethnicity; but I will only take one example of a myth from our philosophical imaginary – the stock of images, myths and other symbolic relations which structure, largely unwittingly, how we think and act.

The contemporary British philosopher Mary Midgley defends the existence of myth as, in her words, "symbolic stories which play a crucial role in our imaginative and intellectual life by expressing the patterns that underlie our thought."[15] She maintains that anyone who denies that myth underlies their thinking simply has not become aware of "the general background within which all detailed thought develops."[16] Midgley even employs myth and its symbolism to make sense of the significance of philosophy in her own personal life. She introduces her memoirs, *The Owl of Minerva*,[17] with two non-human figures from ancient mythology: the female deity Minerva (Athene is the equivalent in ancient Greek myth), and her owl, representing wisdom. The figure of Minerva is also famously employed by G.W.F. Hegel in the nineteenth century to describe the moment in the history of philosophy when an era would seem to be at an end. We can glimpse the role of this figure in Hegel's own words:

> [...] on the subject of *issuing instructions* on how the world ought to be: philosophy, at any rate, always comes too late to perform this function [...] it is only when actuality has reached maturity that the ideal appears opposite the real and reconstructs this real world, which it has grasped in its substance, in the shape of an intellectual realm. When philosophy paints its grey in grey, a shape of life has grown old, and it cannot be rejuvenated, but only recognized, by the grey in grey of philosophy; the owl of Minerva begins its flight only with the onset of dusk.[18]

Similarly to Hegel, I suggest that Midgley points to "the love of wisdom" being recognized at dusk, at a moment of difficult transition, of loss or death. Her choice of the imagery of Minerva and dusk later in her own life, as well as in the wake of the philosophical life which she shared with her husband who is deceased,[19] tells us something about her view of "the love of wisdom": it emerges in difficult or darkening times. Minerva's owl symbolizes the capability of seeing – wisdom – in the dark at the end of a day or of an era. So the owl sees in the dark. Yet I would like to stress that the darkening at dusk is not permanent; nor is the imagery of dusk alone adequate for a fair picture of Mary Midgley's philosophical wisdom.

Returning to my new mythical persona, Dawn, we know that each night is followed by a new *dawn*. The break of day, the rising of the sun, the beginning of a new day, and similar images constitute imagery for thinking after – for instance – the long dark night of late twentieth-century post-modernism. Speaking metaphorically, this is the night when the light of modernity's reason is eclipsed by uncertainty and obscurity. Moreover, the symbolism of light remains most appropriate to a philosophical imaginary which recognizes a lasting debt to ethically significant aspects of seventeenth- and eighteenth-century Enlightenment philosophy in Europe at least.

And yet we know that Midgley employs imagery from ancient Greek mythology and modern German philosophy to capture the nature of wisdom in the context of the dark difficulties of fear, violence and death: "Going out in the dark brings danger of death. But if you have to go out, then it is surely a good thing to have with you a creature that can penetrate the darkness."[20] In this, she is pragmatic: when things get tough we have to turn to the wisdom in philosophy; thus the wise philosopher is a necessity. And what subject is more difficult to grasp, or is darker in its depths, especially in its loss, than excessive love!

At this point I offer a possibly contentious reading of Midgley's discovery of wisdom in certain philosophical difficulties. This wisdom expressed symbolically as the danger brought about by death could be explained by psycholinguists as the mode of the philosopher who remains in melancholia.[21] To treat this as one possible explanation, consider Julia Kristeva's psycholinguistic description of the woman who has successfully shifted her attachments away from the security of maternal love:

> [...] shifting the symbolic *at the same time* as [shifting] to a sexual object of a sex other than that of the primary maternal object represents a gigantic elaboration in which a woman cathexes a psychic potential greater than what is demanded of the male sex. When this process is favourably carried out, it is evidenced by the precocious awakening of girls, their intellectual performances often more brilliant during the school years, and their continuing female maturity. Nevertheless, it has its price in the constant tendency to extol the problematic mourning for the lost object [...] not so fully lost [...][22]

Melancholia, as represented by the young girl in Kristeva's account (above), which follows after the loss of love, can generate, according to Kristeva, great psychic potential for intellectual performance. But to use Kristeva's other well-known imagery of the "black sun," this darkness haunts the wisdom of a melancholic woman; this is the woman who is unable to grieve. Recall that Butler insists that we submit to a transformation in the process of mourning ... – again Butler does not see this as a choice, but resistance seems to be the obstacle: one resists when mourning is not allowed to happen.

Previously I have explored critical problems with Kristeva's *Black Sun*. Yet for one additional aside, the late feminist philosopher of religion Grace M. Jantzen might well have argued that Midgley remains caught up in the masculinist symbolic of death which displaces both beauty and natality insofar as she remains within the darkness of death. Instead, Jantzen advocates that we embrace natality rather than mortality as life-affirming.[23] But none of these other women approach the large ontological question which has bothered me. Is there a choice to be made concerning selfhood and relationality?

A less contentious reading than Kristeva's or Jantzen's psycholinguistic readings would recognize, in the texts of Western philosophy, the myths of patriarchy – which have shaped our philosophical imaginary and configured Western relations between men, women and the divine. Under patriarchy love's capability is configured in ways which variously empower love's characters; patriarchal myths have given authority on matters of ethical wisdom to fathers and sons over mothers and daughters, as well as men generally over other women and young girls. Think of the ways in which the myth of Oedipus determined twentieth-century accounts of familial and other love relations. Think of the unforgettable myth of Eve's eating the forbidden fruit of the tree of knowledge of good and evil. In the patriarchal telling of these myths, love is portrayed both to liberate and to constrain relationships, according to gender differentiation. Ultimately, the patriarchal "resolution" of the gender constraints on sexual relations has over time eclipsed the ethical wisdom of many women.[24]

Le Doeuff demonstrates, with a creative discovery of a liberating myth, the (constant) need to unearth the obstacle in relations between women and everything or everyone else. The difficulty is the identification of the obstacle: "that barely perceptible reality which does not speak its name."[25] In this paper my contention is that we should seek to create, or recreate, myths which can liberate that eclipsed capability which has been hidden by oppressive or dark forms of love. This means liberating our gendered forms of love according to the specificities of the lives of actual women and men who are each distinguished by age, race, class, ethnicity and sexual orientation. *Agape* (charity), *philia* (friendship), *eros* (desire) and other affections each contain an element of that capability[26] which is integral to yet often enslaved by human love.

In his last writings on memory, forgiveness and love, Paul Ricoeur describes how human capability has been wounded by painful affection.[27] His mythical descriptions of *the enslavement of the triad freedom–goodness–love assume the loss of human capability*.[28] In various ways across the course of his writings, Ricoeur contends that the symbolic and mythical language of slavery expresses this loss as an enslaved freedom (or as "the captive free will" which is enslaved to evil). Nevertheless, we can and should recover freedom's more primordial (original) ground of goodness.[29]

In one sense, our myths about love are timeless. But in another sense, the myths which structure our love stories are about time and the variable relations of human subjects to eternity and divinity. In my writings on feminist philosophy of religion, I have been repeatedly struck by how much philosophy has relied unwittingly or wittingly upon myths to support its gender norms.[30]

Midgley presents a highly relevant account of imagery concerning wisdom. But I contend that the imagery of Minerva's owl is only part of the picture of wisdom. A network of symbolic relations certainly constitutes the structure of myths, portraying wisdom. This network gives significance to stories and to a whole range of interrelated imagery. In addition, a myth is cultivated by composing narratives which make sense of the lived experiences of individuals; this composition brings together the rational, attentive and conative[31] capability of individual women and men. I employ "capability" in line with the later writings of Ricoeur to describe human subjects in terms of their potentiality, especially the power which enables us to relate and to love as moral beings.[32] Ricoeur's own final portrait of the capable human being is neo-Aristotelian and Kantian (but not intentionally post-Hegelian).[33] His self-description is revealing, but it also fits nicely with the picture developing here.

a myth for wise lovers: the joyful and hopeful symbolism of enlightenment

It is Le Doeuff who has uncovered – for me at least – a significantly different symbolic figure and myth from Minerva and her owl, from Psyche and Cupid, and from Eve and Adam. In her 2006 Weidenfeld Lectures, Le Doeuff demonstrates the ethical significance of a highly distinctive myth for twenty-first-century men and women.[34] Essentially the significance of this myth is its message: in order to gain reciprocal affections, we should take care not to force a girl to grow up to be a goddess of maternal love with sacrificial and tragic relations to men, to other women, to gods and goddesses. An original (classical) story told by Le Doeuff lends itself to a recreation of a timely contemporary myth about a young girl, Dawn, whose *vulnerability* needs to be *enhanced*, in order for her *heart* which is reason to enlighten us. Here, affection becomes mutual insofar as we allow Dawn's vulnerability to provoke in us qualities of both tenderness and firmness, attentiveness and wise generosity, joy and enjoyment, in those who love her. Here I will end with encouragement: that we can and should recognize the critical role of affects and affections in vulnerability and love; this is necessary, I submit, in order to rethink our relations to Dawn, that mythical persona who enlightens each daybreak, with new possibilities for freeing the so-called vulnerable – that separated and denigrated group – from the constraints of fear and violence, in order to transform our socially constituted bodies into love and vulnerability.

Le Doeuff's reference to "the heart" of Dawn derives from her own reading of the Spanish philosopher Maria Zambrano's symbolic poetics. Zambrano portrays Dawn's heart as significantly different from either the mind or the body, of either eternal male or eternal female essence. Instead, the heart encompasses aspects of both the incorporeal and the corporeal. But the heart is not exactly the soul either. Yet it is clearly significant for the distinctive identity of the young girl prior to her adolescence, at which time her self-identity becomes challenged by her changing body, her sexuality, her female beauty, her sexually specific pleasure – a joy which will be more than sexual. We might compare Dawn's joy with Spinoza's intellectual love of God. In this light, the heart is a fundamental and encompassing term for what needs to be protected in the young girl as she grows up, generating the wisdom of love. Le Doeuff leaves us to wonder whether the heart of a young boy is more easily protected from the illusions and oppression of imposed social-sexual stereotypes.[35]

Le Doeuff herself discovers the main elements of this story from her reading of another woman writer: Maria Zambrano.[36] Zambrano was educated in philosophy, wrote fiction and non-fiction in Spanish, and contributed to a conception of poetic reasoning in which the symbolic has a philosophically significant role. Le Doeuff picks up crucial elements from what becomes "*la philosophie imaginaire*" of Zambrano to challenge traditional stereotypes about young girls, reason, mature women, motherhood and divinity; "Dawn" does have both classical and religious (or, at least spiritual) origins. In telling Dawn's story, Le Doeuff appropriates Zambrano's poetic reasoning about a girl whose heart is reason, in order to create an ethical figure of hope for women and men in philosophy. The heart becomes a symbol for a fresh understanding of a human soul in loving reciprocal relations. If we extrapolate a bit more, then this mythical language about a young girl's heart begins to personify liberated love – not the bonded love of a female deity, whether a goddess of wisdom or of motherhood. (Here I think of Etty Hillesum who describes how, in her words: "Much has been changed in my relationship with my parents, *many tight bonds have snapped, and as a result I have gained the strength to love the more genuinely*.")[37] Le Doeuff asserts that Dawn should not be forced to become divine.

My own contention is that Le Doeuff's retelling of Dawn's story offers us a new Enlightenment narrative. Of course, other narratives could be created and/or similarly reconfigured to avoid the pernicious dangers in apotheosis, but in the present context consider this retelling of a (mythical) story about Dawn. Each dawn begins anew, offering us hope for each woman and each man to be attentive and tender to one another; to learn to love this young girl involves practising tenderness, not unthinking force. A revised ethics is implicit in a new enlightenment narrative, whereby a young girl holds out a promise for practical wisdom, while women and men create new ethical dispositions (e.g., tenderness) in being drawn to the vulnerability of Dawn. Le Doeuff insists that European Enlightenment philosophy was unethical when it came to women and the potential of a woman's ethical wisdom. Yet Le Doeuff's new myth, unlike Midgley's memoir, does not take its starting point from the symbolism of dusk. Instead, dawn is the starting point of this alternative myth, which comes after "the dark": whether this imagery refers to the era of medieval or of post-modern darkness Dawn brings light to certain unfathomable difficulties, especially to the sexual violence and living death which have enslaved women.

Le Doeuff is not preoccupied with any post-modern imaginary or any assumed death of Enlightenment philosophy, which can arguably be read as melancholia. In sharp contrast to either a medieval or a post-modern imaginary, Le Doeuff's story is about a new Dawn who/which has the capacity to enlighten; to teach us unwittingly how to protect a heart which symbolizes un-enslaved reason. This Enlightenment narrative does not oppose reason to love, or mind to body. Instead, reason, like a pre-adolescent heart, if it is cultivated, can enlighten love in others, too. Thus the mutually produced wisdom of love comes with Dawn, at the break of day, and not exclusively with Minerva at dusk.

Elsewhere I have pointed out that Le Doeuff draws productively on the imagery in women's writings to make sense of a movement for women's recognition.[38] She focuses on the imagery of dark and light in the movement of waves as they break seemingly between sea and sky. Perhaps unaware of the result, Le Doeuff nevertheless shifts an imaginary relationship from dusk and darkness to the dark and light oscillations reflected on the sea at dawn. For example, she appropriates the imagery with which Virginia Woolf begins her twentieth-century novel *The Waves*: "The sun had not yet risen. The sea was indistinguishable from the sky, except that the sea was slightly creased as if a cloth had wrinkles in it. Gradually as the sky whitened a dark line lay on the horizon dividing the sea from the sky and [...]"[39]

In this way, Le Doeuff reveals her own enlightened preference for hope, even when the political climate is dark or darkening. Consider her references to joy and hope in the light which continues to dawn across the horizon of the sea every morning:

> The waves of hope rise and fall: "The grey cloth becomes barred with thick strokes moving, one after another, beneath the surface, following each other, pursuing each other, perpetually. As they neared the shore each bar rose, heaped itself, broke and swept a thin veil of white water across the sand. The wave paused, and then drew out again, sighing." These opening sentences from Virginia Woolf's *The Waves* might well contain the poetics of our collective historical experience. Successive waves of women have joyfully fought, convinced that once we had at last gained the right to, for example, a job, education, citizen's rights, or a sexuality freed from the chains of reproduction, something fundamental would have changed in the general female condition. A thin veil of white water across the sand: those gains have hardly even yet been gained and the radical transformation that we expected along with civil equality or birth control has not come. Besides, like harbour pools governed by a complex system of locks and sluices, particular social spaces open to us and then close off again.[40]

Le Doeuff confirms that each woman's joyful struggle to express her own wisdom is shaped around the collective history of an ethical movement for reciprocal equality, or recognition.[41] This history includes the ebb and flow of the imagery and political ideas of each woman. Here feminism is implicit as a politics constantly moved forward by both successes and failures of women individually and collectively. This movement creates shifts in what Le Doeuff has articulated as the philosophical imaginary: this is essentially the symbolic and narrative patterns of thought which shape (often unwittingly) philosophical texts. For Le Doeuff, Woolf becomes a paradigmatic figure of and for a woman's writing speaking profoundly to her readers, even in this new century, about how patriarchy has dis-inherited women.[42] This lack of inheritance means that women have mainly been separated from their own ideas which have been given away, or cast off, without any rightful recognition of their ownership by or origin in a specific female thinker.

The imagery of the waves is a case in point. To illustrate how the failure of inheritance might be reversed, Le Doeuff picks up and exploits the metaphorical and mystical language making up Woolf's novel, in order to express the rise and fall of hope in a woman's collective inheritance. This exploitation means that Le Doeuff makes suggestions with this imagery which go beyond the intended significance in *The Waves*. But she also disagrees with Woolf's writings on women when the latter fail to recognize ideas which have been generated by women from past centuries.[43] So "waves of feminism" present themselves on a political scene as historical movements of individual women: they are like the recurring lines rising and falling on the sea waters each dawn. Thus the imagery of waves gives expression to the complex patterns and shifts in the relations of *each* woman to each other and to all of those others whom they love. Love relates them individually and collectively to the larger reality of patriarchy.

The crucial point is that Le Doeuff would find any exclusive stress upon the grey on grey, whether taken from Woolf or Hegel, as missing the significant light shed on the crest of waves. The symbolism and myth of this ethical wisdom emerge like the light shining from the lives of each woman who is part of a vibrant, if hidden, collective historical experience. The task is to claim each woman's wisdom as part of our philosophical inheritance; that is, an inheritance of the ideas of past women whose writings were quickly cast off. My present argument takes support from Le Doeuff to contend that *love's capability* can be found in both the imagery of kindly cultivating a young girl's heart and the larger picture of our collective inheritance. So, the philosophical imaginary would no longer picture a woman exclusively in the shadow of a man: not just Geoffrey Midgley with Mary, or Hegel with the owl of Minerva, but Mary Midgley with the wise men and women who have learned to liberate love's capability; perhaps they have learned about love from a reason freely expressed and a heart tenderly received.

"Not a goddess, she!" is Le Doeuff's crucial cry. If Dawn grows up *without* having *imposed* those humanly impossible, patriarchal gender roles which enshrine a goddess in bonded love and stereotypical beauty – and yes, ethereal beauty can also be sexist – then her reason will enable non-oppressive love and so goodness to shine upon humanity and its relations. This myth implies that a woman's oppression begins in adolescence, at which point the myths of patriarchy enslave the relations of men and women. Yet liberation can be achieved when the young girl develops an adolescent heart which is treated tenderly; but this must be prior to her (maternal) sacrifice to the god(s).

There are plenty of good reasons to reflect upon the wisdom of love rather than the love of wisdom. My argument is that such wisdom derives from "liberated love" rather than "bonded love" – a distinction which, however contentious, I employ from the outset of this paper. It is also my view that the practical wisdom of contemporary women and men finds itself at a moment when our critical reflections should be compelled to reject the bonded love which is associated both literally with violence and symbolically with death. To support this, it is imperative to reject the symbolism of a self-destructive bonding to an unenlightened other and begin to recognize the nature of liberated lovers. Looking closely at symbols and myth is a highly abstract exercise; nevertheless, this is substantially supported by cutting-edge work like that of Le Doeuff on "the philosophical imaginary"[44] – the decisive significance of which should become clear.

To end this critical reflection, consider two claims:

> Liberated love is superior to bonded love: Wise lovers are not only more joyous, but more effective and beneficent than unenlightened lovers.[45]

> By refusing to accompany her father in his blindness, by saving herself and her child

instead of obeying her husband, by opening her eyes and seeing with whom she is living, Psyche has walked out of the Oedipus plot.[46]

The first quotation (above) concerning liberated love assumes that love can and should be freed from a certain sort of bondage. This is a huge and contentious assumption. Can and, if so, should love be liberated? It might be thought that by its very nature love binds those who love to others – so that love is always in some sense bonded – and certainly love which requires obedience to a higher authority is in bondage to, say, a divine or absolute law. For the sake of my argument let us suppose that love can be liberated; and see if I can persuade you. The question is, from whom or what precisely – and to what degree – is love freed? At the very least love can be freed from total passivity.

The second quotation (above) suggests an answer in the interpretation of mythical imagery: the blindness of a familial relation, as portrayed in this case by the plot of the Oedipus myth, renders these bonds of love less effective by preventing the daughter from seeing reality; she only "knows" the man-made structures of authority and obedience in love. Roughly, we will see that the young girl, Psyche (who is mentioned in the quotation and is taken from the Cupid and Venus story), has the capability to reject the plot in which the man literally or symbolically marries his mother and the woman simply accepts the patriarchal authority. The first quotation points out that wisdom liberates and creates "enlightened lovers." But from where does the wisdom of love arise?[47]

I have tried to argue that a new philosophical imaginary – which would no longer connect vulnerability exclusively to fear and violence – would motivate us to liberate love's capability, especially from the bondage of patriarchal myths (those of blind obedience to a higher "authority"); and that liberated capability is expressed in the retelling of the stories about the gendered relations between human beings themselves, between human and divine, and humans and their internal and external environment. In the telling and retelling of love stories, we try to imagine how the vulnerability which remains latent in the mythical configurations of these relations both affects and is affected by love's capability. Remember that this capability is the openness to mutual affection which I would like to rename vulnerability.

notes

Completion of this paper was made possible through the support of a grant from the John Templeton Foundation, via the Enhancing Life Project. The opinions expressed in it are those of the author and do not necessarily reflect the views of the John Templeton Foundation. The paper will eventually be part of a monograph on *Love, Vulnerability and Affection: New Concepts to Live By* … or, *Enhancing Vulnerable Life: Love, Confidence and Affection* …

1 Editors' note: we have restricted editorial changes to the correction of typographical errors and the amendment of clear infelicities of "draft" style. In Anderson's original text, some passages were highlighted in yellow, others were typed in red, and others were typed in bold. In none of these cases was there any indication what the rationale for the typographical device was. We have registered her use of yellow highlighting by means of underlining, her use of red type by means of **bold**, and her own use of bold (which it seems clear was just her way of emphasizing material) by means of *italics*.

2 Here I am thinking of myths which have been constructed by "the philosophical imaginary" (cf. Michèle Le Doeuff, *Recherches sur l'imaginaire philosophique* (Paris: Payot, 1980); *The Philosophical Imaginary*, trans. Colin Gordon (London: Athlone, 1989; Berkeley: Stanford UP, 1990; republished London: Continuum, 2002); cf. Max Deutscher, ed., *Operative Philosophy and Imaginary Practice: Michèle Le Doeuff* (New York: Humanity, 2000)), especially those about fathers and their daughters, wives, mothers; when living by patriarchal myths, we are motivated by hierarchical, asymmetrical affections, including violence, fear and vulnerability.

3 Le Doeuff, *The Philosophical Imaginary*.

4 Michèle Le Doeuff, "Not a Goddess, She!," Lecture 4 of "The Spirit of Secularism: On Fables,

Gender and Ethics," Weidenfeld Professorial Lectures, University of Oxford, Trinity Term 2006. See also Friedrich Nietzsche, *Daybreak: Thoughts on the Prejudices of Morality*, trans. Maudemarie Clark, Brian Leiter, and R.J. Hollingdale (Cambridge: Cambridge UP, 1997).

5 Paul Ricoeur, "Ethics and Human Capability: A Response" in *Paul Ricoeur and Contemporary Moral Thought*, eds. John Wall, William Schweiker, and David Hall (New York and London: Routledge, 2002) 284.

6 For another example of a new story of vulnerability and loving attention, which liberates – "tames" (from the French verb *apprivoiser*) – love, see Antoine de Saint-Exupéry, *The Little Prince* (Harmondsworth: Heinemann, 1945; rpt. by Puffin, 1962) 79–84.

7 Ibid. 83–84.

8 See Judith Butler, *Notes toward a Performative Theory of Assembly* (Cambridge, MA: Harvard UP, 2015); *Precarious Life: The Powers of Mourning and Violence* (London: Verso, 2004).

9 See the unnumbered note at the head of this Notes section.

10 The present attempt to expose the contradiction of "selfing and un-selfing" should be distinguished from the concerns of Weil and of Murdoch, who each have slightly different conceptions and conclusions concerning love of self from my own and each other. Yet both Murdoch and Weil have a common reaction to their European contemporary philosopher Jean-Paul Sartre, whose conceptions of unbearable freedom and self-deception render genuine love impossible. For discussion of Sartre's influence on Murdoch, see Maria Antonaccio, *Picturing the Human: The Moral Thought of Iris Murdoch* (Oxford: Oxford UP, 2000) 62–75; and again, see my discussion of Newton-Smith's reading of Sartre in "'Moralizing' Love in Philosophy of Religion" in *Philosophy of Religion for a New Century*, eds. Jerald T. Wallulis and Jeremiah Hackett (Amsterdam: Kluwer, 2004) 235–37.

11 Compare this search to Le Doeuff's account of the "I" who seeks identity which is not that proposed by social representation. Le Doeuff illustrates this with the choice of the ancient woman philosopher of mathematics, Hipparchia, seeking knowledge rather than remaining "at the loom" where society expected her to be: see Michèle Le Doeuff, *Hipparchia's Choice: An Essay Concerning Women, Philosophy, Etc.*, trans. Trista Selous (Oxford: Blackwell, 1991) 206; 2nd ed. and rev. trans. (New York: Columbia UP, 2007); this could be explored further as the (un)selfing necessary for doing philosophy, that is, for both finding oneself and losing oneself in the wisdom of love.

12 Iris Murdoch, *The Sovereignty of Good* (London: Routledge, 1970) 47. Concerning a woman who "unfinds herself" through exile from her social identity, see Le Doeuff, *Hipparchia's Choice* 206.

13 At the same time, if we follow Le Doeuff's argument, then this multiplicity of specific concrete situations of (un)selfing would be most evident in the times and places in history when and where women's "identity" in reality makes up "a collective disarray": Le Doeuff, *Hipparchia's Choice* 207.

14 Mary Midgley, *The Myths We Live By* (London: Routledge, 2004) xi, 1, 2, 5.

15 Mary Midgley, *The Ethical Primate: Humans, Freedom and Morality* (London: Routledge, 1994) 109: Midgley asserts that "Myths are not lies, nor need they be taken as literally true," and gives a highly useful, philosophical definition of myth; this basic, relatively uncontentious treatment renders mythical symbolism a necessary addition to scientific facts. For her initial use of the term, see Mary Midgley, *Wickedness: A Philosophical Essay* (London: Routledge, 1984) 10–12, 162. For the more technical use of myth, see Midgley, *The Ethical Primate* 109, 117–18; the latter is repeated and elaborated ten years later in Midgley, *The Myths We Live By* xi, 1, 2, 5.

16 Midgley, *The Ethical Primate* 117; more generally 109–20. To read more from this: the way in which myths work is often very obscure to us. But, besides their value-implications – which are often very subtle – they also function as summaries of certain selected sets of facts (117) … When we attend to the range of facts that any particular myth sums up, we are always strongly led to draw the moral that belongs to that myth. But that range of facts is always highly selective. It is limited by the imaginative vision that lies behind that particular story. This vision can, of course, generate actual lies, which is what makes it plausible to think of the myth itself as a lie. Thus, myths about the inferiority of women, or of particular ethnic groups, have supported themselves

by false factual beliefs about these people (ibid. 117–18).

17 Mary Midgley, *The Owl of Minerva: A Memoir* (London: Routledge, 2005) x–xii.

18 G.W.F. Hegel, *Elements of the Philosophy of Right*, ed. Allen W. Wood; trans. H.B. Nisbet (Cambridge: Cambridge UP, 1991) 23.

19 If one wanted to make this argument, a premise would need to be defended; that is, Mary's memoirs testify to Geoff Midgley's wisdom which lives in the various forms of her love and her practices of philosophy. But it is unfair to push the argument this far. The reverse is more likely to be true: Mary is the source of inspiration for Geoff's wisdom.

20 Midgley, *The Owl of Minerva* xi.

21 Cecilia Sjoholm, *Kristeva and the Political* (London: Routledge, 2006) 50, 54–58; cf. Julia Kristeva, *Black Sun: Depression and Melancholy*, trans. Leon Roudiez (New York: Columbia UP, 1989) 27–30.

22 Kristeva, *Black Sun* 30.

23 Grace M. Jantzen died on 2 May 2006. So this present claim extrapolates from the project on which she was working – a first volume of which is published: Grace M. Jantzen, *Foundations of Violence: Death and the Displacement of Beauty*, vol. 1 (London: Routledge, 2004) 11–20.

24 For the examples and implications of this eclipse, see Le Doeuff, *Hipparchia's Choice* 28. Cf. Michèle Le Doeuff, *The Sex of Knowing*, trans. Kathryn Hamer and Lorraine Code (New York and London: Routledge, 2003), especially Part 1, "Cast-Offs."

25 Le Doeuff, *Hipparchia's Choice* 28; cf. Le Doeuff, *The Philosophical Imaginary* 100–28.

26 Paul Ricoeur, "Ethics and Human Capability: A Response" in *Paul Ricoeur and Contemporary Moral Thought*, eds. John Wall, William Schweiker, and David Hall (New York and London: Routledge, 2002) 280, 282, 284.

27 Paul Ricoeur, *Memory, History, Forgetting*, trans. Kathleen Blamey (Chicago: U of Chicago P, 2005) 460.

28 Ibid. 459–66.

29 Ricoeur, "Ethics and Human Capability" 284; cf. Paul Ricoeur, *Fallible Man*, trans. Charles A. Kelbley (Chicago: Regnery, 1965); rev. trans. Kelbley with a new Introduction by Walter J. Lowe (New York: Fordham UP, 1986) 9–15, 144–45; *The Symbolism of Evil*, trans. Emerson Buchanan (New York and London: Harper, 1967) 152, 156–57.

30 Pamela Sue Anderson, *A Feminist Philosophy of Religion: The Rationality and Myths of Religious Belief* (Oxford: Blackwell, 1998), especially 4, 21–22, 113–14, 138–43, 245–47; Pamela Sue Anderson, "Myth and Feminist Philosophy" in *Thinking Through Myths: Philosophical Perspectives*, ed. Kevin Schilbrack (New York and London: Routledge, 2002) 101–22. Midgley's understanding of symbolism and myth in the wisdom of our living, learning and knowing bears similarities to Le Doeuff, *The Philosophical Imaginary* 1–20; cf. Midgley, *The Myths We Live By*, especially 1–5, 88–93, 97–101.

31 The adjective "conative" recalls Baruch Spinoza's conception of *conatus* as the human striving to persist in one's own being.

32 Ricoeur, "Ethics and Human Capability" 282–83.

33 Paul Ricoeur, *The Course of Recognition*, trans. David Pellauer (Cambridge, MA: Harvard UP, 2005) 91; and more generally chapter 2.

34 See note 4 above.

35 For a crucial backdrop to Le Doeuff's thinking on "le coeur," see Maria Zambrano, *Les Clairières du bois*, trans. from Spanish Marie Laffranque (Paris: L'Éclat, 1989) 65–80; see also note below.

36 Maria Zambrano is born in 1904 in Andalusia, attends the University of Madrid where she studies philosophy and dies in 1991. Zambrano wrote numerous books in Spanish – one of which inspired Le Doeuff with a story about Dawn who remains human, unlike the goddess "Dawn" of classical literature. For the challenge of "la philosophie imaginaire" in Zambrano to the traditional gender stereotypes of divine women, see Maria Zambrano, *De l'Aurore*, trans. from Spanish Marie Laffranque (Paris: L'Éclat, 1989).

37 *An Interrupted Life: The Diaries of Etty Hillesum*, ed. J.G. Gaarlandt (New York: Washington Square, 1985) 119. [Editors' note: Etty Hillesum (1914–43) was a Dutch Jewish victim of the Holocaust.]

38 Pamela Sue Anderson, "Feminism and Patriarchy" in *The Oxford Handbook of English Literature*

and Theology, eds. David Jasper, Andrew Hass, and Elizabeth Jay (Oxford: Oxford UP, 2006) 810–26.

39 Virginia Woolf, *The Waves*, Biographical Preface by Frank Kermode, ed. with an Introduction and Notes by Gillian Beer (Oxford: Oxford UP, 1992) 3. For an example where Woolf moves from the light–dark imagery of waves rising and falling to the figure of a rider on a proud horse who faces a dark enemy advancing against her or him, see ibid. 247–48.

40 Le Doeuff, *Hipparchia's Choice* 242–43; cf. Woolf, *The Waves* 3. For a contextualization of French feminism in terms of waves, see Lisa Walsh, "Introduction: The Swell of the Third Wave" in *Contemporary French Feminism*, eds. Kelly Oliver and Lisa Walsh (Oxford: Oxford UP, 2004) 1–11.

41 For more on recognition, or reciprocal equality, see Le Doeuff, *Hipparchia's Choice* 278–79; Pamela Sue Anderson, "Life, Death and (Inter)subjectivity: Realism and Recognition in Continental Philosophy," *International Journal of Philosophy of Religion* 13, Special Issue, *Issues in Continental Philosophy of Religion* (2006).

42 Hamer and Code translate Le Doeuff's French term *déshérences* as "cast-offs": see Le Doeuff, *The Sex of Knowing* 18. Instead, to emphasize the lack of inheritance in this context, the (albeit awkward) "dis-inherited women" is the present translation.

43 For example, Le Doeuff points out that Woolf fails to recognize any renaissance or medieval woman writer; so Le Doeuff singles out a counter-example: Christine de Pisan is a fourteenth-century woman writer who did much to demonstrate the crucial significance of the imaginary for the successful living and thinking of women; see Le Doeuff, *The Sex of Knowing* ix–x, 119, 135–38. Cf. Christine de Pisan, *The Book of the City of Ladies*, trans. and with Notes by Rosalind Brown-Grant (London: Penguin, 1999).

44 Concerning the urgent need for a feminist imaginary, see also Penelope Deutscher, "When Feminism is 'High' and Ignorance is 'Low': Harriet Taylor Mill on the Progress of the Species," *Hypatia* 21.3 (2006): 147.

45 Amélie Rorty, "Spinoza on the Pathos of Idolatrous Love and the Hilarity of True Love" in *Feminism and the History of Philosophy*, ed. Genevieve Lloyd (New York: Oxford UP, 2002) 222; cf. Spinoza, *Ethics*, trans. and ed. G.H.R. Parkinson (Oxford: Oxford UP, 2000) 314–16.

46 Carol Gilligan, *The Birth of Pleasure: A New Map of Love* (London: Chatto, 2002) 40.

47 For the claim that philosophy is "the wisdom of love in the service of love," see Emmanuel Levinas, *Otherwise than Being*, trans. Alphonso Lingis (The Hague: Nijhoff, 1981) 162. For a gloss on Levinas's statement on "the Said said in the service of the Saying, the 'justified Said', in which wisdom has learnt from love, or in which politics is not uninformed by ethics," see Stella Sandford, *The Metaphysics of Love: Gender and Transcendence in Levinas* (London: Athlone, 2000) 91.

1 reorienting ourselves

In 1949 Simone de Beauvoir wrote the following about female mystics:

> Il y a des femmes d'action comme […] Jeanne d'Arc, qui savent fort bien quels buts elles se proposent et qui inventent lucidement les moyens de les atteindre: leurs révélations ne font que donner une figure objective à leurs certitudes; elles les encouragent à suivre les chemins qu'elles se sont tracés avec précision. Il y a des femmes narcissistes […] qui, à bout de silencieuse ferveur, se sentient soudain "dans un état apostolique".[1] Elles ne sont pas très précises sur leurs taches; et – tout comme les dames d'œuvres en mal d'agitation – elles se soucient peu de ce qu'elles font pourvu que ce soit *quelque chose*.[2]

Today I will argue that there is a third alternative for women in philosophy: a new kind of creative freedom. First of all, I would like to propose that we, feminist philosophers, aim to reorient ourselves in the thought of Michèle Le Doeuff, looking closely at a particular passage concerning "feminine intuition" in *The Sex of Knowing*.[3] We will find that Le Doeuff considers the revaluation of women in philosophy; she turns to philosophers – like Henri Bergson – who have given "fair value" to intuition as an intellectual faculty. Could women who follow Bergson be given fair value along with intuition – with which they have frequently been associated? Second, with this philosophical question concerning women and intuition clearly in mind, I would like to turn from Le Doeuff's writings on intuition to writings by Bergson and by Beauvoir. Third, I will return periodically to Le Doeuff. Finally, my overall

pamela sue anderson

edited by nicholas bunnin

REORIENTING OURSELVES IN (BERGSONIAN) FREEDOM, FRIENDSHIP AND FEMINISM

intention is to reorient ourselves in (Bergsonian) freedom, friendship and feminism.

Normally, when "feminine intuition" is mentioned in the history of Western philosophy it has been a pejorative reference to women who are not able to be philosophers or, simply, not able to reason. So, intuition has been associated with something non-rational, or perhaps worse, the irrational. However, as Le Doeuff points out, Bergson (with some similarity to Schopenhauer) might initially be a counter-example in raising the status of intuition to that of a philosophical method. In Bergson's case this method is associated with only a few "great souls," or artists, who are able to exercise intuition as superior to scientific analysis.

Artists as great souls gain knowledge by intuition of what Bergson calls "real time." In fact, the artist who intuits is supposedly like the mystic who grasps the absolute in the dynamic process of actual and virtual life. Bergson calls this process "pure duration": it is real time. Unlike "time" as conceived by philosophers from Descartes to Kant and to contemporary Kantians, Bergson's "real" time is not spatial, external and static. According to Bergson, intuition as a method requires a leap into pure duration. But in his philosophy, intuition is not only a method; it is also a faculty. As such, intuition is a faculty superior to that of the intellect. At times this intuition has been referred to as intellectual sympathy, or empathy. If following Bergson, intuition becomes both the superior faculty and the superior method for complete, true knowledge.

Le Doeuff points out the problem with this Bergsonian account of intuition for women in philosophy, especially for contemporary feminist philosophers: once intuition is attributed to the great souls of artists, then women are no longer associated with it. Such a failure to revalidate women's intellectual faculties is re-enforced by Bergson's own conversion of intuition into a superior philosophical method: this conversion is accompanied by his substitution of "feminine sensibility" for what might have revalued women intellectually.[4] Might intuition as feminine (have) become the superior method and faculty in philosophy? Le Doeuff gives her answer in a critique of "epistemological inequalities"; and she elucidates a complex issue for "intuition" and for "women's intellectual worth"; that is:

> [T]o return to the example of intellectual faculties, we sometimes hear it said that if intuition, or empathy (its modern equivalent), were given fair value, then women would *ipso facto* be revalued. And likewise housework, mothering, and so on.
> Such a project is vulnerable to all manner of critique: to begin with, the concept of intuition is unstable; it is impossible to claim that anything that might be called intuition exists in itself, prior to any epistemological theory, no matter how imprecise [...] [T]he constitution and distribution of modes of knowing does depend on the theoretical frame of reference you choose. You can have binary theories or theories comprising more than terms; "intuition" may or may not be part of the nomenclature; sharp divisions, oppositions, or simply hierarchies may separate the various modes. As a result, the idea of reclaiming the value of intuition, with the promise that we will revalidate women in so doing, has no fixed point; its term of reference – intuition, to be reclaimed – does not function outside a general theory of the ordering of modes of knowledge.
> Moreover, the idea of recognizing the value of women by restoring respect for intuition is invalidated by the following [...] counterexample: Bergson [...] foregrounds intuitions; you might imagine that he draws first-rate conclusions about women's intellectual worth and that philosophically he rehabilitates the mode of cognition that is supposedly ours. *Don't imagine anything; read him!*[5]

So, I have read Bergson.

2 a woman's intuition: mysticism and/or feminism

This section will consider queries which arose in reading Bergson. What would a woman in philosophy say if she were to find Bergson construing Joan of Arc (*Jeanne d'Arc*) to be a "heroine" of mystical intuition? As a reading of his *The Two Sources of Morality and Religion* shows, Bergson presents Joan of Arc as a heroine and a mystic.[6] But could this fifteenth-century woman have *actually* employed intuition as a method, in the same sense as the intuition of a Bergsonian philosopher or mystic? And if so, would we – as Le Doeuffian feminists – find it constructive for women in philosophy to say that Joan of Arc both acts on feminine intuition and provides a model for the thought and action of a woman mystic or philosopher today?

Alternatively, we might instead agree with Le Doeuff that "feminine intuition" is meaningless "outside a general theory of the ordering of modes of knowledge" and that these theories must be looked at carefully, since they have yet to revalidate a woman's capability for philosophy. Now, allow me to demonstrate more about philosophy, especially salient philosophical distinctions, in the threesome of Bergson, Beauvoir and Le Doeuff.

I would like to propose tentatively that Bergson himself attempts to revalidate the intuition of a woman, Joan of Arc; and that this revalidation of a woman's intuition happens on the basis of her capability to intuit immanent rather than transcendent life. With her intuition, then, a woman (Joan) expresses a "dynamic" and "open" project. Here Bergson's use of "dynamic" describes the evolving quality of becoming in project(s) which are "open" to life and love. Bergson also distinguishes dynamic from "static" groups; that is, static can be the characteristic of a group (of men), which remains without change, as in a "closed" style of morality, say, in the fixed moral lifestyle of a hyper-traditional social world. So, in Bergson's sense of a dynamic rather than a static project, Joan of Arc acts heroically, moved by a creative energy (love) – to which she remains open.

In one of her discussions of Simone de Beauvoir's *Le Deuxième Sexe*, Le Doeuff herself describes sexists, in Bergsonian terms, as a group which is closed within a static project.[7] In contrast, neither Beauvoirian nor Le Doeuffian feminists constitute a group which is closed by their own fixed norms. Instead, the dynamic projects of these feminists generate confidence in, and openness to, actual and virtual life; "virtual" means the continually dynamic past–present which, as Bergson writes, "gnaws into the future."[8] This requires a view of past–present–future life as a continuous, virtual and actual process which, as seen already, means pure duration in Bergson.

From Le Doeuff's appropriation of Beauvoir's use of Bergson's distinctions of open and closed, dynamic and static, it should follow that the opposite of sexism is an open group, with a dynamic project, like that (potentially) of feminism. Moreover, the open, creative and dynamic qualities of (Bergsonian) freedom are, I suggest, significant for feminism today. My contention is that feminists, who follow after Beauvoir and Le Doeuff, encourage an open morality; this means generating creative emotions (as energy) and dynamic projects for constructive action. This openness is very different from the preoccupation of other contemporary feminist ethicists, political theorists and moral philosophers, with the conflicts, paradoxes and analyses making up the philosophical "problem of freedom." Most characteristic of the latter, theoretical problem is the popular, polarizing debates for and against either libertarianism or determinism. My additional contention is that the freedom implicit in Le Doeuff's feminism is, in contrast, not a matter of mere choice. Instead, her expressions of freedom are closer to Bergson's conception: freedom is a human capability for both making (creativity) and doing (activity).

Here I take Bergsonian freedom to be the capability for, and the energy in, living our projects openly and loving creatively. This freedom is consistent with the creative energy shaping and re-shaping our lives; and this means, at times, becoming undone by others in love and loss, and at other times, becoming once again confident in recognizing our freedom in human capability: that is, in our creative activity.

My recent turn to follow Le Doeuff's imperative, "Don't imagine anything; read him!," has meant reading Bergson alongside Beauvoir's apparent readings of his texts. His philosophy, which was initially popular in 1920s–30s France, has guided me back to the 1949 publication of Beauvoir's *Le Deuxième Sexe*.[9] This text suggests, for example, an open morality, unencumbered by debilitating forms of hyper-traditional life. Furthermore, I read Beauvoir as Bergsonian in advocating that we evolve beyond a hyper-traditional personal life as found in a closed form of mysticism. For instance, the apotheosis of a female mystic, as presented in *The Second Sex*, encloses her within, and subjects her to, a submissive love for her "Father" God. Whether read as narcissistic or masochistic this apotheosis, becoming a divine woman, is a regressive movement – or, so I suggest – following Beauvoir's text.[10]

Elsewhere I have argued that a Bergsonian openness is implicit in the freedom and feminism of Beauvoir; and this is most notable when it comes to her reading of female mystics.[11] Beauvoir describes, and argues against, female apotheosis because it subjected a woman lover – and/or a female mystic – to a submissive love of her man and/or God as her superior, since patriarchal, authority; and this illustrates what I have read as Bergson's "closed morality." In other words, Beauvoir rejects what I would call "a hyper-traditional form of female mysticism" as incoherent, if not self-defeating. Basically, to require a transcendent man-God to bestow freedom upon a female mystic already assumes her dependence on the bestowal of freedom by the patriarchal figure; and hence, this dependent relationship renders creation of "her" own freedom (autonomy) impossible.[12]

3 interpreting freedom: in folds, unfolding and enfolding

I admit having become personally intrigued by the ways in which Le Doeuff uncovers Beauvoir's appropriation of ethically and politically salient distinctions from Bergson's *The Two Sources of Morality and Religion*. My discovery of intertextual connections derives from Le Doeuff's distinctive and skilful unpicking of the ways in which Beauvoir's text appropriates Bergson's philosophy, in order to conceive – and to enact – freedom, friendship and feminism. As I have already noted, two of Bergson's sets of distinctions, which appear in *The Second Sex*, are closed and open groups (of morality) and static and dynamic projects (of religion). Re-conceiving these distinctions as overlapping relations (and not oppositions), Beauvoir herself points to an additional but often unnoticed dimension of Bergson's conception of the self. He acknowledges the existence of not only a "superficial," but also a "profound" self.[13]

I have come to understand that Le Doeuff would never accept "naturalizing" a so-called profound self – let alone, a soul! This would be to assume the existence in some deep and obscure place of a static self-soul. Instead, as a contemporary twenty-first-century woman philosopher, Le Doeuff would be much more likely to rethink the misleading distinction of profound and superficial self, which Beauvoir takes from Bergson, with new concepts and imagery. In fact, we might imagine, instead of a self that is split between profundity and superficiality, the surface of one's life is "complex" rather than "simple." This interpretation of a life's surface as complex is made possible by the philosopher Gilles Deleuze, who interprets the surface of freedom in terms of "folds," "unfolding" and "enfolding."[14] In part at least, the Deleuzian interpretation of a surface with folds, which is continually unfolding, folding and enfolding, takes a lead from his own contemporary Michel Foucault, in developing a style of writing which *shifts*. As Tom Conley explains, this shifting is a constantly evolving life-force, where concepts and figures "are metamorphosed," showing

> that in Deleuze's world everything is folded, and folds, in and out of everything else. The development of the fold demonstrates that philosophy finds in the fold the expression of a continuous and vital force of being and of becoming.[15]

I might conclude that the assured confidence in a dynamic project of freedom assumes a world where everything is folded, folds, and is enfolded in a creative energy: this is what might be called "love."

Returning to Beauvoir's appropriation of Bergson's philosophical distinctions, the latter ironically penetrate the mystical matters of *The Second Sex*. This is "ironic" because philosophers tend to steer clear of mystics. Philosophers, perhaps too often, dismiss anything "mystical" for its connotation as irrational, say, as a description of hysteria. This Bergsonian irony concerning mystical matters is manifest in Beauvoir's own portrait of the distinctive creativity of Joan of Arc. Basically, Beauvoir follows Bergson in calling Joan "a mystic." However, this use of the term does not presuppose a Christian theological, or a contemplative, form of mysticism, but rather a form of mysticism in which the mystic – Joan of Arc – becomes a heroine of love for her country.

Of course, we, feminist philosophers, might ask: isn't her motivation really Joan's love of her prince (who becomes king, the supreme authority, for whom she gives and loses everything)? If so, how does this hierarchal pattern of love differ from submission in love to God the Father? Does Joan of Arc love (her own) life? Does redefining mysticism and attributing it to Joan of Arc actually revalidate a woman's intuition as a method or faculty of philosophy? In other words, could Beauvoir's appropriation of Bergson's mystical intuition generate a serious alternative to Le Doeuff's account of feminine intuition as failing (in Bergson) to revalidate a woman's philosophical faculties, and so the role of a woman in philosophy?

Informed by Deleuze's *Bergsonism* more can be said about the mystic heroine in Bergson's philosophy, and by implication, in Beauvoir's. As two prominent commentators – Keith Ansell Pearson and John Mullarkey – writing on both Deleuze and Bergson explain, "Bergson [...] calls these heroes 'mystics', though, again, the notion of some ascetic contemplative is far from what he has in mind. These mystics are creators, transgressing boundaries of life, mind and society."[16] First, Bergson describes "complete mysticism" as "true, complete, active mysticism [which] aspires to radiate, by virtue of the charity which is its essence"; and "heroism itself is a return to movement, and emanates from an emotion – infectious like all emotions – akin to the creative act."[17] Second, Deleuze acknowledges the extraordinary role of the mystic in Bergsonian "philosophical intuition." Consider Deleuze's explanation of mysticism giving "an envelope or a limit to all the aspects of method":

> [T]he great souls – to a greater extent than philosophers – are those of artists and mystics (at least those of [...] mysticism that Bergson describes as being completely superabundant activity, action, creation).[18] At the limit, it is the mystic who plays with the whole of creation, who invents an expression of it whose adequacy increases with its dynamism [...] Everything happens as if that which remained indeterminate in philosophical intuition gained a new kind of determination in mystical intuition – as though the properly philosophical "probability" extended itself into mystical certainty [...] [I]t is precisely the existence of mysticism that gives a higher probability to this final transmutation into certainty, and also gives, as it were, an envelope or a limit to all the aspects of method.[19]

When a woman in philosophy (like Beauvoir) thinks of a limit to knowledge, or thinks of intuition as a faculty, she will have Kant in mind; and she won't be wrong either, if she imagines Kantian limits to Bergsonian philosophical intuition, even while the mystic's creative and dynamic life offers a kind of "certainty."

Twentieth-century French philosophy in Paris, especially between the two world wars when Bergson was publishing his later philosophical works, was fairly firmly placed in a French tradition of neo-Kantian philosophy. Furthermore, mysticism was claimed to be necessary for moving dynamically at the Kantian limits of knowledge and thought. This mystical dimension of Bergson's philosophy was, however, in the process of being replaced by French Hegelianism. In fact, some commentators will insist that the "French Hegel" replaced the popularity of Bergson in Paris.[20] It was, then, Deleuze alone who famously revives Bergsonian philosophy in the late 1960s, when the Latin Quarter in Paris was buzzing with French appropriations of Hegel, Husserl and Heidegger. Normally Beauvoir is associated with the latter, three German philosophers. However, Le Doeuff's originality is to point out the highly significant passages in *Le Deuxième Sexe*, which point back to the former, French philosopher; that is, she directs us back to read Bergson.

Most significant is Le Doeuff's bold comment in which she criticizes the preoccupation of the French appropriators of the German phenomenologists – presumably phenomenologists from Hegel to Husserl and to Heidegger – for what she discovers in Beauvoir concerning "a way out of" self–Other relations. This way out takes a path both (first) backwards to, and (next) forwards through, Bergson. I will return to show how Le Doeuff's Beauvoirian key to this exit from French Hegelianism generates new life for Bergsonian freedom, but also for friendship–love and feminism. Allow me to say more on Bergson's ironic use of a certain female mystic.

4 a mystic life: intuition enveloping its object

In the previous section we discovered the distinctive role of folds in Deleuze's style of writing philosophy, notably in his later writings on Foucault and Leibniz.[21] In *The Two Sources of Morality and Religion*, Bergson argues that "if the fringe of intuition surrounding intelligence is capable of expanding sufficiently to envelope its object that is the mystic life."[22] Bergson's imagery of enveloping anticipates Deleuze's folding; the imagery of envelopes and folds expresses the philosophers' ways to overcome the splitting of a self into a transcendent reality and a superficial or empirical self. Remember intuition in Bergson is the method and faculty for conceiving reality within an immanent process, that is, in pure duration.

According to the Bergsonian philosopher, in order to intuit virtual reality, mystical intuition has to make what is dead come to life again in pure duration. By intuiting the virtual (past), what is asleep awakens in actual life; and by inciting our capability for loving we expand human reality intuitively, cognitively and affectively. A Bergsonian intuition moves and is moved by this mystical life; as Bergson himself also makes clear, philosophical intuition is as rare as mystical experience. Despite the inexpressibility of such experience, intuited life shows itself in an ontology of becoming; and philosophical intuition of a constantly evolving, creative ontological process manifests itself in transformations of life.

So, when exactly is intuition not just philosophical, but also mystical? An intuition appears mystical when its activity is transformed into a liberating creativity rather than into reactive emotions. Bergson finds this creativity in "a heroic act," moved by the creative energy of love.[23] Bergson's *The Two Sources of Morality and Religion* generates positive conceptions of both the heroine and the female mystic as follows: (i) the mystic acts heroically out of her love of humanity (it is not clear whether "humanity" here is gender specific, that is, "man");[24] (ii) the heroine shows freedom to be the capability for continuous creativity; this capability manifests itself in an immanent dynamism, bringing together virtual (past) and actual (present) life; and ultimately, (iii) the mystic's love erupts in transformative change.

In my earlier essay I proposed that Bergson's mysticism, especially as he sees it lived by Joan of Arc, manifests itself as confidence in the intuitive power of love.[25] However, we might well ask: does Joan of Arc actually liberate herself from a (blind) devotion to her dauphin (whom she helps to become king)? The Le Doeuffian feminist would question Joan's love for the one whom she makes the most significant figure of patriarchal authority within her world. Does Joan in fact make the ultimate act of self-sacrifice for her king alone?[26] Whatever the case, for some feminist activists Joan of Arc might – nevertheless – be reconfigured as a lesbian, or transgender, icon for cross-dressing; that is, she is a mystic and heroine who transgresses sexual, social and work boundaries.[27]

Furthermore, Bergson places mystical intuition in an evolutionary line, alongside scientific method, in which the mystic leads:

> In order to carry [a line of evolutionary development] further otherwise than by mere guesswork, we should simply have to follow the lead of the mystic. That current of life which traverses matter, and which accounts for its existence, we simply took for granted. As for humanity, which stands at the extremity of the main line, we did not ask whether it had any other purpose but itself. Now, this twofold question [concerning two lines of evolving life] is contained in the very answer given to it by mystical intuition, Beings have been called into existence who were destined to love and be loved, since creative energy is to be defined as love.[28]

But let us return to Le Doeuff as she teases out and applies Bergson's distinctions between a closed and open morality in the Introduction to *The Second Sex*. We have already noted that Beauvoir describes sexism as remaining within a closed system of misogynist norms.[29] These "moral" norms enclose members of the group in duty to those who are the same. Moreover, as Le Doeuff argues persuasively,

> [Beauvoir] [...] lets us feel a moral reticence: the antagonism between the same and the other wouldn't exist if human reality were the locus of friendship [...]
>
> The source of this moral reticence is most probably Bergson: the phrase "immediate data of the social" in Lévi-Strauss seems also to be a transposition of a title of Bergson's: *Time and Free Will: An Essay on the Immediate Data of Consciousness*. In fact, Bergson's philosophy could be deemed a major but veiled source of inspiration for the whole introduction to *The Second Sex*. Bergson's *The Two Sources of Morality and Religion* offers a distinction between a closed morality, attachment to the group to which one belongs and obligation to the members of the closed community to which one belongs, and open morality, a humane and dynamic love of humanity in general that goes beyond the interests of the closed group. [As mentioned already] this distinction could be applied to the view that Beauvoir has of men: most of them remain within sexism, which is closed.[30]

The crucial feature of Le Doeuff's reading of Beauvoir's moral reticence is the decisive rejection of the category of the Other as an essential feature of human relations.[31] The love of the transcendent One, to which the woman submits, re-enforces closure and restricts freedom to something "bestowed" on the other by the One. Or, is it the divine man projected by the same (man)? Instead of differentiating freedom from its bestowal, the love of friendship is immanent, reciprocal and open. This immanence in friendship–love is generative of a self-making freedom, creative of equality, not reactive to the Other, but interactive within life's immanent relations, and generative of new movements in actual and virtual life; that is, in Bergsonian duration. Notice the stress on immanence rather than transcendence in Bergson's philosophy. A positive focus on immanence marks a significant difference for Bergson and Deleuze, in contrast, to French existential phenomenologists.

5 differentiation within immanence

In his extremely influential writings on immanence, Deleuze himself draws from both Spinoza and Bergson; and these philosophers inspire Le Doeuffian feminism not only because of the role of becoming in their philosophies, but because of their more marginal location in the dominant canonization of the history of philosophy. Obviously, this location provokes similar questions to those concerning marginalization in philosophy due to gender. Le Doeuff questions women's place in philosophy. For example, she draws points for her feminist conception of "dialogue" from Deleuze's *Dialogues II*, with a woman intellectual, Claire Parnet.[32] Le Doeuff asks rhetorically, what happened to Parnet? For us, the question might well be, why are there so few dialogues between a man and a woman in philosophy? Why is it that the man in philosophy will be remembered, while it is uncertain about the woman with whom he is in dialogue? Not that Deleuze has explicit answers to this line of questioning, yet he does help philosophers to turn away from the transcendent values which have been obstacles for women (and other marginalized subjects) in philosophy.

In particular, as already suggested, Deleuze turns philosophers away from transcendent forms of mystification, and towards immanence, creative energies and emotions within actual and virtual life. It is no coincidence that Deleuze was inspired by Bergson, amongst others, to turn the focus of twentieth-century philosophy towards actual-material and virtual life. Admittedly a philosophy of immanence would be dismissed by more traditional Anglo-American philosophers (of religion): whether a contemporary perspective on immanence or a modern European one, immanent thinking for many philosophers remains a dubious strand in the history of European philosophy. Nevertheless, my point is that Deleuze draws on Bergson; and our unpicking of ethically salient distinctions and differences in their texts can inspire, or perhaps is already inspiring, a new wave of feminist philosophy in and beyond France. This wave differentiates free subjects within an immanent, creative process.

By this point, we have begun to glimpse how it is that Bergson, Beauvoir, Deleuze and Le Doeuff inspire a movement within immanence. This movement is dynamic, since immanence is life and life is immanence, differentiating itself within a creative process. Immanence is not (like transcendence) lack. Transcendence had locked the one, or the self-same, and the other within an enclosure of narcissism and submission. Or, at least this is what I have been arguing on the basis of Le Doeuff's philosophical insights. Although in twentieth-century French thought it is Deleuze who revitalizes Bergson's philosophy, it is Le Doeuff who helps us – women in philosophy – to reorient ourselves in thought and life. This reorientation turns towards an alternative genealogy of immanent life, creative emotions and affections; this dynamic genealogy is necessary for a feminism of friendship (love as *philia*). We are, then, able to move away from the endless tensions, or conflicts, of oppositional relations. To repeat, not unlike Deleuze, Le Doeuffian feminism suggests to me taking Bergson's philosophy of (actual) present and (virtual) past–future life to support a sharp turn away from the Hegelian, Heideggerian or Sartrean phenomenology which had been dominated by struggles between the One and the Other. Le Doeuff wants nothing to do with, in her exact words, "a French style of German phenomenology" which became a "dogma" on the Left side of the Seine at some point after the 1930s in Paris.[33] Instead of struggling endlessly with self–other relations, Le Doeuff calls for the multiplications of difference: those which differentiate a life.

The "dogma of the other" as a necessary category, which remains at the heart of a French, *non*-Bergsonian form of mysticism – or, indeed, of mystification – traps philosophers within the either/or relations of the other to the One or the Other to the same. The subjection of "the one" (gendered man) by a wholly transcendent Other (the divine man) devalues immanence; and transcendence transcends the body in a disembodied consciousness. Subjection, on the one hand, was inevitable in that French style of phenomenological mystification. For instance, within Sartrean phenomenology, "no exit" exists out of "the hell" which is one's movement towards (his) transcendence and against (her) immanence. On the other hand, Deleuze and his co-author, Félix Guattari, in *What is Philosophy?* are well aware that any philosophical movement of immanence which celebrates life fully, rejecting the hierarchy of values in oppositional thinking, faces strong criticism from the main tradition in the history of philosophical argumentation. Nevertheless, the opposition of self–other and of transcendence–immanence is to be replaced by "transcending transcendences," especially by transcending "religious authority." Consider their sobering words:

> Putting their work and sometimes their lives at risk, all philosophers must prove that the dose of immanence they inject into world and mind does not compromise the transcendence of a God to which immanence must be attributed only secondarily [...] Religious authority wants immanence to be tolerated only locally or at an intermediary level, a little like a terraced fountain where water can [flow] [...] briefly immanent on each level but on condition that it comes from a higher source and falls lower down [...] Immanence can be said to be the burning issue of all philosophy because it takes on all the dangers that philosophy must confront, all the condemnations, persecutions and repudiations that it undergoes. This at least persuades us that the problem of immanence is not abstract or merely theoretical. It is not immediately clear why immanence is so dangerous, but it is. It engulfs sages and gods.[34]

This passage about immanence also contains what I have elsewhere argued is the decisive difference between Luce Irigaray's hyper-traditional mysticism of female apotheosis (transcendence) and Beauvoir's mysticism of creative activity (immanence). While a mysticism of sexual difference finds the sexually specific transcendence determining male and female lives fundamentally, independent of each other, a mysticism of creative energy finds immanence in a mystical life which is not divided on sex, or sexist, lines. The latter – immanence – could mean, if following Deleuze, that a life is creative in friendship and dynamic in freedom.[35]

Moreover, although a sexual-difference mysticism is aimed at sensible ecstasy in union with either the transcendent (hu)man or the transcendent male divine, I contend that, in contrast, only a mysticism inspired by a vital impetus (*élan vital*) will generate a creative emotion and a life energy (love). But are "a heroic love" and "a mystical intuition" (in Bergson's philosophy) virtually and actually open to life's continual creative process within immanence?

6 on subjection and bergsonian freedom

My previous defence of the distinctive strand of mystical life, which erupted in the Bergsonian philosophy of early twentieth-century Paris, was built (in part at least) on a critique of an Irigarayan imperative to become divine.[36] My critique was intended to expose the closure of female apotheosis; this closure locks lovers into asymmetrical relations of the one (human) to the Other (divine); and the other (woman) to the same (man). So, what about Joan of Arc and her dauphin (whom she will help to make king, while he will let her be burned at the stake)? In following Beauvoir and Le Doeuff, I want no part in any subjection of a woman to the One (king), or (wo)man to the Other (God). Instead, following Deleuze's *Bergsonism*, I propose that we should continue to extend Le Doeuffian feminism and Bergsonian freedom into a dynamic openness; open projects would resist subjection within the closure of self–other relations. The task would, then, be to create (global) friendships which, in turn, would encourage "a cosmic Memory"[37] liberating virtual (past) and actual (present) life. This is Bergsonian freedom in Deleuze's words:

> The little interval "between the pressure of society and the resistance of intelligence" defines a variability appropriate to human societies. Now, by means of this interval, something extraordinary is produced or embodied: creative emotion [...] [W]hat is this creative emotion, if not precisely a cosmic Memory, that actualizes all the levels at the same time, that liberates man from the plane (*plan*) or the level that is proper to him, in order to make him a creator, adequate to the whole movement of creation? [...] [T]o each member of a closed society, if he opens himself to [this liberation, this embodiment of cosmic memory in creative emotions...], it communicates a kind of reminiscence, and excitement that allows him to follow. And from soul to soul, it traces the design of an *open* society, a society of creators, where we pass from one genius to another, through the intermediary of disciples or spectators or hearers.[38]
>
> [...] the great souls – to a greater extent than philosophers – are those of artists and mystics (at least those [...] that Bergson describes as being completely superabundant activity, action, creation). At the limit, it is the mystic who plays with the whole of creation, who invents an expression of it whose adequacy increases with its dynamism.[39]

For Bergson, freedom expresses integral experience. Free acts both express us and transform a life, gathering together the whole – integral life – of the universe within pure duration. In other words, we freely enact what transforms us. As we have seen, Bergsonian freedom is not a quality or property of an individual subject, not either free or determined. Instead of freedom as deliberation about our individual choices, Bergson proposes that indetermination is the principle of freedom; and indetermination becomes the true principle of life, as the condition for the open-ended projects of creative beings. With this creativity, freedom appears immanent in the relations of all living beings, within an integrated whole. Thus, an open project is capable of free and dynamic relations, while material, or "matter," always contains the indeterminacy of life. Put simply, indetermination is a crucial characteristic of actual and virtual life within a dynamic, open process; and this is crucial for Bergsonian freedom.

So, my reading is that indetermination as the principle of freedom is in sharp contrast to the conception of freedom in the second half of the twentieth century by French and German phenomenologists: that of a subject's freedom to choose. But an individual's freedom (of choice) is precarious. In contrast, the revitalization of a Bergsonian freedom liberates a superabundant activity, creativity, of life: "the feeling that certain souls have [...] [of] love for every human being [a]s equal."[40] This creative energy of love equalizes the principle of freedom in friendship.

Against subjection (to the One [man] or the Other [god]) Bergsonian freedom demonstrates a distinctive openness, and the vital impetus (*élan vital*), in the creative love of humanity. A Bergsonian thread appears in philosophical writings in twentieth-century France on freedom and friendship: this thread traces the survival of images of love as *philia* in virtual life. Love between friends affects the interaction of actual (material) and virtual life; and so, actual and virtual affection recalls what Deleuze calls "cosmic Memory."[41] We can also understand how Bergson accounts for both the survival of images and the recognition of enduring images in pure duration: this virtual process in living freely generates the highly dynamic projects of loved and loving friends.

7 conclusion

A Bergsonian kind of mystical intuition runs through French thought (even today): it exists in the soul of an artist, mystic or creator who acts, inspired by a generative love. However obscure Bergson's own writings on mysticism appear to contemporary philosophers, a revitalization of confidence in a creative process motivates the feminist, open and dynamic project of friendship–love for, and within the lives of, women and men.

In the end, a picture of freedom, friendship and feminism emerges from virtual (in Deleuze's Bergsonian sense of being part of a cosmic memory) readings of Bergson, Beauvoir and Le Doeuff. This is a portrait of confident and capable interactions in creativity and dynamic projects, which transform our becoming within life. Let us assume here that the love of friendship is between like-minded, embodied and interrelated selves. The question is whether we transform our lives in freedom and in love between friends. I admit that human – and equally, humane – solidarity in freedom of "great souls" or, more carefully revalidated, intuition of a free self[42] is highly attractive; as in Beauvoir's women of action, with whom I began this paper. Instead I urge an incisive Le Doeuffian critical caution against naturalizing a timelessly abstract female soul for contemporary feminist philosophers. After this caution, I would like to conclude the present reorientation of ourselves with an image of living life freely *for* and *with* friends of Le Doeuffian feminism today.

notes

This publication of my research into Bergson's conception of the freedom of "a life" – as the human capability for becoming creative in, and open to, love – was made possible through the support of a grant from the John Templeton Foundation for the Enhancing Life Project. It is a revised version of a paper presented on 19 September 2015 in Paris. The opinions expressed in this publication are those of the author and do not necessarily reflect the views of the John Templeton Foundation.

1 Mme Guyon.

2 Simone de Beauvoir, *Le Deuxième Sexe, tome II* (Paris: Gallimard, 1949) 584. In English translation:

> There are women of action like [...] Joan of Arc, who are well aware of the goals they

set themselves and who lucidly invent the means to reach them: their revelations merely give an objective form to their certainties; they encourage them to take the paths they have carefully planned. There are [also] women narcissists [...] who, at the limit of silent fervour, feel suddenly "in an apostolic state". They are not very precise concerning their tasks: and – like patronesses seeking excitement – they do not care too much what they do as long as it is *something*. (Simone de Beauvoir, *The Second Sex*, trans. Constance Borde and Sheila Malovany-Chevallier (London: Cape, 2009) 733–34)

3 Michèle Le Doeuff, *The Sex of Knowing*, trans. Kathryn Hamer and Lorraine Code (New York and London: Routledge, 2003) 15–16; *Le Sexe du savoir* (Paris: Aubier, 1998) 43–45.

4 Le Doeuff, *The Sex of Knowing* 16.

5 Ibid. 15–16; emphasis added.

6 Henri Bergson, *The Two Sources of Morality and Religion*, trans. R. Ashley Audra and Cloudesley Brereton (Notre Dame, IN: U of Notre Dame P, 1977) 53, 227–28.

7 Michèle Le Doeuff, "Toward a Friendly, Transatlantic Critique of *The Second Sex*" in *The Legacy of Simone de Beauvoir*, ed. Emily R. Grosholz (Oxford: Oxford UP, 2004) 22–36.

8 Henri Bergson, *Creative Evolution*, trans. Arthur Mitchell (Mineola, NY: Dover, 1998) 4.

9 For reference to female mystics in Beauvoir's *Le Deuxième Sexe*, see note 2 above.

10 Beauvoir, *The Second Sex* 726–34.

11 Pamela Sue Anderson, "An Eruption of Mystical Life in Feminist Action: Mysticism and Confidence after Bergson" in *Mysticism in the French Tradition: Eruptions from France*, eds. Louise Nelstrop and Bradley Onishi (Farnham: Ashgate, 2015), especially 39–45, 48–50.

12 Creating one's own freedom could be re-stated as becoming autonomous in self-governance; rational and sensible human subjects liberate themselves, give themselves autonomous life, with their own capability for making and doing, that is, for making sense of life and for loving it by actually and virtually living it.

13 Henri Bergson, *Time and Free Will: An Essay on the Immediate Data of Consciousness*, trans. Frank Lubeck Pogson (Mineola, NY: Dover, 2001) 231–32.

14 This interpretation is informed by Michel Foucault's conception of "subjectivation" as the relation to oneself, which continues to create itself; see Gilles Deleuze, *Foucault*, trans. and ed. Sean Hands (London: Continuum, 2006) 80–101. In Deleuze's own words:

> [S]ubjectivation, the relation to oneself, continues to create itself, but by transforming itself and changing its nature [...] Recuperated by power-relations and relations of knowledge, the relation to oneself is continually reborn, elsewhere and otherwise. (86)

and

> The struggle for a modern subjectivity passes through a resistance to the two present forms of subjection, the one consisting of individualizing ourselves on the basis of constraints of power, the other of attracting each individual to a known and recognized identity, fixed once and for all. The struggle for subjectivity presents itself, therefore, as the right to difference, variation and metamorphosis. (87)

15 Tom Conley, "Folds and Folding" in *Gilles Deleuze: Key Concepts*, ed. Charles J. Stivale (London: Acumen, 2005) 180.

16 Keith Ansell Pearson and John Mullarkey, *Henri Bergson: Key Writings* (London: Athlone, 2002) 42.

17 Ibid. Cf. Bergson, *The Two Sources of Morality and Religion* 53; Anderson, "An Eruption of Mystical Life in Feminist Action" 37–57.

18 Deleuze refers his readers at this point to Bergson's *The Two Sources of Morality and Religion* where "the three mysticisms" of the Greeks, the Orientals and the Christians are discussed; see Bergson, *The Two Sources of Morality and Religion* 216–34.

19 Gilles Deleuze, *Bergsonism* [1966], trans. Hugh Tomlinson and Barbara Habberjam (New York: Zone, 1991) 112.

20 The "French Hegel" refers to the highly idiosyncratic, yet influential appropriations of Hegel in France from 1929, when Jean Wahl first published *Le Malheur de la conscience dans la philosophie de Hegel* (Paris: Rieder, 1929); the latter was followed by two more highly significant books on Hegel, by the French philosophers Jean Hyppolite and Alexandre Kojève; each of their distinctive French readings of Hegel would shape how French philosophy developed, especially in 1960s Paris. For more historical, bibliographical and philosophical details about French readings of Hegel, see Michael S. Roth, *Knowing and History: Appropriations of Hegel in Twentieth-Century France* (Ithaca, NY: Cornell UP, 1988); and the more recent account in Bruce Baugh, *French Hegel* (London: Routledge, 2003).

21 Deleuze, "Foldings, or the Inside of Thought (Subjectivation)" in *Foucault* 80–101; and Gilles Deleuze, *The Fold: Leibniz and the Baroque*, trans. Tom Conley (London: Continuum, 2006).

22 Bergson, *The Two Sources of Morality and Religion* 268.

23 Ibid. 53; Anderson, "An Eruption of Mystical Life in Feminist Action" 37–57.

24 Bergson, *The Two Sources of Morality and Religion* 53.

25 Anderson, "An Eruption of Mystical Life in Feminist Action" 43–44, 54; Pamela Sue Anderson, "Confidence in the Power of Memory: Ricoeur's Dynamic Hermeneutics of Life" in *Hermeneutics and the Philosophy of Religion*, eds. Ingolf U. Dalferth and Marlene A. Block (Tübingen: Mohr Siebeck, 2015) 51–70.

26 Is this merely another example of what Le Doeuff diagnoses as the Héloise complex? See Michèle Le Doeuff, "Long Hair, Short Ideas" in *The Philosophical Imaginary*, trans. Colin Gordon (London: Athlone, 1989) 102–10, 119–20.

27 For an example of appropriating Joan of Arc to make a case for transgender, see Tia Michelle Pesando, *Why God Doesn't Hate You* (Bloomington, IN: Balboa, 2014).

28 Bergson, *The Two Sources of Morality and Religion* 257.

29 Le Doeuff, "Towards a Friendly, Transatlantic Critique of *The Second Sex*" 33–34.

30 Ibid.

31 Pamela Sue Anderson, "The Other" in *The Oxford Handbook of Theology and Modern European Thought*, eds. Nicholas Adams, George Pattison, and Graham Ward (Oxford: Oxford UP, 2013) 83–104.

32 Gilles Deleuze and Claire Parnet, *Dialogues II*, 2nd ed., trans. Hugh Tomlinson, Barbara Habberjam, and Eliot Ross Albert (London: Continuum, 2002); *Dialogues II*, new ed. (London: Continuum, 2006) 11–12, 113–14, 120 n. 5, n. 7, n. 8. Michèle Le Doeuff, "Women in Dialogue and in Solitude," *Journal of Romance Studies* 5.2 (2005): 1–15. See also Pamela Sue Anderson, "In Dialogue with Spinoza and Others: Deleuze, Le Doeuff and the *Ethics*," *Paragraph* 37.3 (2014): 341–55.

33 Michèle Le Doeuff, *Hipparchia's Choice: An Essay Concerning Women, Philosophy, etc.*, trans. Trista Selous, 2nd ed. (New York: Columbia UP, 2007) 107. Cf. Pamela Sue Anderson, "Believing in This Life: French Philosophy after Beauvoir" in *Intensities: Philosophy, Religion and the Affirmation of Life*, eds. Katharine Sarah Moody and Steven Shakespeare (Farnham: Ashgate, 2012) 34–37.

34 Gilles Deleuze and Félix Guattari, *What is Philosophy?*, trans. Graham Burchell and Hugh Tomlinson (London: Verso, 1994) 45. Cf. Gilles Deleuze, *Pure Immanence: Essays on A Life* (Brooklyn, NY: Zone, 2001) 18–19.

35 Deleuze, *Pure Immanence* 18–19.

36 Anderson, "An Eruption of Feminist Action in Mystical Life" 37–58.

37 See next note for reference.

38 Deleuze, *Bergsonism* 111.

39 Ibid. 112.

40 Bergson, *The Two Sources of Morality and Religion* 311; also 99–100, 213–15, 227–38, 244–49. See also Le Doeuff, *The Sex of Knowing* 16–18, 199–208.

41 See note 40 (above); see also Pamela Sue Anderson, "Shadows of the Past: Phantoms of the Negative and Traces of the Affective," *Literature and Theology* 28.4 (2014): 371–88.

42 Beauvoir writes in her *Diary*, on 9 August 1926, about Bergson's account of a profound self; see Beauvoir, *Diary of a Philosophy Student*, vol. 1 (Urbana: U of Illinois P, 2006–) 60.

pamela sue anderson

edited by nicholas bunnin

SILENCING AND SPEAKER VULNERABILITY
undoing an oppressive form of (wilful) ignorance

As I stand before you today, I can hear the voices of women resounding from my own past, especially women's voices from the last decade of the twentieth century in Durham. In the present, I know of women in philosophy who might have been silenced by their audiences; and I must also confess to hearing women philosophers' voices whose mutual vulnerability (with my own) I did not recognize.

On International Women's Day 2016, I would like to admit, in particular, my "wilful ignorance" of speaker vulnerability – an ignorance which I will explain later in this talk. But it is enough to say from the outset that in my own attempts to gain confidence in speaking and developing reciprocal relations in philosophy I had disavowed my own vulnerability; this was self-deceptive. Teasing out the paradox surrounding speaker vulnerability in philosophy is part of my task today; the other part is "arguing" that mutual vulnerability in philosophical relations is what should characterize collective work in philosophy – or, at least, in feminist philosophy.

At the turn of the century, on 8 November 2000 (to be exact), I myself had the good fortune – or, perhaps, the not so "good" experience – to speak to Durham University Philosophers on the question "Is feminist philosophy a contradiction in terms?" I had a rather large audience for my talk in the Philosophy Department on that day, because most of them – male students and male philosophers – had mistaken my name for someone else: thinking it referred to the Other Pamela Anderson whose name right through the 1990s tended to appear regularly in newspapers. This confusion of interest in "me" had been encouraged by the appearance of a blonde-haired figure of a sexy woman, alongside my name and my title, on the poster announcing my philosophy talk for that day?!? Needless to say, this blonde figure was an addition to the original poster notifying philosophers of my talk. In the 1990s, especially, I was often not believed to be a "philosopher," when my name was seen ... So, was the name, with the addition of another woman to the poster, a joke?! Whatever the case, it remains a fact that on that particular 8th of November in Durham I was, first, not imagined as coming to speak about "philosophy" because of my name, but I was, second, not believed to be "feminist" because of what I actually said!! Instead I was accused, by one of the then prominent male philosophers, of "disappointing" the assembled audience, for speaking in abstract terms about feminist epistemology which, that male philosopher claimed, "in no way could be 'feminist,' since lacking the particularity, concreteness and relationality required for women, and so, for 'feminism'"!

I was quickly defended by the woman friend-philosopher "Chair" on that occasion, Dr Soran Reader ... who came out of her role as chair in order to respond to the so-called "disappointment" at hearing me. And yet, on reflection, I have realized since then something about speaker vulnerability and the silencing which confronted me as a woman in philosophy and a speaker who was not heard because at least some of the audience did not identify me as "a knower" with authority on feminist philosophy.

Today I might wonder what "I" as a speaker could have done differently in relation to my audience ... Indeed, was my intention on that day to seem "invulnerable" – like the philosophers who confidently discuss abstract issues in epistemology without any hint of vulnerability – in order to be taken seriously as a philosopher? But perhaps, even if I had spoken about particularity, concreteness and relationality on that day, I would still *not* have been heard speaking as a philosopher. I have to conclude that the situation was unresolvable by me alone.

However, since that occasion I have learned something extremely significant about what the feminist philosopher Michèle Le Doeuff in 1980 had called for: "collective work." Le Doeuff claimed that this work is "plural" and necessary for women seeking access to the philosophical. A collectivity was – and is – needed, despite the fact that access to philosophy had traditionally been mediated – for a philosopher – by the supposed "invulnerability" of one great mentor-philosopher. Following Le Doeuff, instead of relying on "one great man" in philosophy to pave the way, I would like to advocate (for younger women and men in philosophy) a new reliance on collective work, modelled on our mutual vulnerability as speakers and audiences; the aim is to cultivate reciprocal relations to the "unknown." Plus, this collectivity means today that my present talk can draw generously from a range of women in philosophy in and beyond my own group; this includes Michèle (Le Doeuff), Soran (Reader), Jennifer Hornsby, Rae Langton, Nancy Tuana, bell hooks, Judith Butler, Ann Murphy, Kristie Dotson and Simone de Beauvoir.

How different would my experience have been, together with Soran, if a collective group of women had supported us in the audience on 8 November 2000 in Durham Philosophy?

I collective work and the unthought: following after le doeuff

My own implicit awareness of a collectivity of women in philosophy began gradually in the last decade of the twentieth century, as the late Soran Reader and I organized various occasions for Philosophy here in the North East of Britain. Most notable is the occasion in 1994, when we hosted Michèle Le Doeuff's visit to Durham – at which time Le Doeuff gave a Royal Institute of Philosophy (RIP) lecture – for which we had a vastly different audience than I had as "Pamela Anderson"; but Le Doeuff, a woman in philosophy, our invited speaker in 1994 for the RIP in the North East, is part of another story, about a different audience, which I will leave for another time!

Much earlier, in 1980, Le Doeuff had described the lesson of collective work in her now classic essay "Long Hair, Short Ideas." The lesson is, in Michèle's exact words, "that 'I do not do everything on my own', that I am a tributary to a collective discourse and knowledge, which have done more towards producing me than I shall contribute in continuing to produce them" (Le Doeuff 127) – and also that

> [T]he only [...] attitude which makes collective work possible and necessary [is] a "collectivity" whose scope obviously extends beyond the "group" of people working together. (128)

As Le Doeuff goes on to explain,

> The belief which has emerged from my still very recent experience [prior to 1980] of collective work is that the future of women's

struggle for access to the philosophical will be played out somewhere in the field of plural work [...] Here, one has the impression of experiencing a new rationality, in which a relationship to the unknown and to the unthought is at every moment reintroduced. (Ibid.)

Thus, Le Doeuff forecasts the significance of a collectivity, which she discovers in twentieth-century women's struggle for access to the philosophical; but she also continues to teach us about the role of "the unknown" and "the unthought." The latter – the unthought – will play a crucial role in my accounts of both "speaker vulnerability" and a fundamental "ignorance of vulnerability."

2 silencing and speaker vulnerability

The vulnerability of a (woman) speaker follows from her dependence upon an audience; if she is to be heard, her dependence requires an audience who is both willing and capable of hearing her as a speaker and a knower. As (feminist) philosopher Jennifer Hornsby also explains, in her essay "Disempowered Speech," reciprocity between speaker and audience is essential. In Hornsby's words, "The existence of reciprocity is actually a perfectly ordinary fact, consisting in speakers being able not only to voice meaningful thoughts but also to be heard" (134).

Again, the Le Doeuffian idea of collective work should be brought into projects seeking more or better reciprocity in philosophical relations; and I take, as my focus, a speaker's relations to her philosophical audience as crucial here – for addressing the unknown, but also for seeking what has remained unthought; that is, the mutual vulnerability of relations of dependence (and affection), such as speaker and audience reciprocity. We must not go too quickly on this point: the fact of communicative reciprocity and the implicit dependence of a speaker on her audience still does *not* mean that these needs – of reciprocity and of interdependence – for the speaker's relations are easily met in philosophy. As many young women in philosophy today know (perhaps better than I thought when young), philosophical relations have tended to be built upon an assumption of the "invulnerability" to decisive attack.

Yet, as I have come to learn from other feminist philosophers – notably from those engaging with "an epistemology of ignorance" – philosophers who claim an invulnerability (in speaking) are self-deceived. Instead, every speaker – whatever their sex or gender – is *vulnerable* precisely because they are also dependent on an audience not only to hear them but to recognize them as a knower. So, to repeat, a philosopher is open to not having her speaker's needs met; this means vulnerability. Silencing is the risk a speaker runs, since an audience might not hear her or recognize her as a knower. But there can be different forms of silencing a speaker.

My concern is <u>both</u> that the audience actually needs to be willing and capable to hear what a speaker says <u>and</u> that the speaker must perceive this audience-competence, if silencing is to be avoided. A mutuality is required for successful communicative reciprocity; if not, silencing happens. To explain this briefly, I will appropriate a distinction from a 2011 *Hypatia* essay, "Tracking Epistemic Violence, Tracking Practices of Silencing," where Kristie Dotson identifies two forms of speaker-silencing: "quieting" and "smothering." On the one hand, a speaker is vulnerable to quieting, if an audience refuses to listen. In general, this means that the speaker is not treated by their audience as a knower (Dotson 242–43). Feminist epistemologists have identified quieting as a form of oppression in silencing women of colour, in particular (cf. Collins 69–81).

For example, the African-American feminist author bell hooks is perhaps the best known black feminist in the twentieth century to have demonstrated, in her now classic feminist text *Ain't I a Woman: Black Women and Feminism* (1981), the way in which black women speakers in the United States were undervalued not only by male audiences, but were not recognized as knowers by white feminists either. bell hooks continues to write about lack of recognition. In her 2012 essay "True Philosophers: Beauvoir and bell," she includes women in philosophy such as the white woman Simone de Beauvoir, and the black woman bell hooks *herself* (hooks, "True Philosophers" 227–36). Basically, the undervaluing and misrecognition of women in and outside of philosophy reflect how specific dependencies of women as speakers have not been met. But the *range* of women who have been silenced – by quieting – and the precise *nature* of their speaker vulnerability remain underexplored.

On the other hand, a speaker is vulnerable to "smothering," as a second form of silencing, when the speaker truncates her own voice and so the content of her message; that is, the speaker silences herself (Dotson 244). In fact, smothering as a self-silencing is a coerced silencing, when the speaker realizes her audience would not understand and/or not accept certain content; this smothering silences content for which the audience's competence is lacking, or, which the speaker knows is too risky to express to that particular audience. Many instances of coerced silencing exist: smothering a speaker is the only example of self-silencing I will mention, insofar as it is helps me to illustrate speaker vulnerability. And this vulnerability risks an audience's ignorance which, as a result, does not meet a speaker's needs. The speaker cannot depend on her audience to hear her; and the audience could not undo her silencing.

In contrast to smothering, quieting as the first form of silencing is determined by controlling images – such as those making up the philosophical imaginary, as uncovered by Le Doeuff. This quieting and its philosophical imaginary produce stereotypes as fixed images, built upon ignorance of a woman as a knower. In quieting, individuals and groups are treated as "not-knowers." Furthermore, this ignorance, which is maintained by an audience in cases of quieting, has been built on a more fundamental form of *wilful* ignorance.

3 vulnerability and wilful ignorance

The American feminist philosopher Nancy Tuana defines "wilful ignorance" as "a systematic process of self-deception, a wilful embrace of ignorance that infects those who are in positions of privilege, an active ignoring of the oppression of others and one's role in that exploitation" (11). For example, philosophical excavation of "a racial contract" has disclosed a direct link connecting systematic racial oppression and wilful ignorance (cf. Mills 18). This ignorance is not the opposite of knowledge. Instead, it is an active disavowal of one's own and another's vulnerability. Moreover, such active ignorance of a speaker as a knower produces violent acts of silencing, which infect the self-deceptive who deny life's vulnerability. A black woman's speaker vulnerability is materially and socially open to this violence, insofar as her life is dependent on others who are wilfully ignorant of oppressive relations; and an audience, which is privileged by race and gender, exploits this systematic process of self-deception.

No one has done more in recent years than the American feminist philosopher and queer theorist Judith Butler to show the myriad ways in which we all – whether lesbian, gay, queer, trans- or hetero-sexual – are dependent on others and vulnerable due to "precarious life" (Butler, *Precarious Life* 128–51). Life is, according to Butler, precarious because, roughly, we are dependent on others, and beside ourselves when undone by loss of the other (ibid.; cf. *Frames*; *Notes*). But, in fact, it is also bad faith (that is, self-deception) to expect – unthinkingly – a safe movement from this shared vulnerability as embodied speakers to a reciprocal, ethical accountability as a protection of one's vulnerability from violence. Moreover, the potential of vulnerability as openness to affection is denied in violent forms of self-deception.

To illustrate the problem of speaker vulnerability and violence, due to wilful ignorance, allow me to read some passages from bell hooks's own account of what I suggested above is an audience quieting her as a speaker. She is vulnerable to an audience's disavowal of her as a knower. In fact, bell hooks herself describes how she had to learn that self-silencing takes place; and it did for her. After being disavowed – quieted – by a white audience in her academic life she learned to perceive when it is too risky to discuss her views (as a black woman), when it is too dangerous to tell the truth! In a few lines from bell hooks's *Ain't I a Woman: Black Women and Feminism* (1981), we can see when and where bell herself explores the silencing of a black woman speaker by an audience of white men and white women. Also, in a few lines from bell hooks's account of her own first failed attempt to pass an oral examination for her Ph.D., in *Wounds of Passion: A Writing Life* (133–34), we can see when and where she learns that self-silencing is required; and I suggest that this is so because she is vulnerable as a speaker to wilful ignorance.

4 an example: bell hooks

4.1 racial oppression as the wilful embrace of an ignorance which infects those who ...

So, first of all, let us hear how bell hooks describes a nineteenth-century black woman speaker Sojourner Truth in the United States:

> [T]he white man who yelled at Sojourner, "I don't believe you really are a woman," unwittingly voiced America's contempt and disrespect for black womanhood. In the eyes of the 19th century white public, the black female was a creature unworthy of the title woman; she was mere chattel, a thing, an animal. When Sojourner Truth stood before the second annual convention of the women's rights movement in Akron, Ohio, in 1852, white women who deemed it unfitting that a black woman should speak on a public platform in their presence screamed: "Don't let her speak! Don't let her speak! Don't let her speak!" (hooks, *Ain't I a Woman* 159)

Thus, in *Ain't I a Woman*, bell hooks portrays the black female figure of Sojourner Truth as a figure who exposes these white women and the white men, who are aiming to silence a black woman for not being a woman! Yet Sojourner Truth moves the truth forward, by exposing a collective silencing – as a systematic process of self-deception – infecting nineteenth-century slave owners. In this reciprocal exposure of the audience's vulnerability and the speaker's to the truth of a black woman, Sojourner actually bears her breasts to her audience; and so we see the undoing of an oppressive form of ignorance. The mutual vulnerability of the female slave who speaks out and the audience who is forced to see the reality of a black woman's life equally forces a change, at the very least in perception, of womanhood (159–60 ff.). We glimpse here the potential in vulnerability for transformation.

Second, bell hooks admits not only the quieting which continues in racism and sexism after slavery in the United States but also the smothering of her own voice. She herself experiences the coercion into silencing her voice, not unlike the voices of other women of colour, in the nineteenth and twentieth centuries. In other words, bell hooks, born 1953, will recall that at nineteen years of age:

> [W]e were by and large silent. Our silence was not merely a reaction against white women liberationists or a gesture of solidarity with black male patriarchs. It was the silence of the oppressed – that profound silence engendered by resignation and acceptance of one's lot. (1)

Thus, this smothering of speakers exposes their vulnerability in both the self-silencing of black women and the silencing of black feminism.

Allow me to read more about how it was that bell hooks spoke openly at her first oral Ph.D. examination. At the same time, an audience's quieting was already at play preventing five white examiners from hearing bell hooks as a knower. In fact, the white examiners failed her for answers which they did not want to hear; she told the truth about race and gender, and they refused to listen to what she knew all too well. Now, let us listen to bell hooks as she captures a wilful ignorance of her vulnerability in telling the truth about race and gender. Notice the speaker vulnerability which the Ph.D. examiners exploit by wilfully embracing ignorance of racial oppression, or at least of bell hooks's account of it in teaching:

> I pass hours of written exams. My orals take place in a small room with five white people present. When I am asked how I will teach James Joyce, I respond that I have no intention of teaching his work and give my reasons why. I am totally honest. I make it clear that I have read Joyce but am unmoved by his writing and that of many of the so-called great white male writers. I speak about the need to have an unbiased curriculum, one that is diverse and varied. Since I have so clearly read everything required of me and indicate that in the discussion, I believe I have done well. When they tell me with smiles that I have failed, that I can try again in so many months, I am stunned. I know I will never willingly face them again. (*Wounds* 133)

bell hooks reflects on herself – that stunned self – retrospectively and writes the following in the third person:

> *By the time she walked the short distance home from the exams, brushing the tears from her eyes, she understood the way the system worked and was reconciled. She would have to start over somewhere else.* (133–34)

Of course, I might well ask myself, at this point, if I had been one of those white examiners, hearing bell hooks speak, would I have passed her, when it could be said that she did not exactly answer the question in her oral examination about teaching James Joyce? This question is about knowledge. However, it might reflect a disavowal – refusal – to grasp the actual vulnerability in relations between students and examiners, speakers and audiences, philosophy students and philosophy teachers. As audiences, do we, examiners, teachers, mentors ... actively deny our own relational needs for reciprocity and inter-dependence in philosophy? There continues to be a great need for us to learn about race and gender in philosophy.

Later, at another graduate school, bell hooks would understand how to answer the questions as required! At the same time, she still felt the need to have her views – what she perceived as the truth – heard! Her way forward resists complete self-silencing by speaking out in her graduate classes. But listen to her disappointment, as she reflects that, even in her intimate relation to an otherwise attentive boyfriend, who was also supportive of her writing life, he clearly did not understand her yearning to be heard:

> [...] [H]e doesn't understand why I need to share my ideas in the classroom, why I need to be heard. He thinks I would spare myself a lot of pain if I would just sit in these classrooms and be silent. (207)

In demonstrating how she manages not to be completely silenced, bell hooks avows herself; that is, she accepts her vulnerability as a speaker and as a black woman who wants to change both her life and the lives of those others around her. So, she continues, struggling with (her) speaker vulnerability in classrooms and in her writing life. We might say that she looks for mutual affection in vulnerability.

Clearly, in sharp contrast, I have never suffered as a woman of a non-privileged race from either the long and shocking history of slavery and ongoing racism in the United States or from racial and ethnic oppression in the world. Nevertheless, I have questioned how I might have been silenced in trying to speak as a (feminist) philosopher. Without a doubt, I have tried to protect myself by denying my own vulnerability as a speaker and as part of an audience in philosophy (e.g., as an autonomous thinker). And yet I am readily aware that it is never easy to be heard in philosophy; and much in the world of philosophy is structured for, and by, men who automatically claim for philosophy a privileged sort of "invulnerability" – but of course, I am suggesting that this will mean that we deceive ourselves about our own vulnerability, even in autonomous philosophical relations. A collectivity strengthens a woman speaker.

Now, returning to my opening example, I was vulnerable as a speaker – as a feminist philosopher – in that particular seminar in Durham's excellent Philosophy Department. Did I try to protect myself from criticism by not doing philosophy the way the men in philosophy expected "a woman" – or a "feminist" – to think and to speak? Whatever answers we might give about this, I did want to be taken seriously as a woman philosopher. So I might have silenced myself, smothering my expression of the full reality of feminist epistemology. Or, I might have been silenced, in the sense of quieted, by the prominent male philosopher who claimed I had disappointed my audience. Why couldn't the abstractness of my philosophy talk be "feminist," too? I have already agreed that collective work is necessary for women's access to the philosophical, enabling a mutual vulnerability in philosophical relations.

But I should be clear: my contention is that speaker vulnerability derives from dependence on an audience. This vulnerability is compatible with philosophers who think autonomously, whether great thoughts or not. My modelling of philosophical relations on speaker–audience reciprocity is just a relational model for philosophers' lives; but I am also trying to generalize this relational model to all of life's relations. This is to assume an inter-dependence of our lives which, as Butler has demonstrated, is seen most acutely in loss of love, loss of health and loss of life itself. Moreover, Butler adds our relations to organic and inorganic things, too. But if we stay with my focus, a speaker's dependence on an audience renders both sides of this mutual relation vulnerable; and this mutuality, I propose, is of great significance not only for those who have been marginalized, or dismissed (say, women), as if only they are "the vulnerable" in philosophy.

In fact, we are all vulnerable to being undone by the other when our needs cannot be met. We see this on a large scale in the loss of a loved one – on whom we have been dependent – but we are equally deceiving ourselves if we disavow our speaker vulnerability as philosophers. It would seem that vulnerability as an openness renders our relations to the world, to others' lives, and to life in general vulnerable to either violence or affection. Vulnerability is literally being liable to wounding, to openness or exposure; this vulnerable relationality makes us liable to harm and infection, but also to mutual affection.

5 undoing an oppressive form of wilful ignorance

My current research involves arguing for an "ethical" vulnerability; this would require striving for mutual affection; but this affection can be disavowed by oppressive forms of ignorance. Nevertheless, my intention in this research is to demonstrate that vulnerability – of any kind – is not reducible to an exposure *to violence only*; and so vulnerability is not merely a woman's problem – as in the violation of a woman's body. It is not fair to assign vulnerability to a separate class, a different gender, another race or a group of disabled persons ... who are said to make up "the vulnerable"! We are all vulnerable, so marginalizing or instrumentalizing "the vulnerable" reflects, instead, an oppressive form of wilful ignorance. In response to such wilfulness, we should avow vulnerability as an openness to the potential (capability) for inter-relational affection. I will return to this avowal, but my argument confronts serious opposition due to the harsh realities in life.

Returning to the theme of today's conference, "Resounding Voices: Women, Silence and the Production of Knowledge," I would like to extend my brief exploration into speaker vulnerability in order to explore, all too briefly, what is deeper (more primordial) than the exposure of women's voices to, and the speaker's dependence upon, the violence of silencing. There exists a fundamental ignorance of vulnerability itself.

The critical question raised in my concern with philosophical relations of vulnerability is the nature of a speaker's openness to self and other affection. On the one hand, speaker vulnerability is an openness to affection, leading to positive changes in one's knowledge or to becoming undone and eventually transformed, especially through one's loss of affection by way of violence. That is, due to life's precariousness, we are undone in becoming natal and mortal; birth and death involve changes for good and for not good in our relations to the world, which we carry with us in all our relations. On the other hand, speaker vulnerability is an exposure to, and dependence on, an audience, which can be wilfully ignorant of our mutual vulnerability, in silencing a woman's voice in philosophy. There is silencing of, in more technical feminist philosophical terms, a woman's "testimony" of the very idea of corporeal vulnerability, in *not* recognizing a female speaker as a knower who is trustworthy and whose vulnerability is highly significant for understanding our precarious lives together.

Extending this understanding of vulnerability to all of life we can understand, as Butler has shown, life's precariousness; and this recalls the Le Doeuffian idea of a collectivity. Collective work by feminist philosophers has unearthed the reality of human vulnerability, which nevertheless has been wilfully disavowed. To repeat, as Tuana says, "*a wilful embrace of ignorance infects*" those privileged audiences and privileged speakers. One problem, which surfaces again and again as we dig deeper into this matter, is the wilful ignorance of vulnerability itself; that is, the vulnerability of the speaker, as well as a more fundamental ignorance of vulnerability, becomes obvious in the precarious ways in which human lives are or are not oppressed.

Again, it is Butler who has led women – who are lesbian, gay, queer, straight, trans ... and so on – in philosophy, in ethics, in politics to an awareness of this deeply problematic ignorance of vulnerability. Her writings on precarious life, and the precarity of lives differentially located, expose often tragically those bodies on a political edge of life. Becoming aware of bodily vulnerability, however, does not necessarily lead to affection. Instead, all too often, responses to bodily vulnerability erupt into, as Butler argues, militaristic politics. Retribution all too naturally follows violent exposure to one's own vulnerability.

Globally the wilful ignorance of vulnerability itself has (ironically) given some people reasons for violence. Consider the situation in the United States where an escalation of gun violence happens far too easily. One example of an American news report tells us that a twenty-nine-year-old man shot a woman in a cinema in Seattle, Washington, when his concealed gun accidentally went off. He was carrying the weapon, he said, because of his fear of mass shootings. This strange logic generates an ending that is precisely the opposite of what was desired: rather than offering protection, his gun made the world less safe.

The man was striving for invulnerability. Like many US citizens, he thought his bodily vulnerability could be overcome with possession of a gun. But the data is very clear: the very presence of more and more guns continually increases the violence. Striving for invulnerability – whether as the man with a gun for "self-protection" or the philosopher with an argument for his shield against his vulnerability – puts us at a serious human risk. And it misses the opportunity that vulnerability can offer.

Ultimately the challenge in my arguing for ethical vulnerability is indicated in various ways by Butler's many publications on precarious life, precarity and vulnerability (Butler, *Precarious Life* 28–29; cf. *Frames*; *Notes*). Butler points out that an increased sense of vulnerability is one that is often accompanied by a similarly increased sense of violence; this is re-enforced by there being nothing in the recognition of one's own embodied vulnerability that necessarily inspires generous love, empathy or tolerance. Nevertheless, Butler claims that recognition of our lives as dependent on others – especially in grief, desire or rage – could be the ground on which we might build non-violent affection – such as non-militaristic political action; but this would require us, in Butler's words, "to attend to, abide by" (*Precarious Life* 29), what I have suggested is "the unthought"

(Le Doeuff 128). In other words, we must think of our dependence on others, "by staying with the thought of corporeal vulnerability itself" (Butler, *Precarious Life* 29). Butler associates vulnerability in politics with grief or mourning, which motivates either retaliation or other action forcing us to change. Facing such loss, loss of health, of life, of love, never leaves us unaltered.

To conclude, I began my talk on International Women's Day 2016 with women's voices resounding and Michèle Le Doeuff's provocation for collective work in gaining access to philosophy, the unknown and the unthought, which need to be reintroduced continually, in order to avoid a fixation on the completeness of one's knowledge. I also admitted that as a woman in philosophy I have wilfully disavowed my own vulnerability as a speaker in philosophy: above all, I wanted to be an autonomous thinker – not a "vulnerable" woman. However, I suggested at the outset that this was a self-deceptive, if not a self-defeating, stance for a philosopher to take. I have endeavoured to demonstrate how speaker silencing takes place in both "quieting" of a speaker, as a not-knower, by an audience and "smothering" of a speaker by her own self, whether coerced or not. In exploring how bell hooks's writings offer accounts of both the quieting and smothering of women of colour, I suggested that Nancy Tuana has helpfully pointed out the way in which a disavowal of vulnerability itself needs to be undone as an oppressive form of wilful ignorance. This undoing, I suggest, should take place by recognition of our mutual vulnerability instead of an acceptance of a systematic process of self-deception that "infects those who are in positions of privilege," whether these positions are that of the great mentor-philosopher or that of the white examiners of an African-American woman Ph.D. candidate.

In the end, I must admit that there is nothing to compel the philosopher to accept my challenge – to recognize their vulnerability in philosophical relations. Nevertheless, no one can deny in all honesty that they will not be undone by others in love, bereavement or rage. Thus, I urge us to increase our collective work on relations of mutual vulnerability as, at the very least, a philosophical task worthy of anyone who is at all serious about the production of knowledge by and for women in philosophy.

note

My writing of this keynote address for the International Women's Day Conference, Durham University, UK (8 March 2016) was made possible through the support of a grant from the John Templeton Foundation, via the Enhancing Life Project. The opinions expressed in this paper are those of the author and do not necessarily reflect the views of the John Templeton Foundation.

bibliography

Butler, Judith. *Frames of War: When is a Life Grievable?* London: Verso, 2009. Print.

Butler, Judith. *Notes toward a Performative Theory of Assembly.* Cambridge, MA: Harvard UP, 2015. Print.

Butler, Judith. *Precarious Life: The Powers of Mourning and Violence.* London: Verso, 2004. Print.

Collins, Patricia Hill. *Black Feminist Thought: Knowledge, Consciousness and the Politics of Empowerment.* New York: Routledge, 2000. Print.

Dotson, Kristie. "Tracking Epistemic Violence, Tracking Practices of Silencing." *Hypatia: A Journal of Feminist Philosophy* 26.2 (2011): 236–57. Print.

hooks, bell. *Ain't I a Woman: Black Women and Feminism.* Boston: South End, 1981. Print.

hooks, bell. "True Philosophers: Beauvoir and bell." *Beauvoir and Western Thought from Plato to Butler.* Ed. Shannon M. Mussett and William S. Wilkerson. Albany: State U of New York P, 2012. 227–36. Print.

hooks, bell. *Wounds of Passion: A Writing Life.* New York: Holt, 1997. Print.

Hornsby, Jennifer. "Disempowered Speech." *Philosophical Topics* 23.2 (1995): 127–47. Print.

Le Doeuff, Michèle. *The Philosophical Imaginary.* Trans. Colin Gordon. London: Athlone, 1989. Print.

Mills, Charles. *The Racial Contract.* Ithaca, NY: Cornell UP, 1997. Print.

Tuana, Nancy. "The Speculum of Ignorance: The Women's Health Movement and Epistemology of Ignorance." *Feminist Epistemologies of Ignorance.* Spec. issue of *Hypatia: A Journal of Feminist Philosophy* 21.3 (2006): 1–19. Print.

editorial note

In the final year of her life, Professor Pamela Sue Anderson was engaged in a new phase of her research in philosophy of religion – linking reflections on human vulnerability with analysis of the nature of love within religion. The context was two research projects, both funded by the John Templeton Foundation, in which she was participating; she found that each enriched the other, while she brought a distinctive integration to the two. First, she was a Senior Scholar in the Enhancing Life Project based at the University of Chicago, where her theme was "Vulnerability and a Liveable Life." At the same time she was a Co-investigator in the "Love in Religion" project at Regent's Park College, University of Oxford, which had its origin in a proposal from Muslim scholars (in an open letter to world Christian leaders called "A Common Word") that the double love-command of the Christian Gospels and the Torah – love of God and love of neighbour – could be common ground between religions. Her development of the theme of vulnerability in the two contexts of "enhancing life" and "love of God and neighbour" broke new ground for the philosophy of religion.

Professor Anderson made her research in that last year accessible through a series of seminars and lectures as she was able. During May–June 2016 she led a graduate seminar in the Philosophy Faculty of the University of Oxford, introducing a series of texts from women philosophers on the theme of vulnerability, including the work of Judith Butler, Anne Murphy, Alison Assiter, Jackie Scully, Julia Kristeva, Catherine Keller and Elizabeth

pamela sue anderson

edited by paul s. fiddes

CREATING A NEW IMAGINARY FOR LOVE IN RELIGION

O'Donnell Gandolfo. The seminars attracted a remarkably high and sustained attendance, largely because through them she was sharing insights from her own research. Her work was also disseminated through papers at four international conferences: an "International Women's Day" conference in the Philosophy Department of the University of Durham (March 2016); a conference on "Relation, Vulnerability, Love: Theological Anthropology in the Twenty-First Century" at the University of Leuven (September 2016); a colloquium on "Cutting-Edge Issues in the Study of Love" at the University of Oxford (November 2016) as part of the "Love in Religion" project; and a British Academy conference in London on

"Vulnerability and the Politics of Care" (February 2017). Anderson was not well enough to attend the first and last of these events, and her paper was read by a former pupil. Each time her work evoked considerable interest and a lively response from the participants, there being a general consensus that a truly original argument was being advanced which was reaching deeply into human experience.

In the following paper I was aiming, with Anderson's own consent and encouragement in conversations with her, to make some of the results of her research for both the "Enhancing Life" and the "Love in Religion" projects more widely accessible by combining parts of her papers given for the events at Oxford and London, with some light editing. The sections which come from her paper delivered at the "Love in Religion" colloquium have already appeared on the website of the project,[1] but here they take on new significance in the context of her reflections on what she called "speaker vulnerability." In brief, she was urging the creation of a new social imaginary in recognizing vulnerability.

The theme of vulnerability is usually discussed in the context of violence, either analysing violence inflicted on certain groups with the aim of defining vulnerability, or urging (more positively) that fear of violence should not become the occasion for denying or avoiding a universal vulnerability. Anderson's aim was to shift the framework of discourse altogether, and to consider vulnerability as a means of developing bonds of affection that would enhance life. While this project has some affinities with the work of Judith Butler, the way that Anderson has developed it has (in my view) unique features. First, she has taken the instance of "speaker vulnerability," experienced especially by women, as an illuminating paradigm for exposure to either violence or affection in dependence on an audience. Second, she has related vulnerability to the feminist concerns for recognizing wilful "epistemological ignorance" and for cultivating a true openness to the "unknown"; and third, she has explored vulnerability, in its fostering of affection, as a distinctively religious experience throwing light on religious ideas of love.

The interaction of these three areas promises much for the promotion of both "enhancing life" and "love in religion," and the conclusion of the essay that follows is a kind of manifesto showing that the two concerns are in fact one. So Professor Anderson lays out a track for future development that she herself, in her own vulnerability, was not able to follow any further.

From my general observations, the Abrahamic religions today tend to be pulled in two directions – towards love or towards vulnerability. The first often motivates an obedience to law, and the second often motivates either the inflicting or evasion of violence in an effort at self-defence. Neither perspective would seem to escape problematic myths which block our exposure to giving and receiving true "neighbour-love," a form of love which ought to be shared by Jews, Christians and Muslims. Let us assume for the sake of argument that "myths" are, as Mary Midgley explains: "symbolic stories which play a crucial role in our imaginative and intellectual life by expressing the patterns that underlie our thought."[2] I propose that myths in our imaginative and intellectual life need to be explored openly and critically for their impact on the place of love in religion.

I love and religion

Opposing perspectives concerning love in Judaism, Christianity and Islam are recognizable in the conceptions of, on the one hand, "a personal God" of love, whose followers have access to "their" God's words, derived from the law of the prophets, *and*, on the other hand, a distinctively "mystical God" of love, who is imagined not through words or laws, but felt as a mysterious, incomprehensible gift of gracious love. For adherents to the latter, love comes directly from God. But when we think critically about these images, the former, a personal God, can become a grave liability for persons in the Abrahamic religions, insofar as their God is limited by the very fact of being treated as "a person." For instance, this God would be limited by a man's projection of his own gender onto God as a divine person.[3] Moreover, the supposed guidance of a personal God who apparently condones acts of atrocities in the name of Christianity, Judaism or Islam obscures any concrete practice of love across religions. On the other hand, recognizing the dangerous limitations of human projections of God as a person ("He"), the Abrahamic religions have at times attempted to transcend any personal conception of divine love by turning to a "mystical God" of infinite and ineffable love. Such a God, however, would be able to give *no* cognitive guidance for the practice of love in religion.

I have thus found both of these personal and mystical conceptions of "the one God of love" inadequate for practices of neighbour-love; each "myth" falls short of other contemporary accounts of human affections and spiritual practices by moral and evolutionary psychologists, neuroscientists and affect theorists. Actual contemporary religious practices of love are what I would like to explore: we need to discover how love might be performed openly and creatively, and how love is (or has been) imagined in the myths we live by.

From my present standpoint, it is difficult to imagine what our contemporary global world might look like if the Abrahamic religions *actually* shared – *in* current *practice* – the two love commandments and the one God who is love itself. In Mark 12.28–31 it is written,

> "Hear, O Israel, the Lord our God, the Lord is one. And you shall love the Lord your God with all your heart [affection], with all your soul [conation], with all your mind [cognition] and with all your strength [vital force]." This is the first commandment. And the second, like it, is this: "You shall love your neighbour as yourself." There is no other commandment greater than these.

In his essay "The 'Rule of Law of Love'," the Islamic philosopher HRH Prince Ghazi bin Muhammad of Jordan quotes these verses from the Gospel of Mark, as well as similar statements of the two love commandments in Matthew and Luke, while referring back to their Old Testament source in Deuteronomy 6, Leviticus 19 and other relevant biblical verses.[4] Prince Ghazi argues that the two love commandments, when combined with the "Golden Rule" ("Do to others what you want them to do to you" – Luke 6.31), offer common scriptural ground for love in Judaism, Christianity and Islam. If we follow these love commandments then we will (at least) have in mind the relationships which God creates by way of the prophets.

The central concepts for analysis in the three Abrahamic religions, are "shall" (obligation), "love," "neighbour" and "yourself." The second-person references in "you shall love [...] your God with all your heart [...] soul [...] mind [...] and all your strength" also imply human capacities for love. Conceptual and theological differences between religions are, however, reflected in the patterns which underlie thinking about the obligation: "you shall love your neighbour as yourself." Two significant differences, for example, that have to be taken into account in finding "common ground" for love in religions are displayed in the contrasting thought of two philosophers – the Jewish twentieth-century philosopher Emmanuel Levinas and the Christian nineteenth-century philosopher Søren Kierkegaard – in their understandings of both "love" and "neighbour," while they share the sense of obligation ("you shall") implicit in the love commandments.[5] All too briefly, neighbour-love in Levinas appears more demanding ethically than Kierkegaard's neighbour-love which is enabled by divine love (implying a duty to remain in love's debt to God's grace).[6] Levinas shows ambivalence about the meaning of love, which leads him to treat "love" as "responsibility," and "the neighbour" as "the Other (who commands the I)," writing typically that "the I before the Other is infinitely responsible,"[7] so that the face of the other commands us.[8] Kierkegaard claims that neighbour-love is always dependent on God's gracious gift through which we are capable of loving "the neighbour" – as we have been loved – and the neighbour is potentially anyone else. It is clear that the Levinasian asymmetrical relation of self–other and the Kierkegaardian reciprocal relation of self–neighbour derive from their respective theological assumptions; these may prove decisive for their saying very different things about "neighbour-love."

Action-guiding concepts, as well as human capacities, are thus given different meanings depending on how we understand our religion and our relationship to "the Lord our God." These differences raise serious questions concerning our ability to communicate with other religions, using the same words which have significantly different religious significance for guiding practices of neighbour-love. So, it becomes obvious that love in Judaism, or love in Islam, is not always understood as "love" is in Christianity; furthermore, within each religion, there will be different understandings of love. In the light of these conceptual difficulties, I turn in our present-day context to consider one practice which offers occasion for love, but which also has a problematic myth informing it, no less than love in religion.

2 vulnerability, love and enhancing life

In recent months, I have been researching the use of "vulnerability" and its portrayal by our social or, as I prefer to say, our "philosophical" imaginary. Let us imagine vulnerability as the wound-ability of heart, soul, mind or strength, which will affect our overall capability for love, for good or for bad. I have made the ambitious proposal to change our philosophical imaginary when it comes to certain mythical patterns of thought – and concepts – we currently live by. In particular, this would mean re-imagining vulnerability by transforming an exclusively dark myth of fear and violence, which dominates our social imaginary, into (re)new(ed) concepts for love and vulnerability. This would make a contribution, I believe, to the human project for enhancing life. The dark myth has penetrated the philosophical concepts which structure our argumentation about "the vulnerable" on religious, political and ethical matters.

The problem (as I see this underlying pattern of thought) is that the myth immediately associates vulnerability with violence; and this creates a pattern for human relations where vulnerability generates fear, which in turn generates violent forms of self-protection and/or self–other control; eventually, terror turns nations in on themselves and escalates the global conflicts which will (unwittingly) eliminate "the weak." One damaging response has been to name marginalized groups of people who are devalued and, often, excluded "the vulnerable"; this marginalization involves a projection of vulnerability onto an inferior other by an imaginary belief that the invulnerable have a superior life. It is, then, simply assumed that fear – as in terror – undermines the real goal in political, religious and ethical life, which is *in*vulnerability. We can surely see this myth personified on the political landscape around us, whether in the United States or the United Kingdom.

The critical question is, what exactly motivates people to respond to vulnerability by closing themselves off, and using violence for protection, instead of an openness to love and loving efforts for mutual affection? Why do we, as human, allow an open wound to bleed rather than to care for it? After all, wounds can be openings for healing relations. The dangerous message that we need to overcome vulnerability at all costs is simply counterproductive, since it leads to interminable violent separations and conflicts as seen in global terrorism. Of course, charitable organizations and health-care professions readily focus on caring for the vulnerable; yet a dark social imaginary continues to stigmatize those needing to be cared for as a drain on an economy, carefully separating "the cared for" from those who are thought to be "in control" of their lives and of the world. As the political myth suggests, "we" do not want too many of "them," for example migrants and refugees.

3 the example of speaker vulnerability

To explore the "dark myth" of vulnerability further, I propose to take as a paradigm the particular vulnerability that many speakers in front of an audience experience. This situation is especially acute, I have observed, in the case of a woman philosopher. We readily see that her vulnerability follows from her dependence upon an audience; if she is to be heard, her dependence requires an audience which is both willing and capable of hearing her as a speaker and a knower. As (feminist) philosopher Jennifer Hornsby also explains, in her essay "Disempowered Speech," reciprocity between speaker and audience is essential. In Hornsby's words, "The existence of reciprocity is actually a perfectly ordinary fact, consisting in speakers being able not only to voice meaningful thoughts but also to be heard."[9]

Here I have learned something extremely significant about what the feminist philosopher Michèle Le Doeuff in 1980 had called "collective work" in her now-classic essay "Long Hair, Short Ideas." The lesson is, in Michèle's exact words, "that 'I do not do everything on my own', that I am a tributary to a collective discourse and knowledge, which have done more towards producing me than I shall contribute in continuing to produce them."[10] As she goes on to explain,

> the future of women's struggle for access to the philosophical will be played out somewhere in the field of plural work [...] Here, one has the impression of experiencing a new rationality, in which a relationship to the unknown and to the unthought is at every moment reintroduced.[11]

A collectivity is needed, despite the fact that access to philosophy had traditionally been mediated – for a philosopher – by the supposed "invulnerability" of one great mentor-philosopher. Following Le Doeuff, instead of relying on "one great man" in philosophy to pave the way, I would like to advocate a new reliance on collective work, modelled on our mutual vulnerability as speakers and audiences. At the same time, what Le Doeuff calls the "unthought" plays a crucial role in my accounts of both "speaker vulnerability" and a fundamental "ignorance of vulnerability": the aim is to cultivate reciprocal relations to the "unknown."

I take a speaker's relations to her philosophical audience as crucial here – for addressing the unknown, but also for seeking what has remained unthought: that is, the mutual vulnerability of relations of dependence and affection, such as speaker and audience reciprocity demonstrate. Speaker vulnerability models the possibility of turning from violent actions (such as silencing or undermining the speaker) to the creation of affectionate relations. We must not go too quickly on this point: the fact of communicative reciprocity and the implicit dependence of a speaker on her audience still does *not* mean that these needs – of reciprocity and of interdependence – for the speaker's relations are easily met. As many young women in philosophy today know (perhaps better than I thought when young), philosophical relations have tended to be built upon an assumption of the "invulnerability" to decisive attack.

Yet, as I have come to learn from other feminist philosophers – notably from those engaging with "an epistemology of ignorance" – philosophers who claim an invulnerability (in speaking) are self-deceived. Instead, every speaker – whatever their sex or gender – is *vulnerable* precisely because they are also dependent on an audience not only to hear them but to recognize them as a knower. So, to repeat, a philosopher is open to not having her speaker's needs met; this means vulnerability. Silencing is the risk a speaker runs, since an audience might not hear her or recognize her as a knower.

No one has done more in recent years than the American feminist philosopher and queer theorist Judith Butler to show the myriad ways in which we all – whether lesbian, gay, queer, trans- or hetero-sexual – are dependent on others and vulnerable due to "precarious life."[12] Life is, according to Butler, precarious because, roughly, we are dependent on others, and beside ourselves when undone by loss of the other.[13] But, in fact, it is also bad faith (that is, self-deception) to expect – unthinkingly – a safe movement from this shared vulnerability as embodied speakers to a reciprocal, ethical accountability as a protection of one's vulnerability from violence. Moreover, the potential of vulnerability as openness to affection is denied in violent forms of self-deception.

I have already argued that collective work is necessary for women's access to the philosophical, enabling a mutual vulnerability in philosophical relations. I should be clear: my contention is that speaker vulnerability derives from dependence on an audience. This vulnerability is compatible with philosophers who think autonomously, whether great thoughts or not. My modelling of philosophical relations on speaker–audience reciprocity is certainly a relational model for *philosophers'* lives, but I am also trying to generalize this relational model to all of life's relations. This is to assume an interdependence of our lives which, as Butler has demonstrated, is seen most acutely in loss of love, loss of health and loss of life itself. Moreover, Butler adds our relations to organic and inorganic things, too. But if we stay with my paradigm, a speaker's dependence on an audience renders both sides of this mutual relation vulnerable; and this mutuality, I propose, is of great significance not only for those who have been marginalized, or dismissed (say, women), as if only they are "the vulnerable" ones.

In fact, we are all vulnerable to being undone by the other when our needs cannot be met. We see this on a large scale in the loss of a loved one – on whom we have been dependent. It would seem that vulnerability as an openness renders our relations to the world, to others' lives, and to life in general vulnerable to either violence or affection. Vulnerability is literally being liable to wounding, to openness or exposure; this vulnerable relationality makes us liable to harm and infection, but also to mutual affection.

4 wilful ignorance of vulnerability

The critical question raised (above), in my concern with relations of vulnerability, is the nature of a speaker's openness to self and other affection. On the one hand, speaker vulnerability is an openness to affection, leading to positive changes (in one's knowledge), or, to becoming undone – and eventually, to becoming transformed by those changes. This is especially poignant when one's loss of affection is by way of violence; that is, due to life's precariousness, we are undone in becoming natal and mortal; birth and death involve changes for good and for not good in our relations to world, which we carry with us in all our relations. On the other hand, speaker vulnerability is an exposure to, and dependence on, an audience, which can be wilfully ignorant of our mutual vulnerability, in silencing a woman's voice. There is silencing of, in more technical feminist philosophical terms, a woman's "testimony" of the very idea of corporeal vulnerability, in *not* recognizing a female speaker as a knower who is trustworthy and whose vulnerability is highly significant for understanding our precarious lives together.

Extending this understanding of vulnerability to all of life, we can understand, as Butler has shown, life's precariousness; and this recalls the Le Doeuffian idea of a collectivity. Collective work by feminist philosophers has unearthed the reality of human vulnerability, which nevertheless has been wilfully disavowed. The American feminist philosopher Nancy Tuana defines "wilful ignorance" as "a systematic process of self-deception, a wilful embrace of ignorance that infects those who are in positions of privilege, an active ignoring of the oppression of others and one's role in that exploitation."[14] Such "a wilful embrace of ignorance" infects audiences and speakers who think of themselves as privileged exceptions. One problem, which surfaces again and again, as we dig deeper into this matter is the wilful ignorance of vulnerability itself. The vulnerability of the speaker, as well as a more fundamental ignorance of vulnerability, become obvious in the precarious ways in which human lives are, or are not, oppressed.

Again, it is Butler who has led women – who are lesbian, gay, queer, straight, trans ... and so on – in philosophy, in ethics, in politics to an awareness of this deeply problematic ignorance of vulnerability. Her writings on precarious life and the precarity of lives differentially located expose often tragically those bodies on a political edge of life. Becoming aware of bodily vulnerability, however, does not necessarily lead to affection. Instead, all too often, responses to bodily vulnerability erupt into, as Butler argues, militaristic politics. Retribution all too naturally follows violent exposure to one's own vulnerability.

Globally the wilful ignorance of vulnerability itself has (ironically) given some people reasons for violence. Consider the situation in the United States where an escalation of gun violence happens far too easily. To take one example, an American news report tells us that a twenty-nine-year-old man shot a woman in a cinema in Seattle, Washington, when his concealed gun accidentally went off. He was carrying the weapon, he said, because of his fear of mass shootings. This strange logic generates an ending that is precisely the opposite of what was desired: rather than offering protection, his gun made the world less safe. The man was striving for invulnerability. Like many US citizens, he thought his bodily vulnerability could be overcome with possession of a gun. But the data is very clear: the very presence of more and more guns continually increases the violence. Striving for invulnerability – whether as the man with a gun for "self-protection" or the philosopher with an argument for his shield against his vulnerability – puts us at a serious human risk. And it misses the opportunity that vulnerability can offer.

Butler claims that recognition of our lives as dependent on others – especially in grief, desire or rage – could be the ground on which we might build non-violent affection, such as in non-militaristic political action; but this would require us "to attend to, abide by" (Butler's words)[15] what I have suggested (after Le Doeuff) is "the unthought."[16] In other words, we must think of our dependence on others, "by staying with the thought of corporeal vulnerability itself."[17]

5 conclusion: vulnerability and the two love commandments

Having explored, with the aid of the paradigm of speaker vulnerability, the need to revise our myths of vulnerability, we return to the myths of love with which we began. We might take the view that love is shown in the personal relationship of a prophet to his or her personal God. That might also involve (as it often has), concluding that showing love to other persons – for instance, in doing to others what you would do to yourself – is a mere human portrayal of divine love. In sharp contrast to these conclusions, we might conceive divine love as mysterious, ineffable and, in the end, unknowable, and yet this can make "love" too vague, and "neighbour" too broad a category to guide our religious practices.

Nevertheless, in venturing to bring together Christians, Muslims and Jews in a shared love of the one God, it is assumed that a common thread (of love) exists to unite the Abrahamic religions with "their" God. There seems to be some hope in the air that we can be united in love and, especially, by the two love commandments which the three religions share. I have argued that, if we are concerned with enhancing life, we need to give attention to actual practices of love (though practices are shaped by concepts), and one significant practice of love is in reacting to vulnerability (such as speaker vulnerability) by creating bonds of affection. Renewing our social imaginary of vulnerability may then enable us to clarify our concepts of love and to assess the myths of love we live by.

If we return to the scriptural passage from Mark 12.28–31 quoted above, we might find four ingredients for true neighbour-love. First, we need to show how love means both caring for and caring about the wound (*vulnus*) which opens us up to the possibility of mutual affection ("your heart"). Second, we need to strive to know a one God whose love reveals the world as it actually is ("your soul"). Third, we need to show that shared or collective knowledge in religion is a knowing whom to love as the neighbour, and how to love that person ("your mind"). Fourth, we need to discern how we have the capacity for this love ("your strength"). With these needs as a guide, we can return again to the two love commandments and create an opening for a transformed myth of love and vulnerability.

notes

1 Pamela Sue Anderson, "Love and Vulnerability: Two Love Commands and One God," available <https://loveinreligion.org/resources/> (accessed 21 Nov. 2019). Used by permission.

2 For her early use of "myth," see Mary Midgley, *Wickedness: A Philosophical Essay* (London: Routledge, 1984) 10–12, 162. For her more technical definition of myth, see idem, *The Ethical Primate: Humans, Freedom and Morality* (London: Routledge, 1994) 109, 117–18; the latter is repeated and elaborated ten years later in idem, *The Myths We Live By* (London: Routledge, 2004; Routledge Classics, 2011) xi, 1, 2, 5.

3 Here, gender is socially and materially constructed by intersecting mechanisms of discrimination, including race, ethnicity, sex and class; so, the gender of a white, South African, transsexual, upper class "woman" will differ in multiple ways from a black, African-American, heterosexual, lower class "woman" or "man." For an early statement of gender's intersectionality, see Kimberlé Crenshaw, "Demarginalizing the Intersection of Race and Sex," *The University of Chicago Legal Forum* 140 (1989): 139–67.

4 HRH Prince Ghazi bin Muhammad, "The 'Rule of Law of Love'" in *Within the Love of God: Essays on the Doctrine of God in Honour of Paul S. Fiddes*, eds. Anthony Clarke and Andrew Moore (Oxford: Oxford UP, 2014) 29–46.

5 Concerning the obligation to "love your neighbour as yourself," my thinking has been helped by M. Jamie Ferreira's method of reading Emmanuel Levinas and Søren Kierkegaard on biblical love commandments; see M. Jamie Ferreira, "Kierkegaard and Levinas on Four Elements of the Biblical Love Commandment" in *Kierkegaard and Levinas: Ethics, Politics and Religion*, eds. J. Aaron Simmons and David Wood (Bloomington: Indiana UP, 2008) 82–98.

6 Søren Kierkegaard, *Works of Love*, ed. and trans. Howard V. Hong and Edna H. Hong (Princeton: Princeton UP, 1995).

7 Emmanuel Levinas, "Existence and Ethics" in *Proper Names*, by Emmanuel Levinas; trans. Michael B. Smith (Stanford: Stanford UP, 1996) 74.

8 See Emmanuel Levinas, *Otherwise than Being, Or Beyond Essence*, trans. Alphonso Lingis (Pittsburgh: Duquesne UP, 1997) 111–16.

9 Jennifer Hornsby, "Disempowered Speech," *Philosophical Topics* 23.2 (1995) 127–47 (134).

10 Michèle Le Doeuff, *The Philosophical Imaginary*, trans. Colin Gordon (London: Athlone, 1989) 127.

11 Ibid. 128.

12 Judith Butler, *Precarious Life. The Powers of Mourning and Violence* (London: Verso, 2004) 128–51.

13 Ibid. 21–23.

14 Nancy Tuana, "The Speculum of Ignorance: The Women's Health Movement and Epistemologies of Ignorance," *Hypatia* 21.3 (2006) 1–19 (11).

15 Butler, *Precarious Life* 29.

16 Le Doeuff, *Philosophical Imaginary* 128.

17 Butler, *Precarious Life* 29.

I have to confess that it is only now that she has gone that I have found myself reading any significant amount of Pamela's more recent writings in what may be called the philosophy of religion, but which, in her case at any rate, I should be more inclined to call the philosophy of the understanding of life. There was, however, a time – as long ago as the early 1980s when I was acting as supervisor of her doctoral thesis on the philosophy of Paul Ricoeur – when I read and discussed with her virtually everything that she was then writing. What stands out for me as I read these much later texts is not only the sheer contrast or discontinuity between the controlled assurance of their writing and the hesitations and confusions of her papers when she first came to work with me, but also the continuity of her most persistent philosophical and existential concerns – one of which, of course, was the nature of the deep connections between them.

Thus, as a leading example, human vulnerability and what she came to see as its essential connection with openness to others. Pamela, as I remember her, was remarkable in the ways in which she knew and faced up to her own vulnerabilities. When I first met her all those years ago, she was already some considerable way through what should have been her overall time as a graduate student. But, for whatever reason, she had somehow failed to connect with her previous supervisor, who in his turn had clearly failed to pick up on just what was going on – or not going on – in the papers that she would bring for his appraisal. She came to me – in some desperation, it has to be said – simply because I was at that time just about the only member of the then Sub-

alan montefiore

PAMELA ANDERSON AND "VULNERABILITY"

Faculty of Philosophy in Oxford who not only happened to know Ricoeur personally but also just a little about his philosophical background and work. What Pamela had to show me at our first encounter was – it has also to be said – really something of a mess. I remember having to explain to her why, if we were to work together, she would have to accept the need to re-start, as it were, by going back to assure herself of a well-founded background understanding first of Hume and then of Kant, and that this would almost certainly mean her taking at least a year longer than she had originally counted on before her thesis would be ready for submission. What really impressed me – and still impresses me – was how readily and understandingly she accepted the need to return in that unplanned-for way to the securing of a certain basic philosophical groundwork; and how well she succeeded in securing it, despite all the initial confusion.

So yes, certainly, the Pamela whom I first got to know was in what one might well call a situation of double or reciprocal vulnerability: of philosophical vulnerability, so to speak, as that of an Oxford graduate student already quite substantially embarked on a thesis project for which she now found herself to be lacking much of the necessary grounding (and the confidence which comes with it); and of existential vulnerability as that of someone, far from her home base and thus already not altogether secure, finding herself in what for anyone would be an unexpectedly uncertain situation in their own personal life.

As things turned out, of course – or, perhaps I should say, as Pamela, being the kind of person that she was, made them to turn out, she was able to emerge from that situation of double uncertainty and vulnerability with what from its initial perspective was a quite remarkable degree of double achievement. Having taken the necessary steps back to secure its philosophical foundations, she persisted in reworking her thesis to its successful doctoral conclusion – a version of which was indeed subsequently published as her first book, *Ricoeur and Kant*, in 1993 – and then going on to a notably successful academic career, ending up, as Adrian Moore put it in his *Guardian* obituary for her, "as an international figure whose work broke important new ground."[1]

Vulnerability was, then, a condition that Pamela knew only too well as an inescapable feature of her own experience of herself. At the same time, she was able to see, and to feel, that vulnerability not simply as a condition peculiar to her or to her own particular situation but as characteristic in one way or another of the human condition as such. As such – and this, of course, was a theme that she was very much working on towards the end of her life – vulnerability was not to be understood or experienced as a reason for shutting oneself off in an effort to build for oneself walls of protection against others but rather as a ground of openness towards them in a spirit of reciprocal comfort and support – in short, in a spirit of what Pamela did not hesitate to call love.

If this came to be one of the most notable themes of her later work, it remained very much bound up with other themes of long persisting and deeply intertwined concern to her. The "feminist" theme of the many practical and self-relational problems of what it is to be a woman in what was – and in many ways no doubt still is – a largely man-dominated world; the theme of how best to order a proper understanding of one's relationship to the religious tradition of one's own background, and of its stance in regard to those of other faith communities; and the theme of how thinking philosophically can and should make a positive difference to the ways in which those who engage in it might both conceive of and live their own lives.

It is obviously true of all writers, philosophers included, that certain themes will preoccupy them above all others at certain periods of their lives, and even in many cases throughout the whole of their working and thinking careers. But a primary concern for the exploration and elaboration of themes as contrasted, for example, with one for the ins and outs of conceptual analysis and for detailed argument structures may help to explain Pamela's evidently natural feeling for philosophers and philosophy in the so-called Continental tradition. For in that tradition or family of traditions (if I may risk a somewhat wild thematic generalization) there is indeed much to be found by way of insistence and variations on themes as compared with attempts to substantiate or to pin them down by way of detailed formal or so-called informal logic.

To take one example, one which I remember having discussed with Pamela herself. She was, it is evident enough, proud to regard herself as being in some important sense a feminist philosopher. But when asked whether she thought that the criteria of good and bad reasoning, of sound argument or of accurate conceptual analysis should be considered as being in any way different depending on whether the philosopher in question happened to be male or female, she was quite clear that his or her gender could have nothing to do with the matter. Feminists were as such quite generally (and rightly) concerned with what I have just called "the many practical and self-relational problems of what it is to be a woman in what was – and in many ways no doubt still is – a largely man-dominated world"; and feminist philosophers would naturally have a particular concern for the status and treatment of women by and within the institutions and communities of philosophy and philosophers at large. In that sense, a man could perfectly well be counted as a feminist philosopher. It is wholly understandable, however, that women philosophers should in general have a far more immediate and urgent feel for the importance and significance of this theme than the overwhelming majority of their male colleagues. And while argument and careful analysis of what may be the relevant facts are obviously crucial to any proper setting out and endorsement of a theme such as this, there is, equally obviously, much more to its practically effective exposition and advocacy than logical demonstration alone.

Pamela sought to understand our general vulnerability as human beings not as a reason for people to try and protect themselves by shutting themselves off from the threats that all may be felt to present in one way or another to each other, but rather as one both to offer and to find mutual support in a communality of reciprocal relations. She was – as a matter of her own personal experience, no doubt – particularly sensitive to the different forms of stress that may be experienced by speakers before expectant but as yet unknown audiences and those, conversely, felt by members of those very audiences, uncertain of whether they would be able to follow what was being said. They were in this way dependent on each other; and thus, as she had come to see it, provided a model for how people in general should learn to see themselves in relation to each other. As she herself put it in one of her unfinished papers: "My modelling of philosophical relations on speaker–audience reciprocity is certainly a relational model for *philosophers'* lives, but I am also trying to generalize this relational model to all of life's relations."[2]

This is a philosophy of "Look at it in this way rather than in that" rather than one of insistence on the intricacies of fine conceptual distinctions and chains of would-be logically constraining arguments. This is, no doubt, the same philosophical sensitivity at work as that to be found in Pamela's treatment of that other theme so persistently important to her, that of the importance of religious traditions and the problems of how to understand and relate to the different, and often at least prima facie conflicting, beliefs and practices of the communities built around them – including, of course, that from which one may oneself have come and to which one may in some important sense still belong, whatever one may have come to think of oneself as "believing." Here too Pamela was very much in natural philosophical sympathy with the Bergsonian idea of an intuitive metaphysical insight into certain deep but ineffable truths – whose very ineffability should in principle, one might suppose, prevent them from functioning as barriers of potentially hostile doctrinal separation between one religious tradition and another: an insight not open to strictly rational proof as such but which may, on this view, be both enabled and strengthened by informed philosophical meditation.

My meeting with Pamela first came about, then, thanks to her committed interest in the philosophy of Paul Ricoeur. One of his leading ideas of particular significance to her was that the way in which one may think of a person's continuing identity over time is in effect constituted by the narrative which we or others, or indeed the person himself or herself, may come to construct of his or her life. Other philosophers have sought the assurance of a continued personal identity in that of memory or in the continuous spatio-temporality of the individual body – attempts which, notoriously, can both run into difficulties and paradoxes of their own. For myself, I am not sure that there is any one satisfactorily conclusive solution to this deeply personal conundrum. What one can say with fair certainty is that our relations both with ourselves and with others are built upon and held together by the identity-narratives that we construct about ourselves and each other. One of the most poignant passages in Pamela's writings runs as follows: "Any continuous relation to the other can be destroyed by death. And yet the thread of life continues, however fragile, in being remembered."[3] Pamela herself was shockingly still much too young to die as early in her life as that. Yet the thread of her life does somehow continue as we remember her in our no doubt many different ongoing narratives of Pamela today.

disclosure statement

No potential conflict of interest was reported by the author.

notes

1 A.W. Moore, "Pamela Sue Anderson Obituary," *The Guardian* 24 Mar. 2017, available <https://www.theguardian.com/theguardian/2017/mar/24/pamela-sue-anderson-obituary> (accessed 20 Nov. 2019).

2 Pamela Sue Anderson, "Creating a New Imaginary for Love in Religion," ed. Paul S. Fiddes, in *Love and Vulnerability: Thinking with Pamela Sue Anderson*, ed. Pelagia Goulimari, Spec. issue of *Angelaki: Journal of the Theoretical Humanities* 25.1–2 (2020): 51.

3 "'A Thoughtful Love of Life': A Spiritual Turn in Philosophy of Religion," *Svensk Teologisk Kvartalskrift* 85 (2009): 119–29 (123).

laurie anderson sathe

VULNERABILITY AS A SPACE FOR CREATIVE TRANSFORMATION

My sister, Pamela Sue Anderson, encouraged us to conceive of our lives as a process of creative transformation, and to believe that transformation is initiated by an openness to vulnerability. She argued for recreating our perception of vulnerability as a capability: to understand it as that which is positive in our process of transformation. We are innately vulnerable to experiences that distress or disorient us; however, when seen as a capability, vulnerability opens a space for our creative transformation.

Throughout her career, Pamela wrote to understand the experiences in her life. This was never truer than when she was working on the Enhancing Life Project through the Templeton Foundation during her journey with cancer. Through her own growing awareness of her loss of health and impending loss of life, she revealed to us wisdom to enhance our lives through love, vulnerability and creative transformation.

I come to this exploration of transformation both as an academic and as Pamela's sister, exploring my own lived experience of vulnerability and love as a result of her passing, and seeking to understand her concept of creative transformation and how it might allow me to be open to something new. In the space created by my grief, I find myself in a process of transformation, and writing this paper provides an opportunity to engage with her work, as well as with the work of other theorists, to understand the role of vulnerability in creative transformation.

On the Enhancing Life Project website there is a short video clip of Pamela explaining that,

> In a world torn apart by violence and fear, I would like to open up people's lives in considering what makes a life worth living [...] In particular, I would like to encourage vulnerability to open us up to mutual love, affection and relationship. (Enhancing Life Project)

As she describes them, transformative experiences happen within social and political contexts, even as they happen within our personal lives. Consequently, as individuals change, their worlds, small and large, also change. In a similar way, I also explore how individual change relates to broader social change or transformation. I draw from the imagery of *The Dance* by Matisse, used in my previous work on women's transcendence, as an apt imagery for the creative transformation of individuals and communities. In this painting, human figures move freely, as though floating, each moving in their own way and yet their hands are clasped, creating a circle of dancers. I describe the way that "The imagery of Matisse's *Dance* is a metaphor for people who are always in a flowing movement, enabling constantly different shapes. Like an amoeba, these [...] figures dance together changing themselves and their worlds" (Anderson Sathe 326).

In this paper, I explore how lives might be creatively transformed through an openness to vulnerability. I begin with an exploration of vulnerability and love. Next, I look at the spaces of vulnerability through the metaphors of a threshold, a liminal period or a margin. Finally, I describe examples of creative transformation.

vulnerability and love

Joan Halifax, a Buddhist nun, who works with those who support people in their dying process, creates an image of vulnerability as having a "soft front and strong back" (Halifax 16). Through this embodied metaphor of balancing the front and back sides of our bodies we can imagine being both vulnerable and strong in the face of change. In this context, being vulnerable relates to being open and strong as an inner strength or courage. Like Pamela, Halifax sees love as crucial:

> All too often our so-called strength comes from fear not love; instead of having a strong back, many of us have a defended front shielding a weak spine. In other words, we walk around brittle and defensive, trying to conceal our lack of confidence. If we strengthen our backs, metaphorically speaking, and develop a spine that's flexible but sturdy, then we can risk having a front that's soft and open. (17)

A piece missing from Pamela's work is what Halifax describes as the strength it takes to be open to change and to experience the spaces of vulnerability.

spaces of vulnerability

Pamela writes that "vulnerability locates us in a space of freedom; that is, we are *free for* enhancing life as dynamic, affective and transformative" (Anderson, "New Concepts" 2). As we explore this space where we can respond creatively we can draw from metaphorical descriptions of this space as a "threshold," as Pamela does (Anderson, "Enhancing Life Project Proposal" 6); or "liminal," as educational philosopher Jack Mezirow puts it (Mezirow 3–33); or a "margin," as feminist theorist bell hooks describes it (hooks 149). I am intrigued by this space of vulnerability where we are free to choose our response.

When we are confronted with an unanticipated choice, it can be uncomfortable. The space created is not a calm, peaceful place but a place that disorients and can be dark and uncomfortable. Here we sit with our wounds. This space of vulnerability may create a sense of yearning or longing for something different, where we are no longer what we were but are in the process of becoming something different. Pamela described this space as a "threshold," a temporary space or opening to move through. She explains: "the imagery of the threshold helps us to imagine a space for both life's enchantments and its possibilities" (Anderson, "New Concepts" 2).

Mezirow developed the theory of transformative learning and its key concept of disorienting dilemma (Mezirow 3–33). From this perspective, education for children tends to be informative – helping them to form their perspective, while adult learning is transformative, helping adults to question and reassess their perspectives based on their life experiences. Disorienting dilemmas are those experiences that are disruptive and disorienting and create liminal space for transformation. According to Mezirow, it is in this liminal space that people make changes in their worldview and in their actions. In many ways, this terminology is similar to Pamela's use of the word threshold but helps to further the idea of a space where one is neither here nor there: a space perhaps before the threshold, a space of reflection, angst and discomfort. It is a space ripe for creative transformation.

hooks, an African-American woman, describes the space of being in the margins socially. In this case, the space is life-long and based on the structures of oppression that determine spaces where one can physically be. This space represents limited opportunity and oppression. hooks, however, describes choosing to be in the margins, outside of mainstream thoughts and ideologies. It is in this space that she can develop her own voice and ideas. She describes this space as vulnerable but also creative and life giving (hooks 149). She helps us to see how space for creative transformation can be created by a response to oppressive structures.

A threshold, a liminal period or a margin all can be seen as metaphors for space that provides the freedom for a creative response or transformation.

creative transformation

Pamela describes that "life is dynamic insofar as a continuous, creative process" ("Enhancing Life Project Proposal" 8). When life is seen as a creative process of transformation, then in the dark, disorienting and marginal spaces we are free to respond spiritually and creatively. To help us imagine possible responses, I draw from three stories of vulnerability and creative transformation. Matthew Sanford, from the space of loss and disability, helps people to connect to their bodies and their own healing story through yoga; Judy Chicago stands in the space created by patriarchy and tells women's stories through her art exhibits; and Ananya Chatterjea, in the space of injustice for women of color, choreographs dances of transformation drawing on social justice themes for women.

Sanford was in a car accident with his family when he was thirteen years old. They hit a patch of ice on the road and the car rolled over the railing that was protecting them from the edge of the road. His father and sister were both killed and he suffered multiple injuries including a severed spinal cord, which left him paralyzed from the chest down. From his hospital bed, in the midst of unimaginable grief and pain, he made a choice to live and to ultimately thrive. Reflecting back on the experience in an interview thirty years later, Sanford explains:

"Things happen, you know, even loss of childhood innocence, anything [...] a death of a loved one – where suddenly the world changes its shape and you have to confront how are you going to connect back to the world" (Sanford). After the initial instruction to focus on his mind and his intellect as the way to respond to his loss, Sanford found that it was the connection to his body through the practice of yoga that helped him to move forward and allowed for his transformation. In a space of vulnerability, yoga helps individuals not only to ground in their own body and healing story but to a sense of shared humanity and connection. Sanford created a yoga studio that offers adaptive yoga for people living with disability; it is in this way that his transformation has initiated the transformation of his community, which has now become international in scope.

Chicago was marginalized as a female artist in the 1960s when women's artistic abilities were not recognized as mainstream. Through a period of darkness and frustration she persevered and transformed herself and women's role in the art world in the process. She created a space where women artists could be vulnerable to explore their feelings of oppression from patriarchy and to create a response together. She advocated for women to know themselves and their stories through a feminist process of working together. In addition, she chose what had been traditionally called women's crafts, ceramics and needlework as her form of creative expression. Her major works include *The Dinner Party*, a depiction of women in history through a place setting of an embroidered table runner and a ceramic plate in the image of a vagina, and the *Birth Project* and subsequently the *Birth Project: Born Again* depicting women's stories of childbirth and women's creative spirit (Chicago, *Birth Project*; *Through the Flower*).

Ananya Chatterjea, a dancer, choreographer and a scholar, embraces the vulnerability of the injustices that women experience around the world and responds with powerful dances of transformation. Growing up in Kolkata, India, she learned about women's injustices early on. Dance became a space for transformation. She describes that the purpose of her company, Ananya Dance Theatre, is to allow

> the layering of our different histories (to) enable us to see each other in important ways, and to ask the question at the heart of the project: How do we show up for each other? How can we stand for justice, with each other in the name of love? (Ananya Dance Theatre)

In her production "Shaatranga: Women Weaving Worlds":

> women work painstakingly and innovatively to sustain and transform our worlds, reimagine painful pasts, and materialize hopeful futures [...] Repeatedly, our creative process for this work has been rocked by news of violence and injustices from across the world. We hold this pain, struggle and devastation in our hearts as we dance Shaatranga. (Ananya Dance Theatre)

This exploration of vulnerability and creative transformation reveals that Pamela's work on vulnerability can be applied to creative transformation broadly. The stories of Sanford, Chicago and Ananya embody vulnerability and transformation in the practices of yoga, art and dance. Each of these individuals changes themselves and their worlds. I too know that I am in a process of creative transformation and that I am now able to see Pamela's work in a new way.

During the weeks that I cared for Pamela before her death, her academic work about vulnerability became real and embodied. We both felt vulnerable in not knowing what was next and certainly not wanting the inevitable change that was before us. Following her death, I experienced profound sadness and grief. I turned to her writing for solace. At first, in my grief, I could only read a few sentences, but with time I was motivated to re-read more and more. I found that I understood her writing in a new way and could see how it related to the transformation I was experiencing. I realized that my deep love for my sister and my vulnerability in her passing created a space for an expansion of myself to respond creatively and spiritually to my loss and also to the everyday experiences in my life and in my teaching and writing. In my work that encourages a mind–body–spirit view of health and healing I can see how Pamela's conception of vulnerability as a capability opens us to a creative response for healing. As with the stories I used of Sanford, Chicago and Ananya I continue to explore the role of story, listening and relationship as a part of that creative response. I realize that we respond to life in a continuous creative process of creating a life worth living. I return to Matisse's imagery and join the circle of dancers. In this circle, we each might represent vulnerable dancers open to the potential for change as we hold hands connecting with love, allowing each other to grow, transform and create new worlds together.

disclosure statement

No potential conflict of interest was reported by the author.

bibliography

Ananya Dance Theatre. "Shaatranga: Women Weaving Worlds." Program.

Anderson, Pamela. "New Concepts to Live By: Affection, Dispossession and Transformation." Collection of Pamela Sue Anderson, 2015.

Anderson, Pamela. "Pamela Sue Anderson on the Relevance of the Enhancing Life Project." 12 Jan. 2017. Web. 20 Nov. 2019. <https://www.youtube.com/watch?v=24iuEk45wbE>.

Anderson Sathe, Laurie. "Creating a Space for Practical Wisdom: The Dance of Transcendence Incarnate." *New Topics in Feminist Philosophy of Religion: Contestations and Transcendence Incarnate.* Ed. Pamela Sue Anderson. Dordrecht: Springer, 2010. 319–28. Print.

Chicago, Judy. *The Birth Project.* New York: Doubleday, 1985. Print.

Chicago, Judy. *Through the Flower: My Struggle as a Woman Artist.* 1975. New York: Authors Choice, 2006. Print.

"The Enhancing Life Project Proposal." Collection of Pamela Sue Anderson, 2015.

Halifax, Joan. *Being with Dying: Cultivating Compassion and Fearlessness in the Presence of Death.* Boston: Shambhala, 2008. Print.

hooks, bell. "Choosing the Margin as a Space of Radical Openness." *Yearning: Race, Gender and Cultural Politics.* 1990. New ed. Abingdon: Routledge, 2015. 145–54. Print.

Mezirow, Jack. *Learning as Transformation: Critical Perspectives on a Theory in Progress.* San Francisco: Jossey-Bass, 2000. Print.

Sanford, Matthew. "The Body's Grace." Interview. *On Being with Krista Tippett.* 2006. Web. 20 Nov. 2019. <https://onbeing.org/programs/matthew-sanford-the-bodys-grace/>.

susan durber

PAMELA SUE ANDERSON – WITNESS TO THE GOSPEL, PROPHET TO THE CHURCH
what might the church hear from her work?

I first met Pamela in 1979 when we were both new students at Mansfield College. Our two lives overlapped and interwove in many different ways over the decades since then and I so much valued this friendship that was of such long standing and in which so much did not need to be spoken because it was simply shared.

My own journey has included the study of theology, ordination to ministry in the church, becoming a feminist and reflecting on how to be a feminist within and for the church, marriage, divorce, re-marriage, loss and bereavement, motherhood, preaching, writing, speaking, living, loving and friendship. Pamela accompanied me through all these things. I have, as many others have, a trail of books given as gifts on significant occasions, books inscribed with thoughtfulness. She was bridesmaid at my first wedding. I spent a year living in her home town of Minneapolis attending a seminary of the Lutheran church of her upbringing while being much supported by her parents. Pamela came to my ordination, she befriended my daughter, she was sometimes a part of the congregation I served in Oxford and she was a faithful friend over decades.

Pamela's relationship to the church was more ambivalent and complex than mine, but I am left now with a sense that her thinking and her work were considerably shaped by her upbringing within and her (sometimes ambiguous) belonging to the church. I am convinced that the church needs to be shaped by her insights. Her relationship with the church, as with much else, was not simply about intellectual convictions or doubts but was also shaped by very particular relationships and experiences. She knew in her own life both how wonderful and how terrible the church, or the people in it, could be. She understood from the inside how the church can be anything from profoundly welcoming and affirming to deeply flawed and abusive. She was often fiercely critical of the church (I suspect more forthrightly with some than others) but she never decisively left it or abandoned it. I don't think she could find it in herself to do that. She had been shaped by the church and she wanted to shape it too. At times, it seemed clear that she believed that her work, as a feminist philosopher of religion, was what she did as an offering of service to the church. It was what she had to give. And so it's important that that offering continues to be received.

Pamela was continually fascinated by religion, faith and (to a lesser extent) the church. But it was a kind of fascination that could also include being appalled, even while her narrative about her own life, and her own death, were shaped by the Christian narrative. I think that there are many signs that while her thinking and writing were in many ways critical of some streams of theology and faith, they were also indelibly created within it. She grew up in the Lutheran church in Minnesota. As I spent a year of my own life immersed in a Lutheran context, indeed very much in *her* Lutheran context, I would come to see how many themes in her writing and reflection owe something to the preoccupations of that tradition. A Lutheran service often begins (really absolutely begins) with confession of sin and the search for forgiveness. Lutheran theology is often rooted in a theology of the cross, in an understanding of the essential vulnerability of Jesus. Luther's writing and Lutheran theology often dwell on questions of freedom and the will. And, at what I would regard as its best, Lutheran theology focuses on that grace of God that comes to us in profound and overwhelming love. She did find a home for a while in her younger days in a Baptist church, at a time when I think she may have been searching for a form of religion that was more lived, more emotional, more feeling. And when in Oxford she found herself at various times living between the Lutheran tradition as it found expression and presence for a while at Mansfield College, in the United Reformed Church at St Columba's and for the last sixteen years of her life within a Baptistic ethos at Regent's Park College. In none of these settings was Pamela ever, I think, either completely at home or completely engaged, but faith was important to her, and certainly not only as an intellectual exercise.

But if Pamela did intend her work to be her contribution to the life of the church, what is it that we should make sure that the church continues to hear? If Pamela was a witness to the Gospel and an almost prophetic figure, speaking truth to God's people, to what shall we listen?

When my daughter was confirmed at about age thirteen Pamela gave her a book as a gift. It was a collection of sermons by Marilyn McCord Adams, entitled *Wrestling for Blessing*[1] and Pamela wrote in the front page:

> To Grace. I am not sure if these sermons will touch you at this stage of life – at your confirmation – but I want to give you God's blessing for now and the future.

I think that this gesture and gift say much about Pamela's legacy for the faith community of the church. She was always keen that young *women* should be educated and empowered, particularly in their encounter with faith. She wanted my daughter and all our daughters to have their eyes opened and to be rightly critical of a patriarchal church. She wanted to make sure that she read the words of a radical woman who was preaching with passion. Marilyn McCord Adams was someone who, like Pamela, was not afraid to say that the church is misogynist. But Pamela could also offer God's blessing for now and the future. She did not believe that the church is so broken that it is without hope. She believed that it was possible, and even desirable, to offer God's blessing. She recognized, as does the title of the book, that blessing sometimes has to be wrestled for, that it has to be fought for from a sometimes even corrupt and broken church, but that the God who is the source of all blessing can nonetheless be found. I remember being very moved that my daughter's confirmation was marked in this way as a significant event, and that Pamela brought to it that note of both critique and blessing. She had a hermeneutic of suspicion about the church, but also, I believe, a hermeneutic of trust in the God who is a source of blessing. In doing that she makes it possible for those of us who are more committed to the institutional church than she was herself to continue to serve there in the hope that we might be part of that wrestling of blessing. She offers the hope that the church does not have to be left to the patriarchs, but can, through all sorts of wonderful subversions, become a place of blessing.

Pamela also brings to the church, I believe, a reminder of the need to value its own traditional wisdom and the possibility that knowledge and truth are not only situated in thought and in the mind but that bodily experience, intuition and feeling can be real sources of knowledge and wisdom. Pamela's conviction that love is not only an emotion and a feeling but also a source of knowledge has much to encourage a faith that puts love at the centre. I have often had the experience, in secular settings, where sometimes people think of love only in terms of hearts, flowers and romance, as a "soft" kind of thing, of needing to defend the possibility that love could be strong (stronger than death one might say), a source of knowledge and a matter of the will, of decision and conviction. Pamela wrote so movingly about love. She pleaded with us, and showed us, that love is about emotion becoming *intelligent*, that we don't have to choose between passion and reason but that each can make more beautiful the other. She refused the idea that love is simply a mysterious gift that comes from somewhere outside ourselves, or that it's something we just fall into. It is something we can give and make and improve. She taught us to believe that we can be intelligent about love, that it can be a form of *knowledge*. She knew, from her own life, that our loving is imperfect, but she believed that love can be perfected. I heard in her an echo of the Christ who *commands* us to love, who says we can choose to love by doing and enduring, by disciplining duty with delight. I think that Pamela was saying something about the love of *God*, but I can also hear her rebuking me and saying that it was *her* love, and that I must claim and take responsibility for the love *I* feel and think and act upon too. She called us all to cultivate love as a *virtue*; habitual, reliable, consistent. I think that when those who reflect on faith often feel the need to think in abstractions and ideas, Pamela offers the church a kind of confidence in its commitment to love as something strong and practical, a source of knowledge, a matter of the will. She claims the philosophical ground for Christianity's most familiar language and offers us the possibility of walking there more bravely.

Pamela also offers to the church, I suggest, another way of reflecting on the passion of Christ, on his incarnation, suffering and death. One of her most stunning and compelling intellectual moves is to take the thing for which feminists have often criticized the world and the church for pressing upon them and to turn it round by re-imagining it. So, for example, feminism has often taught us not to make ourselves vulnerable, to protect ourselves against the dangers of the world and the church's call to service and sacrifice and to find a new strength. Pamela, taking a different stand, looks hard at vulnerability and finds within it (rather than in overcoming it) a true source of wisdom. She writes of us being undone by the love of others and of how we are all vulnerable and dependent on others. Our strength and our path to a life well-lived do not lie in rejecting vulnerability but in embracing it. Vulnerability is one source of the bonds of affection that will enhance life. A "thoughtful love of life" will include this kind of vulnerability.[2] Ironically, perhaps, Pamela shows how vulnerability can be our profoundest strength on the path to life. "We are all vulnerable to being undone."[3] I don't think it can be entirely coincidental that this comes from someone long fascinated by a faith that celebrates the Christ who became vulnerable for love of us, who humbled himself, who stood silent and vulnerable before Pilate, who gave himself up even to death. A Christian faith that is rooted in a theology of the cross knows much about the wisdom and the power and the potential of vulnerability.

Pamela also believed that any way of thinking or being should be judged by its potential to enhance life. She thought that philosophy of religion, and I would suggest Christianity itself, should be changed and transformed by life itself, in all life's reality and complexity. She urged that thoughtful reflection on our lives (and that's what I think we do or should do every Sunday in church) can be transformative, full of the energy of joy, part of a love of life. Philosophy of religion, and faith itself, should certainly not focus only on questions to do with truth claims about whether God exists, or whether we are free, but about how we are living and loving. She wrote about a faith practice that is deeply engaged and committed to narrating honestly the truths of our lived experience. Pamela believed that life was a gift and a potential joy, even while it was also open to great suffering, and she really felt in herself how important it is to be able to account for how you were living your life, if not at a last judgment then certainly in each moment that you have life to live. She believed that being vulnerable was something that we, all of us (not just some separate category of "vulnerable people") might inhabit, and that this was properly life-enhancing. She wrote that

> the task for contemporary philosophy of religion is not only to become, but to remain, life-giving and whole-making.[4]

That is a task that I would love to find the church seizing on too, to become, and to remain, life-giving and whole-making. Pamela's own experience of the church was not, I think, that this was always so.

Pamela's critique of too-easy forgiveness, of forgiveness that separates itself from justice, is also one that needs to continue to be heard in the church. She is brave in recognizing that it can be too easy to urge forgiveness on the victim when, first, reparation and restoration need to be made and justice found. But her immersion in the church is so deep that she can also glimpse the possibility of those times when forgiveness can be saving and healing, and can be done out of the strongest and most resilient yet vulnerable kind of love, even when broken from justice.

I cannot claim to be sure that I have represented Pamela as she might want to have been. I cannot claim fully to have understood or grasped all her insights. But I want to celebrate her work and its implications for the church that she saw herself serving through her work and writing. What she did was far more than offer the kind of critique that may be obvious and just, but not necessarily helpful. What she did, I would suggest, is find within the resources of the church's faith and some of its most ancient wisdom the sources of its own redemption. She honoured love in a way that strikes powerful notes today. She fathomed vulnerability in new ways. She lifted up experience and intuition to find true wisdom there. She sought and succeeded to wrest blessing where many might have given up hope.

Pamela once said, in a sermon preached before the University of Oxford, "Let a unity of virtues, connected by love, shape the stories we read and write about our lives."[5] It's a phrase characteristic of her; beautiful, poignant, drawing connections, not quite transparent, inviting thought. Pamela, like many of us, was reading and writing about her own life as she did her work. That life was shaped by the church and, I pray, will in turn continue to shape the church, restore it, heal it and bless it. We should be encouraged that some of Pamela's profoundest insights do find echoes in words spoken or sung in churches regularly. A hymn by the theologian William Vanstone[6] and his book *Love's Endeavour, Love's Expense*[7] are particularly powerful examples. The final verses of his hymn draw us back to central themes in Pamela's writing about the nature of the vulnerability of love. May her song, even more than his hymn, continue to echo in the church.

> Love that gives gives ever more,
> Gives with zeal, with eager hands,
> Spares not, keeps not, all outpours,
> Ventures all, its all expends.
>
> Drained is love in making full;
> Bound in setting others free;
> Poor in making many rich;
> Weak in giving power to be.
>
> Therefore He Who Thee reveals
> Hangs, O Father, on that Tree
> Helpless; and the nails and thorns
> Tell of what Thy love must be.
>
> Thou art God; no monarch Thou
> Thron'd in easy state to
>   reign;
> Thou art God, Whose arms
>   of love
> Aching, spent, the world
>   sustain.

disclosure statement

No potential conflict of interest was reported by the author.

notes

1 London: Darton, Longman and Todd, 2005.

2 Pamela Sue Anderson, "'A Thoughtful Love of Life': A Spiritual Turn in Philosophy of Religion," *Svensk Teologisk Kvartalskrift* 85 (2009): 119–29.

3 Pamela Sue Anderson, "Creating a New Imaginary for Love in Religion," ed. Paul S. Fiddes, in *Love and Vulnerability: Thinking with Pamela Sue Anderson*, ed. Pelagia Goulimari, Spec. issue of *Angelaki: Journal of the Theoretical Humanities* 25.1–2 (2020): 51. The phrase "being undone," as Pamela acknowledges, comes from the work of Judith Butler.

4 "'A Thoughtful Love of Life'" 129.

5 University Sermon, 3 March 2003.

6 "Morning Glory, Starlit Sky" in *Rejoice and Sing* (Oxford: Oxford UP, 1991), hymn number 99. Reproduced by permission of the copyright holder, Maureen Smith.

7 London: Darton, Longman and Todd, 1977.

With your leave, I shall endeavour to explain how it feels, for a non-believer, to read the Bible.[1] I first discovered the Book as a twenty-four year old, hence hopefully as an adult and as someone supposed to be fully trained in philosophy, except that philosophy is a field in which you may gladly be a lifelong beginner. At any rate, when I first started reading the Bible I was already teaching philosophy, hence in charge of young people's intellectual lives, a responsibility to be taken very seriously. I was already a feminist too, more precisely an activist for reproductive rights and also a reader of Simone de Beauvoir. As a result, when I first opened the Bible, I was positioning myself as an equal because I felt mature and perfectly independent of the writings I was about to discover. None of them would be binding for me, no more so than say Hesiod's poetry, which I loved. There may be various forms of equality and the concept has more than one sense. In this piece, I shall mostly refer to the minimal idea that a version of equality is achieved when there is no relation of power between the parties involved, when submission of one to the other – structural, traditional or otherwise – does not exist. This is the notion of equality you can sense being used within many feminist movements. When we discuss the question of equal pay, we do of course refer to arithmetic equality (the same amount of money on your payroll when equal work has been performed) but there is another fundamental cord that is vibrating in harmony with this: if women are paid less, many will have to enter matrimony in order to avoid poverty or to secure the basic lifestyle they expect, hence they will have to accept submission to a

michèle le doeuff

EQUALITY AND PROPHECY

better-off partner. When discussing equal pay, you frequently feel that this anger (about the necessity to get or remain married obliquely written on your payslip) is emotionally the deepest aspect of the debate.

On the other hand, when reading the Bible I was not mistaking myself for the pure, 100 per cent organic reason, unadulterated by any religious creed, a pure reason which could therefore stand as a touchstone, and a touchstone for what, anyway? I simply wanted to meet the works of archaic bards with a free mind, moreover to enjoy these works, to value what would be valuable in them, even perhaps to feel lifted by them as I had been by some of Hesiod's verses. Just as the Parthenon and Notre Dame south rose window, seen from the outside when arriving from the Left Bank, always give me a kind of upward joy or suddenly make a heavy heart lighter. Or just as a fine production of a play by Shakespeare has the magic effect of making me disregard my own concerns for a while, as if these were trivial things really. And when, in the 1980s, a group of architects built L'Institut du Monde Arabe, springing lightly from a smallish plot of ground, a triumph of skill and momentum over meagre circumstances, they also created a building that was able to cheer up many different people. I have heard taxi drivers give genuine, enthusiastic praise to it. You do not need to be of Arabic descent to have received any higher education, or to identify with a given faith to exclaim a sincere "Ahhh!" and elaborate: "This is my favourite sight of Paris!" or "I can't see enough of it!" There is a space for Ancient and Modern achievements, an open space in which admiration, jubilation, and recognition may take place, far beyond what a membership to a given nation or denomination dictates in terms of aesthetics. I would definitely feel sorry for you if you never experienced the discovery of beauty, "Ahhh," outside your own parish or clan. Aren't exclamations the truest form of aesthetic acknowledgement, when they are the raw expression of surprise, gusto or elation?

Was my expectation of reading splendour-endowed works fulfilled when I first read the Bible? It was, not continually perhaps and I did skip a few pages, but I want to mention the writings attributed to King Solomon and, in the New Testament, the unforgettable promise, "Truth will make you free."[2] "Vanity of vanities," "all is vanity and grasping for the wind."[3] Indeed, you can measure the power of the Word, the power of words, by the fact that Ecclesiastes survived translations and, at least in Latin, English or French, still has the strength to move someone. Does it mean the force to move us towards pessimism and the assumption that everything is done in vain? Perish the thought, this would be propaganda! Or that the wise and the fool will die and be forgotten in the same way? Well, don't we have to accept that, from time to time, we share the same situation as all our neighbours, wise and fools alike? On an election day, people who believe that they are wiser than the average have to know that their vote will have exactly the same weight as the vote from anybody, including someone they see as quite foolish. Democracy requires that we accept such an assumption – moreover, that we anticipate all sharing the results of a ballot, perhaps after having done our humble best to spread a view (which rightly or wrongly we deemed enlightened) of what is at stake. Yes, there are reasons to be moved by Ecclesiastes, which does not mean to be influenced by it. You do not need to strictly identify with these writings to realize that you truly wanted to be acquainted with them and would have missed a lot if some narrow-mindedness of yours had prevented you from opening the Bible. You may be a downright optimist, you may believe in progress, scientific progress, human rights and women's rights progress, you may think highly of wisdom, just as King Solomon did by the way, and still appreciate Ecclesiastes' passages, written in a low key and yet so grand. It means that even if you devote your energy into making progress happen, and/or into becoming wiser, you still have to accept, at least as a hypothesis, that, at the end of the day, it all might amount to nothing. Prima facie, it may sound simply like a challenge: are you able to face such a possibility? Then, it is like a counterpoint which you may want to insert among the manifold possibilities within your own world-view, though perhaps a music frequently to overcome but still to be kept as precious, a music sometimes crucial "for a while." When you are a committed intellectual, there are moments of minor or major frustration, hence of discouragement. It is not a bad thing then to turn to the poetics of Ecclesiastes and to murmur a few lines of sorrow; this will help you gamely to start afresh soon because the form given to the disappointment here is beauty in itself. And is this not a much better option than to blame other activists for the lack of success of a given project? In short, it is a valid form of sublimation and it may teach us something about sublimation in general: when life is difficult you may want to borrow forms of solace from any culture that can provide them, from other cultures as well as from your own: in such an adjustment, you don't need to stress the otherness of the culture from which you borrow a perspective helping to give shape to your disappointment, you are not looking for something exotic *because* it is exotic. The distinction between cultural otherness and cultural sameness is not relevant when you simply need some means to overcome a bad time in a positive way. "If you sleep on the back of a tiger, if you sleep long enough and soundly enough, the tiger will end up falling asleep with you." This might be a Taoist saying; my memory is not clear about the origin of it, and again it does not matter, since we are not looking for exoticism here. It first sounds like a joke, a quirky indication of an impossible remedy for some dreadful situation. But it may happen that you want to numb your emotions for a period of time and simply carry on mechanically in order better to tackle or outlive a problem, and then the saying will appear witty, not to say cardinally full of humour, and you will feel grateful that somebody somewhere, and you can't remember who, coined it.

As for "Truth will make you free," you may take this short sentence out of context as much as you want, you may feel it is even better when taken out of context, you may quote it while writing on many topics, from psychoanalysis to journalistic responsibilities or climate change, you may give it to your beloved students for an essay ("'Truth will make you free': discuss."), it is still full of meaning. It encapsulates the presupposition all of us should adopt and assume when writing or teaching, namely that there is a "you" somewhere and that a "you" (any "you") always matters, a you who will be set freer, at least in some respects, by what we are to say, if what we say contains some truth. It's a promise and a bet, it's a prophecy, at least in the sense of Proverbs 31, which refers to "the prophecy that King Lemuel's mother taught him." In this passage, the word "prophecy" describes a moral teaching – don't drink, don't give your strength unto women – followed by the portrait of the ideal wife, whose value is above rubies, a portrait you may endorse as such or not. When "prophecy" means moral teaching or the description of what is held as appropriate mores by the speaker, you are at liberty to question it, to disagree, you may analyse it even in the light of common and garden psychology: this is a mother talking to her son, isn't it? And she is setting the bar so high for her portrait of the strong woman that perhaps she is not going to get a daughter-in-law anytime soon. And, because "Truth will make you free," I offer you this reading not as a quip but as an opportunity for everyone, women and men of all persuasions or none, to wonder and possibly free themselves from a time-honoured portrait. For who, among us women, does not want or indeed need to be a strong woman? But the content of the concept is still open to free discussion. And if we evoke the theory of "culture shock," as Kalervo Oberg put forth in 1954 (and this during a talk at the Women's Club of Rio de Janeiro – I'm not making that up), this theory will make us acknowledge that the first contact between, say, biblical writings and feminist thinking may not be utterly smooth; it can be a shock to start with, eventually a productive one, but there is now some reciprocity: I might have been like Oberg's immigrant when I first read the Bible, but now you can well be the immigrant when first reading Mary Wollstonecraft and Simone de Beauvoir or kindly attending the present lecture. Derived from the Gospels, there is a saying attributed to Gloria Steinem, "The truth will set you free but first it will piss you off," which may now work both ways.

At any rate, prophecy is not necessarily about predicting the future. One can safely leave that to the Sibyls, haruspices and Ancient Pythia, or, in politics, to people who are good at deciphering a given situation and infer from that where it is heading, including scientists who study the climate with scientific tools and calculate the point at which we shall all be burned, roasted, toasted and cooked. I would plead for a strictly secular concept of prediction, very distinct from biblical writings like Jeremiah or Lamentations. For I suspect that some people today dismiss important predictions (particularly about the climate) as if these predictions belonged to the same *genre* as writings attributed to Jeremiah or rather as predictions by Hananiah, another prophet whose views, according to Jeremiah, were not inspired by God. The notion of "false prophets" was included in the genre straight away. I very much fear that scientists, activists and the politicians we manage to persuade of the urgency of environmental issues are seen through this cliché of false prophets and then all we say is deemed silly jeremiads, no more, which is very unfair.

But if prophecy is not necessarily about predicting the future, what is it? That has been my question while writing this paper. The Conference organizers might have to explain why they invited such a non-typical reader of the Bible as myself to take the floor. As for me, my responsibility, as I see it, is to give an account, as candid as I can, of my experience. I feel grateful to Regent's Park College and to Paul Fiddes for the invitation, and we should consider it as deeply significant of a historical move taking place in our times. The idea that interfaith gatherings are necessary seems to be well rooted nowadays; sometimes, these reunions include atheism as well as the many forms of monotheism. This most welcome change may be a belated effect of the Second Vatican Council, but one may feel tempted to say that for years feminists have found it deeply congenial to adopt the idea that interfaith discussions are important and should involve atheists too.

I became aware of that around 1990 while living in Geneva and having productive discussions with a woman pastor. I could have already sensed something at the beginning of 1966 when the Catholic group in my class in Brest asked me to exchange views with them, at the time the Second Vatican Council had just concluded its work. Perhaps they could not find a Protestant, a Muslim or a Jewish fellow pupil to carry out what the Council had ordered, but there was at least a tame and sweet atheist in the vicinity. The first question I asked them was: "What is this story about Adam's rib?" as if the pre-condition of a dialogue was that they dismissed the unsavoury implications of such a metaphor. The most learned of them replied: "'Rib' is a mistranslation; in fact it was a whole side."[4] Better, of course, but only just. I had not read Simone de Beauvoir yet, I had probably not heard the word "feminism" at all, so this is, I'm afraid, the most genuinely personal version of what I thought of religions in general when I was seventeen, namely that they contain narratives that make women feel small. I had still to discover that the problem is not specific to religions only and that patriarchy is everywhere. Simone de Beauvoir turned me into a more tolerant person, by writing that "Lawmakers, priests, philosophers, writers, and scientists have gone to great length to prove that women's subordinate condition was willed in heaven and profitable on earth [...] Men have put philosophy and theology in their service." Etc.[5] I think it is true: patriarchy is more or less everywhere, except that some domains may prove more plastic to our efforts to improve the situation than others. I have occasionally claimed that there is little point in being an atheist if it does not lead you to be a feminist, or at least a bit more of a feminist than your church-going neighbour. Nowadays I would not word it this way but we may still reason in terms of psychological economy: if you take back some energy from any system of symbolic creed you used to adhere to, the crucial question is what use you then make of this reclaimed strength.

At any rate, the idea of "interfaith gatherings," that would include atheism too, seems to have found a good soil in feminist philosophy. Perhaps you are already conversant with Pamela Sue Anderson's work or hopefully you will soon be. Let us turn to the volume our late and much missed friend edited, *New Topics in Feminist Philosophy of Religion*.[6] In the Introduction, she writes that interfaith philosophical discussions, including works by philosophers who happen to be atheists, is the right framework from which to challenge "sexism, idolatries and oppressive forms of spiritual practice [...] still deeply entrenched in world religions."[7] Pamela and I were close friends and we cooperated in philosophy throughout a quarter of a century. She was a believer, while I never was one. None of us ever tried to convert the other to her own creed. It would have been pointless not to say strictly irrelevant. The project we had in common was to track down traces or indeed whole structures of patriarchy, misogyny and masculinism within the philosophical canon and beyond, while also analysing some very bad habits still extant within the philosophical community as we know it. Once, we explicitly disagreed about Kant, we argued, we tried to reach some mutual understanding and probably failed. But we never discussed the respective values of being a believer or an atheist, in my case a third-generation free thinker, which means that I did not choose atheism in the first place, I received it in my cradle and then gladly "chose" it with hindsight as a young adult. In the volume Pamela edited, all the contributors had also dropped the old competition between faiths: please stop wasting your energy standing up for the superiority of your faith over other faiths or absence of faith, when we all have to emancipate creeds, systems of thought and behaviour from sexism and oppressive relations.

But then, why did I start reading the Bible in the first place? The main reason was that I hoped better to analyse and understand the ethos of the culture in which I lived, say Christianity or the Judeo-Christian heritage as the dominant (or no longer so very dominant?) culture in my own surroundings. Patterns of action or behaviour, ways of feeling may first originate in some religious constructions and then become usual schemes within a culture where a given religion is pregnant, and this with the same meaning or not. Here comes an example: Pamela and I spent many studious holidays together and I quickly noticed that we had a form of behaviour in common: work until you drop! She was worse than me in that respect and sometimes I thought it necessary to try to moderate her, to no avail ever. At any rate, we both enjoyed ourselves a lot while at the same time believing in what we were doing; fits of laughter were frequent. It is not difficult to trace Pamela's hard-working attitude back to the Lutheran upbringing she received in Minnesota. As for me, I was brought up in a context created by the founding fathers of secular schooling in France: these nineteenth-century men were Calvinists or Freemasons. At primary school, first thing in the morning, we were given a brief moral lesson, through some edifying story. A large proportion of this teaching was about doing your job properly, about being thorough and exact, often with the idea that other people's lives or quality of life were at stake. No wonder Pamela and I had such behaviour in common! All the same, for both of us, working hard had a meaning far beyond what Protestant or Freemason ethics may have had in view. As women, we had won our freedom through being seriously dedicated to our work, hence getting degrees and jobs thanks to that: economic independence, which is not granted to every young woman in any culture, had come to us that way. And we both considered that economic independence for girls, along with some education, are among the first steps towards freedom; indeed, we knew this with certainty through lived experience, surely not as a part of any traditional religious teaching, even the much laicized version of Calvinist ethics I received. Mirth while working hard, and holding your sides frequently, might also be something quite foreign to religious ethics in general. Cheerful, strong-minded and happy to be independent: should we not consider that a productive dialectics may take place, and this with utterly original and most welcome results, when you start from within the framework of what a given upbringing may enforce, and then move much beyond that? In other words, any upbringing can give you patterns of action, which you may then use to achieve goals quite unforeseen by those who gave you your initial training.

So, my reading of the Bible had first been based on intellectual curiosity, like taking the plunge into the archaeo-ethnography of the region of the world in which I was living, and possibly based too on a personal question:

what sorts of ideas have been smuggled into my atheist mind by this context without my even being aware of it? There was also the small matter of fairness: I had read Homer, Hesiod, the Greek philosophers, Virgil, Shakespeare, and many others. Why bypass another important root of our mainstream culture? If this was out of some atheist narrow-mindedness, call it anticlericalism *à la Française*, if you like, one does not want that! True, as a child, I was not constantly above the aforesaid anticlericalism, which occasionally flourished in my family, never for long but always for good reasons. I remember witnessing verbal aggression directed at my mother by the local priest, while she and I were digging up the last bed of potatoes in the school garden. He had no right to come there, only parents were admitted in the school courtyard, not even in the classrooms, but he had come, this man whom I saw as a menace.[8] No right either to lay down the law to my mother: "Of course, Madame Le Doeuff, you will not prevent the children from attending catechism, will you? And of course, Madame Le Doeuff, you will not dissuade them from being Christians, will you?" and so forth and so on. Impugning hypothetical intentions, but in the negative, hence with a good dose of *praeteritio* in it, what an amazing scene to witness! My mother was a primary schoolteacher and the head of the small state-run, secular, school for girls in the village. Very strict national legislation applied to that schooling. All children had Thursdays off, so that they could attend catechism if their families wanted them to do so, and this without any need to broach the topic with anyone. Besides, if there was a rule well enforced in all state-run, hence secular, schools at the time, it was this one: "Thou shalt not discuss religion within the premises." This ban applied first and foremost to the teachers and second if necessary to the children, although I can remember only one incident. As a result, some history classes were delivered in a well-guarded and toneless voice. When teaching the History of France, you can't avoid giving at least one lesson on the Crusades and one on the massacre of Saint Bartholomew's Day, can you? But the teachers were supposed to do so in a neutral and minimalistic way, because the whole idea of secular schooling was to make it possible for children of all persuasions, or of no persuasion at all, to grow up together, learn together, play together, away from conflicting world-views, and all this free of charge because it was the State's duty to give some instruction to the young in the most egalitarian way the teachers could achieve. Therefore, if I developed an early allergy to the Crusades and to any conflicts between religious groups, this must have been my own doing and my own responsibility, for no one ever taught me such a distaste, even at home.

The village priest's invasion of the school space was both illegal and unnecessary. It was also violent and it staged a clearly gendered scene. For he was invoking all his weight as a male authority while questioning a woman, whereas he never dared go to the village school for boys and speak to the headmaster. No wonder I then adhered to the anticlerical mood (as I knew it) until I realized that anticlericalism is just a reaction; it will never get you anywhere, whereas secularism is an idea which may structure a large project. Silly, nasty clerics will produce anticlerical people by the dozen, and that's the end of it. One had better rise above that. As a result, reading the Bible was also an exercise and an effort in that direction. I wanted to overcome what had been left in my mind and in my heart by more than one appalling encounter with the religious world.

I first experienced the possibility of mutual recognition between women of different persuasions or none when a journalist working for a Catholic monthly came to interview me after *L'Etude et le rouet* [*Hipparchia's Choice*] was first published. She made it plain that she wanted to say "thank you" to the women of my generation who had fought the battle for contraception, and she knew that Catholic women had been (to put it mildly) under-represented among the activists, although I knew one, namely Thérèse Clerc. She was very gracious while I was the dumb one: what do you say in an interview to someone who expresses gratitude at length and states how right you are to be the person you are? Then, when I was in Geneva, I enjoyed a number of discussions with Isabelle Graesslé, a Calvinist pastor. A few years later, when in charge of the whole Calvinist community of the Republic, she was to hold the view that Christianity is like a river carrying along in its wake a lot of things, historical or cultural, which have nothing to do with the pure water of the faith. This is a powerful image, with an important outcome, for her main examples of garbage in the river were homophobia and the subjection of women. As a result, she declared herself in favour of equality between gays and heterosexuals, and in favour of women's access to abortion. Needless to say, from my point of view, women's access to contraception and abortion is, among other things, a matter of equality, because it means that a woman's opinion is as valuable and relevant as anyone else's opinion, and then a bit more, considering it's her own life which is at stake. Isabelle and I could agree about a definition of civil rights, moreover about a humanistic vision of life, since she also declared that she believed there is a life before death, which is much more than just stating a belief: it is like sketching a demand. If there is a life before death, let us make it as humane as we can for everyone. And if this implies some political and legislative change, no problem, we are also ready to act for that.

Now, I'm mentioning people, friends like Pamela and Isabelle, whereas I had first embarked on reading written material because I wanted to find out what the dominant ethos of my local culture was. The least I can say is that my initial inquiry was not straightforward. After all, if any religion is a historical entity, then it is only to be expected that people throughout the centuries have added views of their own making to what may have been the original institution. Perhaps St Augustine, along with a few others, is more relevant a source than the Old Testament and the Gospels to understand what my childhood neighbours experienced? Some discrepancies are blatant: St Anne is not mentioned at all in the New Testament, whilst she is such a cult figure in Brittany. Christ with no granny, poor thing! Or perhaps he had one but that aspect was censored? Years later, some of my Catholic friends and I were to discover "Celtic" (needless to say apocryphal) legends we truly relished together. You didn't know that St Anne was a Breton lass, did you, unfortunately married to a brute who used to beat her up so badly that angels took pity on her and moved her to Palestine where she met another man called Joachim and started an unwedded relationship with him? Well, now you know, and you have an idea of what sort of togetherness my still Catholic friends and I found when they started turning away from their chaplain's teaching. One of them explained to me that I had played a role in her emancipation because, she said, I maintained that morality does not need religion as a foundation and proved it. But I would say that the main force which led them to disinvest the priest's teaching was sex. For he kept talking (ill) about it, and about flirting – how awful it is – thus stimulating some drives while at the same time claiming they should be inhibited.

On the whole, it is not self-evident to assume the existence of a connexion between a religious text and a religion as you may encounter it in real life. Sometimes it works a bit and will give you food for thought. Reading the story about Noah's ark in Genesis enables you to discover where this piece of nursery lore came from, except that what you knew was a much-abridged version. And it stops being the same story when God appears (that could not happen in secular nursery schools!) and orders Noah's family to be fruitful and multiply. Now, what is the importance of such an injunction, which echoes what Adam and Eve had first been told? And you must further wonder: is this the reason why "*they*" (many male doctors, politicians, etc.) were so difficult in the 1970s when we demanded contraception and safe access to abortion? And is this why women churchgoers were so ashamed to ask for contraception or even to accept it when offered for free? For this was an issue for a few decades in France – past history, now, I am very glad to say. Let me insist, in case it could be helpful in other countries today, such as Latin America. For years, it was harder to recommend contraception to Catholic women than to provide them with good access to abortion when they needed one. You may of course consider this is begging the question, since they turned to us precisely when they wanted a termination. And they only used the language of needs, "needs must," not the language of freedom, choice, women's rights nor did they refer to any project for them to plan a family. Contraception still appeared as "sin" to them, something forbidden combined with premeditation, hence more than they could cope with. I am glad to say that all this seems over now in France, after years of discussion with us, activists who held some counselling services: not only did we maintain that contraception is a much better way to avoid unwanted pregnancies but we also explained that we were concerned that the group of women who felt guilty about contraception was the one in which "second abortions" happened more frequently. Catholic or not, the new generation's view of reproductive rights, family planning – more importantly, of their own good and their fundamental right to define their own good themselves – has become less blurry. It is as if a "blocking message" had been in the way of such a necessary perception, as if a smokescreen has now been removed.

"Be fruitful and multiply": is there a connexion between such a biblical order and what many women experienced throughout the centuries? This pertains to a more global question: is it possible at all to measure the weight of a textual injunction, in this case deemed to be a divine decree, in the fashioning of a collective behaviour and a form of sensibility? Causality is something often difficult to grasp, and even more so to prove. This is true in many domains. It is certainly a patriarchal view that women should produce as many children as possible, even if it is not a good thing for their health, their own lives, their well-being, the well-being of the entire household, and their own projects. The fact that women's lives, health and well-being should be simply ignored, and this for the sake of a father's glory, for there are traditions of glorifying prolific fathers and flattering their manhood, seems to be the signature of the patriarchal order. God's writ, twice issued in Genesis, to be "fruitful and multiply" can then be seen as a knot: it knits together a patriarchal structure and a religious command. This, in its turn, may mean that patriarchy is not a stand-alone entity. It needs props, and by the way you could read *The Second Sex* as an exploration and inventory of the many props patriarchy has forged to preserve itself, religions and philosophy being included in the list of artificial props.

But then, what was knitted can also be unknitted: such an operation was carried out in the seventeenth century by a French woman, namely Gabrielle Suchon, who had reclaimed this power from within her philosophical readings. She tackled the question of the order given to Adam and Eve to be fruitful and multiply (hence, for people to get married so as to have children). From her point of view, such an order made sense at the time it was issued, because the earth was then empty. But nowadays, with the earth well populated, it is no longer apposite; as a result, leading a single life is now permissible. Now, if you found the title of my piece, "Equality and Prophecy," intriguing, kindly consider that I am a reader of Gabrielle Suchon and also encouraged Pamela to become one too. The idea that there could be a best before date on God's injunctions had both of us rolling with laughter (before praising the depth of Suchon's perspective), especially Pamela, who still deplored that "in Minnesota, you marry, you have children and you cook." Now, equality and prophecy: when a woman analyses a well-known prophecy and deems it to be apposite at a time and then obsolete in her (our) times, she is positioning her own intelligence as an equal to something registered in the Bible, no less. And, because this prophecy is now obsolete, women may remain single and childless, if they want to. This is what I mean by unknitting: she removed a prop, a fragment of patriarchal ideology pressing women into matrimony, an unhappy situation according to her, and forcing them to marry so as to produce children and as many of them as the husband may fancy.

I could further acclaim Suchon's views by pointing out that overpopulation in our times is among the factors destructive of many humanistic efforts to overcome poverty, pollution and warlike tendencies. Reproductive rights are first of all women's human rights, increasing the amount of freedom where they have been conquered, but in addition to that they potentially have beautiful effects, lovely to contemplate. I certainly want to endorse the idea that producing children is not (any longer) compulsory. But I must acknowledge that Gabrielle Suchon baffled me, by introducing a contrast between archaic times and the present, so as to emancipate the present from what happened at the very beginning. This does not tally with what I thought I knew of Christianity and its idea that the present should conform as much as possible to the exalted times of foundation, an *in illo tempore* marking the outstanding status of the origin. I must have got it wrong and shall have to (gladly) revise this view. What is more, I may also have to revise my poor opinion of interpretations in general. When reading a piece of philosophy or literature, my rule always was to read the text in itself and for itself (needless to add: for myself). You do not turn to commentaries and you don't want interpretations. But Gabrielle Suchon's writings tell a different story. Claiming that "Be fruitful and multiply" was valid only at the time the earth was empty does seem to be an interpretation and one I do welcome even though I don't believe in interpretations (no more than in biblical injunctions). How am I going to make sense of this?

Perhaps we should note that Suchon's goal is to contradict the opposite view, namely that this command or prophecy would be valid for ever, which was also already an interpretation. This interpretation had been around for centuries and she is opposing it with another view, which is logically of the same nature, thus providing an interpretation against another interpretation. She puts forth her own understanding of the text against the received understanding of it. She is not challenging the text itself but a mistaken interpretation that had become canonical. One could also say that she had entered into a dialogue with this divine writ and had grasped something which had escaped previous commentators, namely the connection between the injunction and the situation of emptiness of the earth. She heard something in the prophecy which had never been perceived, or perhaps we should say she was the true prophetess.

An interpretation against another one: I should like to compare Suchon's position with a well-known passage in Plato's *Symposium*. Diotima, who is described as a prophetess, has made the point that "Love is neither beautiful nor good" and Socrates is a bit too quick to exclaim: "What do you mean, Diotima? Is Love ugly, then, and bad?"[9] He has readily inferred that "neither beautiful nor good" meant "ugly and bad," in short he has offered an interpretation (and a particularly mistaken one) of what Diotima was setting forth. Diotima replies something which sounds like a scolding and she uses a word much discussed in the literature and of interest in linguistics too. The verb *euphemein* may mean to keep quiet or to pronounce auspicious words. In Plato's translations, it is sometimes rendered by "Peace, for shame!" or "No blasphemy!," translators being uncertain about what amount of sacredness is to be attributed to Diotima's retort. You could even understand it as simply a "Can't you shut up for a minute, Socrates?" because his inference is not only wrong but also *in the way* of what Diotima is developing. She has then to reclaim the floor and launch into a monologue, whereas up to then the intellectual scene had been structured as a dialogue. Plato had been a playwright before turning to philosophy. You would be within your rights to assume (or not) that Diotima was a fictional character and that deeming her a prophetess simply helps add authority to her silencing of Socrates, in short that the theatrical setting is perfect as such. All the same, the lesson is about logic and not theology: there is more than one inference possible here, the crass one which young Socrates offered without taking the time to ponder and another one, subtler, and at risk of being blocked by the silly one. As a result, the silly one is briskly to be swept away so that the subtler theory can be voiced and explained.

Hasty interpretations are in fact familiar to us all. When reading a book, hopefully we do not swallow it roundly like a host. There always is some possibility of a dialogue with the text while you read it. But this possibility has to be held back a bit if you want to reach the next paragraph, the next page, the next chapter. You need to silence your own objections, or your answers for a while, if you want to reach the end of the story. You will remember the main ones, the relevant ones. You will then return to them and at the end of the day a fruitful dialogue between the text and you will have taken place. This is, as a rule, how it works for me when reading philosophy.

And the same while reading the Bible? No, not utterly. But let me take an example: I did stop short in front of a passage, and I still do, which means that an astonishment never was silenced. I am referring to the phrase about the "jealous God." A jealous God, now what is this? True, I had previously come across such a phrase in *Les Contemplations* by Victor Hugo, but I had thought it was poetic licence, probably heretical, an expression of the grief which had made the poet lash out at God, and basically a downright calumny. In human beings, jealousy is a pathology, a misfortune, perhaps a moral failure. It creates a lot of harm to the jealous person in the first place and to everyone around, particularly when it is a permanent character trait. But how could a God be jealous? Aristotle's prime mover was not likely to experience such a feeling. Anselm of Canterbury's "most perfect being" couldn't possibly be blemished by such an imperfection. Sophie Seban, a former student and a great friend, after pondering the matter, returns her diagnosis: "Michèle, you mix up the philosophers' God with the Biblical one," and any reader of Pascal knows that this is not to be done. Point taken, yes, I had a preconception derived from reading philosophy. But it does not solve the problem: what is this idea, verging on blasphemy, doing in the Bible? Perhaps it is just anthropomorphism? Or perhaps those who drew up the text used the word "jealous" for lack of a better term to describe the way a monotheism may claim an emotional monopoly of the worship people offer? I recently had the curiosity of Googling "*Dieu jaloux*" to see if someone had solved what I still see as a problem. This is what I found (in French; my translation): "Perhaps a practical example will help. If a husband sees another man flirting with his wife, he will have grounds to be jealous, because only he has the right to do so. Such jealousy is not a sin, it is even perfectly appropriate." Such an example does not help: do you first have to imbibe the structure of monogamy (and the appropriation, by a man, of a woman) in order to make sense of Exodus?

Is this any of my business, as an atheist, you may wonder? Surely I could leave this question to believers and urge them to hurry up and develop an interpretation which would make this notion harmless. Harmless, I say, because, as it is, this notion is dangerous. If, as Bacon claimed, wars of religion derive from this fact (and Bacon considered it a fact, that "the true God is a jealous God"[10]), then the problem is anyone's business and mine. Wars of religion are a plague (along with all sorts of wars) and they tend to affect everybody, non-believers included. Moreover, when a war erupts, which is not based on religion in the first place, a religious language may be used for bellicose campaigns. When a certain American administration decided to launch a war on Iraq, followed by the British government and many of its citizens, but not by their French counterparts, a phrase was used which turned the French into enemies: "Who is not with us is against us." The powers-that-be who launched that war didn't bother to mention that this was a recycled phrase from Matthew, "He that is not with me is against me."[11] It rang powerfully, and no wonder spin-doctors loved it. No wonder the phrase, in the plural, had already found its way into a popular film, *Magnum Force*, as the rallying cry of a group of policemen turned into a gang of serial killers, when they try to force Clint Eastwood to get involved. Denying other people any right to disagree, or any right to simply keep away and abstain ...

Is jealousy a form of hatred that demands to be shared? This is again a question I am laying at your feet for I cannot solve it. While reading Augustine's *City of God*, I was amazed by the amount of material pointing out that no one in the Pagan world was likable, neither the deities nor the famous men. No one was truly moral either. The author does his best to share a form of hatred for Pagan civilization; he seems to be organizing his readers into a crowd fighting back another culture, as if loyalty to Christianity demanded that not even the smallest bit of your heart went to the rival culture. There are even scarier examples than Augustine. In 1205, Pope Innocent III wrote to the king of France, Philip Augustus, that he would show the fervour of his Christian faith by persecuting the Jews (*in eorum demonstret persecutione fervorem quo fidem prosequitur Christianam*),[12] which the king did. The same king also launched a war against the Cathars and, all in all, wrote one of the most terrible pages in French history. We do need a deep and thorough analysis of jealousy even if the idea that harming a rival can be a token of love may sometimes appear in history more as an excuse than as the real motivation. Even if one must suspect that a shallow notion of "national unity" may bring about as many shameful troubles as a given religion.

At any rate, and to conclude, I don't think it is a good thing always to stress the alterity between a culture to which you belong and another culture. My own field, namely philosophy, is not radically devoid of similarities with the New Testament and I want to acknowledge that. When I first read the New Testament, my main reaction was: "But this is Greece!," as if Jesus and his twelve disciples would be like your typical philosophy school. Kindly reread Diogenes Laertius, the stress on love, or *philia*, and to the friendship among members of a given school, but surely not for members of other schools, who all had deplorable mores! "He who is not with me (or with us) is against me (or us)" could be the axiom deeply engraved in every philosophical school in Antiquity. They were sects, all of them, each with a set of principles and beliefs, and little love lost between them. Jesus, the founder of the group, was sentenced to death; perhaps he (nor those who compiled the Gospels) had not heard of Socrates' manner of death, though I would find it difficult to assume. At any rate, the Romans had: in the Ancient Greek and Roman world, they would not mind issuing a death warrant or a banishment towards a philosopher who taught young people; witness what had happened to Carneades and, later on, was to happen to Epictetus. Just as what happened, many centuries earlier, to Protagoras, who had to run away in order to save his life, because he had written that he was unable to know whether Gods existed. Apparently, the Greeks and then the Hellenized Roman Empire feared what independent intellectuals could bring about in the City, particularly when endowed with charisma. One may wonder if the narrative of Jesus' life and death was not written down in Alexandria and not just translated into Greek somewhere. It could have become a chapter in Diogenes Laertius. Even the importance of a mother is not un-Greek at all. Socrates had one to whom he respectfully refers. Moreover, Pythagoras (who claimed to be Hermes' son) had one too and there is an anecdote about him which may ring a bell for you:

> On coming to Italy, he made a subterranean dwelling and enjoined on his mother to mark and record all that passed, and at what hour, and to send her notes down to him until he should ascend. She did so. Pythagoras some time afterwards came up withered and looking like a skeleton, then went into the assembly and declared he had been down to Hades.[13]

No one knows when this anecdote found its way into the common wisdom about Ancient philosophers and then into the *Lives of Eminent Philosophers*; no one even knows when Diogenes Laertius lived and wrote. He claims he found it in Hermippus, a third-century man who allegedly spent his days reading in the Library of Alexandria. It is thus impossible to tell if the story about Protagoras predates the New Testament. In any case, this was the Middle Sea and Alexander's (ex-)dominions, a tremendous site where different cultures merged or perhaps stemmed from a common background and then developed each in its own direction. It is stating the obvious to say that philosophy lives on a Greek legacy; but there are also Greek aspects in Christianity. Take the question of miracles, quite central in the Gospels: it is a Greek notion whereas you will not find many occurrences of miracles in the Old Testament. Some Talmudists today even maintain that it is not acceptable at all to believe in miracles. I don't anyway, but this does not prevent me from using this notion quite frequently in everyday life. Imagine: the dishwasher is out of order but, while trying to move it, you give it a jerk and lo and behold, it starts working again. This is really an occasion to rejoice, hence ironically to exclaim: "And 'They say miracles are past'!," a famous line turned into a quip against my own parish.[14] But then a Talmudist friend will remind you straightaway that he shouldn't countenance hearing such things. I learned something on that day and no one had to do the dishes.

Another time, we shall discuss the passage about Martha and Mary. Because, if it has some theological or ideological importance, we just can't afford to accept the meaning it seems to have. And, another time, I shall tell you how, when Pamela died, and the village where I spend my summers shared my grief, it was a Muslim neighbour who endeavoured to console me through telling me a story about Prophet Nouh.

disclosure statement

No potential conflict of interest was reported by the author.

notes

1 This paper was presented at the "Prophetic Word Conference," 13–16 September 2017, at Regent's Park College, Oxford.

2 John 8.32.

3 Ecclesiastes 1.14.

4 A few years later I met Vladimir Jankélévitch, who deemed that story simply unmentionable in polite company.

5 "Introduction" in *The Second Sex*, trans. Constance Borde and Sheila Malovany-Chevallier (New York: Knopf, 2010) 11.

6 Dordrecht: Springer, 2010.

7 *New Topics* xi.

8 Only parents and only in the courtyard: this maximal limitation was due to TB prophylaxis, an important issue at the time.

9 Plato, *Symposium*, 201e, trans. Alexander Nehamas and Paul Woodruff, in *Plato on Love*, ed. C.D. Reeve (Indianapolis: Hackett, 2006) 63.

10 Francis Bacon, "Of Unity in Religion" in *The Works of Francis Bacon*, eds. James Spedding, Robert Leslie Ellis, and Douglas Denon Heath (London: Longman, 1861) VI: 381.

11 Matthew 12.30. Contrast with Mark 9.40: "For he that is not against us is on our part."

12 Letter, "Etsi non displiceat."

13 Diogenes Laertius, *Lives of Eminent Philosophers*, 2 vols., trans. Robert Drew Hicks (London: Heinemann; Cambridge, MA: Harvard UP, 1980) 2: Book viii, section 41.

14 Shakespeare, *All's Well That Ends Well*, Act II, Scene 3.

I

I want to provide an oblique, and perhaps obsessively blinkered, approach to Pamela Sue Anderson's unified vision of our vulnerability to violence, need for and openness to love, and reflective self-understanding. If we restrict ourselves to a level of robust common sense, Pamela can be seen as working out separate conceptions of human vulnerability, love and reflective self-understanding and then connecting them externally to one another through some kind of unifying theory. I will try out the more radical idea that she was seeking to locate an underlying metaphysical and ethical unity that makes our human vulnerability, love and reflective self-understanding both possible and intelligible.

My essay traces only one path towards Pamela's rich and diverse thinking on these matters, and I look forward to other pathways and appreciations explored in this volume. In trying out the idea that she was seeking an original unity, I draw on many discussions with her about her own thinking, puzzling, drafting, doubting, reconsidering, and creatively progressing – all of which I hope reflect what our conversations revealed about her own dialogues with herself, her "internal dialogues" with historical figures and her actual dialogues with contemporaries. We all know that talking with Pamela was so much fun, full of life, excitement, perplexity and unstuffy discovery, leaving us joyful, contented, inspired, and, if circumstances of sadness, anxiety or grief required, comforted.

My thought is that Pamela was pursuing something fundamental about being human, although that is not quite right because her

nicholas bunnin

VULNERABLE SELVES AND OPENNESS TO LOVE

account of humanity is one of open, creative, fluid and risky *becoming* rather than *being*. Her quicksilver ability to move between the mundane and the metaphysical can mislead us if we do not grasp her approach to the metaphysical. Stated baldly, Pamela was deeply influenced by our mutual friend Adrian Moore's version of metaphysics as making sense of things, including making sense of ourselves, where the ordinary is not displaced but returned to and transformed by a reflective sensibility. Parenthetically, my own thinking owes so much to trinary conversations with Pamela and Adrian.

To move towards what I am suggesting, let me allude to Erwin Schrödinger's notion in quantum mechanics of entanglement, where some apparently distinct spatially separated phenomena must be understood with reference to one another, although for my philosophical purposes the entanglements are within and between ethics and metaphysics rather than within physics, although also lurking in the background are the dangerous and delightful physical and emotional human entanglements of love.

You might reasonably grumble that in citing Schrödinger I am seeking to clarify something *difficult* to understand, a fundamentally entangled ethical and metaphysical unity of vulnerability, love and self-understanding, by something *impossible* to understand, a fundamentally entangled unity of quantum-mechanical phenomena – that I am seeking to explain the obscure by the more obscure.

But my strategy is one of juxtaposition rather than clarification, showing the centrality of entanglement within a philosophy of the humanities rather than by mimicking insights about entanglement within a philosophy of science and mathematics. I try to trace the theme of underlying unity and, hence, moral and metaphysical entanglement, in Pamela's philosophical imaginary to resonances or retrievals from three philosophers who featured in her "internal dialogues": Spinoza, Kant and Levinas. Her thinking certainly does not reduce to any of these or other suggested influences, but I hope to persuade you that this backward-looking procedure throws light on the tasks Pamela set for herself and can perhaps help us to deal with these predecessors as well. With regards to her feminism, Pamela did not dismiss reading male philosophers, but from the beginning of her career reread them with her own individually creative feminist sensibility.

2

From Spinoza, I focus on love in the *Ethics* as offering liberation from the bondage of the emotions. For Spinoza, our freedom is constituted by rational understanding of our place in nature, where achieving this kind of knowledge allows our actions to arise from reason rather than from emotions, and hence for us to be internally free. This freedom could be protected from others in a harmonious society governed by a rational legal order. For Spinoza, we are vulnerable to the bondage of our own emotions, which result from our ignorance, but also vulnerable to the external violence of the emotionally driven actions of the ignorant, who evade the constraints of the rational legal order.

In Spinoza's account of psychology, emotions can be overcome not by reason but only by stronger emotions, all of which are grounded in ignorance except for love, which can be grounded in knowledge. At its pinnacle, love as the intellectual love of God is identified with the intuitive knowledge of God, thus allowing even lesser love to be rational to a degree and for this reason to be capable of combating irrational emotions and the vulnerability to which they give rise.

Although we can question each and every facet of this standard narrative, we can also see in Spinoza a path towards thinking of love and vulnerability together. Of course, Spinoza's rigorously expounded and fiercely defended account of substance leads to fundamental unities of God and nature and of mind and body, unities that are hidden from us in our ordinary confinement to knowledge of inferior kinds but open to rational discovery as our knowledge becomes adequate. I think that Pamela found Spinoza's rigour misplaced and his account of the best way of living clunky and unpersuasive, but that she felt kinship to his thinking of vulnerability and love together and his vision of underlying unities to make sense of ourselves. I suggest that this gathering of themes from Spinoza offered materials for the humanistic understanding of the human entanglements that I find in Pamela's work.

3

The next stage of my essay focuses on Kant. I turn first to the *Critique of Pure Reason*, where Kant's critical metaphysics rejects and overcomes the metaphysics of Spinoza and other of his predecessors. At the heart of this work, the categories and the transcendental unity of apperception, the "I think" that accompanies all our representations, emerge together. The transcendental deduction of the categories turned out to be a unified deduction of the possibility of objectivity *and* subjectivity, a Kantian insight that structures and guides the whole further elaboration of his critical thought. This austere "I think," however, is a wretched non-entity, incapable of either vulnerability or love, not even a shadow of the Cartesian thinking thing rejected by Kant, but merely a mode of combining representations. It is the forebear of Wittgenstein's metaphysical subject in the *Tractatus*, which was not an object in the world but rather reduced to a point as a limit of the world.

I turn now to Kant's moral philosophy. It would seem impossible to fit up the minimalist subject of the "I think" to be the self in the version of the categorical imperative that implores each of us to treat humanity, whether in oneself or others, not merely as a means but also as an end in itself. Kant repeatedly doubled back to consider the self in his critical writings, either as random addenda and afterthoughts or as an orderly progress through the various methods he considered to be appropriate to the different domains of his investigations. We are likely to find lucidity and order in his accounts of the self the more we think his programme succeeds and to find collapse and ruin the more we think it fails, but I am going to consider a touchstone of his moral philosophy, discussed by Christine Korsgaard, that enhanced my habit of thinking about Kant and Pamela together. For Korsgaard's Kant, culminating in her 2001–02 John Locke Lectures, *Self-Constitution: Agency, Identity, and Integrity*, the origin of normativity lies in a capacity to construct in the same acts the moral law and ourselves as reflective moral agents, a capacity we have as human selves capable of practical reason. I would go on to say that the joint origin of the objectivity of moral law and the subjectivity of our moral agency explains why the moral law is a law for us rather than a heteronomous imposition. It is not only the law; it is our law. But even if the moral law is our law because we make it together with our moral agency, it is not clear why we should care about its injunctions.

If we are merely protecting our capacity for practical reason, why not amend the "humanity" version of the categorical imperative (Kant, *Groundwork of the Metaphysics of Morals* (Cambridge: Cambridge UP, 1997) 4: 429) to an injunction "to treat *practical reason*, whether in oneself or others, not merely as a means but also as an end in itself"? This emended version might fit Spinoza's fear of our rationality being enslaved by the emotions, but I suggest that Kant chose to treat our *humanity*, rather than our practical reason, as an end in itself because he had a richer sense of our human vulnerability, and this richer sense gave compelling urgency to our concern as human moral agents for the moral law. If this makes sense, we have a metaphysical and moral enrichment of the First Critique's merely schematic unity of deducing objectivity and subjectivity. In addition, the injunction to treat our humanity in ourselves and others not merely as a means but also as an end in itself places a fuller human vulnerability, self-love and the love of others within the scope of this original unity.

A further aspect of our reflective self-understanding as crucial to Kant's discussion of "treating humanity as an end in itself" can be elucidated by considering his later account in the *Critique of Judgement* of our subjective but inevitable use of reflective judgement to treat organized beings as beings in which the relations of parts to one another and to the wholes of which they are parts are mutual relations not merely of means but also of ends. With Kant, we are closer to a humanistic understanding of human entanglements that I find in Pamela's work, but the dangerous and delightful physical and emotional entanglements of love still lurk at the margins.

4

Although Pamela was no more a Levinasian than she was a Spinozist or a Kantian, with Levinas we are closer to the heart, or rather heartbeat, of Pamela's perception of vulnerability and love and her conception of gendered human selves living lives of complex becoming rather than of being, where first philosophy is neither Husserl's epistemology nor Heidegger's ontology but a fusion of morality and metaphysics. For Levinas, fully human entanglements are both possible and intelligible because for each of us the Other and the Self are not fixed beings but rather open becomings. The implications for my chosen pathway towards Pamela's thinking can be found in the unity of Levinas's post-phenomenological deduction of subjectivity and saying (rather than the said) in *Otherwise than Being, or Beyond Essence*. A fuller exploration of Pamela's possible engagement with Levinas's writings on vulnerability is provided by her former student Xin Mao's contribution to this volume.

5

I conclude by suggesting that Pamela drew on resources discovered in her own internal dialogues with Spinoza, Kant and Levinas, that these had some part in intensifying her confidence in her philosophical vision of the gendered unities of mind and body, reason and emotion, and fact and value underlying this last profound phase of her thinking. Her thinking was not completed, but so very sadly broken off, but I hope this prelude to her thinking reveals reflective trajectories that are open for us to pursue.

When I outlined my plans for this essay to Adrian Moore, I confessed worries that I might be imposing my own preoccupations on Pamela's thinking. He reassured me that my worries were most likely fully justified, but at least the essay would show how talking with Pamela could stimulate fresh thinking in others. I hope I have reached at least this minimal standard.

disclosure statement

No potential conflict of interest was reported by the author.

This essay, in honour of my friend and kindred spirit Pamela Sue Anderson, is an evocation which bypasses the usual evaluations and arguments that often prevail in philosophical conferences. Our friendship dates from the year 1990, when we met at a conference, entitled *Meaning in Texts and Actions: The Questions of Paul Ricoeur*, that was organized by another Ricoeur scholar, David Klemm, and held at the University of Iowa. It was our shared passionate interest in both the philosophy of Paul Ricoeur and the status of women, especially in connection with philosophy of religion, that sealed the bond of our friendship.

We kept in touch over the intervening years, meeting often at conferences and publishing articles in edited volumes that we both published. One question that was often asked of us, given that we both identified as feminists, was why we were particularly interested in the work of Paul Ricoeur. This was because, at that time, Ricoeur was not regarded as exhibiting any feminist sympathies. Nevertheless, we discerned a generosity in this humble man who was both supportive of and interested in our work. Pamela and I both journeyed with Ricoeur at the same time that we pursued our feminist commitments. I will not be able to do justice to the many rich and varied topics we both encountered following in the footsteps of Ricoeur's celebrated detours, where hermeneutics, narrative, and ethics were the most important. Instead, I intend to focus first on Pamela's work, followed by certain of Ricoeur's commitments, and end with a selection of ethical stances where their paths intersected.

morny joy

PAMELA SUE ANDERSON'S JOURNEYING WITH PAUL RICOEUR

the kantian period

One of the most fascinating observations that Pamela Anderson made appears in an interview with Sophia Blackwell for *The Oxford Muse* in 2002. It summarily reflects the time and place of Oxford in the first years of her D.Phil. studies in the 1980s. Pamela recalls that she was often asked: "Why are you here if you are working on a French philosopher (i.e., Ricoeur)?"[1] Pamela admits that, at that time, she could not think of a suitable response for her attraction to the philosophy of religion, and especially to the work of Ricoeur. She later acknowledged, however, that it was a stimulating exercise to engage with challenging issues that she viewed as still relevant for her teaching. In the same article, Pamela acknowledged the wise guidance of her tutor, Alan Montefiore.[2] She praises him as not only an "excellent enabler of Oxford students" but also "a bridge builder between 'so-called Continental' philosophy and Anglo-American analytic philosophy."[3] In addition to supporting her work on Ricoeur, Montefiore also encouraged her to study modern philosophy, especially the work of Immanuel Kant. This was fortuitous because Ricoeur was also an admirer of Kant, and he is on record in the 1980s as announcing that Kant was his preferred master in the study of philosophy of religion:

> Kant's approach in *Religion within the Limits of Reason Alone* seems to me exemplary in this regard: here we see the philosopher thinking at the limit, proposing an autonomous rational interpretation of figurative contents that reason does not draw out of itself.[4]

Pamela persevered in her thesis studies and in 1989 she received her D.Phil. for the thesis: "Paul Ricoeur's Philosophy of the Will: Temporal Experience, Sin, and God." This work was not published, but in 1993 it appeared in a somewhat revised form as *Ricoeur and Kant: Philosophy of the Will*, which caught the attention of Ricoeur scholars.[5] Basically the book was an analysis of Ricoeur's philosophy of the will, and the influence of Kant on Ricoeur's developing ideas. In time, however, Pamela would gradually move away from Kant, although she still referred to him on particular issues, and published another book together with Jordan Bell in 2010.[6] The work of Ricoeur became her principal focus. Again, in her interview in *The Oxford Muse*, Pamela provided an outline of this period in the 1990s and its formative importance for her intellectual life:

> Both Ricoeur and Kant led me to a more secure position in my knowledge of the history of philosophy – as well as knowledge of the most contemporary developments in the field. That is, I have read on questions of freedom, justice, evil, goodness, God, personal identity and love precisely because of following the works of Ricoeur.[7]

a feminist philosophy of religion

It was also in the early years of her teaching career during the 1990s, both in the United States and Britain, that Pamela became increasingly aware of the problematic situation of women in philosophy. At that time, well-qualified women were struggling to obtain and maintain teaching positions. During this period Pamela was drawn toward feminist philosophy. She reflected:

> My areas of expertise and teaching competence became increasingly focused on the areas of ethics and feminist questions in philosophy, especially epistemological questions. My research in epistemology included work on women and knowledge, as well as questions about the rationality of religious belief.[8]

It was her publications and presentations in this area that led to an invitation from Blackwell's to write her ground-breaking volume *A Feminist Philosophy of Religion* (1998).

This volume marked the first critical book published by a woman on the topic of philosophy of religion. It was in this book, together with an article that appeared in *Ars Disputandi*,[9] that Pamela launched her investigations into the status of women in the discipline of Philosophy of Religion. A comment made by Pamela in the *Ars Disputandi* article, describing what prompted her to undertake this initiative, was especially challenging. In this context, Pamela referred to the discipline of Philosophy of Religion as a "strange discipline." She then offered the reasons why she chose this phrase and its relevance for her work:

> The intention is to render strange the conceptions which are, or have been, all too familiar in order to see the exclusive nature of a now traditional perspective. In particular, there is too much familiarity, and so unquestioning acceptance, accompanying the classical model of traditional theism.[10]

At issue for Pamela was the very strangeness of the nature of an immortal God whose very existence continued to be debated, and of the qualities such as omniscience, omnipotence, and omnibenevolence that were attributed to such a Being.

For Pamela, the theoretical emphasis devoted to these issues, with their ensuing proofs and truths, seemed to be at a far remove from the lives of many women.[11] It was in response to this lack of sensitivity that Pamela declared that her intention would be to develop a transformative mode of philosophy in relation to religion. Central to her approach was an acknowledgement of the "deeply gendered – often sexist and racist – nature of our social and physical locations."[12] Such an approach, she believed, would encourage an awareness of the importance of the notions of sex and gender, as well as the diversities of race, class, ethnicity, and sexual orientation, which she considered to have been neglected.[13] At the same time, Pamela understood only too well that this demanding task would not be realized without a constructive epistemological strategy. She described this as involving a process of "thinking from the lives of others, and reinventing ourselves as other."[14] In this exercise Pamela appealed to the work of other women scholars to help her develop her views on this topic.

The term "otherness" is one that was used frequently in the timeframe from the 1970s to the 1990s, with its phenomenological and deconstructive connections that referred to practices of exclusion as well as the attempts made to help eradicate such practices.[15] Pamela adapted this term, appealing to a number of feminist thinkers who helped her to hone her position. She then clarified and refined this ambitious undertaking in a number of books, articles, and interviews in the following years.[16] Two women scholars in particular, Sandra Harding, a leading proponent of "standpoint theory,"[17] and Michèle Le Doeuff, with her explorations of the "philosophical imaginary,"[18] were acknowledged by Pamela as major influences.

At this stage of her work, Pamela defined her approach as basically an "epistemically informed perspective." This position was directed to thinking about the lives of other people, especially those who have been relegated to the margins by prevailing epistemological standard concepts. Pamela's words reflect her own passionate opposition to this practice: "A feminist standpoint is an achievement – i.e. the achievement of an epistemically informed perspective – resulting from struggle by, or on behalf of women and men who have been exploited, oppressed or dominated."[19] As a result, a standpoint analysis cannot be considered as linked to a position of absolute objectivity. Instead, it is a reflexive move that strives to ameliorate the living conditions of those human beings regarded as "others" and whose voices have not been heard. Pamela did not restrict this position of "standpoint analysis" solely to women, and welcomed a wider application, though her main focus was that of women.

There is, however, another important factor to be considered. In Pamela's opinion, being born a woman does not automatically qualify one to adopt the status of a feminist standpoint. Nor could a woman simply claim to have achieved "an epistemically informed perspective." Such a stance has to be earned by application and experience. In Pamela's view, negative myths and rational concepts can interfere with one's behaviour and attitudes. In order to correct such potentially aberrant behaviour, Pamela introduced analyses of certain myths, aided by the philosophical imaginary, as part of a necessary process of imagining how people's lives could be conceived differently. She describes her strategy:

> [I]t *begins with taking* the privileged readings of female figures or images of women in *patriarchal texts* out to the margins in order to reconfigure them *from the standpoint of others*. In this way, the familiar in philosophy of religion is rendered strange; and it becomes apparent that a self-conscious awareness of our sex/gendered perspectives (with all the sexual and social factors that go with these) moves us to change conceptions of ourselves, i.e. to reinvent ourselves as other than we have been.[20]

reconfiguring a gendered philosophy of religion

Yet it would seem such procedure is easier said than done, and it is for this reason that Anderson appealed to the work of the French philosopher Michèle Le Doeuff. In her understanding of the "philosophy imaginary," Le Doeuff acknowledges the images, symbols, and other fragments of a non-rational nature can be extremely influential. "Imaginary" here does not bear any relation to psychoanalytically based theories in the manner of either Lacan or Irigaray but refers to a certain form of a philosophical excavation, involving the imagination, that Anderson, following Le Doeuff, appreciates as both evaluative and restorative.

In Anderson's adaptation of Le Doeuff's work, she invokes the work of the imaginary in philosophy as not simply an ornamental additive but as a device that operates effectively in a manner that is crucial to a person's self-image. This is achieved by carefully examining images and the words they evoke in order to assess their relevant ideals and worth. This is followed by what Pamela names as a "reconfiguring" of harmful images and ideas, especially those indicting women philosophers.

Le Doeuff herself does not prescribe any definitive method for detecting the means by which women have been excluded from the hallowed precincts of philosophy. In keeping with Le Doeuff's reluctance to prescribe a definitive method, Anderson will adopt her own particular approach. It first involves an investigation of certain female mythical figures, e.g., Antigone,[21] as she has been interpreted by men in the past, then followed by more recent re-evaluations. Pamela will also reinforce these moves with explorations of women's desires, especially that of "yearning," as a way to confirm women's restoration of their role and identities.

"Yearning" is a word that Pamela adapts from the African-American scholar bell hooks. Anderson appreciates hooks's use of this term that implies a passion, that is, particularly for Pamela, a "cognitive passion." She regards it as a rational passion that seeks to achieve a parity or worth in a society that has for many centuries deprived women of access. Pamela quotes from bell hooks's work: "[U]nder the heading *Yearning* [...] I looked for *common* passions, sentiments, shared by folks across race, class, gender, and sexual practice, I was struck by the depths of longing in many of us."[22] In describing this "passionate longing" as women's reaction to their exclusion from being able to flourish, Pamela is very careful in this move not to diminish in any way the force of hooks's call for an end to social injustice for African-American women. Nor does she distance herself from the necessary concrete struggles required to end all such forms of oppression. As a confirmation of her commitment, Pamela affirms:

> I employ the specific term, yearning, to stress the cognitive and political nature of a common passion for equalitarian reciprocity. This cognitive passion unites subjects across gender, sexual, racial and class divides. But *the yearning for* recognition ensures both the realism and the risk of intersubjectivity.[23]

In addition, Pamela will also endow "yearning" with her own special interpretation, whereby yearning takes on both personal and political dimensions for women philosophers. Pamela states: "My contention is that the ultimate goal of a woman's philosophical search for identity is mutual recognition, even if unreachable. The struggle for recognition serves as a guiding ideal, it also ensures a realism."[24] She describes this passion for recognition as also "evident in sexual desire, political rage, unavoidable grief and self-giving/self-created love."[25] In support of such an aspiration, especially as it includes women philosophers, Anderson invokes Judith Butler's (post-)Hegelian reading of "longing" in her work "Longing for Recognition."[26] Yet Pamela is well aware of the risks involved in this wager of intersubjectivity. Le Doeuff has alerted her to the fact that women need to remain extremely conscious that they do not, in their turn, initiate a new form of exclusivity, by establishing a women's-only mode of philosophizing.

At the heart of Pamela's quest in philosophy, it is imperative that women retain the responsibility to see themselves "as if" through the eyes of others, i.e., in a self-reflexive and impartial manner that does not presume that they have access to any ultimate truth. In this way, Anderson seeks to modify the claims to a purely objective knowledge that presumes to provide a God's-eye view or to assert that rationality alone dictates the terms of philosophical or theological knowledge.

ricoeur's ethical turn[27]

In 1992, Paul Ricoeur surprised many people by publishing a book on ethics: *Oneself as Another*.[28] As a result, he moved from theoretical discussions of philosophical problematics – though he had always been concerned with matters pertaining to everyday life, i.e., the "life-world" or the *Lebenswelt* of Husserl – to struggle with more pronounced ethical and practical issues. It marked a progression that would inform the last thirteen years of his life. There had been, however, indications in earlier essays and interviews that a change was imminent. Ricoeur had expressed a growing dismay at the undiminishing amount of violence that human beings continued to inflict on one another. For Ricoeur, this was a manifestation of suffering in the form of unjustified harm perpetrated on innocent people. One example of his reflections was expressed in an interview with Charles Reagan in 1988:

> It is this speculative problem of action and passion but also the problem of victimization – the whole story of this cruel century, the twentieth century – and all of the suffering imposed on the Third World by the rich, affluent countries, by colonialism. There is a history of victims that keeps accompanying or reduplicating the history of the victors. But the history I try to revive has a strong ethical debt to the victims.[29]

In the same interview, he also admitted: "I must say that in my previous work there is very little about ethics and politics."[30] Ricoeur's decision to move toward ethics and political thought in order to help alleviate the existence of human suffering was no doubt informed by his personal religious orientation. In his later writings, however, Ricoeur was concerned with providing cogent grounds as to the inability of abstract philosophical reasoning, or even of speculative explorations, to provide conclusive answers to the problem of evil and suffering in the world. While Ricoeur still conceded that the different religions could provide assistance for a suffering humanity,[31] he nonetheless remained anguished that they could not solve the problem either of evil's origin or its prevention. Ricoeur's compassion for all humanity became patently obvious. He described his own personal diagnosis and strategy to address the situation:

> It is at this point that the distinction to which I am most attracted – that between, on the one hand, fragility, vulnerability, fallibility – in short, finitude – and, on the other, the historical effectiveness of evil already present – constitutes the primary resistance that I oppose to the temptation of mastery that thought claims to achieve, before considering any project of liberation, and this is so as early as the work of delimiting and identifying the problem of evil.[32]

In this context, Ricoeur places himself at a distance from philosophical arguments, which do not provide sufficient insight into the predicament of human fragility. Instead, Ricoeur will appeal to his own understanding of wisdom to aid in his exacting task:

> Wisdom, which is no longer to develop arguments or even to accuse God but to transform, practically, emotionally, the nature of desire that is at the base of the request for explanation. To transform desire practically means to leave behind the question of origins, toward which myth carries speculative thought, and to substitute for it the question of the future and the end of evil.[33]

fragility and vulnerability

In making this statement, Ricoeur confirms his vital engagement with the notions of both fallibility and fragility as aspects of human finitude. Yet, in the course of Ricoeur's investigations into instances of human suffering, a noticeable distinction between these two terms, "fallibility" and "fragility," began to appear.

In his early work in the 1960s on *Fallible Man*, Ricoeur's use of the term "fallibility" had been employed as identical with that of "fragility." In this context, it witnessed to a weakness or intrinsic fault in humanity, "the primordial weakness from which evil arises."[34] In contrast, during the late 1980s and 1990s, Ricoeur began to employ the words "frailty" and "fragility," together with "vulnerability," as being indicative of the instances of undeserved suffering in the world that so troubled him. He struggled to discern a way to protect human beings from such grievous suffering. Rather than seek to determine the human fault or weakness that can lead to such behaviour, the question had changed for Ricoeur. It became: "What shall we do with this fragile being, what shall we do for her or him? We are directed towards a future of a being in need of help to survive and to grow."[35] This statement graphically portrays the impetus that informed Ricoeur's turn to ethics.

As he began to develop an ethical orientation in *Oneself as Another* (1992), in order to support his aim of helping human beings to live "with and for each other in just institutions," Ricoeur undertook two separate tasks.[36] One was to establish the most important activities that designate what Ricoeur terms a "capable human being" (*homo capax*).[37] He justified his approach in this way:

> I would like [...] to underscore my emphasis, since *Oneself as Another*, on the importance of the idea of *homo capax* as integrating a wide conceptual field. With this theme I have tried to bring together those diverse capacities and incapacities that qualify human beings as acting and suffering human beings.[38]

Ricoeur also undertook a phenomenological description of *homo capax*, of the four capabilities that he considered indispensable to the constitution of human well-being. He introduced these capacities:

> the power to designate oneself as the speaker of one's own words; the power to designate oneself as the agent of one's own actions; the power to designate oneself as the protagonist in one's own life-story; and finally the capacity to accept responsibility for the effects of one's actions.[39]

These capacities clarified the requisite activities for participating in what he considered to be the good life. It is in the interference or abolition of such capacities to act, i.e., when people are denied the right to exercise these capacities/capabilities, that fragility becomes apparent.

It could appear that, with the introduction of this model of *homo capax*, Ricoeur was making amends for what he regarded as his previous shortcomings. He acknowledged that:

> I left unclear the face of impotence owing not only to those infirmities of every sort that may affect the human body as the organ of action, but also the interference of outside powers capable of diminishing, hindering or preventing our use of our abilities.[40]

Ricoeur's addition of capability or "imputation," a term he amended from Kant to indicate responsibility, allowed him to strengthen his position. Ricoeur states that: "Imputation and responsibility are synonymous, the only difference being that it is actions that are *imputed* to someone and it is persons that are held *responsible* for actions and their consequences."[41] It is in exercising his or her responsibility that a human being can guard against duplicity and the exploitation of fragile fellow beings. This particular notion of fragility, which Ricoeur aligns with vulnerability, however, differs markedly from Ricoeur's earlier usage where fallibility and fragility were described as indicators of a susceptibility to evil. A subtle change in his usage has become evident. Ricoeur introduces a revised definition of a fragile and suffering human being:

> The vulnerability that stands in counterpoint to responsibility can be summed up in the difficulty that everyone has in inscribing his or her action and behaviour into a symbolic order and in the impossibility a number of our contemporaries have in comprehending the meaning and necessity of this inscription, principally those whom our socio-political order excludes. If we have been able to see in this capacity something that we presume every human being is capable of as human, now it is in terms of incapacity that we have to speak of the corresponding fragility.[42]

There are many more issues that could be explored in Ricoeur's encounters and analyses, such as the fragility of the symbolic order, Ricoeur's work in *The Course of Recognition*,[43] and issues of justice. What I have tried to convey in abbreviated form, however, are the most significant aspects of Ricoeur's journey as he came to appreciate the delicate intricacies of human fragility and vulnerability. I have focused mainly on specific facets of his work that resonate strongly with Pamela's work.

engaging with vulnerability

Pamela's concern for those whose lives had been damaged and her subsequent search for ways to mitigate the ensuing conditions that limit their lives – both theoretically and practically – are witness to Pamela's profound compassion. It is then not surprising when she turns her attention to the subject of vulnerability. In the years since Judith Butler's work *Undoing Gender* (2004), "vulnerability" has become a topic of significant consideration, especially for women philosophers. Pamela allows that her own writings were galvanized by the work of Judith Butler, especially her writings on "precarious life, precarity, and vulnerability."[44] She declares that her own intention will be one of "transforming an ignorance of vulnerability into a distinctively ethical avowal."[45] In this way, Pamela will venture to provide a more effective appreciation of vulnerability that also promotes enhancement.

vulnerability and the ethical turn

One of the first appearances of the term "vulnerability" can be found in "Autonomy, Vulnerability, and Gender,"[46] an essay that Pamela published in 2003. In this context, she is not yet investigating the dynamics of vulnerability as they will appear in her future work, although there are definite intimations of her intended project. In her article, Pamela is worried about the implications of Kant's attitude toward women which she understands as imposing authoritative moral rules. She is also challenging Kant's understanding of autonomy, which she views as excluding women from exercising their rational capacity, and from being authors of their own lives. To counter these limitations, introduced by what she describes as "moral rationality," Pamela suggests that there is a need to recognize human contingency. In illustrating this aspect of existence, she proposes "the incorporation of ethical practices previously devalued by their association with vulnerability, such as attention, affection and relationality."[47] While these qualities are not necessarily consistent with the attributes Pamela will later associate with vulnerability, they are indicative of a disposition that accepts the contingencies of human existence while not conceding ground to extremes of assertive demands or self-indulgent sentiments.

There are other more recent publications where Pamela advances her thoughts in favour of "a distinctively ethical vulnerability." However, it is in her article "Arguing for 'Ethical' Vulnerability: Towards a Politics of Care?"[48] that she presents her most cogent and compelling insights. One of these is her determination to rescue "vulnerability" from what she understands as a negative reading. Pamela expresses her diffidence toward Judith Butler's statement that "an increased sense of vulnerability is one that is often accompanied by a similarly increased sense of violence."[49] She is also troubled by Butler's remark that there is no impetus in the "recognition of one's own embodied vulnerability that necessarily inspires generous love, empathy or tolerance."[50] Finally, Pamela is hesitant about Butler's explanation of "the sense of dispossession" which can result from grief or "becoming undone" by the loss of a beloved person.[51] Pamela observes that in Butler's work "there seems to be no clear or certain path from the reality of corporeal vulnerability to a normative ethics or a just politics, since there is nothing specifically normative in recognition of becoming undone."[52]

In her own response to these obstacles, Pamela attempts to provide an alternative way of appreciating or "reconfiguring" vulnerability. Rather than simply linking vulnerability with a possible violent reaction, as Butler does – and which Pamela regards as an ambiguous and ambivalent situation – she dissents. Pamela's rejoinder introduces vulnerability as enabling "a life-enhancing capability that can inculcate an openness to affection, change, and affirmation of life."[53] This appears to be something of a tall order, especially as Pamela intends to position her suggested solution within an ethical framework, as distinct from a moral one. Unfortunately, there is insufficient space to describe in detail the many complex arguments Pamela provides, but I will endeavour to examine the most vital of her proposals.

Pamela begins by describing two distinct levels that will undergird her strategy. The first is the level of phenomenology, which she posits as disclosing "the materially specific lived experience of intimacy [...] while also admitting affection could generate negative effects of fear, shame or rage."[54] As such, Pamela affirms that while phenomenology may reveal a receptivity to love and to attachment, she also admits that it can, simultaneously, indicate loss and harm. In this latter observation, Pamela seems to agree with Butler's seemingly negative stance, but she also intends to explore ways of moving beyond this impasse.[55] This is where Pamela's second level of ethics is introduced. It is in this context that she intends to insert a revised form of ethics that can intervene in support of vulnerability. In this way alternative ways of assessing justice can also be realized. Pamela declares: "A phenomenology of bodily vulnerability is a precondition for repairing injustice; this should enhance a dynamic process for rendering vulnerability ethical."[56] Such a weighted statement needs further in-depth commentary, but basically what Pamela was also hoping to achieve is a rebuttal of what she considers as the harsh utilitarianism that has dominated much of recent moral theory and even virtue ethics.[57]

In order to accomplish her goal, Pamela first examines what she views as an "excessive moral demandingness" whereby a moral subject is confronted with an "impossible moral obligation."[58] She also adds a further observation which reveals her own evaluation, where, in its utilitarian form, "contemporary moral theory has tended to interpret vulnerability as a condition of need, dependency, or, simply, a lack which requires a moral response."[59] It soon becomes obvious that Pamela's specific aim is to distinguish her understanding of ethics from such a moral theory. She provides the reasons for her harsh criticism:

I am distinguishing "moral" from "ethical" in order to show that what I have called "moral" has an unethical sense, insofar as it results in a paternalistic, controlling and oppressive treatment of (those pejoratively called) the vulnerable; and this latter would have a moralizing sense which is, moreover, unjust precisely when it comes to claiming a deceptive "moral invulnerability" as superior to ethical vulnerability.[60]

relational accountability

The ethical position that Pamela endorses does not necessarily reflect a definitive feminist orientation. She is quick to state that there is no longer one stable or viable version of feminism but a diversity of definitions. Nevertheless, Pamela does concede that there is a deeply shared concern among many women scholars on topics such as justice, vulnerability, and forgiveness.[61] Surprisingly, she also recognizes the contribution of Carol Gilligan's book, published in 1982, *In a Different Voice*,[62] which, in that era, did allow women a voice on certain issues. What Pamela has come to realize, however, is that the "ethics of care" movement that subsequently emerged initiated what she calls "a rather crude binary of care and justice,"[63] solidifying male and female stereotypes. In comparison, it appears to Pamela that, given the volatility in present-day conflicts of claiming identities, with an accompanying proliferation of genders, and variant types of relationships, all such stark binary divisions are no longer tenable.

It is at this stage of her analysis that Pamela returns to phenomenology and ethics to help her negotiate the items needed to support her own position. She first engages with the phenomenological level of experiencing vulnerability, which entails divergent positions of both a positive and negative nature. For Pamela, however, it is a revised ethical component that can, as it were, temper such diverse experiences. To counter the negative element of vulnerability, Pamela proposes that vulnerability also has the capability to provide an "opportunity for relational accountability."[64] As a result, rather than have an abused person simply retreat in hurt and anger, Pamela supplies a bold intervention. She suggests that one can summon the needed strength for openness, for mobilizing an appeal directed at another person to emphasize their unethical, if not destructive, behaviour. Such a move can advance the possibility of a creative encounter. Yet this activity can be exacting, even dangerous, and Pamela does not insist that women must necessarily undertake such activities. Nevertheless, she offers her own profound reflections of this tentative step that could enable women to seek remedial action for unmerited abuse.

This mediation attests to a decisive move made by Pamela in her own journey toward realizing not only the disparate effects of vulnerability but the possibility of an enhancement of life in this world.[65]

a shared commitment

As I was writing and deliberating on the above proposals presented by both Pamela and Paul Ricoeur it occurred to me that their respective contributions have much in common from a certain perspective – especially their dedication to alleviating human suffering. Both were seeking a form of justice that was compatible with their own ethical framework, yet their specific aims and approaches differed. Pamela's contribution was focused mainly on the distress of women whose lives had been shattered by dismissals and abusive relationships. Such intrusions occurred because of the restrictions and prejudices that have confined women within what could be called "benighted gender ideologies." Ricoeur's scope was somewhat wider, lamenting the unmitigated anguish of displaced and mistreated human beings, be they victims of war, of colonialism, or of unlawful expulsions. Each of them tried to ameliorate the dire conditions of existence suffered by their fellow human beings. The principal terms that they employed – "vulnerability," "fragility," "responsibility," and "accountability" – all contributed to their intent to instigate a concerted response that would galvanize change.

conclusion

It is difficult to determine the precise influences that Ricoeur had on Pamela's later writings, apart from the work on vulnerability. She did continue her close readings of Ricoeur's later explorations, as is evident from her bibliographical references, which include a review of the book that marked his move to ethics, *Oneself as Another* (1992).[66] In addition, Pamela explicitly draws Ricoeur into conversation in an essay titled "Ricoeur in Dialogue with Feminist Philosophy of Religion" (2016).[67] However, it did seem particularly fitting when, in the final year of her life, Pamela suggested that we submit a joint panel to be presented at the annual meeting of the Society for Ricoeur Studies in Chicago on the later work of Ricoeur, who had died in 2005. It was accepted, but Pamela was unable to attend because of her failing health. In concluding this paper, I would like to present a section of Pamela's own proposal that expresses her respect and admiration for the work of Paul Ricoeur and also the topics he addressed that had captured her attention.

As a final tribute to both Pamela and also to Ricoeur, I will quote short sections of her proposal for this conference where she expands on the topic of "Ricoeur, Vulnerability, and Friendship":

> Our panel would like to take as its focus, a bold, and especially confident, affirmation that our emphasis must be on friendship as a source of enormous vulnerability. This statement is taken as a provocation for us to assess the nature of an open – vulnerable – life, which would be marked by the great dynamism of memory and the mutual affection of friendship. Such a vulnerable life is inspired by Ricoeur's writings but also by his own life. A mutuality in vulnerability underlies his understanding of "The good life with and for others,"[68] its relations and its fragility. We will, however, stress specifically the distinctiveness of this "Ricoeurian" vulnerability.
>
> Many of us tend to assume that "vulnerability" – being capable of wounding and being wounded – is something to overcome. As vulnerable we are susceptible to wounding, whether an injury, a violent attack, a disease, or a loss of love. Our proposal, however, is

that being vulnerable – given that all of life is – does not necessarily need to be reduced to a negative condition, requiring protection (and paternalism). Instead, being vulnerable manifests a positive need for affection, generating a creative freedom for each of us, to begin something new. In particular, we aim to demonstrate how vulnerability as an opening to mutual affection has a crucial role to play in our understanding and practice of friendship.

It seems more than appropriate for us to celebrate the implicit and explicit work of Ricoeur on vulnerability ten years after his death, with a panel on friendship, precisely because of one thing that stands out – perhaps most of all – since Ricoeur's death. This is the incredible number of people who would say that Ricoeur touched them as a friend! Clearly Ricoeur himself had a great ability to touch individuals, and so, to nourish friendship. What we hope to demonstrate is that this capability for friendship is also a matter with a distinctively Ricoeurian inspiration. It is readily known that in *Fallible Man*, he develops the notion of human fragility, but what has been less noticed in passages often missed or unstudied in Ricoeur's texts is the very significant stress placed upon the self's opening, unfolding and enfolding in a celebration of life and friendship.

That said, we are not proposing merely to present Ricoeur's precise account of friendship, or of vulnerability. Instead it is very significant to us that we intend to re-configure a "distinctively" Ricoeurian vulnerability for today. We are not merely presenting, or repeating, Ricoeur's view at one point in his life. What we are trying to convey is what Ricoeur himself did best in his engagements with other philosophers; that is, in a Ricoeurian spirit, we would encourage the ongoing critical reflective openness to the worlds which his writings and practices have opened for us.

Our proposed outcome for this panel discussion is to create a model, by way of *philia*, of friendship-love with ever-new beginnings. This love would be a good model not only for mutual affection in our ethical relationships, but for political transformation through affection.

In turn, this means an ethical life, well-lived, with an openness – vulnerability – exposed to wounding, unfolding and enfolding life's complexities.

This new model would generate the mutuality of a vulnerability which is open to reciprocity and need, at one and the same time. So, this vulnerability would not be reduced to the violation of either the other by the one, or the one by the other. Ultimately, our contention is that friendship-love would not be an oppositional conflict between self and other, if vulnerability plays its proper role. The task is to take seriously the "enormous vulnerability" that accompanies a clear Ricoeurian possibility.

As I reminisced while writing this paper about Pamela's friendship and our work together on Ricoeur, I have become deeply aware of Pamela's own commitment to live her own life as very much in keeping with the ideals that she cherished: epistemic justice, recognition, vulnerability, friendship, and love. I am deeply indebted to her for the innumerable ways that she has enriched my own life and work, as well as that of many, many others.

disclosure statement

No potential conflict of interest was reported by the author.

notes

1 Pamela Sue Anderson, "In Conversation with Sophia Blackwell," *The Oxford Muse*. See <https://www.oxfordmuse.com/?q=node/147> (accessed 22 Nov. 2019).

2 Pamela contributed an essay to a book in honour of Alan Montefiore on his eighty-fifth birthday. See Pamela Sue Anderson, "The Subject's Loss of Self-Confidence in its Own Ability to Understand Itself" in *Life and Philosophy: Essays to Honour Alan Montefiore on his 85th Birthday*, eds. Catherine Audard-Montefiore et al. (Oxford: FEP, 2011) n. pag.

3 Montefiore was also responsible for introducing Pamela to the work of French philosopher Michèle Le Doeuff, whose ideas would also have a strong impact on her work.

4 Ricoeur further declares: "Philosophy has attempted in various ways to colonize this outside entirely for its own benefit and to make it its own. Renouncing this *hubris* seems to me the first stage," and being "prepared to recognize its Other and to be instructed by it." Ricoeur in *The Philosophy of Paul Ricoeur*, ed. Lewis Edwin Hahn (Chicago: Open Court, 1995) 472.

5 Pamela Sue Anderson, *Ricoeur and Kant: Philosophy of the Will* (Atlanta: Scholars, 1993).

6 Pamela Sue Anderson and Jordan Bell, *Kant and Theology* (London: T&T Clark/Continuum, 2010).

7 Anderson, "In Conversation with Sophia Blackwell."

8 Ibid.

9 Pamela Sue Anderson, "The Case for a Feminist Philosophy of Religion: Transforming Philosophy's Imagery and Myths," *Journal of Philosophy of Religion: Ars Disputandi* 1 (2001): 1–17, available <https://doi.org/10.1080/15665399.2001.10819707> (accessed 22 Nov. 2019).

10 Anderson, "The Case for a Feminist Philosophy of Religion" 1.

11 Pamela did acknowledge that men could also encounter problems, but her main focus was the lives of women.

12 Anderson, "The Case for a Feminist Philosophy of Religion" 3.

13 This acknowledgement is an early reference to what today is named "intersectionality." See Kimberlé W. Crenshaw, "Mapping the Margins: Intersectionality, Identity Politics, and Violence against Women of Color," *Stanford Law Review* 43.6 (1991): 1241–99.

14 Anderson, "The Case for a Feminist Philosophy of Religion" 5.

15 See Morny Joy, "Encountering Otherness" in *Continental Philosophy and Philosophy of Religion* (Dordrecht: Springer, 2012) 221–46.

16 See especially Pamela Sue Anderson, "'Standpoint': Its Rightful Place in Realist Epistemology," *Journal of Philosophical Research* 26 (2002): 130–53; "Autonomy, Vulnerability and Gender," *Feminist Theory* 4.2 (2003): 149–64; *Re-visioning Gender in Philosophy of Religion: Reason, Love and Epistemic Locatedness* (London: Routledge, 2012).

17 Pamela met Sandra Harding in her first teaching position in the United States at the University of Delaware. See Sandra Harding, *The Feminist Standpoint Theory Reader* (New York: Routledge, 2004).

18 Michèle Le Doeuff, *The Philosophical Imaginary*, trans. Colin Gordon (London: Continuum, 2002).

19 Anderson, "The Case for a Feminist Philosophy of Religion" 5.

20 Ibid. 6.

21 See Pamela's evaluation of Ricoeur's work on Antigone in "Lost Confidence and Human Capability: A Hermeneutic Phenomenology of the Gendered, yet Capable Subject," *Text Matters* 4.4 (2014): 35–38.

22 bell hooks, *Yearning, Race, Gender and Cultural Politics* (Boston: South End, 1999) 12–13.

23 Pamela Sue Anderson, "Life, Death and (Inter)-Subjectivity: Realism and Recognition in Continental Feminism," *International Journal for Philosophy of Religion* 60.1–3 (2006): 43.

24 Ibid.

25 Ibid. 44.

26 See Judith Butler, "Longing for Recognition: Commentary on the Work of Jessica Benjamin," *Studies in Gender and Sexuality* 1.3 (2000): 271–90, doi:10.1080/15240650109349159. Anderson also acknowledges that her work on recognition owes a debt to Beauvoir's reading of Hegel and the influence it had on a certain stream of French feminism. See note 7. "Life, Death and (Inter)Subjectivity" 43.

27 Certain sections of this paper on Ricoeur's work have been previously published in *Symposium: Canadian Journal of Continental Philosophy* (Spring 2016). These sections are reprinted here with permission from the journal Editor.

28 Paul Ricoeur, *Oneself as Another*, trans. Kathleen Blamey (Chicago: U of Chicago P, 1992).

29 Paul Ricoeur in Charles Reagan, ed., *Paul Ricoeur: His Life and Work* (Chicago: U of Chicago P, 1996) 114. Although the interview occurred in 1986, Reagan's book of interviews was not published until 1996.

30 Ibid.

31 Paul Ricoeur in *The Philosophy of Paul Ricoeur*, ed. Lewis Edwin Hahn (Peru, IL: Open Court, 1995) 475.

32 Ibid. 473.

33 Paul Ricoeur, "Evil" in *The Encyclopedia of Religion*, vol. 5, editor-in-chief Mircea Eliade (New York: Macmillan, 1987) 199–208 (207).

34 Paul Ricoeur, *Fallible Man* [1960], trans. C.A. Kelbley (Chicago: Regnery, 1986) 146.

35 Paul Ricoeur, "Fragility and Responsibility" in *Paul Ricoeur: The Hermeneutics of Action*, ed. R. Kearney (London: Sage, 1996) 15–22 (16).

36 Ricoeur, *Oneself as Another* 172.

37 Ricoeur understood *homo capax* as the cornerstone of his philosophical anthropology. He describes four capabilities as indispensable to the constitution of human well-being, and introduces them with four verbs: "*I can speak, I can do things, I can tell a story*, and *I can be imputed*, as an action can be imputed to me as its true author." See Paul Ricoeur, "Ethics and Human Capability: A Response" in *Paul Ricoeur and Contemporary Moral Thought*, eds. John Wall, William Schweiker, and W. David Hall (New York and London: Routledge, 2002) 280.

38 Paul Ricoeur, "A Response by Paul Ricoeur" in *Paul Ricoeur and Narrative: Context and Contestation*, ed. Morny Joy (Calgary: U of Calgary P, 1997) xxiv.

39 Ricoeur in *The Philosophy of Paul Ricoeur* 367.

40 Ricoeur, "A Response by Paul Ricoeur" xi.

41 Paul Ricoeur, "The Human Being as the Subject Matter of Philosophy" in *The Narrative Path: The Later Work of Paul Ricoeur*, eds. T. Peter Kemp and David M. Rasmussen (Boston: MIT P, 1989) 89–101 (101).

42 Paul Ricoeur, "Autonomy and Vulnerability" in *Reflections on the Just*, trans. David Pellauer (Chicago: U of Chicago P, 2007) 85–86.

43 Paul Ricoeur, *The Course of Recognition*, trans. David Pellauer (Cambridge, MA: Harvard UP, 2007).

44 Judith Butler has defined these terms as follows: "'Precariousness' is a figure used to designate the fragility of life to call attention to the vulnerability that constitutes the human condition" (*Frames of War: When is Life Grievable?* (London: Verso, 2009) 79).

45 Pamela Sue Anderson, "Silencing and Speaker Vulnerability: Undoing an Oppressive Form of (Wilful) Ignorance," ed. Nick Bunnin, in *Love and Vulnerability: Thinking with Pamela Sue Anderson*, ed. Pelagia Goulimari, Spec. issue of *Angelaki: Journal of the Theoretical Humanities* 25.1–2 (2020): Abstract (online only). This was presented initially at a celebration of International Women's Day at Durham University, on 8 March 2016. The conference was entitled "Resounding Voices: Women, Silence and the Production of Knowledge."

46 "Autonomy, Vulnerability and Gender," *Feminist Theory* 4.2 (2003): 149–64.

47 Ibid. 149.

48 "Arguing for 'Ethical' Vulnerability: Towards a Politics of Care?" in *Exploring Vulnerability*, eds. Heike Springhart and Günter Thomas (Göttingen and Bristol, CT: Vandenhoeck, 2017) 147–62. This article was published posthumously.

49 Ibid. 162. This particular paper resulted from Pamela's participation in the "Vulnerability Group" of the Enhancing Life Project that was supported by a grant from the John Templeton Foundation.

50 Ibid.

51 Ibid.

52 Ibid. It is unfortunate that Pamela was not able to read certain of Judith Butler's later works where she qualifies some of her earlier views. In one of her recent books Butler observes:

> I wish to point out that even as public resistance leads to vulnerability, and vulnerability (the sense of "exposure" implied by precarity) leads to resistance, vulnerability is not exactly overcome by resistance, but becomes a potentially effective mobilizing force in political mobilizations.

While Butler's work is more involved with politics than Pamela's philosophical analyses, Butler's revision of vulnerability from possible conflict to a mode of activism could establish grounds for a certain compatibility or comparison with Pamela's creative reading of vulnerability. See Judith Butler, "Rethinking Vulnerability and Resistance" in

Vulnerability in Resistance, eds. Judith Butler, Zeynep Gambetti, and Leticia Sabsay (Durham, NC: Duke UP, 2016) 14.

53 "Arguing for 'Ethical' Vulnerability" 149.

54 Ibid. 147–48.

55 Again, Butler, this time with her two co-editors, poses a question that could lead beyond the impasse of inaction or negation that worries Pamela. They ask:

> What follows when we conceive of resistance as drawing from vulnerability as a resource of vulnerability, or as part of the very meaning or action of resistance itself? What implications does this perspective have for thinking about the subject of political agency? (Judith Butler, Zeynep Gambetti, and Letitia Sabsay in "Introduction" in *Vulnerability in Resistance* 1)

56 "Arguing for 'Ethical' Vulnerability" 148.

57 Ibid. 151.

58 Ibid. 149.

59 Ibid. 151.

60 Ibid.

61 Ibid. 152.

62 Carol Gilligan, *In a Different Voice* (Cambridge, MA: Harvard UP, 1982). Pamela also remarks that this book was crucial in identifying women's modes of care relationship in contrast to the rule of justice, and, in one sense, provided women with a form of recognition and agency.

63 "Arguing for 'Ethical' Vulnerability" 159.

64 Ibid. 153.

65 "Enhancement" is a term that Pamela encountered when she participated in the Enhancing Life Project. In a late interview she discusses her own understanding of the phrase. She says:

> I see enhancing life as a process. It is not static. Change is constantly happening. Enhancing life would be creative and give confidence; it's about striving. And striving is a kind of vulnerability because you're open and reaching for something that isn't there yet [...] My focus on vulnerability is on transformative experiences [...] when people have been able to discover not only their openness to possible harm or pain, but also an openness to change and growth. (See "Life-Giving Philosophy: A Q&A with Dr. Pamela Sue Anderson," 2 Feb. 2016, available <http://enhancinglife.uchicago.edu/blog/life-giving-philosophy-a-q-and-a-with-dr-pamela-sue-anderso> (accessed 22 Nov. 2019))

66 Pamela Sue Anderson, Review of Paul Ricoeur, *Oneself as Another* in *Journal of Literature and Theology* 8.3 (1994): 328–30.

67 Pamela Sue Anderson, "Ricoeur in Dialogue with Feminist Philosophy of Religion: Hermeneutic Hospitality in Contemporary Practice" in *Feminist Explorations of Paul Ricoeur's Philosophy*, eds. Annemie Halsema and Frenanda Henriques (Lanham, MD: Lexington, 2016) 199–220.

68 Ricoeur, *Oneself as Another* 172.

enhancing life

At the time of her death in March 2017, Pamela Sue Anderson was working on research funded by the Templeton Foundation under the overall title Enhancing Life.[1] In introductory remarks to their proposal, William Schweiker and Günter Thomas describe this project as a response to the challenge of making life better. One of their contentions is that "religious" and "spiritual" traditions should not be dismissed for being too caught up with the world beyond to be useful in a project about the enhancement of life in the here and now. Instead, they suggest that the "conceptions of a counter-world (broadly understood)," fostered by these traditions, can be of great value. They wonder how people can "open up" these "spiritual" resources and impact on people's lives – how they can become "spiritually guided stewards for the enhancement of life."[2]

What I am interested in exploring here are the ways in which Anderson sought to fulfil this remit. She did not see herself as a theologian – though she had a good awareness of theology and engaged with theologians[3] – and was generally reserved about issues of personal faith or about identifying herself with any particular "faith community" or Church, calling herself a free thinker.[4] It is hard to imagine her, for example, beginning to write from the perspective of as theologically resonant a term as "counter-worlds," yet she was increasingly occupied with the notion of bringing about a "spiritual turn" in philosophy of religion.[5] This is not to suggest that the Enhancing Life Project was not concerned with the kind of philosophical and ethical enquiry with which

alison jasper

MORTAL VULNERABILITIES
reflecting on death and dying with pamela sue anderson

Anderson was identified. It is more to ask about what Anderson meant by "enhancing life" and how she might have seen herself as "a spiritually guided steward" for this. A consideration of some of the embedded themes with which she was concerned during her career will, I believe, bear out the suggestion that Anderson's approach very much fits this bill. But it is perhaps the idea of vulnerability, most of all, that crystallizes for me the distinctiveness of her approach and addresses the aims of the Enhancing Life Project, but also brings *this* feminist philosophy of religion – as well as her person – most powerfully to mind. In particular I am interested in the way in which, through this focus – and as a philosopher often concerned with a "thoughtful love of life" – she also allows us to attend seriously to death (including her own), invoking the positive and enhancing implications of our unavoidable vulnerability for practices of rational affection, without losing sight of our vulnerability to the violence of loss and mourning.

gendering the philosophy of religion

One way to sum up Anderson's work over the years, using her own words, is to say she was involved in a project of "gendering" the philosophy of religion.[6] It will be easily agreed that she saw herself very much as a philosopher in the analytic tradition, albeit one who sought to bridge the gap in the light of perceived differences between this and the Continental approach. This emphasizes the significance of clear and rigorous thinking about the terms and measure of any concept or argument without, at its best, reducing it to a mere "game of logic."[7] She did not see this as an approach that was opposed to feminist reasoning where the aim was, according to bell hooks's definition, "to end sexism, sexist exploitation and oppression."[8] If it could be used to identify and oppose the unexamined premises or the faulty assumptions and logic of any argument leading to oppressive thought or actions then it was good to use. She was also rooted, from her doctoral studies onwards, through her reading of Kant as it impacted on significant notions such as morality, freedom knowledge, understanding and, of course, reason and rationality.[9] She took what she called an "Enlightenment view,"[10] because she believed that the exercise of reason was a powerful practice for calling out sexism, sexist exploitation and oppression, recognizing, none the less, that reason itself was bounded by contingencies, not least the contingencies of human embodiment and gender. She continued to read and adapt Kant but without being blind to his shortcomings,[11] including dismissive remarks about women and sweeping gendered generalizations.[12] However, she defended him because his work provided "tools for radically questioning and carefully judging the foundations of thought itself – even the gendered nature of that thought."[13]

As a philosopher of *religion*, she admitted she struggled to find her place in respect of Christian philosophy in Oxford during her time there in the 1980s when she was a doctoral student, and to accept the philosophical expectations – perhaps "red lines" would express the idea – of some Christian philosophers.[14] She continued to oppose this emphasis, wanting to move away from "theoretical debates about traditional theism" to a "distinctive philosophical practice [...] to do with the self's relations."[15] But in 2011 she was "constantly uncovering problematic norms such as the omni-attributes of the traditional theistic God which still dominate[d] the field."[16] Thus from early on in her career she also embraced the different philosophical trajectories of, for example, Continental thought through Hegel and Marx to the Frankfurt School, drawing attention to material and social issues underpinning understandings of justice as well as of God and reality.[17] In particular, Paul Ricoeur's phenomenological approach to hermeneutics gave her scope to engage with texts in which a variety of people spoke in different ways about "freedom, justice, evil, goodness, God, love [...] personal identity,"[18] and hope.[19] In his work, Anderson found resources for her own thinking that addressed the limitations of philosophy of religion as she had first encountered it. Whilst the traditions of a certain kind of analytical philosophy – especially in the period of Anderson's doctoral work – were out of sympathy with Ricoeur's interests in theology and literature[20] and insisted on the familiar patterns of philosophical argumentation within Christian theism,[21] Anderson clearly found the work of this philosopher profoundly nurturing – perhaps "life-enhancing" would not be an inappropriate description. In the first instance, for the young scholar, the attraction was perhaps driven by a love of French literature and a wish (in Oxford) to have ideas of her own![22] However, Ricoeur's work undoubtedly remained important to her because of its characteristic invitation to bring philosophy into contact with a much wider range of human experience. And, from fairly early on, this included the liberating experience of reading about feminism and gender that she was able to integrate into her work, for example in adapting his practices of mimetic reading and suspicious hermeneutics to a feminist hermeneutics of Christian mythology.[23]

Her first encounters with feminist philosophy occurred when she took up a post at the University of Delaware and thus came into contact with the work of Nancy Hartsock on "standpoint theory" and Sandra Harding's notions of "strong objectivity."[24] With their attention to the social, material conditions of thought, she was finally able to begin articulating "the serious and generally hidden obstacle to recognizing oppressive gender-bias"[25] and to address her "primal scene" in which "a voice inside my head paralyzed my well-warranted confidence, saying 'Lutheran girls don't have ideas of their own, they are respectful of (male) authority!'"[26] Through her encounter with feminist philosophy she arrived at a point where she could begin to voice her own ideas about what might constitute a philosophy of religion that took into account and challenged the efforts of philosophers over centuries to deny her, alongside most other women, space to read and engage with these "forbidden texts."[27]

Of course, as with Kant, Anderson's undoubtedly very fruitful relationship with Ricoeur in respect of his philosophy of religion was not all plain sailing. She has admitted that she found it odd, to say the least, that in the course of a very long academic career of addressing all kinds of philosophical challenges, Ricoeur never engaged with feminism. Although it was not difficult to adapt his ideas and thoughts to what she wanted to say, she had to complete the work of reconciling his work, in this way, herself.[28] Even from a feminist perspective, her distinctive project of gendering philosophy of religion was not a straightforward task. The context of modern feminism in the West – from the late nineteenth century onwards – has evinced in many ways a strong sense of ambivalence about the discourse of "religion" – presumably because it has generally been identified with Western forms of Christianity and dismissed as merely a way to sacralize Western patriarchal and colonial structures.[29] And it is notable that there is little explicit sense of either positive or negative engagement with this discourse of religion within the group of feminist and gender theorists and philosophers whom Anderson most admired, such as Sandra Harding, Seyla Benhabib, Michèle Le Doeuff, bell hooks or Judith Butler. It is true that Butler has been willing to enter the discussion in respect of her own Jewish heritage,[30] but it would be eccentric to refer to her as a feminist theologian or even a scholar of "religion." In relation to feminist theology too, Anderson has found herself to some degree at odds with a strong tendency in the field, linked with the psycholinguistic approaches of the so-called "French feminists" and Luce Irigaray in particular. Her responses, though well informed and thoughtful, perhaps reflect the ambivalence of a – still significantly – analytical philosopher. However, she has continued to identify herself as a feminist philosopher of religion, setting out what this means, more systematically, in two volumes in particular: *A Feminist Philosophy of Religion*[31] in 1998 and *Re-visioning Gender in Philosophy of Religion: Reason, Love and Epistemic Locatedness* in 2012.[32] And in the last ten years and more of her life, there was a definite strengthening of themes in her work that focused on a "spiritual turn" to the philosophy of religion by which she implied that philosophy and philosophers should be involved in a practice that was transformative, a fully embodied form of reflection.[33] In the last years of her life, and especially in work on the Templeton-funded project, the idea of vulnerability comes ever more into focus, expanding and illuminating the broad characteristics of her feminist philosophy of religion in terms of this direction towards philosophy of religion as centrally concerned with a transformative practice towards the enhancement of life.

vulnerability as a pathway to "enhancing life"

However, Anderson's focus on the issue of vulnerability within the Enhancing Life Project did not come out of nowhere. She had already given the matter her attention in some earlier contexts. Once again drawing on her reading of Ricoeur, she had discussed this in an article about understanding autonomy as a gendered concept.[34] This was an attempt to address a problematic, historical denial of women's autonomy, resting on their association with vulnerability as a gendered quality.[35] But this argument was also a challenge to any idea that a fully transparent knowledge of ourselves as rational agents was possible without due attention to our vulnerability – to the relationships on which we depend.[36] Her conclusion was that autonomy as a good did not have to do simply with a capacity to narrate our own personal stories but to narrate stories in which we find ourselves already located.[37] In other words, Anderson had, very much in parallel with Ricoeur,[38] already begun to associate vulnerability with how we see ourselves in relation to others to whom we are necessarily bound by practices of attention and affection. By the time it became the theme of her last public lecture on silencing and speaker vulnerability in 2016 (and 2017),[39] Anderson was perfectly clear that vulnerability was not merely a negative circumstance to be avoided at all costs or associated with the paternalistic categorization of certain groups of people but that it identified a necessary human capacity, transcending gender binaries, and that "[l]ike *la mauvaise foi* of the French existentialists, *in*vulnerability is a form of self-deception."[40] This is not to deny that "vulnerability" could be cause for profound concern. In this paper Anderson begins with the very evident struggle faced by women philosophers as they attempt to give expression to new knowledge or to "the unknown."[41] She illustrates the issues involved in this process through the subtle but nevertheless debilitating violence directed towards both herself and the African-American philosopher bell hooks, as speakers in Western academic contexts. She describes the way in which women's ability to be accepted as qualified knowers is attacked and undermined. Unlike definitions of violence against women in terms of "patriarchal terrorism" or "coercive control,"[42] where violence is linked to the desire for power over women and girls, Anderson connects both the "wilful ignorance"[43] of those who will not listen and the "unthought" or unrecognized threat to listeners to her discussion of vulnerability. In different incidents, both Anderson and hooks are misrecognized and dismissed as incapable of thinking or writing philosophically. Anderson draws here on Kristie Dotson's notions of "quieting" and "smothering"[44] to expand our understanding of what is at stake. "Quieting" is illustrated in relation to a first response, by (white) examiners, to hooks's doctoral work. As speaker, in this context, hooks does not fulfil the expectations of her listeners who will not listen to her reasoned argument that she would not teach James Joyce because of his status within a curriculum that fails to reflect the diversity of her community. Their assumptions about the normative nature of philosophy and the literary canon are "quieting." Though Anderson suggested she might equally well have responded to a Ph.D. student in this context similarly, in view of the fact that hooks had not actually answered the examiners' question about how she would teach James Joyce, she accepts that this response itself is a kind of refusal to address the unequal and thus "quieting" nature of the relations between examination committee and student.[45] Anderson's own experience concerns the attempt to deliver an academic lecture to an audience of philosophers and students in Durham, England in 2000. In this example, pre-lecture publicity was hijacked and doctored by some members of the audience to draw attention to the coincidence that she shared her name with a popular American/Canadian glamour model of that era. Subsequently she was subjected to questioning by a male member of the audience who judged her paper unfavourably because, in his view, it disappointed expectations of what a "feminist" philosophy paper would be like. In various ways, then, the audience quieted or remained closed to what she had to say as a philosopher.[46] Anderson reflects on whether this could also have been an example of "smothering" in which pre-recognition of an audience's likely inability to hear something causes a speaker to silence her or himself –

not to say what they think or believe. It is a loss of confidence that one will be heard or, worse, that one has anything worth saying. The debilitating effect in this case was that Anderson herself was uncertain to what extent her vulnerability to these effects – quieting and smothering – had impacted on what she had sought to share with her listeners.

However, what is equally important to Anderson's argument, moving in a more positive direction, though it might not seem so at first, is that quieting is the consequence of an active disavowal – a "wilful" ignorance – of the hearer's own "unthought" vulnerability to both violence *and affection*. The point is that both speakers and listeners have the capacity to recognize their mutual vulnerability to each other, and their need, if gaining knowledge in terms of ethically justifiable relations is genuinely their aim, to be wilfully, thoughtfully open to and/or affected by "the unknown." This additional qualification of vulnerability *to affection*, which challenges both the quieting audiences and smothered or despairing speakers of her examples, is both unexpected – when our thoughts are fully focused on avoiding unwarranted violence – and absolutely crucial to Anderson's argument. In an article originally written for the alumni magazine of Regent's Park College, Oxford, where Anderson taught for many years,[47] Lara Coleman refers to Anderson's suggestion that "the embrace of vulnerability might provide a means, not only of countering sexism and epistemic violence in academia, but also of 'enhancing life' in general."[48] Coleman agrees with Anderson that to ignore the capacity to be affected or wounded by each other and to pretend to a kind of invulnerability is a "systematic process of self-deception."[49] Anderson herself was uncertain whether she could actually compel philosophers to recognize or address their vulnerability in philosophical relations,[50] but Coleman acknowledges how pertinent the critique remains of academic contexts in which speakers continue to be expected to perform invulnerability "in tried and tested fashion." Coleman gives a further example of her own vulnerability in this sense. Having performed the role of speaker invulnerability, by besting a male member of the audience, Coleman is then subjected to his unwanted sexual advances outwith the lecture room.[51] For Anderson, as for Coleman, the problem here is not only that a woman is not being seen as a capable philosopher but that her desire to engage meaningfully at the highest level of scholarship is reduced to an entirely unphilosophical contest in which the aim, on both sides, has to be to humiliate or defeat an opponent.

And so, in response, Anderson wants to say that the problem of wilful ignorance can and should be addressed in terms of an "ethical vulnerability"[52] whose ultimate goal is not to label people as vulnerable but to enable them to be open "to self and other affection."[53] We can see here how Anderson's work speaks clearly to the remit of the Enhancing Life Project and its aim to make life better more broadly, through her appeal to more collective approaches. Drawing on Michèle Le Doeuff's term "a collectivity,"[54] Anderson describes something that is not a clique or coterie of like-minded people but rather a group seeking knowledge extending beyond what it knows (or imagines it knows) already.[55] As Le Doeuff had stated earlier, her work was "a tributary to a collective discourse" composed of "many scholars and thinkers who have done more towards producing me than I shall contribute in continuing to produce them."[56] Le Doeuff discusses the emergence, in these terms, of "a new rationality"[57] in which the relationship to the unknown and to the unthought is at every moment reintroduced. In the light of these insights, Lara Coleman suggests an alternative "life-enhancing" role for the work of the university – of higher education – as a whole. Rather than continuing to turn a blind eye to the kinds of oppressive behaviours illustrated in the various examples cited in Anderson's lecture and Coleman's response, it might instead acknowledge its responsibilities towards the wide academic collectivity. It could then commit itself to a role that would:

> involve a collective commitment to what anthropologist David Berliner calls "getting rid of your academic fake self", including

that we "substitute a politics of competition for an ethics of care" because, as Berliner puts it, "science is about collaborative knowledge and not a massacre."[58]

forever mortal – vulnerability to finitude

In her final lecture on silencing and speaker vulnerability, Anderson thus gives due attention to the ways in which women and men are still routinely subject to devastating forms of suffering through our human vulnerability to violence before going on to describe how, within the context of our necessary relationality, we could access this as a means to enhance lives. Giving greater resonance to this discussion, she cites an essay by Judith Butler.[59] In "Violence, Mourning, Politics,"[60] Butler evokes intransigent obstacles to the enhancement of (all) lives (equally) that, like Anderson's examples, are based on a failure to recognize how irreducibly interrelated our lives are, and that from the very beginning we are "given over to the other."[61] In Butler's words:

> each of us is constituted politically in part by virtue of the social vulnerability of our bodies – as a site of desire and physical vulnerability [...] Loss and vulnerability seem to follow from our being socially constituted bodies, attached to others, at risk of losing those attachments, exposed to others, at risk of violence by virtue of that exposure.[62]

Just becoming aware of our vulnerability does not lead to an open or affectionate response, of course.[63] Rather than enabling us to understand that we have a mutual capacity to wound and/or support each other, as both Anderson and Butler agree, what tends to happen in the life of nations is that "responses to bodily vulnerability erupt into [...] militaristic politics. Retribution all too naturally follows violent exposure to one's own vulnerability."[64] Butler was writing in the aftermath of the attacks of 9/11 on New York and Washington and in some ways as a response to them. What is exposed in Western responses to these attacks, echoing Nancy Tuana's term once again, is a wilful ignorance of our vulnerability (to violence and affection). The refusal to acknowledge its wounding leads to further violent wounding.[65] As Anderson notes, it is, similarly, often the fear of bodily vulnerability that results, in the US context, in the violence of gun crime when people who arm themselves in order to give themselves protection inadvertently increase the likelihood of harm. Rather than allowing our own affective response to the violence to make us consider how others may be suffering, we try to "will away this vulnerability"[66] and choose to remain ignorant.

But Butler is also concerned in the cited essay with questions of grief and mourning occasioned by death as another form of violence to which we are all unwillingly and sometimes wilfully unknowingly, vulnerable. Butler says we cannot "argue against" the "dimensions of human vulnerability"[67] that are our exposure to this. In the context of her lecture on silencing and speaker vulnerability, Butler's reflections on death were not Anderson's primary focus. But, particularly in respect of the 2017 version of the lecture, it prompts the reader to imagine the interplay between Anderson's own experience of vulnerability to the unarguable violence of sickness and the threat of death, and her obligations, as a philosopher committed to a "thoughtful love of life," towards the Templeton-funded project on Enhancing Life. There may well be intended significance to Anderson's reference, evoking the precariousness of life and a form of violent loss and grief which cannot be explained as the consequence of ethically unjustified but willed human behaviour. But of course what may also have been intended is the reference to Butler's response, in which the work of mourning – the acceptance of our vulnerability (to affection in Anderson's terms) – is still expressed in terms of an ethical imperative that allows for a response attuned to human relations, or in other words makes "a distinctively ethical avowal."[68] Even in the case of the death not caused by wilful ignorance or malice "one accepts that by the loss one undergoes one will be changed, possibly for ever [...] a transformation (perhaps one should say *submitting* to a transformation) the full result of which one cannot know in advance."[69] This work of mourning as submitting to (accepting one's vulnerability to) transformation is the acknowledgement that being affected, and having to mourn or grieve, is in the nature of human being, whereby we are always vulnerable to relations with others. It occasions Butler's exhortation to face the fact that "[w]e're undone by each other. And if we're not, we're missing something."[70] From this understanding of the ways in which we are both dependent on the care of others – vulnerable to possible violence – and also vulnerable to the violence that come with the loss of our necessary attachments, Butler develops a general conception of the human in ethical terms through the question "What *makes for a grievable life?*"[71] Butler's implication, of course, is that some lives are seen as being less grievable than others because, to return to Anderson's use of Nancy Tuana's expression, we – continually – remain wilfully ignorant of the ways in which our lives are interdependent.

vulnerability to finitude: towards enhancement of life in the philosophy of "religion"?

Anderson's paper on silencing and speaker vulnerability was focused primarily on the exposure of women to the violence of quieting and smothering in an academic context, beset by what is unthought by wilful ignorance and with an eye to enhancing life through a greater acknowledgement that invulnerability is a toxic myth. However, the question of our vulnerability to death and finitude does seem to have been raised at least obliquely in this lecture by a philosopher committed to the "thoughtful love of life" who was mortally sick at the time. She thus raises questions not only about the scandal of women routinely facing "quieting" and "smothering" but also about what makes life bearable when we are constrained by the loss of those we love and the thought that we have such a short time to live ourselves. Whilst Butler is clearly cited here because of her contribution to feminist and queer scholarship and activism, I believe Anderson also uses her work to reference vulnerability in relation to the violence of death and finitude in this lecture because it is something else to which she had necessarily been giving thought. This last lecture demonstrates in full measure the energy and commitment of what one could call Anderson's philosophical activism – her robust interrogation, on the basis of her prescribing a value for life, of all forms of sexism and sexist oppression. It is also an expression of her philosophical reflectiveness that proposes rational grounds for hopefulness in this mortal predicament that also invokes our vulnerability to the affection that follows from our interrelatedness and interdependence. Let us turn then, finally, to one further way in which Anderson's work gives us ways in which to think about our vulnerability to the condition of grievable and grieving mortals in the light of the realization both that "[a]ny continuous relation to the other can be destroyed by death" but also that "the thread of life continues however fragile in being remembered."[72]

Anderson's understanding of her job as a feminist philosopher of religion strongly favours Ricoeurian phenomenological hermeneutics[73] or critical reflection on lived experience. She acknowledges the power of an identified hermeneutics of suspicion[74] that has paved the way for the sort of restorative feminist process[75] that she links with Adrienne Rich's term re-visioning. However, as she argues about Ricoeur, her interest is also indicative of a "deep and passionate commitment to human life and to living it together" that goes beyond winning the argument.[76] It could be said that our mortality is a primary example of an argument that cannot be won. This is not to suggest that Anderson was interested in any strictly theological issue such as theodicy. She does not try in an apologetic sense to "defend the ways of God to man (sic)."[77] Like Ricoeur, she maintains her independence as a philosopher and within her work "the question of God, as a philosophical question, itself remains in a suspension."[78] In common with some feminist theologians, she is also suspicious of the whole metaphor of divinity and of the apotheosis of invulnerability that remains so characteristic of our current social system focused on making nations "great again" or "taking back control." It is clear that, for Anderson, metaphors of might and invincibility are part of the problem, reflecting the kind of posture she identifies in her lecture on silencing and speaker vulnerability as self-deception, false consciousness and the wilful ignorance of the unthought. Rather than reflecting confidence in transcendence and meaning, they simply reflect an all-too-human failure to recognize our mutual human vulnerability either to violence or to affection. And, of course, this approach is entirely consistent with the philosophical work she has done over many years in subjecting the gendered myths and metaphors of our past to critical feminist analysis mobilizing such feminist philosophical tools as miming (Irigaray) or re-visioning (Rich).

However, clues to her interest in and understanding of rational (in the sense of "substantive reason" or "embodied thinking which remains attached to the substance of desire and bodily life"[79]) hope, love and affection, based on the acknowledgement of mutual vulnerability and capacity to be undone by loss and grief that are very much on display in her last lecture, can also be found in various other earlier works, including her most recent monograph, *Re-visioning Gender in Philosophy of Religion: Reason, Love and Epistemic Locatedness*[80] and also in connection with continuing references to the work of Ricoeur. Her deep seriousness on the subject of death and dying goes back a number of years, for example to a review[81] of a book[82] written by Hanneke Canters and completed for publication in 2005 by Grace Jantzen. Anderson writes a careful and caring appreciation of this book – both of whose authors had died before the review was published in 2007 – in which, as she reads it, a woman philosopher (Hanneke) tries to find and give voice to an authentically sexuate identity. Her reading is, predictably, generous, and sensitive to what she understands as its feminist aim to construct a new kind of philosophy, one which refers to both human passions and the elemental flow of our cosmic existence, rating the fluid process of becoming natals more significant than a traditional preoccupation with (im)mortality. But it is clear, too, that aside from some characteristic ambivalence about Irigaray's psycholinguistic approach in general, she also had reservations about what the book proposes as a solution to the problem of sexist or misogynistic structures in "religion," which, as she reads it, dismisses the question of death as simply the violent, death-obsessed stories of masculinity (including divinity) in the Christian West. It seems that the emphasis on life and natality – characteristic not only of work by Irigaray, Jantzen and Canters but a subject on which Anderson herself writes[83] – leaves her unsatisfied in this context, where the emphasis on life is so strongly marked and yet neither author – friends and colleagues for whom she grieved – was any longer alive. She recognizes the struggle for love and the book's call to resist a hostile and barren necrophilia. But there is also the hint of a critical probing as well as unavoidable poignancy to her question, "but are we not allowed to struggle with death?"[84]

Moving forward in time but remaining with the subject of Anderson's continuing and profound reflections on being open or vulnerable to the undoing of grieving and death, Ricoeur's writing on memory and traces of affection, the subject she addressed in 2014, in Dublin, on the centenary of his birth, marks a significant high point in this theme. At that date, before her own diagnosis of cancer, she had not fully embarked on the Templeton-funded project relating to enhancing life. Yet in this article it is clear that she is thinking about how reflecting on our experiences of loss and mortality had life-enhancing potential. In the published version of her Dublin lecture[85] she drew on Ricoeur's mature understanding of memory as it speaks to our ability to have confidence "in the human capacity to express 'the joy of yes in the sadness of the finite'"[86] instead of "merely accepting life's inevitable march towards death."[87] She explores how Ricoeur's work on memory, through sometimes conflicting readings of Bergson, Deleuze and Proust, comes to express a predominantly Bergsonian understanding of the intuitive power of memory to grasp images of the past, as opposed to

Proust's notion of memory as involuntary; the lost time to which the title of his great work refers, regained only through the identity of the work of art. Anderson shows that, for Ricoeur, the path from the intuitive power to grasp images of the past, in order to achieve the kind of recognition that delivers confidence in this capability, is laid out in the traces of affection with which it is imbued, driving and sustaining the work of making meaning. It is with this Bergsonian-inflected understanding of our intuitive capacity to grasp the past marked by (vulnerability to) affection, our capacity to feel, love, change, that she argues Ricoeur ends his own life:

> [...] celebrating friendship and other close relations. The love of friendship (*philia*) involves mutual trust, enabling confidence in the power to love, to forgive and remember.[88]

Here, in this close-worked piece on Ricoeur's account of memory as an intuitive human capacity, Anderson finds something durable and hopeful to share with her audience and readers for resisting the negative phantoms of human evil or the shadows of the past that is time lost, and for finding meaning "despite loss, suffering and death."[89] In this sense, then, we return to the ambitions of the Enhancing Life Project with which this paper began in order to show that Anderson's work can indeed be described as "spiritual" in the terms she had laid out;[90] not doctrinally Christian and avoiding mystifications of any kind, but profoundly concerned with what makes any particular life meaningful, given the vulnerability to violence and affection of our interrelated and interdependent lives. It embodies the distinctive philosophical/spiritual practice, in other words, of the ongoing narration of our action, relations and life with others in which we are to be accountable.[91]

conclusion

Anderson's philosophical journey started, perhaps, with the primal scene of her undergraduate experience when she first tried to do philosophy as a woman, and could be summed up – drawing on her final lecture on silencing and speaker vulnerability – as a coming to terms with and finding ways to articulate her vulnerability as a human being to violence *and affection* as a basis for transformative thinking in contexts of finitude where we face the painfulness of change: "[E]ven female subjects will have to confront death, the dying and the dead."[92] This is to say that in the course of her academic career, Anderson seems to have developed an increasing sense that, in spite of real and ever-present violence, including the wearisome nature of sexist oppression and the loss of (all) grievable lives, our "vulnerability" is in fact our ethical and rational as much as our embodied capacity to be open to relations of affection, the memory of which sustains us in the face of our own mortality and the loss of those we love. This is mediated through the kind of reason she called "substantive," i.e., attention to rationality and critique that is not detached from desire and bodily life including the sense in which we are dispossessed and undone by each other. Death is not something we can overcome or to which we are invulnerable or can become immune but, along with the protest against exploiting vulnerability, Anderson, as a philosophically and "spiritually guided steward," rests her hopes for enhancing ever-changing lives on our capacity to be affected, to remember this affection and to be remembered with affection. As, of course, she is!

disclosure statement

No potential conflict of interest was reported by the author.

notes

1 See <http://enhancinglife.uchicago.edu/> (accessed 23 Nov. 2019).

2 William Schweiker and Günter Thomas, "The Enhancing Life Project: Templeton Foundation Proposal." Topical bibliography with introductory comments, available <http://enhancinglife.uchicago.edu/sites/545eb5a85918adb390000bac/pages/5460849d2c1cc4b90a008400/files/Bibliography_Initial.pdf?1481481241> (accessed 23 Nov. 2019).

3 See Anderson's discussion within the interdisciplinary space of philosophy of religion and feminist theology in "A Story of Love and Death: Exploring Spaces for the Philosophical Imaginary" in *New Interdisciplinary Spaces*, ed. Heather Walton (London and New York: Routledge, 2011) 167–86.

4 Pamela Sue Anderson, "Engaging the 'Forbidden Texts' of Philosophy: Pamela Sue Anderson Talks to Alison Jasper," *Text Matters* 1 (2011): 312–28 (315).

5 Pamela Sue Anderson, "'A Thoughtful Love of Life': A Spiritual Turn in Philosophy of Religion," *Svensk Teologisk Kvartalskrift* 85 (2009): 119–29. In this context it is worth noting that from 2007 to 2014 she was engaged in a project with the theologian Paul Fiddes at Regent's Park College under the name "Critical Theory and Spiritual Practice" – a title that she herself formulated.

6 Anderson, "Engaging the 'Forbidden Texts' of Philosophy" 325.

7 Ibid. 323.

8 bell hooks, *Feminism is for Everybody: Passionate Politics* (London: Pluto, 2000) 1.

9 See, for example, Pamela Sue Anderson, "Canonicity and Critique: A Feminist Defence of a Post-Kantian Critique," *Literature and Theology* 13.3 (1999): 201–10.

10 Anderson, "Engaging the 'Forbidden Texts' of Philosophy" 319.

11 See ibid. 321; "Canonicity and Critique" 204.

12 Anderson notes this tendency in respect of Kant's gendering of the key eighteenth-century concepts of the beautiful and the sublime in ibid.

13 Ibid. 205.

14 Anderson, "Engaging the 'Forbidden Texts' of Philosophy" 323.

15 Anderson, "'A Thoughtful Love of Life'" 123.

16 Anderson, "Engaging the 'Forbidden Texts' of Philosophy" 315.

17 Ibid. 322.

18 See Pamela Sue Anderson, "In Conversation with Sophia Blackwell," *The Oxford Muse*, available <https://www.oxfordmuse.com/?q=node/147> (accessed 23 Nov. 2019).

19 See also Paul Ricoeur, "Freedom in the Light of Hope" in *Essays on Biblical Interpretation*, by Paul Ricoeur, ed. Lewis Mudge (London: SPCK, 1981) 155–82.

20 Anderson, "Engaging the 'Forbidden Texts' of Philosophy" 314.

21 Ibid.

22 Ibid.

23 See Pamela Sue Anderson, "Myth, Mimesis and Multiple Identities: Feminist Tools for Transforming Theology," *Literature and Theology* 10.2 (1996): 112–30.

24 See, for example, Nancy C.M. Hartsock, *The Feminist Standpoint Revisited & Other Essays* (Boulder: Westview, 1998); Sandra Harding, *Whose Science? Whose Knowledge? Thinking from Women's Lives* (Ithaca, NY: Cornell UP; Buckingham: Open UP, 1991).

25 Anderson, "Engaging the 'Forbidden Texts' of Philosophy" 312.

26 Ibid. 315.

27 Ibid. 316.

28 Pamela Sue Anderson, "Paul Ricoeur in Dialogue with Theology and Religious Studies: Hermeneutic Hospitality in Contemporary Practice," Spec. issue of *Svensk Teologisk Kvartalskrift* 91.1–2 (2015): 202.

29 For a summary of some approaches, see Alison Jasper, *Because of Beauvoir: Christianity and the Cultivation of Female Genius* (Waco, TX: Baylor UP, 2012) 20–26.

30 See, for example, Judith Butler, "Is Judaism Zionism?" in *The Power of Religion in the Public Sphere*, eds. Eduardo Mendieta and Jonathan Vanantwerpen (New York: Columbia UP, 2011) 70–91.

31 Pamela Sue Anderson, *A Feminist Philosophy of Religion: The Rationality and Myths of Religious Belief* (Oxford: Blackwell, 1998).

32 Pamela Sue Anderson, *Re-visioning Gender in Philosophy of Religion: Reason, Love and Epistemic Locatedness* (Farnham: Ashgate, 2012).

33 Anderson, "'A Thoughtful Love of Life'" 123.

34 See Pamela Sue Anderson, "Autonomy, Vulnerability and Gender," *Feminist Theory* 4.2 (2003): 149–64.

35 Ibid. 153.

36 Ibid.

37 Ibid. 149.

38 See Paul Ricoeur, "Autonomy and Vulnerability" in Ricoeur, *Reflections on the Just*, trans. David Pellauer (Chicago: U of Chicago P, 2007) 72–90.

39 Pamela Sue Anderson, "Silencing and Speaker Vulnerability: Undoing an Oppressive Form of (Wilful) Ignorance," ed. Nick Bunnin, in *Love and Vulnerability: Thinking with Pamela Sue Anderson*, ed. Pelagia Goulimari, Spec. issue of *Angelaki: Journal of the Theoretical Humanities* 25.1–2 (2020): 36–45. This version of the paper was read for Pamela Sue Anderson at the British Academy conference on "Vulnerability and the Politics of Care: Cross-Disciplinary Dialogues," 9–10 February 2017. By this time she was too ill to deliver the paper in person. An earlier version was given as the keynote speech at the "International Women's Day Conference," Durham University, 8 March 2016.

40 Anderson, "Silencing and Speaker Vulnerability" Abstract (online only); emphasis added.

41 In her paper, Anderson takes the term "the unknown" from the work of Michèle Le Doeuff, *The Philosophical Imaginary*, trans. Colin Gordon (London: Athlone, 1989).

42 See, for example, Michael P. Johnson, "Patriarchal Terrorism and Common Couple Violence: Two Forms of Violence against Women," *Journal of Marriage and Family* 57.2 (1995): 283–94; Evan Stark, *Coercive Control: How Men Entrap Women in Personal Life* (Oxford: Oxford UP, 2007).

43 Anderson took this term from the work of Nancy Tuana. See "The Speculum of Ignorance: The Women's Health Movement and Epistemology of Ignorance" in *Feminist Epistemologies of Ignorance*, Spec. issue of *Hypatia: A Journal of Feminist Philosophy* 21.3 (2007): 1–19.

44 See Kristie Dotson, "Tracking Epistemic Violence, Tracking Practices of Silencing," *Hypatia: A Journal of Feminist Philosophy* 26.2 (2011): 236–57.

45 Anderson, "Silencing and Speaker Vulnerability" 38–39.

46 Anderson, "Silencing and Speaker Vulnerability."

47 Lara Coleman, "Speaker Vulnerability and the Patriarchal University: A Response and Tribute to Pamela Sue Anderson," available <https://thedisorderofthings.com/2017/11/02/speaker-vulnerability-and-the-patriarchal-university-a-response-and-tribute-to-pamela-sue-anderson/> (accessed 23 Nov. 2019).

48 Pamela Sue Anderson, "Enhancing Life: Vulnerability and a Liveable Life," *Regent's Now* (Alumni Magazine) (2016): 36–37.

49 Anderson, "Silencing and Speaker Vulnerability" 39.

50 Anderson, "Silencing and Speaker Vulnerability."

51 Coleman, "Speaker Vulnerability and the Patriarchal University."

52 Anderson, "Silencing and Speaker Vulnerability" 42–43.

53 Ibid. 42.

54 Le Doeuff, *The Philosophical Imaginary* 128.

55 Pamela Sue Anderson, "Silencing and Speaker Vulnerability" 37.

56 Le Doeuff, *The Philosophical Imaginary* 127.

57 Ibid. 128.

58 Coleman, "Speaker Vulnerability and the Patriarchal University."

59 Anderson, "Silencing and Speaker Vulnerability" 39.

60 Judith Butler, "Violence, Mourning, Politics" in *Precarious Life: The Powers of Mourning and Violence*, by Judith Butler (London and New York: Verso, 2004) 19–49.

61 Ibid. 31.

62 Ibid. 21.

63 Anderson, "Silencing and Speaker Vulnerability" 43.

64 Ibid.

65 Butler, "Violence, Mourning, Politics" 29.

66 Ibid.

67 Ibid. 19.

68 Anderson, "Silencing and Speaker Vulnerability" Abstract (online only).

69 Butler, "Violence, Mourning, Politics" 21; emphasis in original.

70 Ibid. 23.

71 Ibid. 20; emphasis in original.

72 Anderson, "'A Thoughtful Love of Life'" 123.

73 Pamela Sue Anderson, "Ricoeur in Dialogue with Feminist Philosophy of Religion," *Svensk Teologisk Kvartalskrift* 91.1–2 (2015): 199–220.

74 Ibid. 200.

75 Ibid.

76 Ibid.

77 John Milton, *Paradise Lost* (1667), line 26.

78 Paul Ricoeur, *Oneself as Another*, trans. Kathleen Blamey (Chicago: U of Chicago P, 1992) 24.

79 Anderson, "Myth, Mimesis and Multiple Identities" 116.

80 See note 32.

81 Pamela Sue Anderson, "Forever Natal: In Death as in Life," *Literature and Theology* 21.2 (2007): 227–31.

82 Hanneke Canters and Grace M. Jantzen, *Forever Fluid: A Reading of Luce Irigaray's Elemental Passions* (Manchester: Manchester UP, 2005).

83 Anderson, "'A Thoughtful Love of Life'" 120–22.

84 Anderson, "Forever Natal" 228.

85 Pamela Sue Anderson, "Shadows of the Past," *Literature and Theology* 28.4 (2014): 371–88.

86 Ibid. 385.

87 Ibid. 371.

88 Ibid. 381.

89 Ibid. 385.

90 See Anderson, "'A Thoughtful Love of Life'" 123.

91 Ibid.

92 Anderson, "Forever Natal" 230.

When, in May 2001, Pamela Sue Anderson came to Regent's Park College, Oxford for interview as a candidate for a Fellowship in Philosophy and Christian Ethics, she chose to give her "sample lecture" on the theme of forgiveness. I later discovered that she had recently written a chapter on "A Feminist Ethics of Forgiveness" for a book titled *Forgiveness and Truth*, which was to be published later in that same year.[1] I had myself written on the Christian approach to forgiveness in a book on the idea of Atonement in 1998,[2] and had recently published a development of my argument in a book on experience of God as Trinity.[3] As a theologian, as well as Principal of the college, I was naturally interested to discover what Pamela had to say about the subject from the distinct perspective of a feminist philosopher of religion.

From that time onwards, indeed for the sixteen years remaining of her too-short life, Pamela and I held a sustained conversation about the nature and practice of forgiveness. Our talking together, in the Senior Common Room and over meals, marked our friendship, and seeped into print, both explicitly and implicitly. Perhaps the climax of the conversation came in the participation of both of us in a symposium on the place of forgiveness in the practice of Restorative Justice (RJ), organized by another Fellow of Regent's Park College (Myra B. Blyth) as part of her research project, held in June 2014. Both our contributions, suitably revised, were published in the *Oxford Journal of Law and Religion* in 2016, and there we took the occasion to enter into more public debate. Then, in the last year of Pamela's life, the theme of forgiveness took a slightly new form in the context of her

paul s. fiddes

FORGIVENESS, EMPATHY AND VULNERABILITY

an unfinished conversation with pamela sue anderson

developing ideas on the place of vulnerability in love.

In this paper I briefly want to re-trace the stages of her thought on forgiveness, through a series of six articles or book chapters that she wrote, beginning with the piece from 2001 and ending with her final unpublished work. At the same time, I intend to hold a dialogue between her ideas on forgiveness and my own, thus re-creating our conversation and finding new insights within it that were not apparent at the time. It is an exercise in that kind of memory which – as she emphasized – can "enact every situation anew" and "forge new links with the future."[4] My only regret and deep sadness is that she is not here to share in the conversation, and with her quicksilver critique to point up the "ethics of memory" and so prevent any manipulation of my memories of *her* to my own advantage. I am grateful for the continuation of our warm and close friendship that this exercise offers, as well as the opportunity to honour her pioneering thought from which I have learned so much. Inevitably, however, the conversation remains unfinished.

1 forgiveness as a struggle

The first emphasis that Pamela Sue Anderson[5] wanted to make is that forgiveness is a *struggle* that cannot be short-circuited. Here, I begin with the book chapter that she had written just as she came to Regent's Park College in 2001, titled "A Feminist Ethics of Forgiveness." Her point of departure is a critique of what she regards as a traditional Christian notion of forgiveness, and while it is not the only approach it is admittedly widespread. Her "hermeneutic of suspicion" involves a two-fold objection: first, forgiveness of wrongdoing is expected, even required, from people, especially women and marginalized others; and second, it is assumed that forgiveness is always possible since it comes as a divine gift. Thus, she protested, forgiveness is used to reinforce the lack of self-respect suffered by oppressed persons, while the sense of self-respect is a rational good.[6]

In contrast to this Christian account (as she sees it), she insists that forgiveness is always a struggle. The experience of enslaved persons in African-American history suggests that if a wronged person is no longer to feel resentment then there needs to be a painful emotional transformation. She writes that it is difficult to create "stories recounting forgiveness that do not involve the lack or loss of rational self-respect," and so "there is a struggle to create new narratives of forgiveness and promise."[7] The conflict is between forgiveness and justice, since justice entails the development of self-respect, and this in turn requires a righteous resentment against certain forms of wrongdoing such as sexual abuse. Anderson sees the dilemma thus: "how can the soul and its emotions be transformed to achieve forgiveness without a loss of self-worth in the face of massive wrong-doing?"[8]

Anderson's insistence on forgiveness as a difficult process of emotional transformation in the victim seemed to me at the time to have affinities with the idea I had been developing, that forgiveness is a costly journey. Forgiveness can never be demanded of a victim, but the one who *wants* to forgive, I had written, needs to embark on a voyage of experience with two stages to it. First, there is a journey of *discovery* as the forgiver has to expose the truth of what has been done to her, rather than forget about it, and second there is a journey of *endurance* as the forgiver absorbs the hostility and anxiety of the offender.[9] The aim of this two-fold journey of empathy is to create a response in the offender, who needs to face up to the truth of his actions and to be won to the forgiveness which is being offered. The one who has offended is more likely to come to self-realization and reconciliation if he or she experiences the one forgiving as an accepting rather than a judgemental person. From a Christian perspective, the victim who aims to forgive participates in the journey of forgiveness which God has taken universally through the life and death of Christ. The forgiver takes an initiative which relies upon the initiative taken by God in making the deepest journey of empathy into human lives.

As I talked this over with Anderson during the years to come, the question which always arose was whether my idea of forgiveness as a journey of empathy with the offender allowed sufficiently for expression of the righteous resentment which the victim rightly felt. Did it sufficiently reflect the struggle between forgiveness and justice? Yet in this early piece on the theme, Anderson felt that oppressed persons *do* want to let go of the resentment they feel, however righteous it is, because of the toll it takes on them. Forgiveness, she believed, was characterized by "overcoming certain potentially destructive emotions like resentment."[10]

Expanding her second critique of a Christian approach, Anderson asks in this paper why some enslaved persons were able to exemplify the virtue of forgiveness, and comments that "Personally I do not see how a mere reference to [...] Christian forgiveness or grace, could be a sufficient explanation."[11] The struggle could not, and cannot, be short-circuited by an easy divine gift, and so she makes the challenge that it is necessary to develop what she calls a "secular" understanding of forgiveness in which self-worth is retained within a difficult process. There is, she writes, "something about emotional transformation that [...] [a Christian] perspective on forgiveness" cannot achieve.[12] In response, I would (and did) say that when Christians receive the gift of entering into the journey of God's own forgiveness,[13] this is indeed sharing in a struggle of feelings and responses and is no superficial view of grace.

Forgiveness, Anderson urges, involves a process of emotional and rational transformation of the person in order to achieve release from resentment without loss of self-respect. Here, she appeals to a number of witnesses who were important to her thought during the course of her writing. First, there is the narrative account developed by bell hooks, expressing her struggle with the stereotypes which restricted the possibilities for black women's identities in African-American contexts; hooks, noted Anderson, came to an inner transformation in a "gradual release from these stereotypes" which became part of "a redemptive process of 'a writing life.'"[14] This painful process of "refiguring the past" and creating "an imaginary domain" in which persons can relocate themselves in relation to a past of pain and oppression, means that "forgetting is not the same as forgiveness."[15] This is an insight that is also central to my own model of a journey of forgiveness,[16] and it raises the place of memory in a feminist ethics of forgiveness which Anderson was to explore more thoroughly in her next piece on the theme.

Another witness for Anderson to the need for transformation through emotional and rational struggle is Gillian Rose, who points to the "intense work of the soul, that gradual re-arrangement of its boundaries" that is involved in the process of mourning; in the paradigmatic Greek stories of Phocion and Antigone, this is a mourning which makes experiences of past injustice "visible and speakable," so that "mourning draws on transcendent but representable justice."[17] Anderson suggests that there is a similar process going on in forgiveness, where "release from resentment" occurs as the person grieving over a transgression against her "recognizes justice [...] in representations (and new acts) of justice."[18] Yet a further witness here is Paul Ricoeur, whom Anderson makes a conversation-partner throughout her work. Anderson proposes that "re-enacting" narratives of the past anew in relation to justice here and now can reshape the identity of a culture or individual when there is a deliberate "struggle" with the difference of others from oneself. She sees Ricoeur as explaining this "shaping of narrative identity" in terms of "the 'entanglement' of an individual's story with the story of others."[19] A feminist ethics of forgiveness, she concludes, will take responsibility for the life stories of the other, "through the exchange of narratives in imagination and empathy."[20]

Again, this seems close to my understanding of forgiveness as a journey of empathy into the life of another, but we must not miss that the empathy Anderson had in mind was between victims and others who are oppressed, not between victim and oppressor. She might say, if she were here: why should empathy include the transgressor? And I would reply – that it depends on whether one wants to achieve reconciliation with the other as well as freedom from one's own resentment.

2 forgiveness as making a new future

Anderson's next paper that reflected on forgiveness, titled "An Ethics of Memory: Promising, Forgiving, Yearning" (2005), took its point of departure from the question of how a person's identity might be retained in face of the challenge of the postmodern view of the "death" of the self. It was in fact written for the *Blackwell Companion to Postmodern Theology*. Drawing on the thought of Ricoeur and

Hannah Arendt, she proposed that our identity through time consists in the making and keeping of promises. It is through this that we are the same person. Forgiveness thus becomes necessary as a way of dealing with the broken promises of others, opening up a shared future.

The paper repeats the presentation of forgiveness from the 2001 piece as a difficult process of emotional and rational transformation, but there is no direct statement of a struggle between forgiveness and justice. Elaborating the theme of memory from the earlier book chapter, the struggle is now portrayed as being between the past and the future, and it takes the form of a yearning to create just memories which will move beyond the past to forge new links with the future. She writes: "The struggle leads to personal and social transformation only insofar as the response to the injustice of broken promises involves forgiving others and yearning for the transformation of life's narratives."[21]

The process or struggle is defined here as a "yearning," including the "mourning" which appeared in the earlier piece.[22] Anderson proposes that we make "narrative sense of life" through three acts which involve memory in one way or another: there is the making and keeping of promises, the forgiveness of broken promises and yearning (for love and justice) which holds together promise-keeping and forgiveness.[23] Again she writes, "The ultimate aim of my project is to apply an ethics of memory to the feminist problematic of philosophy of religion," explaining that "What needs to be retrieved are the shattered promises, the ability to forgive and the yearning which leads to transforming melancholia into love and justice."[24] In fact, the triumvirate of forgiveness, promising and yearning was not to play a substantial part in Anderson's future working out of her "project," though it merits a page or so in her later *Re-visioning Gender*.[25] In that study she is interested in the "moral force of love" in constructing a feminist epistemology and ethics, in which "yearning" for love plays a substantial part, and promise-keeping is replaced by the "commitment" of love, without the same reflection on forgiveness.[26] If she were here now I would want to ask her why forgiveness was apparently downplayed in what she intended as a major book on the gendering of philosophy of religion: it seems that it no longer had the significance in the making of human identity that she had given it earlier.

In this book chapter, forgiveness *is* still closely bound to the elements of promising and yearning, in making a story of the self with an openness to the future grounded in memory. Promise-making and promise-keeping achieve self-constancy in their continuing through the changes of time. This, Anderson stresses, is not just an individual act but a communal act of commitment, a mutual promise as the basis for shared convictions, rules, norms, customs and beliefs.[27] Forgiving is linked with this phenomenon in freeing us from a past of broken promises. Admittedly, the forgiveness here relates to broken promises, not explicitly to the abuse, violence or oppression that is in view in the first paper. However, Anderson probably thinks that the principles of forgiveness are the same in all instances, since this piece develops the "ethics of memory" she had proposed in the paper of 2001. After all, the breaking of a communal promise, or a social contract, often does involve oppression of particular groups, and she suggests in *Re-visioning Gender* that the breaking of personal promises can be emotional abuse and involve a threat to self-respect.[28] In the 2005 book chapter, the yearning for justice and lost love is also inseparable from forgiveness, since it is in "forgetting or forgiving" that the yearning which is bound up with promising finds the freedom to be "unbound" from promises that have failed to deliver.[29] Anderson's associating of "forgetting" and "forgiving" in this context need not mean, of course, that she has neglected the difference between them that she registered previously.

The significance of forgiveness to both promising and yearning seems here to derive from Anderson's debt to Arendt, who proposes in *The Human Condition* that we gain our narrative identity as agents who promise and forgive. Promise-keeping and forgiveness respectively "bind" and "unbind" us in time.

Promising offers a remedy for the unpredictability of behaviour, and forgiveness offers the remedy for "the predicament of irreversibility," i.e., being unable to undo what one has done.[30] Anderson also gains from Arendt the perception that the disclosure of "who" we are takes place when a new beginning – natality – is established through an action such as promising or forgiving which "falls into an already existing web of relationships."[31] Thus, a single life story affects the life stories of all. Anderson goes on to find similar themes in Ricoeur who, like Arendt, considers promise-keeping to be an example of "the highest expression of selfhood."[32] Anderson notes his obligation to Arendt's idea of "natality," and points out that for Ricoeur such "births," together with memory, establish coherence between past, present and future in the narrative of the self, and that acts of promising always take place "within a web of relationships."[33]

In this piece Anderson does not consider Ricoeur's own handling of forgiveness, as she will do in a later one. She does reflect on Ricoeur's understanding of involvement in the "web of relationships," and here draws attention to Ricoeur's caveat that this does not mean we can actually relive the life of others: she quotes him to the effect that "It is a matter of exchanging memories at the narrative level where they are present for comprehension."[34] This process is portrayed in somewhat cognitive terms as "an ability to *think* from the standpoint of others," and the influence of Ricoeur here may account for Anderson's tendency to establish boundaries to empathy in forgiveness, and her suspicion of my own model of forgiveness as a journey of identity into the life of another. Nevertheless, she repeats from the 2001 paper that an ethics of memory takes responsibility for the life stories of the other, "through the exchange of narratives in imagination and empathy."[35]

Anderson's ethical concern for the opening up of the future in a changed life narrative has parallels with the aims of RJ, a process which brings together offender and victim in a conversation either inside or outside the criminal justice system, in which the victim can confront the perpetrator with the effects of his or her offence.[36] In this meeting, a key aim is to find a way forward together into the future on which all the stakeholders are agreed, and which will involve some kind of change in all who are involved. Later, as we shall see, Anderson *did* comment on RJ, but this was not part of her thinking in 2005.

In my own conversation with her, I raised the question of the place of a loving God within any process in which restoration and the making of a new future is in view. Oddly, contributing as she was in 2005 to a volume on postmodern *theology*, she does not say anything about God. But I wanted to urge that in shaping the future God is also open to change as a participant in the healing of broken relations. God, as a divine forgiver, must be vulnerable, open to suffering and mutable. This is the corollary of a process of forgiveness which is a journey of identification with the other, and which in God's own story is a voyage into all human lives, reaching the most intense pitch in the life and death of Jesus Christ.[37] There can, of course, be no alteration in God's character of goodness and faithfulness, or we would no longer be talking about "God" at all, and neither is the change any movement from reluctance to forgive into being forgiving. Instead, we can conceive of God's taking new experience into the divine life through the death of Christ for the sake of creation, enabling God through empathy to win offenders into reconciliation and achieve transformation.

3 forgiveness as exceeding justice

In a paper by Anderson of the following year, titled "Unselfing in Love: A Contradiction in Terms?" (2006),[38] my own stress on the passibility of God does appear in her dialogue with me. However, this is not where she begins. The point of departure is the idea of "unselfing," a term that Anderson takes and converts from Iris Murdoch's notion of unselfing.[39] Forgiveness then becomes relevant in several ways.

First, an *unhealthy* kind of unselfing would be the "loss of self" in the sense of "self-emptying," loss of self-worth and self-dignity. She maintains that, whatever ambiguities there might be in the idea of "unselfing," the very idea "presupposes a self capable of loving relationships: that is, a self who can decreate in order to find herself in loving another."[40] What Anderson had learnt from Kant's ethics of autonomy remained with her throughout her life as a defence of a woman's power of self-determination. Picking up the theme of her first paper, the demand that someone should forgive seemed to her to foster this kind of destructive unselfing. It ignored the necessary struggle between forgiveness and justice.[41]

But forgiveness appears again in Anderson's view of a *healthy* kind of unselfing, which is marked by a de-centring of the self in giving "attention" to the other. She writes: "I see the essence of love simply in an arresting attention to [...] [a person's] particular existence."[42] Here, she is indebted to Murdoch, and through her to Simone Weil, for the idea of unselfing as turning from mere absorption in the self to attend to another, citing Murdoch's acknowledgement that she has borrowed the word "attention" from Weil "to express the idea of a just and loving gaze directed upon an individual reality."[43] Such attention requires a self "capable of intimate relations," and the result in turn of attending to the other is the creation of enriched relations.[44] In this context she approves bell hooks's notion of awareness of the reality of ourselves,[45] and thinks that a proper self-love might be best expressed as "oneself inasmuch as another."[46] The essence of love remains "in the quality of the self's attending to another, including oneself as another."[47] Now, while the main theme of this paper is "love" in the widest sense as unselfing, Anderson focuses the discussion on one particular loving act of attention to the other, namely forgiveness: "forgiveness becomes the crucial example of an ethical act done in order to sustain loving relationships." It is crucial, she will go on to explain, because "today the act done for the sake of love alone which raises serious questions about love's capability is forgiveness."[48] We shall come in due course to these "serious questions."

Again following Murdoch, Anderson suggests that a further aspect of healthy "unselfing" is the loss of illusions cultivated by the self.[49] "Unselfing" means seeking to rid oneself of self-deceptions concerning the reality of self-love and other-love. One of these illusions, she suggests, is that love is merely benevolence, an altruistic "doing good" to others which neglects the reality of the desires of the self. While benevolence to others is a proper human disposition to be encouraged, it can become distorted into "acts of charity" which mask the unjust discrepancy between the situations of rich and poor in society. It can cease to be a specific act of goodwill towards another, and become "a non-specific act of charity in giving to the personally unknown, less well-off as a duty."[50] In line with Kant, Anderson finds "a duty to love" to be an absurdity, since love is a "feeling," so that if love is regarded as mere benevolence it undermines itself. At this point, Anderson's discussion takes a theological turn, detecting a sanctioning of this human distortion of benevolence in the religious image of an omnibenevolent God.

This is also the point where Anderson appeals to my own insistence on the mutability and passibility of God. A healthy theology of unselfing, she argued, will challenge the view of a God whose love is reducible to benevolence to all; in traditional terms, this is the image of a God of pure *agape* or self-giving love, with no aspect of *eros* or desire. Appealing to my own theology, she suggests that proper human unselfing will be prompted by the view of a God who "unselfs" by ridding God's self of the illusion of invulnerability and impassibility that is pervasive in classical theology:

> What emerges in Fiddes' case is the relational capacity of love. He argues that since human beings are the objects or subjects of the searching love of God, relationship [...] with them must satisfy the desire of God and complete divine joy. Fiddes moves a great distance from both the classical view of divine love as the ideal of invulnerable gift and the human ideal of disinterested self-giving.[51]

Thus (with some theological originality) she proposes that the image of a God who rids God's self of the illusion of disinterested benevolence will challenge our own distortions of benevolence, and awaken us to our proper desires. For God and human beings, unselfing and maintaining the self are to be held in tension: here she approves my claim that "we become more truly ourselves when we give ourselves away [...] self-giving love is in the end a self-realization."[52] Anderson does not here – as I do – explicitly relate this vulnerability of God to the process of forgiving, even in the form of a religious image that might motivate human forgiveness. There is an *implicit* connection in so far as Anderson has already taken forgiveness as the paradigm example of "the relational capacity of love," but it is in another example of ridding oneself of illusions that she brings a discussion of forgiveness to the fore.

According to Anderson, another illusion to be discarded in "unselfing" is that love is a kind of distributive justice, in which love is to be given to everyone impartially. Love cannot be required on the grounds of justice, she writes, to be distributed equally, to intimates and strangers alike. Woman especially cannot distribute love equally, since this destroys a sense of self, and "historically women and marginalized men have not been allowed to create a sense of self in the first place."[53] Making love a form of distributive justice fails to create a proper self-love which is essential for making relationships. It is here that the act of forgiveness, as a paradigm of loving relations, raises the "serious questions" to which Anderson referred earlier. It is clear that "forgiveness [...] must be done out of love, not duty or distributive justice":[54]

> For forgiveness to remain different from forgetting or reparation, it would have to be incompatible with the rules of distributive justice which seek reparation in the form of punishment for crimes or injustices committed. In other words, one forgives precisely because the injustice cannot be repaired.

Forgiveness is the key example of the tension between love and distributive justice: in the case of an offence committed, justice requires reparation, and yet no injustice can be fully "repaired" and so calls for forgiveness. "One forgives the unforgivable for the sake of love," she asserts, "not distributive justice." The implication is that forgiveness exceeds justice, as she had written earlier in her 2005 book chapter: "the cemetery of past promises can be transformed by a love that *goes beyond* morality in forgiveness."[55] Yet, at the same time, Anderson insists that if a victim of injustice denies her own self in forgiving the one who has hurt her, she has little sense of the reality of love.[56] We are back with the struggle between love and justice in the act of forgiveness that occupied Anderson in the first paper above. The development in this piece is to illuminate that struggle by placing it in the tension (even the apparent "contradiction") between "selfing" and "unselfing" in love, but Anderson does not attempt to supply any easy resolution.

Putting forgiveness in the larger context of "unselfing in love" does, however, make it a practice of the "wise lover" who attempts to "confront the egoistic enemy of the good life without neutralizing or denuding the self."[57] The two "egoistic enemies" Anderson has identified in this paper, or "the fat relentless ego[s] in modern ethical theory,"[58] have been an overconfidence in benevolence and distributive justice, but it has been easier to name them than to resolve the tension of which they are symptoms. Rather as she had earlier discerned the need for a slow process of emotional and rational transformation in the process of forgiveness, here she admits that "one may not be able to single out accurately any examples of the wise lover"[59] and that the "perfection of love [...] remains humanly impossible." In the face of a tension that "verges on contradictions" one can only hold a "vision of sheer delight in an arresting attention to the reality of oneself, other selves, and our world."[60]

Anderson's phrases about "forgiving the unforgivable" and perfected love as "impossible" have overtones of the treatment of forgiveness by Jacques Derrida, and in her first paper above Anderson does refer to Derrida in a footnote, recording that he rejects any notion of forgiveness as a duty.[61] He formulates the act of forgiveness in terms of its sheer unconditionality.[62] For Derrida the whole point of forgiveness is that it rises above all mechanisms of reciprocation and the market-place. Forgiveness is not about calculation, or balancing the accounts:

> There is in forgiveness a force, a desire, an impetus, a movement [...] that demands that forgiveness be granted even to someone who does not ask for it, who does not repent or confess or improve or redeem himself.[63]

Forgiveness, he stresses, is always of the unforgivable.[64] For Derrida, unconditional forgiveness is "impossible," but there can be no other kind, or we buy into a mere economy of exchange. I myself also stress that forgiveness itself is unconditional; it does not require repentance or remorse in the offender, since that would undermine the dynamic nature of forgiveness as initiating a response in those who are reluctant to accept pardon. Above all, the forgiveness of God expressed in the death of Christ is unconditional.[65] However, in Derrida's view, forgiveness to be pure must be offered without any hope, *expectation* or intention that the offender will in due time face up to his or her crime, be repentant, seek reconciliation, offer reparation and be transformed. Even holding hope for the offender is, in Derrida's view, entering an economy of exchange. In my approach, while forgiveness is unconditional, the *completing* of forgiveness in reconciliation between those who are alienated (whether between people or between human persons and God) is conditional upon an appropriate response.[66] It does not deny unconditional forgiveness to hope for this response, though it can never be *demanded*. Derrida's view seems to arise from associating forgiveness radically with forgetting,[67] rather than with an empathy that relies on memory.

Despite an apparent echo of Derrida's language, in this piece Anderson appears to reject unconditional forgiveness, remarking that "the moral theologian's insistence on unconditional, spontaneous and selfless love becomes self-contradictory."[68] Certainly, to the end of our conversations, Anderson was unhappy about the idea. It seemed to her to undermine justice and self-worth, and especially to put the woman back in the position of victim. I urged that forgiveness was not the end of the process of healing broken relations. I suggested that reconciliation between victim and oppressor must be conditional on the repentance of the offender and his making of reparation; forgiveness, as unconditional, has the power to create such an ethical response. I wonder whether in this paper, with her urging of the "forgiving of the unforgivable" there is just the seed of a possible agreement. She would have to say.

4 forgiveness as a hope

Some five years later, in a short paper titled "A Feminist on Forgiveness" (2011), Anderson returned to the conflict between forgiveness and justice, as flagged up in the first and third papers considered here. Indeed, this is the point of departure for her piece, which is the transcript of an oral presentation.[69] She says, "Love might say, forgive! But justice may not!"[70] She asks, "Can forgiveness be unjust?"[71] and maintains that "The feminist argues that in the case of an abused woman with a weak sense of self-respect, the danger of forgiveness is to condone injustice."[72] In short, she is sketching out the situation indicated by the subtitle of the piece: "When (Where?) Love and Justice Come Apart."

In the light of this struggle between love and justice it is appropriate that the talk, published in a book designed to honour Paul Ricoeur, takes as its repeated motif Ricoeur's phrase about "difficult forgiveness." Indeed, Anderson judges that "one half-century of philosophical reflections on evil were simply a prelude" to Ricoeur's account of forgiveness in the epilogue to his *Memory, History, Forgetting*, titled "Difficult Forgiveness."[73] As previously, she proposes that the dilemma of forgiveness can be resolved only through a process of transformation in which the struggle is fully recognized and worked through. She refers to a "long process" with forgiveness "a long way down the line,"[74] and cites bell hooks as writing that "confronting myself with compassion, I *learn* to practice the art of forgiveness."[75] She also gives at least qualified approval to the particular Christian view that the pronouncement "I forgive you" is "not an act at all, but is a description of a process; that is, forgiveness involves a process of changing one's emotion." As in her first paper above, she certainly rejects an alternative Christian view that "forgiveness is both necessary and possible as a miraculous gift from God," deriving from a forensic understanding of atonement in Christ as paying an offender's debt.[76]

In exploring the difficult "process" of forgiveness, she finds it to be characterized by both memory and hope. For the aspect of memory she is indebted to Ricoeur's discussion of "recognition" as "a small miracle of memory," when someone suddenly exclaims "That is her! That is him!"[77] Forgiveness, suggests Anderson, is characterized by the same recognition of the truth of what has actually happened in a past act of offence, so that forgiveness depends on "seeing and remembering."[78] It is in memory that the wrong done is recognized, but through memory also that the necessary encounter with someone can happen. Anderson affirms that "in the place where the person is recognized, the spirit of forgiveness becomes manifest."[79] Such a "spirit of forgiveness" only becomes possible through a "fundamental premise" that, as she gladly acknowledges, both she and Ricoeur have gleaned from Immanuel Kant: that innocence is more original than guilt, and goodness more original than evil.[80]

Here, Anderson (in a footnote)[81] makes what she calls a "detour" to describe "how it is I have arrived as a moral philosopher – and a philosopher of religion – to my view of forgiveness." She explains that she is following Ricoeur in his own debt to Kant on the nature of good and evil: that while evil is radical as a propensity of human action, innocence is more original than evil or guilt.[82] Thus there is what Ricoeur calls a "spirit of forgiveness" inscribed in human willing, within the very capability of humans to act both to do right and wrong, and "a capability not only to do wrong but for that wrong doing to be undone." It is this Kantian–Ricoeurian insight that gives Anderson the hope that, despite the struggle between love and justice that cannot be easily resolved, forgiveness is still possible. Ricoeur, she continues, draws the conclusion that the act of forgiving is "an unbinding of evil from the guilty agent" so that the act of evil can be distinguished from the agent who is "potentially restored to his or her original innocence." While Anderson appears to approve this account, we are bound to notice that it leads Ricoeur to equate forgiving with forgetting, as the fault is separated from the agent and sent into oblivion, while the agent is remembered only as an innocent person. Ricoeur believes that this kind of forgetting of faults in the past, or what Ricoeur calls an "unbinding of debt from fault,"[83] can promote the healing of relations; it can, he thinks, prevent an obsessive repetition or commemoration of the past, unblock a situation of conflict in memory, remove melancholia and so make forgiveness possible.[84] Unfortunately, it can also undermine the very process of "transformation" of the person that Anderson herself is commending, in which person and act are bound up in one reality that has to be faced openly by both forgiver and offender. The Kantian insight into original innocence need not inevitably lead to the conclusion that agent and act can be separated, and if forgiveness is to be unconditional (as Derrida perceives),[85] they cannot be. The offence done does not derive from a kind of parcel of evil that can be detached from an agent but from destructive attitudes that have to be changed in the person through a painful voyage of experience.

In this piece Anderson does in fact link my own conception of a journey of forgiveness to her concern for a process of rational and emotional transformation. In a long footnote attached to a comment about forgiveness as a "complex process" she writes:

> Roughly, a Christian moral theologian would probably introduce an account of the stages of atonement – or, as Paul Fiddes describes,

the journeys of forgiveness. Elsewhere I have given attention to the intriguing work done by Fiddes on forgiveness – he has an interesting take on [...] the process of repairing broken relationships in the journey of forgiveness: of discovery and endurance.[86]

Anderson is correct here that I relate the journey of forgiveness to atonement – in the sense that God in the death of Christ takes the furthest voyage into human desolation and isolation in order to awaken human persons to their situation, and to create response to God's forgiving love.[87] However, I do not, as she implies, follow the sequence of the particular stages of atonement she goes on to outline – recognition of wrong, repentance, forgiveness and penance. The whole point of the empathetic journey taken by the Creator into creation is that unconditional forgiveness has the power to prompt repentance and reparation, and that this issues in reconciliation.[88]

I venture to suggest that this kind of pattern, in which human beings participate through their own acts of forgiveness, may offer an answer to another problem that Anderson raises. Alongside the struggle between justice and love in forgiveness, Anderson sets what she finds to be a rational or logical conundrum. On the one hand, forgiveness would be "unjustified" if the wrongdoer has not made reparation. On the other, the act of forgiveness is "pointless" if the wrongdoer has already made adequate reparation.[89] While she offers the slow process of transformation, taking the issue of justice seriously, as the only way through the struggle, she does not appear to have any solution to the conundrum. It ceases to be so acute, however, if we distinguish between unconditional forgiveness and conditional reconciliation as I have done earlier: forgiveness *prompts* reparation rather than following it, and lack of reparation would make unjustified not forgiveness but reconciliation.

The second major characteristic of the process of forgiveness which Anderson discusses in this piece (the first being memory) is that of hope – grounded, as we have seen, in a conviction that innocence and goodness have priority over evil. Here, Anderson expands an idea that she first mentioned in her 2001 paper on forgiveness, prompted by the writing of Drucilla Cornell, that we should conceive a new imaginative space of freedom, an "imaginary domain" in which exploited peoples can recover and relocate themselves in relation to a past of pain and oppression.[90] Beyond Cornell's exposition, she asserts that forgiveness can create that space through love, and, as before, she sees bell hooks as "working to conceive a space [...] where forgiveness breaks down the divisions between our private and public lives in order to open up both to love and justice."[91] But here she goes a step further in seeing the hope for this space as meeting a set of questions about forgiveness which she herself poses, such as: how can forgiveness be justified when victims are no longer alive? When injustice is still taking place against a people, a race, a sex? When the victim cannot forgive?[92] When the victim is not conscious, or gone away, or estranged?[93] Her answer is that at times when forgiveness is impossible, there remains "hope for the place where love and justice will be able to create a new future."[94]

I myself raise almost exactly the same questions about forgiveness, and also offer hope for a "future space" of reconciliation where forgiveness can be practised.[95] However, my account is deliberately theological in a way that hers is not. The image of a journey of empathy directed towards the creation of response to the offer of forgiveness seems especially problematic when someone refuses to be reconciled, or is not present to be reconciled because they have died, or the situation is such as to make it unsafe for someone who has been abused to make any contact with the abuser at all. In such cases, I urge, the one who wants to forgive can still set out in imagination on a path of empathy towards the other, so becoming the kind of person who is freed from the chains of the past. A Christian hope is based not only in a Kantian positive view of human nature but also in an eschatology where all will experience the judgement of having to face the truth about themselves, and have the opportunity to be reconciled with Love.[96]

Belief in a God who is engaged in the same kind of journey as human beings means that our own journey becomes part of the journey of a God in whom all persons "live and move and have their being."[97] Our hopeful imagination thus has persuasive power in creating reconciliation in the world as our created love is added to the uncreated love of God which is a constant pressure towards human flourishing. We cannot know what this will achieve, either in the one with whom we desire to be reconciled or in others who need to be reconciled and of whom we are quite unaware.

5 forgiveness and restorative justice

A paper published by Anderson in 2016, and originally written for a colloquium on Restorative Justice in 2014, has a similar title to the previous one, being "When Justice and Forgiveness Come Apart."[98] The departure point here is the practice of RJ, and the highly contested question, among practitioners of RJ, as to whether forgiveness should play any part in the process. Along the lines of previous pieces, this essay continues to assert a conflict between forgiveness and justice – or between love and justice in the act of forgiveness – and to underline the "difficult" nature of forgiveness.

The article develops the argument, however, by making explicit that the process of forgiveness may, and will in the case of women suffering abuse and "intimate violence," call for a *withholding* of forgiveness at least for a period, not least during the practice of RJ.[99] Time will be needed to cultivate emotions of righteous anger. This "withholding" may well be implied in the "process of transformation" set out in earlier papers, but is not so stated there.[100] In dialogue here with Martha Nussbaum, she maintains that anger, in the form of resentment and contempt, is a cognitive emotion which plays a positive role in withholding forgiveness from the offender, so creating both distance (with space for ethical accountability) and time for the injuries to be recognized. Withholding also allows for the suitability of the positive affective emotion of love, motivating forgiveness, to be assessed.[101]

Forgiveness is to be withheld in the name of self-respect. Resentment and contempt need to be acknowledged if a victim is to be able to know what and how to forgive, or to express any just emotion. Forgiveness, she stresses, is a vice when it maintains injustice. In this circumstance love can be a *negative* cognitive emotion, setting up "unethical love relations."[102] Women can be "too forgiving or too loving to be ethical or just," and "unquestioning trust in a personal religion of love is a deeply-embedded obstacle to justice in the lives of oppressed subjects under patriarchy."[103]

Anderson's hesitations about the practice of RJ is that it might not allow for this exercise of the proper cognitive emotions of anger, and this failure would be exacerbated if acts of forgiveness were included within the process. These would make RJ prone to misunderstanding the cognitive role of human emotions, in the form of both love and anger, which motivate our interactions. Thus RJ might exploit the forgiving nature of those women (and men) who are vulnerable to being treated unjustly precisely because of being too loving.[104] Taking up an earlier theme, Anderson stresses that unconditional forgiveness is not an ethical requirement in *every* situation for *every* person, since it is necessary to take time to address cognitive emotions.[105]

In my own approach to the place of forgiveness within RJ, I agree strongly with Anderson[106] that the survivor of intimate violence has no duty to forgive. Rather, in line with my model of a "journey of forgiveness," I suggest that the exercise of forgiveness can be *encouraged* in the process of RJ, with the effect of creating a response in the offender, without either *requiring* or *expecting* it.[107] Using the language of John Braithwaite, forgiveness can be regarded as one of the "standards" that can be "maximized" as appropriate in the process of RJ.[108] Braithwaite himself prefers to regard forgiveness as an "emergent value," developing out of the process, but in his discussion with me he admits that the issue might be really about the definition of "maximizing."[109] By contrast, Anderson remains apprehensive about introducing forgiveness into practices of RJ at all. In RJ, she affirms, we can learn how to recognize when cognitive emotions such as contempt have a salient role in alerting us to injustice. We must begin the process of restoring trust in oneself in the face of self-denigration before we can hope to restore justice. Forgiveness, she admits, is often the decisive step needed to generate the possibility of repairing ethical accountability, but it is not an easy step to take, and it will probably need to be withheld initially.

Anderson is also apprehensive about certain practices of "caring" relationships. Like RJ, these can run the danger of ignoring ethical *vulnerability* and *accountability* in the name of "caring about" the other's reparation more than one's own.[110] She notes that twentieth-century feminist debates have sometimes distinguished between an "ethics of justice" supposedly typical of men, and an "ethics of care," supposedly typical of women.[111] She judges that the debate has been right to suspect that these two types of ethics have been assigned to the public and private spheres respectively, with the result that an ethics of justice in the public sphere has failed to achieve the restoration of personal relations, while an ethics of care has promoted loving and forgiving relations only in private life.[112] Anderson affirms that it has been a good thing to unearth an ethics of care in the decision making of women, but she agrees with more recent feminist philosophers in disputing any sharp gender distinction between care and justice, writing that "we have many new understandings of gender, transgender and other sexual relations."[113] Stereotypes which divide ethics into men (justice) and women (care) have to be challenged. She also warns against slipping into a sharp distinction between public and private life, since the separation of two spheres of life is highly problematic for forgiveness. Women who suffer intimate violence – within family life – have been taught to forgive immediately and unconditionally. There is decisive risk of injustice in regarding forgiveness as unproblematic within the private sphere of life, and she finds this to be typical of the traditional Christian (pre-modern) community.

The article shows that at this advanced stage of our conversation on forgiveness there is convergence between Anderson and myself in so far as Anderson increasingly associates my understanding of the "journey" of forgiveness with the "process" of transformation she envisages herself. Here, she deliberately links her own account of "taking time to address cognitive emotions" with what she calls my own "dynamic process of forgiveness," and thinks that both can be related to a proper process of RJ.[114] In fact she makes a point of preferring what she identifies as my "late modern Christian theology of forgiveness as a dynamic process" to Braithwaite's suspicion that modernity (and the autonomy it cultivates) is a hindrance to RJ, opposing his desire to return to what she regards as dangerous "ancient traditions" of relationships.[115] Her difference from me is about the stage in the "journey of forgiveness" where forgiveness becomes appropriate, at least in the case of women suffering intimate violence.

For my part, in the paper I contribute to the colloquium, I try to place her advocacy of withholding forgiveness within my own image of forgiveness as a journey of empathy. I have learned to take seriously her insistence that withholding may be necessary, especially in extreme cases of harm such as abuse, to preserve the integrity, well-being and freedom of the victim as well as to make clear to the abuser the terrible depths of the harm inflicted. So I suggest that persons who cannot forgive at a particular moment, and yet who do not have a fixed unforgiving attitude, might *begin* the journey of forgiveness and so escape being trapped in resentment by imagining conditions in which they *might* take a first unconditional movement of forgiveness. They might envisage a situation in which they themselves were in a better position to take this move, or in which the offender were in a different frame of mind or attitude. The very willingness to imagine that forgiveness *might* be possible, though it is impossible at present, is – I suggest – taking one's place in the empathetic journey of God which can in proper time enable further steps to be taken.[116]

A similar step in imagination is commended by the philosopher Charles Griswold, who suggests that when forgiveness seems inappropriate we can nevertheless construct in our minds an "imaginative and credible narrative" about an offender, finding reasons to think that conditions for forgiveness such as remorse might have been or might be fulfilled in a different situation than obtains at present.[117] The advantage I see in the theological context I propose is that the "imaginative narrative" participates in the story of a God who is actually moving in the world to create love and justice ahead of us.

6 forgiveness and vulnerability: in conclusion

The final paper I am considering[118] appeared posthumously in a publication of the Enhancing Life Project at the University of Chicago (2017). Some of the same themes are repeated from the 2016 article – in fact about seven pages[119] are close transcriptions of it – especially the need to withhold forgiveness[120] and to cultivate cognitive emotions of righteous anger in order to achieve just relations. However, this piece triangulates forgiveness with an ethics of care and an ethics of vulnerability, where the latter two themes made only a slight appearance in the former article.

The need to demolish barriers between private and public spheres is taken further, in the light of a situation where offences against women are often relegated to the private or family realm, creating a demand on women to forgive their intimate abusers. Anderson insists on a "*politics* of care," or care in the public space, characterized by the development of reciprocal accountability,[121] a note already sounded in the fourth of the papers I have gathered together.[122] But the most significant expansion from her previous article on forgiveness is her treatment of vulnerability, prompted (it seems) by a dialogue with the notion of universal human "precarious life and corporal vulnerability" in the work of Judith Butler.[123]

The "ethical vulnerability" which Anderson had briefly mentioned in the former paper is "clarified" as existing on two levels. First, there is a "phenomenological level" of experiencing vulnerability, prior to taking any ethical action. This is "a primary capacity for being wounded, or a potential wounding," and includes "a range of positive to negative vulnerable experiences," from loving affection in sexual intimacy to injurious violence that occurs in intimate relations.[124] Anderson also describes this phenomenology as presenting "specific, lived experiences of intimacy, as an openness to love and affection, while admitting affection could generate negative effects of fear, shame or rage."[125] In her previous article she had urged the need for time to come to terms with cognitive emotions arising from these experiences of vulnerability before forgiveness becomes possible.[126] Second, there is an "ethical level" of vulnerability, where "wounding" or the potential for being "wounded" is not something to be eliminated or thought of as a mere liability but adopted as a basis for relational accountability which has within it an openness to change, "of calling one another to account for immoral, non-moral or ethical wounds." Ethical vulnerability opens up an opportunity to restore justice or to repair the horrendous pain of wounds, and such "ethical repair" will need to work with the just emotions of resentment and contempt.[127]

As she makes clear in a coda of deliberate engagement with Butler, Anderson's desire is to shift the experience of vulnerability away from issues of violence, where it often belongs. The human response to vulnerability usually takes the form of a social mythology where violence is either to be avoided or imposed on others. But rather, we should allow vulnerability to lead us into an "openness to loving affection"[128] and accountability in relations. This project was to take initial form in her proposal for a new "social imaginary" of vulnerability in two final, unpublished papers which are now published in this journal.[129] But forgiveness does not feature explicitly in her outline of this imaginary, any more than it takes centre stage in the paper of 2017.

Through six papers we have traced Pamela Sue Anderson's understanding of the impasse, and yet the possibility, of forgiveness. A constant feature has been her urging, in face of the struggle between forgiveness and justice, or between love and justice in forgiveness, to give time and space for a process of cognitive and emotional transformation to happen in which forgiveness can gradually emerge. Though in increasing convergence with my own view of the process of forgiveness, she has remained suspicious of accounts of the "journey" that make forgiveness too much of an initiating action, out of concern that this imposes demands upon women who are abused and oppressed. Her account seems to belong, in terms of this final paper, to what she calls a "phenomenological level" of vulnerability. If Pamela were here, I would ask her what place she finds for forgiveness in the active, "ethical level" of vulnerability within her social imaginary. And I would like to know whether, as a philosopher of religion, she sees a place for a vulnerable God within a new narrative by which we can live. The conversation must now remain open-ended, but then the best conversations always are.

disclosure statement

No potential conflict of interest was reported by the author.

notes

1 Pamela Sue Anderson, "A Feminist Ethics of Forgiveness" in *Forgiveness and Truth*, eds. Alistair McFadyen and Marcel Sarot (Edinburgh: Clark, 2001) 145–56.

2 Paul S. Fiddes, *Past Event and Present Salvation: The Christian Idea of Atonement* (London: Darton, 1989) 171–89.

3 Paul S. Fiddes, *Participating in God: A Pastoral Doctrine of the Trinity* (London: Darton, 2000) 191–223.

4 Anderson, "Feminist Ethics of Forgiveness" 154.

5 Following my personal introduction about "Pamela" I will henceforth refer to her in a more academic way.

6 Anderson, "Feminist Ethics of Forgiveness" 145, 147.

7 Ibid. 148–49.

8 Ibid. 152.

9 Fiddes, *Past Event and Present Salvation* 173–75; Fiddes, *Participating in God* 192–97.

10 Anderson, "Feminist Ethics of Forgiveness" 151, cf. 152.

11 Ibid. 152.

12 Ibid. 155.

13 For an account of this shared journey, see Fiddes, *Participating in God* 206–10.

14 Anderson, "Feminist Ethics of Forgiveness" 149, citing bell hooks, *Wounds of Passion: A Writing Life* (New York: Holt, 1997) v.

15 Ibid. 151, 150.

16 Paul S. Fiddes, "Memory, Forgetting and the Problem of Forgiveness. Reflecting on Volf, Derrida and Ricoeur" in *Forgiving and Forgetting*, eds. Hartmut Von Sass and Johannes Zachhuber (Tübingen: Mohr Siebeck, 2015) 130–33.

17 Anderson, "Feminist Ethics of Forgiveness" 152–53, citing Gillian Rose, *Mourning Becomes the Law: Philosophy and Representation* (Cambridge: Cambridge UP, 1997) 35–36, 104.

18 Anderson, "Feminist Ethics of Forgiveness" 153.

19 Ibid. 155, citing Ricoeur, "Reflections on a New Ethos for Europe" in *Paul Ricoeur: The Hermeneutics of Action*, ed. Richard Kearney (London: Sage, 1996) 6–7.

20 Anderson, "Feminist Ethics of Forgiveness" 155.

21 "An Ethics of Memory: Promising, Forgiving, Yearning" in *The Blackwell Companion to Postmodern Theology*, ed. Graham Ward (Oxford: Blackwell, 2005) 243.

22 Ibid. 239–40. Women's "yearning" was already a prominent theme in Pamela Sue Anderson, *A Feminist Philosophy of Religion: The Rationality and Myths of Religious Belief* (Oxford:

Blackwell, 1998): see, for example, 171–75, 213–15, 225–26.

23 Ibid. 233.

24 Ibid. 234, 235. She notes (239) that Julia Kristeva affirms forgiveness as a "solution to the inertia of melancholia": see Kristeva, *Black Sun: Depression and Melancholia*, trans. Leon S. Roudiez (New York: Columbia UP, 1989) 189–90.

25 Pamela Sue Anderson, *Re-visioning Gender in Philosophy of Religion: Reason, Love and Epistemic Locatedness* (London: Ashgate, 2012) 104–05.

26 Ibid. 106–10, 142–46.

27 Anderson, "An Ethics of Memory" 234.

28 Anderson, *Re-visioning Gender* 105.

29 Anderson, "An Ethics of Memory" 234.

30 Ibid. 237, citing Hannah Arendt, *The Human Condition*, 2nd ed. (Chicago: U of Chicago P, 1998) 236–37.

31 Ibid. 236, citing Arendt, ibid. 183.

32 Anderson, "An Ethics of Memory" 237–38. See Paul Ricoeur, *Oneself as Another*, trans. Kathleen Blamey (Chicago: Chicago UP, 1992) 266–68.

33 Anderson, "An Ethics of Memory" 238.

34 Ricoeur, "Reflections on a New Ethos" 7.

35 Anderson, "An Ethics of Memory" 242.

36 See John Braithwaite, *Restorative Justice and Responsive Regulation* (Oxford: Oxford UP, 2002) 3–28.

37 Paul S. Fiddes, *The Creative Suffering of God* (Oxford: Oxford UP, 1988) 157–63.

38 Pamela Sue Anderson, "Unselfing in Love: A Contradiction in Terms?" in *Faith in the Enlightenment? The Critique of the Enlightenment Revisited*, eds. Lieven Boeve, Joeri Schrijvers, Wessel Stoker, and Hendrik M. Vroom (Amsterdam: Rodopi, 2006) 257–61.

39 Iris Murdoch, *The Sovereignty of Good* (London: Routledge, 1970) 84; cf. "the long task of unselfing" in Iris Murdoch's novel *Henry and Cato* (London: Chatto, 1976) 143. Anderson, "Unselfing in Love" 247–49.

40 Anderson, "Unselfing in Love" 249.

41 Ibid. 253, 260–61.

42 Ibid. 246.

43 Ibid. 255, citing Murdoch, *Sovereignty of Good* 34.

44 Anderson, "Unselfing in Love" 258.

45 Ibid. 255, citing bell hooks, *Yearning: Race, Gender and Cultural Politics* (Boston: South End, 1990) 111.

46 Anderson, "Unselfing in Love" 257, referring to Ricoeur's phrase "oneself inasmuch as being other" in Ricoeur, *Oneself as Another* 3.

47 Anderson, "Unselfing in Love" 255.

48 Ibid. 253.

49 Ibid. 248.

50 Ibid. 251–52.

51 Ibid 257. Cf. Fiddes, *Creative Suffering of God* 71–76.

52 Paul S. Fiddes, *Freedom and Limit: A Dialogue between Literature and Christian Doctrine* (Macon, GA: Mercer UP, 1999) 160–61, cited by Anderson, "Unselfing in Love" 255–56, 255 n.

53 Anderson, "Unselfing in Love" 260.

54 Ibid. 261.

55 Anderson, "An Ethics of Memory" 236.

56 Anderson, "Unselfing in Love" 260.

57 Ibid. 264.

58 Ibid. 260.

59 Ibid. 264.

60 Ibid. 265.

61 Anderson, "A Feminist Ethics of Forgiveness" 152 n.

62 Jacques Derrida, "To Forgive: The Unforgivable and the Imprescriptible" in *Questioning God*, eds. J.D. Caputo, M. Dooley, and M.J. Scanlon (Bloomington: Indiana UP, 2001) 25–30.

63 Ibid. 28, cf. 8.

64 Jacques Derrida, *On Cosmopolitanism and Forgiveness* (New York: Columbia UP, 2001) 32.

65 Fiddes, *Participating in God* 217–19; for an insistence on conditionality in forgiveness, see Richard Swinburne, *Responsibility and Atonement* (Oxford: Clarendon, 1989) 83–85, 148–52, 160–62.

66 Fiddes, "Memory, Forgetting and the Problem of Forgiveness" 126–27, 132–33. Nigel Biggar, *In Defence of War* (Oxford: Oxford UP, 2013) 61–69, similarly identifies an unconditional "compassion-forgiveness" and a conditional "absolution-forgiveness."

67 Compare Miroslav Volf, who argues for eschatological forgetting: Volf, *The End of Memory: Remembering Rightly in a Violent World* (Grand Rapids, MI: Eerdmans, 2006) 203. For a criticism of Volf, see S. Hauerwas, "Why Time Cannot and Should Not Heal the Wounds of History But Time Has Been and Can Be Redeemed," *Scottish Journal of Theology* 53 (2000): 42–43.

68 Anderson, "Unselfing in Love" 260.

69 The address was given at Mansfield College, Oxford, in a series whose theme was *Getting it Right: Moral Issues of Today*.

70 Pamela Sue Anderson, "A Feminist on Forgiveness. When (Where?) Love and Justice Come Apart" in *Paul Ricoeur: Honoring and Continuing the Work*, ed. Farhang Erfani (Lanham, MD: Lexington, 2011) 107.

71 Ibid. 108, 112.

72 Ibid. 109.

73 Ibid. 114 n., referring to Paul Ricoeur, *Memory, History, Forgetting*, trans. Katherine Blamey and David Pellauer (Chicago: U of Chicago P, 2004) 457–506.

74 Anderson, "A Feminist on Forgiveness" 109.

75 Ibid. 112; my emphasis. See bell hooks, *Remembered Rapture: The Writer at Work* (London: Women's P, 1999) 119.

76 Anderson, "A Feminist on Forgiveness" 115–16 n.

77 Ibid. 108; Ricoeur, *Memory, History, Forgetting* 495.

78 Anderson, "A Feminist on Forgiveness" 107.

79 Ibid. 112.

80 Ibid. 108.

81 Ibid. 114–15 n.

82 See also Pamela Sue Anderson and Jordan Bell, *Kant and Theology* (London: Clark, 2010) 62–65.

83 The narrator always owes an "unpaid debt" to the past, the need to render past events their due by rendering them truthfully: Ricoeur, *Memory, History and Forgetting* 363–64; see also Paul Ricoeur, *The Reality of the Historical Past* (Milwaukee: Marquette UP, 1984) 25–27.

84 Ricoeur, *Memory, History and Forgetting* 502–03.

85 Derrida, *On Cosmopolitanism and Forgiveness* 34–39.

86 Anderson, "A Feminist on Forgiveness" 116.

87 Fiddes, *Past Event and Present Salvation* 178–79.

88 For more detail, see Fiddes, *Participating in God* 216–19.

89 Anderson, "A Feminist on Forgiveness" 110.

90 Ibid. 109; cf. Anderson, "A Feminist Ethics of Forgiveness" 151. See Drucilla Cornell, *At the Heart of Freedom: Feminism, Sex and Equality* (Princeton: Princeton UP, 1998) 8–17, 182–86.

91 Anderson, "A Feminist on Forgiveness" 109.

92 Ibid. 110.

93 Ibid. 111.

94 Ibid. 113.

95 Fiddes, "Restorative Justice and the Theological Dynamic of Forgiveness," *Oxford Journal of Law and Religion* 5.1 (2016): 64–65; Fiddes, *Participating in God* 209–10.

96 Fiddes, *Participating in God* 210.

97 Acts 17.28.

98 Pamela Sue Anderson, "When Justice and Forgiveness Come Apart: A Feminist Perspective on Restorative Justice and Intimate Violence," *Oxford Journal of Law and Religion* 5.1 (2016): 113–34.

99 Ibid. 116–18.

100 See Anderson's acknowledgement, in ibid. 118 n., of the similar idea in Joram Graf Haber, "Feminism and Forgiveness" in *Norms and Values: Essays on the Work of Virginia Held*, eds. Joran Graf Haber and Mark S. Halfon (Lanham, MD: Rowman, 1998) 146–47.

101 Anderson, "When Justice and Forgiveness Come Apart" 114–16. She references (114 n.) Martha Nussbaum's John Locke Lectures on

"Anger and Forgiveness" at the time (2014) in Oxford.

102 Anderson, "When Justice and Forgiveness Come Apart" 117.

103 Ibid 123.

104 Ibid 134.

105 Ibid. 123.

106 Ibid. 116.

107 Fiddes, "Restorative Justice" 56.

108 Braithwaite, *Restorative Justice and Responsive Regulation* 14–16.

109 John Braithwaite, "Redeeming the 'F' Word in Restorative Justice," *Oxford Journal of Law and Religion* 5.1 (2016) 84–86.

110 Anderson, "When Justice and Forgiveness Come Apart" 130.

111 Ibid. 118, referencing Carol Gilligan, *In a Different Voice* (Cambridge, MA: Harvard UP, 1982).

112 Anderson, "When Justice and Forgiveness Come Apart" 128.

113 Ibid. 129.

114 Ibid. 116 n., 131 n.

115 Ibid. 121.

116 Fiddes, "Restorative Justice" 64.

117 Charles Griswold, *Forgiveness: A Philosophical Exploration* (Cambridge: Cambridge UP, 2007) 124.

118 Pamela Sue Anderson, "Arguing for 'Ethical' Vulnerability: Towards a Politics of Care?" in *Exploring Vulnerability*, eds. Heike Springhart and Günter Thomas (Göttingen and Bristol, CT: Vandenhoeck, 2017) 147–62.

119 Ibid. 154–61.

120 Ibid. 158.

121 Ibid. 148–51.

122 See Anderson, "A Feminist on Forgiveness" 106.

123 Anderson, "Arguing for 'Ethical' Vulnerability" 161, citing (for example) Judith Butler, *Precarious Life: The Powers of Mourning and Violence* (London: Verso, 2004).

124 Anderson, "Arguing for 'Ethical' Vulnerability" 153.

125 Ibid. 147–48.

126 Anderson, "When Justice and Forgiveness Come Apart" 115.

127 Anderson, "Arguing for 'Ethical' Vulnerability" 154, cf. 147–48.

128 Ibid. 150.

129 Pamela Sue Anderson, "Towards a New Philosophical Imaginary," eds. Sabina Lovibond and A.W. Moore, in *Love and Vulnerability: Thinking with Pamela Sue Anderson*, ed. Pelagia Goulimari, Spec. issue of *Angelaki: Journal of the Theoretical Humanities* 25.1–2 (2020): 8–22; Anderson, "Creating a New Imaginary for Love in Religion," ed. Paul S. Fiddes, in *Love and Vulnerability: Thinking with Pamela Sue Anderson*, ed. Pelagia Goulimari, Spec. issue of *Angelaki: Journal of the Theoretical Humanities* 25.1–2 (2020): 46–53.

It is a great honour to contribute to this collection of essays in memory of my friend Pamela Sue Anderson. Of course the circumstances mean that the pleasure of doing so is mixed with sadness. Anderson and I spent many happy hours discussing philosophy together. It is impossible for me to convey how much I miss our discussions.

In her written work Anderson generously paid a good deal of critical attention to my own. This is especially true of her last book, *Re-visioning Gender in Philosophy of Religion*.[1] I hope it will not appear too self-indulgent if I use this occasion to respond to some of what she said. I believe that she was guilty of certain errors, both exegetical and philosophical. But only someone who was a stranger to philosophy, and indeed to Anderson herself, could think it the least paradoxical that I choose, as my tribute to her in this context, to dwell on what I take to be such errors. The discussion will eventually turn into a more general reflection on the nature of philosophy. What I have to say at that point will be more speculative. It will concern issues about which I am altogether less confident what the implications of Anderson's views are and how, if at all, I would oppose them – though it speaks volumes about the richness and interest of Anderson's work that it so much as leads us in that direction.

Much of my own work has revolved around a number of dualities. In particular, much of it has revolved around the following five dualities:

(1) true/false
(2) absolute/perspectival
(3) effable/ineffable
(4) sense-possessing/sense-lacking
(5) finite/infinite.

a.w. moore

THE CONCERN WITH TRUTH, SENSE, ET AL. – ANDROCENTRIC OR ANTHROPOCENTRIC?

Before I go any further, I want to make brief comments about the fourth and fifth of these. I begin with a comment about the fourth. This comment is largely terminological. I would *like* to have characterized this fourth duality by simply writing "sensical/nonsensical." But standard English, notoriously and maddeningly, does not give us "sensical." (Or at any rate, it does not *yet* give us "sensical." I suppose it is just a question of time. People are increasingly availing themselves of it.) Would "meaningful/meaningless" have suited my purposes here – or, for that matter, "meaningful/nonsensical"? No. This is because I like to distinguish between that which has sense and that which has meaning: the latter, for me, is a broader notion.

For reasons that I am about to sketch, I believe that there are ways of putting language to use which, on the one hand, exploit the meanings of the words involved but which also, on the other hand, result in something that is strictly speaking nonsensical. And when language *is* put to such use, I see some rationale for classifying what results as having meaning but lacking sense. "Meaningful nonsense" is therefore not, on my lips, oxymoronic.

Concerning the fifth duality, I have a comment about the order of the two terms. Looking at how I have couched the other four dualities, you may suspect that I intend an alignment of sorts. In particular, you may suspect that I see some sort of priority of the first term over the second in each case, or some sort of superiority of the first term to the second. And you might then be surprised that I have not written "infinite/finite" in the fifth case. This would be quite wrong. For one thing, I intend no such alignment in the first four dualities. Secondly, even if I did, it would be entirely unstraightforward how the finite and the infinite related to it. I shall come back to both of these points.

Now Anderson discusses all five of these dualities, largely in the context of two others about which I say very little:

(6) male/female

and, perhaps differently,

(7) masculine/feminine.

Why perhaps differently? Well, here I must tread with caution. There are three reasons for this. First, and most basically, I have no expertise in this area. In particular, I have no expertise in feminism, where any distinction between the sixth duality and the seventh is liable to be especially significant. Secondly, and disconcertingly, I am nevertheless aware that practically *nothing* in this area is uncontroversial. Moreover, much of the controversy is not between feminists and those whose ideas they are critiquing, but among feminists. Thus it is controversial to what extent there really is any serviceable, robust, and objective distinction between the male and the female; to what extent there is any such distinction between the masculine and the feminine; and to what extent there is any such distinction between these two dualities themselves, or, more broadly, between sex and gender, of which this is supposed to be an instance.[2] Thirdly, I find it hard to know where exactly Anderson situates herself with respect to these controversies or how this relates to her discussion of my own work.

But I do know that underlying Anderson's discussion of my work is a constant concern with how evaluation infects our philosophical discourse, and in particular with how it does so through the use of what Bernard Williams calls "thick" concepts, that is to say concepts that have both an evaluative aspect and a descriptive aspect. (A standard example of a thick concept is the concept of infidelity. This has an evaluative aspect inasmuch as, in calling someone unfaithful, you censure that person. But it also has a descriptive aspect inasmuch as you are not entitled to call someone unfaithful unless that person has gone back on some relevant agreement.)[3] The question arises – for anyone, but particularly for anyone with Anderson's interests – what sort of thickness, if any, there is in any of the concepts involved in these seven dualities. And this in turn obviously relates back to the issue of what sort of alignment there is among them. As I have already indicated, I assume no privileging of the first term in each duality over the second, not even when attention is confined to the first four dualities. In fact I assume no interesting alignment at all. This is not to deny that the concepts involved are thick. But, if they are, the thickness is in each case far from straightforward; and the relation between the thickness of each to the thickness of all the others is further still from straightforward.

I hope I will be forgiven if, as a prelude to amplifying on these remarks, I give a lightning sketch of some of my central views about the first five dualities.[4]

Directly relevant to all but the fifth is what I call a representation. By a *representation* I mean anything which has content and which, because of its content, is either true or false.

(Representations thus include assertions, thoughts, judgements, theories, and the like.) Here already the true/false duality is in play. But only the most extreme of philosophical sceptics would deny that it has any right to be, or that it has any significant claim on our attention. Anderson would certainly not deny either of these things.

Among representations – and this is where I invoke the second duality – I distinguish between those that are absolute and those that are perspectival. Absolute representations are not coloured by the feelings, concerns, or values of those who produce them. Nor does their content depend on their location, in any literal or metaphorical sense (in the way, for example, in which the content of a tensed representation depends on the time at which it is produced). In other words, absolute representations are not from any *point of view*. Perspectival representations are. Representations of both kinds, I argue, are possible. I also argue that it is representations of the former kind that scientists, and more specifically physicists, aspire to produce; and that if ever anybody does produce such a thing then it will have to be couched in scientific, and more specifically physical, terms. *If* ever anybody produces such a thing ... I am not committed to the view that anybody ever actually has done so or will do so.

The first two dualities cut right across each other. Absolute representations can be true or false. Perspectival representations can be true or false. Whatever privileging there may be of the true over the false, it does nothing to encourage a privileging of the absolute over the perspectival. Nor, in my view, does anything else. The aspiration to produce absolute representations has its rationale in a certain scientific context. Outside that context it has no rationale whatsoever. In particular – this is important for what will come later – it has no rationale *in philosophy*. Nor is the scientific context itself in any relevant sense privileged.

The third duality is between the effable and the ineffable: this applies within states of knowledge. A state of knowledge is effable if and only if it is a representation, in other words if and only if it has content which makes it true or false – in fact true, given that it is a state of knowledge. But there are, I believe, states of knowledge, indeed important and familiar states of knowledge, that are not of this kind, states of knowledge that lack content and are therefore ineffable. Someone who has ineffable knowledge thereby knows how to do certain things, or knows what it is for certain things to be the way they are, or something of that sort; but he or she does not thereby know *that* anything is the case.[5]

If anyone were to attempt to put such ineffable knowledge into words, then the attempt would be a failure. But the result might be of interest for all that. And indeed I believe that, if the attempt were suitably executed – which admittedly raises some large questions about what would count as a suitable execution, though I shall not dwell on these questions now – then the result would serve to individuate the knowledge, and might even serve to convey it. Even so, the result would, strictly speaking, be a piece of nonsense: this is where the fourth duality is pertinent. (It is also what I had in mind when I spoke earlier of meaningful nonsense.) What would be an example? One example, I argue, would be the sentence: "Absolute representations are not possible." But why do I say that this would be a piece of nonsense, rather than simply false? Because, granted the soundness of my argument that absolute representations *are* possible, or in other words that it is false that they are not, this sentence could not serve its function without being hedged with qualifications that prevented it from being interpreted as *that* falsehood; and indeed, crucially, that prevented it from being interpreted at all.

Another example would be the sentence: "The infinite exists."[6] Why would *this* be nonsensical? Because our very notion of the infinite precludes its existing. It is as if the infinite is too great for that.[7] Or, in Wittgensteinian terms more conducive to the current point, it is as if the very "grammar" of the word "infinite" prevents it from directly characterizing anything in reality.[8]

Am I myself producing nonsense in peddling these ideas, and (in particular) in specifying the sort of nonsense that accrues from attempting to express the inexpressible? I do not think so. I think I can avail myself of the distinction between discussing nonsensical uses of words and indulging in such uses. It is not necessary to talk nonsense in order to talk *about* nonsense: one can say, quite truly, "'Brillig' has two syllables." I aspire, in my discussion of these issues, to produce nothing but sense, and indeed to produce nothing but the truth.

In a conference on the work of Derrida in which I participated and which is the focus of much of Anderson's own discussion (see ch. 4), I gave this some context by saying that the kind of philosophy that I practise, which I called "conceptual philosophy," "has a commitment to the truth."[9] But it is a commitment of a distinctive sort. Derrida, in his reply, pointed out that there are other, quite distinct sorts of commitment to the truth, including a sort that he saw as part of the kind of philosophy that *he* practised. One can be committed to the truth by questioning it, indeed by questioning its very possibility, and by taking nothing for granted about how it relates to language or to sense.[10] So be it. The key point, to repeat, is that I aspire, in my discussion of these issues, to produce nothing but the truth.

Now I briefly relate all of this to the sixth and seventh dualities in my book *Points of View*.[11] I admit there that current scientific theories may, in Sandra Harding's phrase, "bear the mark of their collective and individual creators," and that the creators in turn may "have been distinctively marked as to gender, class, race, and culture."[12] This does not trouble me. As I have already made clear, my argument is an argument for the *possibility* of absolute representations, not for their actuality. I also admit that some of the crucial concepts that I myself use to frame this discussion, including some of the concepts that appear in the first five dualities, contain an element of perspective.[13] This is because they cannot be exercised except from some interpretative point of view. I would be happy to go further and admit that some of them contain an element of thickness, and that they cannot be exercised except from some evaluative point of view. But, if that is so, it has no implications for how I view either the sixth or the seventh duality. There is, as I have been at pains to insist, no presumed alignment in the first five dualities. *A fortiori* there is no presumed alignment that extends from them to the other two; or to the duality between what is to be valued and what is to be disvalued; or, heaven forefend, to all three. For, as I emphasize in my book, although there undeniably has been an ideological alignment of the true and the absolute and the scientific with what is to be valued and with what is either male or masculine (a kind of veneration of scientific practice as a detached, authoritative, rational domination of mother nature), I want no part of it. And I see no reason why the dualities themselves should not survive any such (false) ideology.

But Anderson recoils. She attends to each of the first five dualities and suggests that there is, in my work, an implicit privileging in each of them of the first term over the second; and that this privileging, in fact my very concern with each of these dualities, betrays my gender, precisely what I am keen to deny.

Before I go any further, I want to note straight away that Anderson's discussion becomes somewhat muddied in the case of the fifth duality. This is not a criticism. It relates back to peculiarities of the infinite: the subject matter itself condemns whoever engages with it, at least in this sort of context, to a kind of unclarity. In fact I applaud what Anderson says in this connection. In a section of her book titled "The infinite and gender: an ancient question" (75–79) she discusses Grace Jantzen's interesting classification of the urge for infinitude as "a masculine or male obsession," and then notes that, at the beginning of Western philosophy, most notably among the Pythagoreans, it was the urge for finitude, or the privileging of finitude, that had the (far) better claim to that title. Indeed, Anderson makes significant capital out of such ambivalence, capital that directly subserves her project. For, as she further says, "considering why the infinite is given this or that gender will give us new understandings for the re-visioning of gender" (79). This all strikes me as fundamentally correct – though I also think that the muddying of this part of Anderson's discussion, despite how much of it depends on peculiarities of the infinite, should make us wary of expecting any engagement with the first four dualities to escape the same fate.

Still, let us return to what Anderson says about the first four dualities and to my discomfort with it. Adverting to the conference on the work of Derrida that I have already mentioned, she comments on the all-male list of speakers and remarks that "the philosophical assumption seemed to be one of arguing from a gender-neutral perspective, yet the maleness was conspicuous from another perspective" (67). Later there is a characteristically teasing passage where she suggests that, in my own talk of ineffability – of that which cannot be put into words – I may in fact mean no more than that which cannot "be put into the words of a particular (privileged) perspective within the dominant conceptual scheme" (72). And later still we find discussion of the fact that I, in contrast to Derrida, want to eschew nonsense in favour of what not only has a sense but is true:

> [Moore] [...] distinguishes himself from Derrida in insisting that the affirmation of truth is an ultimate concern [...] Moore is only willing to play with nonsense [i.e., Moore is only willing to engage in playful talk *about* nonsense – he is not willing to produce it himself], while Derrida ironically seems far more serious about nonsense! [...] Moore does not aim to produce nonsense, *or to engage seriously with it.* (73–75; emphasis added)

She expands on this in relation to the early Wittgenstein:

> Wittgenstein's relation to [...] nonsense [...] as set out in his *Tractatus*[14] begins to seem closer to Derrida's relation to nonsense (since he takes it very seriously) than Moore's detached play with nonsense. (81)

Much of chapter 6 of her book develops this idea, dealing as it does with the privileging of truth over falsehood and nonsense.

But I demur. To anyone who knows how great my admiration for Wittgenstein is, this reference to his *Tractatus* should already give pause. As Anderson herself correctly insists later, "it could be that the negative connotations of 'nonsense' should be ignored" (84). Indeed they should. There is an irony here. The passage in which Anderson says this involves a rather spectacular failure of proofreading: it is presented as though it were a quotation from me, whereas it is Anderson's own text, written *in propria persona* and supposedly contra me. The irony is that what she says here is something which in fact, as I have just indicated, I would be only too happy to endorse.[15] I shall come back to this.

But there is more. It is not just that Anderson represents me as denigrating nonsense. She also thereby, however implicitly, represents me as denigrating the female and/or the feminine. For the whole thrust of the chapter from which I have been quoting is that the ineffable, and likewise the nonsensical that attends it, are to be thought of in female or feminine terms. Anderson talks about female mystics, and about the nonsense that they produce. She distances me from them. She writes:

> Moore does not intend to produce nonsense. Instead, he aspires to produce truth. Yet [...] doesn't Moore belie his own gender bias, opting for the sense of effable knowledge, when the female mystic's know-how and the wise woman's tales fail to produce sense – and so truth[?] (84–85)

She goes on to cite how Irigaray makes nonsensical play with images of infinitude; and how Jantzen recognizes the importance of stretching language to represent the "inexhaustible fecundity" of the divine (85). Finally, at the very end of the chapter, she says that we must move beyond "traditional answers to the philosophical question of ineffable knowledge," which are "inadequate insofar as they have failed to acknowledge a necessary tension in our gendered relations to the finite and the infinite, as both corrupting and enabling" (87). She continues:

Philosophy of religion as practised by both those who aspire to produce truth and those who engage seriously with nonsense [...] can acknowledge this tension as the first step towards new ethical and epistemological relations between women themselves, men themselves, and women and men, of different material and social perspectives. (Ibid.)

All of this, I confess, leaves me bemused.

There is, in my discussion of these issues, no privileging of sense over nonsense. True, I aspire in any such discussion to produce only the former, as I have already said. In fact I aspire, whenever I write philosophy, to produce only the former. But this is not because I disparage the production of the latter, or at any rate not all of it. *Some* of it I disparage. Indeed, most of it I disparage. So would Anderson. The production of nonsense that is effectively nothing but a botched attempt to produce sense is certainly to be disparaged. But that is not what Anderson is concerned with here. She is concerned with something of the sort that I described earlier: the creative production of nonsense in a suitably executed attempt to put into words knowledge that cannot be put into words, the sort of thing that may even serve to communicate the knowledge, the sort of thing that I have indicated I am prepared to count, despite its nonsensicality, as meaningful. I do not go in for that practice myself: I confine my engagement with such nonsense to quotations either of other people's work or of certain very elementary examples. But this is not because I disparage the practice. It is because I take myself to be *not very good at it*. Other philosophers are very good indeed at it. Thus I believe that Wittgenstein's *Tractatus* consists largely in the production of such nonsense; also that it is one of *the* great philosophical texts; and indeed, if you were to press me, that it is one of the great works of art. The reason why I aim in my own philosophical practice to produce nothing but sense, and more specifically nothing but the truth, is simply that such is the style of philosophy that I take to be my own *métier*. I do not deny that other styles are possible. And I do not say that other styles are inferior.

It seems to me, then, that Anderson is imposing an unhelpful grid here. In particular, I find her use of the categories of male and female unhelpful. In fact I think there is a real issue, ironically, about what, if anything, prevents us from classifying it as sexist. The thought that it is sexist connects, I believe, with the controversies to which I adverted earlier concerning the sixth and the seventh dualities. There is a threat of self-stultification hereabouts: the threat of meeting an unacceptable stereotyping in regard to such categories with more of the same. Evading this threat, for anyone who seeks to champion the cause of women, means striking a delicate balance. For one staple of championing the cause of women is, precisely, fighting an unacceptable stereotyping of women; but fighting it too hard, in particular fighting it hard enough to undermine any sort of essentialism concerning the category of women, may mean that there is nothing left to champion. To quote Mari Mikkola:

> If feminist critiques of the category *women* are successful, then what (if anything) binds women together, what is it to be a woman, and what kinds of demands can feminists make on behalf of women?[16]

There are, to be sure, various tactics that suggest themselves for confronting this dilemma, including deliberately embracing a kind of sexism in a spirit of deconstruction. I certainly do not mean to suggest that I have found some insuperable objection to what Anderson is doing with the categories of the male and the female in this chapter of her book. I simply say that I do not find it helpful.

Now there is, of course – and this is something that I concede in *Points of View*[17] – a very obvious, very basic, and potentially very damning objection to these attempts of mine to deflect Anderson's critique, and it would be crass for me not to acknowledge it. I mean the objection that I am simply betraying my own male point of view once again. Anderson herself makes some telling points that pertain to this objection in a later chapter where she contrasts ways in which male thinkers manage to make themselves heard with ways in which female thinkers struggle to do so, implying that a certain lack of self-consciousness is integral to the former (see, for example, 126 ff.). Later she refers to "a keen sense of injustice which is often not noticed by a privileged thinker who seems to be reasoning about abstract matters" (137). Obviously it would be unacceptable for me simply to dismiss such thoughts. I would face my own threat of self-stultification if I did.

Nor do I. Such thoughts constitute a crucial caveat to all that I have been saying. If I have been saying it from a male point of view, and if I have been doing so in such a way that I count as benighted, *and* if the situation is remediable, then I am, I hope, receptive to whatever remedy is available. If the situation is *not* remediable, and if this is not due simply to some limitation of mine, then that is itself of real philosophical significance. Either way, more needs to be said, even if it cannot be said by me.

At any rate I not think of myself as saying what I have been saying from a male point of view. Nor do I think that the kind of philosophy that I practise can be practised only from a male point of view. If I could be persuaded that this were the case then it would force me to rethink my whole conception of the discipline.

I want to close by saying a little more about that conception.[18] As I remarked much earlier, I deny that it is the business of philosophers to produce absolute representations. Philosophers have to pursue their discipline from some point of view. And I can see the appeal of the idea that they would do well to pursue it from a female point of view, at least to a greater extent than they currently do. Such an idea might even appear to sit well with my denial that the kind of philosophy that I myself practise can be practised only from a male of point. For this denial does not have to be understood as a claim to neutrality. It can be understood as the claim that the kind of philosophy that I practise can be practised *just as effectively* from a female point of view as it can from a male point of view, a claim that encourages practice of it from both. To repeat: I can see the appeal of such an idea. I think it contains an important insight: the insight, to put it in a way that I hope does not sound too flippant, that philosophy needs to be more in touch with its feminine side. Nevertheless, I do not believe that this insight is well expressed in terms of a female point of view. Talk of a female point of view, at least in this connection, still seems to me too close for comfort to what I find unhelpful in the grid that Anderson imposes.

Admittedly, in trying to find a better way to express the insight, I am, in effect, confronting the very dilemma that I said Anderson confronts: that of finding a way to proclaim the feminine in philosophy without being sexist. I cannot, here and now, offer a satisfactory response to this dilemma. But let me sketch what I think such a response would look like. I think it would begin with the thought that what is really important here is not the relation between philosophy and the feminine, or between philosophy and the masculine, or between philosophy and either the male or the female, but rather the relation between philosophy and the *human*. I follow Bernard Williams in conceiving of philosophy as a humanistic discipline.[19] What this means is that philosophy is in an important sense anthropocentric. It is an attempt, by human beings, from their unique position in the world, to make sense both of themselves and of that position. This is to be distinguished from the claim that philosophy is a branch of anthropology. Philosophy is not the scientific study of human beings; nor of any of the peculiarities that mark the way of life of any human beings. For it is not the scientific study of anything. It does nevertheless have a fundamental concern with human beings and with what it takes to be one. And it is properly pursued, at the most fundamental level, from a human point of view. In so far as this has purchase specifically on women, it is because the best philosophy reflects the *varieties* of human experience, both male and female. But the way in which it does this is by making truths about the varieties of human experience available to everyone.

As far as the differences between the male and the female are concerned – or the differences between the masculine and the feminine, if these are different differences – that these are important, and in particular that they are important to philosophy, I do not dispute. Nor do I dispute that they are profound. But their importance and their profundity, within the ambit of the human, seem to me *as nothing* compared with the importance and the profundity of what unites the human, or with the importance and the profundity of the differences between the human and the non-human. In Spinozist terms, and hence in terms that I know would have been congenial to Anderson herself, the *common notion* "human" seems to me incomparably more significant, to each and every one of us than the common notion "male" or the common notion "female."[20] I take that to be a quite general truth. But I also take it to be a truth with a very particular and very significant application to philosophy, for the reasons sketched above.

None of this, I barely need to say in conclusion, constitutes a decisive objection to anything that Anderson was doing in her work, still less to the general tenor of that work. I have rather expressed a certain dissatisfaction with what she was doing, and gestured at some of what I would do instead. Does this betoken a kind of vulnerability? It leaves *me* feeling vulnerable, in particular by challenging my self-image as a philosopher. Anderson would certainly have been sensitive to this and would have wanted to accommodate it in our ongoing conversation about these issues. I only wish that she were here now to continue that conversation.

disclosure statement

No potential conflict of interest was reported by the author.

notes

1 Farnham: Ashgate, 2012. All unaccompanied references will be to this book.

2 See, for example, Anne Fausto-Sterling, *Sexing the Body: Gender, Politics and the Construction of Sexuality* (New York: Basic, 2000); Elizabeth V. Spelman, *Inessential Woman: Problems of Exclusion in Feminist Thought* (Boston: Beacon, 1988); Judith Butler, *Gender Trouble*, 2nd ed. (London: Routledge, 1999); Mari Mikkola, "Feminist Perspectives on Sex and Gender" in *The Stanford Encyclopedia of Philosophy*, ed. Edward N. Zalta, available <https://plato.stanford.edu/archives/win2017/entries/feminism-gender/> (accessed 25 Nov. 2019).

3 See, for example, Bernard Williams, *Ethics and the Limits of Philosophy* (London: Routledge, 2006) 129–30, 140–41. This idea of a thick concept structures much of chapter 6 of Anderson's book. See, for example, 113.

4 What follows draws principally on my *Points of View* (Oxford: Oxford UP, 1997).

5 A possible exception is someone who has knowledge of a necessary truth: see my "Ineffability and Nonsense" in *Proceedings of the Aristotelian Society*, supp. vol. 77 (2003): 169–93 n. 16. I shall ignore that complication in what follows.

6 This is what Anderson is alluding to at 70, where she writes: "According to Moore, ineffability is 'shown' in 'images of infinitude,'" though I would not express it like that. For clarification of my use of the terminology of "showing," see *Points of View* chapter 7, esp. section 3.

7 Cf. Iris Murdoch, *Metaphysics as a Guide to Morals* (Harmondsworth: Penguin, 1993) 508.

8 Cf. Ludwig Wittgenstein, *Philosophical Remarks*, ed. Rush Rhees; trans. Raymond Hargreaves and Roger White (Oxford: Blackwell, 1975) section XII.

9 "Arguing with Derrida" in *Arguing with Derrida*, ed. Simon Glendinning (Oxford: Blackwell, 2001) 59.

10 Jacques Derrida, "Response to Moore" in *Arguing with Derrida* 84.

11 See *Points of View* 101–02, 108–09.

12 See Sandra Harding, *The Science Question in Feminism* (Milton Keynes: Open UP, 1986) 15.

13 See *Points of View* 98–99.

14 Ludwig Wittgenstein, *Tractatus Logico-Philosophicus*, trans. D.F. Pears and B.F. McGuiness (London: Routledge, 1961).

15 I have another, entirely unrelated and frivolous reason for noting this error in Anderson's text. It reminds me of a bizarre mistake of predictive texting in a message that Anderson once sent me, which resulted in much mutual hilarity. In response to my question whether she was able to accompany me to some event at short notice, instead of replying that she could not because she had a graduate student round helping her to proofread, she replied that she could not because she had a graduate student round helping her to procreate.

16 Op. cit. in note 2. For discussion of some of the issues that arise here, see Natalie Stoljar, "Essence, Identity and the Concept of Woman" in *Philosophical Topics* 23 (1995): 261–93; Linda Martín Alcoff, *Visible Identities: Race, Gender, and the Self* (Studies in Feminist Philosophy) (Oxford: Oxford UP, 2006).

17 See 109.

18 One of Anderson's own concerns is with the nature of philosophy. Her specific focus is the philosophy of religion; but it can scarcely be denied that this has, and is intended to have, repercussions for the discipline as a whole: cf. 47–48.

19 See Bernard Williams, "Philosophy as a Humanistic Discipline," reprinted in his *Philosophy as a Humanistic Discipline*, ed. A.W. Moore (Princeton: Princeton UP, 2006). I try to defend the view in "Sense-Making from a Human Point of View" in *The Cambridge Companion to Philosophical Methodology*, eds. Giuseppina D'Oro and Søren Overgaard (Cambridge: Cambridge UP, 2017).

20 See Benedictus de Spinoza, *Ethics* in *Spinoza: Complete Works*, ed. Michael L. Morgan; trans. Samuel Shirley (Indianapolis: Hackett, 2002) Pt. II, Props. 37 and 40, Scholium 2. See also ibid. Pt. IV, Props. 35–37 (couched admittedly in what would now be classified as sexist terminology).

In her most recent work, my sadly missed friend Pamela Sue Anderson was engaged in a creative rethinking of the facts of "mutual vulnerability in philosophical relations."[1] The idea of vulnerability usually has negative connotations: to be vulnerable is to be exposed to violence. In order to follow Pamela here, however, we have to think of it as potentially positive too – that is, as a condition of openness to the love of one's neighbour, and as an ability to form "bonds of affection that would enhance life," as Paul Fiddes puts it in a helpful commentary.[2] For certain academic purposes, a valuable approach to the formation of such bonds may be found by venturing out of the study or library and towards a more collective way of working, as advocated in particular by Michèle Le Doeuff in her classic paper "Women and Philosophy."[3] This is a source from which Pamela will have drawn abundant inspiration, not least because she and Michèle had a track record of collaboration extending over many years.

Of course, any attempt to picture the experience of vulnerability as *life-enhancing* may initially strike us as fanciful, or as lacking in sensitivity to life's "harsh realities."[4] Pamela is aware of this difficulty, but wants to take a step back and derive some general existential insight from our particular moments of disorientation and abjection – to give due weight to the *ever-present* possibility of being cut loose by one's audience when one presumes to speak; of being ridiculed or ignored. This involves a bold imaginative projection on to the recognized bearers of intellectual authority of the kind of thing that happens routinely to people who don't look or sound right for the

sabina lovibond

VULNERABLE AND INVULNERABLE
two faces of dialectical reasoning

setting in which they undertake to express themselves – for example, by reason of skin colour (like bell hooks[5]); or by simply being female, which seems to be at the root of Pamela's appalling account of the quasi-pornographic humour, or pornographic quasi-humour, she met with herself on a visit to the philosophy department at one of our leading universities.[6] An admonition is, in effect, being issued here. Don't forget, master-thinkers: no one is in a place of absolute safety as regards credibility; you, too, depend on the civil and respectful attitude of those you are addressing, an attitude which you perhaps take for granted; you might do well to ask yourselves how it would be if this were withdrawn.

I want to suggest that Pamela's embrace of the idea of vulnerability, or of the "precariousness" of life, can be understood – at any rate in its application to philosophy – as pointing to our alienation from the founding values of the discipline we are supposed to be practising: that is, from philosophical enquiry in the tradition we inherit from Plato. As I will try to explain, what I have in mind is not the transient experience of some kind of sour mood but a general or structural condition of alienation.

Again, this suggestion may appear counter-intuitive. Some of Pamela's remarks on the emotional incentives at work in philosophy sound highly critical in relation to the mainstream: for example, when she says that "Striving for invulnerability – whether as the man with a gun for 'self-protection' or the philosopher with an argument for his shield against his vulnerability – puts us at a serious human risk. And it misses the opportunity that vulnerability can offer."[7] These criticisms are far from being groundless. It is true that military imagery (the ideal of immunity to any possible attack) is in the forefront of Plato's mind as he develops his world-historic conception of "dialectic" – that is, "conversation" in a specialized sense, capable of leading us to the stable possession of truth. Most importantly,

> If a man can't define the form of the good and distinguish it clearly in his account, and then battle his way through all objections [*hôsper en machêi dia pantôn elenchôn diexiôn*], determined to give them refutation based on reality and not opinion, and come through with his argument unshaken, you wouldn't say he knew what the good in itself was, or indeed any other good.[8]

This quest for argumentative "immunity" is obviously informed by an awareness that our current opinions or modes of reasoning may turn out to be faulty – and hence vulnerable to attack – in all kinds of unforeseen ways. If that is the case, we must be prepared to amend them accordingly, or to get rid of them. (There is no disgrace in changing one's mind; only, one should try to do so lucidly and not in a way that generates muddle.[9]) But the point of these principles is to guide one towards an epistemic condition that will remain "unshaken" by any further criticism.[10]

And yet it is worth looking back at the ordinary (incomplete, imperfect) paradigm of conversation from which this idealized version emerges. What could be more "vulnerable" than the sacrificial figure of Socrates – and this, too, is a Platonic construct – who does not claim to *know* anything, since he concludes that "human wisdom has little or no value" and that the closest we can come to wisdom is to achieve an awareness of our own incapacity? And who claims to have dedicated his life to the service of God – even at the price of being reduced to extreme poverty?[11] Others may represent themselves as experts and earn fees for their teaching, but Socrates' contribution consists in the much less marketable activity of discrediting various people's false intellectual pretensions, an activity which (in principle, at least) does not even lend itself to impressive speeches but relies on the succinct exchange of question and answer.[12] I think it is fair to say that the attitude celebrated here, through the portrayal of Socrates as intellectual gadfly with no worldly status to defend, is precisely one of vulnerability – not just because it will never make him rich, but also by virtue of his acceptance of a state of constant exposure to the hazards of criticism and refutation; and fair to say, too, that the recommended mode of enquiry is collective – the quest for understanding in a setting of affectionate, often homoerotic friendship, though this can always be disrupted by scornful and hostile intruders. At all events, "Socrates" as we meet him at his trial seems to gesture towards those very realities of philosophical discussion – the contingency of our social experience, the chronic negativity and inconclusiveness of what is achieved – which "Socrates" in the *Republic* is seeking to transcend.

There are these two sides to the dialectical encounter as pictured at the outset of our tradition: on one hand the confession of ignorance, *aporia*, being-at-a-loss; on the other, the desire to rise above or escape from that state, to be *no longer* at a loss because rendered immune through critical discussion to the objections that could be levelled against one's earlier views. Both sides are integral to the picture. The intellectual defence reflex is integral, because it is not actually *pleasant* to be at a loss: this is a condition for which one will want to find a remedy. Yet this condition, if fully experienced, is our mode of access to intellectual improvement:[13] without a consciousness of the "precarity" of my present state of understanding, I will not be motivated to engage with others to fortify it.

It's arguable, then, that the theme of vulnerability or precarity has been – at least implicitly – present in European philosophy almost from the beginning. But if that is so, the question arises as to why writers like Pamela (or like Judith Butler[14]) still take themselves to have so much critical work to do. One part of the answer to this question will be that Plato himself, with his craving for stability and permanence, all too readily loses sight of the positive value of what is "precarious" in our thinking. But we may also feel that the idea of precarity in its ancient (Socratic) guise is too abstract to express the concerns of "interloper" contributors to philosophy – I mean of those who, for one reason or another, don't find themselves welcomed into whatever in our own social experience has replaced the circle of affection (and diffuse eroticism) formed by Socrates and his young male friends. These concerns do not take up the entire space of Pamela's recent thought, but they do provide one of its starting-points.

Ultimately, says Pamela, the aim of her current research is

> to set out possibilities for a new philosophical imaginary, in which *vulnerability is (re)conceived as a capability for an openness to mutual affection* [...] In particular, developing reciprocal affections in vulnerability would help to revise a weak concept of love: reciprocity would facilitate loving affection in mutual, self and other relations. But this affecting needs to be learnt by allowing ourselves to attend to each other [...] "tenderly," respectfully, sincerely and so, lovingly.[15]

In passages like this, she seems almost to be speaking the language of exhortation or prophecy – proposing not merely a code of good practice for the academic philosophy seminar as we know it but a full-scale philosophical anthropology based on the idea of "vulnerability as a universal," although the "concrete manifestations [of vulnerability] will be socially and historically differentiated."[16]

I don't myself have a very clear idea of what it would be like to go beyond a mode of philosophical conversation answerable to the familiar imperatives of civility and unprejudiced attention – which, after all, are hard enough to live up to – and to move on to the development of "reciprocal affections in vulnerability" as described by Pamela. But I can certainly enter into the motivation for her project as it relates specifically to philosophy: namely, the wish to effect a change of heart towards the "interloper," whether represented by oneself or by another. Viewing this project in terms of "concrete manifestations," it's clear that the post-1968 period was a time of real curiosity about the working of academic institutions and their accessibility (or otherwise) to socially subordinate groups: here we may think not only of Le Doeuff's path-breaking work but also, for instance, of Pierre Bourdieu's *Homo Academicus*, which deals in massive statistical detail with the determinants of progress in the French academic career structure, though it focuses almost exclusively on matters of class and geography.[17] A reawakening of that curiosity today might be signalled by some fresh thinking of a practical, Le Doeuffian nature about what actually constitutes the vulnerability of women (and other non-privileged participants) in the current context of philosophical discourse.[18] I assume Pamela would agree that those already discernible forms of vulnerability or precarity induced by the institutional politics of higher education – by being subject to sexual harassment, intellectual inattentiveness, social exclusion, inadequate mentoring, and so forth – will need to be addressed before we can do justice to the more utopian aspects of her vision. (And there may be colleagues and students working under various kinds of ideologically oppressive regime who would greet the list just offered, sobering though it is, with a murmur of "first-world problems.")

However, a more fundamental difficulty now suggests itself. One might put it to Pamela: is it, in fact, possible to eliminate the ideal of invulnerability from the practice of philosophy? After all, you yourself were a colleague – you, too, had to make it your business to transmit the principles of our craft to a younger generation, who can be pictured as undergoing a certain kind of apprenticeship in thinking. Some aspects of this apprenticeship are indeed of an ethical nature – for example, one learns that there is more to making progress in philosophy than merely winning arguments or keeping one's initial position intact; and one takes on board the "principle of charity," meaning that before embarking on criticism of other people's views one had better expound or reconstruct them in the most favourable terms permitted by the available evidence, rather than wasting time on some self-serving travesty. All this belongs to the "open" spirit of philosophical sociability. But then – you too (Pamela) spent a large part of your working life preparing students for exams and advising them on their essays or theses. And in doing so you could hardly avoid the normal, and required, investment in values of *immunity to criticism* – of argumentative force, coherence, non-contradiction, validity, sound selection of premises, and so forth. Of course, cognitive "invulnerability" without qualification is a mere regulative idea, not something one expects to achieve within any noticeably adventurous or interesting line of reflection. You aptly cite Le Doeuff on "the unknown and the unthought, which need to be reintroduced continually, in order to avoid a fixation on the completeness of one's knowledge."[19] Still, the project of anticipating criticism and preparing to meet it effectively – this does not really seem detachable from philosophy per se, on any reasonably consensual understanding of that term. The acceptance of vulnerability does have an important role in philosophical thinking, but mainly (one might argue) in enabling the thinker to tolerate uncertainty, perplexity, the state of coexistence with unresolved questions or problems – and, of course, with the irreducible "otherness" of other enquirers. This state leaves one vulnerable to the familiar, but unnerving, experience of being forced (on pain of dishonesty) to reply to a question by saying "I don't know": even if the question relates to the very thing about which one has ventured an opinion. The demands imposed by this unnerving experience set a test of character; and they contribute also to the *formation* of character, since they help to implant a sceptical and self-critical spirit that will remain with us through life, regardless of any strictly academic involvement. So the value of the experience lies at least to some extent beyond itself, in the power to hold open a space for renewed enquiry in future – a space that can easily be shut down by boredom, impatience, or some other form of discouragement.

But with regard to philosophy as a self-conscious exercise, the question to which we seem to be directed by Pamela's discussions is that of the relationship between a more purely epistemological and a more empirical interpretation which can be given to the terms "vulnerable" and "invulnerable." The point made just now about immunity to criticism (as a value internal to philosophy) belongs on the epistemological side of this divide. And to make that point is not to minimize the massive scope that there surely is for doing philosophy differently, and especially for finding ways to allow ourselves more of the pleasure of meeting and conversing in (at least comparative) freedom from abusive tendencies such as "quieting" and "smothering."[20] A lot of brave and resourceful work has gone into the description of these social tendencies – which, qua social, are a proper object of empirical record, but this is not to say that their operation is just *obvious*. (Compare the case of "sexual harassment," a term invented at a quite specific moment in the late 1960s, but promptly and widely experienced as meeting an unfilled hermeneutic need.) That work needs to be remembered and developed, and it also needs to be supplemented by a consciousness of the ceaseless moral and intellectual encouragement which some people are fortunate enough to get from their earliest years, and others are not. This (ambient, structural) encouragement, too, is a social phenomenon. As Le Doeuff puts it, some people "receive *too much* support and, from time to time, learn the terrible lessons of impudence and lawless will."[21] Though when it comes to the belief that "the invulnerable have a superior life" – is this belief really an "imaginary" one, as Pamela suggests?[22] It seems plausible enough to me, except in so far as one is led to picture the invulnerability of this or that privileged group in unrealistically absolute terms.

In the end, however – assuming I'm right about the "dialectic" of vulnerability and invulnerability which characterizes philosophy a priori – the conclusion I would draw is that when we think about our discipline in a spirit of institutional critique, we have to do (unsurprisingly, relative to the business of critique) with a certain mismatch, or lack of fit, that exists between the a priori and the empirical: in this case, between the dialectic just mentioned and, on the other hand, the lived experience of vulnerability about which some practitioners of the subject know so much more than others. This is an experience which is evidently close to Pamela's heart in her later work.

disclosure statement

No potential conflict of interest was reported by the author.

notes

1 Pamela Sue Anderson, "Silencing and Speaker Vulnerability: Undoing an Oppressive Form of (Wilful) Ignorance," ed. Nicholas Bunnin, in *Love and Vulnerability: Thinking with Pamela Sue Anderson*, ed. Pelagia Goulimari, Spec. issue of *Angelaki: Journal of the Theoretical Humanities* 25.1–2 (2020) 36. All references to Pamela in the present discussion are to material contained in a dossier of unfinished writings compiled shortly after her death. I am very grateful to Pelagia Goulimari for making this work available, and for the leading part she played in organizing the March 2018 conference at Mansfield College, Oxford, dedicated to Pamela's memory. Thanks also to everyone who took part in discussion of this paper in its earlier form as a talk delivered on that occasion; and to Alison Assiter for written comments.

2 Pamela Sue Anderson, "Creating a New Imaginary for Love in Religion," ed. Paul S. Fiddes, in *Love and Vulnerability: Thinking with Pamela Sue Anderson*, ed. Pelagia Goulimari, Spec. issue of *Angelaki: Journal of the Theoretical Humanities* 25.1–2 (2020) 47.

3 Reprinted in *French Feminist Thought: A Reader*, ed. Toril Moi (Oxford: Blackwell, 1987).

4 Anderson, "Silencing and Speaker Vulnerability" 42. The phrase "harsh realities" is Pamela's. For some topical input on these realities, see *The Guardian* (G2) 26 July 2017, where a woman Labour MP is quoted as saying (about the recent murder of her colleague Jo Cox): "We don't have bodyguards, we don't wear flak jackets; we are completely vulnerable." See also *The Guardian* 6 Sept. 2017: "Diane Abbott received almost half of all the abusive tweets sent to female MPs in the run-up to the general election, an Amnesty International study reveals."

5 Anderson, "Silencing and Speaker Vulnerability" 38.

6 Ibid. 36–37.

7 Ibid. 43.

8 *Republic* VII, 534bc, trans. Desmond Lee (Harmondsworth: Penguin, 1974).

9 Another Platonic observation: *Republic* I, 345b.

10 Even Wittgenstein, for all the radicalism of his later method, continues to aspire to a state of "*complete* clarity," meaning that the problems of philosophy should "*completely* disappear" (*Philosophical Investigations*, 3rd ed., trans. G.E.M. Anscombe (Oxford: Basil Blackwell, 1967), section 133; emphasis added).

11 See *Apology* 23ac, trans. Hugh Tredennick (Harmondsworth: Penguin, 1969).

12 Compare *Protagoras* 329b.

13 Compare *Meno* 84bc.

14 See, for example, her *Precarious Life: The Powers of Mourning and Violence* (London and New York: Verso, 2004), especially chapter 5.

15 Pamela Sue Anderson, "Towards a New Philosophical Imaginary," eds. Sabina Lovibond and A.W. Moore, in *Love and Vulnerability: Thinking with Pamela Sue Anderson*, ed. Pelagia Goulimari, Spec. issue of *Angelaki: Journal of the Theoretical Humanities* 25.1–2 (2020) 8; emphasis in original.

16 Anderson, "Towards a New Philosophical Imaginary" 9.

17 *Homo Academicus* [1984], trans. Peter Collier (Cambridge: Polity, 1988; first published in French).

18 I am expressing myself speculatively here because I do not feel qualified to report on relevant discussions actually in progress at the present time – but, of course, this is not meant to imply that they are not happening.

19 Anderson, "Silencing and Speaker Vulnerability" 44.

20 Pamela credits these terms to Kristie Dotson (Anderson, "Silencing and Speaker Vulnerability" 38–39). She explains that "quieting" takes place when an audience refuses to listen, while "smothering" involves the self-suppression or "coerced silencing" of a speaker; either way, communication fails because the speaker is not recognized as a "knower" by the relevant audience.

21 *Hipparchia's Choice: An Essay Concerning Women, Philosophy, Etc.*, trans. Trista Selous (Oxford: Blackwell, 1991) 281–82; emphasis added.

22 Anderson, "Creating a New Imaginary for Love in Religion" 49.

introduction

In a recent article, Michael McGhee draws attention to the connection between personal experience and the themes pursued by the individual philosopher.[1] Suggesting philosophy is never purely "objective" or "detached" is not new. Feminist scholars have long identified the importance of the personal for philosophical reflection. As Patricia Hill Collins notes, the theoretical and the practical are intimately connected in feminist politics.[2] This article develops that connection by considering friendship as a vital way of constructing philosophical practice as a means of enabling wisdom. It is also written as a response to the death of my friend and sometimes collaborator Pamela Sue Anderson in 2017.

Pamela and I met at a conference held towards the end of the 1990s. We had known of each other through our common interest in feminist philosophy of religion. Pamela was in the final stages of writing the book which was to become a landmark publication in this area.[3] Common interests brought us together; her openness, warmth, and naughty sense of humour ensured we became friends. That friendship deepened through the time we spent together, through a miscarriage I suffered in 1999, and then, later, through the illness and death of her partner Paul. It was also framed by working together on a collection of essays in feminist philosophy of religion.[4] You learn a lot about someone when editing, and I remember fondly sitting together in the spring of 2003 as we put that volume together. As is common with a lot of friendships – particularly in the frenetic climate of the contemporary academy – we went through periods of seeing

beverley clack

WISDOM, FRIENDSHIP AND THE PRACTICE OF PHILOSOPHY

each other a lot, and then not that much. During the last months of her illness we renewed the depth of our friendship. Our last conversation inspired this paper, during which we talked about the potential of friendship to be transformative.

Pamela's last paper, given *in absentia* at a British Academy conference on vulnerability, finds her reflecting on the problem of being a woman in philosophy.[5] She highlights the isolation, the belittling of women's ideas, the problems of being a sometimes solitary female voice in a discipline dominated by men. Alongside these somewhat sad reflections is the call for solidarity between women, for this is one of the ways in which we can ensure the voices of women are heard. To show solidarity is to support each other; and this means taking practical steps to challenge those who would dismiss the things that women have to say. Feminist philosophy emerges as a grounded practice *demanding* solidarity.

The boldness of this last paper makes it a fitting conclusion to Pamela's philosophical work. Her philosophy steps out of the shadows to reveal aspects of her life, weaving the two intimately together. My article picks up on a theme implicit in Pamela's paper: friendship. How might the practices of friendship enable renewed thinking about what it is to be a philosopher in the twenty-first century? It is impossible to think about the practice of philosophy without considering the shape of the university that invariably provides the context for its practice. Philosophy is that part of the academy that *should* more than any other subject provide a space for the critical engagement with thought; but it also promises more than that, for it offers a space for thinking explicitly about how our thought enables the development of wisdom.

To talk of wisdom might seem old-fashioned. It is not necessarily the first word we think of when attending to the demands of the twenty-first-century university. The university has not escaped the trend of the last forty years in Western societies to view everything through the lens of the economic. Structured in response to neoliberal concerns with financialization, utility, and employability, the contemporary university is not necessarily amenable to ideas of what it is to be wise. This is particularly problematic for philosophy, given that wisdom is its central, organizing principle. Philosophers do many things, partake in many different fields, and focus on many different themes; yet informing these practices is the implicit assumption that something vital is performed when we think philosophically that reveals the nature of being human. To be human is to have the capacity to think seriously about life and how best to live. As Pamela puts it, philosophical practice revolves around this question: "Can one make sense of one's life while living it?"[6] In what follows, I suggest that shaping philosophical practice through the lens of friendship invites a reframing of the university as a place which enables the cultivation of wisdom: an idea sadly at odds with its current economic framing, but with the potential to revitalize both philosophical enquiry and the university.

the problem of the neoliberal university

It is tempting to consider the practices of philosophy as if they are unaffected by the political framing of the university as an institution. This will not do, for the form the university takes has considerable impact on the practice of the philosophy taught and researched within it, as I intend to show. In considering the pressures on philosophical practice arising from its placing in a specific political time and place, my comments emanate, necessarily, from the context of the United Kingdom; there is, however, likely to be considerable overlap with the practices of universities in other places, given that the agenda shaping UK universities is one transcending national boundaries.

Recent commentators on the challenges facing universities include Stefan Collini,[7] Martha Nussbaum,[8] and Bob Brecher.[9] If Collini uses John Henry Newman as his conversation partner, the political philosopher Michael Oakeshott, writing in the 1950s, acts as a helpful interlocutor for the framing of my reflections when he sets out the problems facing the academy of his day:

> The university will have ceased to exist when its learning has degenerated into what is now called research, when its teaching has become mere instruction and occupies the whole of an undergraduate's time, and when those who have come to be taught come, not in search of their intellectual fortune, but with a vitality so unroused or so exhausted that they wish only to be provided with a serviceable moral and intellectual outfit; when they come with no understanding of the manners of conversation but desire only a qualification

for earning a living or a certificate to let them in on the exploitation of the world.[10]

Some seventy years on, this description fits rather too well with the experience of those teaching and researching in many (perhaps most) British universities. (Members of "elite" institutions may not recognize their experience in the words of this passage; this is unlikely, I think, given the role government frameworks have played in shaping the practice of *all* Higher Education institutions since the 1980s.[11]) In post-1992 universities, certainly, Oakeshott's fears reflect the situation all too accurately. Academics' work is fragmented into "research" and "teaching," with hours assigned to each as if they constitute discrete tasks. Students are encouraged to visualize their relationship to their tutors as that of customer to service provider: a model which is hardly surprising, given that the fees structure suggests they are indeed paying for the "services" of their tutors. The question of whether they are getting "value for money" inevitably arises. Is the student (or their parent) getting a good return on their financial investment? Will the student be able to achieve a well-paid "graduate" job? The implication of asking such questions is illustrated in reports in 2018 that Hull University was to close its Philosophy programme. We might expect recruitment to be the issue. This was not, however, the case: students *wanted* to study philosophy at Hull. When pressed to explain the university's proposal, Hull's registrar explained that the intention was "to ensure that [a student's] qualification holds value over time," as well as that the university "meets the needs of our students, research and business partners."[12] In other words, philosophy must go as its graduates are not the kind of workers required by today's businesses, and certainly not by those businesses where they are likely to make the most money.

This example suggests something of just how far reaching are the consequences of framing the university and what happens within it through the lens of the economic. We might well see in this example Oakeshott's fears about what happens to the university when it is understood solely as a means to an end. What is *the function* of an education? What is a university *for*?

Oakeshott focuses explicitly on that last question. Writing in the aftermath of the Second World War, and against the backdrop of a post-war Labour government anxious to shape a new, fairer society, he directs his attention to the problem of shaping of the university as a tool for achieving governmental goals. The ideals shaping this government's policies might seem benign, their aim to develop a more inclusive, socially just society. Yet Oakeshott is worried about the effect of prioritizing a set of political imperatives. The very idea of what constitutes "the university" is undermined by such an approach. His account of what makes for a university shows why he thinks this. The university is "not a machine for achieving a particular purpose or producing a particular result; *it is a manner of human activity.*"[13]

To define the university as "a manner of activity" is to understand the university as an ongoing conversation, a place for talking and thinking. It is a community bound together by a shared conversation. The aim of the university is thus to promote "the pursuit of learning as a cooperative exercise."[14] There is no end point to such a vision, no handy cut-off point for this ongoing conversation. The university is "not a machine"[15] committed to producing a uniform and clearly determined end. To even ask what the university is *for* is to fall prey to forces that would reduce all forms of value to questions of usefulness. To be part of a university is to be part of an ongoing conversation that cannot be so neatly circumscribed. For Oakeshott, this conversation has a particular form, for it involves dialogue with the historical texts that have shaped "our" culture.[16] He is explicit as to the nature of the culture to which he refers. The university is concerned with explaining and communicating a set of specific historical texts that form the basis for a shared cultural life. The conclusion is, he claims, that the university is "unavoidably conservative."[17]

Here, the liberal academic, working in a *multi*cultural context, may well feel uncomfortable, for Oakeshott, presumably, will have no truck with ideas of broadening the canon, or challenging the whiteness or maleness of the curriculum. His university is a "conservative" institution. Before rejecting such an idea out of hand, however, it is worth thinking a little more about what exactly we might want to "conserve" when we consider the university. What happens if it is framed as an institution through "progressive" ideals? Oakeshott's contention is that it is *the practices* of the university that require conservation. Historically, the university has been shaped as a place for thinking and talking: no more, no less. Oakeshott's anxiety centres on what he sees as the politicizing of the academy. Viewed from the vantage point of 2019, the concerns of the 1945 Labour government with which Oakeshott takes issue may well be ones we wish to endorse. Attempting to create a more equal society out of the rubble of the Second World War, and thus to see the universities as important motors for social change, seems all very laudable. Yet what Oakeshott identifies are the problems that arise when the university is seen primarily from the perspective of *governmental* concerns to address wider social issues. Claims about its *use* – the ends to which it should be directed – come to define the work of the university, *not* its historical shaping as a place of ongoing conversation into which students are inducted.

If Oakeshott was bothered by the political shaping of the university of his day we have cause to be even more concerned by political interventions which would determine the function of a university education. Today's university is not even seen as an institution that can address entrenched social injustice. If it were, maintenance grants for the very poorest students would not have been scrapped in 2016, nor attempts at cultivating "lifelong learning" shunted to the sidelines. The university of *our* times is shaped by economic imperatives that see it as valuable only if it contributes to the work of wealth creation, or when its resources are directed to training the skilled workers required by business. There are dangers when defining a university education through its function, for invariably functional accounts force it to amend its core activities to whatever political ideas are in vogue at the time. These might be laudable, but, then again, they might not. Either way, they distort what the university *should* be.

To understand the politics which shapes the universities of our time, it is necessary to interrogate the dominant political and economic ideology of the last forty years: neoliberalism. If Enlightenment thinkers conceived the individual as rational, autonomous, free, capable of choice, the contemporary iteration of that account of the human subject locates the individual in an explicitly *economic* setting. Emerging in the late 1940s as a response to the perceived threat of the Keynesian State for individuals and for business, the ideas of this "new liberalism" came into their own as politicians sought new solutions to the political crises of the 1970s.[18] The triumph of neoliberalism in the governments of Ronald Reagan in the United States and Margaret Thatcher in the United Kingdom involved instigating economic policies which would free up business through the cutting of red tape and the curbing of the public sector. But this was never just a political movement consisting of a set of discrete economic policies. More dramatically, the aim was "to maximise competition and competitiveness, and to allow the market to permeate all aspects of life."[19] This "financialisation of everything"[20] required areas previously located outside the scope of business and the market – health, education, social services – to be understood through the needs of business and the imperative to create economic growth.[21] As Wendy Brown notes, neoliberalism is not simply an economic policy but rather "a governing rationality that disseminates market values and metrics to every sphere of life."[22]

"Every sphere of life" is to be subjected to a business ethos. "The Market" becomes a *regulatory* tool that transcends the messiness of human relationships. While human beings are subjective and open to bias, the Market is objective and neutral.[23] Economic assessment becomes the principal criterion for assigning meaning, with right- and left-wing governments accepting this framing of reality. Not only are institutions to be viewed through an economic lens. The new economics requires a new kind of individual: one shaped as an economic unit, detached from community, capable of responding to the demands of a new, global, and connected world. The individual is a mini-business, a human resource, an entrepreneurial subject,[24] capable of shaping their own social, economic and political destiny. In a series of lectures given in the late 1970s, Michel Foucault provides a neat name for this new human being: "homo economicus" or "Economic Man".[25]

Education is not immune from this extension of the economic. How do you ensure citizens have the right skills for successfully negotiating a world which demands flexible employment? As funding models changed, so universities could not escape engaging with this question. The university began to be modelled as if it were a business. Vice Chancellors took on the character of CEOs; self-governance gave way to managerialism. Targets were routinely set, and competition enshrined as the mechanism for determining where funding should go. Collini provides some key dates which enabled this shift in the nature of the university. The year 1981 saw savage cuts to university funding. In 1986, funding for research was tied to the first Research Assessment Exercise. The year 1988 saw changes to the legal status of academic tenure, with university funding now dependent on delivering reforms and meeting targets. In 1992, "new universities" were created out of the old polytechnics: in part to further "diversify" the kind of university education on offer to students. The expansion in student numbers seen during this period was, crucially, not accompanied by increased investment, with the result that the "unit cost" of Higher Education was driven down.[26] Accompanying these structural changes was a shift in how the student was encouraged to view their experience. No longer shaped through studying a subject for its own sake, "being a student" now involved learning a set of skills *through a subject* that would enable them to become the adaptable worker needed by the broader economy.

Being an academic in such a context also changed. "Quality Assurance" measures ensured that "learning outcomes" and "learning objectives" determined the end point of teaching. Attention to transferable skills shifted the gaze from the content of disciplines to the creation of "flexible" learners. Subject to the forces of competition, all academics could not but be aware of the external factors governing their research. Consider the effect of attaining a coveted 4* rating in the regular "Research Excellence Framework" exercises. This grading never simply denotes the quality of one's work, but is required if one's institution is to attain the funding it needs. Fail to achieve the funding and there is a very real possibility that your department or subject area will close as economically unviable.

It would be a mistake to see competition as completely alien to the academy. Literary representations of academics as solitary, arrogant, obsessed with attaining some treasure or besting some rival would not be so commonplace if they did not reflect to some degree the reality. If we return to Oakeshott, a rather different view of our relationship, one with the other, emerges: "The pursuit of learning is not a race in which the competitors jockey for the best place, it is not even an argument or a symposium; *it is a conversation.*"[27]

The apparently nebulous notion of a conversation might lead philosophers – already on the back foot under the imperative to see everything through the lens of the economic – to avoid this framing for justifications of their discipline. The "value" of philosophy might be attempted on economic grounds: its "transferable skills" of critical thought enable students to "think outside the box," a quality that comes from philosophical study and that businesses report liking.[28] This approach may be pragmatic, but it implicitly accepts the claim that only in the economic is meaning to be found.

Stefan Collini provides an alternative approach which reflects Oakeshott's claim that conversation provides a more fitting model for the university. His advice is simple: resist offering reductionist economic answers to the meaning of the university by stating over and over the *practices* of academics and what it means to be *educated*. The university is "a protected space in which various forms of useful *preparation for life* are undertaken in a setting and manner which encourages students to understand the contingency of any packet of knowledge and its interrelations with other, different forms of knowledge."[29]

The university is *a space that allows for preparation for life*. Framing a subject like philosophy economically ignores this broader placing. Restating what education involves enables resistance to be made to the functionalist accounts misshaping it. Here, Oakeshott's model of conversation does more than suggest the place of philosophy in the life of the university. Modelled as a conversation, philosophical enquiry also looks rather different. "It has no predetermined course, we do not ask what it is 'for', and we do not judge its excellence by its conclusion; it has no conclusion, but is always put by for another day."[30] We might well return to the existential questions with which the philosopher was once intimately engaged: why are we born? Why do we love? Why do we suffer? Why do we die? How do we make sense of our existence? These are questions that can never be concluded, for they arise from human experience and thus always require fresh engagement.

Feminist philosopher Michèle Le Doeuff suggests a similar vision of the philosopher as engaged in an open-ended conversation. To be a philosopher does not involve joining a particular school of thought; nor does one become a philosopher through finding a master to whom one could become a disciple. Rather, it is *practising* philosophy that makes one a philosopher.[31] In thinking critically for one's self, something else happens. One's world is opened up as that which we take for granted is challenged.[32]

The Neoliberal University, by way of contrast, is framed by the desire to close down, to find that end point which the philosopher should resist. Philosophical practice modelled as conversation involves opening up one's engagement with life. It also suggests the significance of relationship for the practice of philosophy, for to converse requires someone with whom to speak. What happens if this model is pursued: for philosophy, but also for the university?

friendship and becoming wise

Here, we must return to a discussion of the significance of relationship for philosophy, and particularly to consideration of the practices conducive to the development of wisdom. Pursuing this thread offers the possibility of challenging the functional and constrained model of intellectual enquiry dominating neoliberal universities. If we consider the meaning of "wisdom," we find that is not synonymous with the study of philosophy, for it goes beyond acquiring a particular set of facts, or even engaging in the clarification of ideas. To talk of wisdom is to describe a way of being in the world which emerges from deep reflection on the nature of things. If we reflect on the history of philosophy, a close connection can be discerned between epistemology and ethics. Critical thinking is viewed as enabling better understandings of the world, which themselves provide the basis for better living.[33]

Artistic representations of "the philosopher" resist suggestions that there is any one way of construing the relationship between thought and the practice of living. Notably, there is little agreement on the role that relationship might play in enabling the development of a wise perspective on life. Gerard van Honthorst's painting "The Steadfast Philosopher" (1623)[34] portrays the philosopher, surrounded by "his" books, in the act of shunning the attentions of a scantily clad woman who is attempting to seduce him away from his studies. Relationship – or at least sexual intimacy – would seem to be at odds with the solitary work of philosophical reflection. Edward Hopper's "Excursion into Philosophy" (1959) may be painted some three hundred years later, yet it suggests that a similar detachment is necessary for the work of philosophical reflection.[35] A man sits on a bed, a discarded book by his side. Behind him, a woman is lying on her side, her buttocks exposed to the viewer. The physical world, connected with Woman, is to be rejected in favour of reflection.

Both paintings reflect the problematic place of Woman in the history of Western philosophy. The male, associated with thought, mind and rationality, is defined in distinction to the supposed female characteristics of physicality, body and emotions.[36] Philosophy, practised by the male, reflects this sense of detachment. But there are other ways of portraying philosophical work, ways which acknowledge the importance of conversation for reflection, and which make engagement with others absolutely necessary for the kind of philosophy that enables wiser ways of living in the world.

An image suggesting an alternative mode of reflection is presented by Stanley Spencer in his "Consider the Lilies" (1939), one of the paintings in his series *Christ in the Wilderness*.[37] Given the title of this series, we might anticipate a similar idea to that of van Honthorst and Hopper. To be wise or to cultivate deep reflection involves entering the wilderness, detaching oneself from world and others. Christ's attitude in Spencer's painting could not be further from this claim. Surrounded by daisies, Christ is attending to these flowers with the entirety of his being. He's looking at them; he's thinking about them; he's really engaging with them. Pamela Sue Anderson described wisdom as "the thoughtful love of life," and in this picture that notion is expressed perfectly. A connection is made between Christ and the flowers to which he is attending. It is not difficult to see in his posture Anderson's definition of what this thoughtful love of life would involve: it would be "a love which is informed by thinking about life, *perhaps about the biological*, but even more about a way of life for relational subjects who in living generate a collectivity of thinkers."[38]

That latter point suggests something of the intensity of attention. Rather than see it as dependent on isolation, Anderson suggests that it requires connection. A similar claim informs the perspective cultivated by the Ancient Hellenistic Schools. Philosophy is a critical discipline embedded in life.[39]

Connecting philosophical practice with life *as it is lived* is a perspective found in both the Epicurean and Stoic Schools. For Epicurus, wisdom requires avoiding empty argument or rhetorical flourishes. Taking his lead from Aristotle, and modelling philosophy as a form of medicine, its practice must be focused on relieving the anxiety and suffering that inevitably accompanies life in this world: "empty is that philosopher's argument by which no human suffering is therapeutically treated."[40] The Stoic Seneca offers a similar vision of philosophy: it is not the same as wisdom, but its practices are directed at this goal.[41] Working at a correct understanding of the nature of the universe is important and, once this is attained, one must align one's actions with it. The concern of philosophy is, as a result, "not with words, but with facts."[42] But this is not the acquisition of facts for their own sake. A better understanding of the nature of things opens up better ways of living. Elaine Fantham's recent translation of Seneca's letters gets at this rather well: philosophy "does not consist of words but deeds."[43] If Seneca's critics have accused him of rather too great a love of words,[44] the point remains. Something more is required than the love of words if the philosopher is to help us live well.

An important aspect of this "something more" is friendship. To become a philosopher requires a kind of intimacy. Solitary philosophical practice is not by itself sufficient for the attainment of wisdom. The practices of the Ancient Schools reveal this most clearly. Epicurus' students gather around him in a place that sounds not dissimilar to a commune, for the pursuit of wisdom *requires* a life together.[45] Given the communal context of Epicurus' "Garden," it is not surprising that friendship should be viewed by Epicurus as vital for a deeper engagement with other and the world: "Of all the means which are procured by wisdom to ensure happiness throughout the whole life, by far the most important is the acquisition of friends."[46] The Stoics mirror something of the high value placed on friendship. It is a gift from God which allows for the exploration of the things necessary for the pursuit of wisdom.[47] The role of dialogue and letters in Seneca's work suggests something of how it enables this. Philosophy is an intimate practice, something we do together, as the tone of his letters to his friend Lucilius suggests.

The high place given to friendship reflects the indebtedness of the schools to Aristotle. Here, perhaps, we get an indication of the problems arising when friendship is identified as vital for the development of wisdom. Aristotle, his ideas shaped by the rigid distinctions between class and sex in his society, makes the highest forms of friendship dependent on equality of status.[48] He is not alone in this, and seems to be drawing on the ideas of his mentor Plato. Sure, wisdom is developed in the context of friendship, a perspective to which Plato draws attention in his *Symposium*. But the kind of friendship Plato has in mind requires a mature relationship of equals if it is to enable a shared exploration and contemplation of the Good.[49] It is *male* companions of equal standing who are able to share ideas, who are "*mentally pregnant*,"[50] and who are "filled with the offspring you might expect a mind to bear and produce."[51] These mental offspring are immortal, not prey to death and decay in the way that physical children, created out of a man's love for a woman, are.[52] Only a relationship of (male) equals makes possible the creation of philosophical ideas.

The philosophical schools which followed Aristotle were far more open, broadening out the conditions that make for such companionable relationships.[53] Feminists, likewise, have explored the possibilities of friendship in ways that reconfigure the claims of Plato and Aristotle.[54] Julie K. Ward, in particular, argues that Aristotle's writing on *philia* opens up possibilities for feminist accounts of female friendship.[55] But before turning too quickly from the limitations of their constructions, it must be acknowledged that Aristotle and Plato highlight the difficulty of placing personal connection at the heart of philosophical practice. If friendship enables the kind of philosophical practice vital for the goal of attaining wisdom, isn't this to ground it in a practice that by its very nature is exclusive? Friendships inevitably emerge from common experiences that necessarily exclude others. Before addressing the problems of friendship, let us say something about its transformative possibilities, for it is these virtues that make grappling with its problems worthwhile. While pursuing friendship suggests grounding philosophical practice in relationship, it also suggests a vision of the university that could not be further from the economic concerns which currently shape it.

the model of friendship for philosophical practice

Rather than think of philosophy as thought-in-isolation, making friendship the context for its practice allows something more intimate and personal to emerge. In the experience of friendship, the other person is met, and in that meeting an openness develops to life in all its varied hues and tones. The philosophical practice which emerges from friendship is first and foremost personal. "Lived experience" is not something to be ashamed of, nor is it to be factored out of our discussions. There need be no separation between one's life and one's philosophical pursuits. If anything, the experiences of life lend themselves to the philosophical questions to be pursued. So Michèle Le Doeuff relates her experience of sexism in French schooling to a broader discussion of the historic and continuing problems women face in being taken seriously as scholars.[56] Likewise, Lawrence Hatab links his careful scholarly work on Nietzsche's eternal recurrence with the sense of relief he felt when encountering Nietzsche's writings for the first time. Confronted with a philosopher who battled physical and mental illness in life and in his work, Hatab felt less alone, finding in Nietzsche's struggles with mental and physical illness something of his own sense of alienation from life. Rather than see this felt connection as something to be overcome by an appropriate philosophical detachment, he makes this intimacy central to his analysis of Nietzsche's writing: "I think I can say that I know Nietzsche's sentences 'by heart.'"[57]

Acknowledging the personal well-spring for enquiry returns us to the existential questions once deemed central to philosophical enquiry. The practice of philosophy encompasses not just the preoccupations of the trained philosopher but also the experiences of all human beings. "Why was I born?" "What is it to love?" "What does death mean?" "Why do we suffer?" As we journey through life with our friends we are likely to find our conversations including these questions as we encounter the visceral human experiences which give rise to them. A philosophy framed in response might be less technical, more connected to the desires and fears of those outside the academy. Questioning, critical thought meets the ordinary experience of being human.

Existential questions require serious engagement. This is about more than clever argument: it is about how we are *to live*. The experiences that give rise to them propel us – often against our will – into a deeper engagement with life in this world. As Paul Tillich notes, "there can be no depth without the way to depth."[58] The encounter with failure, loss, suffering, and grief acts as a provocation to go beneath superficial understandings of ourselves and the world. These are the times when we are "questioned by life,"[59] to use Holocaust survivor and logotherapist Viktor Frankl's reformulation of what happens when we are confronted with suffering. This is about more than an abstract philosophical problem. As mutable beings, we cannot escape this questioning. But rather than be swamped by events we can reflect upon them, interrogate them, explore them. It is no surprise to find philosophical preoccupations mirroring personal experience and, often, those things which are most troubling and upsetting.

The jewel at the heart of a philosophy modelled through friendship is that such painful themes need never be explored alone. Sara Maitland is quite right to resist the intrusion of noise into all aspects of life.[60] This noisy world leaves precious little time for the solitude necessary for a proper engagement with one's place in the world. Philosophical enquiry requires space for quiet reflection; but as relational beings we also require the space to talk with others, to share thoughts, to refine ideas and to change them as the other person is encountered.

This is the power of friendship. A friendship of sufficient duration is likely to encounter joy, laughter and the delight of maturity; but also, inevitably, depression, disappointment, failure, and loss. As Pamela Sue Anderson develops her feminist philosophy of religion, she is at pains to note that it is not enough for the feminist to focus on life, for "we are given a life, but each of us also dies."[61] This is the inescapable reality that frames existence. The deepest friendships reflect this, for they are never framed just by an ability to share good times. Confronted by the pains of existence, it is then that there is the possibility of deepening the relationship through the sharing of such experiences.

While this makes sense in the realm of friendship, we might wonder how this would shape the experience of the philosopher in the contemporary academy. Maggie Berg and Barbara Seeber provide a helpful account of its potential in their challenge to the culture of speed in the academy.[62] Against the backdrop of an academy shaped by process, where "downtime" is seen as inefficiency, and where achieving targets limits the time that can be spent thinking in depth about anything, Berg and Seeber reflect on their experience of collaboration. Working together offers the possibility of resisting a view of education defined by the lauding of competition that accompanies marketization. It is a subversive form of activity. Reflecting on the experience of collaborative writing led Berg and Seeber to more than just the production of a co-authored text. In the process of writing, their friendship was deepened. This happened particularly in moments when they felt daunted by the task of writing together. Confessing to each other how inadequate they felt to the task, talking about their fears of failure, had a surprising result. Their work improved. It was not just that these moments of vulnerability acted as epiphanies for deeper relationship; they also allowed for the creation of better ideas, co-created in their conversations. "Collaboration is about thinking together";[63] it is a form of intimacy.

Thinking together in the way Berg and Seeber describe suggests a different form of practice from the mechanisms that would enshrine objectivity in the assessment of academic work. There is a significant difference between the reflections of the "anonymous reviewer" of the peer review and the interventions of a friend:

> When one of us considered an idea or sentence as not working, she was able to say so without crushing the other in the way that peer review often does. The underlying trust and respect made it possible to have an open exchange of ideas: we listened to each other in an attempt to understand rather than to find the weaknesses we had been trained to do. *The result was the same.*[64]

Trust, respect and the willingness to listen did not lead to sloppy thinking: quite the contrary. Collaboration led to better reflections and clearer expression.

Before we adopt too-rosy a view of this kind of working, we should return to the problems of modelling philosophy on friendship and personal connection which were identified in Plato's and Aristotle's models of friendship. There, the kind of friendship crucial to the developing of ideas was seen as possible only between equals. There is a truth here, for our friends are likely to be self-selecting, reflecting common occupations, based in common neighbourhoods or leisure activities or past histories. There is, then, a danger for a philosophy based on the practices of friendship. Feeling comfortable with a group of like-minded peers can all-too-easily erode the place for critical enquiry. Our subjects and our reflections extend only to the desires and preoccupations of one particular group of people like us. Against the backdrop of university structures, it is easy to identify philosophy departments where few perspectives are offered outside those of the white, the male, and the middle class.[65]

If philosophical conversation is not to be limited and narrow, the voices of groups excluded from it must be actively encouraged into the academy. Here, my conversation with Oakeshott enters difficult waters, for his account of the university explicitly rejects the intervention of government in higher education, and so would resist policies aimed at widening participation. There is, however, no easy fix to the limited nature of much academic conversation. Even if policies were in place to address the problems of cronyism and implicit bias, identified most recently by Jennifer Saul,[66] there may still be good grounds for feeling uneasy about placing relationship at the heart of our philosophical practice. Friendships are not immune from the distortions of power, envy, and betrayal. They do not always make us more resilient, but can make us more vulnerable. Michèle Le Doeuff's analysis of the famous conversation between Jean-Paul Sartre and Simone de Beauvoir in the Luxembourg Gardens reveals a more disturbing side of intimacy. Beauvoir recounts this sad meeting in her *Memoirs of a Dutiful Daughter*. "Day after day" she measured herself against Sartre. Friends and companions, she excitedly shares with Sartre her nascent philosophy. He listens; and then "rips it to shreds." Crushed, Beauvoir decides that she is not a philosopher. Ever after she would say that she "left the philosophy to Sartre."[67]

Beauvoir and Sartre may be friends and collaborators; but that does not stop Sartre enacting the kind of intellectual bullying common in the academy. The very fact of their friendship probably makes Beauvoir *more* inclined to accept his conclusions about her work. Yet there is something in acknowledging the personal and its potential for a deeper kind of philosophical enquiry that makes me loath to give it up, even in the face of such an upsetting example of the limits of friendship.

friendship, risk and the neoliberal university

Given the complexity, even the messiness, of friendship, it might seem easier to retreat into the more comfortable territory of the solitary philosopher, a formulation that also sits rather well with neoliberal accounts of the atomized subject. The scholar as individual rather than collaborator becomes a unit whose research can be graded, whose engagement with the subject can be defined according to "its" outcomes. Yet the vulnerability of friendship suggests something of why it might be particularly important when constructing an ideal for academic enquiry.

The cultural critic Marshall McLuhan describes the difficulty of *seeing* – *really* seeing – the cultural ideals and practices that surround us. We take our "environment" for granted, much as we take for granted the air that we breathe.[68] Academics have become used to framing the university through neoliberal values. The language of economics, metrics and targets permeates every aspect of the twenty-first-century university. To recalibrate academic enquiry through the lens of friendship challenges the resulting complacency, acting as a reminder that institutions are not natural phenomena that cannot be framed in any other way. Institutions result from human decision making. The functionalism of the contemporary university is not a fact of life; it can be disrupted, and emphasizing the importance of relationship for the shaping of wisdom can go some way to enabling this change in perspective.

Consider the fears that make the uncertainty of human relationships something requiring management. Hannah Arendt's critique of bureaucracy identifies this preoccupation. Bureaucratic systems reflect desires to contain and control that which is experienced as unpredictable and uncontrollable. Systems and processes attempt to manage the uncertainty of human relationships. But something vital is lost in the attempt to make safe that which can never be rendered certain. What is lost is the "startling unexpectedness"[69] of human creativity. As spontaneous creatures it is always possible for human beings to "begin something new out of their own resources."[70]

Spontaneity brings with it risk. To allow for the spontaneous, to make room for the unpredictable, requires giving up ideas that the end of any particular endeavour is predictable or assured. When we act, we always do so in relation to others, and the way in which others respond is not something that can be circumscribed.[71] This might make us uneasy, and it can seem preferable to apply models of production derived from the factory to all areas of human life and activity. The apparent certainty of this way of proceeding goes some way to explain the tenacity of neoliberal forms: they offer a comforting simplicity to the shaping of experience. Faith shifts from what happens between human individuals to the pleasing objectivity and cleanness of numbers. Financial models, metrics and statistics "come to take political precedence over the aesthetic, the affective and the hermeneutic."[72] All can be contained through assigning discrete numbers or clear lists of outcomes.

Something is lost when faith in the system defines the activities of our institutions. For Arendt, what is lost is the possibility of spontaneous action; for me, it is the proper acknowledgement of the role that relationship plays in the flourishing human life. The personal opposes the supposed objectivity of the economic.[73] Yet promoting the complexity and messiness of relationship can seem ill-advised. We deceive ourselves, however, if we think adherence to "the System" will ensure the end of abuse or prejudice or unkindness. Risk remains an issue for the university, despite the application of such managerial tools. Far from eradicating unhappiness and vulnerability, the Economic University creates stress, unhappiness, and the conditions for bullying. The suicide of the biologist Stefan Grimm in 2014 is a case in point. Subjected to strict performance management systems, his death exposed the unbearable pressures staff were under in a target-driven university.[74] Placing the System above the relational does not ensure the university as a place for flourishing.

Anxiety about possible abuses dogs pedagogical perspectives that would make relationship a vital aspect of teaching. Paul Tillich's writing is inspiring; but he has been exposed for having inappropriate relationships with his students and their partners.[75] No university should turn a blind eye to abuses in the name of relationship, but to factor out the role of the relational in learning is to lose some of the most profound moments that happen incidentally, in an after-class discussion, or in an activity not obviously connected to the class materials. Good teaching never just involves the transferring of material from teacher to taught; it also involves "being interested in the pupil himself, in what he is thinking, in the quality of his mind, in his immortal soul, and not in what sort of school master or administrator he can be made into."[76]

This comment from Oakeshott raises, again, the importance of the open conversation. The limits of our own perspective are acknowledged; we listen to what the other has to say. The other is met as a *person*, not just as a fellow worker or someone who sits in a class. We talk with someone who may not share our views. To meet the other as a fellow human being requires honesty, and the ability to have our positions challenged. To listen is thus as important as it is to talk. In attentive listening we hear the other person into speech: an image that is a central ideal for feminist theological engagement.[77]

Embracing the risk of the personal requires two concepts that emerge from Arendt's account of the human condition: promising and forgiveness. In the promise, we attempt to provide some security for the other.[78] Promises are serious because they attempt a degree of certainty in the realm of human relationships: I will behave in the way I tell you I am going to behave. The possibility of forgiveness is a necessary correlate to the promise, for it holds out the prospect of a future if actions are bad or go wrong.[79] Forgiveness is not easy to give or to receive, and its difficulty acts as a reminder of the painful realities of a world where human beings are not perfect but are forged through the pain, as well as the joy, of lived relationship. How much richer our lives if we pay attention to these things which frame our experience, and which provide the basis for the kind of maturity necessary if a wiser perspective on life is to be cultivated.

conclusion: beyond the neoliberal university

Paying attention to the role of friendship in the practice of philosophy suggests a vision of the subject that does not disconnect it from the totality of life, nor from the practice of living. Here is philosophy as the practice that enables wisdom, as it offers a space for grappling with the experiences of life and finding ways of coming to terms with them. It is difficult to see how the university as it is currently structured can provide the kind of space conducive for such practices. Yet exposing the paucity of its vision of education might go some way to demanding new visions of what might happen if the university returned to its historical place as a community engaged in collaborative thinking. We might note that, despite the last forty years of prioritizing the economic, the vision of the university as a *community* has not entirely been expunged. In January 2018 the University of London was the focus for a campaign aimed at ending the outsourcing of services such as catering and cleaning. Behind this action was the vision of the university as a community, where the work of all its members is vital for creating a setting where we flourish together through the practices in which we engage. When UCU took strike action to protect staff pensions, the union similarly refused to make its campaign just about the concerns of one group of workers. Instead, it also highlighted the pernicious effects of short-term or zero-hours contracts on the lives of younger academics. In both actions, students were overwhelmingly supportive of staff, and a new image of what the university could be is starting to emerge from the acknowledgement that something is lost when the university as a community is lost.

Placing the human at the heart of our endeavours acts as a reminder of the vulnerability of our humanity. When I reflect on my friendship with Pamela Sue Anderson I cannot forget the fragility of the conversations we had. They were passing, just as we are passing. Perhaps it is that very fragility that contributes to the longing to formalize, to set in stone, to reduce to words on a page. Sure, I can look at the printed words we framed together; I can conjure up her presence as I read her articles and books. Yet it is the traces of the conversations we shared that live most: walking through University Parks during a solar eclipse, gossiping and laughing over drinks in Oxford pubs too numerous to name. In these memories, I find her presence as she heard me into speech. These remembered traces of our friendship continue to inspire me: delicate as flowers, ephemeral as mist. It is a difficult thing to come to terms with our transience as human beings. At its best, philosophy makes space for us to grapple with these realities. Here is where the possibility of wisdom is found. At its best, the university can provide a space for engaging with the deeper possibilities open to human beings which transcend cultural obsessions with work or money. Here is where the practice of philosophy finds its importance, for it offers a space for meeting each other as real human beings, caught in the joys and sorrows of life. We are not economic units, we are creatures seeking to make sense of our lives, striving to find ways of living well together. In our practices as philosophers we can model these attempts, and in embracing the notion of an open-ended conversation we might even be able to create a university prepared to value what cannot be defined, what is difficult to capture, and what emerges from the fragility of being human.

disclosure statement

No potential conflict of interest was reported by the author.

notes

1 Michael McGhee, "The Voice of Cordelian Ethics: Imagination and the Loss of Religion," *Journal of Scottish Studies* 10 (2018): 52–68.

2 Patricia Hill Collins, *Black Feminist Thought* (London: Routledge, 1991) xii.

3 Pamela Sue Anderson, *A Feminist Philosophy of Religion* (Oxford: Blackwell, 1998).

4 Pamela Sue Anderson and Beverley Clack, eds., *Feminist Philosophy of Religion: Critical Readings* (London: Routledge, 2004).

5 "Vulnerability and the Politics of Care" conference, British Academy, 9–10 February 2017. Pamela Sue Anderson, "Silencing and Speaker Vulnerability: Undoing an Oppressive Form of (Wilful) Ignorance," ed. Nick Bunnin, in *Love and Vulnerability: Thinking with Pamela Sue Anderson*, ed. Pelagia Goulimari, Spec. issue of *Angelaki: Journal of the Theoretical Humanities* 25.1–2 (2020): 36–45.

6 Pamela Sue Anderson, "'A Thoughtful Love of Life': A Spiritual Turn in Philosophy of Religion," *Svensk Teologisk Kvartalskrift* 85 (2009): 119–29 (119).

7 Stefan Collini, *What Are Universities For?* (London: Penguin, 2012).

8 Martha Nussbaum, *Not for Profit: Why Democracy Needs the Humanities* (Princeton: Princeton UP, 2010).

9 Bob Brecher, "Universities: The Neoliberal Agenda" in *Interrogating the Neoliberal Lifecycle: The Limits of Success*, eds. Beverley Clack and Michele Paule (London: Palgrave Macmillan, 2019) 127–42.

10 Michael Oakeshott, "The Idea of the University" in *The Voice of Liberal Learning*, ed. Timothy Fuller (Indianapolis: Liberty Fund, 2001) 117.

11 Collini, *What Are Universities For?* [Kindle ed.] 32–38.

12 Julian Baggini, "If Universities Sacrifice Philosophy on the Altar of Profit, What's Next?," *The Guardian* 21 Dec. 2018, available <https://www.theguardian.com/commentisfree/2018/dec/21/universities-philosophy-profit-business-partners> (accessed 12 Feb. 2019).

13 Oakeshott, "The Idea of the University" 106; my emphasis.

14 Ibid. 107.

15 Ibid. 106.

16 Ibid. 116.

17 Ibid.

18 David Harvey, *A Brief History of Neoliberalism* (Oxford: Oxford UP, 2005) 1–38; Philip Mirowski, *Never Let a Serious Crisis Go to Waste: How Neoliberalism Survived the Financial Meltdown* (London: Verso, 2014) 27–88.

19 Guy Standing, *The Precariat: The New Dangerous Class* (London: Bloomsbury, 2011) 1.

20 Wendy Brown, *Undoing the Demos: Neoliberalism's Stealth Revolution* (New York: Zone, 2015) 28.

21 William Davies, *The Limits of Neoliberalism: Authority, Sovereignty and the Logic of Competition* (London: Sage, 2014) 20–23.

22 Brown, *Undoing the Demos* 176.

23 Davies, *The Limits of Neoliberalism* 22.

24 Thomas Lemke, "'The Birth of Bio-politics': Michel Foucault's Lecture at the Collège de France on Neo-liberal Governmentality," *Economy and Society* 30.2 (2001): 190–207 (199).

25 Michel Foucault, *The Birth of Biopolitics*, ed. Michel Senellart; trans. Graham Burchell (London: Palgrave Macmillan, 2008) 268.

26 Collini, *What Are Universities For?* 33–34.

27 Oakeshott, "The Idea of the University" 109; my emphasis.

28 Jessica Shepherd, "I Think, Therefore I Earn," *The Guardian* 20 Nov. 2007, available <https://www.theguardian.com/education/2007/nov/20/choosingadegree.highereducation> (accessed 12 Feb. 2019); "What Can You Do with a Philosophy Degree?," *Times Higher Education Supplement* 17 Nov. 2016, available <https://www.timeshighereducation.com/student/subjects/what-can-you-do-philosophy-degree> (accessed 12 Feb. 2019); Nicholas Miller, "5 Reasons Why Philosophy Majors Make Great Entrepreneurs," *Entrepreneur* 5 July 2017, available <https://www.entrepreneur.com/article/295699> (accessed 27 Nov. 2019).

29 Collini, *What Are Universities For?* 56; my emphasis.

30 Oakeshott, "The Idea of the University" 109–10.

31 Michèle Le Doeuff, *Hipparchia's Choice: An Essay Concerning Women, Philosophy, Etc.* [1989], trans. Trista Selous (New York: Columbia UP, 2007) 59–60.

32 Michèle Le Doeuff, *The Sex of Knowing*, trans. Kathryn Hamer (London: Routledge, 2003).

33 Thus Lucretius' *De Rerum Natura* ("On the Nature of Things") is both a discourse on the nature of the universe and a reflection on how to live well in that world.

34 <https://commons.wikimedia.org/wiki/File:The_Steadfast_Philosopher,_by_Gerard_van_Hondhorst.jpg> (accessed 8 Feb. 2019).

35 <http://www.edward-hopper.org/excursion-into-philosophy/> (accessed 8 Feb. 2019).

36 Genevieve Lloyd, *The "Man" of Reason* (London: Methuen, 1984); Beverley Clack, "Introduction," *Misogyny in the Western Philosophical Tradition: A Reader* (London: Macmillan, 1999).

37 Mark Oakley's article "Invitation to Contemplate" in *The Church Times* 1 Feb. 2013 includes a reproduction of this painting and a helpful commentary on the contemplative function of the series of paintings of which it is a part. See <https://www.churchtimes.co.uk/articles/2013/1-february/books-arts/reading-groups/invitation-to-contemplate> (accessed 28 May 2019).

38 Anderson, "'Thoughtful Love of Life'" 120.

39 Pierre Hadot, *Philosophy as a Way of Life*, ed. Arnold I. Davidson; trans. Michael Chase (Oxford: Blackwell, 1995).

40 Quoted in Martha Nussbaum, *The Therapy of Desire* (Princeton: Princeton UP, 1994) 13; see also 121.

41 Seneca, *Moral Letters to Lucilius*, LXXXIX, "On the Parts of Philosophy" line 6, available <https://en.wikisource.org/wiki/Moral_letters_to_Lucilius/Letter_89> (accessed 15 Feb. 2019).

42 Seneca, *Letters from a Stoic*, trans. Robin Campbell (London: Penguin, 1969) 64.

43 Seneca, *Selected Letters*, trans. Elaine Fantham (Oxford: Oxford UP, 2010) 31.

44 F.H. Sandbach, *The Stoics* (Indianapolis: Hackett, 1994) 162.

45 Nussbaum, *Therapy of Desire* 119–20.

46 Epicurus, "Principal Doctrines," trans. P.E. Matheson, in *Greek and Roman Philosophy after Aristotle*, ed. Jason Saunders (New York: Free, 1966) 53–57, 55–56.

47 Seneca, "On Favours" in *Moral and Political Essays*, eds. and trans. John Cooper and J.F. Procopé (Cambridge: Cambridge UP, 1995) 288.

48 Aristotle, *Nicomachean Ethics* 8–9; *Politics* 1.13 on women; also Nussbaum, *Therapy of Desire* 54–56.

49 Plato, *Symposium* 209b.

50 Ibid. 209a, trans. Robin Waterfield (Oxford: Oxford UP) 52.

51 Ibid. 209a, 52.

52 Ibid. 209c–d.

53 Epicurus was the first to open his school to women: Nussbaum, *Therapy of Desire* 117. Nussbaum also sees Lucretius as framing his ideal of marriage as a form of *philia*: ibid. 187.

54 For a variety of explorations of friendship, see, for example, Marilyn Friedman, *What Are Friends For?* (Ithaca, NY: Cornell UP, 1993); Mary Hunt, *Fierce Tenderness: A Feminist Theology of Friendship* (New York: Crossroad, 1991); Melissa Raphael, *The Female Face of God in Auschwitz* (London: Routledge, 2002).

55 Julie K. Ward, "Aristotle on Philia: The Beginning of a Feminist Ideal of Friendship?," *Feminism and Ancient Philosophy*, ed. Julie K. Ward (London: Routledge, 1996) 155–71.

56 Le Doeuff, *Hipparchia's Choice*.

57 Lawrence Hatab, *Nietzsche's Life Sentence: Coming to Terms with Eternal Recurrence* (London: Routledge, 2005), esp. 111–13 (113).

58 Paul Tillich, *The Shaking of the Foundations* [1949] (Harmondsworth: Penguin, 1962) 61.

59 Viktor Frankl, *Man's Search for Meaning*, trans. Ilse Lasch (London: Rider, 2004) 12.

60 Sara Maitland, *A Book of Silence* (London: Granta, 2010.)

61 Pamela Sue Anderson, "Life, Death and (Inter)-subjectivity: Realism and Recognition in Continental Feminism," *International Journal for Philosophy of Religion* 60.1 (2006): 41–59 (41).

62 Maggie Berg and Barbara Seeber, *The Slow Professor* (Buffalo: U of Toronto P, 2016).

63 Ibid. 89.

64 Ibid. 88; my emphasis.

65 For critiques of academic cronyism, see bell hooks, *Where We Stand: Class Matters* (London: Routledge, 2004); Patricia Hill Collins, *Black Feminist Thought* (London: Routledge, 1990).

66 Jennifer Saul, "Implicit Bias, Stereotype Threat, and Women in Philosophy," *Women in Philosophy: What Needs to Change?*, eds. Katrina Hutchison and Fiona Jenkins (Oxford: Oxford UP, 2013) 39–60.

67 Le Doeuff, *Hipparchia's Choice* 136.

68 Marshall McLuhan, *The Relation of Environment to Anti-Environment* (Berkeley: Gingko, 2005).

69 Hannah Arendt, *The Human Condition* [1958] (Chicago: U of Chicago P, 1998) 178.

70 Hannah Arendt, *The Origins of Totalitarianism* [1948] (New York: Harcourt, 1968) 455.

71 Arendt, *Human Condition* 182–84.

72 Roger Burrows, "Living with the H-Index? Metric Assemblages in the Contemporary Academy," *Sociological Review* 60.2 (2012): 355–72 (358).

73 For problems with the supposed objectivity of statistics, see Ian Hacking, *The Taming of Chance* (Cambridge: Cambridge UP, 1990).

74 Chris Parr, "Imperial College Professor Stefan Grimm 'Was Given Grant Income Target,'" *Times Higher Education Supplement* 3 Dec. 2014, available <https://www.timeshighereducation.com/news/imperial-college-professor-stefan-grimm-was-given-grant-income-target/2017369.article> (accessed 25 Feb. 2019).

75 Hannah Tillich, *From Time to Time* (New York: Stein, 1973).

76 Oakeshott, "The Idea of the University" 113.

77 See Catherine Keller, "The Apophasis of Gender: A Fourfold Unsaying of Feminist Theology," *Journal of the American Academy of Religion* 76.4 (2008) 905–33.

78 Arendt, *Human Condition* 243–47.

79 Ibid. 237.

dorota filipczak

THE DISAVOWAL OF THE FEMALE "KNOWER"
reading literature in the light of pamela sue anderson's project on vulnerability

Allow me to begin by describing my discursive position in dialogue with the philosophy of Pamela Sue Anderson. I am a literature scholar, not a philosopher of religion, though both disciplines share a variety of concerns among which the interest in the cultural imaginary is crucial. Hence I have chosen to structure my argument around Anderson's two texts on the imaginary and her paper entitled "Silencing and Speaker Vulnerability: Undoing an Oppressive Form of (Wilful) Ignorance." These particular works encapsulate the ideas that have preoccupied me ever since I realized how important it was for me as a female scholar to speak about literary works while engaging with sexual difference.

My first experience of Pamela Sue Anderson's approach to the feminist philosophy of religion was a privileged one. In September 1994 I was chairing a session at a conference organized by David Jasper at the University of Glasgow, during which Anderson presented her paper on Antigone. The paper immediately stimulated my emotional and intellectual response, because I was then concerned with the feminist voices of dissent, female counter-narratives and the attempt to dislodge the rigid stance on canonicity within academia. At that stage I was becoming acutely aware of the widening gap between the ways in which I experienced literary texts as a woman and the gender agenda structured around them by mostly patriarchal literary theory. As such, I was looking for "a gender-sensitive approach" to literature, to use a phrase from Anderson's article on "Gender and the Infinite" (192). At the same time I had reached a stage of disillusion with difference feminism, and those feminist approaches that reinforced the already entrenched binaries that women had been enmeshed in. Anderson offered a much more constructive approach by reclaiming rationality for women, and by creating a concept of rational passion which did justice to reason while not denigrating desire.

By refiguring Antigone as an embodiment of dissent and marginality Anderson's philosophy inspired me to interpret the condition of those female protagonists whose dilemmas were crucial for my analysis of literature. I contend that the focus on Antigone in the early writings which matured into *A Feminist Philosophy of Religion* paved the way for this feminist philosopher's concern with the vulnerability of the female speaker. As a person sentenced to "living death" (*A Feminist Philosophy of Religion* 197) for the rationality of her belief (202), Anderson's Antigone encapsulates the condition of a female knower who refuses to be silenced, but who is silenced nevertheless. Her plight can be subsumed by what Anderson elucidates while discussing the position of a female philosopher in academia:

> Her vulnerability follows from her dependence upon an audience; if she is to be heard, her dependence requires an audience which is both willing and capable of hearing her as a speaker and a knower. ("Creating a New Imaginary" 50)

Let me apply the above to the literary characters starting with Anderson's preferred heroine. Aware of her precarious position, Antigone embodies the vulnerability which Creon consciously disavows when he inflicts oppression upon the culprit. Complicit with Creon's dictate due to fear, the audience of the *polis* will not "identify" Antigone as a knower. Only in unofficial private discourse in the households is she declared to be in the right. Creon tries to make Antigone play his game by asking her if she knew about his decision to leave the body of the enemy brother unburied, but Antigone confirms that what she did was done with full awareness of the consequences. Therefore she will be coerced into the silence of death and left unmourned when she takes her own life in a walled-in cave. Through this final act of resistance she will still affect Creon by exposing the vulnerability that he has to confront after his son's and wife's respective suicides. Antigone's "living death" enacts "a return to the womb" and "a new relationship with the maternal" (Anderson, *A Feminist Philosophy of Religion* 202). As the philosopher points out (after Irigaray), Antigone stood in for the absent mother when mourning the brother who was considered the enemy of the *polis* (196). Goddess of the underworld or a symbol of the buried maternal, Antigone "speaks female desire" and thus disrupts patriarchal configurations of the most important relationships (200).

Anderson's refiguring Antigone in the nineties is matched by her refiguring vulnerability in the writings that came into being before the philosopher's untimely death in March 2017. As Lovibond and Moore contend in the Abstract to her work which they edited: "Anderson urges us to reimagine our vulnerability as a condition not merely of exposure to violence but of openness to mutual affection, love, and friendship" ("Towards a New Philosophical Imaginary" Abstract (online only)). This considerably extends the potential of human relationships in the world and in literature which attempts to engage with lived experience. In light of this interpretation, Creon finds himself undermined by the loss of those who were dear to him, because he failed to open himself to "mutual affection" at the moment that might have proved decisive for the fates of his son and his son's beloved – Antigone.

Literary research has taught me about vulnerability and its disavowal in patriarchal society. In order to explore the precarious position of the female knower who risks being discredited on account of her gender, my analysis will focus on selected literary examples from the nineteenth and twentieth centuries. I return again to the novels that have had the greatest impact on me: *The Mill on the Floss* by George Eliot, which I analysed more than a decade ago in light of Michèle Le Doeuff's philosophy ("Is Literature Any Help?" 118–19), and *The Diviners* by Margaret Laurence, which became crucial for me because I am a writer of literary texts in my native Polish. Anderson's work on vulnerability allowed me to approach these texts again from a different perspective. I will start with Eliot's *The Mill on the Floss*, whose heroine, Maggie Tulliver, is not the only woman who rebels as a child only to be restrained and moulded into submission as an adult woman. As Anderson cautions us, referring to Le Doeuff: "a woman's oppression begins in adolescence, at which point the myths of patriarchy enslave the relations of men and women" ("Towards a New Philosophical Imaginary" 18).

Little Maggie with her unruly hair and wayward comments is a continual source of frustration to her mother, while her father tacitly disapproves of too much intelligence in a woman. The crucial scene in Eliot's strongly autobiographical novel hinges on the moment when this very intelligent heroine is finally reconciled to social expectations, much to her mother's pleasure:

> Her mother felt the change in her with a sort of puzzled wonder that Maggie should be "growing up so good"; it was amazing that this once "contrairy" child was becoming so submissive, so backward to assert her own will [...] The mother was getting fond of her tall, brown girl, – the only bit of furniture now on which she could bestow her anxiety and pride. (299)

Kristie Dotson's definitions of quieting and smothering discussed in Pamela Sue Anderson's paper "Silencing and Speaker Vulnerability" (38) correspond with the formation of womanhood in the Victorian epoch. Firstly, Maggie is quieted by the incessant efforts of her mother and brother to deprive her of initiative. This, however, would not have been successful without Maggie's decision to smother her own message which the community finds inappropriate. The protagonist who starts out as a highly perceptive knower is shown maturing towards what Anderson terms "sacrificial and tragic relations to men" ("Towards a New Philosophical Imaginary" 15), which springs from the community's "wilful ignorance," defined by Nancy Tuana as:

> a systematic process of self-deception, a wilful embrace of ignorance that infects those who are in positions of privilege, an active ignoring of the oppression of others and one's role in that exploitation. (Qtd in Anderson, "Creating a New Imaginary" 51)

Maggie's openness to "mutual affection" is misinterpreted and misused by her despotic brother, who considers himself the man in charge of her life and attachments.

Interestingly, George Eliot was greatly impressed by Sophocles' Antigone, which she discussed in 1856, that is, before the publication of *The Mill on the Floss* (Semmel 76). In her view, the tragedy showed the conflict between "custom, tradition and personal feeling on the one hand, and obedience to the state on the other" (ibid.). Critics perceive affinities between Antigone and Maggie Tulliver, notably in the Victorian heroine's inner conflict between familial duty towards Tom and compassion for Philip, the son of her family's enemy, and passion for Stephen, her cousin's fiancé (McDonagh 52). Röder Bolton notes Maggie's readiness to admit that she violated Tom's demand that she should not see Philip. Like Antigone, Maggie is ready to take the consequences for her disobedience to male rule (Röder Bolton 61). Yet the above criticism follows George Eliot's own handling of Antigone too closely and uncritically. Hence it obscures the writer's emphasis on the loss of an individual female voice as a result of familial and social pressure.

It is useful at this stage to invoke Anderson's comment on "the 'I' who seeks identity which is not that proposed by social representation. Le Doeuff illustrates this with the choice of the ancient woman philosopher of mathematics, Hipparchia, seeking knowledge rather than remaining 'at the loom' where society expected her to be" ("Towards a New Philosophical Imaginary" 20). In contrast, Maggie Tulliver reverses Hipparchia's choice under the pressure of the community's "wilful ignorance" of her emotional and intellectual needs. As a child she hates wasting her time on patchwork where fragmented material must be sewn together again and again in a futile and repetitive exercise. As an adult she renounces all her books and finds masochistic pleasure in poring over elaborate stitches, an alteration that is greatly welcome by her mother. Maggie loses her voice and self in the process of renunciation.

Thus, "self-silencing" (Anderson, "Silencing and Speaker Vulnerability" 39–41) becomes the literary heroine's ideal. Only then can the family and community relinquish their arduous task of making her quiet for her own good. Whether this has deadly repercussions for her is nobody's concern. Maggie Tulliver's death in the embrace of her domineering brother in the waters of the flood that they are both trying to navigate is a bitter enough coda to quieting the message that the female character may have wanted to share. The social contract in Victorian times allocates invulnerability to men, and this means that authority can never be granted to a female speaker who is in constant threat of having her needs and thoughts misrecognized or suppressed. Yet the irony of the ending in *The Mill on the Floss* is that Maggie's brother, who denied vulnerability, shares his sister's fate. Tom ignored "an openness to affection" (Anderson, "Creating a New Imaginary" 51) which would have allowed him to relate to his sister in order to understand and not oppress.

Eliot's novel about the waste of a female genius by the community can be reinterpreted today in the light of Anderson's insights into the conflict between justice and unconditional forgiveness ("When Justice and Forgiveness Come Apart" 116). Controlled by her brother who denies her the right to socialize with the only intelligent interlocutor, confined in the stereotype of a fallen woman after her boat trip with Stephen who fell in love with her, deserted by the community that keeps slandering her, Maggie is just one of the many victims of what Anderson calls "intimate violence," which denotes "physical, sexual, emotional, financial, psychological and/or spiritual abuse by (stereotypically speaking) male heterosexual subjects of female subjects" (131). Maggie's decision to unconditionally forgive her brother and oppressor for his mistreatment is indeed a vice that she is prevented from perceiving because of her religious and patriarchal indoctrination. The oppressor dies with the oppressed at the end of the novel, which is mistakenly seen as an image of reconciliation between siblings, whereas in fact it is an image of loss and irremediable harm. Maggie was the one who managed to reach her old home in order to rescue her punitive and disapproving brother, and not the other way around. Yet she was silenced by the waters of death. Her death with her brother was reclaimed by the community as an ideal image of love between the siblings, a smug patriarchal legend for those who deny their own emotional violence, and protect warped relationships by silencing the oppressed women.

Women's need to be heard was continually disavowed in response to their growing demands for access to education and professions in the nineteenth century. The problem of single women unaided by men and desiring equal rights gave rise to heated debates. A section of *Anna Karenina* by Leo Tolstoy focuses on men's debate about the possibility of changing women's status, thus summed up by the prominent Canadian writer Aritha van Herk: "The dangers of educating women, they'll know too much, become uncontrollable, then what is to be done with them?" (131). The idea of women's liberation is derided at the party held at the estate of Prince Shcherbatsky, the father of three unimaginative daughters, who dare not reach for higher aims. Offering a supposedly witty argument against women's access to civil service, the prince asks whether he would be eligible as a wet nurse at the Foundling House. Shcherbatsky quotes the stereotypical proverb "her hair is long because her wit is ... " (Tolstoy 684) as the only justification of his dismissal of the woman question. As such, instead of an argument, the privileged male speaker uses "the controlling image," that is, a stereotype "built upon ignorance of a woman as a knower" (Anderson, "Silencing and Speaker Vulnerability" 39). Complying with their father's "controlling image," the Shcherbatsky sisters try to fare in the world on the strength of their good looks and wifely duties which do not leave room for knowledge other than that which is connected with the needs of husband and children.

Predictably enough, it is the social endorsement of "wilful ignorance" that does not permit Anna Karenina to be accepted as a female knower despite her immense intelligence. Van Herk draws attention to the fact that Anna becomes a self-taught expert in a number of fields, much to the amazement of her lover Vronsky, who disbelieves her as a knower but is unable to prove her wrong. Yet Tolstoy clearly suggests that Anna's reading interferes with her maternal role and ruins her marriage. The connection between reading and adultery is well established in literary works by men focusing on women, to mention only *Madame Bovary* by Gustave Flaubert, or one of its twentieth-century reinterpretations, Brian Moore's *The Doctor's Wife*, which rewrites the motif in order to expose its patriarchal injustice (Filipczak, *Brian Moore's Eponymous Heroines* 74, 88–89). Female writers in the twentieth century were bound to confront this negative legacy and to attempt to undo "the oppressive forms of wilful ignorance."

Morag Gunn, the protagonist of *The Diviners*, written by one of the founding mothers of contemporary Canadian literature, Margaret Laurence, starts out like Maggie Tulliver: a rebellious and intelligent child who questions certitudes and speaks her mind. All this changes when she begins her education at the university and falls in love with an English literature professor many years her senior. Morag smothers her insight and turns from a knower of myths, stories and truths into a passive object of worship, then into a docile wife, whose chocolate cake is beyond compare. She dutifully arranges appointments with the hairdresser so as to keep her hair the way her husband likes it. A post-Victorian "angel in the house," Morag Gunn silences herself like Maggie Tulliver, whose rebellion was just a stage to be overcome on the way towards maturity, which in women's case often implies being quieted. Maggie's unruly hair was a cause of distress to her mother just as her opinions were. When Maggie relinquished her intellectual independence she also handed her image over to the maternal care, and accepted an old-fashioned Victorian appearance.

When Morag Gunn is married to Brooke Skelton, a handsome university professor, born in colonial India, his frequent term of endearment to her is "hush, child" (Laurence 243). Morag finds herself paralysed with fear that her husband might reject her on account of her past which was far from his "controlling image" of a mysterious blank page; however, since Brooke does not identify her as a knower, either in an intellectual or a sexual sense, she has to smother the story of her underprivileged childhood and teenage love. *The Diviners* is Laurence's response to Joyce's *Portrait of an Artist as a Young Man*, as it poses the question of what happens when a young artist is a woman (316). Joyce's modernist self-absorption in the idea of exclusively male genius remains an instrument of "wilful ignorance" that patriarchally minded audiences use in order to silence female artists. Joyce's text, in which women surface only as mothers or sexual fetishes, is troubling for a feminist reader, who can either find it totally irrelevant to her experience in the way that bell hooks did (as Anderson reminds us in her paper "Silencing and Speaker Vulnerability" 41) or else rewrite it from a female point of view.

The reason why I find Laurence's insights crucial and dovetailing with the project on vulnerability pursued by Anderson is precisely because Anderson (in philosophy) and Laurence (in fiction) set out to reclaim genius, reason and creativity for femaleness. At the very same time both thinkers realized that women had been enmeshed in the negative vision of their own vulnerability which signified being prone to harm. This, in turn, rendered them unsuitable for the demanding experience of creativity, be it connected with literature, art, science or philosophy. This perspective is very much a part of my personal legacy. I grew up in the country where the only scientist awarded the Nobel Prize was a woman (Maria Skłodowska-Curie won it for physics in 1903, and for chemistry in 1911), and yet for years I had heard and accepted the opinion that women were not capable of abstract thinking. Thus, even though a book on Maria Curie was on my shelf, I was discouraged from pursuing sciences at the slightest obstacle. What I knew in theory was effectively undermined by sexist practices.

As a female poet I had to confront the stereotype that a woman should not write but should only be written about: defined rather than in charge of definitions. In the greatest examples of Polish literature, the author is more often than not a knowledgeable man whose agenda and authority make it impossible for a woman to respond to his legacy on equal terms: that is, as a writer. Laurence's portrayal of a class that her heroine attends offers a case in point from a different cultural context. When faced with the male lecturer's analysis of "The Canonization" by John Donne starting with the words "For God's sake hold your tongue, and let me love" Morag is unable to accept or accommodate the message (Laurence 208). She will not hold her tongue – or will she? That is precisely where theory and practice may come apart. Though self-conscious and talented, Morag will go underground (though not for good) when her favourite handsome lecturer becomes her husband. What Laurence powerfully exposes is how women who dismantle sexist assumptions in theory can still find it possible to abide by them in their lived experience. That is why for years I have lived by the concepts from Anderson's feminist philosophy. She drew my attention to the fact that women who often started out brilliantly ended up like Antigone: that is, symbolically entombed and cut off from any chance of self-realization. Let me turn back to Laurence in order to complete my point.

In Morag's case we encounter a female artist who is torn between the role of a wife and the desire to write. It turns out that in her marriage it is not possible to combine both of these roles, for Brooke makes Morag quiet not only by means of his term of endearment ("child") but also by disapproving of her as a potential knower. The proposal of marriage does not allow for her development as a postgraduate student. Brooke assures her that she can read at home, because education is not about getting a degree. This situation sounds all too familiar when we recall Anderson's comment on Le Doeuff's argument about Héloïse and her erotically charged relationship to her mentor, which was the only possible way of accessing knowledge: "a woman's admiration for her own mentor […] prevents her from seeing the value of her own thinking" (*A Feminist Philosophy of Religion* 50).

When Brooke's students come over to debate some issues at home, Morag wants to take part in the discussion. Insecure about what she said, she seeks Brooke's approval later, but he accepts neither her message nor the role that she unexpectedly took. Eventually Morag begins to work on her novel while Brooke is busy teaching. She wants to be heard and recognized as a knower outside her relationship. Her confidence is strengthened when she discovers that she can defend what she has written in front of the publishing reviewers. Aware of Brooke's condescending attitude, she avoids sharing her work with him:

"I'll take a quick run through it if you like," Brooke says.
"Well, thanks, but that's pretty well settled, the changes."
"I see. My reactions aren't any longer welcome to you."
"It's not that. It's – I know you know a lot about novels. But I know something, as well. Different from reading or teaching."
"With that insight, perhaps you'd like to take over my English 450 course in the Contemporary Novel? I am sure it could be arranged." (281)

The passage sums up Morag's relationship with Brooke; he is her teacher-husband, for whom she was a member of the audience, but there was no possibility of this dynamic becoming reciprocal as a result of Brooke's refusal to treat her as a knower. Rather, Brooke exploits Morag's insecurity and need for approval. Brooke's "self-deception" resides in the conviction of his own invulnerability. The child of an indifferent father and a mother who never raised her voice to him, Brooke has taught himself to cope with the childhood trauma of emotional abandonment by the parents. He "remains ignorant of his own wounding," to quote Anderson ("Silencing and Speaker Vulnerability" Abstract (online only)), and will project vulnerability on to Morag. This, however, means infantilizing her and refusing to recognize her as a knower.

For philosophers such as Anderson and Le Doeuff the crucial issue is that women gain access to philosophy; for writers such as Eliot and Laurence access to education and creativity was the vital thing. However, the disavowal of a female knower also lies at the heart of the ban on female priesthood in the Catholic Church. These three areas have been interconnected throughout the centuries, which has considerably damaged female potential and resulted in women's vulnerability to oppression. Michèle Roberts's novel *The Secret Gospel of Mary Magdalene* constitutes an imaginative attempt to reconstruct the processes through which women who followed Christ began to find themselves gradually removed from the important functions in the early church.

The novel recounts the growing conflict between Christ's disciples Mary Magdalene and Simon Peter. Up to the moment of crucifixion, Roberts's Mary Magdalene, who is also the beloved of Jesus in the literal sense, can make her message heard with his approval. Jesus welcomes her words and vision in which the first likeness of God is feminine. Roberts interprets the old concept of Sophia from wisdom literature as the Mother aspect of the divine (Cole, Ronan, and Taussig 50). In Mary Magdalene's vision, Sophia gives birth to a son, who considers himself perfect: "Sophia named him Ignorance because he forgot who made him" (Roberts 80). Characteristically, Mary terms the followers of misogyny "children of Ignorance" (81). In the novel Jesus approves of Mary's "gender-inclusive" vision that accommodates God as the Father and the Mother. He interprets Mary Magdalene's dream in the following way:

> The children of Ignorance are the adversaries of God, because they prevent the man and the woman from living out the fullness of God. (84)

Roberts's message connects with Anderson's refiguring of vulnerability as an openness to mutual affection, as she emphasizes the necessity of reforming relationships circumscribed and monitored by "wilful ignorance" which has so far guaranteed the self-perpetuation of patriarchy.

Roberts re-creates the beginnings of Christian community and sees their entanglement in the sexism that followed from women's ritually unclean status in Jewish religion and from their being devalued as defective and inferior in Greek culture. After Christ's death, Roberts's Mary demands her rightful position among the disciples, but this is how Simon Peter responds to her:

> In the eyes of God all of us are equal [...] But at the same time we live in the world, a wicked and corrupt world where women are at risk of being exploited and abused by sinful men. How can we allow our sisters to go about in public and expose themselves to this danger?
> – If we were priests I said through my tears, it would be far less likely to happen. (141)

Mary Magdalene's contention is that equality signifies access to authority and public space. Only on equal terms with men can women voice their own testimony, but Peter remains invincible in his illusion of male invulnerability. There is no possibility of connecting womanhood and discipleship. Peter's comment explicitly conflates vulnerability with gender and openness to violence. Roberts's portrayal of Christ's successor alerts the reader to the fact that "the vulnerable" – that is, women – are treated as "an inferior class, or problematic/pitiful people" (Anderson, "Towards a New Philosophical Imaginary" 9). The Christian community "commits an act of an injustice" by giving its women "lesser social identities," which reduce their humanity (ibid.). As Anderson points out in "An Epistemological-Ethical Approach" in a much earlier book, although the woman was the first to realize Christ's resurrection, "none of the (male) disciples believed the female testimony" (90). In Roberts's novel Mary Magdalene, Martha, Jesus' mother and Salome decide to leave their land and offer their testimony elsewhere. Roberts's Mary Magdalene is ready to do it because she experienced vulnerability refigured as "openness to mutual affection" ("Towards a New Philosophical Imaginary" 8) in her relationship with Christ. As such, she is able to pass it on with her message. Roberts's vision of alternative

Christianity is gender inclusive, non-hierarchical and certainly not realistic even at the present moment.

The disavowal of woman as knower is repeated throughout all the texts highlighted here, even those in which the female characters awaken to "their cognitive and non-cognitive" potential (Anderson, "The Subject's Loss of Self-Confidence" 5). Morag Gunn tells her husband Brooke "I am not your child, I am your wife" (Laurence 243) because she is mature enough to reject the lesser identity conferred on her by her patronizing husband. Though a gifted student, Morag is consigned to Maggie Tulliver's situation where reading/writing takes place on the sly and in private, and must not be unduly publicized, lest it undermine her socially constructed femininity, as in the case of Anna Karenina. Hipparchia's choice is never approved, as the patriarchal communities close ranks in their "disavowal" of thinking and the unthought. This is most poignant in the case of Roberts's protagonist. The writer argues that the exclusion of female testimony means the exclusion of the Mother and everything she stands for. Mary Magdalene is silenced like the female tradition within Christianity.

Mary Magdalene's message goes underground in the novel like the seed in the biblical parable: "I shall bury it in a stone jar under this tree where I have spent so much time waiting for the voice of God" (197). Or else, her message goes underground like the buried maternal, or Antigone, whom Mary Magdalene and two other Marys mime when they rush to the tomb with spices in order to anoint Christ's body (Mark 16.1). Roberts's Mary Magdalene says: "my mission [...] is to warn you against Ignorance, and to preach an idea" (197–98). This message forms a parallel to the feminist philosophy of religion pursued by Pamela Sue Anderson. Her reformist project on vulnerability offers a deeply ethical warning against the "wilful ignorance" that has so often damaged female potential and human relationships. As such, her work will continue to share the message of love in defiance of "living death."

disclosure statement

No potential conflict of interest was reported by the author.

bibliography

Anderson, Pamela Sue. "Creating a New Imaginary for Love in Religion." Ed. Paul S. Fiddes. *Love and Vulnerability: Thinking with Pamela Sue Anderson.* Ed. Pelagia Goulimari. Spec. issue of *Angelaki: Journal of the Theoretical Humanities* 25.1–2 (2020): 46–53. Print.

Anderson, Pamela Sue. "An Epistemological-Ethical Approach." *Critical Readings: Feminist Philosophy of Religion.* London: Routledge, 2004. 87–102. Print.

Anderson, Pamela Sue. *A Feminist Philosophy of Religion.* Oxford: Blackwell, 1998. Print.

Anderson, Pamela Sue. "Gender and the Infinite: On the Aspiration to Be All There Is." *International Journal for Philosophy of Religion* 50 (2001): 191–212. Print.

Anderson, Pamela Sue. "Silencing and Speaker Vulnerability: Undoing an Oppressive Form of (Wilful) Ignorance." Ed. Nick Bunnin. *Love and Vulnerability: Thinking with Pamela Sue Anderson.* Ed. Pelagia Goulimari. Spec. issue of *Angelaki: Journal of the Theoretical Humanities* 25.1–2 (2020): 36–45. Print.

Anderson, Pamela Sue. "The Subject's Loss of Self-Confidence in its Own Ability to Understand Itself." *Life and Philosophy: Essays to Honour Alan Montefiore on his 85th Birthday.* By Catherine Audard-Montefiore. N.p., 2011. MS.

Anderson, Pamela Sue. "Towards a New Philosophical Imaginary." Ed. Sabina Lovibond and A.W. Moore. *Love and Vulnerability: Thinking with Pamela Sue Anderson.* Ed. Pelagia Goulimari. Spec. issue of *Angelaki: Journal of the Theoretical Humanities* 25.1–2 (2020): 8–22. Print.

Anderson, Pamela Sue. "When Justice and Forgiveness Come Apart: A Feminist Perspective on Restorative Justice and Intimate Violence." *Oxford Journal of Law and Religion* 5 (2016): 113–34. Print.

Cole, Susan, Marian Ronan, and Hal Taussig. *Wisdom's Feast: Sophia in Study and Celebration.* Lanham, MD: Rowman, 1996. Print.

Eliot, George. *The Mill on the Floss*. London: Penguin, 1994. Print.

Filipczak, Dorota. *Brian Moore's Eponymous Heroines: Representations of Women and Authorial Boundaries*. Berlin: Lang, 2018. Print.

Filipczak, Dorota. "Is Literature Any Help in Liberating Eve and Mary?" *New Topics in Feminist Philosophy of Religion*. Ed. Pamela Sue Anderson. Dordrecht: Springer, 2010. 117–26. Print.

Laurence, Margaret. *The Diviners*. Toronto: McClelland, 1988. Print.

McDonagh, Josephine. "Early Novels." *The Cambridge Companion to George Eliot*. Ed. George Levine. Cambridge: Cambridge UP, 2001. 38–56. Print.

Roberts, Michèle. *The Secret Gospel of Mary Magdalene*. New York: Pegasus, 2007. Print.

Röder Bolton, Gerlinde. *George Eliot and Goethe: An Elective Affinity*. Amsterdam: Rodopi, 1998. Print.

Semmel, Bernard. *George Eliot and the Politics of National Inheritance*. Oxford: Oxford UP, 1994. Print.

Tolstoy, Leo. *Anna Karenina*. Trans. Constance Garnett. Planet. e-Book.

Van Herk, Aritha. *Places Far From Ellesmere*. Red Deer: Red Deer College P, 1995. Print.

During my first year of postgraduate study, I was fortunate enough to be supervised by Pamela Sue Anderson. At the time, I was working as a bartender in a pub to support my study and my research sought to abstract and critique my experience of being required to perform my white, middle-class femininity in this role through the performance of vulnerability. Front-facing bar work, I argued, was a form of affective labour where the embodiment of vulnerability was a carefully codified, subtly inscribed, requirement of the job. Job descriptions asking for "enthusiasm," masculine management's positive responses to heteronormative flirting practices, and customers' demands for emotional labour through refrains such as "cheer up" – occasionally rewarded in tips – all pointed towards the necessity for a particular performance of femininity in order to succeed in the role. Taken together, I found that customer-facing service-sector roles were more readily occupied by white, middle-class women able to perform a specific type of femininity-as-vulnerability.

However, as my research took a critical perspective on the performance of vulnerability, what I encountered in my supervisions with Pamela, I now realize, countered the possibility of such a narrow understanding of the concept. As I, in a slightly cocky, enthusiastic, postgraduate manner, sought to systematize and codify vulnerability as gendered, racialized and classed, and to criticize the concept on such a basis, the intellectually enriching character of my supervisions and the friendship that ensued were made possible on the basis of Pamela's own performance of vulnerability-as-generosity.

This idea that vulnerability cannot be reduced to such an overdetermined, negative

emily cousens

ANDERSON'S ETHICAL VULNERABILITY
animating feminist responses to sexual violence

meaning is one that Pamela not only performed as a friend, supervisor and committed member of the academic community, but began to theorize in her later work. In both life and writing, she demonstrated the transformational character of vulnerability: its implication in violence but also in generative relationalities such as love and friendship too. In "Arguing for 'Ethical' Vulnerability: Towards a Politics of Care?" (2017) Anderson writes: "let me note at the outset that my paper, instead of reducing vulnerability to an exposure to violence, *aims to say* something life-enhancing about vulnerability" (148–49). It is this contention – that there is a positive dimension to vulnerability, and one which is ethically and politically significant – which I shall interrogate. My aim in this essay is to develop Anderson's insight regarding the transformational character of vulnerability, exploring it first in the context of sexual violence theory and then applying it to the recent #MeToo movement. My argument is that vulnerability as theorized by Anderson has an unacknowledged but significant contribution to make to the philosophy underscoring intersectional feminist responses to sexual violence.

vulnerability and violence

In recent years, Anderson has been one of a number of feminist philosophers reconsidering both the value of vulnerability and the nature of its relation to violence (see also Ferrarese; Gilson; Mackenzie; Murphy; Oliviero). The term, as Alyson Cole explains, has been resignified through an emphasis on its universality and generative capacity (260). Influential in this turn, for Anderson among others,[1] has been Judith Butler's articulation of a "'common' corporeal vulnerability" (*Precarious Life* 42) as the potential ground for a universal ethics of non-violence. For Butler, the condition has the capacity to furnish "a sense of political community of a complex order" (22) through its exposing of the interconnectedness and interdependence of embodied existence. "From where," she asks, "might a principle emerge by which we vow to protect others from the kinds of violence we have suffered if not from an apprehension of a common human vulnerability?" (30). For Butler, then, attending to vulnerability has the potential to transform how we respond to the violence that vulnerability permits. The possibility of non-violence[2] emerges "from an understanding of the possibilities of one's own violent actions in relation to those lives to whom one is bound" (Butler, "Reply" 194) and thus recognition of the vulnerability of the Other is central to a politics of non-violence, as this recognition constitutes the means by which interdependence becomes apparent.[3]

Anderson builds on Butler's reconceptualization of the relationship between vulnerability and violence, exploring what such an ambivalent ontology of vulnerability may facilitate for a politics of accountability. For Anderson, if, as Butler argues, vulnerability includes susceptibility not only to violence but a whole host of more positive intersubjective affective relations ("'Ethical' Vulnerability" 147), then what connects the range of experiences that result from vulnerability is transformation.

Anderson elaborates that there are two levels to vulnerability: the phenomenological and the ethical. The phenomenological level is close to Butler's ambivalent corporeal ontology. It refers to the "materially specific lived experiences of intimacy, as openness to love and affection, while admitting affection could generate negative effects of fear, shame or rage" (147–48) and echoes Erinn Gilson's conceptualization of vulnerability as "a basic kind of openness to being affected and affecting others in both positive and negative ways" ("Vulnerability, Ignorance, and Oppression" 310). The transformation at this phenomenological level is largely unintentional and unwilled. Phenomenological vulnerability is both an effect of and directs us towards the ontological character of vulnerability, and as such I will occasionally refer to "ontological vulnerability" in place of "phenomenological vulnerability" in order to maintain a direct dialogue between Anderson and contemporary feminist philosophers who are engaging and building on Butler's thought.

In contrast to the uncontrollable character of phenomenological vulnerability for the subject experiencing it, at the ethical level this openness can be actively mined in the pursuit of positive relations with others. Anderson writes that "an ethical level of vulnerability would be an openness to affective relations between subjects who interact; ethical openness to change and to being changed would be positive insofar as enabling relational (overcoming asymmetrical) accountability"[4] ("'Ethical' Vulnerability" 148). Thus ethical vulnerability is an active, necessarily reciprocal, practice of embracing transformation in self and others, derived from a more foundational vulnerability of the constitutive corporeal variety present in the work of Butler and Gilson. Accountability, as will become apparent, ensues as the means by which ethical vulnerability can be practised.[5]

Rather than posing a static actor, one who rationally decides between a more or less morally good course of actions, as the basis for the ethical subject, the constitutive character of vulnerability, as a condition of transformability, implies a becoming subject whose existence is always in excess of any action they have done or been subject to. The ethical character of this subject lies not in their capacity to choose between a more or less harmful or virtuous course of action but in their openness to being changed: "what I advocate as distinctively ethical vulnerability acknowledges and activates an openness to becoming changed," writes Anderson, and "this openness can make possible a relational accountability to one another on ethical matters" ("'Ethical' Vulnerability" 150). Accountability as a basis for justice presumes that victim and perpetrator (i) are temporary ascriptions and (ii) that moving positively beyond the injustice involves both parties engaging with, listening to and affirming one another in their complexity. As such, a subject characterized by openness to change through others is characterized by exactly the same dynamic, relational ontology that engenders the possibility of accountability.

This ontology of transformation gives rise to two ethical imperatives. Regarding the self, it compels one to open oneself to such change, "enabling forward movement in life, moving from what we take ourselves to be to what we are becoming" (149), and regarding the Other, it entails carving a space for forgiveness of a complex order. If, for Derrida, the impossibility, or at least paradox, of forgiveness – "forgiveness forgives only the unforgivable" (32) – lies in the unchanging ethical content of the act to be forgiven, for Anderson, it is not the ethical content of the act but of the actor which occasions the possibility and importance of forgiveness. If the ethical subject is one underscored by an ontology of transformation, then responding to an act of violence entails focusing not on the unchangeable event but on the actors. Securing a future for a subject based on what they have done, or have been subject to, fixes the future from the perspective of the present. By contrast, Anderson's focus on the actors involved in an instance of violence instead of the act itself exemplifies Sedgwick's reparative insight that "to realize that the future may be different from the present" necessitates entertaining such "profoundly [...] relieving, ethically crucial possibilities as that the past, in turn, could have happened differently from the way it actually did" (146). Ethical vulnerability entails a dynamic temporality which holds out the reparative possibility for renewed relationality between those where harm has been done.

Anderson appeals to vulnerability in the context of violence in order to underscore a politics of ethical responsiveness. Openness to being changed is a relational ontology, it is through others that transformation takes place, and it is from this basis that accountability becomes central to responding to violence: "this openness can make possible a relational accountability to others on ethical matters" ("'Ethical' Vulnerability" 150). Thus if injury has taken place, "ethical vulnerability opens up an opportunity to restore justice, or to repair, the horrendous pain of wounds (vulnerabilities) [...] with relational accountability" (153). Accountability therefore becomes central to ethical responsiveness, and is a precondition for forgiveness ("Justice and Forgiveness" 117). Anderson has applied this ethics in the context of what she terms "intimacy wounding," the situation in which a person has experienced "intimate violence," which "denotes physical, sexual, emotional, financial, psychological, and/or spiritual abuse which is perpetuated [sic] by, for example, adult males on adult female partners in close, personal relations" (116). For her, in such instances, ethical accountability must be prioritized in the pursuit of restorative justice. In what follows, I extend the application of ethical vulnerability, contending that Anderson's insights are highly relevant to the difficult question for feminists of how to respond to sexual violence.

feminism and sexual violence

Sexual violence represents both a principal concern for feminists and a challenging topic to respond to. It is a principal concern because it is as gendered and sexed beings that sexual violence happens. Whilst there are divergent theories on the nature of sexual abuse – is it a question of sex or power for instance? (see Cahill 15) – it is empirically the case that trans, non-binary and female-presenting individuals experience sexual violence at disproportionately high rates across the world (see Teays 132; James et al. 198). As such, gender is clearly a relevant factor. In addition, the choice of sex as the vehicle for violence again makes it an issue for feminists, given that one of the most enduring legacies of feminisms since the abolition movement has been the politicization of sex as a microcosm of broader power relations (see Rutherford; Millett).

Yet sexual violence is also a highly contentious issue for feminists. The difficulties it raises fall into two categories:

(1) problems of identification;
(2) problems of response.

Problems of identification include defining sexual violence and naming one's experiences as sexual violence. The lines between rape, sexual assault and non-problematic sex are not clearly delineable in advance. Where some theorists have argued for a continuum approach in identifying violence (e.g., MacKinnon; Dworkin; Gavey) others have advocated a "victim-centred approach" where the experience or testimony of the victim[6] is what counts (e.g., Bourke; Cahill; Mardorossian). Whilst many writing from academic feminist perspectives are critical of the mainstreamed liberal contract approach where the presence of "consent" determines the line between good and bad sex (e.g., Alcoff; Razack, "Consent to Responsibility" 893), for others the widely recognized feature of this approach renders it at least politically useful (see Hunter and Cowan). These are important discussions. However, in this essay what I am pursuing is the usefulness of Anderson's "ethical vulnerability" for addressing problems pertaining to the second question: once a wrong has been identified, how should feminists respond?

Questions pertaining to how to respond to sexual violence traverse feminist theory and activism. Feminist theorists have grappled with the question of how to avoid essentializing the identities of those involved in an instance of sexual violence by reducing them to their status as "victim" or "perpetrator" (Lamb 3). The insights of deconstruction highlight the fallaciousness of such tidy, oppositional categories in the first place; meanwhile, psychoanalysis has demonstrated that such discrete, unchanging subject positions are neither stable nor reflective of an individual's subjectivity. Descriptively, too, these categories are idealized oversimplifications which have the unintended effect of obscuring the ways in which perpetrators frequently have a history of victimization themselves; meanwhile, victims are complex individuals who can rarely meet the standards of "innocence" associated with membership of that group (Lamb 158; Phillips 67). The category of "victim" has come under additional scrutiny for its apparent evacuation of women's agency, with some posing the term "survivor" as a less passive alternative (Mahoney 59). In addition, the racialized, classed norms by which an individual may be intelligible as a victim at all have also led to problems with the category (Phipps, "Rape and Respectability"). All this is to say that feminist theorists have struggled to theorize how to respond to sexual violence, even once it has been established that an injurious event of this nature has occurred, given the ontological and political questions that such discourses raise.

Feminist activists face a different, although not unrelated, set of problems in responding to sexual violence. These pertain to what "justice" might involve. Whilst some, typically white, feminists have argued for greater rates of prosecution and longer sentencing lengths for perpetrators in order to address the patriarchal undervaluing of women's lives and the lack of belief that accrues to women's testimony, these strategies have been met with convincing criticisms. Anti-carceral feminists point to the structural racism of the justice system and question the investment in a prison complex which has no proven record of addressing crime or violence (Davis 25). Indeed, in the case of sexual violence, the move to incarcerate is almost a move to return the initial violence in a different scene, given the ubiquity of physical violence, including sexual violence, in prisons. Jackson elaborates that "incarceration is itself an act of racialized sexual violence, one enabled by the mobilization of fantasies of violent black male sexuality" (198). Given that few inmates will leave prison without having experienced any physical violence, and studies on the problem in men's prisons in the United States have reported the rate of "sexually coercive behaviours" to be as high as 20 per cent (Struckman-Johnson and Struckman-Johnson; Wooden and Parker), the idea that prison addresses violence has been found wanting. It seems that incarceration amounts to an outsourced justice of revenge, and one with no tangible benefit for the victim, the assailant or the community. To the contrary, in an economy in which violence begets violence, if anything, carceral solutions seem to contribute to the problem. The most readily available response to sexual violence then, the state and its penal complement, the prison, is one which is particularly fraught for feminists given its discriminatory and violent operation (Gilmore 14). In short, given that "the criminal justice system is now far more racist than it is sexist in adjudicating victim claims" (Haaken 785), responding to sexual violence through prison sentences is a highly contested move.

ethical vulnerability and sexual violence

Whilst I have demonstrated that Anderson posits a necessary link between ethical vulnerability and accountability, how does such an ethics inform the question of how to respond to sexual violence? In the remainder of this essay I propose that Anderson's ethical vulnerability can allay some of the difficulties just outlined facing both the academic and the activist attempts to *respond* to sexual violence. To summarize, these pertain first to the problems of essentializing the categories of victim and perpetrator and second to the ineffective and racialized logic of the pursuit of judicial justice. If ethical vulnerability is able to address both these problems, then it must also be tested against the following minimum requirements for a response to sexual violence to be intersectional: (i) power relations rather than the cultural or social identities of the actors involved are appealed to, and (ii) it refuses the privileged position of valuing protection for some over protection for all.

To elaborate on each of these intersectional requirements, identifying power relations precludes individualized, pathologized explanations for sexual violence which function to obscure what Nicola Gavey refers to as "the cultural scaffolding for rape" (2) in their exceptionalizing of the incident. Focusing on power relations also refuses the logic of "cultural deficit" (Razack, "Imperilled Muslim Women" 131) explanations for sexual violence, where if the actor was from a minority culture then culture rather than gender is put forward as an explanation. Given that intersectionality insists on a "consideration of gender, race, and other axes of power" (Cho et al. 787), responding to sexual violence intersectionally necessitates illuminating and interrogating such interlocking vectors of oppression. Second, refusing the protection of some over the protection of all means that to oppose sexual violence entails opposing the institutions that foster and enable it. Given the disproportionately high rates of violence in prison, this entails a critique of the prison-industrial complex alongside a critique of sexual violence (see Phipps, "Feminists Fighting"). Thus, in addition to eschewing essentialism and judicial-based justice, responding to sexual violence intersectionally entails identifying power relations and refusing the displacement of violence from some bodies onto those deemed more socially disposable.

Anderson's ethical vulnerability provides a framework for responding to sexual violence which addresses the problems that feminists have faced and incorporates these fundamental intersectional criteria. Ethical vulnerability entails eschewing essentialism as appealing to a common, corporeal vulnerability is an inherently non-binary move which dispels the possibility of discrete categories of victim and perpetrator categorized by vulnerability and invulnerability respectively. Discrete, oppositional categories such as these also tend to be static ascriptions, a characteristic that Anderson's ontology of transformation inherently repudiates. For Anderson, neither victim nor perpetrator can be conceived as pre-determined categories which means that, for embodied, living beings, becoming does not end with an instance of sexual violence, no matter how serious, damaging and exploitative.

This reparative, anti-essentialist insight, that neither victim nor perpetrator can be reduced to such fixed identities, is relevant too for addressing the problem of denying women's agency. As a fixed, negative state, "agency is regarded as incompatible with vulnerability, which is conceived as a hindrance, and thus, by definition the vulnerable person is weak, incapable, and powerless" (Gilson, "Vulnerability and Victimization" 74). However, by reconceptualizing vulnerability as an openness available to all, Anderson intervenes in such a binarizing logic, underscoring the denial of women's agency and its complementary logic of paternalism.

In addition, collapsing the dualistic logic of vulnerable/invulnerable underscoring categories of victim and perpetrator is relevant for addressing the politicized and racialized means through which the category of perpetrator will become fixed. Bitsch finds that in Norwegian rape cases, "nationality or ethnicity is mentioned as a relevant fact when it involves minority men but not majority men" (946). As a result, where minority men are subject to "stigmatic" shaming by society, majority men are subject to "reintegrative" shaming. Extrapolating from her findings indicates that whether the identity of a perpetrator becomes fixed and essentialized will often be in keeping with racialized practices equating non-whiteness with sexual threat. This reproduces a history of racialized masculinities being framed as threats to the white female body (Ware 4–5), which comes to stand in for the nation, and is in keeping with a US-centric logic of "sexual exceptionalism" (Puar 79) where to be a racial other is to be a sexual other. The benefit of Anderson's appeal to a common vulnerability here lies in the ability of such a move to dismantle the ontological grounds for an equation between invulnerability, racialized masculinity and sexual threat. If the perpetrator was not predetermined as such, on account of their individual pathology or racialized/sexualized otherness, then we are forced to ask – in keeping with Anderson's becoming subject – how they came to be, and how they could be otherwise. As such, the related problems, when responding to sexual violence, of essentializing the categories of victim/perpetrator and appealing to a justice system which perpetuates race and class inequalities are addressed by a relational ontology in which the subject is always becoming and accountability rather than blame is prioritized.

When Anderson opposes relational accountability to asymmetrical accountability ("'Ethical' Vulnerability" 148, 151) she is gesturing towards the place of power relations in ethical relationships, which may serve to favour some over others, highlighting the necessity of attending to and acknowledging these as a precondition for ethics. Similarly, in refusing individualized or cultural-deficit explanations for violence, which are underscored by dichotomized accounts of vulnerability – some are vulnerable and deserving of protections, others predatory and deserving of prosecution – Anderson redirects a focus towards the power relations that produce victims and perpetrators in any one instance. Ontological vulnerability highlights the shared, largely ambivalent character of the condition. Yet if, at the level of lived material experience, some are disproportionately liable to negative instances of vulnerability (i.e., violence), then this raises the question of what social, political and economic conditions are at work. Unequal vulnerability to violence, when not understood as a property of a particular group, emerges as an effect of concrete institutional policies and power inequalities. For instance, the vulnerability of transwomen to violence in public spaces is an outcome of discourses, such as those which frame trans subjecthood as a question or debate, which circulate alongside concrete policies of marginalization such as restricted access to services, employment and medical support. Together, these combine to make public space a highly dangerous environment for transgender individuals (Namaste). Applied to sexual violence against gender nonconforming individuals, transwomen and cisgender women, the institutional enablers of rape culture, the discourses that surround it as well as the systemic underpinnings of these – specifically patriarchy and heterosexism – are brought into relief by an approach which neither naturalizes nor negates the unequal distribution of negative instances of vulnerability. Anderson's ethical vulnerability has intersectional insights, then, as it directs a focus away from individuals or social identities and towards power inequalities instead. Discrepancies between the shared ambivalent ontological vulnerability and the more decisively negative lived experiences of the condition point to the necessity for an intersectional critical analysis of power. For these to be fully realized, of course, more context-specific detail is required and the essay will end with one such application of Anderson's thought to contemporary sexual violence politics.

Anderson's contention that accountability follows from her characterization of the ethical subject is one which also resonates with intersectional feminist sexual violence politics. Recognizing, as Wendy Brown also argues, that the call for judicial redress "casts the law in particular and the state more generally as neutral arbiters of injury rather than as themselves invested with the power to injure" (27), women of colour feminists have long sought extra-judicial avenues for justice (see Davis 25; Thuma 55; INCITE!). Lisa Marie Cacho highlights that "when [American] law targets certain people for incarceration or deportation, it criminalizes those people of color who are always already most vulnerable and multiply marginalized" (Cacho 4), and her arguments regarding the racialized inequality governing criminalization extend globally (Penal Reform International 16). As such, responses to violence which position the state as innocent with regard to the production of violence have been found wanting. In their place, community accountability has emerged as a key component of intersectional, transformative justice movements led by women of colour and queer anti-violence activists seeking alternatives to state-led responses to violence (Generation Five; Armatta 15).

Aspiring towards accountability and transformation rather than blame and incarceration is both central to the reparative logic that holds out the possibility for renewed future relations and one that has always been central for queer communities and communities of colour who seek to protect their members from the violence of larger society, at the same time as needing to address violence from within the community (see Collins; Schulman). Anderson's contribution to this rich history of women of colour organizing is that vulnerability is both an unwilled, phenomenological condition and a promising ethical practice. Taken together, Anderson offers an account of accountability, where the rationale for accountability is derived from the characterization of the ethical subject herself. As such, she expands the rationale for accountability as a response to violence by locating it in the transformability of the subject, thereby providing the philosophical foundations for an accountability oriented approach to justice. I will end with an examination of the recent #MeToo movement in order to test these arguments regarding responsiveness in light of recent developments in sexual violence politics.

ethical vulnerability and the #metoo movement

In recent years, the question of responding to sexual violence has become an increasingly pertinent one. Since 2017, the landscape of sexual violence politics has become saturated by the #MeToo movement. The movement in its viral version emerged in 2017 after the actor Alyssa Milano penned a tweet encouraging spreading the hashtag #MeToo. This was a phrase first used by African-American activist Tarana Burke in 2006, who had been working in communities of colour to counter the stigma and silence around sexual violence and to build a community of survivors equipped and empowered to support one another. Burke's coinage of the phrase and longstanding activism has been, if belatedly, widely recognized. However, the viral movement is one which departed from Milano's tweet and has a political life that exceeds, and does not always complement, the politics and ambitions of Burke's grassroots movement. As such, where I speak of the viral or mainstream version, it is to the aftermath of Milano's tweet – the sharing of stories online and the media reporting of the most high-profile accusations – that I refer. By contrast, when I discuss the grassroots Me Too movement, I am referring to Burke's community of colour-focused sexual-violence activism both before and after the viral movement took off.

The mainstream movement was catalysed into existence in 2017. Milano's aim in penning the tweet was to make apparent the widespread character of sexual harassment and sexual violence after the issue became newsworthy following high-profile sexual-abuse allegations against Harvey Weinstein from women in the film and media industry in October 2017. The hashtag went viral. "In just one year, the #MeToo hashtag has been used more than 19 million times on Twitter alone" (Chan in Burke, "'Our Pain'") and has circulated in eighty-five countries beyond the Global North.[7] Indeed, "#MeToo has become a global phenomenon, spreading from the United States to the United Kingdom, Canada, Australia, Israel, India and beyond" (Davis and Zarkov 3). Sara Ahmed's image of the domino effect that follows when the lid is lifted on what it is permissible to articulate in the context of sexual harassment – "a 'drip drip' becomes a flood" (30) – is particularly apt, as millions of women across the world retweeted the hashtag, often accompanied by stories or discussion of their experience(s). Now, over eighteen months after Milano's first tweet, the movement or stories associated continue to occupy headline news regularly, and media commentators have framed it as marking a "watershed moment" or signalling "a reckoning," shifting the terms of sexualized interactions between men and women, particularly in the workplace.[8]

Feminist commentators have been less emphatic in their response to the movement, pointing towards the "ambiguities and dilemmas" (Zarkov and Davis) that the viral movement has raised. Interestingly, despite the mainstreaming of feminism in recent years, #MeToo is being presented as a movement independent of feminism (Serisier 94). Whilst, as Ann Pellegrini writes, "Experiences of sexual harassment and sexual assault are hardly new. Nor are feminist movements to confront such misconduct new. Even more importantly, disagreements among feminists are not new either" (262), media engagements with the topic suggest otherwise. Mainstream reports participate in an "outrage economy" (Phipps, "Reckoning Up" 1) which frames sexual harassment as a recently discovered problem. This functions simultaneously to depoliticize the issue as it is dislocated from a structural analysis of power relations and erase past lives of feminist sexual-violence activism.[9]

Moreover, in its viral and mainstream iteration, the movement meets neither of the criteria for an intersectional sexual-violence politics laid out above. As Virginia Goldner observes, "every time it seems we have exhausted our supply of top-tier sexual harassers, another one bites the dust" (235), reflecting the dominant currency of the discourse as a movement of identifying perpetrators rather than illuminating power relations. In addition, #MeToo prioritizes the protection of those with a voice over those without. Stories of sexual assault in prisons and detention centres, for instance, do not appear within the discourse. As such, rather than illuminate the broad tapestry of violent sexual relations and the accompanying institutional policies and frameworks which enable it, the movement in its most media-friendly version effaces such interrogation of the "broad structures of power" by focusing on "individual bad apples case by case" (Duggan, "The Full Catastrophe"). Indeed, whilst in the United Kingdom, for instance, widespread cuts to women's refuges are largely ignored, one is compelled to question the investment of media outlets and their readers in stories of sexual assault with their accompanying images of white feminine vulnerability, which arguably trade in the same violent eroticization which enabled such abuse in the first place (a question posed by Rose).

In fact, in as far as the viral movement has focused on testimony and "speaking out" (Serisier), it has offered little in terms of a politics of how to "respond" to sexual violence. This marks a departure from Burke's movement, where "empowerment through empathy" was at the centre of a movement of and for survivors.[10] In what follows, I will argue that in contrast to the contentions raised by the viral version of the #MeToo movement, examining Burke's grassroots movement in light of Anderson's "ethical vulnerability" framework illuminates much of its strength. Consequently, I propose that the two can inform one another, highlighting key philosophical and practical priorities for the pursuit of intersectional feminist responses to sexual violence.

Tarana Burke's initial formulation of the Me Too movement was about creating a community of survivors who could find strength in the knowledge that they were not alone. "Me Too," she explains, "became the way to succinctly and powerfully, connect with other people and give permission to start their journey to heal" (Burke, "We Spoke"). Ethical vulnerability is present in the way that Burke's emphasis is on the transformation of the victim so that in naming an injustice they can begin to move past it: "we want to turn victims into survivors and survivors into thrivers" (Burke, "Empowerment through Empathy"). The agency as well as the ontological becoming of the subject of violence is at the heart of Burke's distinctly non-paternalistic politics. Ethical vulnerability is also apparent in the potential for repair between perpetrators and victims:

> people who are perpetrators, (which is largely men) need to be talking about accountability and transparency and vulnerability. They need to be standing up and saying, "this is what I'm going to do to change", or, "I apologise". Everybody needs to do their work on their own. (Burke, "We Spoke")

In focusing on the potential for both victims and perpetrators to move past an injustice, Burke's Me Too movement exemplifies a pragmatic yet radical politics of responsiveness to injury.

As such, Burke's activism around responding to violence employs the insights of ethical vulnerability regarding embracing transformation of both self and other. In contrast to the mainstream movement with its vilification campaigns, Burke explains that "The reality is, if we really want to really look toward ending sexual violence, we have to examine all of our behavior [...] This is across the board, however you identify on a gender spectrum" ("Our Pain"). Change requires interrogating the way in which the scaffolding for structural vulnerabilities is located throughout the fabric of quotidian behaviours and institutions; in other words, complicity in rape culture is social rather than individual. The logic of Burke's anti-violence politics is that of "an economy predicated on the principles of transformative empathy" (Rodino-Colocino 99). Thus, as with Anderson's "ethical vulnerability," Burke's politics of "empowerment through empathy" shares an ontology of transformation which makes possible a reparative responsiveness and avoids essentialized ascriptions of victimhood or blame.

Burke's Me Too movement is intersectional in its foregrounding of complex power relations. Indeed, she is operating in the long history of women of colour anti-violence organizing in which to appeal to the state is to endanger the community. As Burke highlights,

> There are nuances in our community around sexual violence that are informed by centuries of oppression and white supremacy, but we have to confront them. Across the board there's shame, but in our community there's shame on top of fear on top of ostracization – there are layers of things we have to unpack. (Burke, "#MeToo Should Center")

It is in this sense that it serves an intersectional feminist goal, attending to the meaning of sexual violence within a specific history and community and focusing on both the confluence of power relations as well as the way in which they are lived. Burke emphasizes that making accountability the prerogative of the few obscures the systemic character of sexual violence. Yet, at the same time, she acknowledges the nuances involved in attending to instances in their particularity:

> Narrowing our focus to investigations, firings and prison can hinder the conversation and the reality that accountability and justice look different for different people. We need to refine our approaches for seeking justice to reflect that diversity. Sexual violence happens on a spectrum, so accountability has to happen on a spectrum. And that means various ways of being accountable are necessary. (Burke, "On the Rigorous Work")

In this way, Burke refuses to prioritize the protection of some over the protection of others. Accountability is as widespread as the vulnerability that demands it, yet both are, as Anderson also highlighted, "materially specific, lived experiences" ("'Ethical' Vulnerability" 147) which demand sensitivity and cultural and historical awareness.

In directing her focus to power relations and all, rather than the most privileged, victims, Burke criticizes the way in which, in the mainstream movement, certain experiences are amplified at the expense of others. In 2018, she says that whilst she launched the Me Too movement in 2006 "because I wanted to find ways to bring healing into the lives of black women and girls [...] those same women and girls, along with other people of colour, queer people and disabled people, have not felt seen this year" (Burke, "On the Rigorous Work"). Intersectional responses to violence necessitate attending to the experiences of all, something the mainstream movement, with its dualistic postulation of some as vulnerable, others as perpetrators, has failed to achieve. By contrast, Me Too as a term for connecting survivors with one another has the capacity to function, as Lee and Webster explore, as "a multimodal mobile social amplifier" which involves participants simultaneously "handing [themselves] over to the multitude and the heterogeneous" (250). Indeed, Burke's movement utilizes "transformative empathy" which Rodino-Colocino explains "promotes listening rather than distancing or looking at speakers as 'others'. It requires self-reflexivity and potential transformation of one's own assumptions" (97). Empathy for Burke is thus a transformative intersubjective affect made possible on the basis of a subject underscored by an ontology of transformation. It is a precondition for the "reciprocal accountability" advocated by Anderson and similarly prioritized by Burke:

> without [accountability], there's no clear path for people, especially public figures, to regain the trust of those they've harmed and let down. This is playing out publicly as many of the celebrities and entertainers whose behavior was exposed are now attempting comebacks without having made amends to those they harmed, publicly apologizing, or acknowledging how they're going to change their behavior, industries, or communities to help end sexual violence. (Burke, "On the Rigorous Work")

Accountability is thus a precondition for reparative responsiveness to sexual violence for Burke, just as I have argued it is for Anderson. Whereas carceral justice solutions leave victims with little agency, foregrounding accountability in repair, argue Anderson and Burke, re-inscribes the victim as a complex, dynamic and agential subject. Whilst the reparative insight is that the future can be otherwise, a positive future for victims entails achieving recognition for their harm; this is rarely achieved in carceral responses where justice gets abstracted into sentencing lengths.

Me Too was not conceived as a discourse of outing but rather a strategy of community response and repair, which involved the power of solidarity in reminding individuals that they are not alone (Burke, "Empowerment through Empathy"). In their introduction to *Vulnerability in Resistance*, Butler, Gambetti, and Sabsay write that:

our point of departure is to call into question through the analysis of concrete contexts the basic assumption that vulnerability and resistance are mutually oppositional, even as the opposition is found throughout in mainstream politics as well as prominent strands of feminist theory [...] What follows when we conceive of resistance as drawing from vulnerability as a resource of vulnerability, or as part of the very meaning or action of resistance itself? (1)

This is precisely the insight that Burke pursues when she argues that Me Too, in many ways, is about agency. "It's not about giving up your agency, it's about claiming it" (Burke, "'You Have to Use Your Privilege'"). The movement in its inception was one in which identifying vulnerability was about building a fabric of already-existing resistance. Rather than propose a solution to violence, as if non-violence can be achieved, the task is to negotiate a way of persisting and sustaining liveable lives in the present; and this is precisely the place of accountability.

This essay has discussed how Anderson's engagement with vulnerability contains a phenomenological and an ethical level and that, taken together, these correspond to an *account* of accountability, premised on an ontology of the transformable subject. Through an exploration of the challenges facing feminist responses to sexual violence, as well as the ambivalent status of the viral #MeToo movement for feminists, I have paved the way for a consideration of the centrality of accountability in responses to sexual violence. The intersectional potential of this is demonstrated in Tarana Burke's grassroots anti-violence activism. Eschewing essentialism is a key part of an intersectional response which focuses on power relations rather than individuals and refuses to allow cultural-deficit explanations for violence to stand in for an interrogation of patriarchy and white supremacy. Burke's activism is intersectional and politically promising. What Anderson's theorization of vulnerability offers in addition is an ethical ground for prioritizing accountability and, in the process, it demonstrates the relevance of Burke's model of anti-violence organizing across intersectional lines more broadly, exposing inadequacies of the viral movement in the process.

conclusion

For Anderson, the meaning of vulnerability cannot be reduced to its negative association with injury. On the contrary, as she demonstrated in both her life and her writing, vulnerability entails openness to transformation and this is both a phenomenological condition and one which can be actively mined in the pursuit of "life-enhancing" ethical relations ("'Ethical' Vulnerability" 149). I have argued that in place of the rational, deliberative subject of normative ethics, Anderson poses a vulnerable subject, underscored by an ontology of transformation. This is an ethical subject, one whose emergence in the context of violence – phenomenological vulnerability, our capacity to be affected, underscores the potential for violence – makes possible ethical responsiveness to violence. Echoing Gilson's postulation that "it is precisely because we are vulnerable [...] that we feel any compulsion to respond ethically" (*Ethics* 11), for Anderson there is a normative account of responsiveness which ensues from the postulation of a common, shared vulnerability. Ethical vulnerability, she argues, entails active engagement with openness to being changed and this has both a self- and an other-regarding dimension. A feminist response to violence entails precisely such an "openness to self- and other-affection [...] to a new future as a dynamic process" ("'Ethical' Vulnerability" 147) and such a dynamic, reciprocal process of repair necessitates accountability.

I have argued that the contention that it is as vulnerable beings that we are open to transformation – in both negative and positive directions – has implications for longstanding questions within feminism regarding how to respond in an intersectional feminist manner to instances of sexual violence. When considered in such a context, Anderson's ethical vulnerability meets the following conditions. It refuses essentialized subject positions such as victim/perpetrator as these are at odds with her dynamic ontology of the subject as always becoming and transforming.

In her prioritization of reciprocity and accountability, ethical vulnerability does not pursue judicial justice, which is both ineffective and far from neutral with regards to its logic of which bodies are deserving of protection. Finally, ethical vulnerability is intersectional in its focus on power relations as the cause of violence, rather than pathology or culture. I ended by exposing the shortcomings of mainstream sexual violence discourses which do not incorporate the insights of Anderson's ethical vulnerability. By contrast, Burke's grassroots, community-centred Me Too movement, I demonstrated, does incorporate many of Anderson's concerns. As such, I proposed that each can speak to the other: Anderson's contribution provides the philosophical grounds by which the political merits of Burke's movement can be fathomed. Reciprocally, Burke's necessarily intersectional and embedded context offers a testing ground for Anderson's reflections and locates Anderson's account of accountability within a rich history of women of colour activism.

Anderson's ethical vulnerability can provide a point of departure for an intersectional feminist engagement with sexual violence politics and whilst it is by no means comprehensive, it addresses some of the key challenges that feminists grappling with this question have faced. Ethical vulnerability entails an ontology of the transforming subject and such an ontology is political in its implications for reparative responses to sexual violence.

disclosure statement

No potential conflict of interest was reported by the author.

notes

1 Anderson refers to Butler as "a highly significant dialogue partner for my own work on vulnerable life" ("'Ethical' Vulnerability" 161).

2 Whilst violence of some degree is inescapable for Butler, being the background condition for subject emergence, Butler's normative politics is directed towards "ethical proscriptions against the *waging* of violence" ("Reply" 185). See Gilson (*Ethics*), especially chapter 2, for a thorough discussion of the dual operation of the norm in Butler's thought, as well as its relation to violence.

3 See Lloyd for a discussion of the emergence of corporeal vulnerability in the context of the 9/11 terror attacks and the concept's relation to Butler's earlier thought.

4 Anderson criticizes Utilitarianism ("'Ethical' Vulnerability" 150) as well as the "ethics of justice" (148) for their valorization of moral impartiality and moral invulnerability, and the "ethics of care" for non-reciprocal emphasis on the vulnerability of the other ("Justice and Forgiveness" 130).

5 Anderson stresses the relational character of accountability in order to emphasize that accountability is a two-way process between subjects who interact. Anderson posits a relational ontology in which subjects are bound to and thus dependent on one another. As such, both vulnerability and accountability are necessarily relational. This intersubjective character of both conditions is also what belies their ethical character, and Anderson also refers to "relational accountability" as "ethical accountability." This amounts to a challenge to dominant ontologies of individualism, in which victim and perpetrator can be treated as discrete, independent subjects. In addition, by distinguishing relational accountability from asymmetrical vulnerability, Anderson is highlighting the importance of attending to relationships, power dynamics, structures, processes and complexities which are often obscured in narrow or decontextualized interpretations of accountability. (See Moncrieffe for a discussion of relational accountability.)

6 When I use the terminology "victim" or "perpetrator" it is simply to refer to how subjects' role position in an instance of violence or harm has been articulated. These are not intended as identities, and certainly not as discrete, fixed categories. As I employ the terms, one can be a victim or perpetrator of an attack but not more generally; the terms only signify within a specific context. See Beck et al. and Armatta for discussion of the rates of violence in prison.

7 Including South Korea, Japan, Indonesia and Palestine. See <https://MeToorising.withgoogle.com/> (accessed 4 Dec. 2019); Gill and Orgad. Whilst having a near global reach, the movement

is also culturally specific. See Hasunuma and Shin for a comparison of the impact of the movement in Japan and South Korea.

8 A year after Milano's allegations, Bloomberg reports that "The headlines alone are dizzying. Since the New York Times reported allegations of serial predation by movie mogul Harvey Weinstein a year ago, at least 425 prominent people across industries have been publicly accused of sexual misconduct, a broad range of behavior that spans from serial rape to lewd comments and abuse of power." See <https://www.bloomberg.com/graphics/2018-me-too-anniversary/> (accessed 4 Dec. 2019).

9 In this way it is somewhat reflective of a "postfeminist" discourse. McRobbie characterized the 1990s as a period in which "feminism is decisively aged and made to seem redundant" (255) and, in its mainstream media instantiation at least, sex has become political, but as distinct from feminism.

10 Burke is ambivalent about #MeToo. Whilst she has worked with it and is frequently positive about its ability to reach a large number of people, she also articulates hesitations, particularly with the movement's shift of focus from survivors to high-profile individuals (Burke, "On the Rigorous Work"), as well as its neglect of less privileged groups (Burke, "Our Pain").

bibliography

Ahmed, Sara. *Living a Feminist Life*. Durham, NC: Duke UP, 2017. Print.

Alcoff, Linda Martín. "Discourses of Sexual Violence in a Global Framework." *Philosophical Topics* 37.2 (2009): 123–39. Print.

Anderson, Pamela Sue. "Arguing for 'Ethical' Vulnerability: Towards a Politics of Care?" *Exploring Vulnerability*. Ed. Heike Springhart and Günter Thomas. Göttingen and Bristol, CT: Vandenhoeck, 2017. 147–62. Print.

Anderson, Pamela Sue. "When Justice and Forgiveness Come Apart: A Feminist Perspective on Restorative Justice and Intimate Violence." *Oxford Journal of Law and Religion* 5.1 (2016): 113–34. Print.

Armatta, Judith. "Ending Sexual Violence through Transformative Justice." *Interdisciplinary Journal of Partnership Studies* 5.1 (2018). Web. 4 Dec. 2019. <https://doi.org/10.24926/ijps.v5i1.915>.

Beck, Allen J., et al. "Sexual Victimization in Prisons and Jails Reported by Inmates, 2011–12." Bureau of Justice Statistics, 2013. Web. 4 Dec. 2019. <www.bjs.gov/content/pub/pdf/svpjri1112.pdf>.

Bitsch, Anne. "The Geography of Rape: Shaming Narratives in Norwegian Rape Cases." *Signs: Journal of Women in Culture and Society* 44.4 (2019): 931–53. Print.

Bourke, Joanna. "Foreword." *Theorizing Sexual Violence*. Ed. Renée J. Heberle and Victoria Grace. New York and London: Routledge, 2011. ix–xii. Print.

Brown, Wendy. *States of Injury: Power and Freedom in Late Modernity*. Princeton: Princeton UP, 1995. Print.

Burke, Tarana. "Empowerment through Empathy." *JustBeInc*. Web. 20 June 2019. <https://justbeinc.wixsite.com/justbeinc/the-me-too-movement-c7cf>.

Burke, Tarana. [Interview by Emma Brockes.] "#MeToo Founder Tarana Burke: 'You Have to Use Your Privilege to Serve Other People.'" *The Guardian* 15 Jan. 2018. Web. 20 June 2019. <https://www.theguardian.com/world/2018/jan/15/me-too-founder-tarana-burke-women-sexual-assault>.

Burke, Tarana. "#MeToo Founder Tarana Burke on the Rigorous Work that Still Lies Ahead." *Variety*. 2018. Web. 20 June 2019. <https://variety.com/2018/biz/features/tarana-burke-metoo-one-year-later-1202954797/>.

Burke, Tarana. [Report by Melissa Chan.] "'Our Pain is Never Prioritized.' #MeToo Founder Tarana Burke Says We Must Listen to 'Untold' Stories of Minority Women." *Time* 23 Apr. 2019. Web. 20 June 2019. <https://time.com/5574163/tarana-burke-metoo-time-100-summit/>.

Burke, Tarana. [Interview by Elizabeth Adetiba.] "Tarana Burke Says #MeToo Should Center Marginalized Communities." *The Nation* 17 Nov. 2017. Web. 20 June 2019. <https://www.thenation.com/article/tarana-burke-says-metoo-isnt-just-for-white-people/>.

Burke, Tarana. [Interview by Daisy Murray.] "We Spoke to Tarana Burke, the Woman Who Really Started the 'Me Too' Movement." *Elle* 23 Oct. 2017. Web. 20 June 2019. <https://www.elle.com/uk/life-and-culture/culture/news/a39429/empowerment-through-empathy-tarana-burke-me-too/>.

Butler, Judith. *Precarious Life: The Powers of Mourning and Violence*. London: Verso, 2004. Print.

Butler, Judith. "Reply from Judith Butler to Mills and Jenkins." *Differences* 18.2 (2007): 180–95. Print.

Butler, Judith, Zeynep Gambetti, and Leticia Sabsay, eds. *Vulnerability in Resistance*. Durham, NC: Duke UP, 2016. Print.

Cacho, Lisa Marie. *Social Death: Racialized Rightlessness and the Criminalization of the Unprotected*. New York: New York UP, 2012. Print.

Cahill, Ann J. *Rethinking Rape*. Ithaca, NY: Cornell UP, 2001. Print.

Cho, Sumi, et al. "Toward a Field of Intersectionality Studies: Theory, Applications, and Praxis." *Signs* 38.4 (2013): 785–810. Print.

Cole, Alyson. "All of Us Are Vulnerable, But Some Are More Vulnerable than Others: The Political Ambiguity of Vulnerability Studies, an Ambivalent Critique." *Critical Horizons* 17.2 (2016): 260–77. Print.

Collins, Patricia Hill. *Black Feminist Thought: Knowledge, Consciousness, and the Politics of Empowerment*. 2nd ed. New York and London: Routledge, 2000. Print.

Davis, Angela Y. "Rape, Racism and the Capitalist Setting." *The Black Scholar* 9.7 (1978): 24–30. Print.

Derrida, Jacques. *On Cosmopolitanism and Forgiveness*. Trans. Mark Dooley and Michael Hughes. London: Routledge, 2001. Print.

Duggan, Lisa. "The Full Catastrophe." *Bully Bloggers*. 18 Aug. 2018. Web. 20 June 2019. <https://bullybloggers.wordpress.com/2018/08/18/the-full-catastrophe/>.

Dworkin, Andrea. *Pornography: Men Possessing Women*. London: Women's P, 1981. Print.

Ferrarese, Estelle, ed. *The Politics of Vulnerability*. Abingdon: Routledge, 2018. Print.

Gavey, Nicola. *Just Sex? The Cultural Scaffolding of Rape*. London: Routledge, 2005. Print.

Generation Five. Web. 20 June 2019. <http://www.generationfive.org/the-issue/transformative-justice/>.

Gill, Rosalind, and Shani Orgad. "The Shifting Terrain of Sex and Power: From the 'Sexualization of Culture' to #MeToo." *Sexualities* 21.8 (2018): 1313–24. Print.

Gilmore, Ruth Wilson. *Golden Gulag: Prisons, Surplus, Crisis, and Opposition in Globalizing California*. Berkeley: U of California P, 2007. Print.

Gilson, Erinn C. *The Ethics of Vulnerability: A Feminist Analysis of Social Life and Practice*. London and New York: Routledge, 2014. Print.

Gilson, Erinn. "Vulnerability, Ignorance, and Oppression." *Hypatia* 26.2 (2011): 308–32. Print.

Gilson, Erinn. "Vulnerability and Victimization: Rethinking Key Concepts in Feminist Discourses on Sexual Violence." *Signs: Journal of Women in Culture and Society* 42.1 (2016): 71–98. Print.

Goldner, Virginia. "Sexual Harassment: Seeking the Pleasures of 'Consent' under Duress." *Studies in Gender and Sexuality* 19.4 (2018): 235–40. Print.

Haaken, Janice. "'Toward a New Feminist Theory of Rape': The Seductions of Theory." *Signs: Journal of Women in Culture and Society* 27.3 (2002): 781–86. Print.

Hasunuma, Linda, and Ki-Young Shin. "#MeToo in Japan and South Korea: #WeToo, #WithYou." *Journal of Women, Politics and Policy* 40.1 (2019): 97–111. Print.

Hunter, Rosemary C., and Sharon Cowan, eds. *Choice and Consent: Feminist Engagements with Law and Subjectivity*. Abingdon: Routledge-Cavendish, 2007. Print.

INCITE! *Color of Violence: The INCITE! Anthology*. Durham, NC: Duke UP, 2016. Print.

Jackson, Jessi Lee. "Sexual Necropolitics and Prison Rape Elimination." *Signs: Journal of Women in Culture and Society* 39.1 (2013): 197–220. Print.

Jaffe, Sarah. "The Collective Power of #MeToo." *Dissent Magazine* Spring 2018. Web. 20 June 2019. <https://www.dissentmagazine.org/article/collective-power-of-me-too-organizing-justice-patriarchy-class>.

James, Sandy E., Jody L. Herman, Susan Rankin, Mara Keisling, Lisa Mottet, and Ma'ayan Anafi. *The Report of the 2015 U.S. Transgender Survey*. Washington, DC: National Center for Transgender Equality, 2016. Web. 4 Dec. 2019. <https://www.transequality.org/sites/default/files/docs/USTS-Full-Report-FINAL.PDF>.

Kapur, Ratna. "Pink Chaddis and SlutWalk Couture: The Postcolonial Politics of Feminism Lite." *Feminist Legal Studies* 20.1 (2012): 1–20. Print.

Lamb, Sharon. *The Trouble with Blame: Victims, Perpetrators, and Responsibility*. Cambridge, MA: Harvard UP, 1996. Print.

Lee, Kyoo, and Jamieson Webster. "The Formative Power of Metony#metoo." *Studies in Gender and Sexuality* 19.4 (2018): 249–53. Print.

Lloyd, Moya. "The Ethics and Politics of Vulnerable Bodies." *Butler and Ethics*. Ed. Moya Lloyd. Edinburgh. Edinburgh UP, 2015. 167–92. Print.

Mackenzie, Catriona, ed. *Vulnerability: New Essays in Ethics and Feminist Philosophy*. New York: Oxford UP, 2014. Print.

MacKinnon, Catharine A. *Toward a Feminist Theory of the State*. Cambridge, MA: Harvard UP, 1989. Print.

Mahoney, Martha R. "Victimization or Oppression? Women's Lives, Violence, and Agency." *The Public Nature of Private Violence: The Discovery of Domestic Abuse*. Ed. Marta A. Fineman and Roxanne Mykitiuk. New York: Routledge, 1994. 59–92. Print.

Marcus, Sharon. "Fighting Bodies, Fighting Words." *Feminists Theorize the Political*. Ed. Judith Butler and Joan Wallach Scott. New York and London: Routledge, 1992. 385–403. Print.

Mardorossian, Carine M. *Framing the Rape Victim: Gender and Agency Reconsidered*. New Brunswick, NJ: Rutgers UP, 2014. Print.

McRobbie, Angela. "Post-Feminism and Popular Culture." *Feminist Media Studies* 4.3 (2004): 255–64. Print.

Millett, Kate. *Sexual Politics*. London: Hart-Davis, 1971. Print.

Moncrieffe, Joy. *Relational Accountability: Complexities of Structural Injustice*. London: Zed, 2011.

Murphy, Ann V. *Violence and the Philosophical Imaginary*. Albany: State U of New York P, 2012. Print.

Namaste, Ki. "Genderbashing: Sexuality, Gender, and the Regulation of Public Space." *Environment and Planning D: Society and Space* 14.2 (1996): 221–40. Print.

Oliviero, Katie. *Vulnerability Politics: The Uses and Abuses of Precarity in Political Debate*. New York: New York UP, 2018. Print.

Pellegrini, Ann. "#MeToo: Before and After." *Studies in Gender and Sexuality* 19.4 (2018): 262–64. Print.

Penal Reform International. *Global Prison Trends*. London: Penal Reform International, 2015. Print.

Phillips, Lynn. *Flirting with Danger: Young Women's Reflections on Sexuality and Domination*. New York: New York UP, 2000. Print.

Phipps, Alison. "Feminists Fighting Sexual Violence in the Age of Brexit and Trump." 2019. Web. 4 Dec. 2019. <https://genderate.wordpress.com/>.

Phipps, Alison. "Rape and Respectability: Ideas about Sexual Violence and Social Class." *Sociology* 43.4 (2009): 667–83. Print.

Phipps, Alison. "Reckoning Up: Sexual Harassment and Violence in the Neoliberal University." *Gender and Education* (June 2018): 1–17. Print.

Puar, Jasbir K. *Terrorist Assemblages: Homonationalism in Queer Times*. Durham, NC: Duke UP, 2007. Print.

Razack, Sherene. "From Consent to Responsibility, from Pity to Respect: Subtexts in Cases of Sexual Violence Involving Girls and Women with Developmental Disabilities." *Law and Social Inquiry* 19.4 (1994): 891–922. Print.

Razack, Sherene. "Imperilled Muslim Women, Dangerous Muslim Men and Civilised Europeans: Legal and Social Responses to Forced Marriages." *Feminist Legal Studies* 12.2 (2004): 129–74. Print.

Rodino-Colocino, Michelle. "Me Too, #MeToo: Countering Cruelty with Empathy." *Communication and Critical/Cultural Studies* 15.1 (2018): 96–100. Print.

Rose, Jaqueline. "I Am a Knife." *London Review of Books* 40.4 (22 Feb. 2018): 3–11. Print.

Rutherford, Alexandra. "Sexual Violence against Women: Putting Rape Research in Context." *Psychology of Women Quarterly* 35.2 (2011): 342–47. Print.

Schulman, Sarah. *Conflict is Not Abuse: Overstating Harm, Community Responsibility, and the Duty of Repair*. Vancouver: Arsenal Pulp, 2017. Print.

Sedgwick, Eve Kosofsky. *Touching Feeling: Affect, Pedagogy, Performativity*. Durham, NC: Duke UP, 2003. Print.

Serisier, Tanya. *Speaking Out: Feminism, Rape and Narrative Politics*. Basingstoke: Palgrave Macmillan, 2018. Print.

Struckman-Johnson, Cindy, and David Struckman-Johnson. "Sexual Coercion Rates in Seven Midwestern Prison Facilities for Men." *The Prison Journal* 80.3 (2000): 379–90. Print.

Teays, Wanda, ed. *Analyzing Violence against Women*. Cham: Springer, 2019. Print.

Thuma, Emily. "Lessons in Self-Defense: Gender Violence, Racial Criminalization, and Anticarceral Feminism." *Women's Studies Quarterly* 43.3–4 (2015): 52–71. Print.

Ware, Vron. *Beyond the Pale: White Women, Racism and History*. New ed. London: Verso, 2015. Print.

Wooden, Wayne S., and Jay Parker. *Men behind Bars: Sexual Exploitation in Prison*. New York: Plenum, 1982. Print.

Zarkov, Dubravka, and Kathy Davis. "Ambiguities and Dilemmas around #MeToo: #ForHow Long and #WhereTo?" *European Journal of Women's Studies* 25.1 (2018): 3–9. Print.

chon tejedor

CONDITIONED RESPONSIBILITY, BELONGING AND THE VULNERABILITY OF OUR ETHICAL UNDERSTANDING

This paper is born out of two strands of philosophical conversations I had the good fortune to engage in with Pamela Sue Anderson during the last fifteen years of her life. The first of these – which resulted in a research project for which we received a John Fell Oxford University Press award – focused on what I have come to call the problem of the Individual Ethical Gap; the second focused on the notion of "ethical vulnerability" coined by Anderson and explored so lucidly in her papers "When Justice and Forgiveness Come Apart: A Feminist Perspective on Restorative Justice and Intimate Violence" and "Arguing for 'Ethical' Vulnerability: Towards a Politics of Care?"[1] Although my treatment of this material has evolved over the years and has moved away from some of the ideas we explored together, it seems to me most fitting to be contributing to the present volume with a paper that highlights how very alive those conversations – in her office at Regent's Park College and at the Green Café on St Giles' in Oxford – remain.

I shall begin by introducing the problem of the Individual Ethical Gap as I currently understand it and explore the notion of responsibility in light of it; towards the end of the paper I shall connect this material to Anderson's discussion of vulnerability by introducing the idea of the fundamental vulnerability of our ethics.

I the individual ethical gap

I would like to begin by introducing an ethical problem which is, I think, increasingly pressing, but in view of which ethical philosophy as we currently conceive it presents insufficient resources. The problem I have in mind emerges in situations that satisfy the following three criteria: firstly, the combined actions of numerous individuals cause significant harm; secondly, the actions of any one such individual, in and of themselves, do not cause said harm; and, thirdly, the individuals do not intend the resulting combined harm, even though they may anticipate or expect it.

By "combined actions" I do not mean "coordinated actions" but simply the combination – the mix – of the actions of such individuals. Often the harm in question will simply be the cumulative effect of these actions – I shall refer to this as *aggregated harm*. On other occasions, the harm will result not simply from the cumulation of certain actions but from the way in which they interact dynamically with each other *given the cultural, social, economic or legal practices in place* – I shall refer to this as *dynamic harm*.

Climate change is an example of aggregate harm: it is a form of harm brought about by the cumulation of certain types of action performed by individuals, such as travelling by plane or driving a petrol-guzzling car.[2] In contrast, actions resulting in dynamic harm include: buying cheap clothes when prices are being driven down by production in faraway sweatshops; renting a flat in a misaligned property market where ineffectual social housing policies together with rising demand are pushing prices up and people into homelessness; or applying for a position in a job market where there is a strong racial or gender bias in one's favour and against other groups.[3] Dynamic harm can be subtler and more difficult to spot than aggregate harm, so it is worth spending a moment exploring it. Like aggregate harm, dynamic harm presents key aggregative aspects. Buying cheap clothes in sufficient numbers is harmful in that it contributes to sustaining a market structured around exploitative practices and thus fosters the survival and proliferation of sweatshops. Aggregation does, of course, matter here: if people were not buying clothes in *sufficient numbers*, sweatshops would simply disappear. However, whilst aggregation matters here, this type of harm is not *merely* aggregative: dynamic harm does not come about merely through the cumulation of actions but requires certain dynamics – typically, power dynamics, enhanced or countered by social and cultural practices and by the workings of legal frameworks – to be in place. For instance, if laws protecting against job exploitation were implemented stringently throughout the planet so that it became impossible to run sweatshops anywhere on the globe, buying clothes in large numbers would not (could not) cumulatively result in the proliferation of sweatshops; conversely, when there is a region of the world in which anti-exploitation laws are non-existent or laxly implemented, a comparatively smaller number of purchases can foster the proliferation of sweatshops in that particular region. This type of harm is not therefore merely about *aggregation* but about the aggregative effect of actions performed *against the background of certain (power, social, cultural, legal, etc.) dynamics being in place*. These dynamics are typically socially constructed and therefore in essence fluid, in principle changeable, even though their effects on individuals at given times are often inescapable and their power, in this respect, entirely *real*.

With these preliminary clarifications in place, we can begin to home in on the problem I propose to discuss. The problem can now be described as one which emerges in situations satisfying the following three revised criteria:

i the combined actions of individuals cause significant aggregate or dynamic harm;
ii the actions of any one such individual, on their own, do not cause this harm; and
iii the individuals in question do not intend this harm, even though they may anticipate or expect it.

In the aggregate case relating to climate change, the actions of individuals who travel by plane or drive petrol-guzzling cars can be further specified as follows:

i* the aggregate of their actions causes climate change;
ii* the actions of any one individual (even over a long lifespan) do not cause climate change;
iii* the intention of these individuals is not to produce climate change, even though they may anticipate or expect that, cumulatively, in sufficient numbers, actions such as theirs produce this effect.

Similarly, in the dynamic harm case concerning sweatshops, the actions of individuals buying cheap clothes can be further specified as follows:

i** the aggregate of their actions, in the absence of appropriate legal frameworks, sustains exploitative practices and fosters the proliferation of sweatshops;
ii** the actions of any one individual (even over a long lifespan) do not cause the sustaining and proliferation of sweatshops;

iii** the intention of these individuals is not to sustain and foster sweatshops, even though they may anticipate or expect that, cumulatively, in sufficient numbers, such actions produce this effect.

I shall call situations that meet criteria i–iii (or some of their variants, i*, i**, etc.) *Individual Ethical Gap* (IEG) situations. Individual Ethical Gap situations are characterized by an apparent *gap* in our theoretical ability to account for the responsibility of individuals. In contemporary ethical theory, responsibility is typically couched in terms of either consequences or intentions. In IEG situations, however, individuals cannot be held responsible by virtue of the consequences of their individual actions, since, *pace* ii and its variants (ii*, ii**, etc.), their individual actions, in and of themselves, do not result in or cause the combined harm in question. And individuals cannot be held responsible by virtue of their intentions either since, *ex hypothesi*, *pace* iii and its variants, they do not *intend* the combined harm. We are thus left with a difficulty in framing and accounting for the precise responsibility of individuals (if any) in these situations. I will explore this difficulty in more detail below.

Before I continue, I would like to highlight that not all individuals who drive petrol-guzzling cars, travel by plane, or buy clothes rendered cheap by the existence of sweatshops satisfy the IEG criteria: in other words, not all individuals performing such actions fall within the theoretical framework of the IEG. The leader of a global superpower typically won't, since her political actions will have significant causal impact with respect to these combined harms by virtue of the power invested in her executive role. Similarly, there may be individuals so wealthy and dedicated to buying cheap clothes as to be in a position to sustain or close down, through their individual purchasing habits alone, sweatshops around the globe. Individuals such as these fail to meet criterion ii: they do therefore not face an IEG with respect to the combined harms in question because there is a direct causal link between their actions and said harms; their responsibility can thus be easily traced to the direct impact of their individual actions and poses no special theoretical difficulty. I shall call individuals of this type *high causal impact individuals*. In turn, there may also be individuals so malevolent as to *intend* actively to contribute with their actions to climate change, to the proliferation of sweatshops, etc. Such individuals do not count as facing an IEG either, since they fail to meet criterion iii. For the sake of clarity, I shall refer to individuals falling in this category as *actively malevolent individuals*.

In what follows, I shall not be focusing on the cases of high causal impact or of active malevolence, but on the far more common – I'd go as far as to say overwhelmingly common – cases of individuals who satisfy the IEG criteria with respect to certain combined harms and who therefore face a gap with respect to the possibility of accounting for their individual responsibility with respect to said harms. This gap, I suggest, is of a theoretical nature and typically not a matter of self-deception; in this respect, it is to an extent related to Miranda Fricker's problem of "hermeneutical lacuna."[4] The problem, as we will see, is *not* that self-deceiving individuals fail to apply conceptual tools for correct attribution of responsibility that are in fact available to them; the problem, rather, is that the relevant conceptual tools are not sufficiently clear or not readily available. There is, in other words, a *gap* in our ethical theory – in our understanding of individual responsibility – that needs to be addressed.

2 mind the gap

Let us examine in more detail the question of why precisely the IEG poses a problem. Contemporary ethical theory turns centrally on the idea that individual ethical responsibility derives either from intention or from consequences: I am ethically responsible for an action of mine either by virtue of the manner in which I intended it or by virtue of the consequences that my action produced. As just noted, however, in IEG situations the actions of individuals do not cause harmful consequences, *pace* ii, and wrongfulness of intention is also ruled out, *pace* iii – *ex hypothesi*, the individuals in question do not intend the resulting combined harm, even though they may anticipate or expect it.

An objection may emerge at this stage, in connection to criterion ii and its variants. For one may be tempted to argue that, if each individual action does indeed contribute, albeit insignificantly, to the combination of actions that causes harm, then that individual action should be regarded as causing the harm in question – *contra* ii. This objection does not survive scrutiny, however. For it seems clear that something can be part of the cause of X without itself causing X. Say, for instance, that a large ocean wave causes a ship to capsize. Clearly, the drops of water that make up the wave are part of the cause that produces the capsizing of the ship and yet there is no respect in which any given one of these drops, in and of itself, *causes* the capsizing of the ship.

Perhaps the objection can be revived, however, by appealing to what can be called *threshold situations*. Imagine that we are dealing with a situation in which n number of actions of a particular type causes no harm but, with action n^{+1}, a threshold is reached so that harm ensues. In other words, under normal circumstances prior to n^{+1}, any one action, in and of itself, produces no harm. However, when action n^{+1} occurs, due to its relative position with respect to previous actions and their cumulative consequences, harm is produced. Do threshold cases show that there is a difficulty in framing IEG situations? I suggest that they do not. For all that they really show is that threshold situations are *not* IEG situations: threshold situations are situations in which individual actions *typically* characterized by their causal *insignificance* suddenly acquire, by virtue of their position with respect to other actions, causal *significance*. In other words, threshold situations are situations in which the individual suddenly no longer faces an IEG, since in performing action n^{+1} the individual *is* causally efficacious and does not meet criterion ii.

The notion of a threshold is an important one and certainly deserves close scrutiny. However, appealing to it does not help to dissolve the problem of the IEG: it simply highlights that individuals need to develop an awareness of how they and their actions are positioned with respect to others and how this positioning may alter their degree of individual causal impact – and the nature of their responsibilities – when thresholds are in play.

This leads us to a third possible objection to the IEG. This possible objection, drawing from expected utility consequentialist theory, begins by noting that we need to distinguish between two types of IEG situations: those in which individuals *expect* their combined actions to have harmful consequences and those in which individuals do not expect or anticipate this harm (they simply don't see it coming, as might have been the case in the 1970s with respect to climate change). Following on from this, one may be tempted to use expected utility theory to argue that, in cases where individuals *expect* harmful consequences to result from their combined actions, individuals are responsible by virtue of this expectation. After all, expected utility theory suggests that we are responsible for the expected – not the actual – consequences of our actions. This might be one way to ground the idea that individuals do indeed retain ethical responsibility in IEG situations when certain expectations are in place, in spite of the fact that their individual actions are causally insignificant. Unfortunately, however, this response does not eradicate the problem posed by the IEG either. For the key driver in expected utility theory is the thought that an individual is responsible for the expected consequences *of her individual actions* – not those of others. In the scenarios we are working with, however, it is unlikely that an individual will expect the consequences of *her* individual actions to be anything but negligible: indeed, the actual consequences of her actions *are* negligible by virtue of ii. If the individual did expect her actions to have a more than negligible causal impact, we would quite rightly question the appropriateness of that expectation. Note, however, that the central point here is not that such an expectation would be inappropriate (although it would be) but that it would be surprising for it to form at all in the situations we are envisaging: when facing IEG situations, individuals will *not* typically expect their *individual* actions, in and of themselves, to have causal impact on the combined harm. When an individual is considering whether to perform a particular action, she may reasonably expect and anticipate *both* that her action, in and of itself, will have a negligible causal impact and that the combined result of many such actions, including hers, will be harmful. The question we face is: how precisely do we motivate the idea that the individual retains at least a degree of ethical responsibility *given that* the contribution of her individual action to the harm is – as a matter of fact – negligible and her intentions are non-problematic? We are now back to square one.

One possible move would be to answer the latter question negatively. Perhaps we should simply accept that, in IEG situations, individuals bear *no* responsibility for the resulting combined harm. A version of this response has been defended by John Broome in his *Climate Matters: Ethics in a Warming World*. Broome draws on expected utility theory to argue that, in situations such as this, only governments, corporations and more generally those agents that can be expected to have a genuine impact on the combined harm (i.e., what I have called "high causal impact" individuals) count as responsible for this harm; ordinary individuals whose actions can be expected to have only negligible consequences have no direct responsibility for said harm. In the case of climate change in particular, Broome argues that *individual* responsibility is thus limited to voting in elections for parties likely to adopt measures to counter climate change and to offsetting individual carbon trails.[5]

Broome's approach is thought-provoking, but ultimately, in my view, problematic. For it is unclear that it can deliver even this (much-reduced) type of responsibility for individuals. In particular, it is unclear that it can deliver individual responsibility with respect to voting. From the point of view of expected utility theory, it may make sense to suggest that, as an individual, I am responsible for carrying out those actions I expect to produce sufficient carbon offsetting to compensate for my own emissions. After all, my individual actions do have sufficient causal impact to bring about those particular individual carbon offsetting consequences: they have sufficient causal impact to bring about those results. However, voting does not fit this mould. Typically – i.e., other than in threshold situations where electoral victories hang on minute margins – the consequences (the causal impact) of any one individual vote will in fact be negligible. In these relatively common scenarios, nothing much typically hangs on my individual vote. Nor would it make sense for me typically to *expect* my vote to have anything more than a negligible impact on the electoral result. Clearly, individuals can understand (and rightly expect and anticipate) that the aggregate of votes will produce electoral results that matter; but this does not help with the individual's own decision to issue their particular single vote, since this action, in and of itself, has negligible consequences. To put this in a different manner: large-scale elections are typically – i.e., other than in threshold cases where results hang on very small margins – IEG situations. Broome's approach, extended consistently, would therefore lead to the conclusion that individuals typically have no electoral responsibilities at all. This is a serious matter for concern.

The situation is even more worrying than it may appear, however. For, unless an individual can, in and of herself, have a significant causal impact in persuading a large enough number of other people to join forces or to coordinate their actions directly, she will lack any expected-consequence-based reasons, as an individual, to try to join forces or to coordinate with them. She will lack these even if she does expect and anticipate that *joint action in sufficiently large numbers* would have a crucial causal impact. For the same problem will simply re-emerge at this level: just as the expected-consequences rationale for going out to vote is missing for individuals in ordinary (i.e., non-threshold) situations, so is this rationale missing with respect to trying to organize or persuade others to join forces. The IEG is thus a major stumbling block to the possibility of coordinated – let alone collective – action and therefore a major stumbling block to the possibility of political action. It is clear from this that, far from affecting a small cluster of exceptional cases, the IEG has wide-ranging ramifications: it has the potential ethically to disempower us as individuals in *any* areas of our lives in which sufficiently large levels of coordination are required for causal impact. The impact of the IEG on our ethical agency is far more extensive and less exceptional than might previously have been thought.

3 arendt and young on political responsibility

Both Hannah Arendt and Iris Marion Young have developed theories which, although not directly focused on IEG situations, are relevant to addressing them. Whilst these theories ultimately prove unsatisfactory for our current purposes, they offer important starting points on which to build a theory capable of addressing the problem of the IEG.

In *Responsibility for Justice*, Iris Marion Young explores a phenomenon she calls *structural injustice*. Structural injustice emerges when an ethical wrong occurs that is not attributable to the wrongful actions of an individual agent or of a larger body or institution. Young writes:

> Structural injustice is a kind of moral wrong distinct from the wrongful action of an individual agent or the repressive policies of a state. Structural injustice occurs as a consequence of many individuals and institutions acting to pursue their particular goals and interests, for the most part within the limits of accepted rules and norms [...] [It commonly involves] the unintended consequences of the combination of the actions of many people.[6]

Although Young's understanding of structural injustice differs in important respects from my understanding of an IEG situation, it bears sufficient resemblance to shed light on my investigation. Young starts addressing the question of structural injustice by introducing a distinction she finds in Hannah Arendt's papers "Collective Responsibility" and "Organized Guilt and Universal Responsibility," as well as in Arendt's *Eichmann in Jerusalem*.[7] In these texts, Arendt explores a distinction between, on the one hand, ethical blameworthiness and guilt and, on the other, political responsibility. Arendt argues that, whereas blameworthiness and guilt are connected to the notion of punishment, political responsibility is not. Guilt is backward-looking in so far as it relates to the idea of past wrongs for which one can legitimately be blamed and punished; political responsibility, in contrast, is not about past wrongs but about finding ourselves in a position where we can legitimately be called upon to political action, where such action can legitimately be demanded from us. Unlike guilt or blameworthiness, political responsibility is therefore forward-looking: it is about present and future actions that can be legitimately demanded of us.[8] Young writes that political responsibility is "always now, in relation to current events [...] and their future consequences."[9]

Drawing on Arendt's works, Young uses this distinction to develop a fuller account of how an agent can be politically responsible without being ethically guilty or blameworthy. In the context of her discussion of Eichmann and Nazi Germany, Arendt draws a contrast between the ethical status of two groups of people: those who were guilty of crimes and who were therefore ethically blameworthy (in addition to being legally liable); and those who were not guilty of crimes but who did nevertheless bear political responsibility. In the first category, Arendt includes Eichmann; in the second category, she places Germans of an adult age who did nothing to oppose the genocidal Nazi regime.[10] For Arendt and Young, the latter should be viewed as politically responsible but not ethically blameworthy. Political responsibility without ethical blameworthiness is thus, in their view, a category reserved for people who do not directly contribute to the production of crimes but "whose active or passive support for governments, institutions and practices enables culprits to commit crimes and wrongs."[11]

Out of the cases discussed by Arendt and Young, the one most directly relevant to the question of the IEG is that of *some* of the adult German civilians alive during the Nazi regime who failed to oppose it. I say "some" because some such civilians may have been actively malevolent or high causal impact individuals, in which case they would fail to meet, respectively, criteria iii and ii or to fall within the IEG framework. My focus will therefore be on the subset of German civilians who did not have malevolent intentions and whose individual ability to causally impact the Nazi regime was insignificant.[12] Whether the combined actions and omissions of such civilians did *in fact* cumulatively result in sustaining the genocidal Nazi regime is an empirical matter which we need not resolve here (although it seems plausible that they did). Let us assume, for the sake of argument, that this was indeed the case. In other words, let us assume that there was a large enough number of German civilians such that:

i*** the aggregate of actions and omissions of these individuals (their cumulative failures to resist) caused the Nazi regime to endure;
ii*** in isolation, the actions and omissions of any one of these individuals did not cause the Nazi regime to endure;
iii*** these individuals did not intend the Nazi regime to endure.

According to Arendt and Young, civilians fitting these criteria should not be regarded as ethically guilty or blameworthy; they should, however, be viewed as politically responsible for Nazi crimes.[13] They should not be regarded as guilty or blameworthy because they didn't, through their actions, directly contribute to the Nazi genocidal machinery: they were not directly involved in the perpetration of the crimes. Nor did they *intend* the resulting harm: the intentions behind their actions were other and not obviously culpable; in some cases, the intention might have simply been to keep their families safe. Arendt and Young coincide in concluding that such civilians should nevertheless be regarded as politically responsible, but differ in their reasons for this conclusion. Arendt argues that individuals count as politically responsible (even when they are not ethically blameworthy) by virtue of their membership of the political community that perpetrates crimes in their name.[14] Young disagrees – correctly, in my view – with this understanding of the grounds for attributing political responsibility to individuals. She writes:

> It is a mystification to say that people bear responsibility simply because they are members of a political community, and not because of anything at all that they have done or not done.[15]

Membership of a political community is "too static" a notion, she concludes.[16] Young therefore proposes an alternative criterion for political responsibility. For her, political responsibility arises, in the absence of ethical blameworthiness, not by virtue of static membership but when "active or passive support for governments, institutions and practices enables culprits to commit crimes and wrongs."[17] Young therefore argues that the non-resisting, non-persecuted German civilians were politically responsible (though not ethically blameworthy) for Nazi crimes because:

> they participated in the society and provided the guilty agents with at least passive support that undergirded their power.[18]

> [they] dwell within the social system that enables the crimes and supply that system with at least passive support. In this case, their passivity produces a political vacuum. The attitudes and behaviour of the majority of people is so privatized that there exists little organized public space in which actors can appear to others with their judgments of events, let alone join in collective action to transform them.[19]

From the perspective of our discussion of the IEG there is, however, a crucial problem with the notion of *enablement* at the centre of Young's response. For this notion lends itself to a revised version of the IEG problem – let us call this the IEG enablement problem (IEGE), to distinguish it from the earlier causal version. The IEGE can be summed up as follows:

i(e) the combined actions of individuals enable significant aggregate or dynamic harm;

ii(e) the actions of any one such individual (their failures to resist), on their own, do not enable this harm; and

iii(e) the individuals do not themselves intend the resulting harm, even though they may anticipate or expect it.

Perhaps it may be objected that ii(e) does not fit Young's examples since, in her view, individual failures to resist did enable the Nazi regime to endure. I would like to review the notion of enablement implicit in this view, however. For, whilst the cumulation of individual failures to resist may clearly have enabled the Nazi regime to endure, it is highly unclear that the repeated failures of any one such individual (let alone any one individual failure) would have. Perhaps Young is of the view that, if a number of actions cumulatively enables X, then each of those individual actions must itself count as enabling X. This does not seem to hold water, however. For the enabling relation requires significant causal impact: to enable X is to cause a set of conditions to obtain which in turn facilitate or allow X to obtain. For instance, if I enable someone to come into my house by opening the front door to them, I am causing a set of conditions to obtain (i.e., the opening of my front door) that allow the person to come into the house. Without this, the concept of enablement dissolves into a platitude; it certainly ceases to be robust enough to piggy-back any meaningful understanding of responsibility onto it. This becomes crucially important in the context of IEG situations. For, in such situations, individuals typically find that they can no more *enable* X than they can *cause* X to obtain. If my individual causal impact is insignificant with respect to eliminating climate change, the existence of sweatshops, misaligned rental property markets or biased job markets, it will also

typically be insignificant with respect to furthering or eliminating the conditions that *facilitate* or *allow for* these. I say *typically* because this need not always be the case, of course. There is certainly nothing at the conceptual level to guarantee that a lack of significant causal impact with respect to X *entails* a lack of significant causal impact with respect to the *conditions* that facilitate or allow for X. Still, it seems reasonable to suggest that, in the kinds of scenarios we are exploring, the two will tend to go hand in hand: if I lack significant causal impact with respect to X, I shall also lack significant enabling impact with respect to X – that is, I shall lack significant causal impact with respect to the conditions that facilitate or allow for X. So, although we do need to remain alert to the possibility that, in particular circumstances, lack of causal impact may not result in lack of enabling impact, I think it is safe to conclude that this will, for the most part, fail to hold in IEG situations (or, indeed, in Young's example concerning the Nazi regime). The problem of the IEG cannot thus be erased by moving the focus away from the notion of causal impact to that of enablement.

4 gappy ethical responsibility

As we have just seen, Arendt and Young draw a distinction between, on the one hand, ethical blameworthiness or guilt and, on the other, responsibility. Guilt and blameworthiness, they suggest, are backward-looking: they relate to the idea of a past wrong for which ethical reprobation (i.e., *blame*, as well as, depending on the circumstances, legal liability, punishment, etc.) can be warranted and appropriate. Political responsibility, in contrast, is not about past wrongs but captures the status of individuals placed in a position where they can legitimately be *called upon* to political action, where such action can be legitimately demanded of them. Unlike guilt or blameworthiness, political responsibility is therefore forward-looking: it is about future actions that can be legitimately demanded of us, in the light of present circumstances or events (rather than in response to a past wrong committed by us).

As noted in the previous section, there are difficulties with the grounds provided by Arendt and Young for the view that individuals are politically responsible in this way. There is, in addition, a difficulty with their suggestion that the responsibility in question *must* be amoral. From the point of view of our focus on IEG situations, the question is: should such amoral political responsibility serve as a model for responsibility in IEG situations? Notwithstanding the differences (discussed above) between situations of structural injustice and IEG situations, should we follow suit and argue that individuals in IEG situations are (forward-looking) politically responsible but not ethically blameworthy?

There is certainly something compelling and illuminating about the distinction developed by Arendt and Young between backward-looking blame and forward-looking responsibility. Arendt and Young are, in my view, correct to highlight the crucial difference between my being blamed for something that I have already done (e.g., a wrong or a crime I have perpetrated, as in the case of Eichmann discussed by Arendt) and my being responsible in a forward-looking sense. What distinguishes forward-looking responsibility from backward-looking blameworthiness is that, in the former, I am legitimately called upon to respond or act, not on the grounds of some past wrong or crime of mine but on the grounds of the *conditions* in which I find myself operating. This idea of responsibility arising solely out of conditions – conditions which may not be of one's choosing, of which one may have little or no proper understanding – is, I suggest, fundamental to addressing the problem of IEG situations, and needs to be brought into far sharper theoretical focus. In particular, although Arendt and Young are correct to highlight that this notion of forward-looking responsibility is central, their suggestion that it must always be *amoral* is questionable.

There are, in my view, two important questions that we should be considering in connection to this. Firstly, we should consider whether forward-looking responsibilities can, when unfulfilled, *give rise to* backward-looking responsibility: if I, as an individual, fail to act upon a demand that is legitimately placed upon me, could this failure not count as a wrong of mine (a wrong of *some* sort to be specified: political, legal, etc.) for which reprobation (again, of some sort) *is* warranted in a backward-looking sense? Secondly, we should consider whether forward-looking responsibility must always be *amoral* or whether it can also, at least in some cases, be ethical in nature.

Martha Nussbaum raises the first of these questions in her insightful critical Foreword to Young's *Responsibility for Justice*. She writes:

> it seems to me that what we ought to say is that if A has responsibility R for social ill S, and she fails to take it up, then, when the relevant time passes, she is guilty of not having shouldered her responsibility. I think that this follows quite simply from the logic of ought: Young says that A ought to shoulder the burden; well, that appears to imply that if A doesn't shoulder the burden A has done something wrong.[20]

Nussbaum's line of criticism seems persuasive to me. If the notion of responsibility is to have any bite at all, non-fulfilment of responsibility should, at the very least, justify reprobation of *some* sort (to be specified, depending on the circumstances). If we found ourselves in a situation where it was genuinely *appropriate* to respond to someone's failure to act on a demand by saying "oh well, that's OK then," we should consider whether the demand in question was indeed legitimate – that is, whether the person bore any responsibility at all, in the first place, with respect to it. If I fail to fulfil my supposed responsibility to clear the table at the end of a work meeting and the appropriate response to my failure to do so is "oh well, that's OK then," then it would seem that no genuine *responsibility* had been ascribed to me in the first place: either no demand was placed on me or the demand placed on me was not legitimate. This seems simply part and parcel of the internal structure of the concept of responsibility.

This leads us to the second question, that of whether forward-looking responsibility can be ethical in nature. It seems relatively clear that different forms of forward-looking demands can be placed upon us, some political, others legal, etc. In certain circumstances, *political* action can be legitimately demanded of us – for example, in the form of acts of resistance to authoritarian regimes, such as the participation in protest demonstrations. There may also be circumstances in which *legal* action can be legitimately demanded of us – for instance, when one witnesses a car crash and is later required to tell the truth in court. Similarly, it seems relatively clear that different forms of *reprobation* may be appropriate when I fail to fulfil forward-looking demands: legal penalties may be appropriate if I am found to lie in court; political penalties (such as becoming barred from participation in resistance cells) may be appropriate if I fail to take part in certain key demonstrations, etc. In both of these cases, the reprobation warranted will of course be affected by the conditions in which I find myself. Failing to attend court or to demonstrate because I spend too long getting dressed in the mornings is different from failing to do these things because I have broken my ankle and am in excruciating pain: conditions *shape* the reprobation warranted in each case.

It seems relatively clear, therefore, that there can be different forms of forward-looking responsibility. A forward-looking responsibility will be *merely* political when the nature of the demand and the associated reprobation are exclusively political in nature; legal, when these are exclusively legal, etc. I propose that there can be forms of forward-looking responsibility that are ethical *in addition* to also being, for example, political, legal, etc. A (political, legal, etc.) forward-looking responsibility will also count as ethical if failure to discharge it results in a wrong for which *ethical reprobation* (e.g., blame) is also appropriate.

In order to shed light on this question, let us revisit the IEG case of individuals whose failure to resist the Nazi regime causes it to endure. As we saw above, the following criteria hold in this case:

i*** the aggregate of actions and omissions of these individuals (their cumulative failures to resist) causes the Nazi regime to endure;

ii*** in isolation, the actions and omissions of any one of these individuals do not cause the Nazi regime to endure;

iii*** these individuals do not intend the Nazi regime to endure.

Compare now the following examples of two adults living under the Nazi regime who meet criteria i***, ii*** and iii***: a wealthy individual leading an opulent, luxurious life; and an individual living close to starvation who spends most of her time anxiously searching for work and food to secure survival. Let us assume, as per the IEG hypothesis, that their actions and omissions to act have negligible consequences with respect to the regime's endurance and that they do not intend the regime to endure. Although both individuals are in IEG situations, there seems to be an important difference in the kind of reprobation one may even *consider* as appropriate in the two cases – a difference with a distinctive *ethical* flavour. More precisely, whilst it seems clear that no *ethical reprobation* (no *blame*) is appropriate in the case of the individual living close to starvation, it is at the very least *open to question* whether ethical reprobation is appropriate in the case of the wealthy individual. If a holocaust survivor years later asked "Why did you fail to oppose the Nazis?," being in a position truly to answer "because I spent my days looking for ways to survive and avoid starvation" would help to exonerate the speaker. Replying "because I spent my time enjoying my many luxuries" would clearly not give rise to or justify such exoneration. The fact that there is a difference here at all suggests that there is an ethical dimension at work in this area which arises *out of the differing conditions in which these two individuals are operating*. It shows that there is an aspect of ethical responsibility (i.e., of forward-looking responsibility where failure to discharge warrants ethical reprobation) which arises *solely* from the conditions in which an individual finds herself acting – irrespective of the consequences of or of the intentions behind her actions. This is supported by the above example since we are here, *ex hypothesi*, comparing individuals for whom differences in the nature or degree of responsibility cannot be accounted for with reference to consequences or intentions. The idea that the degree and nature of responsibility might be determined by the conditions in which individuals operate (rather than solely by the consequences of or the intentions behind their actions) may appear problematic. However, it is deeply embedded in much of our ordinary ethical thinking, notably in our thinking concerning mitigating circumstances and situations of self-defence and survival.

In contrast to Arendt and Young, I therefore propose that some forms of forward-looking responsibility are ethical in nature and that these arise not from some abstract notion of *membership* to a political community, as Arendt suggests, or from the fact that individuals *enable* these cumulative wrongs, as Young suggests, but more directly out of *the conditions in which individuals operate*, out of the way in which we are *normatively enmeshed in these conditions*. As we have just seen, this idea of an ethics stemming from conditions is brought into sharper focus by comparing the responsibilities of individuals in IEG situations. As we will now see, however, this ethics out of conditions brings with it a crucial dimension that has been insufficiently explored in the literature: that of the fundamental *vulnerability* of our ethics.

5 the vulnerability of our ethics

It is beyond the remit of this paper to go into the complex task of specifying precisely how ethical responsibility is affected by the conditions of individuals, irrespective of the individuals' causal or enabling impact or of the nature of their intentions. That task I leave for another occasion. It seems reasonable to suppose, however, that – typically – the degree of responsibility arising exclusively from conditions in IEG situations will be lesser than that arising in non-IEG situations involving wrongful intention (e.g., in cases of active malevolence) or harmful individual consequences (e.g., the case of high causal impact individuals).

For my current purposes, it is not necessary to go into the specifics of how such degrees of responsibility might be adjudicated in different circumstances. All I needed was to motivate the idea that conditions alone *can* determine the degree and nature of forward-looking responsibility and make a crucial difference on whether ethical blame is warranted. My proposal is that there are indeed forms of forward-looking responsibility which are ethical and which arise solely from the conditions in which individuals operate, independently of considerations of consequences or intention. This is not to deny that consequences and intention play a central role in ethics but simply to isolate an important, often neglected area of ethical thinking in which *conditions – not* consequences or intentions – are critical. This form of responsibility emerges more clearly in IEG situations precisely because individual intentions and consequences are rendered *ex hypothesi* irrelevant to the attribution of responsibility. This renders self- and other-ascriptions of individual responsibility vulnerable to error in a manner that is often insufficiently recognized in moral theory. For it renders (forward-looking forms of) responsibility dependent on conditions structured in complex, fluctuating ways – conditions that individuals typically do not choose and of which they may have little understanding or even awareness.

Consider, for instance, the example of John, a white man led by family circumstances to move to a new branch of the company he works for, based in a different city. Unbeknownst to John, this branch of the company is blighted by racism and sexism. John himself is neither racist nor sexist; on the contrary, his formative experiences all took place in communities and work environments with high levels of equality, where racism and sexism were simply non-existent. Indeed, John's intentions in taking up this new job were not in any way shaped by racism or sexism but centred on protecting his family from falling into poverty: they were intelligible, reasonable and ethically above board. Imagine now that John is successful in his new position: although his previous job had been somewhat precarious, his position at this new branch quickly becomes secure, partly because he has a skillset which is rare amongst his new co-workers, and partly because he is a white man in a (unbeknownst to him) racist and sexist environment. So he quickly finds himself leading a comfortable and secure life, well paid and with minimal stress, even though he doesn't hold a high-level position within the organization and has no power to influence the way in which it functions. Let us further imagine that, during the first few months on this new job, John is genuinely unaware of the prevailing racism and sexism. In his previous jobs, racism and sexism were non-existent, so he never came to form the expectation that such problems might arise at work. Furthermore, the racism and sexism in this particular branch of the company are so acute and long-standing that the minority of non-white and women staff have learnt to be very cautious: they are reticent to discuss the problem, especially with strangers, and it takes a while before they feel comfortable enough to speak to John about it. Initially, therefore, John has no real understanding of the conditions in which he is operating and, therefore, no understanding of the special demands that may legitimately befall him with regards to supporting his non-white and women colleagues in this branch of the company. This lack of understanding does not mean that no such demands *can* legitimately be placed on him, however, just as ignorance of the law does not void the legitimacy of the demand to tell the truth in court when one has witnessed a car crash. The process of speaking and interacting with colleagues through which John eventually comes to understand the conditions in which he is operating is not a process whereby responsibility is *created*. Rather, it is a process whereby John is brought to *see* a forward-looking responsibility he already *had* by virtue of those very conditions. If the conditions in question did not legitimize certain demands, coming to understand these conditions would not, in and of itself, *generate* responsibility. It is clear that the responsibility in question does not arise from a wrong that John himself has committed but from the conditions in which he finds himself normatively enmeshed – namely the fact that his working life, as a white man, is secure and flourishing in an environment dominated by racism and sexism. During the initial months in which John is unaware of these prevailing conditions, he may well fail to support his non-white and women colleagues in the required ways. During this period, his lack of awareness may well affect the nature and degree of reprobation that these omissions merit: for instance, it may mean that political, but not ethical, forms of reprobation are warranted, such as his being kept away from certain political meetings (e.g., union meetings) where these problems are discussed. His lack of awareness does not, however, alter the fact that the conditions in which *he*, specifically, finds himself operating legitimize demands for support being placed on him. These conditions give rise to a forward-looking form of responsibility: one which may remain merely political whilst he is unaware of these conditions, but which becomes ethical *also* as soon as John gains the relevant understanding of his situation.

The above example shows how a change in one's conditions (e.g., John's move to a job in a new branch of the company) can render one's self-ascriptions of forward-looking ethical responsibility vulnerable to error. In John's case, the relevant change in conditions comes about because of a move that he initiates. However, changes in conditions can happen without our initiating them in any sense – they may simply come upon us. Given the fluidity and complexity of the conditions in which we may find ourselves operating, the scope for error is substantial.

This systematic potential for error is what I have in mind when I speak of the fundamental vulnerability of our ethics. Our ethics are systematically vulnerable in that our self- and other-ascriptions of ethical responsibility are determined partly by the conditions in which we operate – conditions which may, by their very nature, change unbeknownst to us.[21]

If our ethics are indeed vulnerable in this way, the central question becomes: how precisely should we regard this vulnerability? And, crucially: is this problematic? One response, stemming from traditional readings of Kantian ethics, would be to view this form of vulnerability – in so far as it connects to *heteronomy* – as posing a major challenge to the very possibility of ethics: if individuals are systematically potentially in error in their ascriptions of responsibility by virtue of changes in conditions that do not fall within their sphere of autonomy, then the very practice of ascribing responsibility must be in danger. In this view, the vulnerability of our ethics threatens the ideal of autonomy and, therefore, the very foundation of ethics.

There is, however, a different line of response, one that draws both on Anderson's work on ethical vulnerability and on her discussion of Kant's approach to heteronomy.[22] Note indeed that, in John's example, the problem is not that it is *impossible* for him to achieve understanding but rather that it is difficult for him to achieve such understanding *without interacting with others*. That is to say, examples such as John's emphasize the importance of *relationality* in coming to understand the conditions in which one finds oneself operating. It is only by speaking and interacting with all of his colleagues and by watching them in action that John can become able to appreciate the full extent of the problem in his new workplace and the responsibilities that befall him, given the particular circumstances he finds himself in. This means, however, that, far from threatening ethics, an awareness of the vulnerability *of* our ethics renders ethics possible. Honing our awareness of the fact that we *could* be in error in our ascriptions of responsibility – that we could be in error because responsibilities are shaped by conditions that may well be beyond our immediate grasp – can foster a form of openness to others that is, in fact, essential to ethics. Indeed, coming to understand that we depend on interaction and relationality with others for our understanding of the conditions that shape ethical responsibility serves as a bulwark against what is perhaps the most serious threat to ethical practice: the threat of insular and insulated dogmatism. Viewed from this perspective, the real threat to ethics is not so much the uncertainty that comes from the possibility of systematic error but the kind of certainty that can only come from a dogmatic refusal to enter into appropriate relationality with other ethical agents. By bringing to the fore the importance of relationality and of intersubjective connectedness, the vulnerability of our ethics opens the way for a more honest encounter with others and with the world.[23]

disclosure statement

No potential conflict of interest was reported by the author.

notes

This paper was written as part of the research project PGC2018-093982-B-I00, *Intercultural Understanding, Belonging and Value: Wittgensteinian Approaches*, funded by the Spanish Ministry of Science, Innovation and Universities and the European Union.

1 Pamela Sue Anderson, "When Justice and Forgiveness Come Apart: A Feminist Perspective on Restorative Justice and Intimate Violence," *Oxford Journal of Law and Religion* 5 (2016): 113–34; Pamela Sue Anderson, "Arguing for 'Ethical' Vulnerability: Towards a Politics of Care?" in *Exploring Vulnerability*, eds. Heike Springart and Günter Thomas (Göttingen and Bristol, CT: Vandenhoeck, 2017) 147–62.

2 Clearly, responsibility for climate change lies most centrally on high-impact corporations and institutions. For the purposes of the present paper, however, my interest lies primarily in the question of the responsibility of individuals.

3 Iris Marion Young discusses versions of the former two examples in her *Responsibility for Justice* (Oxford and New York: Oxford UP, 2011). However, as we will see below, her treatment of these scenarios is different from mine.

4 Miranda Fricker, *Epistemic Injustice* (Oxford: Oxford UP, 2007) 150–52.

5 John Broome, *Climate Matters: Ethics in a Warming World* (New York: Norton, 2012) 66–68, 73–117.

6 Young 52–53.

7 Hannah Arendt, "Collective Responsibility" in *Amor Mundi: Explorations in the Faith and Thought of Hannah Arendt*, ed. James William Bernauer (Boston: Springer, 1987) 43–50; Hannah Arendt, "Organized Guilt and Universal Responsibility" in *Essays in Understanding, 1930–1954: Formation, Exile, and Totalitarianism*, eds. H. Arendt and J. Kohn (New York: Schocken, 2005) 121–32; Hannah Arendt, *Eichmann in Jerusalem: A Report on the Banality of Evil* (New York: Viking, 1963). For the purposes of this paper, I will leave to one side the complex exegetical question of the extent to which Young captures Arendt's views correctly in full.

8 Arendt, "Collective Responsibility" 43–47; Arendt, "Organized Guilt" 124–26; Young 76–90.

9 Young 92.

10 Arendt, "Collective Responsibility" 45–47; Arendt, "Organized Guilt" 124–29; Arendt, *Eichmann in Jerusalem* 251; Young 76–90.

11 Young 91–92.

12 These would include apolitical adult civilians who went along with the Nazi regime because of considerations of self- and family-preservation. This category includes those "family men" (as defined by Arendt) who, unlike Eichmann, found themselves in a position of insignificant causal impact. For a discussion of this notion of the apolitical "family man," see Arendt, "Organized Guilt" 129; Young 84.

13 Arendt and Young do not restrict themselves to those adult civilians who fit the IEG; their discussion also covers civilians with higher causal impact, for instance. However, it is clear that their discussion includes civilians who fit the IEG profile.

14 Arendt, "Collective Responsibility" 45.

15 Young 79.

16 Ibid. 87.

17 Ibid. 90–92.

18 Ibid. 81.

19 Ibid. 86.

20 Nussbaum, Foreword in ibid. xxi.

21 It is important to note that this notion of "error" need not be associated with a form of realism or objectivity about the conditions that give rise to responsibility. The question of whether there is a form of realism or objectivism at work in my view is a complex one, which cannot be addressed in detail at this stage. Here, suffice it to note that some understandings of pluralism admit of robust notions of error that would be compatible with my view. See, for instance, the notion of "melioristic pluralism" developed in José Medina, *The Epistemology of Resistance: Gender and Racial Oppression, Epistemic Injustice, and the Social Imagination* (Oxford: Oxford UP, 2012) 283–84, 289–97.

22 Notably Anderson, "When Justice and Forgiveness Come Apart"; Anderson, "Arguing for 'Ethical' Vulnerability: Towards a Politics of Care?"; Anderson, "Autonomy, Vulnerability and Gender," *Feminist Theory* 4.2 (2003): 149–64.

23 This idea of *honesty* arising from a clearer understanding of one's position in the world also emerges, albeit in a different form, in Wittgenstein's early treatment of ethics. On this, see Chon Tejedor, *The Early Wittgenstein on Metaphysics, Natural Science, Language and Ethics* (London and New York: Routledge, 2015).

Pamela Anderson argues that our understanding of the human condition would profit from rethinking the vulnerability of love, leaving behind the associate myths of the Western philosophical imaginary. Spurred by Judith Butler's seminal work, Anderson finds herself challenged to rethink her ontological assumptions, away from the traditional conceptions of the self. This essay is an attempt to face this challenge upfront, and come to terms with the kind of vulnerability that Anderson wants to vindicate. I start with distinguishing different contrastive but interlocking pairs of concepts of vulnerability: the ontological and the ethical, the pathogenic and the self-enhancing, the inherent and the circumstantial. I then argue for the relevance of ontological vulnerability and suggest that it reveals the apparent normative structure of human agency and indicates the root of mutual accountability. In this perspective, human vulnerability to love and love's own vulnerability can be appreciated and reassessed as a distinctive drive to cooperative interactions and shared agency, which allows finite and interdependent agents to deal and cope with contingency and temporality, by relying on mutually accountable relations. Focusing on the dynamic reciprocal permeability which is distinctive of love, I concur with Anderson that emotional vulnerability is not the source of burdens and constraints but a precious capacity that enables relations of mutual accountability, shapes human identity, expands individual agency, and shapes integrity in interactive and historical ways.

1 emotional vulnerability as an enabling condition

In a series of recent papers, Pamela Anderson proposes that philosophy should free love and,

carla bagnoli

LOVE'S LUCK-KNOT
emotional vulnerability and symmetrical accountability

in general, vulnerability from the negative construal inherited from the tradition in Western philosophy.[1] This proposal is meant not so much to dismantle an underlying obsolete metaphysics of the invulnerable self as to offer the means for ethical and political transformation. While the specifically normative features of the project remain tentative and uncertain, the task is clearly defined: the object of this transformation is the self, and the basic claim is that the path toward political empowerment, reconciliation, and repair requires a reassessment of its distinctive vulnerability. A basic source of vulnerability of the self is the self's vulnerability to other selves. In traditional settings, vulnerability is often construed in terms of dependency and fragility, as if lovers would themselves be made reciprocally weak, hostages to their lovers and their willingness to reciprocate love – and, ultimately, hostages to contingency and luck.

In order to free love from these associations, Anderson does not recommend that we deny the vulnerability that we all experience, nor does she claim that the work is done by accepting it. Rather, she argues that we should reconceive the vulnerability distinctive of love as a "capability for an openness to mutual affection."[2] This definition is articulated at two levels, which Anderson names the phenomenological and the ethical. The *phenomenological* level of vulnerability describes the subjective experiences of intimacy, in its positive and negative effects, including the susceptibility to love and affection but also the experience of loss, grieving, and wounding with the associated emotions such as fear, shame, or rage. The *ethical* level of vulnerability indicates the openness to affective relations which enables mutual accountability. Pertaining to this level are the susceptibility to change and transformation which is distinctive of interpersonal relations; and the affective capacity for overcoming and correcting asymmetrical accountability.

I find it interesting that Anderson figures out the ethical complexity of love as an emotion in terms of a distinctive kind of openness to change and transformation which is marked by symmetrical accountability and reciprocity. This is a thought that goes against the grain of much recent literature advocating vulnerability, especially as a category opposite to autonomy. The vulnerable subject is often contrasted with an invulnerable rational agent, autonomous and independent, or perhaps showing tough virtues such as autonomy, strength of will, resilience, and grit. By refocusing the discussion onto openness to change and transformation, Anderson emphasizes the positive aspects of the capacities and dispositions that are distinctive of the vulnerable. The implication is that the vulnerable are not victims of specific kinds of wrongs and harms but agents capable of specific kinds of interactions and, in particular, agents disposed to enter personal relations marked by mutual recognition and reciprocity. This perspective sheds light on the fact that vulnerability is a positive feature of agency, rather than a source of impediments and hindrances to it – a fact that is all too often overshadowed by recurrent associations of vulnerability to victimhood, subjection, subordination, weakness, and dependency. To envision a novel political system, love should be set free from the bondage of patriarchal myth, which makes it subordinate and passive, emotional instead of cognitive, disruptive rather than stabilizing, and hence in need to be mastered and controlled by a higher authority, such as that of reason or convention.

Furthermore, by refocusing the discussion of vulnerability on capacities and dispositions that favour reciprocity we recruit the concept of vulnerability in the service of autonomy, and thus place it right at the centre of a longstanding debate in which the notion of vulnerability is, characteristically, absent. Furthermore, the emphasis on reciprocity favours and sustains the attempt to dislodge love from the paternalistic associations to dependency, as well as various other forms of patronizing and controlling affective relations, which challenge moral equality. This choice of words indicates that Anderson uncovers a stable, specific relation between vulnerability and reciprocity, which directs us to the core of mutual accountability.

2 love as a transforming power

Love is a paradigmatic form of emotional vulnerability. In the traditional construal this means that it makes us vulnerable to others, dependent on them, and hence makes us hostages to luck.[3] In Anderson's construal, instead, love is paradigmatic because it is the paradigmatic form of affective relationality, which enables us to relate to others as moral beings. Love is a moral power, and not only because it is a good thing to love others and a virtue to benefit them out of love, but also because love has a transforming effect on both the lover and the beloved.

To fully appreciate the significance of understanding love as a power, and indeed as a transforming power, it is useful to recall that this theme is discussed in relation to Judith Butler. Butler remarks that the increased sense of vulnerability is usually accompanied by the sense of violence, which suggests that there is nothing in the recognition of one's own embodied vulnerability that necessarily inspires or demands love (and its cognates, such as compassion, benevolence, and loving attention).[4] In contrast to the dark and sad philosophical associations of vulnerability, Butler claims that the recognition of mutual vulnerability and dependency – especially in grief, desire, or loss – could provide the basis for non-violent interactions, or perhaps even cooperative and mutually supportive interactions. These suggestions do not appear to be mandatory, however, and Anderson seems to share Butler's inclination to regard vulnerability itself as not normative. Even though it remains mysterious, or at least undetermined, how to build a normative ethics and politics of non-violent, cooperative, or benevolent interactions from this standpoint, it is clear enough that a radical re-orientation toward vulnerability is required in order to reconceive of politics and ethics anew. Like Butler, Anderson urges us to account for vulnerability as a mode of relationality which is differentially visible – according to historical, social, material, and especially economic conditions. She emphasizes that the sort of vulnerability that is constitutive of our bodies is socially constructed and, therefore, socially and politically significant. These claims have various important implications which are worthy of further reflection.

First, vulnerability takes concrete forms and is manifest in various aspects of our life. This means that generalizations are inadequate and often dangerous.[5] The risk is to overlook specific ways in which dispositions and affective powers are manifested and distorted, and also become insensitive to specific ways in which individuals wrong each other, react, and adapt to each other.

Second, there is much about such significance that is outside individual control, often unwanted and felt as inevitable. According to Anderson, Butler shows that our need for mourning loss of life is required of us in different senses, and not a matter of choice. In mourning and grieving we accept the loss but we also accept that the process of mourning and grieving is a necessary part of valuing that we mourn and grieve out of love. If we did not undergo this painful process we would be missing something important about the experience of loving. I would say that this is because mourning and grieving are modes of valuing, and also in themselves valuable features of our vulnerability. We would not want to do without them, even though they are painful to endure. Coming to terms with loss involves grief, and it takes time because conceptually elaborating loss is a personal and affective experience that is structured by time and by personal dynamics. Clearly, the task of grief is not to get rid of the painful experience of losing somebody we loved, thereby lifting a burden and liberating oneself from the bonds of love. In fact, grieving is an activity continuous with loving. It is perhaps very much *like* loving, if under severely different circumstances.

More abstractly, loving and grieving are the same sort of "active passion," under the relevant transformations. The oxymoron "active passion" indicates that entering the process of loving (or grieving) is not something we get to decide. And yet these qualify as activities we undertake, rather than processes we merely undergo. In contrast with other (biological) processes such as, for example, growing hair, the way we undertake these processes is revelatory of the people we are. How we love and how we mourn indicate the relation we had with the beloved, but these attitudes also indicate something important about our selves. Likewise, how we conduct ourselves in the face of loss and how we endure the process is revealing of the kind of people we are and of the relations we can sustain. Enduring passions such as grief and love is an experience of dispossession which is imposed by the circumstances, an opportunity that we are forced to take up unwillingly; but it is also an expression of agency, as much as willing or deciding. This is an instance of the exercise of capacities and strengths characteristic of vulnerable finite rational beings such as we are.

Finally, these considerations about enduring love and grief seem to call into question some ontological presumption about the self and surroundings. According to Anderson, the ontological view that bans vulnerability is markedly Kantian in that it assumes a fundamental ontology of the self, invulnerable to circumstances and contingencies, distinguished by its capacities even though phenomenologically vulnerable. The Kantian self exists prior to our knowledge of external objects, which stands prior to any of our relations and actively unifies and systematizes all our subjective experiences:

> In the past I have rejected the very idea of a relational ontology – assuming, instead, a fundamental ontology of a self was necessary on largely Kantian grounds. However, my more recent reading and thinking about vulnerability, its affects and connections to love, have made Butler's account of relationality – and vulnerability as "a mode of relationality" – a serious challenge to my previous thinking; so much so that I have had to allow myself to be transformed by a new understanding of affects and affections in motivating love, and in reconceiving vulnerability.[6]

The ideal of (ethical and ontological) invulnerability is accepted by many ethical theorists, and especially by Utilitarians. In contrast to these mainstream ethical theories, Anderson points to Butler as marking a turning point in ethical theorizing. To view vulnerability as an ethical concept, capable of grounding a whole agenda of ethical and political transformation, we need to step away from the Kantian account of a transcendental self. Anderson presses a further question about love: is love powerful enough to drive us (politically and ethically)? She concludes that there is no clear path, no unique route from corporal vulnerability to normative ethics and politics, because there is nothing normative in vulnerability.[7] In what follows, I shall argue to the contrary that the Kantian conception of vulnerability is well suited to further her

project and is rich in normativity. The present challenge, as I see it, is to sharpen our concepts so as to come to terms with the relevant sort of contingency, and in a way that reveals how reciprocal emotional vulnerability is empowering rather than limiting, constraining or self-undermining. It is the sort of vulnerability that allows us to share with others in reason and action.

3 constitutive vulnerability and embodied rational agency

In recent debates across Continental and analytic philosophy different concepts of vulnerability have emerged which inform different and often competing ethical programs.[8] It is useful to distinguish two general approaches to vulnerability, one *ontological* and the other *ethical*.

The *ontological* approach to vulnerability calls attention to the human condition, and aims to identify the constitutive features that make all humans fundamentally vulnerable, independently of specific circumstances and contingencies. The ontological concept of vulnerability singles out ontological features, generally grounded in our biology. The main source of reservations against the ontological concepts of vulnerability is that the focus on what is invariant across political and ethical contexts is imperceptive of the particular circumstances of injustice, and thus potentially dangerous in that it tends to make us overlook the social and political origin of injustice. This is Judith Butler's worry, for instance.

The *ethical* approach to vulnerability prevails when the philosophical problem that the concept of vulnerability is meant to articulate concerns issues such as discrimination and the task of the theory is to provide the theoretical means to support and protect vulnerable subjects. Here the concept of vulnerability singles out the categories of agents that are especially susceptible and subjected to harm. Paradigmatically, minorities belong to the category of vulnerable subjects because they are susceptible to suffering wrongful harms. In these cases, the relevant sort of vulnerability is contingent, dependent on the disfavouring circumstances of features associated with the category of vulnerable subjects. Such circumstances include our biology, natural emergencies such as earthquakes, floods, and political conditions such as oppressive regimes, discriminatory policies and racist practices. In so far as the ethical concept of vulnerability helps us to map such ethical problems it is also central to remedial justice and the ethics of reparation. It calls attention to some categories of subjects as vulnerable, and hence it singles them out as the appropriate target of remedial attitudes and redress. In a way, vulnerability is a matter of justice.

Yet there are reservations in accounting for justice starting with profiling vulnerable subjects, partly because vulnerability is associated with victimhood, passivity, weakness, inferiority, incapacity to provide for oneself, pathological dependency, and various failures to meet the threshold condition for attribution of the status as moral and epistemic peers. In my view, this way of opposing the ethical to the ontological misrepresents the challenges associated with vulnerability, in particular by mischaracterizing the tension with the concept of autonomy, and it is also at risk of inducing and implicitly condoning paternalistic attitudes.[9] Anderson's proposal of reconceiving vulnerability as a positive capacity goes in the direction of separating it from victimhood. We learn from Anderson that the negative associations with vulnerability can be tossed out. In fact, the ethical concept of vulnerability regains its descriptive and transformative power when it is disconnected from such associations. By emphasizing the contingent nature of the ethical concept of vulnerability we are able to appreciate that such concepts may apply to different categories of subjects across time and place. It does not nail some categories to a determined political and social destiny. On the contrary, it shows the way for reform, transformation, and repair. In short, the ethical concept of vulnerability is dynamic and relational. It is not fixed and static, and points toward an articulation of justice centred on multiple modes of mutual support and recognition.

In contrast to the ontological concept of vulnerability, Anderson emphasizes that "vulnerability differentiates us socially, historically and materially – in complex, perhaps mysterious ways!"[10] While these worries are genuine, they should not blind us to the positive import of the ontological concept of vulnerability, which helps us appreciate the distinctive resources and capabilities distinctive of the human condition. Narrowing down the significance of the concept of vulnerability to the ethics of discrimination, reparation, and redress is, ultimately, not a good strategy for comprehending the ethical, epistemic, and political impact of vulnerability. In particular, it does a disservice to the project that Anderson defends so passionately and convincingly, that is, the project of transformation driven by the positive appreciation of vulnerability. To be sure, the ontological conception of vulnerability is not all we need for ethical purposes, but it plays a crucial role in a general account of normativity, and this role is crucial for understanding how we function and fail as rational and moral agents.

In order to capture the relevant sort of vulnerability that the ethical and ontological approaches identify, I propose that we deploy an alternative contrastive pair of concepts – circumstantial and constitutive vulnerability – which cuts across the ontological and ethical dichotomy.[11] *Circumstantial* vulnerability names vulnerabilities that are contingent on some external circumstances. Some of these vulnerabilities are pathogenic and make the subjects susceptible to specific kinds of wrongs and harms such as those due to gender and race discrimination, loss of status, loss of citizenship entitlements, lack of recognition, oppression, and deprivation. The ethical approach presented above focuses on these sorts of vulnerabilities since it is preoccupied with defining wrongs and what we owe to the wronged, including remedial attitudes and redress. However, it should be noted that circumstantial vulnerability presupposes ontological vulnerability. For instance, the fact that we all are vulnerable to paternalistic policies depends on the fact that we are embodied and thus susceptible to being affected by patronizing attitudes and paternalistic institutions. Yet this is not to say that being treated in a paternalistic way is a normal or healthy condition for embodied minds. It is a pathological condition, but it is a condition that affects us in so far as we have embodied minds that can be so affected. For the same reason as we are prone to be subjected to wrongs, we are also capable of self-enhancement and gaining autonomy. The ethical concept of vulnerability is often related to the circumstantial.

Constitutive vulnerability indicates a generic capacity to be affected, understood in a very broad sense, and marked by positive and negative valence. It depends on a complex network of dispositions and capacities, for example suffering and enjoyment, frailty and resilience, reliance and dependency, and so on. Other kinds of ontological vulnerabilities are positive, and include psychological endowments, capacities and skills that people develop and refine over time, and which enable them to enter in fruitful (psychological and normative) relations with others. A basic capacity in this regard is the capacity for emotional contagion, that is, the capacity for unintentionally echoing emotions that others display by mimicry and feedback.[12] Other more complex and more mediated mechanisms, which can be named emotional resonance, include modes for being affected by emotions that others feel by sympathy, dialogical reasoning, conversation, hypothetical reasoning, and counter-factual reasoning. All these mechanisms are not as completely unintentional as the term "emotional contagion" suggests, even though large parts of these psychological mechanisms are semi-automatic and operate below the level of personal subjective awareness. This is because they all more or less require subjects to be attentive to others and alert to the context, and attention can be modulated, which means that all the above mechanisms operate with a minimum of deliberative involvement on the part of the subjects. Of course, this is not to say that the various modes of emotional resonance are under deliberative or psychological control, or that they can be enacted at will; but they can be interestingly altered by focusing or refocusing attention. In a way, moral transformation amounts to morally appropriate alteration of attentional worlds refocused onto others.

The concept of constitutive vulnerability makes the complementarity of the different aspects of vulnerability apparent, while the ethical approach tends to hide that they both spring from the same source, that is, embodiment. Embodiment is not the sole dimension of our being that is important in understanding the varieties of human interactions of which we are capable. Yet embodiment is the inevitable starting point from which the inquiry about vulnerability should start. By refocusing the debate on constitutive vulnerability we can identify the general constraints and predicaments that agents face in so far as they are embodied, while appreciating the kinds of capacities, skills, abilities, and practical resources that are distinctively associated with the status of constitutive vulnerability.

4 constitutive vulnerability and love

Constitutive vulnerability can be articulated by focusing on four dimensions. The first dimension is embodiment. The body is the seat of our agency, not only an instrument of it. Embodiment gives human agency the distinctive shape it has. The specific embodiment that characterizes human agency allows us to identify three further dimensions of constitutive vulnerability: the enacted dimension, the embedded dimension, and the extended dimension. Some of these features such as interdependency and the capacities for extended minds and agency are not merely biological necessities but also and, perhaps more importantly, morally valuable features of human life: they contribute to leading a good life, a life that is worth living. Civic and personal friendships and loving relations are shared activities grounded both on reciprocity and mutual dependency. Likewise, we depend on others in the various ways in which we acquire knowledge, search for truth, form beliefs, and learn about our surroundings, but also in the way we feel and become interested in action, and in touch with ourselves, with others and with the world.

As a constitutive feature of the human condition, vulnerability is characterized primarily as an aspect of embodiment, a dimension that humans share with other non-human animals, under some limited description. This characterization of human vulnerability highlights different clusters of problematic aspects of human agency. First, it pairs vulnerability with embeddedness, hence revealing how profoundly human agency is exposed to various forms of contingency. Second, constitutive vulnerability makes the temporal structure of human agency apparent. As all living things, humans are finite, affected by time, and subjected to various sorts of temporal bias. They act and interact in time and are capable of sustaining agency and commitment through time. Finitude and the importance of temporal constraints reverberate at different levels, which concern the very structure of agency, the resources that rational agents can access, and the external conditions of the context of choice in which agents are embedded. Third, when focusing on the corporal dimension of agency, vulnerability is associated with interests, needs, desires, and other conative states. Being the repository of needs and interests, the body makes us susceptible to suffering from deprivation of resources in ways that deplete both the opportunity and the capacity for action.

This particular aspect of vulnerability is a canonical theme in moral philosophy, and for two distinct reasons. First, desires, interests, and needs are traditional sources of resistance to morality, as they generate egoistic and aggressive behaviour, frailty, weakness of the will, and other vices. Second, such needs are also the sorts of things that morality must protect: it is a primary moral obligation to provide shelter, food, and the basic means of survival, and the grounds of such a moral obligation have to do with the preservation and protection of human life.

There is a third reason which can be brought to light by focusing on constitutive vulnerability. Embodiment stands in an interesting relation to the social nature of human animals, which rests on the capacities for emotional contagion and emotional resonance. In this connection, vulnerability relates emotional mutual dependency to the susceptibility to be harmed or helped, obstructed or facilitated, undercut or enhanced, directed or manipulated by other agents. In so far as humans are social animals, they are mutually dependent in profound ways. They depend on each other not only occasionally but systematically; not only strategically but also, and in a pervasive way, for the sake of intrinsic ends, in the ordinary exercise of their cognitive and practical agency. They are endowed with emotions, feelings, and affects. Emotional vulnerability allows humans to develop a complex network of dispositions, skills, and capacities by which to respond to the predicaments of a human life. Fundamentally, I want to argue, vulnerability is the root of shared agency. A paradigmatic case is love.

Love binds, and the binding nature of love often generates actions. I would like to address love's vulnerability in the perspective of agency, something that allows us to extend and enhance our agency. Love is the motive and the reason that explains individual action. But it is also, and more importantly, the motive and reason why we engage in action with others. It is the drive of cooperative actions and of shared actions. These two kinds of actions differ in the following respects. Cooperative actions are individual intentional actions that converge with the individual actions of others in a common pursuit. Shared actions are actions generated by shared intentions, and thus require that each of the agents converges with the other in intending to engage in action, and not only in producing an end that both sides find desirable. A distinctive aspect of love is that it generates shared action without intentions being shared. That is to say, love binds and drives shared action without the mediation of planning and thus bypassing typical ways of collective decision making. This is a significant power of love that is distinctively self-enhancing because it enhances the capacity for agency. This power is also, and at the same time, something that exposes us to luck, and radically so. To sustain shared activities, we radically depend on our beloved. Differently from cooperative interactions, the kinds of shared activities that originate in love radically depend on the beloved because they are our irreplaceable partners. We engage with activities because of the kind of practical subjects we are, and not solely in order to pursue a goal independent of the loving relation we entertain with others. To this extent, love is like the Chinese luck-knot, whose difficult beauty is an achievement that requires understanding, knowledge, and a measure of luck. That love exposes us to luck in profound ways is not enough to represent it as a negative and self-destructive force. The features of love that make it vulnerable to contingencies and expose us to luck are the same features that make love self-enhancing and extend our agency beyond individual boundaries and across time.

5 love, self-discipline, and self-transformation

The claim that love is self-enhancing and expands the sphere of individual agency may be thought to be in contrast to some strands of Anderson's work, which relate to Simone Weil and Iris Murdoch. These philosophers insist that love requires self-discipline to be genuine. In the process of loving, the self must "de-create," in order to either find itself in, or connect itself to, loving relations. The suggestion seems to be that the role of love may be construed as self-constraining rather than self-enhancing, and it may have nothing to do with agency, much less with expanding the bounds of individual agency.

The view of love as self-discipline belongs to a rather traditional vision of the virtuous life, and bears a striking similarity to the Kantian view of moral self-love. Of course, differences are important and, especially in this context, perhaps more important than the similarities. On the Kantian view, moral self-love is rationalized self-love, that is, love that results from the constraining process of reasoning, and it is subjected to and governed by recognition and respect for others as legitimate sources of valid claims.[13] On the Kantian view, the subjective experience of respect reveals the psychological and moral fragility of the self, dependent on the recognition of others to draw boundaries, to raise walls, and protect individuality by establishing separateness.[14] At the same time, it also calls attention to the constitutive relationality of the self: the dependence and reliance on the recognition of others is not only remedial reaction to one's own limitations and fragilities but it is also ontologically constitutive of self. There is no individuated self, prior to and independent of the relation of recognition and respect to other selves. I am disputing the attribution to Kant of the claim that the self is invulnerable.[15]

By focusing on the constraining effects of reasoning on self-love, Kant offers an account of moral transformation, that is, the path from self-regard and self-conceit to rational and moral self-love. Most certainly, this is too narrow an account, which does not bring about the sort of multiform transformation that Anderson envisions. In this regard, the mystic model of Simone Weil and Iris Murdoch may seem more promising in that they represent the transformative power of love that allows us to engage with reality and recognize others for what they are, that in which consists the primal moral experience.

In spite of these similarities, there is a stark contrast between the rationalistic and the mystic models. On behalf of the former, I want to stress that it uniquely intercepts the sphere of agency, that which remains at the margins of the mystic accounts of transformation.[16] My suggestion is that we can retrieve important conceptual tools by reading Kant in contrast to the consequentialist and performative conceptions of action.[17]

6 mutual recognition and the dynamics of reciprocal empowerment

In Kant's view, the constraining role of reason is not equivalent to limiting the agent's opportunities for action, for example by selecting the morally appropriate motives and telling right from wrong. More fundamentally, the idea of the law enables people to legitimately and authoritatively attribute reciprocal powers and responsibilities. This is the sense in which the categorical imperative is both the constitutive form of goodwill and the constitutive norm of rational justification. Differently from specific laws of command and imperatives, which prescribe things to do or prohibit types of actions, the categorical imperative is the constitutive form of certain kinds of activities which enable subjects to conduct and effectively participate in such activities.

The correct exercise of reason can be explained by reference to the merely logical form of the law; but this characterization does not stand alone in Kant's account of the categorical imperative as a norm constitutive of reasoning, and it is insufficient to give justice to the social dimension of reason or its publicity, which best emerges in the third formulation of the categorical imperative. The claim that reason is the sole way to orient oneself in thinking does not lead toward a solitary confabulation, as Murdoch and Butler often suggest. By contrast, it urges that human reasoners cannot think correctly unless free to express their judgements and subject them to public scrutiny. Sharing truths with others, hence certifying truths through reasoning with others, is more important that finding out what these truths are. In short, relationality is at the very heart of Kant's conception of certified knowledge. This is exactly because human reason is not an infallible faculty for detecting truths. In its process of validation, reason does not have dictatorial authority but is itself subjected to public scrutiny.[18] This does not exclude the fact that other rational beings avail themselves of other forms of rationality and have access to truth but urges that humans need a social context to express and correctly perform reasoning aimed at truth. The hypothesis that Kant urges us to take into account is that reason and sensibility can work together, not because they may happen to converge on occasionally shared goals but because they are integrated (under the name of practical reason).

Anderson seems to side with Kant in claiming that morality requires inner transformation, which can be imposed by self-discipline and self-constraint. For Kant, the concept of respect or reverence for the lawmaking capacity of humanity is key to this experience.[19] For Anderson, instead, it is love, again, that provides the primal and paradigmatic experience of morality. But these ways of understanding the experience of morality do not differ as much as might appear at first. In both cases, morality demands an inner transformation and in both cases self-discipline is required to achieve it. The reference to the law in Kant's ethics is constitutive of rationality and it is not a limiting condition. The moral law is constitutive of rational agency but it is a regulative ideal for finite rational agents, in the sense that it is what represents the complete form of rational agency, which they cannot attain but only approximate. However, in so far as it is the standard of rational agency, moral law is not imposed on finite rational agents as if from outside, in the guise of sanctions or threats, but works as their internal criterion of correctness. That is to say that such a standard constrains but internally, giving rise to a transformation. The locus of this inner transformation is rational deliberation, which amounts to ranking the incentives, thereby determining the right motive for action. The subjective experience of rational deliberation is respect, which names a complex psychological activity, comprising pleasurable reassurance that one is able to act as one deliberates, and a displeasing sense of frustration and humiliation resulting from the selection of debased maxims. It is through this activity of the mind that incentives are transformed into motives for action. One might say that this sort of transformation is temporary, since it amounts to a deliberative exercise that the finite rational agent repeats anew any time she engages in action. Respect does not provide any permanent moral discernment, no breakthrough in the moral domain, no direct insight into moral truth. This is correct, in my view, but it does not contradict the claim that rational deliberation is the locus of genuine moral transformation. Even though it is not a mode of moral discernment, the moral feeling of respect and the underlying complex activities bring some cognitive gain. In particular, it conveys the thought of acting on principle. This thought contains the idea of a self-reflective subject that is not automatically driven by impulses, nor is she fully determined by reason, but she is capable of rational deliberation. Under this description, reverence for the law is essential to practical knowledge of what to do, but it is also practical knowledge of oneself as efficacious through one's intention.

7 the dynamics of love

By bringing to light the connection between love and agency, and emphasizing the active aspects of loving relations, I do not mean to underestimate love's receptive features. Love cannot be understood other than in terms of one's emotional responsiveness to one's beloved. Such responsiveness is an important aspect of mutual enhancement. Lovers are capable of enhancing themselves by mutually defining and promoting the wellness and well-being of one other. The root of their mutual strength is also the root of their mutual vulnerability.

As a social emotion, love belongs in a large network of emotional attitudes whose general function is to cope with the predicaments of contingency and embedded agency. Many instances of activity and thinking are assisted and even constituted by forms of affectivity that are social and dynamic. It is because of love that humans are capable of exercising complex forms of agency, namely, shared agency. Thus, love makes us vulnerable to one another, not because it makes us subjected to another will or dependent on it but because it allows us to make plans and contribute to activities that we cannot possibly pursue by ourselves. Love makes us constitutively dependent on our beloved, exactly because it expands the sphere of our agency and enhances our capacities for agency. Rather than being a threat to our autonomy, love is one of the many ways in which we exercise agential autonomy. It requires that we engage with others, constructing with them new attentional worlds that form the background of a communal understanding.

Philosophers have paid special attention to changes that concern the characters of lovers. The fact that love unfolds and develops over time is importantly related to the fact that love is directed to some particular other, creates a personal relation where the lovers deeply impact on one another's emotional life and systematically and reciprocally interfere with their agency and autonomy. A view that has become standard is that love is peculiar because it is historical and it is historical because it binds people in virtue of their being people, rather than as properties-holders. Dynamic permeability fosters changes and mutual adjustments that are merely external to the self or limited to the sort of relation they entertain and the sorts of things they do, but extend more significantly to the sorts of people they become through and by loving.[20]

My proposal is to pay attention to both the practical and ontological dimension of dynamic permeability. From an ontological perspective it says that, through and by love, lovers mutually change their identity and bounds of agency over time. From a practical perspective it says that they mutually change their practical perspective on themselves, and their lives, for example maturing new goals, perfecting others, or abandoning old ones. This view agrees with common understandings of romantic love, which is experienced as life-changing so much that its end is often narrated as a turning point or even a loss of identity. Such mutual permeability exposes each of the lovers to risk and unexpected change. This is to say that love makes lovers vulnerable to different sorts of luck: constitutive luck (in so far as lovers are mutually permeable by love), and circumstantial luck (in so far as they each become susceptible to circumstances in unexpected ways).

In this bi-dimensional perspective we can say that love is primarily self-enhancing rather than self-undermining and undercutting. This is because lovers are not only bound by love, subjected to mutual responsibilities and burdens; they also affect each other in ways that create new opportunities for change and development. Loving relationships multiply the opportunities to exercise personal and agential autonomy, rather than restricting them and they are potentially self-enhancing rather than undermining our status as autonomous agents. The sort of vulnerability that love exemplifies is neither a form of passivity nor receptivity but the basis for important activities that qualify us as practical subjects, that is, subjects capable of practical concerns and mutual recognition.

8 repairing: on the normative aspect of vulnerability

One may object that expanding agency does not necessarily amount to enhancing the self. There are ways of engaging in action that are detrimental to the self, for instance, because they are submissive and self-undermining. The issue is to determine when engagement in agency is protective and expressive of the agent's self, and this is a *normative* issue, which calls for a normative approach to vulnerability. It is often difficult to determine exactly the line between healthy and pathogenic vulnerability in specified contexts, and it can be problematic to argue that such a line is a priori definable or even predictable. These problems can be addressed by centring the present inquiry on the *primary function* of love and other forms of emotional vulnerability, that is, enabling mutual accountability and shared agency, without discounting the fact that things can get very complicated, and there are many ways this function can be fulfilled or impeded. This is a contestable methodology and, in closing, I want to spend a few words in its defence.

Philosophers attentive to miscarriages of justice have argued that we should start with defective instances first, rather than take for granted that there is a paradigm scenario of justice. For instance, Judith Shklar has argued powerfully that "philosophy fails to give injustice its due" when it focuses on the virtues and ignores vices.[21] In her view, it is misleading to presume that one should have featured justice in order to understand the defective instances of it. In a similar vein, Alice Jaggar and Theresa Tobin hold that we should start with non-ideal conditions of justice in order to understand how justice can be brought about.[22] This is because – they claim – what counts as rational justification in an unjust world radically differs from the standards of justice in idealized circumstances.

By contrast, I share the Rawlsian view that ideal theory comes before non-ideal theory, not in place of it.[23] The point in starting with the primary normative function of emotional vulnerability – love in this case – is that we need a systematic understanding of how to intervene on the non-ideal world. By engaging with ideal theory first, we fix the ideal of reference that serves as normative guidance to articulate the normative tasks.[24] In this manner, we can make sure that corrections and interventions in the non-ideal circumstances must be principled and systematic, rather than arbitrary and scattered. The presumption is that the principles that inform ideal theory are not radically different from those that we should pursue in non-ideal circumstances. In fact, the ideal must be able to guide us under non-ideal circumstances in order to be normative. It would fail to be practical if it did not; hence, applicability represents a test of adequacy for ideal theory. This is to point out that ideal theories can be assessed against the standard of descriptive plausibility and applicability. They are not all inapplicable in so far as they are ideal, and they may fail for quite different reasons, which deserve close scrutiny: a general condemnation will not serve ethical theorizing, one way or another.

Ideal theory makes two critical assumptions. First, it assumes that citizens are generally willing to comply with the chosen principles, and that they act in reasonably favourable social conditions, conducive to political cooperation. The second assumption excludes malpractice of reasoning as the one identified above, for example where citizens are so terrified, humiliated, or angry that their capacity for moral reasoning is undermined, bypassed, or overwhelmed. It might be thought that these assumptions make ideal theory impractical in a social world inhabited by vulnerable subjects because such subjects are frail often enough that they fail to comply with principles of justice, even when they choose to do so, and also because they may be deprived of the capacity for reasoning or of the capacity to trust their own reasoning. These are important considerations to monitor how principles of justice should guide institutional settings and personal relations. But to renounce ideal theory leads to adapting to the circumstances of injustice and brings us close to the risk of obtruding the capacity to identify failures of justice.

The appeal to the ethical dimension of constitutive vulnerability as openness to engage in relations of symmetrical accountability serves a crucial role in bridging the gap between ideal and non-ideal theory. The primary function of emotional vulnerability is to enable and favour symmetrical accountability. In a disrupted social world, vulnerability serves a reparative and corrective function, as it contrasts asymmetrical relations of accountability and restores or promotes symmetrical ones. It is a decisive resource for repair and restorative justice, which combines the virtues of justice and care, and may take the form of forgiveness and repentance.[25]

9 conclusion

I have argued that our vulnerability to love is constitutive and represents an important source of self-enhancement and shared agency. In order to capture the importance of love as extending individual agency I have drawn from Kant's conception of rational self-love, which is constituted partly by respect for others as independent sources of valid claims. The kind of shared agency that this form of love provides is principled and yet susceptible to being modulated in various ways. It is a fundamental resource to overcome the limitations of individuals, and to nourish and sustain their practical identity.

disclosure statement

No potential conflict of interest was reported by the author.

notes

1 See, for example, Pamela Sue Anderson, "Arguing for 'Ethical' Vulnerability: Towards a Politics of Care?" in *Exploring Vulnerability*, eds. Heike Springhart and Günter Thomas (Göttingen and Bristol, CT: Vandenhoeck, 2017) 147–62; "Creating a New Imaginary for Love in Religion," ed. Paul S. Fiddes, in *Love and Vulnerability: Thinking with Pamela Sue Anderson*, ed. Pelagia Goulimari, Spec. issue of *Angelaki: Journal of the Theoretical Humanities* 25.1–2 (2020): 46–53; "Towards a New Philosophical Imaginary," eds. Sabina Lovibond and A.W. Moore, in *Love and Vulnerability: Thinking with Pamela Sue Anderson* 8–22; "Love and Vulnerability: Two Love Commandments and One God," available <https://loveinreligionorg.files.wordpress.com/2017/02/anderson-love-and-vulnerability-amended-title-9-1-18.pdf> (accessed 8 Dec. 2019).

2 Pamela Anderson, "Arguing for 'Ethical' Vulnerability" 147; see also Kristine Culp, "Vulnerability and the Susceptibility to Transformation" in *Exploring Vulnerability* 59–70. Anderson draws also on Paul Ricoeur, *Memory, History, Forgetting*, trans. Kathleen Blamey (Chicago: U of Chicago P, 2005) 460; "Ethics and Human Capability: A Response" in *Paul Ricoeur and Contemporary Moral Thought*, eds. John Wall, William Schweiker, and David Hall (New York and London: Routledge, 2002) 280, 282, 284.

3 See Carla Bagnoli, "Autonomy, Emotional Vulnerability and the Dynamics of Power," *Women Philosophers on Autonomy*, eds. Sandrine Berges and Alberto L. Siani (London: Routledge, 2018) 208–25.

4 Judith Butler, *Precarious Life* (London: Verso, 2004) 23, 21–23, 28–29, 51, 128.

5 Anderson, "Arguing for 'Ethical' Vulnerability" 157.

6 Anderson, "Towards a New Philosophical Imaginary" 10.

7 Anderson, "Arguing for 'Ethical' Vulnerability" 162.

8 See Susan Dodds, Catriona Mackenzie, and Wendy Rogers, "Introduction: What is Vulnerability and Why Does it Matter for Moral Theory?" in *Vulnerability: New Essays in Ethics and Feminist Philosophy*, eds. Susan Dodds, Catriona Mackenzie, and Wendy Rogers (New York: Oxford UP, 2014) 4–10.

9 Anderson aims to show that the concepts of autonomy and vulnerability, properly understood and spelled out, are entangled; see "Arguing for 'Ethical' Vulnerability." See also Catriona Mackenzie, "The Importance of Relational Autonomy and Capabilities for an Ethics of Vulnerability" in *Vulnerability: New Essays in Ethics and Feminist Philosophy*.

10 "Towards a New Philosophical Imaginary" 11.

11 On the distinction between the ontological and the ethical conceptions of vulnerability, see Anderson, "Arguing for 'Ethical' Vulnerability" 161. Compare Dodds, Mackenzie, and Rogers ("Introduction"), who distinguish three concepts of vulnerability: inherent, situational, and pathogenic. What I call "ontological vulnerability" corresponds to what they call "inherent vulnerability," while "circumstantial vulnerability" includes both situational (non-pathogenic) and pathogenic aspects of vulnerability. I introduced the contrastive pair constitutive/circumstantial vulnerability in order to stress the analogy with the pair constitutive/circumstantial luck, which belongs in a debate whose main concerns overlap with those central in my account of vulnerability, as argued at length in "Vulnerability and the Incompleteness of Practical Reason" in *Vulnerability and Applied Ethics*, ed. Christine Strahele (London: Routledge, 2016) 13–32. For an alternative account of the role of vulnerability in Kant's ethics, see Paul Formosa, "The Role of Vulnerability in Kantian Ethics" in *Vulnerability: New Essays in Ethics and Feminist Philosophy*.

12 Anderson, "Arguing for 'Ethical' Vulnerability" 161.

13 On the differences between the constraining function of respect and the transformative effect of love, see Carla Bagnoli, "Autonomy, Emotional Vulnerability and the Dynamics of Power." One way to cast the difference relevant in the present discussion is to focus on the standard of proof. For Kant, the standard of proof for morality is the experience of respect, which testifies to the impact of reasoning on our mind, and its efficacy in determining action. For Murdoch, instead, the standard of proof is love. She holds that the transformative power of love allows us to engage with reality and recognize others as they are, independently of our projections and strategic interactions with them. See Carla Bagnoli, "Constrained by Reason, Transformed by Love: Kant and Murdoch on the Standard of Proof" in *Truth and Love*, ed. Gary Browning (Heidelberg: Springer, 2018) 63–88; Iris Murdoch, *Existentialists and Mystics: Writings on Philosophy and Literature* (London: Chatto, 1997) 215.

14 Murdoch, *Existentialists and Mystics* 216, 331. By dissociating emotions and the self, pathological feelings and morality, the intellectualist model deprives us of resources for bringing about significant changes in vision.

15 The self is nothing but a reflexive structure, which fits a distinctive conception of public reason, and a public conception of autonomy; see Carla Bagnoli, "Kant in Metaethics: The Paradox of Autonomy, Solved by Publicity" in *The Palgrave Kant Handbook*, ed. Matthew C. Altman (London: Palgrave Macmillan, 2017) 355–77.

16 Again, this is not without reason, and it has some points of merit, which are best highlighted in contrast to two prominent views of agency, namely, consequentialist and behaviourist views. Murdoch's description of moral transformation ensued by loving attention aims to represent a mode of moral activity that is decidedly alternative to the behaviourist conception of action. Nonetheless, the sphere of agency remains marginal and under-investigated.

17 Murdoch mistakenly treats Kant's conception of action as akin to behaviourism. She conflates Kant's own conception with the Kantian conceptions underlying her contemporary Kantian theories, such as Richard M. Hare's or Stuart Hampshire's. See Carla Bagnoli, "Constrained by Reason, Transformed by Love" 72 ff.

18 Kant, C1 A738/B766. References to Kant's works refer to the Prussian Academy edition and are given using the following abbreviations: C1 *Critique of Pure Reason*; C2 *Critique of Practical Reason*; MM *Metaphysics of Morals*.

19 Kant, MM 6: 465, 389, 379; C2 5: 42, 151–57.

20 Amélie Rorty speaks of love as "dynamically permeable" in that each of the lovers profoundly shapes each other by loving. Lovers affect one

another in ways that "tend to ramify through a person's character"; see her "The Historicity of Psychological Attitudes: Love is Not Love Which Alters Not When it Alteration Finds" in *Friendship: A Philosophical Reader*, ed. N.K. Badhwar (Ithaca, NY: Cornell UP, 1993) 73–88 (77).

21 Judith Shklar, *The Faces of Injustice* (New Haven: Yale UP, 1990) 9; see also Shklar, *Ordinary Vices* (Cambridge, MA: Harvard UP, 1984).

22 Alison Jaggar and Theresa W. Tobin hold that moral justification might be different in an unjust world; see their "Moral Justification in an Unjust World" in *The Routledge Companion to Feminist Philosophy*, eds. Ann Garry, Serene J. Khader, and Alison Stone (New York: Routledge, 2017) 501–14.

23 John Rawls, *A Theory of Justice* (Cambridge, MA: Harvard UP, 1971). Rawls' claim is that we should have completed an ideal vision of what are the normative standards to address one another in reasoning in order to understand how to correct what does not work in non-ideal conditions.

24 Anderson seems undecided on this point. Some remarks suggest that she does not renounce the primacy of political standards: "I am not yet clear whether a politics of care can preserve or achieve this ethical accountability, without some form of justice as our primary political standard" ("Arguing for 'Ethical' Vulnerability" 149).

25 Anderson importantly remarks that in some cases (e.g., cases of intimate violence or "core intimacy wounds") the duty to forgive is a highly contentious matter. Pamela Sue Anderson, "When Justice and Forgiveness Come Apart: A Feminist Perspective on Restorative Justice and Intimate Violence," *Oxford Journal of Law and Religion* 5.1 (2016): 113–34. Compare Lucy Allis, "Wiping the Slate Clean: The Heart of Forgiveness," *Philosophy and Public Affairs* 36.1 (2008): 33–68; Margaret Urban Walker, "Moral Vulnerability and the Task of Reparations" in *Vulnerability: New Essays in Ethics and Feminist Philosophy* 110–33.

introduction: the ambiguity of vulnerability

The first time I met Pamela was at the beautiful campus of Wuhan University in China on a rainy and green summer day, where she taught that year's Philosophy summer school in China on Emmanuel Levinas's *Totality and Infinity*, more than a decade ago. From not knowing much about Levinas to a dedicated Levinasian, her acute intellectual perception and passionate teaching ignited my long-lasting interest in studying the philosophy of Emmanuel Levinas, particularly with a feminist perspective. We were in touch ever since and her generous help, her caring, positive and kind personality shed light on my way to become a scholar myself. I dedicate this paper to her and to my memory of her as my beloved teacher and caring friend.

In the theoretical tradition, the idea of vulnerability has not played a key role in moral or political philosophy until rather recently. Formerly it was posited as the opposing conceptual pole to capability and autonomy; however, the recently emerging "vulnerability theorists" have uncovered that the traditional theoretical perceptions of vulnerability are in fact the production of a series of biases, and that the negative connotation of vulnerability is very often foregrounded because of the subordinate status assigned to corporality and dependency as compared to reason and independence traditionally conceived. With the revival of celebratory social imaginaries of human corporality and relationality, vulnerability has become a key notion for re-imagining human society itself. Especially for feminist thinkers, the negative meaning given to vulnerability

xin mao

THE THREE FACES OF VULNERABILITY
my vulnerability, the vulnerability of the other and the vulnerability of the third

reflects the paternalistic perspective which prioritizes the rationality and capability associated with male character. As Alison Assiter points out, the Western philosophical tradition promotes a dualism wherein the body that is not controlled by mind is only a distraction. She observes acutely: "[i]n so far as civilised society classically recognised embodiment, its citizens frequently possessed male bodies" – which is to say, bodies that are not vulnerable.[1] The vulnerability theorists stress that the traditional paternalistic view ignores the vulnerable reality of a human subject who is born and will die, and does not realize the essential role of vulnerability within human relationality itself. In her last works Pamela Sue Anderson maintains that it is human vulnerability that conditions human intimacy, making affection possible. Vulnerability inspires love, and its openness leads to genuine human relatedness.

Many new dimensions of vulnerability are currently being explored within the expanding theoretical debate and literature on vulnerability: yet, at the same time, the ambiguity of the concept remains of crucial concern. Notably, the notion's positive aspect as promoted by vulnerability theorists is in fact not clearly discerned from its negative side. This question has been touched upon by Ann Murphy in the form of a question about the ethical ambiguity of vulnerability, indicating the gap between an ontological notion of vulnerability and the normative consequences of vulnerability. She argues, based on her reading of Judith Butler and Adriana Cavarero, that the affirmation of the importance of the recognition of vulnerability does not lead to an ethical demand in a prescriptive sense. This is because the "irremediable availability to both care and abuse that constitutes vulnerability is not something that any ethics will ever manage to conceal or negate."[2] She holds that vulnerability as an openness to love and care cannot be the subject of a normative demand, since it can lead to abuse and violence at the same time.

Pamela Sue Anderson treats this ambiguity at a deeper level. She points out that the praised positivity of vulnerability as caring and loving is often seen as associated with the female gender. This association reveals an effort to correct a traditional perception of the feminine, usually labeled as negative and inferior: yet at the same time the image of the vulnerable female who is constantly ready to care and to forgive also confirms that hyper-traditional image of the female. To promote a morality where the female subject faces excessive calls to give love and care to those who are vulnerable can unjustifiably place an extra moral burden upon female subjects, and this in turn makes the female negatively vulnerable to such unjustified moral demands. As Anderson appeals to her reader: "the caring person is often thought of as the loving person; and the vulnerable person is often thought of as the person in need of love, but aren't we all in need of love?"[3] The female, in the hyper-traditional image, is called upon to love and care, but whether she is loved back is not part of the narrative. In this sense, vulnerability as openness to love seems to be positive, but its negative and unjustifiable aspects are never far away.

It is not, however, sufficient simply to explain away this ambiguity by ascribing it to the innate meaning of vulnerability, as this would leave a number of interesting issues unexplored. And indeed when we refer to vulnerability we do seem to be referring to a notion with a unified meaning, which we would rather say has varied implications when situated in different inter-human relationships – for example relations of Eros, ethical relations, or political relations. And in these relations we can also discern whose vulnerability is at stake. In the case above, for example, according to Anderson when women are asked to love and care for those who are vulnerable they themselves become vulnerable to excessive moral demands. Thus, in this scenario we discern that vulnerability has two layers of meaning concerning whose vulnerability is at stake: that is, whether it is the female subject's vulnerability or the vulnerability of the other. And the vulnerability can be seen as positive or negative according to whose vulnerability is at stake and in what relation it is located. Reference to "the vulnerable," those whose vulnerability opens the possibility of love from the female, evokes a subject–other ethical relation. The vulnerability of the other in an ethical relation provokes love and care and in this sense can be viewed positively. Yet the vulnerability of the female who faces an excessive and unjustified moral demand should be seen as located at a social and political level where vulnerability is not distributed fairly. Calling for equal recognition of the moral vulnerability of the female subject, Anderson stresses a justice of care, which is based on an objectively comparable vulnerability in political relations. The unjustified vulnerability in political relations is negative and should be resisted. From this example we can see that when we are able to discern the multiple layers of the meaning of vulnerability, in the sense of whose vulnerability it is and in what inter-human relations the vulnerability is located, some of the ambiguity of vulnerability can be dispelled.

Here we will explore these two intertwined layers of the meaning of vulnerability based on the philosophy of Emmanuel Levinas. Through the triad of the "I," the other, and the third, Levinas provides an in-depth discussion of ethical pre-original relations, Eros relations, political relations of justice and the dynamics among them. Utilizing Levinasian philosophy to explore vulnerability, we can firstly draw inspiration from his direct engagement with the notion of vulnerability in his phenomenology of Eros in *Totality and Infinity* and in his later work on ethical subjectivity in *Otherwise than Being or Beyond Essence*. More important for our present purposes, however, we will adopt Levinas's method, specifically his idea of phenomenological exposedness, in order to investigate the horizon of vulnerability's appearance in these different inter-human relations.

Under the shadow of the complicated relationship between Levinas's phenomenology and the Husserlian phenomenological tradition, Levinas's phenomenological method is often marginalized in mainstream phenomenological discussions. However, Levinas himself insists that "despite everything, what I am doing is phenomenology."[4] Although he acknowledges that he does not follow the Husserlian method in a strict sense, he claims that his method "remains faithful to intentional analysis," which aims to uncover "the locating of notions in the horizon of their appearing."[5] Levinas's phenomenological exploration aims at the horizon that has been "unrecognized, forgotten or displaced," because when one directly perceives a notion, to look at this notion alone absorbs the horizon of its appearing.[6]

In the ways they are represented and theoretically discussed, some notions seem to have a meaning irrelevant to their persona. Yet Levinas's phenomenology reveals that the neutrality of notions presupposes a self-centered movement, where the constitution of the notion is done by the consciousness of the subject, which at an ultimate level confirms a first-person-centered relation. For Levinas, the seemingly neutral activities of cognition and representation in fact reflect the "relationship of oneself with oneself."[7] Thus such activities are innately self-bound and determined by self-interestedness. Levinas maintains that in the Western philosophical tradition "knowledge is in pursuit of itself," where alterity is only grasped as an object of knowledge.[8] In this sense, knowledge based upon representation and consciousness belongs to an egological inclination. After refuting the pretended neutrality of theoretical notions, Levinas shows how to look at notions via the horizon of their appearance within human inter-subjective relations. For example, for Levinas, both death and God are signified by the relation with alterity instead of by their own truth. In death, the subject encounters the absolute alterity: the meaning of death is from a source "other than myself," that is, from my relation with the other who is exterior and who evades my grasp.[9] Similarly, Levinas's claim "for the other man and thereby unto God!"[10] confirms that God is approached through taking responsibility for the other. Levinas comments that the philosophy of the Neuter promotes "the obedience that no face commands."[11] The logos and the Being of beings establish a world of "no one." Such faceless conceptions give rise only to theories that are indifferent and inert. The need for knowledge and understanding is contrasted by Levinas with desire, a desire that is more precisely "a desire for a person."[12]

Thus, in order to apply Levinas's phenomenology to an exploration of the notion of vulnerability, the seemingly neutral notion of vulnerability will be located at its horizon, and more specifically the horizon of relation and dynamics of "my vulnerability," that is, the vulnerability of the subject, the vulnerability of the other, and the vulnerability of the third.

my vulnerability: the pre-original signifyingness

Subjective vulnerability as an exposedness to the excessive responsibility for the other orchestrates the entire sweep of the ethical phenomenology that Levinas explored throughout his life's work. Vulnerability, seen in Levinas as *my* vulnerability, makes its appearance from the horizon of the pre-original ethical relation. Particularly as depicted in *Otherwise than Being or Beyond Essence*, vulnerability, together with related terms such as wound, trauma, and hostage, represents an extravagant hypothesis of a subject passively bearing responsibility for the other, in a way that is necessary for any ethical relation to be possible. Not being a characteristic of the subject, vulnerability actually defines the ethical subject through a sensibility as one for the other and an exposedness to the other. In this sense, the pre-original exposedness is prior to the identity of any individual. My vulnerability to excessive responsibility for the other takes the place of being or consciousness, becoming the "unconditional condition" for subjectivity, and even the meaning of humanity.[13]

The excessive vulnerability that is presupposed by the ethical relations between the subject and the other is nowise a normative moral demand. The key word here is vulnerability as a *pre-original* signifyingness. Unlike what is "original," namely that which is the beginning of a status that can be represented and of actions that can be initiated, the pre-original is "foreign to every present and every representation."[14] The meaning of *pre-* is in fact given by Levinas through the French term *En-deçà*, and this term has been translated by Alphonso Lingis into different English words, all of which are influenced by his own understanding of the term *En-deçà*, which only appears ghost-like in Levinas's own work. One of the translations or interpreted meanings of this term is "prior to": the pre-original is prior to all initiatives and their principles.[15] To be exact, that which is prior to self-consciousness and being is not necessarily a temporal beforehand, yet neither is it a logical precondition. Different from the original which initiates actions, the pre-original signifies a passivity. This passivity is defined in an extreme way as more passive than the passivity of receptivity. For Levinas, receptivity is "capable of assuming what strikes it."[16] The pre-original vulnerability to be responsible for the other is passive in that it is not initiated by any decision.

Levinas defines his notion of sensibility through this vulnerability which is *En-deçà*, prior to any self-consciousness or self-identity. For him, sensibility cannot be associated with consciousness or seen as a lesser degree of cognition. Rather, sensibility is a susceptibility to the relation with the other. For him, the subject is not a spectator who is indifferent to the other but is pre-originally exposed to affectivity, open to being exalted or pained.[17] In fact, the subject is not established prior to this vulnerability such that this suffering can be ascribed to him/herself. The sensibility of the subject is this very vulnerability, in subjecting oneself to the responsibility for the other before any pleasure or pain can be sensed. My vulnerability is the exposedness to the other that exists before any definite wound comes about.

Another translation of *En-deçà* is "beneath" or "on the hither side": this expresses that the signifyingness of ethical subjectivity as vulnerability is underneath presence and gives meaning to all presence. The underneath or hither side of consciousness is more precisely corporeal vulnerability, especially as conveyed in the image or paradigm of a maternal body. Tina Chanter remarks that "the maternal body figures in Levinas as the absolute renouncement of being for the other," and "conveys the sense of Levinas's insistence upon the extreme ethical responsibility that the I bears for the other."[18] Through defining human corporeality as the maternal body, human incarnation is no longer the weight of his/her own existence but the very fact he/she needs to carry the burden of "alien existence."[19] Jennifer Rosato observes that the maternity he emphasizes is more exactly the physical aspect of pregnancy.[20] Indeed, for Levinas, corporeal vulnerability for the other signifies one-for-the-other not only as some beautiful idea but also as a concrete giving – as in to give to the other "the bread from one's own mouth."[21] And it is exactly this giving on the hither side of consciousness – as opposed to knowing or intentionality – which denotes signifyingness to a human subject.

The pre-original vulnerability of ethical subjectivity in Levinas is posited in an extreme sense. It redefines the human subject since it is through this extreme responsibility for the other that the subject begins to form before his/her self-identification. That is to say, the vulnerability not only aims to interrupt the self-centered egoistic movement but also aims to interrupt the very identity of the subject. Levinas refers to this interruption from vulnerability as *dénucléation*, which is conveyed by the strong image of "a fission of the nucleus opening the bottom of its punctual nuclearity, like to a lung at the core of oneself."[22] The vulnerability of the subject exists to a degree that even the form that his/her identity relies on is opened up. In this vulnerability, the subject is torn from itself, and can never escape from responsibility for the other. Prior to and underneath the establishment of an "I," there is "for the other" conditioning and giving meaning to any establishment of the "I."

Why does Levinas need to establish this extreme vulnerability in order to understand the ethical relation between the one and the other? Answers can be given from two perspectives. Firstly, Levinas is suspicious of any hypothesis which posits that the initiation of equal and symmetrical inter-human accountability can lead to ethical human relations and peace. To Levinas, symmetrical relations run the risk of losing sight of the uniqueness of each subject. A symmetrical relation does not support genuine difference, since in symmetrical relations difference is calculated on the "continuous form."[23] The calculation of whether one has given and received the same amount as the others relies on this continuous form where each individual is replaceable by the other. For Levinas, the social order conferred by autonomy, free will and the chain of reason ignores the fact that each of us is created from a relation to the other. When my vulnerability is seen as my subjectivity, this opposes any discourse that is built on the idea of independent and self-centered subjects where movements initiated by one's own interest inevitably lead to conflicts of interest with the other. Through the pre-original excessiveness of "being for the other," justice which promises equality will not be a balance of self-centered interests but will rather be applied by the motivation of responsibility for the others.[24] The subject is not a replaceable unit within a justice system who asks "what can I get from justice?" but an irreplaceable subject who replies: "what do I have to do with justice?"[25] This extreme responsibility sets a different tone for the social-political debate, having as its referential point the idea of responsibility and peace rather than interest and conflict – even though the latter may be unavoidable. We will return to this point in a later section.

Second, this seeking of an extreme notion of vulnerability is the method that Levinas adopts to counter what he calls the "transcendental method" that always seeks foundations.[26] A foundation is a notion drawn from architecture: the transcendental method in philosophy seeks to convey support for a notion via elucidating its foundations. Levinas criticizes this borrowing from architecture, seeking it as importing a worldview based on immobility, where the foundation that supports whatever is above it is motionless and appears as a purely indifferent existence. Such a method cannot produce anything "other" as the foundation limits everything to within itself, formulating a system of the same. In contrast, Levinas maintains, his own method begins with human beings rather than with a world at rest, and especially the human beings who are passive enough to let infinite ideas enter from beyond. His method is thus based on "emphasis" or "overbidding," breaking the limitations of the same in order to welcome the other.[27] The new ideas produced by this method are not justified by the previous idea but by "its sublimation."[28] This method is not one of building up and holding oneself up but rather of exposing oneself, exposing one's idea, and of being vulnerable.

From the above discussions we can see that my vulnerability as excessive responsibility for the other needs to be clearly distinguished from an initiation or action. It is not a foundation that supports our daily behaviors but rather as a sublimation it injects a meaning which breaks the still picture that the logos painted. Levinas once claimed that this ethical excessiveness coincides with the movement for a better society.[29] Yet we need to note that this betterment would not be a situation where everyone satisfies their desire, since that is only betterment conceived as expansion of the same. This betterment is in fact a possibility for peace that addresses the fundamental logics of war, of the same and of self-interestedness.

Despite the excessive pre-original vulnerability of the subject, concerning my vulnerability one needs to acknowledge that Levinas does recognize my vulnerability in a more concrete social political sense. My vulnerability – my corporeal and social vulnerability of "I" as a citizen similar to anyone else who calls for care and protection – is reflected in his discussion of self-love. In *Otherwise than Being* Levinas acknowledges that "my lot is important,"[30] which places my vulnerability on an equal footing with anyone else's. We will discuss the transference of ethical excessiveness into the political objective order later: for now, let us say that as a result of seeing the importance of justice and politics with the entrance of the third party, subjective vulnerability is allowed to be compared with the lots of others, which also enables calls for a self-interested movement so that justice in society can be attained. Through his acknowledgement of the interrelatedness between the "I," the other, and the third, Levinas claims, "Is not the infinite which enigmatically commands me, commanding and not commanding, from the other, also the turning of the I into 'like the others,' for which it is important to concern oneself and take care?"[31]

My vulnerability will be taken care of: yet this does not lead to a purely symmetrical relation. This vulnerability of an "I" who is coexisting with all the others is still distinguished from any objective calculated vulnerability. Levinas introduces a new dimension to the scenario, that is, the aid or grace of God through which the asymmetrical relation can be maintained. This is to say, the symmetrical relation and legitimate self-love is not supported by natural law; rather, Levinas stresses, it is God's grace that guarantees this lot of the "I." When my vulnerability is taken care of, I need to be gracious to the Other, to the exteriority. It needs to be stressed that Levinas is not settling his philosophical puzzle as to how an asymmetrical ethical relation and the moral vulnerability of the subject can survive the concrete social reality by handing over the final word to a mystical God. To explore in detail the significance of God in Levinas would exceed the scope of the present discussion, yet through bringing God's grace to my equal right for care and protection, Levinas gives any self-interested motion an exterior relation, which makes the symmetrical relation among the "I," the other, and the third asymmetrical; and this in turn can sustain his dynamic ethical motions, the restlessness towards the other, and the constant interruption of immanence.

the vulnerability of the other: from eros to immediacy

In examining vulnerability through the lens of the vulnerability of the other within the relation between the "I" and the other, an unavoidable question arises concerning the relation between ethics and Eros in Levinas. Many of Levinas's feminist commentators have questioned the differentiation between the feminine other and the ethical other in his work. Claire Katz closely examines recent feminists' comments on this problematic relation in Levinas,[32] pointing out that the phenomenology of Eros confines the relation to the feminine within a mystic, unethical domain, which provokes critiques on the unequal ethical status assigned to the feminine. Mayra Rivera, for example, points out that Levinas separates the Eros relation from the ethical relation and limits it to the satisfaction of immanent desire in a way that seems to condone violence to the feminine in the Eros relation.[33] Yet Katz herself cautions against the temptation to equate the relation with the other in Eros and ethical relations in Levinas. She calls upon us to go back to Levinas's own notion of ethics,

Eros, from which one can see the necessity of the ambiguous status of Eros, which has the potential for transcendence yet also shows a possibility of being an egoistic movement of the subject.

In *Totality and Infinity*, according to Katz, the relation of Eros, which is not yet an ethical relation, importantly opens the possibility of the ethical relation. In Eros, the vulnerability of the beloved separates the other from the category of totality. From the very beginning of his phenomenology of Eros, Levinas claims that love aims at the other in its frailty. The vulnerability of the other does not define the other as an inferior existence but rather shows the other "at the limit of being and non-being."[34] The vulnerable other, a "raw density," is non-signifyingness, which is exactly an exposure to the light without becoming signification.[35] The difficult images assimilated to the vulnerable other in Eros demonstrate that Levinas fumbles with language in describing something which he considers as neither essence nor nothingness. The vulnerability of the other in Eros is not a weakness, nor is it an exposedness in the sense of the ethical vulnerability we discussed above. The vulnerability of the other in Eros can in fact be seen more exactly as an evasion of ontological categories such as being, essence, or signification; it is an almost nothingness, although this almost nothingness has the potentiality to be the other: "not nothingness – but what is not yet."[36]

The subject cannot grasp the vulnerable other in the relation of Eros, as Eros is not a desire that can be quenched by possession. But instead of the language of justice used in the ethical relation with the absolute alterity, in Eros there is only the language of "laughter and raillery."[37] That is to say, in the relationship of Eros, the I and other have an opportunity to attain an infinite relationship, yet this relation lacks seriousness, which can also lead to an unethical result. To be more precise, without the vulnerability of the other in Eros, the "I"– other relation cannot relieve itself of the immanent violence of the totality. Yet the nudity of the vulnerable other and its status as almost nothing invites new violence. The vulnerability of the other in Eros, described as "a simultaneity or equivocation of this fragility and this weight of non-signifyingness, heavier than the weight of the formless real," signifies a separation of Eros from a projection relation where the "I" is in control of everything, but also the possible abuse of the newly discovered nudity.[38]

Indeed, Levinas does not solve the problem of this possible violence in *Totality and Infinity*. The vulnerability of the other in Eros both provokes ethical responsibility and its possible violation. But in *Otherwise than Being* he does offer a firm alternation. In a footnote, he seems to give the straight answer which the feminists want:

> The sense of this alteration must indeed be clarified in its turn. But it was here important to underline the possibility of the libido in the more elementary and more rich signification of proximity, a possibility included in the unity of the face and the skin, even if only in the extreme turnings about of a face. Beneath the erotic alterity there is the alterity of the-one-for-the-other, responsibility before Eros.[39]

In this footnote, Levinas clearly claims that Eros is conditioned by responsibility, which for him means that the relation of Eros should have excluded any possible violence, as the responsibility that conditions Eros would limit its unethical perspective. In examining this development in Levinas's thought more closely, one can see that the vulnerability of the other, which was discussed as the frailty of the feminine, and her closeness to nothingness, is referred to in *Otherwise than Being* as his/her immediacy to me, devoid of any gender association. This immediacy is designated more precisely as proximity, through which Levinas stresses the urgency of the other's ethical demand towards the subject.

According to Levinas, the alterity in proximity escapes presentation in the sense that it is too weak to be a phenomenon. The contact from the other, that is the other in the immediacy, excludes any essence that is identifiable, and thus always concerns me for the first time.[40] The vulnerability of this alterity is described as "aging and dying," which is not a physical definition but a relation to the subject in a timely manner.[41] The subject is said to be always late in the other's presence, a missing out of his/her past. The subject is blamed for his/her delay concerning the situation of the other. In the presence of the other, the subject is guilty and shameful, and more importantly obsessed by the past, the non-presence of the alterity. The "lapse already lost" disturbs the contemporariness between the subject and the alterity, and the common clock which objectively measures worldly order is opened up to being diachronic.[42] This diachrony contests the historical time that can always be recuperated. In the time of diachrony, the immemorial time, the past, with its effect on us, the wrinkle of skin and mortality, cannot be ignored in the presence of the other in front of me. The youth and beauty that evokes Eros is seen as "already past in this youth."[43] And the diachrony that is underneath the presence of the beauty is more precisely a poverty and wretchedness which, instead of arousing me, calls me and orders me to respond with responsibility.

In the relation of Eros, the subject enjoys the profanation of the other, but in the relation of proximity to the neighbor, Levinas stresses, it is only because of the subjectivity of the subject as "one for the other" that the relation can be one of enjoying or suffering. In this sense, Levinas confirms that the relation of one-for-the-other is pre-original to Eros. The "contact with skin" in Eros is first and foremost a "proximity of a face," where the other, even the feminine other, before entering into the relation of Eros, already demands my responsibility.[44]

From this analysis we can confirm the ethical meaning of the vulnerability of the other, and especially the vulnerability of the other in proximity. The vulnerability of the other conceived of as proximity appeals to the self's responsibility irrespective of his/her concrete situation (e.g., as a woman) or his/her precariousness. When the other is next to me our contact already decides his/her vulnerability, and this immediacy calls upon me to respond. At this level of appearance the vulnerability of the other in proximity does not and cannot provoke violence against the other, as any human contact with the other is already for the other. This equates to saying that the vulnerability of the other is more exactly his/her humanity, and thus before my knowledge of who he/she is, I am already responsible. From this way of understanding we find another reason to oppose the priority given by the traditional view to autonomy or independence, neither of which amounts to the acknowledgement of our common dependency. That is, we are not independent because everyone is burdened by his/her responsibility for the others.

And it can also be seen that the vulnerability of the other as his/her proximity to me does have a prescriptive meaning as regards the relation of Eros. It is only as based upon a responsibility for the other that a genuine enjoyment of Eros can be ascribed. In passing from a potential for an ethical relation to presupposing any ethical relations at all, the vulnerability of the other in Eros and the vulnerability of the other in proximity show an important development of Levinas's idea of alterity from *Totality and Infinity* to *Otherwise than Being*. This development in Levinas's philosophy is significant and should be acknowledged before any criticism is made of his discussions of Eros that is confined to *Totality and Infinity*. Following this development, we can conclude that the vulnerability of the other needs to be understood at the horizon of an ethical relation which conditions Eros and limits possible violence in Eros.

the vulnerability of the third party: the concern of justice

As mentioned in the introduction, with the acknowledgement of the presence of the third, Levinas demonstrates the dynamic transition from ethical duality to the socio-political triad. Through his discussion of the relation between the "I," the other, and the third concerning justice, we can explore the vulnerability of the third party. In particular, we will engage with Martha Fineman's theory of universal vulnerability, which is primarily a socio-political notion that functions as a positive tool for social political criticism, and we will discuss the problems this theory faces. We will then see how Levinas's third-party perspective can help address these problems via a discussion of the vulnerability of the third in the concerns of justice.

Martha Fineman's theory of vulnerability is straightforwardly dedicated to social and political criticism and to improvement within these fields. In brief, based upon her previous studies of dependence and family law, Fineman argues against the Western liberal tradition where the subject in socio-political thought is generally posited as an independent and autonomous individual. For Fineman, the myth of the autonomous liberal subject promoted especially by the neoliberal narrative ignores the "universal and constant vulnerability" of each individual.[45] We are prone to sickness, unfortunate situations, and death; and this common human condition is not properly reflected in the construction of social institutions. By confirming the universality of vulnerability and analyzing the particular forms of this vulnerability in social life, Fineman indicts a neoliberal political ideology which only creates institutions that privilege "liberty in the form of autonomy for the individual and freedom for the market."[46] With this critique, Fineman calls for a responsive state that empowers the vulnerable subject through addressing the "substantive inequalities" in social institutions.[47] The notion of vulnerability is seen as a positive and important "heuristic tool" for socio-political analysis, rather than being relegated to a marginalized individual status.[48]

The traditional liberal (and neoliberal) thinkers who view this responsive state precisely as an authoritarian state cast doubt on Fineman's theory. Even though Fineman has asked her readers to imagine a responsive state that is non-authoritarian, whether this non-authoritarian responsive state is merely a beautiful wish is a serious question. To empower vulnerable individuals, the state certainly also needs the power to re-distribute. If the boundary between the responsive and the authoritarian is only imaginary, Fineman's theory does face problems. Another associated problem is that in opposing vulnerability to autonomy one risks ignoring the importance and universality of autonomy. In his essay "More than Utopia" Morgan Cloud casts doubt on Fineman's emphasis on universal vulnerability over universal autonomy. He maintains that

> [t]he drive for independence emerges in cultures around the world because it is a fundamental part of human nature. Just as most of us need (and desire) connections with society, its institutions, and its people, most of us also have some level of need for freedom from the constraints all societies impose.[49]

Following Cloud's argument, if one's universal desire for autonomy or the liberal right of possession is oppressed or lessened by the responsive state, one may incur a further vulnerability: that is, certain citizens will be vulnerable to the confinement of their needs by the authoritarian state. The boundary between a re-distribution that fits all and a re-distribution that impairs some is not easily drawn. To examine this problem from a Levinasian perspective, we see that it is problematic to define vulnerability as a universal status or character which we all have without acknowledging its meaning within inter-human relations. As a designation of the character of an individual, Cloud quite reasonably opposes the overarching position given to vulnerability and promotes the important character of autonomy, albeit to a lesser degree. Yet if we look at universal vulnerability through a Levinasian lens, that is, from its appearance at the horizon of inter-human relations, the key question is no longer that of the preference of any one of the characters but rather of the human relationality it reveals.

In various works, Levinas investigates the horizon of appearance of socio-political terms through the notion of the third. The notion of the third is given different meanings in *Otherwise than Being* as compared to *Totality and Infinity*. The third appears in *Totality and Infinity* as another who joins the ethical subject in order to build a social asymmetrical ethical space (besides negatively signifying the totalizing third-person perspective). In this sense, it is more social than political, as

Levinas has not addressed in detail the problem of how this asymmetrical space can be realized politically.[50]

In *Otherwise than Being*, the third party has a more specific role, and this is clearly a political meaning, as it is the entry of the third party who calls for justice that introduces the necessity of politics, representation, and calculation. As he points out, with the presence of the third party the question of justice becomes urgent. I cannot be fully responsible for the relation between the other and the third party, and hence "there must be justice among incomparable ones."[51] To achieve justice among the other and the third party, politics is necessary. The appearance of politics at the horizon of ethical relations between the "I" and the other, and between "I" and another other, assigns it a meaning which differs from that of harmonizing different self-centered relations. As Alphonso Lingis explains, by bringing in the dimension of the third Levinas does not aim at pursuing a well-functioning politics but rather at establishing "order among responsibilities."[52]

Indeed, with the acknowledgement of the necessity of politics to justice, Levinas also welcomes back many of the notions that belong to the objective and indifferent areas previously criticized. "Synchronization, comparison, thematization" are the deployment of justice to institute a political terrain common to "I," the other, and the third party.[53] Faces now appear in the light, where their identities and life stories are known. The uniqueness of the others, including their vulnerability, is now calculated objectively. Yet we also need to note that the objective meaning of the notions does not appear as it is given by a neutral initiation; rather, they are signified by the dynamics between the ethical relations and political relations. This dynamic is more precisely the entrance of the third party into the ethical dyad which introduces the necessity of justice and politics, and the reduction of political representation to ethical charity. Levinas utilizes the narratives in the Talmud to illustrate this point: "before the verdict, no face; but once the judgment is pronounced, He looks at the face."[54] The "never-ending" oscillation between ethical relation and political relation[55] is the horizon where notions should be understood. For example, in *Totality and Infinity* Levinas criticizes the primary position given to reason in the Western tradition: "how can a reason be an I or an other, since its very being consists in renouncing singularity?"[56] However, in *Otherwise than Being*, with the entrance of the third party Levinas acknowledges the importance of reason due to the demands of justice and calculation of coexistence. Yet the reason whose importance is recognized in *Otherwise than Being* is ultimately different from the reason protested in *Totality and Infinity*. In *Otherwise than Being* reason suspends the clash of beings in the calculation of justice, which is therefore defined as the "rationality of peace."[57] The rationality of peace does not renounce singularity but rather fulfils the responsibility for each in the manner of a correction of excessive care for one and a judgment of right or wrong.

If we apply this analysis to vulnerability, in order to achieve a just view on vulnerability as mentioned above, my vulnerability and the vulnerability of the other will all become the vulnerability of the third, which can be objectively calculated and compared. In Fineman's theory, this vulnerability is particular to its concrete forms, yet still exists universally, and so an objective analysis of it can enforce the responsive state. Yet this vulnerability should not be seen as a neutral status, whose motionless existence can be presented as an initiation of itself. Rather, the vulnerability of the third should rather be seen as being born from the dynamic between ethics and politics. And with this horizon the calculated coexisting vulnerability comes to be seen as a production of justice. That is to say, rather than a status that is seen as a character of human situations the vulnerability of the third concerns each subject. Levinas stresses that "justice is impossible without the one that renders it finding himself in proximity."[58] It is the commitment of each subject that can deploy justice in respect of the vulnerability of the third: "the forgetting of self moves justice."[59] Justice, for

Levinas, is not a simple process of judging particular cases with general rules. The vulnerability of the third, and a notion of justice, begins with a responsibility for all, calculating "who is right and who is wrong,"[60] that can be understood as a judgment of who has led the third parties into a state of vulnerability and how we can be responsible for it.

With this perspective on the vulnerability of the third, we can address the two problems for Fineman's discussions we mentioned above. The universal vulnerability not only entails a relation with the state which endows another type of value, but comes about from my relationship with the third party. This will lead to a state which is not a responsive state but rather a state that is responsible for the vulnerability of the third. To distinguish between a responsible state and responsive state, first of all, we may say that the responsive state does not concern the horizon of the coming of the vulnerability of its citizens but rather reacts to the result of his/her being already in situations of vulnerability. Yet a responsible state whose existence is a path to justice concerns right or wrong on the hither side of the vulnerability. According to Levinas's limited ideas on its concrete application, we can assume that the state will fulfill its responsibility by judging, correcting and exercising charity concerning the vulnerability of the third. That is to say, it will examine the reason for the vulnerability of the third, correct any wrongs and personally encounter the wrongdoers. Second, a responsible state does not confine its responsibility within the state. Levinas points out that "the State issued from the proximity of the neighbor is always on the verge of integrating him into a we."[61] The responsible state will not limit its responsibility to its own citizens, but exceeds the borders of the state, acknowledging the responsibility of the state beyond its borders. The calling for responsibility for the vulnerable third parties outside of the state interrupts the immanence of the state which is content with its role within a nationalist ideology. With this interruption, the state cannot set itself up as a totality but must be constantly facing the third party abroad.

Concerning the oppositional view on whether the universality of autonomy or the universality of vulnerability is primary, autonomy and vulnerability are not necessarily contradictory to each other, especially when seen through the lens of Levinas's philosophy. The irreplaceable role of the subject in taking responsibility for the other is in fact his/her vulnerability in their immediacy to the other. The irreplaceable responsibility of the self shows itself in an accusative form as one for the other. Yet the order that orders the self to respond to the need of the other is from within oneself, not from any exterior source. The "here I am" that exposes myself to the other, to the other human being's calling for justice and love, is not a response to any oppression or confinement. For Levinas it is the highest autonomy possible, as I am not told what I want by society but am expressing myself in immediacy to another human being. My vulnerability to the other in ethical relations defines my autonomy in politics, which in turn establishes my absolute uniqueness among the vulnerabilities of the third parties. In this manner, vulnerability is a new autonomy, and this new relation between them opens up alternative social political relationalities that call for further investigation.

conclusion

From the above analysis it has been shown that discerning the different "faces" of vulnerability exposes varied dimensions of inter-human relations from which human vulnerability appears, which sheds light on the ambiguity of the conception. As a subjective sensibility prior to consciousness, vulnerability is essential to the human creation that bounds us all. The vulnerability of the other as an immediacy of the other person to the subject presupposes ethical relationship before any other dual relations. The vulnerability of the third, at the level of justice, opens up new perspectives that challenge the priority given to autonomy and self-interestedness in social political critiques. With such clarification, it is possible to search for a prescriptive dimension beyond the ontological description of vulnerability. This prescriptive dimension is more precisely a calling for each person to expose him/herself to the responsibility for the other, to be vulnerable for such an ethical "burden," and an appeal to the social political system for a safe space for such vulnerability to be possible.

disclosure statement

No potential conflict of interest was reported by the author.

notes

1 Alison Assiter, "Kierkegaard and Vulnerability" in *Vulnerability: Reflections on a New Ethical Foundation for Law and Politics*, eds. Martha Fineman and Anna Grear (Farnham: Ashgate, 2013) 30.

2 Ann Murphy, *Violence and the Philosophical Imaginary* (Albany: State U of New York P, 2012) 86.

3 Pamela Sue Anderson, "Arguing for 'Ethical' Vulnerability: Towards a Politics of Care?" in *Exploring Vulnerability*, eds. Günter Thomas and Heike Springhart (Göttingen and Bristol, CT: Vandenhoeck, 2017) 147–62 (158).

4 Emmanuel Levinas, *Of God Who Comes to Mind*, trans. Bettina Bergo (Stanford: Stanford UP, 1998) 87.

5 Emmanuel Levinas, *Otherwise than Being or Beyond Essence*, trans. Alphonso Lingis (Pittsburgh: Kluwer, 1998) 183.

6 Ibid.

7 Emmanuel Levinas, *Totality and Infinity: An Essay on Exteriority*, trans. Alphonso Lingis (Pittsburgh: Duquesne UP, 1969) 34.

8 Ibid.

9 Michael Purcell, "The Mystery of Death Alterity and Affectivity in Levinas," *New Blackfriars* 76.899 (1995): 524–34 (530).

10 Levinas, *Of God Who Comes to Mind* xv.

11 Levinas, *Totality and Infinity* 298.

12 Ibid. 299.

13 Levinas, *Otherwise than Being* 6.

14 Ibid. 14.

15 Ibid. xx.

16 Emmanuel Levinas, *Collected Philosophical Papers*, trans. Alphonso Lingis (Dordrecht: Nijhoff, 1987) 128.

17 Levinas, *Otherwise than Being* xxiv.

18 Tina Chanter, "Introduction" in *Feminist Interpretations of Emmanuel Levinas* (University Park: Pennsylvania State UP, 2001) 1–27 (22).

19 Levinas, *Otherwise than Being* xxvii.

20 Jennifer Rosato, "Woman as Vulnerable Self: The Trope of Maternity in Levinas's 'Otherwise than Being,'" *Hypatia* 27.2 (2012): 348–65 (352).

21 Levinas, *Otherwise than Being* 55.

22 Ibid. 49.

23 Levinas, *Collected Philosophical Papers* 68.

24 Levinas, *Otherwise than Being* 128.

25 Ibid. 157.

26 Levinas, *Of God Who Comes to Mind* 88.

27 Ibid. 60.

28 Ibid. 89.

29 Ibid. 9.

30 Levinas, *Otherwise than Being* 161.

31 Ibid.

32 Claire Katz, "Levinas between Agape and Eros," *Symposium: Canadian Journal of Continental Philosophy* 11.2 (2007): 333–50 (333).

33 Mayra Rivera, "Ethical Desires: Toward a Theology of Relational Transcendence" in *Toward a Theology of Eros: Transfiguring Passion at the Limits of Discipline*, eds. Virginia Burrus and Catherine Keller (New York: Fordham UP, 2006) 255–70 (258).

34 Levinas, *Totality and Infinity* 256.

35 Ibid.

36 Ibid.

37 Ibid. 260.

38 Ibid. 257.

39 Levinas, *Otherwise than Being* 192.

40 Ibid. 86.

41 Ibid. 88.

42 Ibid. 74.

43 Ibid. 90.

44 Ibid.

45 Martha Fineman and Ann Grear, "Introduction" in *Vulnerability: Reflections on a New Ethical Foundation for Law and Politics* 2.

46 Ibid. 24.

47 Martha Fineman, "The Vulnerable Subject: Anchoring Equality in the Human Condition," *Yale Journal of Law and Feminism* 20.1 (2008): 1–23 (19).

48 Fineman, "Equality, Autonomy and the Vulnerable Subject in Law and Politics" in *Vulnerability: Reflections on a New Ethical Foundation for Law and Politics* 20.

49 Morgan Cloud, "More than Utopia" in *Vulnerability: Reflections on a New Ethical Foundation for Law and Politics* 93.

50 Levinas, *Totality and Infinity* 213.

51 Levinas, *Otherwise than Being* 16.

52 Ibid. xli.

53 Ibid. 160.

54 Emmanuel Levinas, *Is it Righteous to Be? Interviews with Emmanuel Lévinas*, ed. Jill Robbins (Palo Alto: Stanford UP, 2016) 9.

55 William Paul Simmons, "The Third: Levinas' Theoretical Move from An-archical Ethics to the Realm of Justice and Politics," *Philosophy and Social Criticism* 25.6 (1999): 83–104 (84).

56 Levinas, *Totality and Infinity* 72.

57 Levinas, *Otherwise than Being* 160.

58 Ibid. 159.

59 Ibid.

60 Emmanuel Levinas, "Ethics and Politics" in *The Levinas Reader*, ed. Sean Hand (Oxford: Blackwell, 1989) 289–97 (294).

61 Levinas, *Otherwise than Being* 161.

alison assiter

ANDERSON ON VULNERABILITY

Two important aspects of the work of Pamela Anderson are her feminism and the attention she has drawn to an aspect of the lives of all of us that contrasts with the work of much philosophy – that of vulnerability, meaning our relationality, our connectedness with others. In a recent article, "Autonomy, Vulnerability and Gender," she re-reads the story of *A Doll's House* by Ibsen.[1] She suggests that the male and female characters *equally* fail to read the relational context of their lives. The female character, Nora, borrows money (she had to forge her father's signature in order to do this as women were not allowed to borrow money) in order, she believes, to help her husband, Torvald. But instead of being grateful he decides she is a liar and a cheat. She realizes that she has been a "doll," first in relation to her father and now to her husband, and she leaves the latter. Both male and female characters, according to Anderson, fail to see the relational aspects of their lives – her husband falsely saw Nora as an innocent doll and she, after the moment when he accuses her, recognizes that she has failed to appreciate the power, first of her father and then her husband, over her. In her decision to leave, on the other hand, Nora takes a step towards self-authorship or autonomy.

Anderson sets out to offer a revised reading of Kant to capture an element of vulnerability alongside autonomy. Anderson suggests that many critics of Kant fail to recognize the partial nature of self-knowledge for him. "I urge that we recognize a Kantian possibility for the female character in Ibsen's play."[2]

She argues that autonomy needs to be revised from the perspective of a personal ideal (as it is proposed in many interpretations of Kant's ethics) to reflect the reality of individuals' lived experience. We can be wrong, according to her and her reading of Kant, about what is right and what we know but also about who we are in relation to our personal and social worlds. Ethics therefore needs to be based upon revisable principles. She claims that if we add what she calls, following her work on Ricoeur, a "narrative identity" to our lives, Kantian ethics can account for self-authorship, gender and vulnerability and it can also recognize the dimension of power in our relationships. Lack of self-authorship of subordinated groups can be remedied by a practical principle of inclusion. She argues that it is possible to revise most interpretations of Kantian ethics.

In another paper of hers, Anderson characterizes vulnerability as "an open-ness to making change possible, enabling forward movement in life."[3] She advocates "moving from what we take ourselves to be to what we are becoming ([...] an aliveness in life)."[4] She critiques the idea of vulnerability as "a weakness, or a disability to be rid of."[5] She expresses scepticism about the "paternalistic morality" that may go alongside the negative conception of vulnerability in so far as it may encourage a false sense of treating the vulnerable as victims – over-indulging a child, for example. Such a sense, she notes, also creates its obverse – an overly strong conception of the "invulnerable" self towards which ethically we are supposed to aim. She suggests a significant caveat to both "justice"-based models of morality on the one hand, and "care"-based approaches on the other. Both, she argues, are too demanding of ethical subjects – in the former case subjects are assumed to be invulnerable, and in the latter they are required to be overly concerned with caring for another. In both cases, there is an over-demanding requirement of the ethical subject.

I think that Anderson's recognition of vulnerability is very important but I'd like to suggest a different way of thinking about this issue from Anderson's. Instead of setting out to modify an account such as that of Kant or that of the "justice" ethicists, I'd like to suggest that there is to be found, in the work of Simone de Beauvoir, an alternative model of the self and of freedom that incorporates an element of vulnerability. Perhaps my account will not accommodate all the significant and subtle elements of Anderson's notion of vulnerability, such as her critical discussion of the emotion of shame and the need to forgive those who abuse, but I hope that it will provide some food for thought.

Firstly, I'd like to note that it is important to distinguish those elements of vulnerability that are normatively desirable from those that are not. There is a difference between the desirable fact of vulnerability in the sense of corporeal and psychological openness to others and forms of vulnerability, on the other hand, such as corporeal or psychological forms – e.g., rape and domestic violence – that are detrimental to the interests of certain social groups. Secondly, I think there are more difficulties than Pamela recognizes with Kant's view of autonomy. It seems to me, in relation to the story above, that the problem is not that both characters fail to recognize their relationality but that the story illustrates the problem with a Kantian-inspired conception of autonomy. Linked to this, I don't think feminists ought to see themselves uncritically as shaped by existing narrative identities that may be detrimental to their interests. Subjects may be "constituted" by injurious social norms. It seems to me that there is an ontological dimension of the problem that makes reconciliation with Kant and with justice ethicists problematic. Kant's view of autonomy leaves no room for vulnerability in Anderson's sense. But further and thirdly, I would like to suggest a more "universal" account of the position of women than Anderson sometimes does.

I'd therefore like to sketch a normative model of freedom, derived from Kierkegaard and de Beauvoir, that allows for relationality. But I'd further like to argue, following Danielle Petherbridge, that there needs to be a political challenge to the unacceptable elements of vulnerability.

I

In a sense, Kant does note something that could be argued to be similar to a notion of vulnerability.[6] For example, in "Answering the Question: What is Enlightenment?" he characterizes enlightenment as the emergence of "men" (*sic*) from their self-incurred immaturity. Indeed, the "fair sex" remain in this state.[7] But the analogue of vulnerability in Kant's work here stems not from a phenomenological state but rather from the lack of courage to deploy one's reason. These are not quite the senses of vulnerability, of course, that Anderson holds.

Famously, in the *Critique of Pure Reason*, Kant defends a notion of self-causation. He articulates the view, in the thesis of the *Third*

Antinomy, that "causality in accordance with laws of nature is not the only causality from which the appearances of the world can one and all be derived."[8] His reason for this is not only that if this were the case then our freedom and autonomy would be compromised but rather that "If everything takes place solely in accordance with laws of nature, there will always only be a relative and never a first beginning."[9] Indeed, he also argues that the idea of a complete determinist system is self-contradictory because it assumes a complete series and this implies both that there must be a beginning of the series (to make it complete) and that every event must have a cause and therefore that there is no beginning. Kant calls the "beginning" an "absolute spontaneity" of the cause[10] and he claims that we, as free beings, act from such a spontaneity. So Kant defends two senses of self-causation – that of an absolute beginning of nature or Being and that of free acts of agents like us.

In the *Groundwork*, Kant suggests that as we are potentially rational beings, so are we potentially free, "as belonging to the intelligible world, [we are] under laws which, being independent of nature, are not empirical but grounded merely in reason."[11] Moreover, as noted above, Kant sees freedom and autonomy as necessarily connected: "with the idea of freedom the concept of autonomy is now inseparably combined, and with the concept of autonomy the universal principle of morality."[12] This is a very strong notion of freedom and autonomy.

In connection to the above, Kant does something else. He identifies the free actions of human beings with following the moral law. When you behave well, you are acting freely. You behave well when you act in accordance with the Categorical Imperative. But this leads to a problem. Kant has difficulty, as many have suggested, explaining the possibility of freely doing wrong, for he frequently argues that freedom and the moral law reciprocally imply one another.

Given this separation between the free and autonomous self and the phenomenal and causally vulnerable self, it is also difficult to provide a Kantian account of the latter that incorporates some element of the former. Kant clearly wanted to uphold a theory that allows for free actions that are morally wrong. But it is difficult for him to do so, on his account of freedom. A further implication is that autonomy – self-authorship – is characterized in such a way as to exclude vulnerability. Autonomy, it seems to me, ought also to be about the very ability of the self to be moral at all. If you define the free self as moral then you are failing to recognize the difficulty involved for human beings in being moral. The way Kant sets out the distinction between the moral self and the causally determined self makes it difficult for him to account for vulnerability.

There is, indeed, a strand in "liberal" second-wave feminism that links with this Kantian view. Agency, on this view, is equivalent to women making autonomous self-willed choices that are not influenced by custom, tradition, or by any patriarchal norm. The good society, one that treats women well, would be, on this view, one that promoted individual autonomy, rationality and self-fulfilment. It should allow individuals the maximum freedom from interference by others. Early liberal feminists, then, such as Mary Wollstonecraft, argued forcefully that women had the potential for full rationality and were as capable as men of moral responsibility.

Some later second-wave feminists, such as Alison Jaggar, critiqued this liberal conception of the self as depending upon "normative dualism." It encouraged, she argued, the view that "individuals are essentially solitary, with needs and interests that are essentially separate from if not in opposition to those of other individuals."[13] Normative dualism encouraged theorists to ignore human biology and to play down the elements of human interaction that depend upon community engagement and dependence. Political society, on the liberal view, must allow individuals maximum freedom to make their own choices, because individuals are the ultimate authorities of their own needs and desires. But this, according to Jaggar and others, including more recently the feminist anthropologist Saba Mahmood,[14] offers an unrealistic and perhaps false view of some women's agency and encourages women who desire something other than individual autonomy of this kind to feel that their agency is undermined.

Mahmood wants to revive a conception of agency that allows that women might choose very differently. Her alternative view of agency sees it as the capacity to "realize one's own interests against the weight of custom, tradition, transcendental will, or other obstacles (whether individual or collective)."[15] She writes:

> Despite the many strands and differences within feminism, what accords the feminist tradition an analytical and political coherence is the premise that where society is structured to serve male interests, the result will be either neglect, or direct suppression, of women's concerns.[16]

Viewed in this way, she argues, what may appear to be a case of deplorable docility and passivity from what she calls a "progressivist" point of view may actually be a form of agency, "but one that can be understood only from within the discourses and structures of subordination that create the conditions of its enactment."[17] She sets out to re-evaluate notions like "shyness" and "piety" as feminist virtues. If a woman chooses to be humble and to cover herself, for example, that may constitute, for her, a form of agency.

The critics of the Kantian view and of the liberal conception of feminism that is inspired by Kantianism, then, would argue that Kantianism is incompatible with a recognition of vulnerability and interdependence. Indeed, it is incompatible also with the view that women can be influenced by norms that shape their actions, outlooks and beliefs, but that don't prevent them from being feminist. Given, then, the significance of autonomous self-willed choice, for this tradition, it seems to me to be difficult to place a view that focuses primarily on vulnerability inside it.

There are certainly "other" Kants than this one. There is, for example, the Kant of the third *Critique* and the Kant of *Religion within the Bounds of Bare Reason*, to take two examples, which set out to reconcile freedom and evil, in particular, or freedom and elements of the causally determined self. But these reconciliations, in my view, come with a dismantling of the very core of Kant's thinking about freedom, in the first *Critique*, which necessarily conceptualizes it as radically distinct from the causally shaped self.

2

In this section I will sketch an alternative model of autonomy and freedom that allows for vulnerability in the sense of openness to others and of relationality. Ironically, though, while I have reservations about using the above aspect of Kant's thought for understanding vulnerability, I do think there is something else in Kant's thinking that is very important and that relates to the issue of vulnerability. That is the notion of a universal humanity – in the ontological and the normative sense. I hesitate to conceptualize this universal in terms of Kantian rationality, yet it seems to me to be vital for both political and ethical ends that there is a universal humanity. Sometimes, as in the analysis of Nora above, Anderson seems to question the notion of a universal humanity. Elsewhere, though, she draws on a radically different conceptual framework of a form of universal humanity deriving from the work of Bergson.[18] While, then, I appreciate Kant's recognition of the importance of thinking of humanity in a universalizing way, I would like, as noted, to challenge the way he understands the universal element of humanity.

There is something very significant, I believe, for conceptualizing a model of universal humanity that incorporates vulnerability, in Bergson's critique of views of matter, like that of Kant, as lifeless and as subject to determinist forces. Instead, Bergson's view of all forms of life as containing some notion of freedom seems to me to be really significant for understanding vulnerability. Darwin, Elisabeth Grosz has argued,[19] has shown how humans emerge from the animal. Bergson adds to this a demonstration of the emergence of the human, also, from the non-human. Moreover, change and movement, rather than stasis, are the characteristics of experience. The present, in Bergson's thought, is infused with the past, with many forms of memory.[20] As he puts it: "there are not two identical moments in the life of a conscious being."[21]

> Take the simplest sensation, suppose it constant, absorb in it the entire personality: the consciousness which will accompany this sensation cannot remain identical with itself for two consecutive moments, because the second moment always contains, over and above the first, the memory that the first has bequeathed to it.[22]

Universalism about humans, then, might be understood in a manner deriving from Bergson, Schelling and Darwin. Both Schelling and Bergson critique the Kantian mechanistic view of nature. Schelling suggests, according to Alderwick, that such a perspective cannot explain subjectivity and freedom nor can it account for the interconnections within nature.[23] A bacterium exhibits a rudimentary degree of freedom, for Schelling, as does a virus. Humans possess freedom to a greater degree than the virus, and freedom may, indeed, constitute an emergent property of humans. But it is not distinct in kind from that of a monkey or a whale.

On this view, then, human nature is continuous with the rest of the animal and the natural world. The "essence" of humanity is not rationality or autonomy but an historically shaped, socially inflected biological core that emphasizes the biological vulnerability humans share with other animals. This does not mean, to clarify the point, that there are not significant differences between human and animal freedom. However, the former, on this view, would emerge from the animal.

Drawing on this tradition, Simone de Beauvoir offers her own critique of models of humanity, like that of Kant, that exclude vulnerability and specifically that describe "woman" as non-human:

> But what singularly defines the situation of woman is that being, like all humans, an autonomous freedom, she discovers and chooses herself in a world where men force her to assume herself as Other: an attempt is made to freeze her as an object and doom her to immanence, since her transcendence will be forever transcended by another essential and sovereign consciousness. Woman's drama lies in this conflict between the fundamental claim of every subject, which always posits itself as essential, and the demands of a situation that constitutes her as inessential.[24]

On the above Kantian view, then, women and other subjugated groups are constituted as non-autonomous. But this is detrimental to the interests and the well-being of all humans.

As lived embodied creatures, we are radically vulnerable and our freedom cannot be purely an internal subjective matter. Moreover, de Beauvoir recognizes that freedom must be characterized as pure openness to the future and cannot be characterized in the Kantian fashion, as being shaped by the moral law.

Simone de Beauvoir, more than her mentor Sartre, drew on the work of Kierkegaard, particularly for her text *The Ethics of Ambiguity*.[25] Kierkegaard, alongside Bergson and Schelling, I believe, offers an ontological model of the human being that can retain the advantages of the Kantian picture while removing its disadvantages. Kierkegaard's self, like that of Bergson and Schelling (one before him and one after), is a natural and vulnerable being. It is not a purely rational being and his view of the self sees it stand dynamically in relations with other selves. Kierkegaard, I have argued elsewhere, provides a dynamical account of the origins of freedom in Adam, in *The Concept of Anxiety*. Freedom emerges from a vulnerability in the self in the Garden of Eden – the fact that the self, even in the Garden, is subject to potential desires and temptations. Eve and Adam become aware of right and wrong after the emergence in them of freedom. The ethical being, then, for Kierkegaard, is not separate from the natural being: "The human being is a synthesis of the infinite and the finite, of the temporal and the eternal, of freedom and necessity, in short a synthesis."[26] Kierkegaard's self is a finite and vulnerable one shaped by forces around it. In *Fear and Trembling*, Kierkegaard writes: "Temporarily, finitude is all what it turns on."[27] There are constant references, in Kierkegaard's work, to time, to finite human emotions and to the fact of death. We are not purely rational beings. We are intertwined with others. We are beings who are born, who live and who die. These events intertwine and shape our rationality in a way that would not be possible on a Kantian view.

De Beauvoir extends Kierkegaard's analysis. Freedom, in her view, consists, as noted, in a recognition of the wide-open character of the future. Freedom is also a matter of recognizing that my freedom does not only concern me. Rather, my freedom cannot be realized without appreciating and recognizing the freedom of others as well. Realizing the freedom of others does not only not negate one's own freedom but it is instead a requirement of one's own freedom. One cannot "will" oneself not to be free, since freedom is a condition, ontologically, of our subject-hood. However, "one can fail to choose oneself as free."[28] Subjectivity, then, is intrinsically and ontologically relational since we will ourselves as free partly through willing the freedom of others. So long as any group of human beings are unfree, as Simone de Beauvoir believed was the case for women, that partially fetters the freedom of all others. One might imagine as an example of this relational freedom a couple like Nora and Torvald, in Pamela's example. Torvald is not fully himself free since he is denying Nora's freedom. He is constrained not to love her as he might, by his views about women's autonomy. She, in her turn, is unable to exercise her own freedom since she is fettered by the views of Torvald and others around her, about women. De Beauvoir, in *The Ethics of Ambiguity*, quotes Ibsen:

> in *A Doll's House*, the childlike naivete of the heroine leads her to rebel against the lie of the serious. On the contrary, the man who has the necessary instruments to escape this lie and who does not want to use them consumes his freedom in denying, them. He makes himself serious.[29]

Here, Torvald represents the "serious man" who denies his own freedom as well as that of others by subsuming his own freedom into the world of a particular ethical universe, that of the party, the church or some other establishment set of values. She argues, though, that the "serious man" is dangerous, for through denying his own freedom he effectively denies that of others. Freedom, however, is never absolute on de Beauvoir's reading; rather, it is a process. Freedom is about gradually being able to surpass what one wants. The existence of others constitutes one of the conditions of my freedom. In other words, for de Beauvoir, freedom incorporates vulnerability.

Women have been constituted as immanent and as lacking some of the crucial conditions that make for freedom. Women are oppressed as women and this is, for de Beauvoir, absolutely wrong. Indeed, some of the norms that constitute women as "other" require political change in order to be eliminated. While Anderson makes an important point in her desire to alter "negative" conceptions of vulnerability, we must also accept that there *are*, as a matter of fact, "negative" aspects of the notion that require political change. Anderson, in her subtle and powerful analysis of domestic violence and of the need and desire for a recognition of the deep hurt of being wronged in this way that requires forgiveness, perhaps pays insufficient attention to the political. The latter was recognized by de Beauvoir as action to chip away at those normative constructions that prevent some from fully realizing their freedom. Setting out to begin to eradicate domestic violence or lower pay for women involves political action. Even childbearing is given a political sense through the way it is experienced by individual women. This need not, as Anderson rightly notes, require "paternalistic" conceptions of "care" that reinforce these negative aspects of vulnerability. However, the socio-historical context that gives rise to unwanted and inappropriate forms of vulnerability, such as rape, warfare and other forms of violence, but also psychological powerlessness such as that exemplified by Nora above, needs to be challenged politically in terms of models of justice. Freedom, in other words, is situated by context.

It is more difficult, de Beauvoir further suggests, for women to identify as women than it is for many social groups, as women's experiences are so variable. As de Beauvoir put it, women lack the resources to identify themselves as a Hegelian "slave" or an "other" and so they label themselves as white women, black women, etc. Extending her analysis, where heterosexual, white and other norms prevail, it is difficult for women to identify themselves with each other. Women tend to forget that they are all women and tend to see themselves instead in antagonistic relations with other women: white women and black women, heterosexual and lesbian and gay, trans and "terf" and so on. In doing this, women unwittingly universalize these various forms of oppression. Particularist criticisms tend, in their legitimate critiques of the exclusion of, for example, black women's experiences from a universal model, to critique all forms of universalizing thinking. De Beauvoir, instead, can be read as articulating the importance (a) of developing an ontological model of humanity that questions the "othering" of any social group and (b) of emphasizing the need for political action that challenges the structures that give rise to this othering. The problem, therefore, with focusing on the "narrative identities" – stories that shape who we are – that partially shape our lives is that some of these are constitutive of the very aspect of the identities of at least some of us that Pamela herself sets out to challenge. De Beauvoir emphasizes universal humanity but she historicizes this universal, and suggests that the form of it suggested by Kant condemns woman to the "Other" of the autonomous ethical being. In turn, the freedom of all is partially denied so long as any group is treated badly. According to her, everyone ought to be interested in the elimination of oppression, the oppressor as well as the oppressed.

Women's emancipation cannot entail "adding" relationality and a recognition of power when there is something wrong with the ontological model that underlies hegemonic masculinity. We require an ontological model that recognizes that human beings ought to combine autonomy with the aspect of vulnerability that recognizes their relationality and that simultaneously critiques those aspects of vulnerability that condemn them to psychological or physical inferiority. No woman, and this includes poor women who do labour work for richer, middle-class women, should be defined against a symbolic construction that characterizes her as a non-ethical being.

If there are women anywhere in the world stuck in domestic labour, or if they are victims of violence, then they are suffering from a form of vulnerability that they ought not to have to suffer. The particularist critics of universalizing feminism omit the normative role of an analysis like that of de Beauvoir. Postmodern-inspired critiques, and there are elements of this in some of Pamela's work, on the other hand, (a) confuse the issue by attempting to describe features of the existing narrative and social reality that still "Others" some women; and (b) remove the universalizing and normative element of feminism altogether. Instead, if dominant and subordinated groups are historically formed, they can contest one form of domination – for example that of women by men – and it will follow that the emancipation, construed in a universalist way, of black women or of trans women becomes a problem for all women. I am offering a challenge, in other words, to any model of the construction of women that assumes that we must "water down" the notion of "woman" because generalizing about all women becomes heterosexist or racist. Instead, the "othering" of any group constitutes, on de Beauvoir's model, a problem for all since the real freedom of each of us is ontologically linked with the freedom of all. There is an ideal of human life, as noted above, that de Beauvoir characterized in *The Ethics of Ambiguity* that involves an ontological challenge to the Kantian model of autonomy. This involves mutual reciprocal recognition of each other's worth and each other's autonomy and vulnerability. To repeat, one cannot be fully autonomous, on de Beauvoir's view, if others are subjugated. Full autonomy is an ideal rather than an actuality.

3 conclusion

I have recognized and appreciated the significance of Pamela Anderson's work on vulnerability. It is a vital corrective to the overemphasis, in some feminist writing, on autonomy. However, there are, I have suggested in this paper, two central difficulties with the adapted particularist understanding of Kant deployed by Anderson (along with many other feminists). The Kantian model, it seems to me, is part of the underlying ontological problematic of women's subordination and of the failure to consider vulnerability. It cannot therefore be adapted, without it fundamentally changing. Secondly, and equally seriously, the particularism of some of Anderson's works, along with that of many post-colonial theorists and others, tends to remove any universalizing egalitarian thinking and therefore remove the normative element from feminist thinking. Ironically, elsewhere in her work, Anderson defends a form of universalism and it is this element of her work, alongside her development of the notion of vulnerability, that I would like to celebrate. Simone de Beauvoir, in contrast to Kant, offers a model of freedom and autonomy that recognizes that I cannot be free without recognizing the freedom of others. This, in turn, presupposes appreciating my own vulnerability as well as that of others.

In setting out properly to critique false universalizing perspectives, which generalize from the experience of white middle-class women to all women, some critics focus on critiquing all forms of universalizing thinking and this, in my view, removes that key egalitarian impetus from feminism.

disclosure statement

No potential conflict of interest was reported by the author.

notes

1 Pamela Anderson, "Autonomy, Vulnerability and Gender," *Feminist Theory* (Aug. 2003): 149–64 (152).

2 Ibid.

3 Pamela Anderson, "Arguing for 'Ethical' Vulnerability: Towards a Politics of Care?" in *Exploring Vulnerability*, eds. Heiker Springhart and Günther Thomas (Göttingen and Bristol, VT: Vandenhoeck, 2017) 149.

4 Ibid.

5 Ibid. 150.

6 I am grateful to Luisa Ribeiro Ferreira for reminding me of this.

7 Immanuel Kant, *What is Enlightenment?* [1784], trans. Ted Humphrey (Indianapolis: Hackett, 1992) 1.

8 Immanuel Kant, *Critique of Pure Reason*, trans. Norman Kemp Smith (London: Macmillan, 1970) A444/B472.

9 Ibid. A446/B474.

10 Ibid. A447/B475.

11 Immanuel Kant, *Groundwork of the Metaphysics of Morals*, Intro. Christine Korsgaard; trans. Mary Gregor and Jens Timmerman (Cambridge: Cambridge UP, 2012) 4: 452.

12 Ibid.

13 Alison Jaggar, *Feminist Politics and Human Nature* (Brighton: Harvester, 1983) 40.

14 Saba Mahmood, *Politics of Piety: The Islamic Revival and the Feminist Subject* (Princeton: Princeton UP, 2004).

15 Ibid. 14.

16 Ibid.

17 Ibid.

18 Pamela Sue Anderson, "Bergsonian Intuition: A Metaphysics of Mystical Life," *Philosophical Topics* 43.1–2 (2015): 239–51.

19 Elizabeth Grosz, *Becoming Undone: Darwinian Reflections on Life, Politics and Art* (Durham, NC: Duke UP, 2011).

20 See Henri Bergson, *An Introduction to Metaphysics* (London: Palgrave Macmillan, 2007).

21 Ibid. 8.

22 Ibid.

23 Charlotte Alderwick, "Nature's Capacities: Schelling and Contemporary Power-Based

Ontologies," *Angelaki: Journal of the Theoretical Humanities* 21.4 (2016): 59–76.

24 Simone de Beauvoir, *The Second Sex*, trans. H.M. Parshley (London: Vintage, 2011) 37.

25 Simone de Beauvoir, *The Ethics of Ambiguity*, trans. Bernard Frechtman (New York: Citadel, 1948).

26 Søren Kierkegaard, *The Sickness unto Death*, trans. Howard V. Hong and Edna H. Hong (Princeton: Princeton UP, 1980) 13.

27 Søren Kierkegaard, *Fear and Trembling*, trans. Alistair Hannay (London: Penguin, 2003) 78.

28 Cristina Arp, *The Bonds of Freedom: Simone de Beauvoir's Existentialist Ethics* (Chicago: Open Court, 2013) 55.

29 De Beauvoir, *Ethics of Ambiguity* 21.

It is in the knowledge of the genuine conditions of our life that we must draw our strength to live and our reason for acting.[1]

This essay considers Pamela Sue Anderson's work on vulnerability in relation to her participation in the Enhancing Life Project from 2015 until her death in 2017. The thesis of this essay is that her notion of a "threshold for enhancing human life" can aid a reconstruction of and critical engagement with Anderson's final written and lived project. Although "threshold" is not one of the "key concepts" that Anderson identifies, it does important work in the formulation of her project.[2] In a 2016 blogpost for the project she explained: "I have hypothesized that vulnerability serves as a provocation for enhancing life by creating a space for transformation. It's an opening for change, whether through loss or joy."[3] "Threshold," "space," and, relatedly, "opening" resonate with the discussions of epistemic locatedness and the intersubjective nature of becoming found elsewhere in her work. Her discussion of a space of transformation is also a point where Anderson's work intersects with a host of other feminists' works, whether "a room of one's own" (Woolf) or the body as a situation (Beauvoir). This essay's engagement with the work of Simone de Beauvoir offers one recognition of those feminist interlocutors.

Engaging certain aspects of Anderson's final work, this essay also gestures beyond it. I begin with a narration of participating with her and other scholars in the Enhancing Life Project. Next, I focus on her treatment of capability and vulnerability, identifying shifts in her approach and bringing theological symbols and

kristine a. culp

A THRESHOLD FOR ENHANCING HUMAN LIFE
anderson on capability and vulnerability

a constructive theological interest to the conversation. Anderson depicted the relation of capability and vulnerability as a "threshold for enhancing human life." This essay evaluates her original post-Kantian conceptualization of threshold in relation to the shifts in her thinking. A sympathetic but more adequate approach can be informed by Beauvoir's phenomenological approach to lived experience and her construal of the body as a lived situation. When vulnerability is interpreted as a situated susceptibility to being changed, for good or for ill, then threshold language can be reintroduced in relation to the intensification, enhancement, and transformation of life, that is, of the "aliveness of life."

1 the enhancing life project and the "vulnerability ladies"

The Enhancing Life Project sought to address one of the most basic human questions – the desire to enhance life. Without necessarily using this language, thinkers have long considered the meaning of enhancing life and its endangerment, ways to enhance life, and judgments about whether life has been enhanced. As the project literature explains, "In our global technological age, these issues have become more widespread and urgent."[4]

Anderson was intrigued when she learned of the project. "The spark was really just the word 'life,'" she explained later:

> I have spent the past twenty years trying to carve out a field called feminist philosophy of religion, and one of the big themes is that women or feminists face a dichotomy: life is opposed to philosophy, like vulnerability is to invulnerability. The logic is that women are associated with caring for life, so feminist philosophy of religion would be life-giving, whereas the philosophy of religion pursued by men has been abstract and detached from life [...] I thought that rather than shutting out our feelings and affections in life, philosophy should become transformed as life-giving.[5]

The Enhancing Life Project was funded by the John Templeton Foundation at the University of Chicago and Ruhr University-Bochum, with William Schweiker (Chicago) and Günter Thomas (Bochum) as the Principal Investigators. It drew together thirty-five scholars from varied fields, including religion and philosophy, the social sciences, medicine, law, and communications. We each pursued an individual research agenda through writing, teaching, and various forms of public engagement, while also developing shared approaches and insights. Interdisciplinary collaborations, particularly those fostered during three two-week summer seminars, allowed the scholars to identify salient concepts and research approaches for enhancing life studies.

In 2014, shortly after Schweiker and Thomas had been awarded the grant, Anderson lectured at the University of Chicago Divinity School. She and I spoke briefly about applying to be part of the Enhancing Life Project – we had already become acquainted through mutual friends and because of intersecting interests. The project represented a rich opportunity for collaboration. She eventually proposed "to develop an ontology of becoming, with a transformed and transformative conceptual scheme, for creating new concepts to live by."[6] She identified capability, confidence, creativity, life, transformative change and transformative experience, and vulnerability as among twenty "key concepts."[7] My own project assumed a construal of vulnerable life and proposed to explore "glory," interpreted as the aliveness of life, as a condensed symbol of the full capacity and integrity of life.[8]

The first summer seminar was convened in Banff, a glorious setting in the Canadian Rockies, in July 2015. The seminars enacted the mantra, "work – converse – enjoy," and enabled us to build a small shared universe of ideas, affections, and vision. Anderson interjected Ricoeur, Bergson, Deleuze, Merleau-Ponty, Le Doeuff, Kant, and Spinoza into the conversation. She manifested "speaker confidence," sometimes having to elbow her way into a conversation and sometimes using her analogical elbows to create an opening that would allow less confident speakers to enter in more fully.

Anderson dubbed fellow Enhancing Life Project scholars Andrea Bieler, Heike Springhart, Sarah Bianchi, me, and herself as the "vulnerability ladies." We shared an interest in the topic of vulnerability – as did several other scholars in the project.[9] For each of us, vulnerability offered a portrayal of intersubjectivity and interdependency and of concomitant possibilities for devastating and/or transforming change. As women theologians and philosophers we also shared a certain solidarity fostered by similar experiences in academic life of, let's just say, vulnerability and capability. In March 2016 we met in Wuppertal, Germany, to discuss our work. That included reading Anderson's January 2016 lecture, "Arguing for 'Ethical' Vulnerability: Or, What is 'a Politics of Care'?," and a draft of her Durham lecture, "Silencing and Speaker Vulnerability: Undoing an Oppressive Form of

(Wilful) Ignorance." I selected chapters from Judith Butler's *Notes Toward a Performative Theory of Assembly* (2015) for our discussion. We explored shifts in Butler's approach to vulnerability and whether Butler's view entailed, in Anderson's phrasing, an "ontological vulnerability."[10]

The vulnerability ladies were to have reconvened in March 2017 in Oxford, but Pamela's cancer had recurred. She had struggled, ever so discreetly, to participate fully during the 2016 summer seminar in Liebenberg and Berlin, Germany. The planned reunion was cancelled as her death drew near. Sarah Bianchi and I had already made travel plans, so we convened in London instead. As it turned out, that allowed us to attend the memorial service at Mansfield College.

The service, led by Susan Durber, was deeply moving, sorrow-filled but ultimately reorienting. Magnificent hymns (including Colin Thompson's setting of Augustine's praise of God's matchless beauty and blazing love from *Confessions*, and Charles Wesley's "Love Divine, All Loves Excelling"), readings of the Song of Songs 8.6–7 and 1 Corinthians 13, a tribute by Adrian Moore, prayers by Paul Fiddes, and a eulogy by Durber, enfolded Pamela's life and work within themes of love, vulnerability, and enhancing life. A reading came from her 2016 blogpost for the project:

> [I]n becoming undone by the loss of a loved one, we are inevitably forced to change. Life can never be the same without that loved one, but the wound of loss makes us recognize the reality of one's love *in that vulnerability*. This recognition gives us the strength to move forward. The hope would be, after recognizing one's vulnerability, that one could live more openly and fully for oneself and others who are equally open.

That remarkable service presented the final lived manuscript of her Enhancing Life Project.

2 enhancing capable life

In this and subsequent sections I follow the development of Anderson's project, reconstructing the shifts that she makes. Her project began with the felt, reflexive awareness of love and loss. One may find oneself thwarted at the core of one's life – susceptible to loss of love, health, confidence, even life itself. And yet recognition of that loss and, more generally, of susceptibility to loss, may also establish a place from which to go on, possibly from which to "live more [...] fully." Accordingly, Anderson's project examines responses to loss and devastation and asks whether life lived in the face of love and loss can become more livable with the help of transformed concepts. More provocatively, she asks what might be learned about enhancing life by paying even closer attention to how we live in and through loss.

In her grant proposal and during that first two-week seminar, Anderson's focus was the relationship of becoming (especially Bergson, Deleuze, Spinoza, Grosz) and capability (Ricoeur, LeDoeuff, Merleau-Ponty). Her project was entitled "Enhancing Capable Life: Transformative Change, Confidence and Creativity."[11] She planned to develop an ontology of human becoming that could offer new ontological and ethical "concepts to live by." She envisioned "a conceptual scheme" that could enhance – that is, undergird, restore, transform – human capability in general and affective, rational, and conative capacities in particular by attending to processes of becoming, duration, and intuition. Referring to Bergson, she argued that such an ontology of becoming would support "an open morality and dynamic religion," which in turn could steer a middle course between a closed religion and static morality that rejects human enhancement, on the one hand, and transhumanism's embrace of radical enhancement, on the other (18–19).

Her proposal identified twenty(!) key concepts. Vulnerability was one of those. It was not (yet) as pivotal or as thickly theorized as capability and becoming. Conversing with Judith Butler's writings on precarious and grievable life[12] and Elizabeth Grosz's picture of life as "forms of competing and coordinating modes of openness" and as processes of becoming and becoming undone,[13] Anderson initially followed

Butler and Grosz in construing vulnerability as "being undone" by love and loss. Accordingly, she interpreted vulnerability as a contingent or "*a posteriori* dimension of human life" (14) – as threatening or diminishing human capability and thus prospects for enhancing life. In other words, at this point in her project, vulnerability appears primarily as a loss of capability, as capability itself being or becoming undone. In her account, "everyday vulnerabilities" including loss "of love, of life, of health, of capacities" (17) and, elsewhere, of confidence, can affect and eviscerate human potential. She observes, however, that being undone may also create openness for new forms of becoming.

She asks, "What is the threshold – the most basic level – for a (truly) human life?" She stipulates capability as "an *a priori* of human life," that is, "as *a priori* potentiality" (17–18). She contrasts this to the capabilities approach in the work of philosophers Amartya Sen and Martha Nussbaum, which Anderson characterizes as specifying lists of basic capabilities. Drawing instead from the work of Paul Ricoeur, Anderson specifies a "generic capability," namely, that "we are all capable as human subjects." This generic capability or "fleshy potentiality" serves as "a threshold for enhancing human life." She elaborates:

> capability is shared by each and every human being, but the specificities of capable subjects will vary depending on their particular capacities for affection, cognition, and conation; it is a generic capability which grounds a confident and full spiritual, ethical, and political life. (18)

In the course of the Enhancing Life Project, Anderson's focus shifts from capability to vulnerability, and she increasingly interprets vulnerability as an openness to becoming as well as to becoming undone. As Paul Fiddes observes, Anderson ultimately considers vulnerability "as a means of developing bonds of affection that will enhance life."[14] This more robust formulation is evident if we revisit her 2016 Enhancing Life Project blogpost:

> [M]y focus on vulnerability is on transformative experiences like critical illness, personal bereavement, or the birth of a child, when people have been able to discover not only their openness to possible harm or pain, but also an openness to change and growth […] [I]n becoming undone by the loss of a loved one, we are inevitably forced to change. Life can never be the same without that loved one, but the wound of loss makes us recognize the reality of one's love *in that vulnerability*. This recognition gives us the strength to move forward. The hope would be, after recognizing one's vulnerability, that one could live more openly and fully for oneself and others who are equally open.

Among the many things one notices in these poignant words is that vulnerability now offers a sort of baseline of "fleshy potentiality." Is she suggesting that capability is known concretely in vulnerability, as vulnerability?

One can speculate on a number of reasons for this shift in Anderson's thinking: facing the reality of her own loss of health, the continued confrontation with "speaker vulnerability" in academic contexts, the continued influence of Ricoeur in relation to Bergson and Deleuze's *Bergsonism*, engagement with Butler's and Grosz's work, the orienting influence of Le Doeuff and Beauvoir, engagement with theological-ethical perspectives and spiritual concerns through the Enhancing Life Project, the prominence of vulnerability in other Enhancing Life Projects, and so forth. Likely it was some combination of these things.

How, then, does Anderson envision enhancing life? This is a project "to restore life's joyful capability" (13), she explained. It is neither a call for radical enhancement of capability with the transhumanists nor to be patient with the status quo but to forge a middle way, to enhance and transform the road we already find ourselves traveling on. She explains: "Thus my crucial aim is not a proposal for radical enhancement, but enhancement to the threshold, which ensures that we do not give up the idea of persons, of self-affirmation, or other-approbation" (19). The enhancement of life's capability and of confidence in one's own capability cannot be ensured by removing vulnerability to loss, by securing invulnerability. Rather, she charts a course of dynamic and creative becoming in which capable life is enhanced through positive transformation. That does not imply greater optimism or a denial of mortality. This project, her final lived manuscript, will cause Anderson to shift towards a construal of vulnerability as a threshold for fleshy, located capability and away from vulnerability as primarily entailing damaging change or as a deprivation of potential, a de-capacitization.

3 thematizing vulnerability

The root of the word vulnerability is the Latin or Middle French "vulnus" or "wound." While this root dates to the sixteenth century, the notion of wound and wound-ability finds more ancient expression in biblical and theological texts. The wounds of Jesus become staples of medieval spiritual devotion; for instance, they are recapitulated in Francis of Assisi's stigmata. Through its linguistic root, *vulnus*/wound, and this deep theological and devotional resonance, the word vulnerability can be understood to be graphically inscribed and inescapably enfleshed.[15] In the early seventeenth century, Caravaggio's "The Incredulity of Saint Thomas," painted in his convention-breaking realist style, offers the pierced side of Jesus as a reality that can be probed to answer early modern skepticism. Around that same time, the prolific German Lutheran composer Paul Gerhardt adapted a medieval meditation on the wounds of Jesus to a hymn setting. The hymn, subsequently translated as "O Sacred Head, Now Wounded," was adapted for a chorale in Johann Sebastian Bach's *St Matthew Passion*.[16] In 1973, the American singer and songwriter Paul Simon underscored the anguish of his own time by evoking and reinterpreting this centuries-old meditation on the wounds of Jesus. Both the hymn setting and its lyrics are repurposed for his song "American Tune."[17] Although he does not use the word "vulnerability," the idea is recognizable. Simon's music and lyrics are redolent with loss, resignation, and the shattering of individual and collective dreams due to assassinations and to the casualties and moral mire of the war in Vietnam. He portrays individual and collective life that sustains profound damage and yet goes on despite having been irrevocably changed and being haunted by both the damage and by the fact of having been changed.

Anderson is profoundly attentive to the ravages of loss and the bodily sting of shame – "wounded, with grief and shame weighed down," as the hymn has it.[18] However, she doesn't turn to such theological or quasi-theological depictions; rather, she relies on the evocative language of being undone by each other used by Butler and Grosz. "[P]assion and grief and rage [...] tear us from ourselves, bind us to others, transport us, undo us, implicate us in lives that are not our own, irreversibly, if not fatally," Butler observes.[19] If Simon's passion scene is the betrayal and aftermath of Vietnam, Butler – who, like Simon, is Jewish – meditates on violence and mourning in post-9/11 America, another time of cultural reckoning and indelible loss. Anderson cites a passage from Butler's 2004 book *Precarious Life*:

> [O]ne mourns when one accepts that by the loss one undergoes one will be changed, possibly forever. Perhaps mourning has to do with agreeing to undergo a transformation (perhaps one should say submitting to a transformation) the full result of which one cannot know in advance. There is a losing, as we know, but there is also the transformative effect of loss, and this latter cannot be charted or planned.[20]

If Anderson appropriates the evocative language of being/becoming undone, she also diverges from Butler's larger project in some important ways. Anderson observes that "Butler might be arguing for an ontology – not an ethics – of embodied vulnerability."[21] Anderson's accent falls on *might*, because she is not convinced that Butler is arguing for an ontology and because Anderson assumes that an ethics is not possible without one. In Anderson's terminology, vulnerability is ontological, meaning that it is "a universal condition for all of life."[22]

Let me tarry a bit longer with Butler in order to explore what Anderson might be reaching for herself. Butler writes that loss, like desire, can remind us "how we are not only constituted by our relations, but also dispossessed by them as well."[23] That is, "we" can be utterly undone – psychically and on the largest social-political scale – such that oneself or others are dispossessed of agency and of the sense of "having" a life as an "I" or a "we." For instance, in war and violence, others' lives may not even appear as "grievable," but rather as objects of torture, ridicule, or "mere" collateral damage. Butler argues that asking "what makes for a grievable life," rather than, say, what makes for an autonomous individual, allows for a more adequate picture of what counts as "liveable life," but "without positing a single or uniform ideal for that life."[24] Arguably, Butler does have an ontology in the sense of a recognition that all human life is shaped by and shares a common condition of bodily dependency – but not one that posits capable personhood. Butler argues that recognition of this constitutive interdependency and precarity "implicates us in a broader political problem of [...] the unequal distribution of vulnerability."[25] She directs attention to how others and institutions "produce and naturalize forms of social inequality" and, more generally, to the social-political production and allocation of value.[26]

Even if Butler offers something like an "ontology of vulnerability," Anderson finds Butler's approach to fall short of what Anderson terms an "'ethical' vulnerability." She observes: "[T]here seems to be no clear or certain path from the reality of corporeal vulnerability to a normative ethics or just politics, since there is nothing specifically normative in recognition of becoming undone."[27] Anderson doesn't dispute the dynamics of becoming undone as depicted by Butler, and she isn't looking to ground an ethics in a notion of autonomy. Rather, she is looking for an ontology of becoming and capability, perhaps one that appears concretely as (or in?) vulnerability. Other thinkers, however, would say there is a hermeneutical path from lived, situated experiences of vulnerability, where ethics and ontology are always already emerging as we make our way with others in the world, reflecting on life and engaging in it.

In everyday use, "vulnerability" is sometimes offered as a recommendation or prescription, viz., to be or make oneself "vulnerable" to another. This (inadequate) notion of vulnerability as an affective state or moral posture towards others that an individual subject chooses can be seen in popular psychological literature about a "wounded healer" as well as in some devotional literature and hymns. Anderson critiques this kind of approach as "excessive moral demandingness" which has been "ambiguously labelled [as] 'care.'" She also critiques "moral invulnerability" or rigorous "impartiality" as another instance of moral demandingness.[28] She depicts these options as often being both polarized and gendered. What Anderson calls for is neither sacrifice or surrender to another/others in the context of non-mutual or unequal relations, nor disregard of the special claims of others, but for restorative justice that is productive of and linked with practices of egalitarian care, affective relations, and accountability that can include appropriate reparation. To use the central terms of her title, she proposes "a *politics* of care" or an "*ethical* vulnerability" (emphasis added) as a critical intervention between an ethics of care and an ethics of justice.

Anderson's proposal for intervention might be better described as an ethics of "relational accountability" insofar as that is actually the parallel concept or norm to care and justice. She is not calling for persons to "be vulnerable" but to recognize their own susceptibilities to damage and to love as they seek relational accountability through appropriate care and restorative justice. Commenting specifically on intimate violence, she writes: "Ethical vulnerability opens up an opportunity to restore justice, or to repair, the horrendous pain of wounds (vulnerabilities) [...] with relational accountability."[29] Interestingly, in this late essay, Anderson now turns to the root language of wounding and woundedness: "Vulnerability is not merely an openness to being wounded; it is not a mere wound which needs to be healed; a weakness which requires strengthening; or a liability to harm or a disability which makes for dependency."[30] She insists that openness to being wounded cannot be separated from openness to affection and love. "Openness" suggests both a capacity for being transformed and a place of devastation or transformation.

4 threshold

The notion of threshold helps us examine how Anderson places capability and vulnerability in relation to each other. Thinking with Bergson's idea of dynamic religion – and also with the Enhancing Life Project's notion of "spiritual laws," or as Anderson interpolates it, "equalizing norms of spiritual life" – she proposed to offer new "spiritual-ethical norms" (that is, to "transform the concepts we live by") that will "knit together the *a priori* of capability with the *a posteriori* experiences of vulnerability" (19). Her (post-)Kantian epistemological terms later seem to give way to the ontological-ethical framework I have noted, in which an ontological capability is assumed for the project of creating an ethical vulnerability in face of the contingent realities of loss and change.

Anderson used the phrase "threshold for enhancing human life" in her twofold hypothesis for her project:

> [...] that (i), *ontologically speaking, we are capable subjects and yet, because of human vulnerability – most notably the precariousness of our bodily lives – human capability can be obscured by loss*; and crucially, that (ii) *capability can serve as the* threshold for enhancing human life, *in a transformative change, when confidence in what we can do, think, and create is lacking.* (12; italics in the original, underlining added)

She focuses on the intersection between capability and vulnerability as a threshold of living and becoming. I do not know the source of Anderson's use of threshold. Her use connotes both a starting point where *a priori* capability crosses over into concrete capacities that are necessarily manifested in relation to the realities of loss and affection, and also a crossing point between *a priori* capability and *a posteriori* decapacitization. Her imaginary is temporal (as in crossing the starting line of a new venture) and spatial (as in crossing through the doorway). In her simplest construals, one crosses over to capability or falls back into lack of capability. As she rethinks vulnerability and argues that both forms of moral demandingness are inadequate to the concrete reality of vulnerability (now as capability for openness or exposure, affection or devastation), multiple crossing points may come into play. The implied shifts in the metaphor are not discussed explicitly. Moreover, a second sense of threshold insinuates itself, that of a level of intensity, magnitude, or concentration at which something becomes manifest or some result comes into effect. Anderson looks to new concepts of becoming that will undergird or even expand (a level of) capability, possibly by using capacities for affection, cognition, and conation more fully, thus reaching a certain magnitude of capacity that one might call "enhanced life." In this second sense of threshold, reaching or sustaining a certain capacity would allow life to be enhanced. However, Anderson does not distinguish between these two senses and neither does her use or her project in general distinguish among epistemological, ontological, and phenomenological keys.

My own proposal is that (1) vulnerability might be better interpreted as the *situation* within which ethical responsibility is interpreted and enacted, not itself as an ethical stance, and also (2) lived, situated experiences of vulnerability are best interpreted and lived in relation to a symbolization of full life, a horizon of possibility or a sense of "the aliveness of life." I take up the former, threshold as situation, in this section, and the latter in the final section.

The language of "situation," of course, comes from Simone de Beauvoir's existentialist phenomenology and ethics.[31] One of the ways I first got to know Anderson was through a shared interest in Beauvoir. And Beauvoir's work comes to mind when I attempt to theorize how transformative change emerges at the intersection of capability and vulnerability.

Beauvoir's depiction of *les données*, "the given" or "given things," in *Le Deuxième Sexe*, may be compared to what Anderson identifies as "ontological." Beauvoir does not write about vulnerability but rather about situatedness, ambiguity, and transcendence, but there are instructive parallels. Beauvoir rejects biological, psycho-sexual, historical/political-economic, and metaphysical reductionism and determinism, while also recognizing features of human life that are shared, enduring, seemingly inescapable, and productive of general features of human existence. These features are unchosen but not deterministic, "given" in the sense of being already operative realities from which one starts; they offer a lived matrix within which, or a "fleshy" sketch from which, human possibilities are enacted.[32]

Consider this passage from Beauvoir's discussion of biological "givens" (the chapter title is misleadingly translated as "Biological Data" in the most recent English translation). Beauvoir launches the chapter with riotous send-ups of sexist anthropomorphisms in so-called scientific studies of non-human species, thereby shredding the scientific pretense of biologistic determinism. In subsequent chapters, her satire and scathing analysis extend to global history, literature, and myth – contexts in which women had neither grievable nor thinkable (contemplated, comprehensible, or richly imagined) lives. Beauvoir shines the spotlight on these "facts and myths" – the subtitle of her first volume. She rejects the notion that "women" are destined by their bodies, desires, or domestic activities – especially by operative theories about them – or by the history and myths we have. She also rejects the idea that women can choose in any simple, once-and-for-all way to negate, overcome, or transcend their bodies, desires, history, culture, etc. "The body is not a thing," she says, "it is a situation." All human individuals are situated in bodies, desires, activity, history, and cultural imaginations. She elaborates: "The body [...] is a situation: it is our grasp [*prise*] on the world and the outline [sketch, *equisse*] for our projects."[33] Beauvoir uses fleshy, physical, and material terms. "Grasp" foreshadows her engagement with historical materialism, her discussion of tool use, and her narrative about difference and psycho-sexual development. "Sketch," together with motifs from sculpture used elsewhere, combines a hint of creative activity with themes from existentialist phenomenology to suggest potential and freedom.

Compare Anderson's notion of "fleshy potentiality" to Beauvoir's "sketch of our projects." Beauvoir points to a given and lived body that is both starting point and matrix for freedom, affectivity, and subjectivity. She identifies her perspective with that of Heidegger, Sartre, and Merleau-Ponty – though Merleau-Ponty's discussion of the lived body, also cited in a footnote within this section, is particularly influential. I suspect this is the section of *The Second Sex* to which Anderson refers in her tribute to Alan Montefiore. Anderson writes:

> Philosophical imagery in the texts of French phenomenology (e.g., key passages in Beauvoir's *The Second Sex*) helped me to elucidate the nature of, in Merleau-Ponty's terms, "the lived body," as if it exists as a kind of (post-)Kantian *a priori*. The lived body's flesh knits human bodies together and to a world. This body is a synthetic form capable of creating unity out of multiple sensations, but also capable of generating differentiations in its relation to the world. The openness and relational ties of a fleshy existence renders the lived body deeply ambiguous, locating the body in a world it did not create and over which it does not have ultimate control.[34]

Anderson seems to follow Beauvoir (and both, Merleau-Ponty) when she imagines "fleshy potentiality." But she transmutes it to "a kind of (post-)Kantian" epistemological framework that diverges from Beauvoir. Is this what Anderson is imagining when she writes about "a threshold for enhancing life"? She planned to develop a concept of capability as a basis for a (truly) human life – "to imagine a space" of possibilities for life's enhancement, a sort of ontological holding place of potentiality – and from which persons can enact and strive towards freedom, love, and becoming.[35] Her concepts and the ontology of becoming that they convey cannot guarantee becoming; becoming can also be undone in concrete actions and relations. But, as Anderson wrote in her blogpost, "The hope would be, after recognizing one's vulnerability, that one could live more openly and fully for oneself and others who are equally open."

Beauvoir's approach is phenomenological; she thinks back from varied situations and instances of situated subjectivity to characterize/theorize these phenomena through a notion of the body as situation. In her influential discussion of Beauvoir's approach as a theory of the lived body, contemporary critic and theorist Toril Moi argues that a renewed focus on the situation and situatedness of persons allows the material facts of different bodies to be thought. "To claim that the body is a situation is to acknowledge that the meaning of a woman's body is bound up with the way she uses her freedom," Moi explains.[36] Moi works through Beauvoir with Judith Butler's deconstruction of the sex/gender distinction in mind. Moi is responsive to Butler's concerns but argues instead for Beauvoir's approach to the lived body as a situation:

> To consider the body as a situation [...] is to consider both the fact of being a specific kind of body and the meaning that concrete body has for the situated individual. This is not the equivalent of either sex or gender [...] [It] is a far more wide-ranging concept than the highly psychologizing concept of gender identity.[37]

As we have seen, Butler's later work on precarity similarly rejects highly psychologizing treatments of mourning and loss in favor of a recognition of bodily proximity and dependencies. A Beauvoirian approach to the body as situation can also inform a non-psychologizing approach to vulnerability as situation and situatedness.

In the paragraph immediately preceding Beauvoir's description of the body as a situation, as "our grasp [*prise*] on the world and the outline [sketch, *equisse*] for our projects," Beauvoir writes about "becoming" and "capacity":

As Merleau-Ponty rightly said, man is not a natural species: he is a historical idea. Woman is not a fixed reality but a becoming [cf. "One is not born a woman, one becomes one"]; she has to be compared to man in her becoming; that is, her *possibilities* have to be defined: what skews the issues so much is that she is reduced to what she was, while the question concerns her capacities.[38]

Beauvoir continues: "Her [woman's] capacities manifest themselves clearly only when they have been realized" (ibid.).

In ancient narratives and tropes, we also glimpse depictions of human life as susceptible to being changed (for good and for ill), as situated, and as lived and shaped among thresholds of transformation. Genesis 32 tells of Jacob wrestling through the night with a mysterious stranger at the ford of the Jabbock. Jacob is injured and marked by the encounter, but he prevails and secures a blessing. He comes to recognize the face of God in the stranger. We might say that Jacob is depicted as not only being susceptible to being harmed but also to striving (conation), blessing (affection), and revelation/(re)cognition. In the New Testament, the Apostle Paul combines images of the human as created from the earth with those found in Jeremiah's prophetic warnings of judgment to portray a community that bears treasure in earthen vessels, "clay jars" as the New Revised Standard Version has it (2 Cor 4.7). This human pottery is capable of being shattered and also of bearing the grace and glory of God. Like the narrative of Jacob wrestling, the trope of earthen vessels reverberates through the history of Jewish and Christian thought as theologians and preachers draw on them to interpret the relation between human and divine agency and among affliction, divine revelation, and human knowing.[39]

Insofar as these later examples also portray what we now call vulnerability, they not only *enflesh* it in Jacob's injury and transformation and in the persecution of early Christians and their ability to bear grace and glory, they *emplace* it. We, the readers of these texts, encounter the possibilities and threats of being changed with Jacob at the ford of the Jabbock and through Paul's address to the community at Corinth. In contrast to the abstractness of some contemporary discourse of intersection and locatedness, these are places, albeit still thickly metaphorical, that are richly imagined and concretely encountered in "fleshy" ways. Hips are displaced from their sockets; clay crumbles or endures.

5 conclusion: vulnerability and the aliveness of life

In *The Second Sex*, Beauvoir attempts to reset the *querelles des femmes*, which she casts as quibbling about what women are like, to a genuine question about what is possible. "What skews the issues so much is that she is reduced to what she was, while the question concerns her capacities," as she put it in the paragraph I cited above. Pamela Sue Anderson argued that the question of capability is (still) the right question for thinking about "enhancing life." In fact, most of the pages of *The Second Sex* chronicle some of the many ways and the many lived situations in which women's capacities are reduced – woman's "wings are cut, and then she is blamed for not knowing how to fly," as Beauvoir puts it.[40] Anderson focuses on that first threshold, occasionally implying something like the second meaning of threshold, a magnitude or intensity of becoming beyond capability. For Beauvoir, possibilities of transcendence, genuine mutuality, and creativity are always on the horizon, if often defeated. Beauvoir concludes the paragraph: "the fact is also that when one considers a being who is transcendence and surpassing [*dépassement*], it is never possible to close the books."[41]

To consider what might enhance – or, conversely, endanger – life, one must be able to picture "life" capaciously. I approach this challenge as a theologian, and through condensed theological symbols more than philosophical concepts. The possibility of human creatures being changed so radically that they become something new – for good or for ill – has long been a topic for theologians. The difficulty of accounting for persons and communities being changed in profoundly negative or positive ways is, effectively, the subject matter in long debates about the relation of nature and grace, the devastation of sin, the power of sacraments, possibilities of social transformation, and justification and sanctification. I first turned to the ideas of vulnerability and glory to interpret the biblical trope of treasure in earthen vessels (clay jars), which itself recasts the language of being earthen creatures on whom and through whom the spirit breathes; call that an "earth-y potentiality."

I have argued elsewhere for an interpretation of vulnerability as the susceptibility to being changed, for good and for ill, and for the rejection of strategies of invulnerability (which have pervaded theology and religious institutions) in favor of a recognition of ambiguity and of lived possibilities of transformation and devastation. Whereas Anderson's project conceptualized a baseline threshold of capability, my own project has looked to the perception and symbolization of the fullness of creaturely life. I turn to a quasi-phenomenological and historical-theological account of "glory" to assist in this task. I have come to follow the second-century theologian Irenaeus, and to refer to glory as "the aliveness of life."

The aliveness of life is intertwined with creaturely vulnerability to being changed, and particularly to perishing. In her poem "Autumn Passage," Elizabeth Alexander considers her mother-in-law's dying, her "suffering, which is real," and how family and community attend to her as she is dying:

> For her glory
> that goes along with it,
>
> glory of grown children's vigil,
> communal fealty, glory
> of the body that operates
>
> even as it falls apart[42]

Here, "glory" is not separated from living. Alexander's poem offers analogies between a singular threshold at the end of life and decisive crossing points in other lives and forms of life.

Her mother-in-law's dying body manifests both suffering and glory in its last living. This picture contrasts with portrayals of human life that either do not admit ongoing creaturely susceptibility to being changed or else attempt to shield creatures from change with strategies of invulnerability.

The poem also attests to "other manifestations of glory," including, in lines I didn't cite, a "dazzling toddler" who displays the full reach of his young linguistic powers: "chrysanthemum," he says when asked for the name of a flower. Go any farther, though, and he would surely tumble over his large words into incoherence. Incoherence haunts other realities in this "autumn passage," including giant "September zucchini" and "other things too big" – such as a nation struggling with the immensity of "vanished skyscrapers." Likewise, the toddler's dying grandmother is at full capacity. Her body, her life, her person, cannot undergo more without turning into "something else."

In this poem and in general, glory signals a threshold where life seems to take on a magnificence that is not self-generated/generating. Correlatively, glory signals a threshold beyond which life may become diminished, begin to unravel, or become endangered. A ripe pear, fragrant with delicate sweetness, is on the cusp of decay. Its glorious taste depends on that threshold, not on the defeat of life cycle. The poem's "dazzling toddler" won't become more glorious when he masters the use of "eggplant" and "chrysanthemum" – but the full aliveness of his post-toddler self may become manifest in different ways.

This quality of aliveness is interconnected with intellection, affection, sensation, loyalty, bodily processes, relationships and social life (possibly also with vegetable life and the life of nations). What appears glorious? Not some sort of embellishment or something superadded to life. Not an invulnerable state beyond suffering and living. Rather, glory is intertwined with the vulnerability of all living things to being changed.

disclosure statement

No potential conflict of interest was reported by the author.

notes

I would like to express my gratitude to Pelagia Goulimari and the other organizers of the conference. With fondness and gratitude, I remember the pioneering and passionate work of Pamela Sue Anderson and her generous, unflagging collegiality. Thanks also to William Schweiker and Beverly Clack for their comments. My participation in the conference was partially supported by a grant from the John Templeton Foundation, via the Enhancing Life Project. The opinions expressed in this paper are indebted to these contexts and conversations, but are my own.

1 Simone de Beauvoir, *The Ethics of Ambiguity* [1948], trans. Bernard Frechtman (Philosophical Library; New York: Citadel, 1991) 9.

2 "Threshold for enhancing human life" and "key concepts" are phrases from Anderson's thesis statement of her Enhancing Life Project proposal. See the discussion of these terms and her proposal below.

3 Pamela Sue Anderson, "The Transformative Power of Vulnerability" (4 Feb. 2016), available at <http://enhancinglife.uchicago.edu/blog/the-transformative-power-of-vulnerability> (accessed 23 Dec. 2019).

4 See <http://enhancinglife.uchicago.edu> (accessed 23 Dec. 2019).

5 Pamela Sue Anderson, "Life-Giving Philosophy: A Q&A with Dr. Pamela Sue Anderson" (2 Feb. 2016), available at <http://enhancinglife.uchicago.edu/blog/life-giving-philosophy-a-q-and-a-with-dr-pamela-sue-anderso> (accessed 23 Dec. 2019).

6 See Pamela Sue Anderson, "Capability, Confidence and Creativity: Transforming the Concepts We Live By" in *The Enhancing Life Project: Scholars and Research Projects*, 2nd ed., eds. William Schweiker and Günter Thomas (n.p.: Enhancing Life Project, 2016) 12.

7 Ibid. See also Anderson's placement of a feminist philosophy of religion in relation to "conceptual and non-conceptual" philosophies in Pamela Sue

Anderson, *Re-visioning Gender in Philosophy of Religion: Reason, Love and Epistemic Locatedness* (Farnham: Ashgate, 2012), especially chapters 4, 6, 9.

8 Drawing on my previous account of vulnerability as the susceptibility to being changed, for good and for ill, I argued that "an adequate consideration of glory should illumine and be illumined by vulnerable life rather than obscure or divert attention from it." See Culp, "Glorious Life?" in Schweiker and Thomas 111; see also Culp, *Vulnerability and Glory: A Theological Account* (Louisville, KY: Westminster John Knox, 2010).

9 See, for example, Heike Springhart and Günter Thomas, eds., *Exploring Vulnerability* (Göttingen and Bristol, CT: Vandenhoeck, 2017). The volume came out of an international symposium entitled "Vulnerability – A New Focus for Theological and Interdisciplinary Anthropology" organized by Springhart and Thomas at the International Academic Forum Heidelberg (IWH), 6–9 September 2015. Contributors include Enhancing Life Project participants Springhart, Thomas, Culp, Bieler, Schweiker, and Dean Bell, Michael Hogue, Stephen Lakkis, among others. Although Professor Anderson did not participate in the symposium, her 2017 essay "Arguing for 'Ethical' Vulnerability: Towards a Politics of Care?" (henceforth cited as "'Ethical' Vulnerability") is included in the volume (147–62). See also, for example, the work of Enhancing Life scholar Michael Ing, *The Vulnerability of Integrity in Early Confucian Thought* (New York: Oxford UP, 2017).

10 We focused on chapters 1, 4, and 6 of Judith Butler, *Notes Toward a Performative Theory of Assembly* (Cambridge, MA: Harvard UP, 2015). See Anderson, "'Ethical' Vulnerability," where she frames this line of inquiry, and my discussion of it below. Her published chapter is slightly revised from the paper she presented at our Wuppertal meeting, and that paper was already revised from a January 2016 lecture at Oxford Brookes University on "Vulnerability and the Politics of Care." Relatedly, note Anderson's Q&A, published on 2 February 2016 and cited above, which revisits "care" in relation to "life-giving philosophy."

11 This section offers a close interpretation of Anderson's proposal as published in Schweiker and Thomas 11–23. The executive summary explains:

> "Enhancing Capable Life: Transformative Change, Confidence and Creativity" intends to articulate a transformed conceptual scheme, with new concepts for humans to live by, for an ontology of becoming. First of all, I stipulate a concept of capability, which is *a priori*: we are created capable. This capability is generic, serving as a threshold for enhancing human life. Second, the concept of vulnerability is grasped *a posteriori*, capturing the precariousness of life as experienced daily; as vulnerable we become undone by one another in grief, rage and desire. Third, the concept of life refers to a continuous process of change; when we are undone by loss a transformative change is not about our choice, but our becoming. Fourth, confidence is a social phenomenon: being utterly changed by grief, we lose confidence in our own capability as bereaved. However, capability is not contingent; we cannot lose it. Yet it can become obscured; if so, it will need to be enhanced. Human enhancement is "measured" by the equalizing threshold of capability, shared by each subject as a birthright. With an engaged grasp of capability, our conceptual scheme can fill out what are variable, human capacities for affection, conation and cognition; these capacities vary according to our social worlds and our bodily specificities. So, we are all capable, even when we are vulnerable and lacking in confidence; enhancing capable life is always possible, not as something we achieve, but as something intuited as the ontological condition for a creative process of life together.

The executive summary is available at <http://enhancinglife.uchicago.edu/people/capability-confidence-creativity-transforming-the-concepts-we-live-by> (accessed 23 Dec. 2019).

12 Anderson cites Judith Butler, *Precarious Life: The Powers of Mourning and Violence* (London and New York: Verso, 2004) 21–23. See the discussion below.

13 Anderson cites Elizabeth Grosz, *Becoming Undone: Darwinian Reflections on Life, Politics, and Art* (Durham, NC: Duke UP, 2011), especially chapter 2, "Deleuze, Bergson, and the Concept of Life."

14 Paul Fiddes, "Editorial Note" in Pamela Sue Anderson, "Creating a New Imaginary for Love in Religion," ed. Paul S. Fiddes, in *Love and*

Vulnerability: Thinking with Pamela Sue Anderson, ed. Pelagia Goulimari, Spec. issue of *Angelaki: Journal of the Theoretical Humanities* 25.1–2 (2020) 47.

15 Much of the theological and devotional background to vulnerability also implies positive transformation in spite of or through loss. For instance, at Anderson's memorial service we sang hymns about excelling divine love coming down in joy and suffusing earthen creatures, fallible, sinful, and stubborn as they may be, rather than of Christ's scorn and affliction.

16 James W. Alexander, trans., "O Sacred Head, Now Wounded," public domain. The hymn opens: "O sacred head, now wounded, with grief and shame weighed down; now scornfully surrounded with thorns, thine only crown; how pale though art with anguish, with sore abuse and scorn!" This 1830 translation of the lyric by Alexander, an American Presbyterian, is well known in the United States and is included in many major hymnals.

17 See <https://www.paulsimon.com/track/american-tune-6> (accessed 23 Dec. 2019).

18 Alexander, "O Sacred Head, Now Wounded."

19 Butler, *Precarious Life* 25. Despite one's best efforts to persevere, "one is undone, in the face of the other, by the touch, by the scent, by the feel, by the prospect of the touch, by the memory of the feel" (24). Cf. Augustine, *Confessions* 10.6, and Colin Thompson's hymn setting of this text, as sung at Anderson's memorial service.

20 Butler, *Precarious Life* 21. Anderson cites this passage in her Enhancing Life proposal. Butler refers to a "common human vulnerability, one that emerges with life itself." Butler is arguing for an alternative conception of the human to that of autonomy (and also to some versions of sociality and relationality) that does not de-politicize the possibilities and realities of dispossession as individual psychic loss. Butler depicts a "primary condition" of vulnerability that "is not a deprivation" but rather the way "in which we are, from the start, even prior to individuation itself and, by virtue of bodily requirements, given over to some set of primary others" (31).

21 Anderson, "'Ethical' Vulnerability" 161.

22 Ibid. See note 26 below.

23 Butler, *Precarious Life* 24.

24 Ibid. 20; *Notes* 209.

25 Butler, *Notes* 210.

26 Ibid. Butler discusses the possibility of morality and the performance of value in chapter 6, "Can One Lead a Good Life in a Bad Life?," with "bad" here meaning a life that is effaced by exploitation and the "unequal distribution of vulnerability."

27 Anderson, "'Ethical' Vulnerability" 162. She writes:

> Butler might be arguing for an ontology – not an ethics – of embodied vulnerability; but this is not clear to me at least, because vulnerability manifests itself in highly materially and socially specific ways; so, basically, vulnerability does not look like the same thing – universally – for everyone. However, even if Butler is unable to establish an ontological vulnerability, which is a universal condition for all of life; she equally does not establish an ethical, or ethics of, vulnerability. (161)

28 Ibid. 149 and *passim*.

29 Ibid. 153.

30 Ibid. 147.

31 See Simone de Beauvoir, *Le Deuxième Sexe: Les Faits et les mythes*, Tome I (Paris: Gallimard, 1949); *The Second Sex*, trans. Constance Borde and Sheila Malovany-Chevallier (New York: Knopf, 2010).

32 Cf. also Beauvoir's choice of *Destin* for the title of the first section, implying a critique of theories that assign a fate and way of being to woman/women, that is, a predestination, while also suggesting (positively) that there is a potentiality for directionality in human existence.

33 *The Second Sex* 46.

34 Pamela Sue Anderson, "The Subject's Loss of Self-Confidence in its Own Ability to Understand Itself" in *Life and Philosophy: Essays to Honour Alan Montefiore on his 85th Birthday*, eds. Catherine Audard-Montefiore et al. (Oxford: FEP, 2011) n. pag.

35 "To imagine a space" is from Anderson's project proposal in Schweiker and Thomas 14. One might compare, favorably, how Anderson turns to vividly imaged spaces at points in *Re-visioning Gender in Philosophy of Religion*, for example to

Adrienne Rich's image of the sunken wreck from her poem "Diving into the Wreck," in the Preface ix–xi, and the image of the descending glow of the day on the water from Virginia Woolf's novel *The Waves* 25–26.

36 Toril Moi, "What is a Woman?" in *What is a Woman and Other Essays* (Oxford: Oxford UP, 2001) 65. See also Iris Marion Young, *On Female Body Experience: "Throwing Like a Girl" and Other Essays* (Oxford: Oxford UP, 2005), especially chapter 1.

37 Moi 81. See Young's discussion of this passage on 18–19.

38 *The Second Sex* 45.

39 See Culp, *Vulnerability and Glory*, for this history of interpretation and for a corresponding construal of theology as involving condensed symbols that take shape in and alter changing sensibilities and interpretations.

40 *The Second Sex* 645.

41 Ibid. 46.

42 Elizabeth Alexander, "Autumn Passage" in *Crave Radiance: New and Selected Poems 1999–2010* (Minneapolis: Graywolf, 2010) 174. Excerpts published by permission of the author.

tapping into an unfinished conversation

In her late work Pamela Sue Anderson became increasingly interested in a concept of vulnerability that is not deficiency-oriented nor focused solely on the negative effects of the capacity to experience psychological and physical harm. She emphasized that "vulnerability is not merely an openness to being wounded; it is not a mere wound which needs to be healed; a weakness which requires strengthening; or a liability to harm or a disability which makes for dependency."[2]

Anderson's philosophical and ethical deliberations can be situated in a larger, ongoing debate on a revised concept of vulnerability that is occurring in various disciplines. I join the conversation as a practical theologian with a particular interest in rethinking theological anthropology and religious practice through a concept of vulnerability that draws on phenomenological insights as well as critical theory.[3]

According to Anderson, an ethical approach to vulnerability ought to be grounded in

> a positive openness to self- and other-affection rather than an exposure to violence only. This implies (a capability for) openness to change through mutual affection. In other words, an openness to a new future as a dynamic process (in becoming) will transform, and always be transforming, life.[4]

She argued that from this openness to mutual affection a relational accountability for a politics of restorative justice could emerge that would overcome the gendered debates in moral philosophy that situate an ethics of care over against an ethics of justice. In her essay "Towards a

andrea bieler

EXPLORING AFFECTIVITY
an unfinished conversation with pamela sue anderson[1]

New Philosophical Imaginary" she claimed that unless we think in reciprocal terms about affectivity we will continue to divide the world into the vulnerable who are dependent and weak and the invulnerable who are strong and care-giving. This division, however, is the basis for a "paternalism that decisively damages the life enhancing capability of the vulnerable."[5]

My final conversation with Pamela circled around a phenomenological exploration of affectivity as a major univocal feature of fundamental vulnerability.[6] We discussed vulnerability as an openness towards the world that finds its gestalt in the reciprocal dynamics of being affected and affecting others. We considered this general claim as a starting point for further deliberations on the dynamics of affectivity. Due to Pamela's illness we never had a chance to continue our common exploration.

In this essay, I immerse myself once again in this unfinished conversation by reflecting further on the dynamics of affectivity. I begin with insights from the work of Maurice Merleau-Ponty and continue by drawing on the work of Thomas Fuchs. In contrast to Anderson's approach, my phenomenological exploration resides in the sphere of pre-ethical deliberation, since it engages with the basic felt sense of embodied living in the world and with the rise of affections prior to any moral or ethical reflection. Also, my phenomenological deliberations strive to inspire theological ponderings.

There is another issue we did not have a chance to discuss further. Following Mary Midgley, Pamela Anderson was interested in exploring the myths we live by that order and direct our thoughts and actions with regard to vulnerability and thus to affectivity. In this context she critically engaged with some tropes of the Jewish-Christian tradition. I will revisit her thoughts on this matter and seek to make an alternative proposal.

Tapping into these unfinished conversations with Pamela, a heightened awareness of the finitude of our lives and the fragmented character of our thoughts arises as one more meditation on the meaning of vulnerability.

affectivity in phenomenological terms

In what follows I propose to understand affectivity as a reciprocal dynamic in which the objectified experience of having a body and the subjective sensation of embodied aliveness constantly intertwine. This creates an oscillation in which I am not able to know my embodied self fully, let alone the other person whom I am encountering. It is in this twilight of not-knowing in which the dynamics of being affected and affecting others occur.

This reciprocal dynamic of affectivity is embedded in a sense of being alive, in existential feelings as background states and in emotions that are driven by affective intentionality and certain action tendencies. These dimensions intersect and overlap in the lived experience. They oscillate as certain aspects are highlighted at particular times. Distinguishing these dimensions helps to nuance our theoretical understanding of affectivity.

Following Maurice Merleau-Ponty, we can say that our bodies are living sensory circuits that constantly relate to others and to a particular social and physical environment. We thus need to explore the reciprocity that is embedded in affectivity. In this vein, the world reaches us or, rather, crashes into us. Merleau-Ponty talks about an ontology of the flesh (French: *la chair*), which describes a rather muted relationship to the world that exists beyond our conscious intentionality.[7] By flesh Merleau-Ponty describes an intercorporeal perception characterized by continuity: the flesh of my body (*Leib-Körper*) is connected with the flesh of the other and with the material world I find myself in. This continuity of flesh fundamentally grounds the necessary precondition of perception. It evokes a reflexivity by which the individual experiences herself as seeing and being seen, as perceiving and being perceived.[8]

The affectable body is the medium through which to sense and perceive the world. As an integrating medium it is not the sum of nature and mind but participates in both. It oscillates between a felt sense of embodied aliveness (*Leib-Sein*) and the perception of the body as object (*Körper-Haben*).[9] The felt sense of embodied aliveness can express itself in a heightened awareness like in moments of physical pain, fear or sexual pleasure. It can also show itself in more subtle senses of discomfort or of feeling well. In moments of modest comfort, the perception of this oscillation might be unrecognized and moves into the background.

The sense of having a body manifests itself as an experience of objectification. This sense of body objectification might arise, for example, through the gaze of others or the diagnostic approach in a hospital. It can be highly ambiguous: a patient's life might be rescued through diagnostic procedures while simultaneously a sense of alienation from her body arises. The gaze of another might be friendly, moved by attraction, or, negatively, taxing. Most of the time this awareness hits a person as an embodied felt sense before it is reflected upon. As such it is a differentiated unity of the active "I" and the passive "me." Amidst this oscillation the perception of the body is fluid, partial and never static.[10] I am thus not able to be entirely aware of myself, and am thus unable to perceive myself fully.

This is obviously also true for my perception of the other person that I am encountering. Intercorporeal affectivity happens in the twilight, as it were; it creates a sensitivity that moves between knowing and not-knowing, recognition and misperception. Accordingly, encountering a person needs to be accompanied by respect for the fact that our perception of one another is always partial, fluid, and changing. This fragmented grasp is the basis for the reflection of profound alterity. The awareness that one cannot fully perceive the other can thus be understood as a prerequisite of further ethical deliberation. It can be conceived as an element of an apophatic anthropology that ponders ways of not-knowing the other as the foundation for respect.

There are various strands in the Jewish-Christian tradition that have emphasized the topic of not-knowing in relation to divine otherness. In this vein, cultivating a faithful self is accompanied by a meditation on the ways of not-knowing God. However, Christian theology has been less interested in developing an anthropology in which not-knowing the other person fully is valued as being fundamental for an ethics of care, a conception of love and justice, and basic reflection on what it means to encounter others.[11] The theologian Mayra Rivera hints at this direction by emphasizing that an analogous relationship with the human other can be informed by apophaticism. The other should then be imagined as "neither univocal as a thing in the Totality of my world, nor equivocal as the absolute exterior either."[12] Grasping the other fully is thus neither possible nor desirable. Simultaneously, claiming a wholly apophatic stance is not appropriate either.

If we take these basic deliberations into account, we can attend in a more nuanced way to the reciprocity of being moved and moving, being touched and touching, being overcome or overwhelmed by affection and loving others. This reciprocity resonates with the experience of being undone by the other as in the experience of loss and grief that Pamela Anderson was reflecting upon.

The described reciprocal dynamics of affectivity as a dimension of vulnerability are embedded in at least three layers: (a) in the multifaceted feeling of being alive, as it is articulated in the felt sense of embodied aliveness; (b) in existential feelings that point to states or moods of how one finds oneself in the world; and (c) in emotions that imply intentionality and a tendency towards action.

The embodied sense of aliveness exists as the backdrop of our cognitive reflections, our actions, and our directed, intentional feelings. Most of the time this sense is unnoticed and unvoiced. Thomas Fuchs states that this embodied sense of aliveness is situated "at the threshold of life and experience, between *Leben* and *Erleben* […] The tacit feeling of life merges in these special and changing emotions without further ado."[13]

Our *Erleben* moves through different states and intensities that range from weak and diminished to heightened and intense. These qualities are captured by the German word *Befinden*. This relates to the lived body as a domain of diffuse ease or unease, relaxation or tension, freshness and vigour, or tiredness and exhaustion:

> These feelings with their basic polarity of *Wohlbefinden* and *Missbefinden* (well- and ill-being) may be regarded as indicators of our state of life in its ups and downs. It can also be subsumed under the term *vitality*. *Wohlbefinden*, such as in freshness or vigour, lets things appear closer, more interesting, and accessible, whereas *Missbefinden*, as in fatigue or sickness, lends a monotonous or vaguely repellent color to the surroundings.[14]

The body functions as the medium with which to experience the world as it oscillates between *Wohlbefinden* and *Missbefinden*.

Particular feelings of vitality can be described as a powerful force that influences and pervades most feelings and perceptions while also structuring experiences in terms of openness and hopeful possibilities. Fuchs states that in feelings of exhaustion or weakness the opposite happens: a sense of distance, numbness, and alienation from one's environment may arise.[15]

The feeling of aliveness in its various shades is connected to the second layer that constitutes affectivity which I have called existential feelings. Existential feelings converge on a basic level with the feeling of being alive and its antonyms: feeling dead, alien to oneself or not fully oneself, feeling like in a dream (derealization), or feeling disconnected from the world vs. fully present to the moment.

Matthew Ratcliffe has coined the term *existential feelings*, drawing on Heidegger's concept of moods. Existential feelings are background states that express how one finds oneself in the world. While Heidegger focused mainly on angst and boredom as existential feelings, there are actually many more possible expressions. Ratcliffe elaborates:

> People sometimes talk of feeling alive, dead, distant, detached, dislodged, estranged, isolated, otherworldly, indifferent to everything, overwhelmed, suffocated, cut off, lost, disconnected, out of sorts, not oneself, out of touch with things, out of it, not quite with it, separate, in harmony with things, at peace with things or part of things. There are references to feelings of unreality, heightened existence, surreality, familiarity, unfamiliarity, strangeness, isolation, emptiness, belonging, being at home in the world, being at one with things, significance, insignificance, and the list goes on. People also sometimes report that "things just don't feel right," "I'm not with it today," "I just feel a bit removed from it all at the moment," "I feel out of it," or "it feels strange."[16]

While Heidegger had the tendency to focus more on the negatively connoted existential feelings, Ratcliffe also makes room for phenomena like feeling at peace, belonging or being in harmony with things. Yet his list also tends towards the negative side. However, for a phenomenology of affectivity it seems significant to acknowledge that the feeling of being fully alive can also be expressed in joy or hopefulness, a sense of freedom, in attentiveness, in warmth and in brightness.

In the Jewish-Christian traditions such existential feelings are expressed in various ways. The psalms, for instance, offer poetic language that gives room for the feelings of freedom and vastness, constraint and sorrow, uncanniness or certainty, belonging or uprootedness, numbness or alertness. Excerpts from Psalm 31 may serve as an example as they are filled with such images that express existential feelings:

> [3] You are indeed my rock and my fortress;
>   for your name's sake lead me and guide me,
> [4] take me out of the net that is hidden for me,
>   for you are my refuge.
> [5] Into your hand I commit my spirit;
>   you have redeemed me, O Lord, faithful God.
> [8b] […] [Y]ou have set my feet in a broad place.
> [9] I am in distress; my eye wastes away from grief,
>   my soul and body also.
> [10] For my life is spent with sorrow,
>   and my years with sighing […]
> [12] I have passed out of mind like one who is dead;
>   I have become like a broken vessel […]
> [16] Let your face shine upon your servant;
>   save me in your steadfast love […]
> [19] O how abundant is your goodness
>   that you have laid up for those who fear you,
>   and accomplished for those who take refuge in you,
>   in the sight of everyone!
> [20] In the shelter of your presence you hide them from human plots;
>   you hold them safe under your shelter from contentious tongues.
> [21] Blessed be the Lord,
>   for he has wondrously shown his steadfast

love to me
when I was beset as a city under siege.[17]

This psalm conveys a variety of existential feelings ranging from trust (vv. 3–5), freedom (v. 8b), gratitude, and hopefulness (v. 19) to deep distress, grief, and feeling dead (vv. 9–12). It thus expresses different degrees of vitality and feeling fully alive in relationship to the divine. Simultaneously the psalmist finds herself in the fragile states that are evoked in a hostile and alienating environment. Although these texts derive from a long-gone historical context, they have the power to immediately express deeply rooted feelings. For those who pray with and through them, these words shape a connection to the world and to the divine. They offer a language for something that is often difficult to express.

Ratcliffe emphasizes that existential feelings constitute a tacit sense of relatedness and offer a blueprint for interpreting experiences by means of an undergirding structure of anticipation. This includes the perception of possibilities that take the form either of habitual certainties or of uncertainty and doubt. In the first example he offers, a person is confident that the ground beneath her feet will not shake and that she will thus not fall into a hole. In the second example, a person experiences uncertainty about whether the person that appears in the dark might be dangerous.[18] In Psalm 31 habitual certainties are anticipated and expressed as trust in God, who is depicted as rock and fortress, as refuge and hiding place. These are juxtaposed with anticipated threats that cause fear and yet also stimulate trust in God.

Besides the dimension of anticipation, existential feelings can also differ in terms of duration. They might linger in the background in relation to certain events or they may exist as a constant sense of being in the world and with others over a longer period of time.

Fuchs stresses that there are existential feelings that are attached to one's self-perception in terms of mental and somatic health: I feel strong or weak, alert or tired, depressed or happy. Or in the words of the psalmist: "I am in distress; my eye wastes away from grief, my soul and body also […] I have passed out of mind like one who is dead; I have become like a broken vessel" (vv. 9–12).

And finally, some existential feelings have a social dimension as when a sense of belonging is generated: I feel at home in a certain place or in the company of old friends. The social fabric of existential feelings also comes to the fore in the ways a person relates to others – either on the basis of general trust or of suspicion.

Existential feelings represent the more diffuse domain of affectivity in which we feel affected by moods and atmospheres that surround us. These have an imprint on how we experience ourselves in the world and in relation to others. They cannot be comprehended in causal modes. We can thus distinguish existential feelings that are rather diffuse, in terms of object relations, from emotions that are intentionally related to persons, situations, or objects.

Emotions are thus the third dimension in the phenomenology of affectivity that I seek to sketch out. Thomas Fuchs identifies three aspects of emotions: affective intentionality, bodily resonance, and action tendency.[19]

Emotions that are driven by affective intentionality tend to encompass ways of weighing the significance of a person or a situation and checking the relevance for the subject. Fuchs refers to James G. Gibson's concept of affective affordances according to which persons or things are experienced as significant, attractive, repulsive, etc. These value judgements should not be understood in terms of propositional attitudes or pure cognitive judgements since they reflect the subjective emotional involvement of the one who is affected.[20] As Fuchs writes:

> Affective intentionality is thus twofold: it discloses an evaluative quality of a given situation as well as the feeling of a person's own state in the face of it. I am attracted by this person (world-reference) might come with a feeling of aliveness (self-reference).[21]

In addition to affective intentionality, Fuchs highlights the action tendency that resides in emotions. Emotions (from the Latin *e-movere*: to move out) encompass the entire body in its moving capacities. Fear might imply the impulse to flee or to hide. Attraction holds a tendency for action towards another person and the desire to be closer, while repulsion might result in a movement in which one turns around and moves away.

Correspondingly, emotions can be characterized in terms of action readiness, according to the different patterns of action which they induce: "approach (e.g., desire), avoidance (e.g., fear), being-with (enjoyment, confidence), attending (interest), rejecting (disgust), non-attending (indifference), agonistic (anger), interrupting (shock, surprise), dominating (arrogance), and submitting (humility, resignation)."[22]

Action readiness is expressed in four basic movements that carry certain emotional qualities. For instance, in affection one tends to move towards the other, while in fear one moves oneself away from the other. Anger or disgust implies the action tendency of pushing the other away from oneself, while when we desire someone we seek to draw the other closer to oneself. These action tendencies are related to the gestures of giving, escaping, removing, and getting.[23]

> These basic movements are connected to a bodily felt sense of expansion or contraction, relaxation or tension, openness or constriction, etc. In anger, for example, one feels a tendency of expansion toward an object in order to push it away from self. In affection, one feels a relaxation, opening, and emanation toward an object or person. Emotions can thus be experienced as the directionality of one's potential movement, although this movement is not necessarily expressed in the outer physical space.[24]

Let me summarize my brief exploration of a phenomenology of affectivity as a basic feature of vulnerability: I began with an apophatic approach to the reciprocal dynamics that are implied in affectivity. Proceeding from this proposal I identified three dimensions of affectivity: the sense of being alive, existential feelings as background states and emotions that are driven by affective intentionality, and certain movement tendencies. These dimensions intersect and overlap in the lived experience. They oscillate as certain aspects are highlighted at particular times. They all contribute to an understanding of affectivity as a central aspect of fundamental vulnerability. They drive the human ability to relate to others in love or in life-diminishing ways. It is useful, however, to distinguish them heuristically in order to develop a more nuanced concept of affectivity.

Besides this phenomenological exploration of vulnerability, it is also useful to reflect on the meaning of affectivity in hermeneutical terms as I pick up Pamela Anderson's proposal to explore in more depth the myths we live by.

the myths we live by: divine affectivity

Anderson refers to Mary Midgley's suggestion to focus on "symbolic stories which play a crucial role in our imaginative and intellectual life by expressing the patterns that underlie our thought."[25] She judged a personal as well as a mythical depiction of God to be insufficient for reflecting on love in the context of religion:

> I have thus found both of these personal and mystical conceptions of "the one God of love" inadequate for practices of neighbour-love; each "myth" falls short of other contemporary accounts of human affections and spiritual practices by moral and evolutionary psychologists, neuroscientists and affect theorists. Actual contemporary religious practices of love are what I would like to explore: we need to discover how love might be performed openly and creatively, and how love is (or has been) imagined.[26]

From a theological point of view, I do not find Anderson's rushed shift from an exploration of the doctrine of God to the realm of moral behaviour fully convincing. Instead, I find an interesting resonance between the phenomenological reflection on human affectivity and embodiment, which was introduced above, and the biblical imagery that portrays the passions and compassion of God. I thus gravitate towards probing biblical myths and how they reflect phenomena of human and divine affectivity. I wish to point to two aspects: the potential of anthropopathic God talk that disconnects divine love from omnipotent control and the counter-intuitive approach regarding affectivity in ethical terms.

From the diverse depictions of how God relates to God's creation and to God's people metaphorical language emerges that portrays divine affectivity. For instance, in the Hebrew Bible we find depictions of a God who cries and who has a lamenting heart (Jer. 16.9–11). God shows remorse in Hosea, and passionate love and disappointment in the face of lost hopes. In particular, the prophet Hosea depicts a movable God in relation to the cosmos of divine emotions.

In this vein, the anthropopathic depiction of God's passion and desire, such as love and tenderness, as well as the wrath of God or the depiction of divine remorse, are of special interest. A range of affections such as disgust and repulsion in the face of injustice and idolatry are portrayed, as are rage and jealousy, when it comes to Israel's breaking of the covenant. The dynamic heart of God pictures the ambivalent cosmos of divine passions and emotions (Jer. 31.20). These ambiguities do not resemble divine arbitrariness yet rather the process of divine self-reassurance that is embedded in a reciprocal relationship with God's people. The prophet Hosea offers a divine soliloquy that expresses divine changeability in affective terms: "My heart recoils within me; my compassion grows warm and tender. I will not execute my fierce anger" (Hos. 11.8 f.).

Accordingly, the image of the moved mover comes to the fore, the one who pours out her or his affection into the created world. Divine affectivity is depicted in anthropopathic language. It is embedded in the reciprocal dynamics of being moved and moving, of being touched and touching. The emotions of God can be portrayed as emotions with action tendency, not as ontological attributes that rest in themselves. The intersection of existential feelings and emotions comes to the fore in the manifold depictions of Jesus' compassion with ordinary people as he is confronted with their suffering – their illness, hunger or social marginalization (Mark 6.34; 1.41). This empathy is situated in the flesh, thus in the embodied sensing of the world. It is expressed with the Greek term *splanchnizomai*, which implies the action tendency of movement towards an other.

In some instances, Jesus is depicted as being moved and affected by the suffering of individuals and groups prior to any rational or ethical deliberation. Jesus senses the collective atmosphere. Jesus is also affected, for example, by the immediate physical encounter with the bleeding woman, or by the challenge of the leper who shouts at him: "if you want, you can cleanse me" (Mark 1.40). In the story of the multiplication of the bread, Jesus' sense that the crowd feels lost and hungry moves him to action.

How shall we read these anthropopathic depictions of God's relation to the world through existential feelings as well as through action-oriented, intentional emotions? Abraham Joshua Heschel suggests that we understand the depiction of divine striving towards love not by means of unmoved and detached mercy but through a relating that is open to affectivity as one dimension of vulnerability.[27]

The incarnation can be depicted as the divine fall into human vulnerability. It is moved by the divine desire to be affected by creation, in all its ambiguities and risks. Accordingly, the gospels give witness to how this entanglement in vulnerability unfolds in the stories of healing and table fellowship, yet also in the trauma of the cross and in the trauma of the resurrection.

When it comes to moral behaviour, we see another strand unfolding. For instance, loving the enemy has to do with acting counter-intuitively, *para physin*, against nature as it were, with regard to expressions of human affectivity. An example can be found in Jesus' demand in the Sermon on the Mount to turn the other cheek if someone hits you. A reframing of impulses is articulated here – a reorientation of affects that is accompanied by reversing common action tendencies. An alternative framework is offered that strives towards an ethics of love. It begins with reorienting human affectivity and asks how we find ourselves in the world and in relation to others. It suggests that reorienting our affects this way gestures towards the practice of love that is not a disembodied fulfilment of a divine command but rather an embodied exercise that transcends self-destructive victimization by creating new possibilities to overcome the logic of violence.

On a similar note, in the early Church Christians were instructed in worship to exchange a sign of peace by kissing each other. This liturgical instruction can also be understood as a counter-intuitive practice which ought to assist in reframing the religious habitus of people who lived in a highly stratified and segregated society in which people from different social classes and genders would normally never kiss each other.

Let me conclude: the phenomenological exploration of the reciprocal dynamics of being affected and affecting others helped to nuance an understanding of affectivity as a basic feature of fundamental vulnerability. In a second move, these considerations offered a helpful frame for thinking about the myths we live by. I focused especially on the theological imagination that is inspired by the Jewish-Christian traditions by pointing to the metaphors and stories that reflect divine affectivity and compassion as well as to the practices that redirect impulses that emerge from being affected by an other.

As my ponderings come to a close, I wonder how Pamela would have responded to my ideas. It seems somehow inappropriate, however, to conclude an unfinished conversation with speculations about her assumed reactions. I would rather not do this. Writing this essay while knowing that there will be no response cannot lead to a well-rounded conclusion but rather provokes a rough ending – in the apophatic spirit that expresses respect, sadness, and gratitude in the face of incompleteness.

disclosure statement

No potential conflict of interest was reported by the author.

notes

1 I encountered Pamela Sue Anderson in the Enhancing Life Project in the summer of 2015. I found her to be a scholar with a particular gift to develop ideas collaboratively. Pamela was an amazing listener who was willing to enter my cosmos of unfinished thoughts. Probably I fell short of being such a listener to her. I felt profound joy in the midst of our conversations. This joy still sticks with me when I think of her. I truly miss her collegial friendship. See <http://enhancinglife.uchicago.edu/blog/remembering-enhancing-life-scholar-pamela-sue-anderson> (accessed 27 Dec. 2019).

2 Pamela Sue Anderson, "Arguing for 'Ethical' Vulnerability: Towards a Politics of Care?" in *Exploring Vulnerability*, eds. Günter Thomas and Heike Springhart (Göttingen and Bristol, VT: Vandenhoeck, 2017) 147.

3 See Andrea Bieler, *Verletzliches Leben. Horizonte einer Theologie der Seelsorge* (Göttingen and Bristol, VT: Vandenhoeck, 2017) 147.

4 Anderson, "Arguing" 147.

5 Ibid.

6 In *Verletzliches Leben* I distinguish between fundamental vulnerability as the dimensions that are constitutive for all of human life and situational vulnerability that arises from particular circumstances (23–66).

7 Maurice Merleau-Ponty, *The Visible and the Invisible*, trans. Alphonso Lingis (Evanston: Northwestern UP, 1968) 136–42.

8 See also Erinn Gilson, *The Ethics of Vulnerability: A Feminist Analysis of Social Life and Practice*, Routledge

Studies in Ethics and Moral Theory (New York: Routledge, 2014) 26: 131–32.

9 See Andrea Bieler, "Enhancing Vulnerable Life: Phenomenological and Practical Theological Explorations" in *Exploring Vulnerability* 71–82. See Bieler, *Verletzliches Leben* 27–32.

10 See Bieler, "Enhancing Vulnerable Life" 78.

11 Chris Boesel and Catherine Keller, eds., *Apophatic Bodies: Negative Theology, Incarnation, and Relationality* (New York: Fordham UP, 2010).

12 Mayra Rivera, *The Touch of Transcendence: A Postcolonial Theology of God* (Louisville, KY: Westminster John Knox, 2007) 73.

13 Thomas Fuchs, "The Phenomenology of Affectivity" in *Oxford Handbook of Philosophy and Psychiatry*, eds. K.W.M. Fulford et al. (Oxford: Oxford UP, 2015) 2, doi:10.1093/oxfordhb/9780199579563.013.0038.

14 Ibid.

15 Ibid. 2–3.

16 Matthew Ratcliffe, *Feelings of Being: Phenomenology, Psychiatry and the Sense of Reality* (Oxford: Oxford UP, 2008) 68.

17 Psalm 31, New Revised Standard Version Bible (1989).

18 See Ratcliffe 67.

19 See Fuchs 7.

20 See ibid.

21 Ibid.

22 Ibid.

23 See ibid. 8.

24 Ibid.

25 Pamela Sue Anderson, "Creating a New Imaginary for Love in Religion," ed. Paul S. Fiddes, in *Love and Vulnerability: Thinking with Pamela Sue Anderson*, ed. Pelagia Goulimari, Spec. issue of *Angelaki: Journal of the Theoretical Humanities* 25.1–2 (2020) 47]. She refers to Mary Midgley, *The Ethical Primate: Humans, Freedom and Morality* (London: Routledge, 1994) 109, and *The Myths We Live by* (London: Routledge, 2004).

26 Anderson, "Creating a New Imaginary for Love in Religion" 48.

27 Abraham Joshua Heschel, *The Prophets* [1962] (New York: HarperCollins, 2001).

introduction

Vulnerability has many forms and facets. It is often seen or experienced as a dark situation in which one finds oneself, a situation which is marked by shame, fear, violence, oppression, stigma and marginalization. But this is not what vulnerability is all about. In this paper I wish to contribute to recent endeavours which seek to reconceptualize and live out vulnerable life in ways which oppose and resist dark, oppressing views and assumptions about vulnerability – views and assumptions that are life-smothering. Such endeavours re-claim vulnerability and explore its empowering, life-enhancing possibilities to be and live well.[1] The paper contributes to these endeavours by offering a phenomenological-ontological approach which suggests that vulnerability pervades human life. On this account, vulnerability is not merely an accidental feature of human existence, a characteristic of certain groups of people, but an essential aspect of our finite nature.

An adequate philosophical reconceptualization of vulnerability involves multiple levels of discussion including ontological, phenomenological, epistemological, ethical and political inquiries. As I mentioned, I focus on certain phenomenological-ontological aspects of vulnerability. I develop a conception of vulnerability as openness which is understood not only as exposure to being wounded but also as openness to transformation and change, which are possible through resilience.[2] The notion of resilience has increasingly come to the fore in numerous recent discussions about human vulnerabilities, but a philosophical systematic account of this concept is still lacking. This paper begins to

roxana baiasu

THE OPENNESS OF VULNERABILITY AND RESILIENCE

address this and provides a starting point for a philosophical approach to resilience.

Different layers of vulnerability, some of which have been mentioned above, are interconnected. It could be argued, perhaps, that a phenomenology of vulnerability, which involves an understanding of how vulnerability is experienced by the vulnerable, is a precondition for an ethical and political approach to vulnerability, a prerequisite for an account of ethical and just treatment of the vulnerable.[3] At the same time, the phenomenological description cannot remain purely descriptive. Certain ethical and political aspects of the problem of vulnerability have to be taken into account by a phenomenology of vulnerability. For example, a phenomenological account has to acknowledge the power relations informing the situation of the vulnerable, power relations which can produce various types of injustices and which, if they do so, need to be challenged or contested in order to make possible a restoration of justice and ethical relations.

the dark myth of given vulnerability[4]

This section offers a sketch of a prevalent, negative, often implicit understanding of vulnerability which pervades common ways of treating and thinking about the vulnerable. The "dark" myth about vulnerability, which is informed by this understanding, perpetuates fear and violence which often appear to be characteristics of many vulnerable people's situations. Vulnerability as experienced, for example, in the loss of love, dignity, or health is often seen as a weakness or deficiency. In general, vulnerability is usually viewed as an accidental and/or temporary feature of individuals or groups. Vulnerability is then something like a label attached to clearly delimited groups of people, who are taken to form a separate "class" or "classes" of "the vulnerable": women, the elderly, the bullied, the chronically ill, the disabled and their carers, etc. For instance, illness or wounding due to bullying are seen as accidental misfortunes which separate the individuals affected by them from the healthy and unwounded people, respectively. Vulnerability becomes a barrier between two social worlds, which isolates and marginalizes the wounded. The Dark Myth establishes vulnerability as something necessarily undesirable, as something one has to get rid of. As I point out in the next section, the Dark Myth involves a lack of understanding of vulnerability, an epistemology of wilful ignorance[5] and, as Anderson also notes, a disavowal of vulnerability which can take various forms.

Vulnerability is seen as something which might call for "protection." This might take the form of a paradoxical manifestation of a disavowal of vulnerability. Misguided or excessively protective attitudes might hide paternalistic, asymmetrical, oppressive power relations which have a damaging effect on the vulnerable and their resilience. Such power relations can be accounted for in terms of a master–slave relation or in terms of the objectification of the vulnerable individual, who is no longer seen as a capable subject but as a mere *object* of observation, care and protection. The vulnerable person is seen as an object over which "the master" has a certain amount of power which enables him/her to control them, and to claim to do so on behalf of them. But this asymmetrical relationship to the vulnerable constitutes just another form of violence which can enhance fear, marginalization and stigma, and can undermine the possibility of genuine social relations; it can thus affect a whole social web constituting the community in which the vulnerable individual seeks, or even struggles, to find or regain their place.

The Dark Myth constructs vulnerability as a mark of inferiority. By enhancing and perpetuating an understanding of vulnerability as a source of shame, fear and violence it has a stigmatizing, disabling and marginalizing impact on what it constructs as the "category" of the vulnerable. It is life-smothering in so far as it reduces or even destroys the possibilities of the vulnerable to be, and live, well.

the gift of vulnerability as openness

Vulnerability can be taken to refer to a wide spectrum of experiences and situations, ranging from negative exposures to violence and fear, to more positive modes of opening possibilities for understanding oneself and the world, for example, through resilience. So vulnerability is not only an openness or exposure to violence and to being wounded but can also be understood as a capability which enables people to be open to others and to the world in positive ways, to be open to change and creative, transformative experiences. Anderson calls it a "life-enhancing capability."[6] This way of thinking about vulnerability can be contrasted with the life-smothering view or attitude towards vulnerability implied by the Dark

Myth. By pursuing this positive line of thinking, in what follows I argue that vulnerability can be conceived as a distinctive openness in relation to our possibilities to be, and live, well as vulnerable beings. I endorse an understanding of vulnerability as an essential aspect of human beings, of who we are: we are all finite and vulnerable. We can never rid ourselves completely of this feature of our existence. It is in this sense a universal characteristic of human beings, although people experience it differently.

Although this approach takes vulnerability to be a universal characteristic of human existence, at the same time it acknowledges the individualizing and particularizing character of vulnerability, its role in differentiating individuals: our own specific vulnerabilities are distinctive features of who we are, which inform our understanding of ourselves, our ways of engaging with the world we live in and with the people we live amongst. Our vulnerabilities pervade our lives.

I suggest that vulnerability can be understood as an intersectional phenomenon: that is to say that vulnerability cannot be conceived simply as an isolated feature of one's life (for example, solely in terms of one's illness) but must be conceived in terms of the intersection of a large number of factors such as physical abilities, gender, race, ethnicity, age, bodily characteristics, cultural or religious values, etc.[7] These factors shape one another and are constitutive of one's vulnerable situation, of how one makes sense of it and of the power relations informing it.

I draw on Martin Heidegger's notion of "openness" to develop in some detail a phenomenological analysis of certain features of vulnerability. Vulnerability can be understood as a form of three-directional openness: an openness to other people (such as, for example, in loss of love or mourning), to the world (as manifest, for instance, in illness when one is coping with the world and everyday life), and to oneself (such as, for example, in losing and finding oneself in mental illness, or changing and transforming oneself through resilience). Certain thinkers, including Anderson, focus on vulnerability as a form of openness or relationality to other people. Other philosophers, such as Carel, seem to focus on vulnerability and illness as openness to the world and the challenges of coping in ordinary environments. In this paper, I would like to draw attention to vulnerability as an openness to oneself through resilience. The differentiation of the three aspects of openness mentioned above does not imply that these are separate from one another. The three-fold structure of openness is taken to be a whole unitary phenomenon: we are always open and related in some way or another to other people, the world and ourselves.

Like Anderson, I take vulnerability to be a characteristic of our embodied being. On this account, vulnerability is an essential aspect of our body, which is constituted not only by material aspects of our "flesh" and biological make-up but also informed by social and political factors. Cultural norms and political forces play an important role in the constitution of basic concepts or criteria for what is considered, for example, to be "normal" or "different," and shape the institutions and practices which enact these basic concepts.

Heidegger conceives of our openness to the world in terms of three interrelated constitutive items: understanding, affectivity (or state-of-mind) and speech (or discourse). He takes these to be essential to any form of openness. The reconception of vulnerability as openness I offer here investigates its distinctive modes of understanding, affection and discourse. These can be analysed in terms of some of their extreme forms, which demarcate a wide spectrum of experiences of vulnerability. Anderson proposes an ethical way of making sense of vulnerability as an openness to *affection* (in particular, compassion and love), which opposes the Dark Myth about vulnerability as exposure affected by shame, fear and violence. Vulnerability also involves distinctive modes of *understanding*, which range from a genuine recognition of vulnerability to wilful ignorance. Its positive distinctive mode of *discourse* can be understood in terms of "communicative reciprocity" which opposes oppressive silencing of the vulnerable. Anderson discusses in detail vulnerability as openness to affection and the discursive situations of the vulnerable,[8] and I consider these below, but I would like to focus then on certain modes of understanding enacted in vulnerable situations of life.

vulnerability as affective openness

As I mentioned above, the account of vulnerability I pursue acknowledges the corporeal side of vulnerability but focuses in this context on its affective side. From this perspective, vulnerability can be understood as the constant possibility of being hurt (by, say, other people, natural phenomena, social or political events). It is the possibility of being exposed to harm brought about by, for example, societal conventions or suffering experienced, for instance, in loss of love or health.

Whether I am aware of it, I am constantly under the threat of being (further) wounded, harmed or hurt in some way or another. This is often not a matter of choice but of something that happens to me and depends on forces beyond my control. I cannot escape the constant threat of getting hurt or being wounded, for example, by loss of love or life. Vulnerability is something like a "fact" which is part of who I am. I find myself having such and such multiple layers of vulnerability (due to social relationships, physical characteristics of my body, my ethnicity, gender, age, cultural context, etc.) which intersect with one another in numerous ways.

The spectrum of affective openness corresponding to vulnerability is wide. A dominant understanding of this, which is characteristic of the Dark Myth, emphasizes negative feelings such as fear, emotional suffering and shame. But there are also positive possibilities of affective openness, such as considerate attention, empathy, compassion, or love (as Anderson points out) which vulnerability can give rise to, and which have not been sufficiently acknowledged and endorsed in everyday life and in theoretical investigations of phenomena of vulnerability. A positive affectivity corresponding to a recognition that we are all vulnerable can motivate ethical relationships in situations in which there is a constant risk of an improper use of power and authority. For example, the carer who genuinely cares about the patient and has a compassionate attitude towards them can oppose an objectifying attitude transforming the patient into a mere physical object of medical investigations and care services.

As Anderson stresses, vulnerability understood as "a capability for an openness to mutual affection"[9] and love makes possible the development of reciprocal relationships. Anderson discusses in detail the transforming power and potential of vulnerability as affective openness, but it is not my task to develop this in further detail here. I now move on to look briefly at distinctive discourse possibilities characteristic of situations of vulnerability.

the discourse of vulnerability

In the context of his phenomenological analysis of our everyday existence, Heidegger points out that speech or discourse is an essential feature of our openness to the world, and that speech, understanding (or our cognitive relation to things) and affectivity are not independent capacities but are interconnected aspects of our openness to the world. Their interconnection is manifest, for instance, in communication, which Heidegger takes to be an essential possibility of speech. Communication involves a sharing not only of a state of understanding but also of an affective state or attunement to a situation. This affective state can be expressed in speech not only by what is said but also through the intonation or the modulation of the voice and the body's emotional "language." Heidegger also notes that hearing and silence are significant possibilities of speech; I consider these below in relation to vulnerability.

Communication and hearing or listening are positive possibilities of speech which are resisted and smothered by the Dark Myth of vulnerability. Silence can have a positive impact when it conveys something in the context of a reciprocal communicative situation, but there are other, dark situations of silence which I would like to consider here. I do so by drawing on Anderson's and Kristie Dotson's feminist approach to the silencing of vulnerable women.[10] I suggest that this feminist approach can be extended and developed as a discussion of speech phenomena characteristic of the situation of the vulnerable in general.[11]

Dotson makes a distinction between the quieting and the smothering of the vulnerable, which Anderson explores further. Dotson points out that vulnerable speakers could be silenced by the listeners' refusal to hear and to understand them, by their wilful ignorance, that is, their refusal to know about the vulnerable individual's experience and situation. The individual is not taken to be competent enough to properly make sense of, and to interpret, their own situation, and is thus not recognized as a "knower." For instance, Anderson, Dotson and other feminists discuss various forms of silencing imposed on women living in patriarchal societies in past and present times, which have had an oppressive impact on their lives. I suggest that a similar way of thinking can be pursued in relation to attitudes in health care. For example, a patient's comments about her experience of her illness might not be taken into consideration by the health practitioner in their diagnosing and treatment of the patient's disease.[12] This could result in inadequate treatment negatively affecting the life of the patient. Consider also another example, namely bullying: audiences and those with power might not hear what the bullied individual says about their experience, and might minimize the situation. Their response and action, in case any is taken in relation to the situation, turn out then to be ineffective and might even worsen the situation and contribute to the proliferation of oppression and marginalization of the vulnerable individual.

Silencing the vulnerable has a serious negative impact on their situation and the actions taken in relation to their situation. This speech attitude corresponds to an oppressive form of intentional or wilful ignorance which reduces vulnerability to mere openness to being wounded and exposure to violence, and ignores its positive possibilities of opening up mutual relations of understanding and affection which can lead to beneficial, life-enhancing courses of action.

Smothering, understood as another negative possibility of speech, can take the form of self-silencing in contexts in which the vulnerable person believes that it might be too dangerous to speak or that those to whom they attempt to talk lack the competence to understand or lack the willingness to hear. Again, this has a negative, stifling impact on the life of the vulnerable which perpetuates the Dark Myth, the shame and fear, the marginalization and oppression which it produces.

There are, however, positive speech possibilities in situations of vulnerability.[13] To be able to live well one should be able to talk freely about one's own vulnerability and to be heard; it is necessary that one's vulnerability is recognized as such, and that the way this is experienced from a first-person point of view is taken into account. As mentioned above, communication is possible through a shared understanding and shared affective state. In the context of the discussion of vulnerability, such a shared understanding does not consist simply in something like "putting yourself in someone else's shoes"; it is impossible to live someone else's life experience of their vulnerability (due, for instance, to a certain illness or disability). But the sharing of understanding and affective state makes possible a mutual relationship and an attitude of empathy and compassion which incorporate a recognition of the vulnerable speaker's competence, their epistemic authority and status of knower of, and "expert" in, the "area" of their own vulnerability. Communication is not an individual undertaking but a reciprocal achievement,[14] perhaps even a collective achievement. Such a solicitous and attentive attitude can motivate right courses of action in particular situations of vulnerability.

understanding, cognition and vulnerability

In the context of his phenomenological analysis of human existence, Heidegger points out that understanding is an essential aspect of our openness to the world. In the context of my discussion of vulnerability, I suggest that understanding or making sense of the world, of oneself, and of one's relationships with other people – finding meaning in all these, whilst being marked by vulnerability – has something to do with what it means to be, and live, well. There is a wide spectrum of possibilities and forms of understanding vulnerability, but I focus here on extreme points of the spectrum corresponding, first, to the Dark Myth, and, second, to a positive, life-enhancing understanding of vulnerability.

The phenomenological analysis of understanding and cognition or knowledge (understood in a broad sense) that I offer here considers two sides of the matter: the first concerns forms of understanding and knowledge of vulnerability from second- and third-person points of view, which are related to the earlier distinction between two opposed forms of speech possibilities, namely silencing/quieting and listening/hearing; the second concerns what it means for the vulnerable person to make sense of things, and this is considered from a first-person point of view. As I mentioned above, although the analysis employs primarily a phenomenological methodology, it acknowledges the role of ethical and power relations, values and culture in shaping situations of vulnerability.

As noted above, the oppressive silencing of the vulnerable manifests a lack of understanding of their vulnerability. This form of ignorance, however, is not merely just not knowing something. As Nancy Tuana argues, in some cases, ignorance is not always as simple as it is typically assumed or claimed.[15] The issue of ignorance is much more complex. There are various forms of ignorance, many of which have a complicated structure and genesis. Tuana offers an epistemology of ignorance, which identifies, and distinguishes between, certain types of ignorance. A basic distinction is between bad and good forms of ignorance. These can be distinguished in terms of their stifling or, on the contrary, enhancing possibilities and opportunities for the vulnerable to live well.

What does it mean that ignorance is not simply just not-knowing, that the lack of understanding is not merely an absence of understanding? To tackle this question let us consider certain bad types of ignorance. For example, somebody might be aware of someone else's vulnerability, but might not be willing to hear more, or even anything, about it or they might pretend they do not hear because they do not care, or care more about their own interests and privileged position which might be challenged, disturbed or inconvenienced by the other person's vulnerable situation. In such cases lack of understanding and not caring protect and enhance the advantaged person's power, and perhaps their economic interests and political privileges. Lack of understanding or ignorance is, in such cases, a form of oppression of the vulnerable.[16] They are aware that they do not know, but they do not care. What they are concerned with is how better to control and subordinate the vulnerable in some way or another and to preserve their power and authority.

Ignorance or the lack of understanding is not always an innocent or passive state but might be an active or even hyper-active productive undertaking or "mechanism" which is put to work to maintain and enhance one's privileges and power. As Elizabeth Spelman says, ignorance is then not something that happens to someone but an "achievement" which requires active work in order, for example, to cover up certain facts, or to minimize or deny some forms of violence targeting the vulnerability that it seeks to disavow.[17]

This form of a lack of understanding is what Tuana calls "wilful ignorance": you do not know and do not want to know. You do not understand things well and are not willing to gain a better understanding of what is at issue and, in particular, to understand it from the perspective of the vulnerable.

Wilful lack of understanding involves systematic and widespread deception. It might involve acts of systematically deceiving the vulnerable. And it also involves self-deception: the oppressor deceives himself by making himself believe that he is invulnerable[18] by virtue, for example, of his power. This wrong assumption of invulnerability is supported by a systematic production of plausible lies that the oppressors tell themselves and other people, and is facilitated by the social or institutional setting which installed them as part of a well-established authority or institution wherein they are regarded as an embodiment of authority, competence and epistemic credibility.

As Anderson notes, the Dark Myth of vulnerability is supported by this sort of ignorance or lack of understanding of vulnerability which blocks its life-enhancing power. Wilful lack of understanding functions as a source of the Dark Myth, which constructs vulnerability as an exposure to violence, fear and shame. The vulnerable person thus becomes exposed to further violence inflicted through a determined lack of understanding which brings about ontological and epistemic injustice. Ontological injustice can be understood in terms of the violence inflicted upon the being of the individual and their identity: it is a force which stifles the possibilities of the vulnerable to be, and live, well. Epistemic injustice occurs when the vulnerable person is denied the status of "knower," epistemic competence and credibility.

As Anderson points out, the task is then to oppose oppressive, wilful ignorance by pursuing a positive recognition and avowal of vulnerability which can make possible positive change and transformation of one's understanding of oneself, of other people and the world. This transformation can be understood as a liberatory force which is constitutive of resilience.

Before I turn to a conceptual and phenomenological analysis of understanding considered from the first-person point of view, I would like to say something about the general concept of understanding I discuss here.[19] This concept is taken in a very broad sense which follows to some extent the ordinary use of the word: it refers not only to our making sense of the meaning of words and other linguistic items but also of people, situations, things in the world. When we understand something we understand its possibilities of being the way it is. To understand something is to make sense of its possibilities.

To understand oneself is to make sense of one's own possibilities and potentiality to be, of one's capabilities to live and "function" in the world. This type of understanding can take the form of being able to set tasks for oneself, to make sense of them in terms of one's own possibilities and the possibilities of things which are relevant for one's carrying out one's tasks. Understanding is an enabling state: it enables one to act in the world and to acquire knowledge about various particular aspects or areas of reality.

I would like to focus now on certain distinctive features of understanding in situations of vulnerability. Vulnerability can change one's understanding of oneself, of the world, and of other people. The transformation can be negative, especially in conditions of violence and oppression produced by the Dark Myth. But this is not necessarily so, at least with regard to some important aspects of one's understanding and life, and especially when vulnerable life is not smothered by manifestations of the Dark Myth. The transformation can become a growth in understanding, as the recent works and vulnerable lives of philosophers such as Pamela Sue Anderson or Havi Carel have shown.

This is not to deny that life and world, and the relation to others, might at some point be about to cease to make sense for the vulnerable individual. But right at the edge, or perhaps even in the middle, of a "breakdown in [...] intelligibility,"[20] right on the verge of losing any meaning, in the middle of a crisis of meaning, a reconfiguration of meaning is always still possible.

Vulnerability can be understood as a loss of possibilities. Let us consider serious illness, understood as a form of bodily vulnerability. In her phenomenology of illness, Havi Carel describes illness as "the loss of opportunities, possibilities, and openness."[21] In illness, one's openness to the world and one's making sense of it through one's actions shrink. The individual with the illness might intend to perform some action, but their illness and vulnerable body hinder or even prevent them from fulfilling their intention. As Carel notes: "in illness bodily intentionality is frustrated, the relation between the lived body and the environment is changed, and [...] possibilities for action shrink."[22] The view of illness as constricted openness to possibilities is also shared by Matthew Ratcliffe in his phenomenological approach to mental illness.[23] So both Carel and Ratcliffe seem to endorse an understanding of illness in terms of a loss of possibilities for connecting with the environment, and as a shrinking of one's openness to the world and others. Using illness as an illustration, I suggest that vulnerability in general can be understood as involving a loss of possibilities of sense-making. The sense-making does not need to be reflective; there are also active, pre-reflective ways of sense-making through one's dealings with things in the world. This shrinking of the possibilities of making sense of the world through one's engagement with the world might bring about, or correspond to, a potential broadening of the exposure to violence or oppression.

Carel further develops her view of illness (or bodily vulnerability) in terms of a phenomenological-epistemic distinction between bodily doubt and bodily certainty. In many illnesses, bodily doubt over one's capability to act limits the range of available possibilities, and increases one's loss of freedom. By contrast, bodily certainty over one's capability to move and act in everyday contexts, which is taken for granted in good health, enhances the openness of possibilities for action and the corresponding sense of freedom.

By using illness as an example, I would like to suggest an understanding of vulnerability as involving a sense-making openness to the world – a distinctive feature of which is that it constantly shelters a serious threat to one's very capacity to make sense of things, to find meaning in one's life and in the world. Vulnerability is an openness to meaning which involves a loss of meaning, and faces us with the threat of a "breakdown in intelligibility," a breakdown of our sense-making capabilities. This threat is covered up in the "normal," smooth running of everyday life. But in vulnerable situations such as, for example, illness, "bodily doubt reveals the extent of our vulnerability, which is normally masked."[24]

This approach, however, is not a rewriting of the Dark Myth of vulnerability as deficiency. Carel also opposes the idea of illness as a deficiency. She points out that in illness "an experience of smooth interwoven experience and action is not a taken-for-granted ground, but *an achievement*"[25] which is the result of daily efforts or even struggle to cope in everyday contexts. These are made possible by the individual's resilience.

Vulnerability understood as loss of opportunities, as a loss of possibilities of sense-making and freedom, is not the end of the story. As Anderson points out, vulnerability can be understood as an openness to change and life-enhancing transformation brought about by loss (e.g., loss of love, health, dignity, etc.). Through resilience, the experience of vulnerability can become a rebuilding process of one's space of possibilities, a profound reconfiguration of one's projects, concerns, interests and values. I propose that this capability to make renewed sense of things is constitutive of what is often called "resilience."

Resilience has been described as the capability to deal with disruptive adverse situations, to adapt and to engage in life, a capability which involves a form of "intelligence." The concept of resilience has recently come to the fore mostly in mental health disciplines (in particular, psychology and psychiatry) but, to my knowledge, it has not received much philosophical attention until now. My intention here is to draw attention to this concept as potentially a central notion of a positive reconceptualization of vulnerability (and related concepts, such as disability), and to initiate a phenomenology of resilience.

In light of the discussion carried out so far, I propose an understanding of resilience as involving a distinctive (perhaps ineffable) understanding of one's situation and place in the world. It is something like a capability or enabling state of being which makes it possible for the individual to make projects, set oneself tasks, act and achieve in seriously adverse conditions. This mode of openness to the world enables one to integrate and organize a more limited space of possibilities in ways that enable one to transgress it, and to transgress certain limitations of one's agency. This capability enables one to develop coping skills enhancing the capacity for action. Vulnerability then becomes a power to make sense of things and to give meaning to things in situations in which one might think all hope and meaning is lost, when life and world and our relations to other people are about to cease to make sense. On the verge of a breakdown of intelligibility there is the possibility of a recovery of meaning and growth of understanding: this is the possibility of resilience, hidden at the heart of vulnerability.

conclusion

Here, I have sought to develop a conception of vulnerability as openness. My approach is phenomenological and ontological. I have pointed out that vulnerability is a "category" of our being – as Anderson says, we are all vulnerable. Whilst she emphasizes that vulnerability is an openness to affection, I have pointed out that vulnerability is also a "cognitive" openness, with distinctive modes of understanding. This might be a starting point for developing a conception of epistemic vulnerability and resilience. In so far as resilience involves a form of cognition or understanding, resilience is something which can be learned, at least to some extent; and this process of learning can be facilitated in various ways. For example, a proper understanding and avowal of vulnerability, recognition of the vulnerable person as a knower, can facilitate their resilience. Furthermore, an understanding of vulnerability as a universal characteristic of human existence, a re-cognition of our own intrinsic vulnerability can be transformative, empowering and liberatory. It can free us from wilful ignorance, stigmatization and auto-stigmatization. The disavowal and lack of understanding of vulnerability not only distort the understanding of the human condition but can have seriously damaging and oppressive effects on the lives of very vulnerable individuals and the people they live amongst.

disclosure statement

No potential conflict of interest was reported by the author.

notes

This is a revised version of my presentation given to the conference in honour and memory of Pamela Sue Anderson to whom the paper is dedicated. I am grateful to Adrian W. Moore for his comments and suggestions, and to Pelagia Goulimari for editorial help and support. Thanks are due also to members of the audience at the conference for some excellent discussion.

1 This is a view pursued recently by philosophers such as Pamela Sue Anderson in her work on vulnerability and Havi Carel in her philosophy of illness. In the last two years of her life, while she was fighting cancer, Anderson developed a life-enhancing, ethical approach to vulnerability understood as openness to affection and, more specifically, love. Following her diagnosis of a serious, life-threatening respiratory illness, Havi Carel has developed a complex and thorough phenomenological investigation of illness, which can be understood as a form of bodily vulnerability. Both philosophers' lives display an extraordinary resilience.

2 My eclectic approach draws on Pamela Sue Anderson's view of vulnerability as openness and Martin Heidegger's ontological phenomenology of "openness" in general.

3 See Anderson, "Arguing for 'Ethical' Vulnerability." In her work on vulnerability, Anderson focuses on such an ethical approach and its political implications.

4 I take over the phrase "dark myth" from Anderson. I draw here on her "Towards a New Philosophical Imaginary."

5 See Tuana.

6 Anderson, "Towards a New Philosophical Imaginary" 9; see also her "Arguing for 'Ethical' Vulnerability."

7 The notion of "intersectionality" has been developed by relatively recent feminist thinking in order to redefine the notion of gender and power relations informing it. I think it can be usefully

employed to tackle the complexity of the notion of vulnerability.

8 See especially Anderson, "Arguing for 'Ethical' Vulnerability"; "Towards a New Philosophical Imaginary"; "Silencing and Speaker Vulnerability."

9 Anderson, "Towards a New Philosophical Imaginary" 8.

10 Anderson, "Silencing and Speaker Vulnerability."

11 See Dotson.

12 An interesting example can be found in Fulford, "Values-Based Practice"; "Facts/Values."

13 See Anderson, "Silencing and Speaker Vulnerability."

14 Cf. Hornsby.

15 Tuana 3.

16 I draw here on Tuana and on Anderson's engagement with it (in Anderson, "Silencing and Speaker Vulnerability"), but use a phenomenological approach.

17 Spelman.

18 Anderson, "Silencing and Speaker Vulnerability."

19 For this sketch of the concept of understanding at issue here, I continue to draw on Heidegger, and to some extent also on A.W. Moore's notion of "making sense of things" and his discussion of ineffable knowledge. See Moore, *Evolution* 5–6; "Ineffability and Religion"; *Points of View* 175–76.

20 I owe this phrase to Stephen Mulhall. See Mulhall 293.

21 Carel 45.

22 Ibid. 68.

23 Ratcliffe 8.

24 Carel 94.

25 Ibid. 105.

bibliography

Anderson, Pamela Sue. "Arguing for 'Ethical' Vulnerability: Towards a Politics of Care?" *Exploring Vulnerability*. Ed. Heike Springhart and Günter Thomas. Göttingen and Bristol, CT: Vandenhoeck, 2017. 147–62. Print.

Anderson, Pamela Sue. "Silencing and Speaker Vulnerability: Undoing an Oppressive Form of (Wilful) Ignorance." Ed. Nick Bunnin. *Love and Vulnerability: Thinking with Pamela Sue Anderson*. Ed. Pelagia Goulimari. Spec. issue of *Angelaki: Journal of the Theoretical Humanities* 25.1–2 (2020): 36–45. Print.

Anderson, Pamela Sue. "Towards a New Philosophical Imaginary." Ed. Sabina Lovibond and Adrian W. Moore. *Love and Vulnerability: Thinking with Pamela Sue Anderson*. Ed. Pelagia Goulimari. Spec. issue of *Angelaki: Journal of the Theoretical Humanities* 25.1–2 (2020): 8–22. Print.

Carel, Havi. *Phenomenology of Illness*. Oxford: Oxford UP, 2016. Print.

Dotson, Kristie. "Tracking Epistemic Violence, Tracking Practices of Silencing." *Hypatia: A Journal of Feminist Philosophy* 26.2 (2011): 236–57. Print.

Fulford, K.W.M. "Facts/Values: Ten Principles of Values-Based Medicine." *The Philosophy of Psychiatry: A Companion*. Ed. Jennifer Radden. New York: Oxford UP, 2004. 205–36. Print.

Fulford, K.W.M. "Values-Based Practice: A New Partner to Evidence-Based Practice and a First for Psychiatry?" *Mens Sana Monographs* 6.1 (2008): 10–21. Print.

Heidegger, Martin. *Being and Time*. Trans. John Macquarrie and Edward Robinson. Oxford: Blackwell, 1997. Print.

Hornsby, Jennifer. "Disempowered Speech." *Philosophical Topics* 23.2 (1995): 127–47. Print.

Moore, Adrian W. *The Evolution of Modern Metaphysics*. Cambridge: Cambridge UP, 2012. Print.

Moore, Adrian W. "Ineffability and Religion." *Language, World, and Limits: Essays in Philosophy of Language and Metaphysics*. By Adrian W. Moore. Oxford: Oxford UP, 2019. 210–23. Print.

Moore, Adrian W. *Points of View*. Oxford: Oxford UP, 1997. Print.

Mulhall, Stephen. "The Idea of Ethical Vulnerability: Perfectionism, Irony and the Theological Virtues." *Love and Vulnerability: Thinking with Pamela Sue Anderson*. Ed. Pelagia Goulimari. Spec. issue of

Angelaki: Journal of the Theoretical Humanities 25.1–2 (2020): 284–96. Print.

Ratcliffe, Matthew. *Feelings of Being: Phenomenology, Psychiatry and the Sense of Reality*. Oxford: Oxford UP, 2008. Print.

Spelman, Elizabeth. "Managing Ignorance." *Race and Epistemologies of Ignorance*. Ed. Shannon Sullivan and Nancy Tuana. Albany: State U of New York P, 2007. 119–32. Print.

Tuana, Nancy. "The Speculum of Ignorance: The Women's Health Movement and Epistemology of Ignorance." *Feminist Epistemologies of Ignorance*. Spec. issue of *Hypatia: A Journal of Feminist Philosophy* 21.3 (2006): 1–19. Print.

1 introductory remarks

Speaking on behalf of William Schweiker of the University of Chicago Divinity School, I would first like to thank the organizers and editors for this opportunity for cooperation, discussion, and remembrance. As the principal investigators of the Enhancing Life Project, we were proud to have Pamela Sue Anderson as a collaborator. Her sharp mind and charm, as well as her outstanding scholarly abilities, brought much to the project. The other thirty-four scholars of the project miss her and will keep her in their memory. That her work resonated with people who work out of very different toolboxes, are on distinct academic journeys and inhabit entirely different epistemic worlds was a powerful testimony to Pamela Sue Anderson's bright mind and winning personality. Admittedly, I am a latecomer to the enriching conversation so many people had with her over the last thirty years. So, I want to thank all those old friends for their intellectual hospitality to the late arrivals.

A short remark on the background of the material presented here appears to be appropriate. First, what follows is, as a matter of fact, a product of generative resonance with Pamela Sue Anderson's writing. For several years, I have been working on issues of medical anthropology which are implicitly related to the theme of vulnerability. Over the last few years, the discourse on vulnerability became a fruitful framing device for what I developed. For this reason, it was a natural fit to cooperate with my colleague Heike Springhart and organize a conference on vulnerability in Heidelberg in the fall of 2015. Pamela could not attend this conference, but eventually contributed her paper to it.[1]

günter thomas

THE RISKS OF LOVE AND THE AMBIGUITIES OF HOPE

The following considerations grew out of a follow-up project on the dynamic relationship between love, faith, and hope both in the Christian faith tradition as well as in cultural processes.[2] The ideas presented here are one piece of a larger puzzle. In terms of social philosophy, I come to Pamela's intellectual environment from another epistemic world. My primary background is in the respective conversations of systems theory and constructive theology and the possibilities of bringing them together. Hence my understanding is grounded in Niklas Luhmann's piercing remark: "Understanding is practically always a misunderstanding without an understanding of the mis."[3] By offering a more phenomenologically oriented perspective on love, I hope to build some bridges between Pamela's work in Continental philosophy and feminist theory and my own.

2 five aspects of love's vulnerability

The focus of this paper is not on the evocative power of vulnerability but on those aspects of vulnerability that are implied in the communication of love. What features of vulnerability are brought centre stage when the communication of love is successful? My question is not whether vulnerability can trigger love but the reverse: what particular aspects of vulnerability are triggered by love? Expressed differently, I want to explore the middle ground between negative and positive evaluations of vulnerability. "Always look on the bright side of vulnerability" – to rephrase Monty Python – does not give the whole picture. There are shadow sides to vulnerability – even if we communicate love. In this respect, this article is a commentary on Pamela Sue Anderson's work. Moreover, in the instances of intensified vulnerability, love is profoundly dangerous in its creative capacity.

2.1 love's willingness to commit foolish risk calculations

Love is ultimately willing to be foolish in its risk calculations.[4] Love does not only reject the risks that risk-averse calculation, aimed towards security, would advise.

Living in the web of life entangles beings with multiple processes of mutual dependency which defy any simplistic idea of autonomy, self-sufficiency, and power.[5] Any mutuality and any form of dependency inevitably open one not only to enrichment but also to the possibility of harm, even destruction, up to the point of death. All cultures are laboratories which seek tools and procedures to manage these dependencies in favour of an excellent shared life: routines of respect and recognition, rules for cautious explorations, or the establishment of the rule of law as a way of securing expectations. That is to say, many tools and processes establish, maintain, protect and secure expectations.

For that reason, risk calculations and corresponding mechanisms of self-protection are woven into the fabric of social life.

Love calls these calculations into question and asks for courageous unilateral action. The double structure of action and observation of the action in terms of its fit into processes of securing expectations is dimmed down or even abandoned.[6] In this respect, the communication of love makes itself intentionally vulnerable. For that reason, the communication of love must always rest on voluntariness.[7] Love is never a calculated and strategic protective strategy for oneself. Just the reverse: love allows one to perceive the vulnerability of the other without an attendant feeling of superiority nor the temptation to take advantage of the other's vulnerability and exploit it for one's own gain.

Any philosophy, theology or social theory which makes love the default mode of social action exempts itself from any serious understanding of social life.[8] Love remains an exception. Love creates a state of exception ("Ausnahmezustand") in a very distinct sense: it can risk beginnings and endings. In calling into question the well-established implicit and explicit mechanisms of risk calculation and securing of expectations, love can have a double effect. It can – through its willingness to risk foolishly – momentarily irritate and intensify social life in favour of heightened sensitivity, a more refined moral outlook and a more gracious perspective on human beings.[9] Love based on this creative aspect of vulnerability shifts the horizons of possibility. Due to its particular type of disregard for caution and distinctly reckless behaviour, love can also destabilize complex networks of expectations – in order to enhance life by providing spaces and times of reorientation.

2.2 love's painful recognition of its limitations

A true spirit of love sensitizes one to others and cultivates the enlightenment of a widened perception. Love graciously discloses the very limitations of life and the markers of its finitude by addressing them. Love transforms perception, both in terms of its depth and its horizon. For true love, the ever-growing and in principle unbridgeable gap between what should be done and what can realistically be done is an element of love's vulnerability. Love opens new horizons and makes imaginable new possibilities. In doing that, love renders the distinction between real possibilities and merely abstract possibilities perceptible.

The expansion of perception, however, comes at a price. How can we love all the distant neighbours who are brought into our realm of concern through the news media?[10] When theologians and philosophers think about the power of love, even of suffering love, they mostly overlook this aspect of vulnerability which consists of a mobilizing but still painful recognition of one's limitations. Hence love forces one to acknowledge one's limitations. Neither Atlas nor Prometheus is a loving figure. Any celebration of the powerlessness of love might be tempted to overlook this selectivity created and intensified by love. For that reason, in the Judeo-Christian tradition love and lament are close neighbours.

2.3 love's conflict with certitude and self-righteousness

Quite some ink has been spilt over the link between love and certitude, courage and the firm will.[11] Whoever communicates love seems to be determined to do the right thing vis-à-vis the hesitant bystander and the uncommitted social *flâneur*. Love and doubt, love and being tempted seem to exclude each other. It is at this point, however, where Friedrich Nietzsche might smile at us and ask whether love needs to inhabit the high ground of self-righteousness and certitude.[12] Is love powered by dedication and commitment just another route taken by the will to power? Much high moralization in public discourse seems to confirm that. In many contemporary debates, people stand on very high moral ground where identities are fortified, and possible alternatives excluded.[13] Hate, disgust and conflict are the dark shadows of public political care for the future.

We need, however, to be honest: self-victimization and self-righteousness often go hand in hand. This insight should not surprise us, but these mindsets and postures bear little resemblance to love.

If love creates a nourishing and stimulating environment for others, a supportive space is opened to new possibilities. Love will allow itself to accept profound differences and maintain a fruitful distance to moral self-righteousness and its communication of certitude. This moral instability and modesty are love's creative vulnerability. That is why love can be so corrosive – in a good sense – to morality. Epistemic tentativeness, the posture of a search for truth and orientation belong to the moral moods of love. Love allows other life to be lived on its own trajectory. Surrounded by a loving environment other life can develop and be enhanced because it can risk being ahead of itself. In love, we transcend our own ideas about the good life and will, not always, but often, accept difference. Thus, love extends freedom. At the same time, the (admittedly difficult) command to love one's enemy is a powerful attack on all forms of self-righteousness.

an intermediate reflection on social ontology

At this point, an in between reflection is necessary. In order to see, unfold and assess the type of vulnerability present in love one must play with open cards concerning what I want to call social ontology.

A number of philosophers, from Ernst Cassirer to Nelson Goodman to Niklas Luhmann, to name just a few, rightly question the idea of a coherent world. They assume very different domains of meaning that form certain "worlds." Each world is characterized by its own symbolic means, codes as distinguishing features or conceptual schemata. Such domains of meaning imply their own dynamic ontology. They are never completely private, although individual experiences play a significant role. Social ontologies are built, cultivated and transformed in communication. Social ontologies consist of at least three "spaces":

(a) what is considered real, (b) what is considered possible and (c) what is considered impossible. From these three "spaces" arise normative and cognitive expectations. The relationships between the three "spaces" are mediated by the willingness to take risks. What are considered real, possible and impossible are usually not simple but highly dynamic objects – which include the formative forces, tensions and goals of life. In many cases where people disagree about the good and the righteous in shaping future life, they live in different moral worlds with different social ontologies. In the encounter of social ontologies love is a transforming force in so far as new things become possible, other features of the worlds seem impossible and even the "given" is re-questioned. Given that love can risk one-sided interventions, it is even more powerful than trust in unlocking and transforming social ontologies.

Why are social ontologies so important to understanding love? In a world of angel-like and well-mannered, rational and like-minded, emotionally passionate and disciplined people the vulnerability of love is almost a triviality. However, we do not live in such a world. We know that. Therefore, we ask questions like, what lies at the root of life? What could be its root metaphor? It makes a difference whether one assumes one is living in the world of Shakespeare or of Winnie the Pooh. Our social ontology is related to questions such as: what forces are living through us? What is the maximum risk I will take for life? Will I get what I need, what I want, and what I deserve in life? What larger forces can we trust? What carries us, when we think we get exploited, mistreated – not just by others, but by life itself and by friends?[14] Even in our academic reflection on love and vulnerability, we more or less explicitly live with assumptions about the forces, goals and tensions of life.

To phrase it differently: acts of love have a hermeneutical and a transformative aspect. They reveal and uncover our social ontologies. At the same time, they have the power to transform social ontologies. Manifestations of love enter or confront a particular social ontology, opening new possibilities and changing what is considered impossible. Communications of love can also reveal a commonality of social ontology – to open a view of a common humanity.[15]

Theologically speaking, we must consider that the thick textures of life, love, hope, and faith always come in a package deal, even in their most mundane or secularized versions and functional equivalents. In short, any conception of love and its place in life carries with it an explicit or implicit social ontology, formatting our spaces of possibilities which frame any deliberate action.

2.4 love and the risk of examining life – the temptation of reflexivity

In the communication of love, other lives are examined in a particular way. Love, which provides a supportive and nourishing environment for others, searches for the good of the other in ways that affect all involved. This caring, benevolent, non-exploitative and non-utilitarian examination of other life asks how the other living being can flourish in its development or be preserved in its disintegration. Adopting such a stance is not without risk for the life of the loving questioner himself or herself.

The risk lies in the temptation of recursive social reflexivity. The widespread moral claim that true love needs to be absolutely oblivious, absolutely without self-reference, is an indicator of the problem and a marker of the risks involved. Whoever examines other persons' lives might start to examine their own life. Processes of reflexivity might go well, revealing a deep sense of satisfaction, gratitude, and responsibility. To perceive oneself – to use a religious term – as blessed is an essential precondition for caring and giving to others in need.[16] This thankful orientation towards others is at the core of the infectious nature of love. It is not the expectation but rather the deeply felt obligation of social reciprocity that drives this constellation of emotion.

However, the examination of one's life in the process of love can lead to the painful recognition of being insufficiently loved by others. Even the most selfless lover will ask – beyond any naive and simplistic idea of immediate reciprocity – by whom he or she is loved. To care for the wounds of others makes one aware of one's own wounds – be they transformed into scars or still open ones. The risk of love is to perceive one's own wounds anew – and this is also an incalculable aspect of love's vulnerability. So one risk of love is the potential of sparking radically one-sided bitterness. "I did enough; I gave so much of my share in life. What is being shared with me?" "When am I taken care of?"[17] Such questions express one's social ontology. In short, love carries with it the risk of more conscious life, the risk of a deeper self-perception.

2.5 love's inability to prevent the triggering of its opposite

Every communication of love enters a space of indeterminate communication and action. In this space, love has a powerful differentiating effect. Love's inability to prevent this differentiating process is part and parcel of its vulnerability, its risk affinity.[18] Without any doubt, love radiates into its environments and is quite literally infectious. Love has an encouraging power. Love can trigger love. Whoever is addressed by love can be transformed so that she or he communicates love too. For that reason, love can be a powerful force for life-enhancing transformations. The caring as well as enabling environment created by love communicates dignity and self-respect and eventually encourages riskier and more loving communication. The investment of attention in the communication of love gives dignity to the neglected ones. Again, much was written on the ability of love to spread and multiply.

This aspect of love, however, is not the whole story. Love cannot determine its effects or responses. The unpredictability of love amid the messiness and ambiguity of life is its vulnerable side. Its creativity, its openness to risk, the truth-seeking, and the high degree of giving attention can trigger its actual rejection. Moreover, beyond any simple I–Thou relationship love radiates into a highly complex and polycontextual world. Put simply, when A loves B, C can find good reasons for hating A and B.

To formulate it pointedly, love "creates," that is to say, unveils, makes visible, evokes and can eventually make present hostility. Such unmasking can take place for at least three reasons. Second-order observations provoked by love often have a relativizing and reorienting effect but can also evoke envy.[19] The reflexivity of love in acts of second-order observations can spark jealousy. Additionally, love might indeed be a destabilizing force for cognitive, cultural, social, and particular moral orders which are keen to protect themselves. The transformative power of love might give rise to new protective strategies. In addition, and again with respect to underlying social ontology, love enters the agonistically structured space of highly conflicting interests. On the very level of social communication, love stirs up the ground of fundamental presuppositions. In a world of stupidity, hate and structural injustice love is often a provocation for which loving ones have paid with their lives. For that reason, the passion of love can lead to the experience of passion as suffering and passivity. The Latin term *passio* encapsulates this dynamic.

3 love in the frame of hope

How is love related to hope? Where does hope come into the picture of risky love? Hope moves to the foreground when the temporal structure of love is analysed.

3.1 love and real future possibilities

Passionate love enjoys the moment and wants to escape the flow of time.[20] However, love that acknowledges, preserves and supports the life of other people in all their situated complexity and their temporality will reach out and include unrealized, but real and temporarily distant possibilities. Passionate love tries to see what other people could be, helps them to reach new possibilities – without using or making a graven image that binds and fixes the other.[21]

As soon as temporal beings include future possibilities into their nourishing care, they *hope for someone*. In the process of reflexivity and recognition, the person or the entity who is hoped for becomes a person who has for herself a *hope in someone*. Relations of love, solidarity and trust are complex webs of "expectations of expectations" in which one hopes in someone, not just at the moment, but in the future. Being loved nourishes the hope that there are moments in which someone will act in supportive ways.

3.2 love and patience

The second way love relates to hope is through patience. Love's deep respect for the other life establishes a very specific posture vis-à-vis its own inability to shape the reality of the other in the way love wishes.[22] When love meets resistance, faces ineffectiveness or less sought-for resonances its reaction differs from a wise calculus or rational-choice calculus. Love does not ask: is it worth the effort? Is the increased investment of time and energy in a sound and rational relation to the delayed or more unlikely goods achieved? Does this justify the effort needed? Am I called to play Sisyphus? We take these postures quite often and for good reasons: we are finite beings and live necessarily, to a certain extent, by rational calculations. Alternatively, resistance sometimes must switch the modus operandi and pull another register: what cannot be achieved by the powerlessness of love might call for the exercise of power. Quite understandably, there is no state which bases its tax system on neighbourly love.

However, love differs from both rational calculations and the exercise of coercive power. Love will accept the limitation of its transformative effect and of not achieving its goals without giving up its intention. Love can temporalize difference and can wait. Patience always implies a double movement: love's patience will accept the current situation and will not deny the current status quo. At the same time, patience will temporalize love's transformative energy. What cannot become real at the moment remains alive as a *real* possibility in the future. Hope as a way of expanding the horizon of action into the future adds time to the work of love. Patient persistence ties love to hope. Love's internal structure simultaneously focuses on the present moment, while making a promise to the future. Those to whom this promise has been made are both forced and invited to trust.

3.3 current limits and the expansion of hope

The third trajectory connecting love and hope is the self-conscious recognition of love's selectivity. We as human beings cannot love the entire world wholly. We cannot love everyone and everything. As already mentioned above, love needs to be selective.[23] In romantic love, this selectivity is taken to be an indicator of love's presence, power and liveliness. Even if we expand the social reach of love in other forms of love, love will still be selective. Inevitably, some criteria of selection remain the *modus operandi* of love. Hence, love always needs a more or less explicit principle of selectivity. The old religious demand "Love your neighbour" is a case in point.

The intrinsic limitation of love can be painful. There is a moment of a suffering love related to the manifest limit of its reach. Love's unavoidable selectivity should not be confused with the notion of a narcissistic slight of love. All true love strives for inclusion and embrace. Even in the most intense forms of romantic love, the lovers long for others to enjoy the same experience.[24] There is a manifest danger that this problem of selectivity will be concealed by a much too broad concept of suffering love. By whatever means the selectivity in the practice of love is rationalized or interpreted, love cannot take joy or satisfaction in its very limitation.

If this recognition of finitude becomes part of the experience and work of love a crucial bifurcation comes into view. Love can add a posture of heroic resignation one can easily find in stoic thought. The lines of solidarity and love have to be drawn to form increasingly intimate circles.

The alternative to heroic resignation in the face of love's obvious social and motivational limitations is the unfolding of hope. Some might say that this is wishful thinking or a Munchausen trick. One might claim that heroic resignation offers nothing other than a desperate realism: "This is just the way the world is!"

4 the ambiguity of hope

A deeper analysis of the communication of love opens the view to two aspects of love – love's power of transformation and love's vulnerabilities and insurmountable risks. This strength and these limits of love put them in a great closeness to hope. Thus, at least at first sight, hope seems to be productive in responding to the inner limits of love.

Not for nothing, for example, in the religious symbolism of the New Testament writings, are love and hope often closely linked. Even though hope addresses, or, one might say, solves some of love's problems, hope remains ambiguous. In truth, the ambiguities of hope illuminate and deepen the risks of love.

Translated into the current conflicts in Western societies, to sustain a vision of a more humane society and culture in the conflicts of the twenty-first century there is no need for discharging but a realistic deepening of our understanding of love and hope.

4.1 deceptive and self-deceptive hope

When we move from the phenomenological structure or the social dynamic of hope to its *content*, we see its ambiguity: there is a real risk that it can be false hope. Deceptive hope is present when human beings do not want to learn from counterevidence. However, this always depends on the specific perspective of the second-order observer.[25] Nevertheless, we should not forget that hope can be deceptive and misleading; not only hope in a *deus ex machina* which is present in some Christian traditions but also hope in the realm of liberal secular humanism.

Looking back to the experiences of the twentieth century, one can see that the most violent, brutal and destructive events were large-scale experiments in human hope. Most of the horrendous evils of the last century were committed by highly committed transformative elites, who benefited from broad consensus among the people. If one looks back to the twentieth century and the history of moral failure, the real challenge to moral theory is the fact that in almost every case the majority of the population – not just a criminal, small minority – were in favour of these policies and practices.

Today's hope in human insight and responsibility, education, foresight and moral agency is as ambiguous and as questionable, or one might say, counterfactual, as most strands of Christian hope. A more disillusioned up-to-date critic of religion might claim that theories of ideal worlds are as useless, or even dangerous, as most religious fantasies.

People committed to a liberal secular humanism (that is all those accused by Charles Taylor of promoting flattened immanence) and those who remain committed to Christian faith find themselves in the same boat: their counterfactual hopes that undergird their strong normative evaluations of this world might be illusory. At the beginning of the third millennium, both groups search for non-illusionary grounds of non-deceptive hope in order to enhance this lived life. Both hope that love and hope will eventually point a way out of the often-tragic structure of life.[26] Hope is necessary to keep necessary utopias alive – beyond their merely rhetorical affirmation.[27]

4.2 desperate hope

The apparent risks in desperate hope should not lead to moral nihilism or the worship of conflicting interests and hoarding up of power, despite the temptations of such postures. The dramatic moral failures mentioned should be a reminder: there is no safeguard against failure, no completely secure foundation, nor certainly any reason for moral arrogance. Moral orientations can be dangerous, cause conflict and create division.

For this reason, hope must be tempered by love. Without love, hope can slip not only into violent impatience but also into moral contempt, moral disgust and utter moral indignation. Each of today's Western societies provides ample examples of this dynamic. Love in its dangerous creativity can dismantle violent hope and break the cycles of self-radicalizing self-righteousness overpowering regard for others.

4.3 hope in divine creativity

The descriptions presented in this essay grow out of a wide hermeneutical circle. They are informed by aspects of love symbolized in the event and person of Jesus Christ. The claim is that this event can shed light on human experience.

Christian hope will always be hope in someone, directly in Jesus Christ and in God's creative spirit. It is not a hope in the return of a warrior as imagined in many audiovisual stories. It is hope, however, in a persuasive power – as persuasive as the warrior – that operates by other powerful means. The question of tragedy and futility remains – evident in every premature death. Christian faith offers no relief from these temptations, but a more comprehensive framework of hope.

Hope in Christ is hope for the full realization, one might say generalization, of the love he lived. This love in someone is not naive personalism but hope in someone whose space of real life-enhancing possibilities transcends our current and finite human space of possibilities. This profound change in the space of possibilities was and is radically manifest in and indicated by the resurrection of Jesus Christ. Suffering love is not enough.[28] It needs to be taken up by the transformative power of God's Spirit. The resurrection indicates divine creativity beyond our individual and social possibilities and beyond the possibilities of suffering love. It is God's ultimate protest against all processes of victimization leading to suffering love. The faithfulness to this earth and the resurrection of Jesus Christ forces Christian faith to hope and lament – in the form of political, spiritual and intellectual practices of love. Both Christian humanists and liberal secular humanists hope that the risks of love will eventually be redeemed. Both hope, under postmodern conditions, without a final anchor point in experience.[29]

disclosure statement

No potential conflict of interest was reported by the author.

notes

This essay was written with the generous support of a grant from the Enhancing Life Project (http://enhancinglife.uchicago.edu/).

1 Pamela Sue Anderson, "Arguing for 'Ethical' Vulnerability: Towards a Politics of Care?" in *Exploring Vulnerability*, eds. Heike Springhart and Günter Thomas (Göttingen and Bristol, VT: Vandenhoeck, 2017) 147–62.

2 A basic assumption woven into the following remarks is the idea that love is not a disposition but happens to be communicated in various media of communication (Günter Thomas, "Die Kommunikation von Glaube, Liebe und Hoffnung als Gestalt christlichen Lebens" in *Liebe: Jahrbuch für Biblische Theologie*, vol. 29, ed. Martin Ebner (Neukirchen-Vluyn: Neukirchener, 2015) 283–301).

3 Niklas Luhmann, *The Reality of the Mass Media*, trans. Kathleen Cross (Cambridge: Polity, 2000) 97.

4 On the differentiation of risk and danger, see Niklas Luhmann, *Risk: A Sociological Theory. Communication and Social Order*, trans. Rhodes Barrett (New York: De Gruyter, 1993).

5 Pamela Sue Anderson, "Lost Confidence and Human Capability: A Hermeneutic Phenomenology of the Gendered, yet Capable Subject," *Text Matters: A Journal of Literature, Theory and Culture* 4.4 (2014): 31–52.

6 The literary tropes of love's naivety, blindness, spontaneity, willingness to be exploited, and eventually to be foolish.

7 An interesting case in point is the command to honour one's parents in Exodus 20.12. Honour and support are enough; love is not asked for.

8 All utopian communities which wanted to abandon the rule of law ended in terror (Keally

D. McBride, *Collective Dreams: Political Imagination and Community* (University Park: Pennsylvania State UP, 2005)).

9 Michael Welker makes a similar point in emphasizing the role of mercy in the development of law. Mercy operates outside of law and at the same time is one of the driving forces for its development – when what is at a given moment just mercy becomes a new law – without destroying the distinction (Michael Welker, "Security of Expectations: Reformulating the Theology of Law and Gospel," *Journal of Religion* 66.3 (1986): 237–60).

10 Lilie Chouliaraki, *The Spectatorship of Suffering* (Thousand Oaks, CA: Sage, 2006); Lilie Chouliaraki and Shani Orgad, "Proper Distance: Mediation, Ethics, Otherness," *International Journal of Cultural Studies* 14.4 (2011): 341–45.

11 Hannah Arendt, *Der Liebesbegriff bei Augustin: Versuch einer philosophischen Interpretation* (Berlin: Springer, 1929).

12 Friedrich Nietzsche, *On the Genealogy of Morality*, 3rd ed., ed. Keith Ansell-Pearson; trans. Carol Diethe (Cambridge: Cambridge UP, 2017).

13 Mark Lilla, *The Once and Future Liberal: After Identity Politics* (New York: Harper, 2017).

14 "With friends like these, who needs enemies?"

15 This insight is spelled out lucidly by Raimond Gaita in *A Common Humanity: Thinking about Love and Truth and Justice* (London: Routledge, 2000) 17–20. Unlike Gaita, we would hesitate to generalize this discovery of the shared basis of humanity as much as he does.

16 Eva Feder Kittay, *Love's Labor: Essays on Women, Equality, and Dependency* (New York: Routledge, 1999).

17 These are the questions one can often hear from people in very old age. Absolutely and radically selfless love is beyond human beings. Conceptually speaking, the conceptual separation of *eros*, *philia* and *agape* – and henceforth the designation of the three elements to different experiences – seems to be misleading. Both religious and secular welfare systems had been very creative in their set-up of a mixed set of awards.

18 One might call this differentiating process a shadow of tragedy. It is the shadow of unintended effects.

19 René Girard's theory is all about this type of second-order observation, also the first murder in the biblical tradition (René Girard, *Violence and the Sacred*, trans. Patrick Gregory (Baltimore: Johns Hopkins UP, 1977); *The Scapegoat*, trans. Yvonne Freccero (Baltimore: Johns Hopkins UP, 1986)).

20 In Goethe's *Faust* (Johann Wolfgang von Goethe, *Faust*, ed. Albrecht Schöne [Sonderausg., textidentisch mit der 4., überarb. Aufl. von Bd. 7/1 der Goethe-Ausg. des Dt. Klassiker-Verl. ed.] (Darmstadt: Wiss. Buchges., 1999)) the eternal moment can be read in two ways. It can be interpreted as the exclusion of any extension of time. It is the intensification of time, the ecstatic moment. At the same time, it can be interpreted as the total extension of time, because this moment is supposed to last for ever and to remain.

21 This is always an open experiment, in which the past is permanently rewritten. Think about divorce counselling, where the most puzzling question often is: if the shared life was always so terrible then why did the couple not stop it in the first place and why did they stay together so long?

22 Even forms of highly selfless love do not remain in the sphere of emotion and contemplation but try to shape reality by interventions.

23 Even contractual relationships – be they real or fictitious ones as in social theories or theories of justice – share this moment of selectivity as a basis of their efficiency and reality. Even if we follow Luke Brunning's plea for seriously analysing the phenomenon of polyamory, the dividing line of selectivity is only shifted. Polyamorous relationships among finite human beings are still based on acts of "discrimination" (Luke Brunning, "The Distinctiveness of Polyamory," *Journal of Applied Philosophy* (2016): doi:10.1111/japp.12240; accessed 10 June 2019).

24 In Friedrich Schleiermacher's eschatology this notion of inclusion leads – against Thomas Aquinas' joy about the suffering crowd in hell – to an utterly empty hell. As long as the believers would enjoy the pain of the non-believers in hell their own love would not and could not be perfected (Friedrich Schleiermacher, *The Christian Faith*, trans. J.S. Stewart and H.R. Mackintosh (Edinburgh: Clark, 1999) section 163).

25 On second-order observation: Niklas Luhmann, *Social Systems*, trans. John Bednarz Jr

with Dirk Baecker (Stanford: Stanford UP, 1995); "Deconstruction as Second-Order Observing," *New Literary History* 24.4 (1993): 763–82.

26 Exemplary is Rowan Williams, *The Tragic Imagination* (Oxford: Oxford UP, 2016).

27 One of these necessary utopias is a thick understanding of human rights. Jürgen Habermas spells out their utopian character in "The Concept of Human Dignity and the Realistic Utopia of Human Rights," *Metaphilosophy* 41.4 (2010): 464–80. With a more pessimistic undertone: Samuel Moyn, *The Last Utopia: Human Rights in History* (Cambridge, MA: Belknap P of Harvard UP, 2010).

28 This is explored lucidly by Paul S. Fiddes, *The Creative Suffering of God* (Oxford: Clarendon, 1988).

29 Pamela Sue Anderson, "Postmodern Theology," *The Routledge Companion to Philosophy of Religion*, 2nd ed., eds. Chad V. Meister and Paul Copan (London and New York: Routledge, 2013) 569–80.

My philosophical conversation with Pamela Sue Anderson starts with the notion of love, and with the cosmic love that one is capable of when one transforms one's ego's boundary and becomes open to love and mutual affection (Anderson, "Towards a New Philosophical Imaginary").[1] My chapter is initially triggered by Anderson's essay "Towards a New Philosophical Imaginary" as a response to Michèle Le Doeuff's Oxford lecture "Not a Goddess, She!" which gradually developed into Anderson's deeper analysis of the philosophical imaginary. I address Anderson's transformative aesthetics on the notion of vulnerability and love, showing how "vulnerability" can be transformed into a positive energy. My interpretation of her writing goes into the deeper reading of her theory of vulnerability and love as a neo-Enlightenment theory having Eastern/Indian philosophical underpinnings. What strikes me most is her spiritual turn in her article "'A Thoughtful Love of Life': A Spiritual Turn in Philosophy of Religion," where she transcends the boundary of mere political and social life and grounds her philosophy in spirituality. Although her theory intersects with Judith Butler's theory of vulnerability and resistance, there is a subtle distinction between the two, as Anderson's approach is more tilted toward spirituality than is Butler's.

le doeuff's complaint against the enlightenment philosophers

Le Doeuff's critique of the Enlightenment philosophers Rousseau and Hegel in *The Philosophical Imaginary* is highly significant. Anderson, however, is especially interested in

ashmita khasnabish

ON THE THEME OF LIBERATED LOVE AND GLOBAL FEMINIST DISCOURSE

the construction of the myth of Dawn in Le Doeuff's "Not a Goddess, She!" and explains the importance of that reference:

> Essentially the significance of this myth is its message: in order to gain reciprocal affections, we should take care not to force a girl to grow up to be a goddess of maternal love with sacrificial and tragic relations to men, to other women, to gods and goddesses. An original (classical) story told by Le Doeuff lends itself to a recreation of a timely contemporary myth about a young girl, Dawn, whose *vulnerability* needs to be *enhanced*, in order for her *heart* which is reason to enlighten us. ("Towards a New Philosophical Imaginary" 15–16)

Recreating the myth, Anderson shows that the image of Dawn, who combines emotion and reason, invites an excursion beyond patriarchy. In this context, I want to ponder Anderson's critique of Mary Midgley's creation of the myth of Owl and Minerva, in which love is recognized or visible only in darkness; under Anderson's interpretation, the idea that love occurs only in darkness or dusk is a paternalistic response. Anderson explains the impact of Western myths like the myth of Owl and Minerva. The effects of such myths, which dominate social life infinitely, are apparent in social media generating political conversation inclined against women. She attributes that discourse quite reasonably and fairly to the impact of Western paternalistic myths, emphatically articulating her grievance that we are controlled by (mythical) gender impositions. Feminist philosophers are all too aware that a philosophical imaginary of violence is "the shameful face" of (Western) philosophy. Anderson ridicules Mary Midgley for suggesting the image of dusk as the symbol of wisdom: she comments that it is because we are so constricted by patriarchy in the West that Midgley follows Hegel in her proposal that "the love of wisdom" is "recognized at dusk, at a moment of difficult transition, of loss or death" and not in everyday life ("Towards a New Philosophical Imaginary" 13).

relational ontology and liberated love

In "Towards a New Philosophical Imaginary" Anderson traces Le Doeuff's reconstruction of the female imaginary as the image of the young girl Dawn, an image adapted from the Spanish philosopher Maria Zambrano's image of Dawn. That source has an oriental undertone, in the unification or synthesis of reason and a purified sense of emotion, as I interpret this idea in my "Conclusion: Political Sublime," in *Humanitarian Identity and the Political Sublime: Intervention of a Postcolonial Feminist*. Anderson writes: "Zambrano portrays Dawn's heart as significantly different from either the mind or the body, of either eternal male or eternal female essence. Instead, the heart encompasses aspects of both the incorporeal and the corporeal" ("Towards a New Philosophical Imaginary" 16). What is notable is this intersection between the corporeal and the incorporeal. She further writes that Zambrano's poetic reasoning is about a girl whose "heart becomes a symbol for a fresh understanding of a human soul in loving reciprocal relations" (ibid.). What I find unique in this development and interpretation of the character Dawn is the portrayal of her personality as a combination of reason and emotion. She is liberated from bonded love, and the love she represents is based on both reason and emotion. Here, I find a connection with my neo-Kantian theory proposed in *Humanitarian Identity and the Political Sublime*. According to Kant, the sublime exists only in the mind. The suggestion that the sublime exists only in the mind is a bit offensive; under Le Doeuff's categorization, following Western culture/philosophy, the mind is associated with men, and the body is associated with women. I further allude to Kant's famous observation in the *Critique of Judgment*: "The Beautiful prepares us to love disinterestedly something, even nature itself; the Sublime prepares us to esteem something highly even in opposition to our sensible interest" (134). I interpret the Beautiful and the Sublime or the senses of emotion and reason in the following way:

> Kantian Sublime makes a permanent divide between the senses and the sublime. Beautiful is associated with the senses and the sublime with the reason. Sri Aurobindo's theory rereads it by suggesting that there is no divide between the two. It is possible to achieve the Sublime (in his own term "supermind" or the supramental consciousness) through ego-transcendence and bring it down to the level of senses. He transcends Freud's theory that ego is the supreme agency. It also sheds light on the ideological difference between the dualism of the West and the non-dualistic philosophy of the East. (*Humanitarian Identity* 142)

I argue here that Eastern/Indian philosophical theory advocates non-dualism, perceived in the modern Indian philosopher Sri Aurobindo's philosophy of supramental consciousness.[2] According to Aurobindo's philosophical theory there are several levels of consciousness, and through mind-control or ego-transcendence one achieves a purified state of mind. After achieving this state, one descends to the material plane of consciousness; through this practice one might conquer one's ego (bad ego) and maintain the pure state of mind in practical life. This notion of ego-transcendence is also the source of my theory of the political sublime. The practice of sublimity in day-to-day life could be defined as the political sublime. Unlike Kantian theory, this theory foregrounds the marriage between the senses and the sublime. Thus, it also sheds light on Zambrano's portrayal of Dawn's heart as combining reason with emotion or senses. Anderson writes: "This Enlightenment narrative does not oppose reason to love, or mind to body. Instead, reason, like a pre-adolescent heart, if it is cultivated, can enlighten love in others, too. Thus, the mutually produced wisdom of love comes with Dawn" ("Towards a New Philosophical Imaginary" 17).

These ideas are very close to those in Anderson's article "Bergsonian Intuition: A Metaphysics of Mystical Life," where she characterizes Bergsonian metaphysical intuition as a mystical experience that unites analysis with non-perspectival sense-making. Anderson's approach also bears a relation to my theory of the political sublime, which is rooted in a critique of the Kantian theory of reason and the divide between the beautiful and the sublime that Anderson addresses in her article on Bergson. Most fascinating is the observation that Kant's resistance to intuition has been challenged by Bergson and Anderson. This in turn underscores an endorsement of mysticism as a source of metaphysical knowledge. Kant opposes intellectual intuition as humanly impossible, whereas Bergson thinks that Kantian thought could be modified under his proposed notion of intuition. Anderson writes:

> I will stress that Bergsonian intuition is "an effort to place oneself in a movement, such as that of philosophy itself," expressing "what is 'living in *philosophers*' rather than what is 'fixed and dead in *theses*.'" This mystical life pushes out the limits set up by Kant for metaphysics (and science) by allowing intuition (with analysis) to reach for absolute, non-perspectival knowledge. ("Bergsonian Intuition" 240; emphasis in original)

When Anderson supports Bergson's paradigm, in which he valorizes intuition and thinks that Kantian thought could be qualified and enhanced by his theory of intuition, we encounter an oriental/Indian philosophical dimension. In Indian philosophy, the Kantian notions of the beautiful and the sublime can be brought together. Similarly, the Kantian theory of reason can be modified by Bergsonian intuition. Anderson interprets reason as metaphysical and mystical and, as a Western feminist, has no reservation about the metaphysical or the mystical underpinnings of Bergson's philosophy and embraces them. It is also profoundly interesting that the Indian philosopher Sri Aurobindo's philosophical theory of supramental consciousness acknowledges and values intuition[3] as one of the steps toward the achievement of the highest level of consciousness. Anderson states clearly that Kant's restriction of intuition to sensibility almost impels European philosophers toward mystical thinking: "some form of mysticism seemed to be the next step after Kant's critique" ("Bergsonian Intuition" 246). Pertinent, too, is Anderson's essay "Metaphors of Spatial Location," in which she adduces the conception of two spaces in Kant's world, one of them knowable and the other unknowable. Alluding to Le Doeuff and Hannah Arendt, Anderson writes:

> To repeat, the extension of Kant's own thinking places Kantian and post-Kantian philosophers in a situation where they cannot express the exact bounds of sense in empirical terms. Nevertheless, they may think that they can place themselves, or imagine their location, in thought on the other side, on these non-empirical, and so sensibly unlocatable, standpoints. ("Metaphors of Spatial Location" 179)

anderson and butler on vulnerability and its intersection with capability

Butler argues, "In my final set of remarks, I want to argue against the notion that vulnerability is the opposite of resistance. Indeed I want to argue affirmatively that vulnerability, understood as a deliberate exposure to power, is part of the very meaning of political resistance as an embodied enactment" (Butler 22). Significant here is Butler's argument that vulnerability can be turned into a positive force. As a matter of fact, vulnerability and resistance can work together under a feminist model, but not through patriarchy or in a paternalistic model. Butler considers the struggles of immigrants and minorities; women, of course, are minorities in almost every society. It is both interesting and startling to note that the battle for women's empowerment is affiliated with the battles of minorities and immigrants. The observation is reminiscent, too, of the theory of capability offered by Amartya Sen and Martha Nussbaum. The theory of capability arose in conversation with and as a critique of the great American philosopher John Rawls's theory of justice and the "First Original Position."[4] Let us look at Sen's comment, discussed in my monograph *Negotiating Capability and Diaspora: A Philosophical Politics*:

> What is amazing to see in Sen's critique is the awareness about the marginalized communities in the Western world – especially the immigrants who constantly readjust and readapt as nomads. Also, notice his following observation, "It is through 'coming to terms' with one's hopeless predicament that life is made somewhat bearable by the traditional underdogs, such as oppressed minorities in intolerant communities." (25)

Like Anderson, Sen connects capability with the power of individual will to transform vulnerability into a political platform on which women and minorities can express themselves. And this is definitely a feminist task because, as Butler also argues, paternalistic power will tend to separate vulnerability from resistance, so that the vulnerable remain helpless and powerless. She suggests that it is the task of the feminists to end that binary opposition and turn it into positive energy and political power. Sen claims that coming to terms with one's hopeless predicament makes life bearable; here, he exposes the harsh reality that the transcendental institutional structures proposed by Rawls do not necessarily afford the transformative power that Butler proposes. Capability deprivation and inequality are part of the vulnerability framework, and it is imperative to combat vulnerability and turn it into freedom through resistance.

intersection between capability and vulnerability

Capability as a tool will expose the difference between the master and the slave, so that there is no possibility of erasure. At the same time, capability offers the strength to create agency. There is a subtle connection between the theory of capability and that of vulnerability and resistance. Under the capability approach, individual freedom is determined by what one has reason to value; under the vulnerability approach, freedom is determined by the strength to turn that vulnerability into resistance and political power. The vulnerable condition is both an existential condition and a socially induced condition, but to invoke sympathy is detrimental. Instead, one has to transform vulnerability into a source of strength. Anderson writes: "In other words, I will follow Butler's lead with a relational ontology, in which vulnerability is a (universal) mode of relationality and not 'the human condition'" ("Towards a New Philosophical Imaginary" 9). Butler strives to transform vulnerability into power and wants vulnerability and resistance to work together in the achievement of political agency. She does not want to blow vulnerability out of proportion by attributing feeling to it and giving birth to a whole new set of "care" values; instead, she would turn it into a political force. Anderson sees in vulnerability an infinite potential for love and turns it into what she calls relational ontology, following Butler; she interprets mourning or grieving as a steppingstone to a better life or a life of transformation. This view resonates with that of the Indian Nobel laureate poet Rabindranath Tagore, who was a great feminist man, as is revealed in his songs. Tagore writes, "*Dukkho jadi na pabeto dukho tomar ghucbe kabe / bishke bsher daha diye marte habe*" (you have to have sorrow in order to conquer sorrow / you have to burn poison with poison) (393; my translation). The sorrow has to be felt; one has to grieve in order to overcome grief. As Anderson asks, "What exactly is missing, if we do not mourn loss of another's life?" ("Towards a New Philosophical Imaginary" 11). When we do not empathize or identify with another's pain, we lose value for or appreciation of life. Let me quote Anderson: "Butler's answer to what is missing seems to be: a life that counts is a life that is valued, and a life that is valued is a life we grieve because it was part of who 'we' were; and this can be no one" (ibid.). In *Humanitarian Identity and the Political Sublime*, I argue,

> this I also define as the "political sublime" where there is no difference between your pain and my pain; I as a human being share your pain, and you as a human being share mine. I love and respect you and you love and respect me and we do not compete and race as animals. We truly discover our ontological roots nationally, internationally as well. We become truly global. (133–34)

In her article "Sublimation and Sublime Meaning," Anderson ponders the sublimation of pain through Fiddes and Kristeva and in dialogue with both of them. She makes a connection between them, on the one hand, relating Kristeva's psycholinguistic sublimation and Fiddes' theological sublimation. The common ground is the mastery of pain, suggested in God's suffering and in Kant's theory of the beautiful and the sublime. Following Kristeva, Anderson is ushering in a space that is a post-Kantian space. The most appealing lines, resonating with my own theory of the political sublime, are the following, where Anderson alludes to Kristeva's theory of sublimation: "But in her psycholinguistic terms, for human subjects both to suffer and to have compassion requires a process of sublimation; and this should culminate in a love of beauty and in sublime meaning for this life" ("Sublimation and Sublime Meaning" 13). When Anderson interprets this process of sublimation that culminates in a love of beauty and the sublime for this life, it resonates with her interpretation of Walter Benjamin's storyteller as philosopher. Anderson writes: "All great philosophers – in so far as they practice a spiritual art of story-telling – 'have in common the freedom with which they move up and down the rungs of their experience as on a ladder'" ("'A Thoughtful Love of Life'" 123). What is important in Anderson's world is the strong connection with what she calls "spirituality." Her philosophy is grounded in spirituality; she defines the spiritual turn as a transformative practice in which one regards not only oneself but also one's relation to social and material worlds. She advocates for the philosophers and the philosophers of religion to move together beyond the debates of traditional theisms. Here, Anderson's approach diverges from Butler's take on vulnerability. The "philosophical imaginary" that she constructs, following and resonating with Le Doeuff, brings to its relational ontology a thoughtful love of life, by which Anderson means spirituality: "The adjective spiritual is meant here to describe relation of the self to self, to other selves, and to the natural, material and social worlds in which human subjects find themselves" (ibid.).

from love to relational ontology

In "Risking Oneself and One's Identity: Agonism Revisited," Zeynep Gambetti brings Arendt into the discussion. Arendt proposes a relationality that Gambetti explains through Greek terms like *agonism*. Gambetti quotes Arendt:

> The agon, the strife of aristeuein [...] is [...] the political equation of reality with appearing to others. Only where others were present, could a specifically human life

begin. Only where one was noticed by others could he, by distinguishing himself, come into his own humanity. (33)

Gambetti is referring to the process as "becoming-human" (ibid.), which resonates with Deleuze's notion of becoming human in *A Thousand Plateaus*. She constructs identity by dismantling power from its institutional and instrumental underpinnings and dispossessing self. To her, the self is nothing without the other, which suggests Butler's theory of vulnerability. This notion of becoming other and acquiring a new identity is addressed later in my discussion of the Indian-American novelist Jhumpa Lahiri's memoir and my theory of virtual diaspora.

Sen, Butler, Arendt, and Anderson strive to give voice to the vulnerable. In this regard, I want to refer to the story of the grandmother's flight dream in Elena Loizidou's essay "Dreams and the Political Subject." The grandmother, who has to flee from a Greek Cypriot village captured by Turkish invasion in 1974, mourns and wants to go back. It is significant that this discourse could turn into a discourse of empowerment, as she returns in her dream. Loizidou writes:

> I recall my maternal grandmother, sitting in the back of the veranda of our house in Nicosia on a low stool, in a loose light black dress, and on various occasions saying: "I had a dream last night. I dreamt I was at the village, in Petra. I saw my home and the church and the river." (122)

This passage captures the fundamental psychological status of a refugee or even an immigrant who can never return to the homeland except through dream. Journeying through dream to the homeland, the grandmother reconciles with her old self, which has been fragmented and broken apart in the pain of separation. Contra Arendt, she ascribes significance to the personal dream that offers a visual entry to a past, and she tries to compensate for her current loss and exile's status. This dream is not a dream to reterritorialize but a nostalgic longing to return to her favorite past.

Along these lines, I want to remark on the Indian-American novelist Jhumpa Lahiri's memoir *In Other Words*; Lahiri's personal story resonates with the stories of immigrants included in Butler's anthology, particularly with the flight dream of the grandmother. I define this condition as a state of virtuality and of virtual diaspora in my Oxford lecture "Virtual Diaspora: A Postcolonial Feminism," offering homage to Anderson. Here, Lahiri experiences the pain of her mother's exile with her own pain; her own state of virtual existence is constructed from that in between space where her mother's state of real diaspora intersects with her own virtual experience.

I must point out here that my theory of virtual diaspora is influenced by Deleuze and Guattari's book *A Thousand Plateaus*, where the main philosophical notion is that of transformation and becoming other: an interpretation, in a way, of Le Doeuff's construct of a philosophical imaginary. It is possible to open the book at any point and encounter the sense of assemblage, fluidity, and a certain kind of becoming or *de-structure*. Lahiri never lived in her mother's country but identified with her pain, and I call this a state of virtuality and virtual diaspora; Lahiri tries to experience this state by imagining a third identity and exploring it through a different language that is neither her mother tongue nor the language she adopted through migration. I am struck by the intersection of the theory of vulnerability and resistance and the notion of virtual diaspora. Consider the narrator's confession: "Because of my double identity I saw only fluctuation, distortion, dissimulation. I saw something hybrid, out of focus, always jumbled" (Lahiri 157). But why does she feel fragmented? It is because of her deep affection for the mother tongue that she does not have.

As she resists her vulnerability when juggling two mothers, Bengali and English, Lahiri triumphs by embracing different languages, thereby growing, and, in Deleuzian terms, not just becoming other but embracing her new identity. As Deleuze and Guattari observe, she "must relaunch for a non-subjective, living love in which each party connects with unknown traits in the other without entering or conquering them, in which the lines composed are broken lines" (189). In the memoir, Lahiri associates herself with the Italian language and seeks a new identity that is universal, resisting any desire for territoriality. At the end of the chapter "Metamorphosis" she confesses that

> it is true that a new language covers me, but unlike Daphne I have a permeable covering, I'm almost without a skin. And although I don't have a thick bark, I am, in Italian, a tougher, freer writer, who, taking root again, grows in a different way. (Lahiri 173)

Where does Anderson's construct of the new philosophical imaginary intersect with the formulation of a stronger political and loving identity? In the end, I want to reflect on Anderson's fondness for the French philosopher Paul Ricoeur's[5] theory of the capability of love, as she references his book *Memory, History, Forgetting* and observes how human capability has been affected by painful affection. Here, she speaks out for the justice and liberated love that she invoked in her vindication of Le Doeuff's creation of the myth of Dawn, and for the vulnerable people discussed here and ranging from women to immigrants, refugees, and all those with minority status: disabled individuals, members of the LGBTQ community, and the wounded. Appealing to the ethics of love, one can claim what one deserves, but strategy is crucial. The dismantling of patriarchal myths is a step forward; Anderson envisions this step and I have pursued it by engaging in discussion with Amartya Sen's theory of capability, which intersects in important ways with Anderson's theory of vulnerability. Finally, Anderson's theory, with its rich potential, liberates me to engage in a global feminist discourse and encourages me to articulate my repertoire of neo-Enlightenment postcolonial cogitations.

disclosure statement

No potential conflict of interest was reported by the author.

notes

1 The lines of Shelley occurred to me, because what is missing in this universe is the sense of cosmic love; let me ponder on the words of the Romantic poet: "The desire of the moth for the star, / Of the night for the morrow, / The devotion to something afar / From the sphere of our sorrow?" alluding to some intangible quality of love that rises with the conquering of sorrow (Shelley 683).

2 The great modern Indian philosopher Sri Aurobindo coined the philosophical term *supramental consciousness*, based on Indian Vedanta philosophy. It involves the processes of the Ascent, where mind goes through the process of ascent via various levels of mind like Higher Mind, Illumined Mind, Intuition, Overmind, to the Supermind or the highest level of consciousness. The journey of Ascent does not stop there; mind, after reaching the Supermind or the highest level of consciousness, descends to the material plane. This is called the theory of supramental consciousness, and it is a spiritual philosophy. Reaching the supramental level of consciousness is also identical with transcending one's ego and reaching the concept of the Brahman or the Absolute, according to ancient Indian philosophy. But we also need to bring down that consciousness to the plane of the body through its descent onto the body.

3 Intuition is one of the steps of Supramental Consciousness, and it comes after Illumined Mind:

> Each level of mind possesses a different level of consciousness in this ascending order. In the Higher Mind, which transcends to a great extent the pulling of the half-light or half-consciousness [...] It is a first step towards the Supermind [...] After this one achieves the Illumined Mind which is "A Mind no longer of Higher thought but of Spiritual light." The next is Intuition, a plane of the mind which is not only a step higher but also one that advances the senses. This stage is part of the Supramental light, but it is also a stage in which the spiritual evolution is still in progress. (Aurobindo Ghose 149)

4 I want to quote here from my monograph *Negotiating Capability and Diaspora: A Philosophical Politics*, where I discuss Amartya Sen's reservation regarding John Rawls's theory of the "First Original Position." I write, interpreting Sen,

The "First Original Position" is problematic because it asks for inculcating the notion of the "veil of ignorance," which means that no one will exactly know the value system of moral or political principle of the other member but will conform for the sake of political justice. (18)

5 Ricoeur says, in the Epilogue of *Memory, History, Forgetting*, interpreting Arendt,

The faculty of forgiveness and the faculty of promising rest on experiences that no one can have in isolation and which are based entirely on the presence of others [...] On this point, Arendt uses to her own advantage the exegesis of the Gospel texts most favorable to her interpretation. These texts say that it is only if humans exchange forgiveness among themselves that they can hope to be forgiven by God as well: the power to forgive is a human power. (487)

bibliography

Anderson, Pamela Sue. "Bergsonian Intuition: A Metaphysics of Mystical Life." *Philosophical Topics* 43.1–2 (2015): 239–51. Print.

Anderson, Pamela Sue. "Metaphors of Spatial Location: Understanding Post-Kantian Space." *Contemporary Kantian Metaphysics*. Ed. Roxana Baiasu et al. London: Palgrave Macmillan, 2012. 169–96. Print.

Anderson, Pamela Sue. "Sublimation and Sublime Meaning: Pain and Passion in an Infinite, Intellectual Love of God." *Within the Love of God: Essays on the Doctrine of God in Honour of Paul S. Fiddes*. Ed. Anthony Clarke and Andrew Moore. Oxford: Oxford UP, 2014. 1–21. Print.

Anderson, Pamela Sue. "'A Thoughtful Love of Life': A Spiritual Turn in Philosophy of Religion." *Svensk Teologisk Kvartalskrift* 85 (2009): 119–29. Print.

Anderson, Pamela Sue. "Towards a New Philosophical Imaginary." Ed. Sabina Lovibond and Adrian W. Moore. *Love and Vulnerability: Thinking with Pamela Sue Anderson*. Ed. Pelagia Goulimari. Spec. issue of *Angelaki: Journal of the Theoretical Humanities* 25.1–2 (2020): 8–22. Print.

Butler, Judith. "Rethinking Vulnerability and Resistance." Butler, Gambetti, and Sabsay 12–27. Print.

Butler, Judith, Zeynep Gambetti, and Leticia Sabsay, eds. *Vulnerability in Resistance*. Durham, NC: Duke UP, 2016. Print.

Deleuze, Gilles, and Félix Guattarai. *A Thousand Plateaus: Capitalism and Schizophrenia*. 1987. Trans. Brian Massumi. Minneapolis: U of Minnesota P, 2005. Print.

Gambetti, Zeynep. "Risking Oneself and One's Identity: Agonism Revisited." Butler, Gambetti, and Sabsay 28–47. Print.

Ghose, Sri Aurobindo. *The Life Divine; Book One and Book Two*. Sri Aurobindo Ashram, Pondicherry, India: All India, 1973. Print.

Kant, Immanuel. *The Critique of Judgment*. Trans. J.H Bernard. Amherst, NY: Prometheus, 2000. Print.

Khasnabish, Ashmita. *Humanitarian Identity and the Political Sublime: Intervention of a Postcolonial Feminist*. Lanham, MD: Lexington, 2009. Print.

Khasnabish, Ashmita. *Negotiating Capability and Diaspora: A Philosophical Politics*. Lanham, MD: Lexington, 2014. Print.

Lahiri, Jhumpa. *In Other Words*. Trans. Ann Goldstein. New York: Knopf, 2016. Print.

Le Doeuff, Michèle. "Not a Goddess, She!" Lecture 4 of "The Spirit of Secularism: On Fables, Gender and Ethics." Weidenfeld Professorial Lectures, University of Oxford, Trinity Term 2006. Lecture.

Le Doeuff, Michèle. *The Philosophical Imaginary*. Trans. Colin Gordon. Stanford: Stanford UP, 1989. Print.

Loizidou, Elena. "Dreams and the Political Subject." Butler, Gambetti, and Sabsay 122–45. Print.

Ricoeur, Paul. *Memory, History, Forgetting*. Trans. Kathleen Blamey and David Pellauer. Chicago: U of Chicago P, 2004. Print.

Sen, Amartya. *The Idea of Justice*. Cambridge, MA: Belknap P of Harvard UP, 2009. Print.

Shelley, Percy Bysshe. "One Word is Too Often Profaned." *The Complete Poems of Percy Bysshe Shelley*. New York: Random, 1994. 683. Print.

Tagore, Rabindranath. *Rabindra Rachanabali, Song*. Vol. 4. Ed. Rabindrakumar Dasgupta et al. Calcutta: Saraswati, 1987. Print.

stephen mulhall

THE IDEA OF ETHICAL VULNERABILITY
perfectionism, irony and the theological virtues

I was very pleased to be invited to participate in the conference on Pamela Sue Anderson's work from which this journal special issue and book has grown. Although Pamela belonged to a different faculty, we did occasionally work together when Oxford students were rash enough to take up positions on the borderline between theology and philosophy, and of course Pamela's charitable and imaginative interest in some of the central figures of what still gets called "Continental Philosophy" offered some reassurance that my own investments in those traditions were not entirely unintelligible. She is very much missed.

When I received that invitation, together with a set of papers representing Pamela's most recent thinking, I had already been working on the theological virtues as part of my contribution to another project – one housed in the School of Philosophy and Art History at the University of Essex – which focused on the ethics of powerlessness.[1] And once I had read Pamela's essay "Arguing for 'Ethical' Vulnerability: Towards a Politics of Care," in which she states "what I advocate as distinctively ethical vulnerability acknowledges and activates an openness to becoming changed" (150), I realized that the material I had been developing for the Essex project in effect converged on exactly the territory Pamela had been attempting to stake out, and so could support and elaborate the goals she was pursuing, and in a theological register that might seem to resonate with her own intellectual orientations.[2] So it seemed to me that working out my own way of reaching conclusions that Pamela reaches in her own way would be a fitting acknowledgement of the enduring significance of this last phase of her intellectual trajectory.

As part of the Essex project's interest in reinterpreting faith, hope and love as theological virtues in modernity, David Batho prepared two substantial and illuminating Green Papers.[3] The first ("Faith, Hope and Love as Virtues in the Theological Tradition": October 2016) explores theological thought from St Paul to Paul Tillich in order to address two central issues: how we should understand the relationship between these three virtues, and whether we should class them as virtues at all. The second paper ("Faith, Hope and Love in Critical Perspective": February 2017) concludes by asking whether these virtues can be secularized, and more specifically whether they are viable in contemporary contexts (i.e., contexts in which a religious framework is at best one optional intellectual horizon for the pursuit of human well-being).

The first set of questions is generated by the fact that Christianity in the West has long distinguished between the moral virtues (within which four have canonical or cardinal status: prudence (i.e., practical wisdom), justice, fortitude (i.e., courage) and temperance) and the theological virtues of faith, hope and love; but it has done so in a way which strongly resists the suggestion that the latter amount simply to an addition or supplement to the former – as if both kinds of character traits belong on the same conceptual or ontological level.

The Catechism of the Catholic Church[4] puts matters this way. The moral virtues are those firm attitudes, stable dispositions, habitual perfections of intellect and will that make possible ease, self-mastery and joy in leading a morally good life; they are the fruit and seed of morally good acts. But the moral virtues are rooted in the theological virtues, which adapt man's faculties for participation in the divine nature: for the theological virtues relate directly to God. They dispose Christians to live in a relationship with the Holy Trinity, the One and Triune God who is their origin, motive and object. The theological virtues animate Christian moral activity and give it its special character. They inform and give life to all the moral virtues; they are infused by God into the souls of the faithful to make them capable of acting as His children and meriting eternal life; they are the pledge of the presence and action of the Holy Spirit in the faculties of the human being.

On this account, it is the divine unity of their object that explains the unity of the theological virtues, and the pre-eminence of love amongst them (since to participate in the divine nature just is to participate in love). And what motivates Batho's worry about categorizing the theological virtues as "virtues" is this account's further claim that a human being's possession of the theological virtues infuses, informs and animates her possession of the moral virtues; for these tropes imply that acquiring faith, hope and love does not add further firm attitudes, stable dispositions and habitual perfections of intellect and will to an individual's existing array so much as it radically reconfigures each and every one of them, remaking them by reorienting the lives of their possessors so that they embody and maintain a relation to God.

In the light of the theological virtues, then, the moral virtues undergo a resurrection or rebirth of significance; the sense and value they possess from the perspective of those whose forms of life are exhaustively structured around them is revealed to be importantly limited or incomplete when viewed from the perspective of those granted possession of the theological virtues: they are imperfectly or inadequately realized or appreciated in the absence of faith, hope and love, and find individual fulfilment in their collective presence. Before, we saw them as in a glass darkly, despite having no reason to doubt the completeness of our comprehension of their nature; now we see them as they truly are (or can be), and so can appreciate how shallow and impoverished that prior understanding actually was (despite all appearances to the contrary). In this sense, the theological virtues are not so much three more (perhaps especially important) human virtues as mutually implicating conditions for the possibility of re-conceiving what it is to live a virtuous life in the first place.

Kierkegaard would call such a re-conception a teleological suspension of the ethical: the knight of faith's true medium remains the ethical, and so requires that he embody the skills of intellect, will and character appropriate to ethical life, but every ethical movement he makes is now suspended from heaven, and so has acquired a new depth or dimension of significance. Abraham's claim to be a father of faith is underwritten by his ability to maintain a loving and hopeful relation both to God's covenant and to his son in a context which appears to make that unintelligible, but which ultimately reveals a radical reconfiguration of the meaning of sacrifice in God's eyes (away from a conception of one's fellow humans as potential sacrificial victims to God and towards a conception of God's love as essentially self-sacrificial, as God substitutes a ram for Isaac, and thereby prefigures the substitution of his only Son, God's Lamb). And just as Abraham and his descendants come to understand the deeper meaning of "sacrifice," so we come to understand the deeper meaning of "prudence," "justice," "fortitude" and "temperance."

What is being exploited here is the fact that virtue terms generally are candidate objects for what one might call growth in understanding – for a kind of comprehension that can intelligibly be characterized not just as the opposite of ignorance but as evaluable in terms of depth and shallowness, profundity or superficiality. It is a familiar aspect of our moral experience with the virtues in general that the further we develop our possession and understanding of them, the deeper and more sophisticated their nature comes to seem to us, the more difficult it becomes to communicate and live out that understanding, and the harder it becomes to feel confident that we have or even could fully realize their potential. Just as Socrates' wisdom is shown most clearly in his knowledge of how far away he currently is from really being wise, so everyday moral life repeatedly discloses broader and deeper ranges of significance in its structuring terms and dispositions, and thereby prepares us for the kind of radical conversion of our concepts that the advent of the theological virtues makes possible. But what is it that makes their advent a genuinely radical conversion of moral significance? Why does it seem to involve not merely a progressive deepening of our grasp of the meaning of the virtues (the kind of development undergone by anyone who begins with the understanding of a child and becomes an adult essentially open to being educated by her ongoing experience) but entry into a new world of significance, one in which we mean every word that we continue to employ in a radically different spirit?

My suggestion is that this is an effect of the unified object of the theological virtues. For that object is the One and Triune God; and He, being the Creator of all that is *ex nihilo*, is not to be encountered simply and solely as one item in the list of all the things that are. Hence, the theological virtues differ from the moral virtues in that the latter's appropriate objects are always intra-worldly. If one attempts to explain what is involved in possessing the virtue of courage, for example, one will do so by characterizing the distinctive ways in which a courageous person will respond to a specific kind of situation (or set of such kinds); the courageous person will recognize that certain situations call for a courageous response, that others are ones in which discretion is the better part of valour, that others again make no claim on us for bravery. And as we mature into human moral life, these discriminations ideally become finer and more sophisticated, achieving greater nuance in their individuating responsiveness to their occasions; but that deepening is always restricted to a finite range of such occasions. By contrast, the theological virtues have no such range restrictions; if they did, their divine object would have to be identifiable with some sub-set of his creations, and they could not infuse, animate or inform all of the other virtues.

This necessary absence of an intra-worldly object need not, however, be interpreted as the necessary presence of an extra-worldly object; it does not presuppose that God is a supernatural or transcendent thing of some kind (however strange). Kierkegaard's pseudonym Johannes Climacus' famous specification of what is involved in relating oneself unswervingly or unconditionally to God in fact supports this point, even though it appears at first to contradict it. For he tells us that establishing such a relation requires us "simultaneously to relate oneself absolutely to one's absolute telos and relatively to relative ends."[5] This can be taken to suggest that we are here talking about two distinct, and hence independently specifiable, relations to different things – one to the Absolute or God, the other to essentially finite or contingent goals and preoccupations – and that establishing the religiously correct relation to finite matters is a correlate or consequence of establishing the religiously correct relation to an infinite being.

However, Climacus' way of glossing these formulations undercuts this appearance; for he restricts himself to defining the God-relation by contrast with its non-religious counterparts. Those counterparts amount to various modes of relating absolutely to what is relatively good – that is, to treating some particular contingent, changeable thing (such as money, power, or talent) as always to be preferred whenever their pursuit comes into conflict with other goods. Hence, we learn by contrast what is involved in relating to such goods relatively; it means treating no such good as absolutely valuable in the above sense but rather regarding them all as possessed of real but finite and relative value, hence as never amounting to something always to be preferred over anything and everything else. To adopt such an attitude to all the ends of finitude is not a consequence of treating one's relation to the Absolute as being of absolute importance, not a supplement to or fall-out from one's relation to God; to relate relatively to relative goods just is to relate absolutely to the Absolutely Good. The two relations are simultaneous not because the one causes or brings about the other but because they are two different ways of describing one and the same relation to one's existence; in so far as one treats every worldly value as non-absolute, then to precisely that extent one is relating to God as the only absolute value.

In other words, Climacus' vision of religious belief, and hence of the transcendent, is exhaustively specified in terms of a certain kind of relation to finitude; and that relation is itself specified in terms of a form of human life that gives a subjective existential reality to a certain way of valuing finite goods and goals. Take the gospel injunction to love one's neighbour as oneself; this formulation does not deny but rather depends upon the fact that we love ourselves. It does not ask us to dismiss ourselves as utterly worthless – to regard ourselves as if we had no rights or moral status to which others have a duty to respond, or to feel that we have no claim upon the affections of those we love. It rather asks us to be prepared to renounce those claims – to relate to them not as absolute but as relative goods. This might mean being prepared to treat those others to whom we stand in such supposedly reciprocal relationships (our relatives, friends, spouses) as they deserve to be treated even when they do not reciprocate, to go beyond what they could reasonably demand or expect of us in the terms such relationships articulate, and to respect and exceed those demands and expectations in the way we treat those who stand in no particular relationship to us, or perhaps only one of enmity or foreignness – those who are simply our fellow human beings, our neighbours. If the believer places no a priori limits on her responses to her neighbour's claims on her, if she does not demand reciprocation or consideration from her, if she does not resent ingratitude, deceit, or betrayal, then her love of her neighbour is independent of the way things happen to go in the world, unchanging and hence immune from defeat. In thereby becoming responsive to her neighbour not because of who or what she is but solely because she is, because of her sheer, contingent existence, the believer at once allows the other to displace herself in her scheme of things, dies to the claims of the self and relates herself to God.

This Kierkegaardian path opens up a number of fascinating possibilities; but on the present occasion, what I want from his pseudonym's strategy is the thought that acquiring the theological virtues is not a matter of acquiring new ways of orienting oneself to specific phenomena either within the world or outside it; it is rather a matter of reorienting oneself to the world as such. This is why the theological virtues are not simply or straightforwardly virtues in the sense in which the moral virtues are virtues; but since such a reorientation to the world as such will infuse our existing modes of orientation within that world, it also explains why they are not simply or straightforwardly *not* virtues.

This strategy also gives us a clearer understanding of how we might go about addressing the question that is central to David Batho's second Green Paper: can we make sense of the idea of secularizing the theological virtues – of establishing their viability in contemporary cultural circumstances? For what my account so far suggests is that any serious candidates for contemporary secular analogues of the theological virtues would have to be discontinuously continuous with the moral virtues in just the sense specified; that is, they would have to be interpretable as taking the world as such as their object, and in such a way as to induce a radical conversion in our understanding of what it might mean to live morally virtuous lives. In the remainder of this paper I will develop what amounts to a three-stage phenomenology of certain familiar but neglected ranges of moral experience in order to show how they might invite and even require the construction of secular analogues of faith, hope and love, and so reveal the moral centrality of love and vulnerability understood as embodying an openness to becoming changed.

I the day after tomorrow: moral perfectionism

Stanley Cavell's version of moral perfectionism – which he distinguishes from others to which that label is often applied by calling it "Emersonian," thereby declaring its distinctively American physiognomy – cuts across more familiar moral preoccupations with doing one's duty or maximizing the general happiness or cultivating one's virtues. It embodies an idea of the individual's faith in or hope for herself or the humanity in herself, but it sees that self-concern as inseparable from a concern with society and the possibilities it holds out for others. For it understands the soul as on an upward or onward journey that begins when it finds itself lost to the world, and it requires a refusal of the present state of society in the name of some further, more cultivated or cultured, state of society as well as of the soul. This species of perfectionism further assumes that there is no final, as it were absolutely or perfectly cultivated, state of self and society to be achieved; rather, each given or attained state of self and society always projects or opens up another, unattained but attainable, state, to the realization of which we might commit ourselves, or alternatively whose attractions might be eclipsed by the attained world we already inhabit.

In that sense, every attained state is (that is, can present itself as, and be inhabited as) perfect – in need of no further refinement; hence, the primary internal threat to this species of moral perfectionism is that of regarding genuine human individuality as a realizable state of perfection (even if a different one for each individual), rather than as a continuous process of self-perfecting (selfhood as self-improvement or self-overcoming). The most extreme version of that threat is realized when an individual's investment in her attained self is so unquestioning that the very possibility of her present state being otherwise is occluded; in such circumstances, overcoming this false sense of perfect self-coincidence (of the self's being identical with its current state) may require a relationship with an other – one who exemplifies in their own lives the possibility of things being otherwise, and exhibits an impersonal interest in recalling particular others to their own ways of becoming other than they currently are.

Cavell's perfectionism thus envisions the self as internally split or doubled, as essentially non-self-identical even when it relates to its attained state as if it could not be otherwise (for to adopt such a relation is itself something that could be otherwise); and part of what is both inspiring and frustrating about this vision of self-perfecting is that our unattained state presents itself as attainable, as within our grasp if we will but admit its attractiveness and turn towards it. Its very closeness to us – the fact that our distance from it is internal to us, hence not strictly speaking a measurable distance from us at all – is what makes its non-realization peculiarly maddening, as well as deeply motivating; but in order to experience that frustration, to reach the point of realizing that a better state might only be a step away, we stand in need of inspiring examples of successfully holding oneself open to self-overcoming – exemplary individuals (Emerson would call them "friends") whose orientation towards their own better selves is realized and displayed to us in such a way as to reveal our present state as dissatisfying and to turn us away from it.

Existing as a self is thus a processual or active business of perpetual nextness to or neighbouring of oneself (or its failure) – what Emerson's disciple Thoreau calls being beside ourselves in a sane sense, and what Nietzsche (himself a lifelong venerator of Emerson) might express as a matter of Becoming (or its refusal) rather than Being. Cavell has recently taken this Nietzschean connection a step further by pointing out that Nietzsche's call for a philosophy of tomorrow and the day after tomorrow deploys a German construction ("morgen und ubermorgen") which parallels his more familiar invocation of the over-man ("ubermensch").[6] If we assume that the man who attains self-overcoming is Nietzsche's way of articulating the Emersonian vision of the self-reliant individual who privileges her unattained over her attained self, and recall the former's intimate neighbouring of or nextness to the latter, then we can infer that the day after tomorrow – the day in which we realize our own and our society's self-overcoming – is itself not a measurable distance away from our present moment but rather haunts each such moment as its better or higher self, from which we are separated by nothing (nothing substantial, no external obstacle, only our own unwillingness to realize it).

An initial point of connection between Emersonian Perfectionism and the theological virtues concerns the former's understanding of the kinds of situation which characteristically prompt a desire to turn away from the attained state of self and society: Emerson thinks of them as conditions of conformity (of which self-reliance is the aversion), Thoreau as quietly desperate forms of living. Cavell's investigations of perfectionism have returned repeatedly to three mythological locales for such experiences: adolescence, mid-life crises and marriage. According to Cavell, adolescence is an epistemologically and politically significant rite of passage:

> When the world's legitimacy comes to rest upon consent – when the public world is something that each individual has at some moment to agree to join – then adolescence is invented as the time for preparing for that agreement and is ended by it [...] The world posed before it, beckoning it, is a field of possibilities [...] [I]nstead of opening secrets to you, it informs you that it has none, that what you see is all there is to it.
>
> You wish to be presented with a world you can want, to which you give yourself. [But] the world as a whole [may] present itself [...] as uninhabitable; [it may elicit] disgust [or] repugnance [...] (TOS[7] 99–100)

The notion of a mid-life crisis is evoked by Cavell in his first attempt explicitly and systematically to characterize Emersonian perfectionism, when – at the outset of *Conditions Handsome and Unhandsome* – he cites the opening lines of Dante's *Divine Comedy*: "At the mid-point of the path through life, I found myself lost in a wood so dark, the way ahead was blotted out."[8] Dante's condition is not best understood as confronting a specific obstacle on his way, or a particular limitation in his character; it is one of general bewilderment, of an absolute loss of orientation, an inability to conceive of himself as having a path to follow at all. And Cavell's treatment of marriage – in the context of his interest in the cinematic genres he entitles "Comedies of Remarriage" and "Melodramas of the Unknown Woman" – identifies an analogous condition.[9]

In comedies of remarriage, the drive of the narrative is not to get the central pair together but rather to get them back together: the fact of marriage in these comedies is not the hoped-for culmination of a tale of young lovers striving to overcome obstacles to their union but an attained relationship currently subject to the threat of divorce, so that a willingness to be married here appears as requiring an unending willingness to remarry. Central to these relationships is the woman's demand for an education of some kind from the man (deriving from her sense that her life asks for some radical transformation, a re-creation that is also a re-creation of the human), and the man's willingness to undergo an investigation of his authority to provide it; his authority is demonstrated and her transfiguration effected by means of their ability to sustain a meet and happy conversation, a mutually appreciative, individuating responsiveness in word and deed. The melodramas, by contrast, concern women who could neither manage nor relish such intercourse with men, and so must achieve genuine existence (or fail to) apart from marriage; they lack a common language with the (always inadequate and often villainous) men of their world, so that their words are pervaded with an isolating irony, often rising to arias of divorce from all around them, to which those around them react with bewildered hostility.

This vision of the crippling loneliness of such (mis-)marriages is at the heart of Milton's sustained pleas for divorce.[10] In the comedies, having suffered a loss of mutual intelligibility and so the possibility that each is in effect divorcing the other, each couple finds a way of overcoming that threat and establishing new terms of conversation; the reality of their shared inhabitation of the world of their marriage is shown to be a matter of their willingness to re-dedicate themselves every day to their meet and happy conversation. By contrast, the route to re-creation or recovery canvassed by the women of the melodramas involves a systematic negation of the existing world's claims upon them, in the name of a higher, unattained state of society in which alone genuine individuality is attainable for them, and apart from which that society's claims upon them are shown to lack any real authority. The price of that aversion is, accordingly, exile from intelligibility.

J.M. Coetzee's protagonist Elizabeth Costello[11] seems to me to resemble these women. Elizabeth is immensely isolated from the world around her, to the point of madness; and just as pretty much every word that the inhabitants of the university town of Appleton utter during her stay (whilst delivering a lecture expressing her perfect disgust for our contemporary treatment of non-human animals) irritates or bruises her, so she perfects the negation of conversation that her exchanges with them represent by declaring and ensuring that every wounding word she utters gives expression to her own woundedness: "I am [...] an animal exhibiting, yet not exhibiting [...] a wound, which I cover up under my clothes but touch on in every word I speak."[12] Her speech consequently takes the form of passionately judging her world: she finds it wanting, in need of radical, pervasive transformation that is no more than a step away (that is, not blocked by material or moral necessities, but essentially available, neighbouring us); but because its currently attained state is such as to render her voiceless (her horrified perception of its present dispensation inarticulable in the terms provided by the dominant conception of rationality – "the great Western discourse of [...] reason and unreason,"[13] any claim she stakes in the name of its unattained but attainable state, and so of her own unrealized but realizable capacity to exist otherwise (to transcend her current haunting of her own life), inevitably takes on the accents of insanity. What to her is a condition of absolute expressiveness is for that very reason also one of absolute inexpressiveness: because everything she says is touched by her woundedness, nothing she says can truly touch her hearers. From their viewpoint, her sense of victimization by what she knows can only appear hyperbolic, inordinate, melodramatic – an apparently excessive response to apparently banal facts or circumstances; what she thinks she knows remains utterly unknown to her interlocutors, and since the trauma of that knowledge constitutes her as the animal she is, she too remains to that extent unknown.

Whether Elizabeth belongs with her comedic and melodramatic sisters, the aspect of their commonality that pertains to our current purposes concerns the ways in which each finds that – as Emerson would put it – every word another speaks might either cheer or chagrin us, not so much because they use those words to make assertions that are true or false in some particular respect, as because they make up an inhabitable discursive universe (one whose inhabitants can render themselves intelligible to one another, and thereby enable each other's achievement of genuine individuality) or fail entirely to do so. Just as with adolescence and the mid-life crisis, the offer of marriage (and the possibility of its refusal, whether on each new day of its continuation or before it can even begin) discloses a world as such (a field of existential and expressive possibilities), and asks whether it elicits our assent or our aversion (in the name of some other available or at least conceivable world, some unattained but attainable city of words).

But I suggested earlier that secular analogues to the theological virtues would not only have to be interpretable as taking the world as such as their object; they would also have to be capable of inducing a radical conversion of our existing conceptions of what it is to live a good life. How might Emersonian perfectionism approximate the second condition? Well: suppose we take seriously its American character, and recall the founding dedication of the United States to facilitating for its citizens "Life, Liberty and the Pursuit of Happiness"; then we might recall the most famous British expression of an analogue to that third goal, Utilitarianism, and ask ourselves how perfectionism might be said to have identified a fundamental threat to its pursuit and so might be thought of as providing a radical reconfiguration of its true meaning and value.

Here is a pertinent passage from John Stuart Mill – as it happens, from his essay "On Liberty" rather than "Utilitarianism":

> In our times, from the highest class of society down to the lowest, everyone lives as under the eye of a hostile and dreaded censorship. Not only in what concerns others, but in what concerns only themselves, the individual or the family do not ask themselves, what do I prefer? Or, what would suit my character and disposition? Or, what would allow the best and highest in me to have fair play and enable it to grow and thrive? They ask themselves, what is suitable to my position? What is usually done by persons of my station and pecuniary circumstances? Or (worse still) what is usually done by persons of a station and circumstance superior to mine? I do not mean that they choose what is customary in preference to what suits their own inclination. It does not occur to them to have any inclination except for what is customary. Thus the mind itself is bowed to the yoke: even in what people do for pleasure, conformity is the first thing thought of; they like in crowds; they exercise choice only among things commonly done; peculiarity of taste, eccentricity of conduct are shunned equally with crime, until by dint of not following their own nature they have no nature to follow: their human capacities are withered and starved; they become incapable of any strong wishes or native pleasures, and are generally without either opinions or feelings of home growth, or properly their own. Now is this, or is it not, the desirable condition of human nature?[14]

The irony of this last question depends upon recalling the strategy Mill adopts in chapter 4 of "Utilitarianism," when attempting to characterize the kind of proof that might intelligibly be given to show that the principle of utility is the first principle of morality. That strategy depends upon the assumption that direct exercises of the faculty of desire might serve as an alternative to proof by reasoning when demonstrating the validity of candidate first principles of conduct, and so assumes that on the most basic level we are desiring creatures – creatures whose ability to judge the world as desirable or otherwise is as fundamental as their ability to represent the state of its affairs. On that basis, Mill claims (first) that no one equipped with such a faculty could plausibly deny that the promise of attaining happiness would (*ceteris paribus*) motivate her to pursue it, and (second) that no one who judges happiness to be pursuit-worthy whenever it is attainable by them could coherently deny its worth to others should they succeed in attaining it. This second step is justified by the following consideration: what is disclosed to us when we encounter or envisage the possibility of being made happy is the value of happiness, not the value of *our* happiness (as opposed to anyone else's), and not its value to *us* (as opposed to, say, society). Since psychological states always have owners, experiences of happiness will always be someone's experiences; but the fact that an experience is mine is not a feature of the experience that distinguishes it from experiences undergone by you: it is rather something that distinguishes me from you, here and now.

Appreciating the moral irrelevance of the metaphysical necessity that experiences of happiness are owned is thus essential to Mill's making the step from acknowledging the value one attributes to the pursuit of happiness in one's own life to acknowledging that the more successful pursuers of happiness there are in the world, the better that world will be. But the passage I just quoted from "On Liberty" discloses a contrasting sense in which the ownership of happiness is absolutely fundamental to its value. For imagine that Mill's diagnosis of his society as in the grip of conformity were true: then such experiences of happiness as it made available to its inhabitants would not really be theirs. Since the activities or modes of behaviour which generate it are not ones for which they take responsibility (not ones they choose whilst fully acknowledging that they might have made other choices, might have experimented with other ways of living), hence not ones in which their autonomous individuality finds expression, then the happiness that results from them remains unowned or disowned — essentially alienated from its putative possessors in the way adumbrated by Heidegger's concept of "das Man" as our average everyday mode of common life.[15] Such happiness as is generated by this society and its inhabitants is thus no one's in particular; metaphysical ownership is negated by moral dispossession.

Now ask yourself: in such a society, what would be the point of attempting to implement the principle of utility as a social policy? You could strive mightily to maximize overall levels of happiness; but at the end of the day, no individual would have had her welfare genuinely enhanced thereby, and if anything the prevailing disorientation or derangement of our faculties of desire — their inability to disclose our attained states of happiness as mere simulacra or counterfeits — would be reinforced. In such a condition, happiness might abound, but there would be no truly happy people to be found; and by analogy, virtuous actions might abound, but there would be no truly virtuous people; and duty might be done, but there would be no truly dutiful people. What the perfectionist sensitivity to conformity thereby discloses is a condition for the possibility of living a genuinely good life — a condition which, if left unsatisfied, renders the supposedly substantial and realized elements of such a life devoid of vitality and significance, mere matter uninformed by value, a present absence. Coming to perceive this threat, and so the need for its overcoming, thereby amounts to a radical conversion of our conception of what is required if — for example — an apparently virtuous life really is to constitute a form of human flourishing.

2 to become human does not come that easily: ironic experience and ironic existence

Another way of articulating Mill's anxiety about conformity and its hollowing out of the satisfaction of desire would be to ask: "Amongst all the pursuers of happiness, are there any pursuers of happiness?" And this takes us to the second stage of my moral phenomenology, which picks up Jonathan Lear's recent making of a case for irony — for ironic experience and ironic existence.[16] Lear argues that we constitute ourselves as human by inhabiting practical identities — descriptions under which we value ourselves, find our actions to be worth undertaking and so our lives to be worth living: examples of such identities would be farmer, artist, teacher. These identities commit their inhabitants to norms — ideals or standards of excellence that they must adhere to in the face of temptation; and those ideals can themselves be the object of reflective inquiry, as when I ask myself not only what they demand of me in a given situation but whether they might be revised in such a way as to better fulfil the good that is achieved by living out the identity they help to constitute.

But such reflective engagement is not enough to engender irony: that arises when we find ourselves confronting the possibility of a radical diremption between the myriad ways in which individuals inhabit this identity (including reflective ways of so doing) and the ideal it aspires to embody. Imagine a teacher, engaging in grading papers and reflecting on how well her department's grading practices match up to their shared goal of developing their students' capacity to learn. Then she is suddenly struck by a sense of vertigo or disorientation in relation to everything that makes up that social practice: the very idea of teaching remains compelling, but it also seems entirely unrelated to how she goes about living out that identity, however reflectively. Phrases like "helping my students to develop their capacity to learn" retain their pertinence, but they have become enigmatic, open-ended, oracular: who her students might be (the ones on the course, the ones who read her books, her colleagues?), what their development might amount to, how anything she can do might contribute to it – these questions have become utterly compelling, but she does not even know how to begin answering them.

Lear calls this a breakdown in practical intelligibility: in such a condition, I can no longer make sense of myself to myself, let alone to others, in terms of my practical identity, and yet this is an expression not of my loss of faith in that identity but of my continued commitment to the ideals that constitute it. It is precisely because I care passionately about teaching that I have come to a halt as a teacher; nothing any longer makes sense to me as the next step I might take *as a teacher*. I retain a strong desire to be and become such a person, but the intensity of that desire is what disorients me; it is my continuing commitment to its ideals that compels me to aspire to transcend altogether the social practices that currently embody it. The uncanniness of such ironic experience lies precisely in the fact that this call to an entirely reconfigured form of teaching life is experienced as manifesting fidelity to an ideal to which I have always been committed. My sense is that all previously received understandings of what it is to be a teacher (and to reflect critically on what it is to be a teacher) fall short of what teaching – in its true significance and goodness – really demands.

It is this kind of would-be directed uncanniness that finds expression in such questions as: "Among all teachers, is there a teacher?" "Among all farmers, is there a farmer?"; "Among all wise people, is there a wise person?"; "Among all Christians, is there a Christian?" And here the connections between ironic experience and Emersonian perfectionism clarify and multiply. Just like the ironist, a perfectionist Mill asks himself "Among all pursuers of happiness, is there a pursuer of happiness?" and a perfectionist Aristotelian might similarly ask "Among all virtuous people, is there a virtuous person?"; both the ironist and the perfectionist are preoccupied with judging the vitality or animation of a moral world as such; both are particularly sensitive to the possibility that such worlds might cease to make sense to us, leaving us utterly disoriented and incapable of making ourselves intelligible either to others or ourselves; and both thereby commit themselves to a conception of selfhood as doubled, because individuals are capable of exhibiting discontinuous continuity, as the very depth of their investment in the ideals incarnate in an attained state of themselves discloses the possibility of an unattained state of self and society that might fulfil those ideals in unprecedentedly deep ways, and so demands that we turn away from what we are to what we might be.

For this is what practice-transcending aspirations (as Lear calls them) ask us to take seriously: the possibility that every aspect of our current realization of a practical identity and its ideals might entirely have lost contact with the telos around which those practices were constituted, so that their inhabitants are – as it were – using all the right words, but their practices of employing them now appear empty or hollow, a mere simulacrum of the meaning their users sincerely believe that they have. To live an ironic existence entails finding a way of living with the ineliminable possibility of such ironic experience; it does not mean trying (impossibly) to live as a teacher entirely outwith the current social practices of teaching, but rather inhabiting them in a way which acknowledges that keeping faith with their constitutive ideals may at any time mean undergoing something more radically self-critical than refining or supplementing its existing array of procedures. Ironic existence means simultaneously being committed to realizing my best reflective understanding of what it is to be a teacher whilst acknowledging that even this understanding might be vulnerable to ironic disruption in the name of the very value it claims to embody.

3 reasoning at the abyss: radical hope

The third step in my moral phenomenology makes a more direct connection between ironic existence and the role of the theological virtues; but taking it requires that we take a step back in the development of Lear's thinking – from his Tanner lectures to his earlier book *Radical Hope*.[17] This book focuses on an analogous instance of a breakdown in practical intelligibility: the cultural devastation inflicted on the Crow tribe by their confinement to a reservation. Before their lethal encounters with the encroaching powers of the US government they were nomadic hunters: their lives centred around hunting buffalo and conducting warfare with other Native American tribes (especially the Sioux), and so the practical identities in terms of which Crow tribespeople understood themselves were fundamentally related (directly and indirectly) to the successful exercise of both activities. Their collective confinement to a reservation stripped away the conditions that made either activity possible, and thereby deprived the Crow tribe as a whole of their cultural world – of the field of practical and expressive possibilities in terms of which they had hitherto made sense of themselves and each other.

In a very real sense, then, things ceased to happen for them: for the Crow lost the concepts with which they might construct the narrative contexts in relation to which any actions they perform acquire their identity, and thereby suffered a breakdown of the conceptual and practical field in which genuinely Crow-like occurrences occur. Or, to put the point in terms of practical identities, and so in a way that brings out the internal relation of this case to cases of ironic experience: once the tribe are ensconced on their reservation, it makes sense for them to ask "Among the warriors, is there a warrior?" or "Among the chiefs, is there a chief?" or even "Among the Crow, is there a Crow?" As Lear phrases it: "Insofar as I am a Crow subject, *I* have ceased to be. All that's left is a ghostlike existence that stands witness to the death of the subject" (RH 50).

This kind of total annihilation of significance is a theme that plainly resonates with Emersonian perfectionists: Cavell's oeuvre persistently returns to anxieties about planetary destruction, whether that be television's monitoring of the world's growing uninhabitability or our apparent willingness either to bring about or to pray for such an end of human time on earth (Cavell twins an analysis of the political deformations inherent in nuclear weaponry and end-time theology in an essay on Emerson presciently called "Hope Against Hope").[18] Prescient in our context, at least, since Lear's primary interest in the cultural devastation of the Crow tribe lies in how their chief at the time – Plenty Coups – attempted to find a viable future for them all. Courage was a central virtue in the earlier Crow form of life, and that ideal was accordingly deeply woven into Crow modes of practical identity; so on the reservation, in order for Crow life to be grasped as continuing, as capable of projection through and beyond its own devastation, a way had to be found of radically reconfiguring what it might mean to live courageously in these new circumstances.

> In such a case, one would begin with a culture's thick understanding of courage; but one would somehow find ways to *thin it out*: find ways to face circumstances courageously that the older thick conception never envisaged. The issue would then be one not simply of going over to the thick concepts of another culture, but of drawing on their traditions in novel ways in the face of novel challenges. (RH 66)

Lear traces in fascinating detail one plausible interpretation of how Plenty Coups did this (by interpreting certain dreams – traditionally used by the Crow to predict the future – and deploying certain familiar figures in Crow religion – in particular, the Chickadee – to authorize the appropriation of skills and values from the culture of the white man in ways that could be understood as maintaining Crow values and ideals in radically different circumstances). On the one hand, this required giving up almost everything the Crow understood about the good life; on the other, this suspension of Crow ethical life is carried out in the name of Crow values, although in the light of a conception of those values that radically transcended their previous social realization. It thus amounts to a teleological suspension of the ethical – a mode of discontinuity suffered and embraced in the name of maintaining continuity. In this sense, Plenty Coups had an ironic mode of existence forced upon him; he exhibited a central virtue of the Crow form of life – that of courage – in finding ways for his people to continue to live courageously in a set of circumstances that were not only radically novel but seemed (in the light of existing Crow forms of self-understanding) to have made the possibility of courageous action unintelligible.

In so doing, Plenty Coups lived out a form of radical hope. He hoped for the revival or resurrection of the Crow form of life, but in a form that was not yet intelligible to him, even in bare outline; in short, he hoped without being able to articulate what he was hoping for. What sustained him in this enterprise was his faith in the Crow God; more specifically, his commitment to that God as embodying the good of the Crow form of life was manifest in his commitment to the goodness of the Crow world as essentially transcending any given attempt to understand or realize it. And acknowledging the possibility that Crow goodness might radically diverge from its current social realization was his way of keeping faith with human knowledge and life whilst acknowledging its vulnerability to radical disruption.

This is one aspect of the finitude of the human condition; but another is equally pertinent here, and equally fully acknowledged in Plenty Coups' stance. This is what Lear, following Plato, calls the erotic aspect of our condition: "in our finite condition of lack, we reach out to the world in yearning, longing, admiration and desire for that which (however mistakenly) we take to be valuable, beautiful and good" (RH 120). In other words, we are fundamentally driven to reach out to the world and make contact with it, both cognitively and evaluatively; despite the vulnerability of our world-directed concepts to disruption by inner and outer forces, we remain oriented towards the world that transcends our finite power to grasp it as nevertheless real and worth grasping. In short, to live well as finite beings is to live hopefully, faithfully and lovingly in relation to the world as such, understood as something whose reality and value is manifest precisely in its capacity to transcend our best available attempts to grasp it.

Since one can think that the goodness of the world outstrips our capacity to grasp it without thinking that this goodness is itself transcendent (transcendentally real or supraworldly), Lear claims that "even the most strenuously secular readers ought to be willing to accept this form of transcendence" (RH 122). My claim is that, in so far as we accept Lear's claim, we are accepting both the feasibility and the necessity of secular analogues to the theological virtues as part of any genuine acknowledgement of human finitude.

disclosure statement

No potential conflict of interest was reported by the author.

notes

1 The project was led by Professor Beatrice Han-Pile and Dr Daniel Watts. The project website is at <https://powerlessness.essex.ac.uk/> (accessed 6 Jan. 2020).

2 Pamela's paper, "Arguing for 'Ethical' Vulnerability: Towards a Politics of Care?," was published in *Exploring Vulnerability*, eds. Heike Springhart and Günter Thomas (Göttingen and Bristol, CT: Vandenhoeck, 2017) 147–62.

3 The two papers can be found at <https://powerlessness.essex.ac.uk/category/research/green-papers> (accessed 7 Jan. 2020).

4 London: Chapman, 1994: Part Three, Article 7.

5 Søren Kierkegaard, *Concluding Unscientific Postscript*, eds. and trans. H.V. and E.H. Hong (Princeton: Princeton UP, 1992) 387.

6 Stanley Cavell, *Philosophy the Day after Tomorrow* (Cambridge, MA: Harvard UP, 2005) 118.

7 *Themes Out of School* (San Francisco: North Point, 1984). Hereafter TOS.

8 Stanley Cavell, *Conditions Handsome and Unhandsome* (Chicago: U of Chicago P, 1990) xxx.

9 Stanley Cavell, *Pursuits of Happiness* (Cambridge, MA: Harvard UP, 1981).

10 Ibid. 58.

11 *Elizabeth Costello: Eight Lessons* (London: Secker, 2003).

12 J.M. Coetzee, *The Lives of Animals*, ed. Amy Gutmann (Princeton: Princeton UP, 1999) 26.

13 Ibid. 25.

14 John Stuart Mill, *On Liberty and Other Writings*, ed. Stefan Collini (Cambridge: Cambridge UP, 1989) 61–62.

15 Martin Heidegger, *Being and Time*, eds. John Macquarrie and Edward Robinson (Oxford: Blackwell, 1962).

16 *A Case for Irony* (Cambridge, MA: Harvard UP, 2011).

17 Cambridge, MA: Harvard UP, 2006. Hereafter RH.

18 For the former, see the essay "The Fact of Television" in TOS; for the latter, see *Emerson's Transcendental Etudes* (Stanford: Stanford UP, 2003).

Index

abortion 72–73
Abrahamic religions 45–46, 50
absolute representations 126–27, 130
academic life 38, 230
accountability 4, 90, 118–19, 164–65, 167–69, 171–74, 204, 234
action-guiding concepts 47
action tendencies 244, 247–49
act of forgiveness 113–14, 116–17
actors 165, 167, 185
adolescence 14, 16, 155, 286–87
affective intentionality 244, 247–48
affective openness 255
affective relations 164, 194, 234
affective state 234, 255–56
affectivity 4, 202, 210, 236, 243–50, 254–55
agency 7, 80, 168, 171–73, 194–95, 198–200, 202–3, 222–23, 234, 260, 276
agents 87, 110, 115, 183–84, 194, 196, 198–99, 222
Ain't I a Woman: Black Women and Feminism 38
alienation 134, 146, 245–46
aliveness 5, 221, 239, 245–47; of life 229–30, 238
alterity 76, 209, 213–14, 245
ambiguity, of vulnerability 207
Anderson, Pamela Sue 3, 34–35, 52–56, 82, 107–8, 145, 147, 161, 163, 193, 207–8, 244–45, 248, 255, 263
Anglo-American analytic philosophy 83
anti-carceral feminists 166
Antigone 85, 109, 154–56, 159, 161
Arendt, Hannah 149, 184–86
"Arguing for 'Ethical' Vulnerability: Towards a Politics of Care?" 88
Ars Disputandi 83
audience 5, 34–42, 45, 48–49, 54, 98–99, 103, 133, 155, 159, 256
Augustine 76
Augustus, Philip 76
"Autonomy, Vulnerability, and Gender" 88

Beauvoir, Simone de 69, 237
Bell, Jordan 83
Bergsonian freedom 23, 26, 29–30

Blackwell, Sophia 82
black women 38–39, 172, 226
bodily vulnerability 41, 50, 89, 100, 258–59
bonded love 14, 16, 274
Broome, John 183
business 75, 130, 136–37, 141–43
Butler, Judith 37, 41, 49, 85, 88, 164, 276

capability 6, 10–11, 13, 16–17, 23, 26, 56, 87, 207, 230–32, 234–36, 238, 258–60, 276, 279
Carel, Havi 258–59
Cavell, Stanley 285
certitude 21, 265
children 7, 57, 71, 73, 157, 160, 282
Christianity 45–47, 63, 70, 72, 74, 76, 77, 97, 161, 282
City of God 76
Climacus, Johannes 283
Climate Matters: Ethics in a Warming World 183
Coetzee, J.M. 287
cognition 22, 46, 209–10, 232, 235, 237, 256–57, 260
Cole, Alyson 164
collective work 2, 34–36, 40, 42, 48–49
Collins, Patricia Hill 139
communication 230, 255–56, 264–67, 269
conflict 23, 28, 89, 91, 102, 114–15, 117, 156–57, 160, 211, 265, 267, 269–70
"Consider the Lilies" 145
constitutive vulnerability 196–99, 204
contemporary feminist philosophers 22, 30, 164
continental philosophy 83
conversation 2–5, 107–8, 111, 114, 118, 120, 131, 134, 140–45, 147–48, 150–51, 229–30, 287
corporeal vulnerability 4, 8–9, 41–42, 49–50, 88, 164, 167, 210, 234
cosmic memory 29–30
Costello, Elizabeth 287
Cousens, Emily 2
creative emotions 28–29
creative process 28, 30, 58–59
creative transformation 56–59
crimes 113–14, 184–85, 187, 288

dark myth 47, 253–58
Deleuze, Gilles 25, 27–28, 30, 102, 230–31, 278
Derrida, Jacques 113–15, 127–28, 165
Deuteronomy 6 46
disavowal of vulnerability 42, 253
discussion of vulnerability 98, 194, 256
"Disempowered Speech" 36, 48
distributive justice 113
divine 12, 14, 17, 27–29, 128, 160, 247, 249
divine affectivity 248–50
divine love 46, 50, 112, 249
The Diviners 155
domestic violence 221, 225
Dotson, Kristie 98, 156, 255
dualities 124–29
dynamic harm 180, 186
dynamic projects 23–24, 30
dynamics of affectivity 244
dynamics of love 202

element of vulnerability 220–21
Eliot, George 155
embodied aliveness 244–45
embodied vulnerability 41, 88, 195, 233
emotional vulnerability 4, 193–94, 199, 203–4
emotions 25, 27, 63, 68, 79–81, 115, 117, 119, 194, 198–99, 244–45, 247–49, 274–75
empathy 4, 22, 41, 88, 107–9, 111, 114, 116, 118, 249, 255–56
enhancement of life 90, 95, 97, 101
enlightenment philosophers 273
ethical concept, of vulnerability 197–98
ethical level, of vulnerability 164, 194
ethical life 47, 91, 282, 292
ethical relations 208, 210–14, 216–17, 253
ethical reprobation 186, 188
ethical responsibility 182–83, 186, 188–91, 213, 235
ethical subject 165, 169, 173, 210, 215, 221
ethical subjectivity 209–11
ethical vulnerability 2, 40–41, 88–89, 119, 163–67, 169, 171, 173–74, 179, 230, 234–35, 281, 281–92; and #Metoo movement 169–74; and sexual violence 167–69
ethical wisdom 13, 15–16
ethics of justice 118, 234, 243
ethics of memory 108–11
"Excursion into Philosophy" 144
existential feelings 244–49
experience of vulnerability 100, 119, 133, 235, 259

faith 62–63, 67, 70, 72, 149, 263, 266, 281–82, 285, 290, 292
Fantham, Elaine 145
female "knower", disavowal of 154–60
feminine 22, 125, 128, 130–31, 160, 208, 212–14

feminine intuition 21–22, 25
feminism, and sexual violence 165–67
feminist philosophy 4, 28, 34–35, 69, 83, 97, 140; of religion 13, 83, 90, 95, 97, 139, 147, 154–55, 159, 161, 230
foolish risk calculations 264
forgiveness 2, 4, 62, 64, 103, 107–20, 150, 157, 165, 204, 208, 221, 225; feminist ethics of 108–9
forward-looking responsibility 187–90
fragility 86–87, 90, 150–51, 194, 200, 213
Frankl, Viktor 147
freedom 21, 23–24, 26–27, 29–30, 57–58, 70, 73–74, 79, 109–10, 215, 221–27, 236–37, 246–47, 259, 276–77
friendship 2, 4, 8, 21, 24, 26–30, 61, 90–91, 103, 107, 139–51, 155, 163; and becoming wise 144–46; neoliberal university and 148, 148–50; for philosophical practice 146–48
fundamental ignorance, of vulnerability 40–41, 49

Gambetti, Zeynep 277
generic capability 232
Gilson, Erinn 164
global feminist discourse 273–79
God 24–25, 28–29, 45–46, 50, 62–63, 72–73, 75–76, 79, 83, 85–86, 96, 107–9, 111–17, 119–20, 159–61, 209, 212, 246–49, 270, 282–84
grief 3, 9–10, 41–42, 50, 56, 59, 75, 77–78, 100, 102, 195–96, 233, 245–47
Griswold, Charles 119

happiness 145, 288–90
Heidegger, Martin 254–56
Hermippus 76
Hipparchia 156
Honthorst, Gerard van 144
hooks, bell 4, 35–39, 85, 97, 109, 115–16, 133, 158
hope: ambiguities of 263–70; deceptive and self-deceptive 269; in divine creativity 270; limits and the expansion of 268
Hopper, Edward 144
Hornsby, Jennifer 36, 48
human agency 193, 198–99
human capability 13, 23, 115, 231–32, 235, 279
humanitarian identity 274, 277
human life 101, 149, 198–99, 226, 232, 234, 236–37, 239, 252, 277, 284
human relationships 142, 149–50, 155, 161
human subjects 13, 142, 207, 210–11, 232, 277
human vulnerability 41, 49, 52, 78, 80, 100, 193, 208, 217, 249, 252

ignorance, of vulnerability 36, 41, 50, 88
illness 4, 139, 249, 253–54, 256, 258–59
imaginary, love in religion 45–51

immanence 27–29, 212, 217, 224
immigrants 68, 276, 278–79
individual actions 180–83, 186, 199
individual ethical gap (IEG) 179–84, 186–89
individual responsibility 181, 183, 189
individual women 13, 16, 225
injustice 7, 58–59, 110, 113, 116–18, 165, 171, 196, 203–4, 249, 253
intellectual life 11, 45, 83, 248
inter-human relations 209, 215, 217
intuition 3–4, 21–23, 25–26, 30, 63–64, 231, 275
invulnerability 48
Islam 47

Jaggar, Alice 203
Jasper, David 154
journey of forgiveness 108–9, 115–18
Joyce, James 98
Judaism 47
justice 64, 82–83, 87, 89–90, 96, 108–20, 165–66, 169, 172, 197, 203–4, 208–9, 211–17, 234, 282–83; love and 110, 113–17, 119–20, 245

Kant, Immanuel 83
Kantian Ethics 191, 220–21
Kierkegaard, Søren 46

Laertius, Diogenes 76
Laurence, Margaret 155
Le Doeuff, Michèle 2, 42, 48, 84–85, 144
Levinas, Emmanuel 46
Leviticus 19 46
liberated love 14, 16–17, 273–74, 279
life-enhancing capability 7, 88, 253
life-smothering 252–53
life's precariousness 41, 49
life's relations 40, 49, 54
life stories 109, 111, 216
"Longing for Recognition" 85
loss of love 12, 40, 49, 90, 231, 253–55, 259
loss of possibilities 258–59
love commandments 46, 50–51
Love in Religion 2, 5, 46
love of friendship 27, 30, 103
love of wisdom 11, 16, 274
love's vulnerability 199, 264–65, 267, 269; aspects of 264
Lovibond, Sabina 155

male philosophers 34–35, 40
Mark 12.28–31 46, 50
marriage 61, 157, 159, 275, 286–88
McGhee, Michael 139
McLuhan, Marshall 149
meaning of vulnerability 173, 208–9, 244
memory 3, 13, 54, 68, 90, 102–3, 107–11, 114–16, 124, 151, 224

#MeToo movement 164, 169–74
Mezirow, Jack 57
mid-life crises 286, 288
Mikkola, Mari 129
mode of relationality 7–10, 195, 276
Montefiore, Alan 83
Moore, A.W. 155
moral invulnerability 89, 234
moral perfectionism 285
moral philosophy 80, 199, 243
moral rationality 88
moral self-love 200
moral virtues 282–85
Muhammad, Ghazi bin 46
Murdoch, Iris 200
mutual affection 156
mutual vulnerability 34–35, 38, 40–42, 48–49, 99, 102, 133, 195, 202
mystical life 26, 29, 275
mysticism 22–25, 28–30, 275
myths 3, 6–16, 45–47, 84, 86, 236, 244, 248, 250, 253–54, 273–74, 279; of love 50; of vulnerability 8, 50

neighbour-love 45–47
neoliberal university 140, 150; problem 140–44
Newman, John Henry 140
New Topics in Feminist Philosophy of Religion 69
nonsense 126–29
non-violence 164, 173
notion of vulnerability 194, 209, 215, 221, 227, 234
Nussbaum, Martha 187, 232

Oakeshott, Michael 140, 150
Oneself as Another 87
ontological vulnerability 2, 164, 193, 196–98, 231
ontology 9–10, 26, 173–74, 230–31, 233–34, 236, 244; of transformation 165, 171–73
openness 23, 40, 49, 52–53, 56–57, 78, 90–91, 119, 160, 164–65, 173, 194, 208, 231–32, 234–36, 243, 252–56, 258–60
The Oxford Muse 82

painful recognition, limitations 264
passionate love 249, 267
patience 268
performance of vulnerability 163
personal life 11, 53
phenomenological vulnerability 164, 173, 252
philosophical activism 101
philosophical enquiry 134, 140, 144, 147–48
philosophical imaginary 2, 6–7, 11–12, 15–16, 37, 47, 84, 273, 277–78; of violence 7, 274
philosophical intuition 25–26
philosophical practice 129, 140, 144–46, 148
philosophical reflection 11, 114, 139, 144

philosophical relations 34, 36, 40, 42, 48–49, 54, 99, 133
philosophy of religion 52, 63, 82–84, 95–97, 110, 129, 230, 273; gendering 96–97
political life 8, 170, 232
political myth 3, 47
political relations 6, 208–9, 216
political responsibility 184–86
political sublime 274–75, 277
Pope Innocent III 76
possible violence 101, 213–14
power relations 166–68, 170, 172–74, 253–54, 257
practical reason 80, 201
practice of philosophy 136, 139–40, 144, 147, 150–51
precarious life 37, 41, 48, 50, 88, 119
principle of freedom 29–30
prisons 166–67, 170, 172
private life 118
process of mourning 9, 12, 109
proper self-love 112–13
prophecy 66, 68–69, 73–74, 135
Protagoras 76
proximity 213–14, 216–17

quieting 36–38, 42, 98–99, 101, 136, 156–57, 256

racial oppression 38–39
radical hope 291
reasoning 14, 130, 134, 200–1, 203–4, 274, 288, 291
recognition, of vulnerability 208, 223, 254
reflective self-understanding 78, 80
reflexivity, temptation of 266
relational accountability 89, 119, 165, 168, 234, 243
relationality 7–10, 12, 35, 191, 195–96, 201, 207, 220–21, 223, 226, 276–77
relational model 40, 49, 54
relational ontology 2, 6–8, 10, 165, 168, 196, 274, 276–77
relation of Eros 209, 212–14
religion: feminist philosopher of 61, 97, 101, 107; feminist philosophy of 13, 83, 90, 95, 97, 139, 147, 154–55, 159, 161, 230
religious traditions 53–54
reparation 64, 113–14, 116, 118, 197
resentment 108–9, 117–19
resilience 4, 194, 198, 252–54, 258–60
responsibility 63, 66, 69, 71, 85, 87, 90, 109, 111, 179, 181–87, 189–91, 209–11, 213–14, 216–18
Responsibility for Justice 187
restorative justice 2, 4, 107, 117, 165, 204, 234, 243
Ricoeur, Paul 87, 232; ethics and 83, 86
risks of love 263–70

role of vulnerability 56, 207
romantic love 202, 268
"The 'Rule of Law of Love'" 46

Schweiker, William 263
self-authorship 220, 222
self-deception 37–38, 42, 48–49, 98–99, 102, 112, 156, 159, 181, 257
self-discipline 200–1
self-giving love 112–13
self-love 80, 112, 200, 212
self-relational problems 53–54
self-respect 108–10, 114, 117, 267
self-righteousness 265
self-silencing 37–38, 156, 256
self-transformation 200
Sen, Amartya 232
sexism 23, 27, 38, 69–70, 96, 101, 129, 146, 160, 189–90
sexual violence 4, 15, 163–74; ethical vulnerability and 167–69; feminism and 165–67; politics 169, 174
silencing 34–38, 40–41, 48–49, 74, 157, 256
situations of vulnerability 217, 255–56, 258
smothering 36–38, 40, 42, 98–99, 101, 136, 156, 256
social imaginary 47
social life 215, 239, 264, 273–74
social ontologies 265–67
social vulnerability 2–5, 100, 212
spaces of vulnerability 57–58
speaker 3, 35–42, 48–49, 54, 68, 87, 98–99, 128, 155, 172, 188
speaker–audience reciprocity 40
speaker's relations 36, 48
speaker vulnerability 3–5, 34–41, 45, 47–50, 98, 100–3, 154, 156–59, 230, 232; example of 47
Spelman, Elizabeth 257
Spencer, Stanley 145
spirit of forgiveness 115
states of knowledge 126
The Steadfast Philosopher 144
Stoic Seneca 145
strategies of invulnerability 238–39
structural injustice 2–5, 184, 187
subjective vulnerability 209, 212
subjectivity 80–81, 210–11, 214, 224–25, 236
suffering love 265, 268, 270
symmetrical accountability 193–94, 204
symmetrical relation 211–12
systematic process of self-deception 37–38, 42, 49, 99, 156

theme of forgiveness 107
theme of vulnerability 45, 135, 263
theological virtues 281–86, 288, 291–92

INDEX

thoughtful love of life 63, 96, 100–1, 145, 277
threshold situations 182–83
Tillich, Paul 147, 149
Tobin, Theresa 203
Tractatus 129
transcendence 27–29, 102, 213, 224, 236, 238, 292
transformation 9, 56–59, 100–1, 109–11, 114–16, 164–65, 168–69, 171–73, 193–94, 197, 200–1, 229, 233, 237–38, 258, 277–78; of life 26, 229
transformative change 26, 230–31, 235
transform vulnerability 276
Tuana, Nancy 37, 41–42, 49, 156, 257
Tulliver, Maggie 156

unconditional forgiveness 114, 116–17, 157
Undoing Gender 88
universal humanity 223, 226
universal vulnerability 45, 214–15, 217

victims 86, 90, 108–9, 111, 113–14, 116–18, 157, 165–68, 171–72, 221, 226
violence 2, 6–8, 16–17, 37, 40–41, 45, 47, 49–50, 98–103, 119, 163–69, 171–74, 225–26, 233–34, 252–54, 256–59; philosophical imaginary of 7, 274
viral movement 170–71, 173
virtual diaspora 278

virtual life 22–23, 27, 30
virtues 25, 63–64, 100, 109, 134, 181–82, 185, 190–91, 194, 202–4, 281–85
vulnerability ladies 230–31

Weil, Simone 112, 200
white women 38, 226
wilful ignorance 3–4, 34, 37–38, 40, 42, 49, 98–102, 156–58, 160–61, 253–54, 256–58, 260; oppressive form of 40, 42, 158; of vulnerability 41, 49–50
wisdom 11–16, 56, 63, 67, 86, 134, 139–51, 274; of love 11, 14, 16–17
wise lovers 13, 16, 113
Wittgenstein, Ludwig 129
women 7–9, 12–17, 21–23, 27, 29–30, 34–41, 49–50, 58, 68–75, 82–85, 88–90, 96–101, 117–20, 129–30, 144–46, 154–61, 169–72, 220–27, 236–38, 273–74; agency 166, 168, 223; of colour 38, 42, 169; philosophers 34, 54, 85, 88, 98; in philosophy 4, 21–22, 25, 27–28, 34–35, 37, 42, 83, 139
word vulnerability 233
working life 136, 190
Wounds of Passion: A Writing Life 38

Young, Iris Marion 184–86